AFRICAN STUDIES
THESAURUS

AFRICAN STUDIES THESAURUS

Subject Headings for Library Users

FREDA E. OTCHERE

Bibliographies and Indexes in Afro-American
and African Studies, Number 29

GREENWOOD PRESS
Westport, Connecticut • London

Library of Congress Cataloging-in-Publication Data

Otchere, Freda E.
  African studies thesaurus : subject headings for library users /
Freda E. Otchere.
    p. cm.—(Bibliographies and indexes in Afro-American and
African studies, ISSN 0742-6925 ; no. 29)
  Includes bibliographical references.
  ISBN 0-313-27437-1 (alk. paper)
  1. Subject headings—Africa, Sub-Saharan. 2. Subject headings,
Library of Congress.   I. Title.   II. Series.
  Z695.1.A37O85 1992
  025.4'9808'89896—dc20   92-12523

British Library Cataloguing in Publication Data is available.

Library of Congress Catalog Card Number: 92-12523
ISBN: 0-313-27437-1
ISSN: 0742-6925

First published in 1992

Greenwood Press, 88 Post Road West, Westport, CT 06881
An imprint of Greenwood Publishing Group, Inc.

Printed in the United States of America

The paper used in this book complies with the
Permanent Paper Standard issued by the National
Information Standards Organization (Z39.48-1984).

10 9 8 7 6 5 4 3 2 1

To the ancestors

Fred Anderson Eldridge and Dorothy (McCann) Eldridge

Frank Demere Eldridge and Rebecca (Patterson) Eldridge
Clarence McCann and Ada (Smith) McCann

William Henry Eldridge and Mary (Davison) Eldridge
William R. Patterson and Annie (Lantz) Patterson
Arthur F. McCann and Ella Jane (Carmichael) McCann
Charles Smith and Mary (Sherman) Smith

John Eldridge and Amelia Eldridge
George McCann and Mary Jane (Martin) McCann
Anaxomander Carmichael and Martha Jane (Spearing) Carmichael

Contents

Foreword

Freda Otchere's wide-ranging index of subject headings related to sub-Saharan Africa is the product of several years of intensive work and is a testimony to her skill and dedication as a librarian. Her request that I write a foreword to her <u>African Studies Thesaurus</u> is an honor and an opportunity.

It is an honor to be associated with an endeavor of this importance and magnitude; my participation in it, limited to the preparation of this foreword, points to the continued interest in Africa within the Montréal academic community and the prospects for growing cooperation between various academic departments in Montréal's several universities.   It is an opportunity to discuss the situation of Africa and Africans, and to point to the need for research into many areas of concern - whether in sociology, history, political science, economics, linguistics, literature studies, or elsewhere.

In the final decade of the twentieth century, Africa occupies an uncertain place in the international community. The reduction of tension between the Great Powers and the political and economic changes under way in the erstwhile Soviet Union and eastern Europe have combined to reduce international competition and concomitantly, strategic interest, in Africa. The Africa of the 1990s is thus less a foreign policy arena than was the Africa of the preceding era, that is, of the Cold War in the 1950s through the 1980s. The institutions, policies, and practices and the leaders who used and applied them in the first thirty years of independence are increasingly seen as a disappointment and are coming under growing challenge both within Africa and in the wider community.   Continuing critical reassessment of this first generation of rulers and of the problems and prospects of their successors is sorely needed.

It is essential that the African cultural experience - prior to, during, and following upon colonial rule - be studied and recounted to the extra-African world. This is especially the case given the ongoing upheaval in the *mores* and practices of social life resulting from colonization and urbanization that have served to disrupt, often in harmful ways, traditional life among the African peoples.   There is much to be learned here - about indigenous societies, about the impact of colonialism, and about its long-term consequences. This thesaurus, which is strong in the rich and complex areas of African culture, religion, language, and literature, will be of particular interest to scholars in these disciplines.

Despite these needs, there is the danger that Africa will be neglected. The political, economic and, as a consequence, academic refocusing on Asia and eastern Europe is taking place simultaneously with the closing of the careers of the first generation of North American Africanist scholars whose long engagement in this field is nearing its end. There is a need for a vigorous turn to Africa by a new generation of North American scholars, who wish to participate in the study of development there.

Ms. Otchere's work speaks directly to these needs. We are fortunate to have it available to us at this time of challenge and opportunity.

John Shingler

Preface

The absence of a comprehensive thesaurus of African subject headings has long inhibited research in this area. <u>African Studies Thesaurus</u> is intended to fill this gap, by identifying nearly 4000 subject heading terms that pertain specifically to Africa south of the Sahara.

The process began with a word-by-word search through the 13th edition of the <u>Library of Congress Subject Headings</u> (<u>LCSH</u>). It continued with the periodic examination of the various publications (<u>Cataloging Service Bulletin</u>, nos. 49-54 (Summer 1990-Fall 1991) and <u>LC Subject Headings Weekly Lists</u> (nos. 01-51 [January 3, 1990-December 19, 1990] and nos. 01-38 [January 23, 1991-September 18, 1991]) put out by the Library of Congress (LC) to inform libraries of corrections to existing subject headings and the creation of new ones. This allowed me to identify those changes that appeared in the 14th edition of <u>LCSH</u>. Most headings were then searched in the UTLAS database, Canada's most comprehensive bibliographical database that includes a copy of the online version of <u>Library of Congress Subject Headings</u>. In many cases, this step allowed me to identify the appropriate Library of Congress classification number, which was then added to the heading. It also served to identify some very recent changes to some subject headings. The thesaurus, then, is current to mid September, 1991 (that is, nearly three-quarters through the 15th edition of <u>LCSH</u>).

After the list of terms was transcribed, I added hundreds of cross-references, primarily broader and narrower terms, to improve consistency throughout the list, and to help the user to more easily identify the term sought. For example, now all languages have broader references to the language family to which they belong and to the countries in which they are spoken, while all African peoples have been linked to the countries in which they live. No new terms were created or changed, since this is a list of terms that are currently in use in libraries across North America, not a theoretical thesaurus. In the same vein, I have chosen not to critique LC's choice of terms, or their occasionally bewildering inconsistencies. Hopefully, this exhaustive listing will identify omissions and will assist in the revision of outdated terms.

Thanks are due to many at Concordia University, including the University for granting the sabbatical leave that allowed me to work full-time on this project; to Audrey Williams of the Research Office for helping to defray the costs of online searching; to Sam Kalb, Associate Director, Technical Services, for his assistance in interpreting WordPerfect 5.0; to Judy Appleby, Head of the

University's Vanier Library, for her valuable comments and suggestions for the Introduction; and to the Interlibrary Loans staff of Vanier Library for swiftly tracking down the obscure titles I needed to verify certain headings. I must also express my gratitude to Dr. John Shingler of McGill University's African Studies Program for graciously agreeing to write the Foreword, and of course to my family for cheerfully tolerating the loss of half of the dining room table for over a year.

Introduction

SCOPE

This thesaurus is intended to be used by students and researchers in African Studies, to help them identify the correct subject heading to use when searching the library's catalog. Since classification numbers are included, it can also be used to browse the stacks.

This is a comprehensive listing of all Library of Congress subject headings that relate specifically to the 41 countries that make up Africa south of the Sahara Desert; that is, all countries in Africa except for those in North Africa: Egypt, Libya, Tunisia, Algeria, Morocco, and Western Sahara. In addition, it contains subject headings for the islands of Cape Verde, The Comoros, Madagascar, Mauritius, Réunion, Saint Helena, Sao Tomé and Príncipe, and the Seychelles.

This thesaurus consists of some 4000 subject headings, including the names of over 600 African peoples and nearly 600 African languages, as well as cross-references from unused synonyms and references to broader, related, and narrower terms. The LC classification number under which most materials are likely to be found on library shelves is also included in square brackets, directly under the subject heading itself.

This Introduction contains instructions on how to use this publication -- both at a glance, and in some detail. The detailed section will be of particular help to students new to a large academic library.

Following the Introduction, you will find two Appendices: an outline of the African history classification (DT) and a table of subdivisions that can be added to geographical subject headings as you see fit, in order to better refine your search. Explanations for all of these concepts are included in the detailed explanation below.

HOW TO USE -- AT A GLANCE

The terms you can ————— **Nigeria** *(Not Subd Geog)* ————— This indicates that a
search by are   [DT 515-DT 515.9]   geographical term (say, a city
indicated in   **--History**   of Nigeria), cannot directly
boldface   **-- --To 1851**   follow "Nigeria"
                              -- --1851-1899
These act as "ditto" ————— **-- --1900-1960**   Suggested LC classification
marks to the term or   NT Senussite Rebellion, 1916-1918   numbers for works on Nigeria
terms in **boldface**   **-- --1960-**
directly above them.   **-- --Coup d'état, 1966 (January 15)**
Thus, this heading   BT Coups d'état--Nigeria   Unused terms. If you look under
should be read as   **-- --Coup d'état, 1966 (July 29)**   them, you are referred back to
"Nigeria--History--   BT Coups d'état--Nigeria   the heading directly above. All
1900-1960"   **-- --Civil War, 1967-1970**   unused terms that relate to
                              [DT 515.836]   this heading are listed in this
Suggested LC classi- —————   UF Biafran Conflict, 1967-1970   column
fication number for   Civil war--Nigeria
works on the 1967-
1970 Civil War

DETAILED EXPLANATION

  Library Catalogs

The key to locating materials in a library is its catalog, which
is an index to the material held within the library. The catalog
itself comes in different formats: cards in a card file, book
catalogs, microform catalogs, and, increasing, computerized (online
or compact disc) catalogs. Occasionally you will find a
combination of catalog formats within a library; for example, a
card file for material cataloged before a certain date, with an online catalog for newer material.

Libraries today collect a wide variety of material in addition to
books: periodicals (journals), audiovisual formats (such as films,
videos, compact discs, software), and so on, all of which are
usually listed in their catalog. Although work is being done on
listing the contents of periodicals (that is, the titles of
articles in the periodicals) in the library's catalog, to date
libraries usually list only the title of the periodical itself (for
example, Journal of African Studies). However, most libraries
provide a detailed catalog entry for each book as well as for each

title in audiovisual format. Throughout this Introduction, I will
speak of the "book" but I use this term to include the broad
spectrum of materials bought by libraries.

If you know the particular author, title, or series title of a work
that you want, you would search under that author or title to
locate the work. But what if you don't have this information;
instead, all you know is that you want to find works on a
particular subject? If that particular subject lies within the
area of African Studies, then this thesaurus was compiled to help
you.

Subjects

Most academic libraries in North America use <u>Library of Congress
Subject Headings</u> (LCSH) as a source for the terms (subject
headings) that they use to describe the subject content of the
books, etc., in their collections. Often, libraries will include
a copy of LCSH near their catalog to help users in their subject
searches; it is currently a large three volume set, bound in red,
and know popularly as "The Red Book." It includes all the subject
headings developed and used at the Library of Congress, plus
references from unused terms (UF), and other references to related
topics, both broader in scope (BT) and narrower in scope (NT), as
well as those related in scope (RT).

Because it contains millions of terms, it can be difficult to find
the term or terms that you are looking for. In addition, you might
not be able to consult this list because someone else is using the
volume you need, or you might be at a catalog that does not have
a copy (such as at a computer terminal accessing an on-line
catalog). A smaller list containing terms specific to one subject
area is certainly easier to consult, and can suggest terms that you
might not have considered using.

Classification

The books in the library are arranged on the shelves by call
number, which consists of a classification number for the subject
area of the material followed by the number for the book itself.
One such classification system, frequently used in public
libraries, is the Dewey Decimal Classification; it begins with a
number and is followed by a combination of letters and numbers for
the author. For example, a history of Uganda for the period 1980
onward written by someone named I. Museveni would have the Dewey
Classification number 967.6104.M87. If your library uses this

classification system, the class numbers that we have included will not be of help to you, although you can still use the book to locate the correct subject heading for searching (assuming, of course, that your library uses LCSH).

The classification system more commonly used by academic libraries in North America was developed by the Library of Congress and is known as the Library of Congress Classification System (LCC). It consists of a letter or letters followed by a number, then a combination of letters and numbers; the book on Ugandan history mentioned previously would have the LCC number of DT 433.285.M87.

As is suggested above, each book on the shelves must have its own unique number to distinguish it from its neighbor. To achieve this, a book number is added to the class number; this book number usually refers to the author of the book. So, although you can find in this book the suggested classification number for the subject term that you want, to get the actual number of an actual book, you will have to look in your library's catalog.

I have included the classification number for those of you who enjoy browsing on the library shelves, or for the (hopefully) rare occasions when the online catalog is down and you need some idea of where to look in the stacks. You should be aware, however, that you cannot be guaranteed that you will be reaching all of the titles that could be of use to you. For example, a book that is written on two subjects (each with its own classification number) can have only one location in the stacks. Thus, you would find it under the classification number for the first subject. If you are looking on the shelves under the classification number for the second subject, you would not locate this book. To do so, you would have to search in the library's catalog under the second subject to get the correct classification number. Or a library might classify all the books in a series together even though individual titles in the series have their own subjects. To get at the classification number of the series, you would have to consult the catalog.

In addition, since LCC has been in use since the turn of the century, the system has undergone substantial modification over time, and a library may well have material on the same subject under somewhat different numbers (libraries rarely have the time and funds to go back and change these superseded numbers to their new numbers). Again, to get the number of the title as used in your library, you should consult your library's catalog.

In 1989, the subject cataloging staff at the Library of Congress introduced a major change in the classification of the history of Southern Africa; they abandoned the span of numbers from "DT 727" to "DT 971" and replaced it with the span "DT 1001" through "DT 3415". More than likely your library will have works on Southern Africa in both areas, and to help you, I have included the appropriate numbers from both spans whenever possible.

In Appendix I, you will find an outline of African history, which is classified in "DT". You could use this outline if you wanted to browse your library's shelves to see what books it has on a particular country.

One area where I have not included any classification numbers is in the discipline of Law. For various reasons, LC has yet to develop classification schedules covering the law of areas outside the Americas and Europe. Individual libraries have developed their own systems to handle this problem.

Subdivisions

A subdivision is a word or term coming directly after the heading itself, and preceded by a double dash (--). It can be specific to the heading (in the example on page v, the subdivision "Coup d' état, 1966 (January 15)" appears only under "Nigeria--History--" since it applies to an event only in Nigeria) or it can be "free-floating"; that is, it can be applied to any heading as desired, to narrow a topic. In the Nigerian example, "History" is a free-floating subdivision in that it could be applied to nearly every subject heading in this book.

There are several hundred free-floating subdivisions that are used in LCSH. In Appendix II, I have listed those that can be applied as desired to the geographical subject headings in this book; that is, to the names of regions (for example, "African, Southern"), countries, cities, etc. These subdivisions can be useful in narrowing a search on a large file under a geographical name, especially in an online search, or for the time when you want a book on a very specific aspect, say, a bibliography on a country.

Black Headings

For the most part, it was not hard to select the subject headings that should appear in this book. I had, though, some difficulty with the subject heading "Blacks" and headings beginning with the

term "Black." In LCSH, these headings are used for works on Black
people outside of the United States (works on the Black people of
the United States are entered under the heading "Afro-American").

There are several pages of headings on Blacks. Some definitely
have been used for books written from the African perspective.
Many have been devised and used for books written on topics as they
pertain to the West Indies, South America, etc. To include the
latter headings in an African subject headings list is misleading
since as far as I can determine, the headings have not been used
for African countries so far. Yet theoretically there could in the
future be books written on these topics from an African
perspective, so I hesitated to leave them out.

As a compromise, I have included all the Black subject headings,
and added at least one African geographical subdivision whenever
I could find it. In the cases where I could locate only non-
African examples, I have omitted geographical subdivisions
altogether.

     Not Included

The nearly 4000 subject headings relating specifically to Africa
south of the Sahara are by no means all of the subject terms under
which you could find works in your library about this area. If you
look in the red LCSH volumes you will find that many of the used
terms are followed by the notation "(May Subd Geog)"; this means
that any geographical heading (for example, "Africa, West," or
"Kenya," or "Zaire--Mombasa") could directly follow the term.

Thus, your library may well contain works with such subject
headings as "Community development--Zambia--Lusaka" or "Foster
parents--Africa, West" (listed in LCSH as "Community development
(May Subd Geog)" and "Foster parents (May Subd Geog)"). In order
to list all of these possible subject headings, I would have had
to list all of the subject headings in the LCSH that contained the
notation (May Subd Geog); this would have amounted to nearly a
duplication of LCSH.

Therefore, if you are looking for material on a general topic as
it applies to Africa, and you cannot locate it in this book, before
assuming that this subject area does not exist, check under the
general topic in LCSH to see if it is listed there as a subject
heading that can be subdivided by a geographical area. If so,
check your catalog under that subject heading, subdivided by the
area or country that you want.

Also omitted in <u>LCSH</u> are all proper names including personal names
and the names of organizations (although I have added in the names
of a few very important organizations, such as the African National
Congress). Also excluded are most geographical headings, such as
the names of cities and provinces or states.

It's Not In My Library

Subject headings are created at the Library of Congress as the need
arises; that is, a person cataloging a new book will examine the
existing headings to identify the one or ones that describe the
subject content of the book. If there is no appropriate one, the
cataloger may choose to use several existing ones that together
cover the subject content, or may propose that a new one be
devised. This means that for every subject heading listed in <u>LCSH,</u>
at least one book has been published on that topic. Therefore, if
you find a subject heading that is exactly what you want, but your
library has no books under that heading, speak to your Librarian
about obtaining the book or books from other libraries through the
interlibrary loan service.

How To Use This Book

In the following list, I have followed the same format found in
<u>LCSH</u>, on the assumption that you will also be using <u>LCSH</u> for
headings that are not included. Therefore, once you are able to
find your way around this list, you should also be able to use <u>LCSH</u>
efficiently.

The list is arranged alphabetically, with numbers at the very
beginning of the list, before the letter "A." A term that you can
use to look under in your library catalog is in **boldface**. If the
term can be followed by a geographical term, that fact is indicated
by the notation (May Subd Geog) directly following the term. Thus,
the heading "Apartheid (May Subd Geog)" could be followed by, for
example, "Namibia" (that is, "Apartheid--Namibia"). On the next
line, I have indicated the classification number for most books in
the subject, which you could use to browse the stacks. In a few
cases, you will find notes about how the heading is to be used; for
example, a detailed note is found after the heading "Blacks."

If there are unused synonyms to the subject heading used in
libraries, then these synonyms are included as "UF" terms, or "Used
For" terms. If you were to look under one of the "UF" terms, you
would be referred back to the subject heading you should use
instead. You may also find "RT" terms (which will refer you to

related terms that you can look under in the catalog), "BT" terms
(which will refer you to broader terms) and "NT" terms (which will
refer you to narrower terms).   In cases where there are several
"UF," "BT," "RT," or "NT" terms, they are listed in a column
beneath the first one, but are not preceded by "UF," "BT," etc.,
each time.   Below these, you might find subdivisions preceded by
a double dash "--."   The double dashes act as ditto marks to the
heading in boldface directly above the dashes.

You should first look under the specific term that you have in
mind, rather than a broader subject term. For example, look under
"Chi (Igbo deity)" rather than the broader heading "Gods, Igbo."
However, if you find nothing under the very specific topic, try
what you think could be the broader term.   If you find nothing
under what you consider to be quite a broad heading, you can try
looking in the LCSH as this may be a very general topic that is not
specific only to Africa.

You can locate African languages by searching under the specific
language, under the family of languages to which it belongs or
under the countries in which they are spoken. The names of African
peoples are found under the specific name of the group, and under
the heading "Ethnology" followed by the name of the country or
countries in which the people live.

African History Classification Outline

This is an outline of the LC classification for African History.
The classification numbers in *italics and round "( )" brackets* are
obsolete as of late 1989, but your library may still have books
under these old numbers.   If you use this list to browse the
stacks, you should search under both the old and the new numbers
if you want to be sure to reach older and newer material.

DT	1-3415	Africa

43-154	Egypt
154.1-159.9	Sudan (Anglo-Egyptian Sudan)
160-177	North Africa
179.2-179.9	Northwest Africa

181-346	**Maghrib. Barbary States**
211-239	Libya (Tripoli)
241-269	Tunisia (Tunis)
271-299	Algeria
301-330	Morocco
331-346	Sahara

348-363.3	**Central Sub-Saharan Africa**

365-469	**Eastern Africa**
367-367.8	Northeast Africa
371-398	Ethiopia (Abyssinia)
401-409	Somalia (Somaliland and adjacent territory)
411-411.9	Djibouti (French Territory of the Afars and Issas. French Somaliland)
421-432.5	East Africa (British East Africa)
433.2-.29	Uganda
433.5-.434	Kenya (East African Protectorate)
436-449	Tanzania (Tanganyika. German East Africa)
450-450.49	Rwanda. Ruandi-Urundi
450.5-.95	Burundi
(451-465	*Mozambique (Portuguese East Africa)*
468-469	**Islands (East African Coast)**
469.M21-.M38	Madagascar
469.M39	Mascarene Islands
469.M4-.M495	Mauritius (Ile de France)
469.M497	Mayotte
469.R3-.R5	Réunion
469.S4-.S49	Seychelles

DT   (611–611.9   Angola)
        (701–720   Namibia (South-West Africa))
        (727–747   Southern Africa)
        (751–779.955   British South Africa)
        (781–789   Lesotho (Basutoland))
        (790–803   Botswana (Bechuanaland
                                  Protectorate))
        (821–848   Cape Province (Cape of Good Hope
                                  Province))
        (850–856   British Central Africa)
        (857–865   Malawi (Nyasaland))
        (866–880   Natal)
            (888   Dutch Republics. Afrikaners)
        (891–909   Orange Free State)
        (911–944   Transvaal. South African Republic)
        (946–960   Rhodesia
            (962   Zimbabwe (Southern Rhodesia)
            (963   Zambia (Southern Rhodesia)
            (971   Swaziland)
            (981   Zambesi River)
            (995   Other regions)

        1001–3415   **Southern Africa**
        1001–1190   Southern Africa
        1991–2054   Cape Province (Cape of Good Hope)
        2075–2145   Orange Free State
        2181–2278   Natal
        2291–2378   Transvaal (South African Republic)
        1251–1465   Angola
        1501–1685   Namibia (South-West Africa)
        1701–2405   South Africa
        2421–2525   Botswana (Bechuanaland)
        2541–2686   Lesotho (Basutoland)
        2701–2825   Swaziland
        2831–2864   British Central Africa (Federation
                                    of Rhodesia and Nyasaland)
        2871–3025   Zimbabwe (Southern Rhodesia)
        3031–3145   Zambia (Northern Rhodesia)
        3161–3257   Malawi (Nyasaland)
        3291–3415   Mozambique

Selected Geographical Subdivisions

The subdivisions listed below may be used as desired under headings for geographic place names including continents; regions; islands; countries; states or provinces; counties and other local jurisdictions larger than cities; and cities. They can be useful for narrowing a search on a large file under a geographic name, especially in an online search, or for the time when you want a book on a very specific aspect, say, a bibliography on a country. The most commonly used subdivisions are in **boldface**.

--Abstracting and indexing
--Abstracts
--Administrative and political divisions
*--Aerial exploration
--Aerial photographs
--Air defenses
--Air defenses, Civil
--Air defenses, Military
*--Altitudes
--Anecdotes
*--Annexation to ...
  Anniversaries, etc.
--Antiquities
--Antiquities--Collection and preservation
--Appropriations and expenditures
--Appropriations and expenditures--Effect of
   inflation on
--Archival resources (May Subd Geog)
***--Armed Forces (May Subd Geog)
***--Armed Forces--Regulations
--Audiotape catalogs
--**Bibliography**
--Bio-bibliography
--**Biography**
--Book reviews
--Boundaries (May Subd Geog)
**--Buildings, structures, etc.
--Calendars
*--Capital and capitol
--Census
--Census--Law and legislation

--Census, [date]
--Centennial celebrations, etc.
--Charters, grants, privileges
--Church history
--Civil defense
--**Civilization**
--Civilization--Foreign influences
--Civilization--Philosophy
--Claims
--Claims vs. ...
--Climate
*--Coast defenses
--Colonial influence
***--Colonies
--Colonization
--**Commerce** (May Subd Geog)
***--Commercial policy
***--Commercial treaties
--**Congresses**
*--Constitution
--Court and courtiers
--Cultural policy
***--Defenses
***--Defenses--Economic aspects
***--Defenses--Law and legislation
***--Dependency on ...
***--Dependency on foreign countries
**--Description
*--**Description and travel**
--Dictionaries
***--Diplomatic and consular service (May Subd Geog)

* = <u>not</u> used under cities ; ** = under cities <u>only</u>
*** = under countries, or regions larger than countries

--Directories
--Discovery and exploration
--Discovery and exploration--English [French, etc.]
--Distances, etc.
--Drama
--Early works to 1800
--**Economic conditions**
--Economic conditions--Maps
*--Economic conditions--Regional disparities
--Economic conditions--Statistics
--**Economic policy**
--Emigration and immigration
--Emigration and immigration--Economic aspects
--Emigration and immigration--Government policy
--Emigration and immigration--Religious aspects
--Emigration and immigration--Social aspects
***--Empresses
--Encyclopedias
--**Ethnic relations**
*--Exiles
--Exploring expeditions
--Fiction
--Film catalogs
--Forecasting
--**Foreign economic relations** *(May Subd Geog)*
***--Foreign public opinion
***--Foreign public opinion, American [British, etc.]
***--**Foreign relations** *(May Subd Geog)*
***--Foreign relations administration
--Gazetteers
--Genealogy
--Geography
*--Gold discoveries
--Handbooks, manuals, etc.
--Historical geography
--Historical geography--Maps
--Historiography
--**History**
*--**History--Autonomy and independence movements**
--History--Blockade, [date]
--History--Chronology
--History--Religious aspects
--History--Siege, [date]
--History--Sources
*--History, Local
--History, Military
***--History, Naval

--Humor
--Imprints
--Index maps
--Indexes
--**Industries**
--Information services *(May Subd Geog)*
--**Intellectual life**
--International status
--Juvenile drama
--Juvenile fiction
--Juvenile films
--Juvenile humor
--Juvenile literature
--Juvenile poetry
--Juvenile sound recordings
--Kings and rulers
--**Languages**
--Languages--Alphabet
--Languages--Law and legislation
--Languages--Texts
--Library resources *(May Subd Geog)*
--Literary collections
--**Literatures**
--Manufactures
--Maps
***--Military policy
--Military relations *(May Subd Geog)*
--Military relations --Foreign countries
*--Militia
--Miscellanea
--Moral conditions
--Name
***--National security
*--Naval militia
--Neutrality
***--Nonalignment
--Officials and employees *(May Subd Geog)*
--Periodicals
--Photo maps
--Photographs from space
--Poetry
--**Politics and government**
--Popular culture
--Popular culture--Economic aspects
--**Population**
--Population--Statistics
*--Population, Rural
--Population density
--Population policy

(May Subd Geog) = Place names may follow the subdivision

--Princes and princesses
***--Proclamations
 *--Provinces
 --Queens
 --Quotations, maxims, etc.
 --Race relations
 --Registers
 --Relations *(May Subd Geog)*
 --Relations--Foreign countries
 --Relief models
 --Religion
 --Religion--Humor
 --Religious life and customs
 *--Republics
 --Research *(May Subd Geog)*
 --Road maps
***--Royal household
 *--Rural conditions
 --Slides
 --Social conditions
 --Social life and customs
 --Social policy
 --Social registers
 --Songs and music
 *--States
 --Statistical services
 --Statistics
 --Statistics, Medical
 --Statistics, Vital
 --Strategic aspects
 --Study and teaching *(May Subd Geog)*
***--Sultans
 --Surveys
 --Telephone directories
 --Telephone directories--Yellow pages
***--Territorial expansion
***--Territories and possessions
 *--Travel regulations
 --Trials, litigation, etc.
 --Voting registers
 --Zoning maps

      * = <u>not</u> used under cities ; ** = under cities <u>only</u>
   *** = under countries, or regions larger than countries

Subject Headings
List for Library Users

1st Chimurenga War (Zimbabwe), 1896-1897
    USE Zimbabwe--History--Ndebele
Insurrection, 1896-1897

1st Street (Harare, Zimbabwe)
    USE First Street (Harare, Zimbabwe)

1st World War
    USE World War, 1914-1918

2nd Chimurenga War (Zimbabwe), 1966-1980
    USE Zimbabwe--History--Chimurenga War,
1966-1980

2nd World War
    USE World War, 1939-1945

1820 settlers (South Africa)
    USE British settlers of 1820 (South
Africa)

1853 Medal (South Africa)
    USE South Africa Medal (1834-1853)

A

A-Bunga (African people)
    USE Bongo (African people)

A.D.B.
    USE African Development Bank

A.N.C.
    USE African National Congress

Ababua language *(May Subd Geog)*
    [PL 8035]
    BT Bantu languages
        Zaire--Languages

Ababua (African people) *(May Subd Geog)*
    [DT 650.A]
    UF Babua (African people)
        Babwa (African people)
        Bobwa (African people)
        Mangbua (African people)
    BT Bantu-speaking peoples
        Ethnology--Zaire

Abahela (African people)
    USE Hera (African people)

Abai River (Ethiopia and Sudan)
    USE Blue Nile River (Ethiopia and Sudan)

Abakuria (African people)
    USE Kuria (African people)

Abaluyia (African people)
    USE Luyia (African people)

Abandoned cities
    USE Cities and towns, Ruined, extinct, etc.

Abarambo language
    USE Barambu language

Abasuba (African people)
    USE Suba (African people)

Abathwa (African people)
    USE Batwa (African people)

Abay River (Ethiopia and Sudan)
    USE Blue Nile River (Ethiopia and Sudan)

Abbai River (Ethiopia and Sudan)
    USE Blue Nile River (Ethiopia and Sudan)

Abbé language
    USE Abe language

Abbey language
    USE Abe language

Abbreviations, Afrikaans
    [PF 861]
    UF Afrikaans abbreviations
        Afrikaans language--Abbreviations

Abdullab (Arab people) *(May Subd Geog)*
    [DT 155.2.A]
    BT Ethnology--Sudan

Abe language *(May Subd Geog)*
    UF Abbé language
        Abbey language
    BT Ivory Coast--Languages
        Lagoon languages

Abia (Rite)
    [DT 571.B47]
    BT Beti (African people)--Rites and ceremonies
        Rites and ceremonies--Cameroon

Abidjan (Ivory Coast). Vridi-Canal
    USE Vridi-Canal (Abidjan, Ivory Coast)

UF = Used for; BT = Broader term; RT = Related term; SA = See also; NT = Narrower term

Abidji (African people) *(May Subd Geog)*
  [DT 545.45.A]
  UF Ari (African people)
  BT Ethnology--Ivory Coast
 --Religion
  [BL 2480.A3]

Abidji language *(May Subd Geog)*
  [PL 8036.A]
  UF Abiji language
      Adidji language
      Ari language (Ivory Coast)
  BT Ivory Coast--Languages
      Lagoon languages

Abidji proverbs
  USE Proverbs, Abidji

Abigar language
  USE Nuer language

Abiji language
  USE Abidji language

Abiri language
  USE Birri language

Abisa (Zambian people)
  USE Bisa (Zambian people)

Abo language (Sudan)
  USE Toposa language

Abolition of slavery
  USE Slavery

Abonwa language
  USE Abure language

Aborigines
  USE Indigenous peoples

Aboure language
  USE Abure language

Abri language (Sudan)
  USE Nirere dialect

Abron (African people) *(May Subd Geog)*
  [DT 545.45.A27 (Ivory Coast)]
  UF Bono (African people)
      Brong (African people)
  BT Ethnology--Africa, Central
      Ethnology--Africa, West
      Ethnology--Ivory Coast

Abu Rof (African people)
  USE Rufa'a al-Hoi (African people)

Abua language *(May Subd Geog)*
  [PL 8036.A85]
  UF Abuan language
  BT Abua-Ogbia languages
      Nigeria--Languages

Abua-Ogbia languages *(May Subd Geog)*
  [PL 8037]
  UF Kugbo dialect
      Ogbia dialect
  BT Benue-Congo languages
      Nigeria--Languages
  NT Abua language
      Odual language

Abuan (African people) *(May Subd Geog)*
  [DT 515.45.A]
  BT Ethnology--Nigeria

Abuan language
  USE Abua language

Abure language *(May Subd Geog)*
  [PL 8039]
  UF Abonwa language
      Aboure language
      Akapless language
  BT Ivory Coast--Languages
      Lagoon languages
 --Phonemics

Abyssinia
  USE Ethiopia

Abyssinian Expedition, 1867-1868
  [DT 386.3]
  UF Magdala Campaign, 1867-1868
      Napier Expedition, 1867-1868
  BT Ethiopia--History--1490-1889
  NT Mak'edala, Ethiopia, Battle of, 1868

Abyssinian language
  USE Amharic language

Abyssinian manuscripts
  USE Manuscripts, Ethiopic

Abyssino-Italian War, 1895-1896
  USE Italo-Ethiopian War, 1895-1896

Accra language
  USE Ga language

(May Subd Geog) = Place names may follow the heading

Accra Plains (Ghana) *(Not Subd Geog)*
   BT Plains--Ghana

Acculturation *(May Subd Geog)*
   UF Culture contact
       Development education
   BT Anthropology
       Ethnology
   NT Blacks--Cultural assimiliation
       Detribalization
 --Africa, West
   [HN 820.A8]
 --Zaire
   [HN 811.A8]

Achanti (African people)
   USE Ashanti (African people)

Acholi (African people)
   USE Acoli (African people)

Acholi language
   USE Acoli language

Acilowe (African people)
   USE Lomwe (African people)

Acoli (African people) *(May Subd Geog)*
   [DT 155.2.A35 (Sudan)]
   UF Acholi (African people)
       Gan (African people)
       Shuli (African people)
   BT Ethnology--Sudan
       Ethnology--Uganda
       Luo (African people)
 --Funeral rites and customs
   UF Funeral rites and customs, Acoli
(African people)
 --Religion
   [BL 2480]
 --Rites and ceremonies

Acoli folk songs
   USE Folk songs, Acoli

Acoli language *(May Subd Geog)*
   [PL 8041]
   UF Acholi language
       Acooli language
       Gang language
       Lwo language
       Shuli language
   BT Nilotic languages
       Sudan--Languages
       Uganda--Languages

Acooli language
   USE Acoli language

Acquired immune deficiency syndrome
   USE AIDS (Disease)

Acquisition of African publications
   [Z 688.A54]
   UF African publications, Acquisition of
   BT Libraries

Acquisition of East African publications
   [Z 688.A54]
   UF East African publications, Acquisition of
   BT Libraries

Acquisition of West African publications
   [Z 688.A54]
   UF West African publications, Acquisition of
   BT Libraries

Acra language
   USE Ga language

Actors *(May Subd Geog)*
   BT Artists
   RT Theater

Actors, Black *(May Subd Geog)*
   UF Black actors
   BT Black theater
 --Africa
   [PN 2969]

Adages
   USE Proverbs

Adaiel language
   USE Afar language

Adamawa dialect
   USE Fula language

Adamawa (Emirate)
   [DT 532.115]
   BT Fula (African people)--History

Adamawa Fula (African people)
   USE Fula (African people)

Adamawa Fulani (African people)
   USE Fula (African people)

Adamawa languages *(May Subd Geog)*
   [PL 8024.A33]
   BT Cameroon--Languages   *(Continued)*

UF = Used for; BT = Broader term; RT = Related term; SA = See also; NT = Narrower term

Adamawa languages *(Continued)*
  BT Chad--Languages
      Niger-Congo languages
      Nigeria--Languages
  NT Bua languages
      Karré language
      Longuda language
      Mbum language
      Mumuye language
      Mundang language

Adampe (African people)
  USE Adangme (African people)

Adan language
  USE Adangme language

Adangbé (African people)
  USE Adangme (African people)

Adangme (African people) *(May Subd Geog)*
  [DT 510.43.A (Ghana)]
  [DT 582.45.A (Togo)]
  UF Adampe (African people)
      Adangbé (African people)
      Adanme (African people)
      Dangme (African people)
  BT Ethnology--Ghana
      Ethnology--Togo

Adangme language *(May Subd Geog)*
  [PL 8043.A3]
  UF Adan language
      Dangme language
  BT Ghana--Languages
      Kwa languages
      Togo--Languages

Adanme (African people)
  USE Adangme (African people)

Adara (African people)
  USE Kadara (African people)

Adari language
  USE Harari language

Adeeyah language
  USE Bube language

Adidji language
  USE Abidji language

Adija (African people)
  USE Bubi (African people)

Adija language
  USE Bube language

Adioukrou (African people)
  USE Adyukru (African people)

Adioukrou language
  USE Adyukru language

Adiukru language
  USE Adyukru language

Adiyah language
  USE Bube language

Adja (African people)
  USE Aja (African people)

Adja dialect
  USE Aja dialect

Adjaua language
  USE Yao language

Adjeur (African people)
  USE Ajjer (African people)

Adjito
  USE Ayo (Game)

Adjukru (African people)
  USE Adyukru (African people)

Adjukru language
  USE Adyukru language

Administration
  USE *subdivision* Politics and government *under*
  names of individual countries, cities, etc.

Adouma language
  USE Aduma language

Adowa, Battle of, 1896
  [DT 387.3]
  UF Battle of Adowa, 1896
  BT Italo-Ethiopian War, 1895-1896

Adultery (Yanzi) law
  BT Law, Yanzi

Aduma language *(May Subd Geog)*
  [PL 8045]
  UF Adouma language
      Douma language
      Duma language

(May Subd Geog) = Place names may follow the heading

BT Bantu languages
   Gabon--Languages
   Zaire--Languages

Adya dialect
  USE Aja dialect

Adyoukrou (African people)
  USE Adyukru (African people)

Adyoukrou language
  USE Adyukru language

Adyukru (African people) *(May Subd Geog)*
  [DT 545.45.A]
  UF Adioukrou (African people)
    Adjukru (African people)
    Adyoukrou (African people)
    Adyukuru (African people)
    Ajukru (African people)
  BT Ethnology--Ivory Coast

Adyukru language *(May Subd Geog)*
  [PL 8046.A22]
  UF Adioukrou language
    Adiukru language
    Adjukru language
    Adyoukrou language
    Ajukru language
  BT Ivory Coast--Languages
    Lagoon languages

Adyukuru (African people)
  USE Adyukru (African people)

Aesthetics
  UF Beautiful, The
    Beauty
    Esthetics
    Taste (Aesthetics)
  RT Art

Aesthetics, African
  [BH 221.A353]
  UF African aesthetics

Aesthetics, Black *(May Subd Geog)*
  UF Black aesthetics

Aethiopian...
  USE *subject headings beginning with the word*
Ethiopian

Afade dialect *(May Subd Geog)*
  [PL 8046.A23]
  UF Affadéh dialect

BT Chad--Languages
   Kotoko dialects

Afan language
  USE Oromo language

Afar (African people) *(May Subd Geog)*
  [DT 411.45.A35 (Djibouti)]
  [DT 380.4.A33 (Ethiopia)]
  UF Afara (African people)
    Danakil (African people)
  BT Cushites
    Ethnology--Djibouti
    Ethnology--Ethiopia

Afar language *(May Subd Geog)*
  [PJ 2465]
  UF Adaiel language
    Danakil language
    Dankali language
  BT Cushitic languages
    Djibouti--Languages
  RT Saho language

Afara (African people)
  USE Afar (African people)

Afoma dialect
  USE Sanvi dialect

Afenmai language
  USE Etsako language

Affadéh dialect
  USE Afade dialect

Africa *(Not Subd Geog)*
  [DT]
  --**Archival resources** *(May Subd Geog)*
    BT Africa--Bibliography
  --**Bibliography**
    NT Africa--Archival resources
      Information storage and retrieval systems--
Africa
  --**Civilization**
    NT Afro-American art--African influences
      Art, European--African influences
      Art, French--African influences
      Arts, Brazilian--African influences
      Arts, French--African influences
      Asia--Civilization--African influences
      Brazil--Civilization--African influences
      Caribbean Area--Civilization--African
influences
      Civilization, Western--African influences
          (Continued)

UF = Used for; BT = Broader term; RT = Related term; SA = See also; NT = Narrower term

Africa
  --Civilization   *(Continued)*
   NT Colombia--Civilization--African
  influences
        Cuba--Civilization--African influences
        Ecuador--Civilization--African
  influences
        Egypt--Civilization--African
  influences
        English literature--African influences
        Europe--Civilization--African
  influences
        Greece--Civilization--African
  influences
        Haiti--Civilization--African
  influences
        Indians of North American--African
  influences
        Ireland--Civilization--African
  influences
        Jamaica--Civilization--African
  influences
        Latin America--Civilization--African
  influences
        Missions--African influences
        Popular music--Great Britain--African
  influences
        Rome--Civilization--African influences
        Trinidad and Tobago--Civilization--
  African influences
        United States--Civilization--African
  influences
        Venezuela--Civilization--African
  influences
        Virgin Islands of the United States--
  Civilization--African influences
        West Indies--Civilization--African
  influences
        West Indies, French--Civilization--
  African influences
   -- --20th century
   -- --American influences
    BT United States--Civilization
   -- --French influences
    BT France--Civilization
   -- --Jewish influences
    BT Jews--Civilization
   -- --Portuguese influences
    BT Portugal--Civilization
   -- --Western influences
    BT Civilization, Western
  --Climate
   -- --Maps
  --Colonization *(Not Subd Geog)*
  --Description and travel
   -- --To 1900

   -- --1901-1950
   -- --1951-1976
   -- --1977-
  --Drama
   USE African drama
  --Economic conditions
   [HC 800]
   -- --To 1918
   -- --1918-1945
   -- --1945-1960
   -- --1960-
  --Fiction
   USE African fiction
  --Foreign relations *(May Subd Geog)*
   -- --1945-1960
   -- --1960-
  --History
   [DT 24-DT 39]
   -- --To 1498
   -- --To 1884
   -- -- --Historiography
   -- -- --Juvenile literature
   -- --19th century
   -- --1884-1918
   -- --1884-1960
   -- --20th century
   -- --1960-
  --Industries
   NT Industrial Development Decade for Africa,
  1980-1990
  --Information storage and retrieval systems
   USE Information storage and retrieval systems--
  Africa
  --Kings and rulers
   -- --Juvenile literature
  --Languages
   RT African languages
       Afroasiatic languages
   NT Afrihili (Artificial language)
       Niger-Congo languages
       Nilo-Saharan languages
   -- --Texts
  --Literatures
   USE African literature
  --Maps
  --Poetry
   USE African poetry
  --Politics and government
   NT Africanization
       Afro-Asian politics
       Pan-Africanism
   -- --To 1945
   -- --1945-1960
   -- --1960-
  --Religion
   NT God (African religion)

(May Subd Geog) = Place names may follow the heading

--Social conditions
-- --1945-1960
-- --1960-
--Strategic aspects
  BT Military geography
--Study and teaching
  [DT 19.8]
  UF African studies

Africa, Black
  USE Africa, Sub-Saharan

Africa, Central *(Not Subd Geog)*
  [DT 348-DT 363.3]
  Here are entered works on the region of Africa that
includes what are now the Central African Republic,
Gabon, Zaire, and the Congo (Brazzaville).
  UF Central Africa
--Description and travel
--1981-
--Economic conditions
  [HC 945]
-- --1884-1960
-- --1960-
--History
  [DT 352.5-DT 353.5]
-- --To 1884
-- --1884-1960
  NT Emin Pasha Relief Expedition, 1887-
1889
--Languages
  NT Bongo-Bagirmi languages
    Central Sudanic languages
    Zande language
--Politics and government
  [DT 353]
-- --1884-1960
-- --1960-

Africa, East *(Not Subd Geog)*
  [DT 421-DT 432.5]
  Here are entered works dealing collectively with
Kenya, Uganda, and Tanzania.
  UF East Africa
--Civilization
-- --Western influences
  BT Civilization, Western
--Description and travel
-- --1951-1980
-- --1981-
--History
  [DT 430-DT 432.5]
  NT Emin Pasha Relief Expedition, 1887-
1889
-- --To 1886

--Literatures
  USE East African literature

Africa, Eastern *(Not Subd Geog)*
  [DT 365]
  Here are entered works on the area extending from Sudan
and Ethiopia to Mozambique.
  UF Eastern Africa
--Civilization
-- --Oriental influences
--Description and travel
-- --1981-
--History
  [DT 365.5-DT 365.8]
  NT Punt Region
--Languages
  NT Makonde language
    Nilo-Hamitic languages
    Nilotic languages
--Politics and government
  [DT 365.59]
-- --To 1886
-- --1886-1918
-- --1918-1960
-- --1960-

Africa, French-speaking Equatorial *(Not Subd Geog)*
  [DT 546.1-DT 546.49]
  Here are entered works dealing collectively with Central
African Republic, Chad, Congo (Brazzaville), and Gabon.
  UF Equatorial Africa, French-speaking
    French Equatorial Africa
    French speaking Equatorial Africa
--Foreign relations *(May Subd Geog)*
-- --1884-1960
-- --1960-
--History
-- --To 1884
-- --1884-1960
-- --1960-
--Politics and government
-- --1884-1960
-- --1960-

Africa, French-speaking West *(May Subd Geog)*
  [DT 521-DT 533]
  Here are entered works dealing collectively with Benin,
Burkina Faso, Guinea, Ivory Coast, Mali, Mauritania, Niger,
Senegal, and Togo.
  UF Francophone West Africa
    French-speaking West Africa
    French West Africa
    West Africa, Francophone
--Description and travel
-- --1981-   *(Continued)*

UF = Used for; BT = Broader term; RT = Related term; SA = See also; NT = Narrower term

Africa, French-speaking West   *(Continued)*
--Economic conditions
  [HC 1005]
--Foreign relations *(May Subd Geog)*
-- --1884-1960
-- --1960-
--History
  [DT 532-DT 533]
-- --To 1884
-- --1884-1960
-- --1960-
--Politics and government
-- --1884-1960
-- --1960-

Africa, German East
  USE German East Africa

Africa, German Southwest
  USE Namibia

Africa, German West
  USE Cameroon

Africa, Northeast *(Not Subd Geog)*
  [DT 367]
  Here are entered works dealing collectively with Sudan, Ethiopia, Somalia, and Djibouti.
  UF Horn of Africa
     Northeast Africa
--Foreign relations *(May Subd Geog)*
-- --1974-
--Politics and government
-- --1900-1974
-- --1974-
--Strategic aspects
  BT Military geography

Africa, Northwest *(Not Subd Geog)*
  [DT 179]
  Here are entered works on the area extending eastward from Morocco, Western Sahara, and Mauritania to include Libya and Chad.
  UF Northwest Africa

Africa, Portuguese East
  USE Mozambique

Africa, Portuguese-speaking *(Not Subd Geog)*
  [DT 591-DT 602]
  Here are entered works dealing collectively with the countries of Angola, Cape Verde, Guinea-Bissau, Mozambique, and Sao Tome and Principe.
  UF Lusophone Africa
     Portuguese Africa
     Portuguese-speaking Africa

Africa, Portuguese West
  USE Angola

Africa, South
  USE South Africa

Africa, South of the Sahara
  USE Africa, Sub-Saharan

Africa, Southern *(Not Subd Geog)*
  [DT 727-DT 747 : old class]
  [DT 1001-DT 1190 : new class]
  Here are entered works on the area south of Zaire and Tanzania. Works on the Republic of South Africa are entered under South Africa.
  UF Southern Africa
--Description and travel
-- --1960-
--Economic conditions
  [HC 900]
-- --1975-
--Fiction
  USE Southern African fiction
--Foreign relations *(May Subd Geog)*
-- --1975-
--History
  [DT 764.5-DT 779.995 : old class]
  [DT 1062-DT 1190 : new class]
-- --To 1899
-- --Mfecane period, 1816-ca. 1840
  UF Difaqane period, 1816-ca. 1840
     Lifaqane period, 1816-ca. 1840
     Mfecane period, 1816-ca. 1840
-- --1899-1975
-- --1975-
--Languages
  NT Khoikhoi language
     Khoisan languages
     Nguni languages
     San languages
     Tswana language
     Zulu language
--Literatures
  USE Southern African literature
--Poetry
  USE Southern African poetry
--Politics and government
-- --1975-
--Social conditions
-- --1975-

Africa, Southwest
  USE Namibia

(May Subd Geog) = Place names may follow the heading

Africa, Sub-Saharan (Not Subd Geog)
  [DT 348-DT 363.3]
  UF Africa, Black
      Africa, South of the Sahara
      Africa, Tropical
      Black Africa
      Sub-Sahara Africa
      Subsahara Africa
      Tropical Africa
  --Civilization
  -- --Indic influences
    BT India--Civilization
  -- --Indonesian influences
    BT Indonesia--Civilization
  --Dependency on foreign countries
  --Dependency on Great Britain
  --Description and travel
  -- --1981-
  --Economic conditions
    [HC 800]
  -- --1918-1960
  -- --1960-
  --Foreign relations (May Subd Geog)
  -- --1960
  --History
    [DT 352.5-DT 363.3]
  -- --To 1884
  -- --1884-1960
  -- --1960-
  --Military relations
  --Politics and government
  -- --1884-1960
  -- --1960-
  --Social conditions
  -- --1960-
  --Strategic aspects
    BT Military geography

Africa, Sub-Saharan, in motion pictures
  [PN 1995.9.A43]
  BT Motion pictures

Africa, Sub-Saharan mythology
  USE Mythology, Sub-Saharan African

Africa, Tropical
  USE Africa, Sub-Saharan

Africa, West (Not Subd Geog)
  [DT 470-DT 504]
  UF Slave Coast
      West Africa
      Western Africa
  --Archival resources (May Subd Geog)
    BT Africa, West--Bibliography
  --Bibliography

    NT Africa, West--Archival resources
  --Civilization
    NT Afro-American quilts--West African
influences
       France--Civilization--West African
influences
  -- --American influences
    BT United States--Civilization
  -- --Brazilian influences
    BT Brazil--Civilization
  -- --French influences
    BT France--Civilization
  -- --Western influences
    BT Civilization, Western
  --Description and travel
  -- --To 1850
  -- --1851-1950
  -- --1951-1980
  -- --1981-
  --Economic conditions
    [HC 1000]
  -- --1960-
  --Fiction
  USE West African fiction
  --History
    [DT 475-DT 476.523]
  -- --To 1884
    NT Bambara Jihad, 1852-1863
       Ghana Empire
       Sokoto Jihad, 1803-1830
       Yatenga (Kingdom)
  -- --1884-1960
  -- --1960-
  --Languages
    NT Bambara language
       Ewe language
       Fula language
       Grusi languages
       Kabre dialect
       Mande languages
       Mandekan languages
       Mandingo language
       Ngombe languages
       Songhai language
       Soninke language
       Tem language
       Uwana language
       Yoruba language
  --Literatures
  USE West African literature
  --Poetry
  USE West African poetry
  --Politics and government
  -- --To 1884
  -- --1884-1960
  -- --1960-   (Continued)

UF = Used for; BT = Broader term; RT = Related term; SA = See also; NT = Narrower term

Africa, West   *(Continued)*
--Social conditions
-- --1960-

Africa in literature
  [PN 56.3.A (General)]
  [PR 149.A37 (English literature)]
  [PQ 145.7.A35 (General French literature)]
  [PQ 307.A45 (20th century French
literature)]
  BT Literature

Africa in mass media *(May Subd Geog)*
  [P 96.A37]
  BT Mass media

Africa in motion pictures
  [PN 1995.9.A43]
  BT Motion pictures

Africa specialists
  USE Africanists

Africaanders
  USE Afrikaners

African aesthetics
  USE Aesthetics, African

African-Afro-American relations
  USE Afro-Americans--Relations with
Africans

African alien labor
  USE Alien labor, African

African American...
  USE Afro-American...

African Americans
  USE Afro-Americans

African art
  USE Art, African

African arts
  USE Arts, African

African-Asian politics
  USE Afro-Asian politics

African authors
  USE Authors, African

African children's literature

  USE Children's literature, African

African children's stories (French)
  USE Children's stories, African (French)

African cookery
  USE Cookery, African

African cooperation
  RT Pan-Africanism

African Development Bank
  [HG 3881.5.A37]
  UF A.D.B.
  BT Development banks--Africa

African drama *(Not Subd Geog)*
  [PL 8010.5]
  UF Africa--Drama
      Black drama, African
      Drama, African
  BT African literature
  NT South African drama
      Swahili drama
      Zimbabwean drama

African drama (English) *(Not Subd Geog)*
  [PR 9343 (History)]
  [PR 9347 (Collections)]
  UF English drama--African authors
  BT African literature (English)
  NT East African drama (English)
      Radio plays, African (English)
      South African drama (English)
      Zambian drama (English)
      Zimbabwean drama (English)

African drama (French) *(Not Subd Geog)*
  [PQ 3983 (History)]
  [PQ 3987 (Collections)]
  UF French drama--African authors
  BT African literature (French)
  NT Radio plays, African (French)

African English
  USE English language--Africa

African epic literature
  USE Epic literature, African

African epic poetry
  USE Epic poetry, African

African fables
  USE Fables, African

(May Subd Geog) = Place names may follow the heading

African fiction *(Not Subd Geog)*
[PL 8010.6]
UF Africa--Fiction
Black fiction, African
BT African literature
NT Somali fiction
Southern African fiction
West African fiction

African fiction **(English)** *(Not Subd Geog)*
[PR 9344 (History)]
[PR 9347.5 (Collections)]
UF English fiction--African authors
BT African literature (English)
NT Short stories, African (English)
Southern African fiction (English)
West African fiction (English)

African fiction **(French)** *(Not Subd Geog)*
[PQ 3984 (History]
[PQ 3987.5 (Collections)]
UF French fiction--African authors
BT African literature (French)
NT Children's stories, African (French)
Short stories, African (French)
West African fiction (French)

African fiction **(Portuguese)** *(Not Subd Geog)*
[PQ 9904 (History)]
[PQ 9908 (Collections)]
UF Portuguese fiction--African authors
BT African literature (Portuguese)

African folk literature
USE Folk literature, African

African folk poetry
USE Folk poetry, African

African gods
USE Gods, African

African hand piano
USE Mbira

African hymns
USE Hymns, African

African **languages**
[PL 8000-PL 8844]
SA *individual languages and groups of languages,*
e.g. Timne language; Bantu languages; and
subdivision Languages under names of African
countries, regions, etc., e.g. Nigeria--Languages
RT Africa--Languages
Afroasiatic languages

NT Blacks--Languages
Khoisan languages
Kordofanian languages
Muana language
Niger-Congo languages
Nilo-Saharan languages
--Clicks
BT Clicks (Phonetics)
--Etymology
-- --Names
NT Names, African
--Names
USE Names, African
--Tone
BT Tone (Phonetics)

African laudatory poetry
USE Laudatory poetry, African

African **literature** *(Not Subd Geog)*
[PL 8010-PL 8014]
UF Africa--Literatures
Black literature (African)
RT Authors, African
NT African drama
African fiction
African poetry
African prose literature
Bantu literature
Children's literature, African
East African literature
Epic literature, African
Equatorial Guinean literature
Ethiopian literature
Folk literature, African
Gabon literature
Kinyarwanda literature
Somali literature
Southern African literature
West African literature
Young adult literature, African
--Cataloging
USE Cataloging of African literature

African **literature (English)** *(Not Subd Geog)*
[PR 9340-PR 9347.5]
UF English literature--African authors
NT African drama (English)
African fiction (English)
African poetry (English)
African prose literature (English)
East African literature (English)
Protest literature, African (English)
Southern African literature (English)
Sudanese literature (English)
West African literature (English)

UF = Used for; BT = Broader term; RT = Related term; SA = See also; NT = Narrower term

African literature (French) *(Not Subd Geog)*
[PQ 3980-PQ 3989.2]
UF French literature--African authors
NT African drama (French)
    African fiction (French)
    African poetry (French)
    Congo (Brazzaville) literature
(French)
    Gabon literature (French)
    West African literature (French)
    Zairian literature (French)

African literature (Portuguese) *(Not Subd Geog)*
[PQ 9900-PQ 9948]
UF Portuguese literature--African authors
NT African fiction (Portuguese)
    African poetry (Portuguese)
    Angolan literature (Portuguese)
    Mozambican literature (Portuguese)
    Revolutionary literature, African
(Portuguese)
--20th century

African Mathematics Program
[QA 14.A4]
BT Mathematics--Study and teaching--
Africa, Sub-Saharan

African mythology
USE Mythology, African

African names
USE Names, African

African national characteristics
USE National characteristics, African

African National Congress
UF A.N.C.
BT Blacks--South Africa--Politics and
government
    South Africa--Politics and government-
-20th century

African newspapers
[PN 5450]
UF Newspapers, African

African periodicals
[PN 5450]
UF Periodicals, African

African philology
[PL 8000-PL 8009]
UF Philology, African

African philosophy
USE Philosophy, African

African poetry *(Not Subd Geog)*
[PL 8010.4]
UF Africa--Poetry
    Black poetry, African
BT African literature
NT Bantu poetry
    Epic poetry, African
    Ethiopian poetry
    Folk poetry, African
    Kinyarwanda poetry
    Laudatory poetry, African
    Somali poetry
    Southern African poetry
    West African poetry

African poetry (English) *(Not Subd Geog)*
[PR 9342 (History)]
[PR 9346 (Collections)]
UF English poetry--African authors
BT African literature (English)
NT East African poetry (English)
    South African poetry (English)
    West African poetry (English)
    Zambian poetry (English)
    Zimbabwean poetry (English)

African poetry (French) *(Not Subd Geog)*
[PQ 3980-PQ 3984 (History)]
[PQ 3985-PQ 3989.2 (Collections)]
UF French poetry--African authors
BT African literature (French)
NT Congo (Brazzaville) poetry (French)
    Gabon poetry (French)
    Zairian poetry (French)

African poetry (Portuguese) *(Not Subd Geog)*
[PQ 9902 (History)]
[PQ 9906-PQ 9906.5 (Collections)]
UF Portuguese poetry--African authors
BT African literature (Portuguese)
NT Angolan poetry (Portuguese)
    Mozambican poetry (Portuguese)
    Revolutionary poetry, African (Portuguese)

African political posters
USE Political posters, African

African portrait sculpture
USE Portrait sculpture, African

African portraits
USE Portraits, African

(May Subd Geog) = Place names may follow the heading

African pottery
  USE Pottery, African

African prose literature *(Not Subd Geog)*
  [PL 8010.6]
  BT African literature
  NT Ndebele prose literature (Zimbabwe)
      Tanzanian prose literature

African prose literature (English)
  [PR 9344 (History)]
  [PR 9347.5 (Collections)]
  UF English prose literature--African
authors
  BT African literature (English)
  NT South African prose literature
(English)

African protest literature (English)
  USE Protest literature, African (English)

African proverbs
  USE Proverbs, African

African publications, Acquisition of
  USE Acquisition of African publications

African radio plays (English)
  USE Radio plays, African (English)

African radio plays (French)
  USE Radio plays, African (French)

African relations
  USE Pan-Africanism

African revolutionary literature (Portuguese)
  USE Revolutionary literature, African
(Portuguese)

African revolutionary poetry (Portuguese)
  USE Revolutionary poetry, African
(Portuguese)

African school songbooks
  USE School songbooks, African

African sculpture
  USE Sculpture, African

African short stories (English)
  USE Short stories, African (English)

African short stories (French)
  USE Short stories, African (French)

African students *(May Subd Geog)*
  BT Students
  --**Foreign countries**
  BT Students, Foreign

African studies
  USE Africa--Study and teaching

African studies specialists
  USE Africanists

African women authors
  USE Women authors, African

African young adult literature
  USE Young adult literature, African

Africanders
  USE Afrikaners

Africaners
  USE Afrikaners

Africanists *(May Subd Geog)*
  [DT 19.5-DT 19.7]
  UF Africa specialists
      African studies specialists

Africanization *(May Subd Geog)*
  Here are entered works dealing with the practice by
  African nations of replacing non-African civil servants,
  businessmen, etc. with local people.
  BT Africa--Politics and government

Africans *(May Subd Geog)*
  BT Ethnology--Africa
  --**Relations with Afro-Americans**
  USE Afro-Americans--Relations with Africans
  --**United States**
  NT Afro-Americans

Africans, West
  USE West Africans

Africans in art
  [N 8232]
  BT Art

Africans in literature
  [PN 56.3.A (General literature)]
  [PR 830.A39 (English literature)]
  BT Literature

UF = Used for; BT = Broader term; RT = Related term; SA = See also; NT = Narrower term

Afrihili (Artificial language)
[PM 8063]
UF El-Afrihili (Artificial language)
BT Africa--Languages
    Language and languages

Afrikaanders
USE Afrikaners

Afrikaaners
USE Afrikaners

Afrikaans abbreviations
USE Abbreviations, Afrikaans

Afrikaans-Arabic dialect
USE Arabic-Afrikaans dialect

Afrikaans authors
USE Authors, Afrikaans

Afrikaans children's literature
USE Children's literature, Afrikaans

Afrikaans children's plays
USE Children's plays, Afrikaans

Afrikaans children's stories
USE Children's stories, Afrikaans

Afrikaans commercial correspondence
USE Commercial correspondence, Afrikaans

Afrikaans drama *(May Subd Geog)*
[PT 6520 (History)]
[PT 6565 (Collections)]
UF South African drama (Afrikaans)
BT Afrikaans literature
NT Children's plays, Afrikaans
    Radio plays, Afrikaans

Afrikaans essays *(May Subd Geog)*
[PT 6575 (Collections)]
UF South African essays (Afrikaans)
BT Afrikaans literature

Afrikaans fiction *(May Subd Geog)*
[PT 6525 (History)]
[PT 6570 (Collections)]
UF South African fiction (Afrikaans)
BT Afrikaans literature
NT Children's stories, Afrikaans

Afrikaans folk songs
USE Folk songs, Afrikaans

Afrikaans hymns
USE Hymns, Afrikaans

Afrikaans language *(May Subd Geog)*
[PF 861-PF 884]
Here are entered works on the language spoken and written by the descendents of the Dutch colonists in South Africa which gradually evolved and differentiated from the Dutch South African dialects of the earlier periods. Works on Dutch South African dialects not conforming to Dutch as spoken or written in the Netherlands are entered under Dutch language--Dialects--South Africa.
UF Afrikander language
    Cape Dutch language
BT South Africa--Languages
--Abbreviations
USE Abbreviations, Afrikaans
--Dialects *(May Subd Geog)*
-- --Arabic
USE Arabic-Afrikaans dialect

Afrikaans literature *(May Subd Geog)*
[PT 6500-PT 6593.36]
UF South African literature (Afrikaans)
RT Authors, Afrikaans
NT Afrikaans drama
    Afrikaans essays
    Afrikaans fiction
    Afrikaans poetry
    Afrikaans prose literature
    Children's literature, Afrikaans
    Quotations, Afrikaans
--20th century
--Competitions *(May Subd Geog)*
-- --South Africa
NT Hertzogprys

Afrikaans newspapers *(May Subd Geog)*
[PN 5479]
UF Newspapers, Afrikaans

Afrikaans periodicals *(May Subd Geog)*
[PN 5480]
UF Periodicals, Afrikaans

Afrikaans philology
[PF 861-PF 884]
UF Philology, Afrikaans

Afrikaans poetry *(May Subd Geog)*
[PT 6515 (History)]
[PT 6545 (Folk poetry history)]
[PT 6560 (Collections)]
UF South African poetry (Afrikaans)
BT Afrikaans literature

(May Subd Geog) = Place names may follow the heading

Afrikaans prose literature *(May Subd Geog)*
[PT 6525 (History)]
[PT 6570 (Collections)]
UF South African prose literature
(Afrikaans)
BT Afrikaans literature

Afrikaans quotations
USE Quotations, Afrikaans

Afrikaans radio plays
USE Radio plays, Afrikaans

Afrikaans satire
USE Satire, Afrikaans

Afrikaans-speaking South Africans
USE Afrikaners

Afrikaans wit and humor
[PT 6530 (History)]
[PN 6222.S (Collections)]
UF Wit and humor, Afrikaans
NT Satire, Afrikaans

Afrikander language
USE Afrikaans language

Afrikanders
USE Afrikaners

Afrikaner loyalists
[DT 777 : old class]
[DT 1896 : new class]
UF Loyalists, Afrikaner
BT South African War, 1899-1902

Afrikaner Rebellion, 1914-1915
USE South Africa--History--Rebellion,
1914-1915

Afrikaner school songbooks
USE School songbooks, Afrikaner

Afrikaner songbooks
USE Songbooks, Afrikaner

Afrikaner students *(May Subd Geog)*
UF Boer students
BT Students

Afrikaners *(May Subd Geog)*
UF Africaanders
Africanders
Africaners
Afrikaanders

UF Afrikaaners
Afrikaans-speaking South Africans
Afrikanders
Boers
South Africans, Afrikaans-speaking
BT Dutch--South Africa
Ethnology--South Africa
NT South Africa--English-Afrikaner relations
South Africa--History--Great Trek, 1836-
1840
--**Ethnic identity**
BT Ethnicity
--**Namibia**
[DT 709 : old class]
[DT 1558.A46 : new class]
--**South Africa**
[DT 888 : old class]
[DT 1768.A57 : new class]

Afro (Hair style)
USE Hairdressing of Blacks

Afro-American-African relations
USE Afro-Americans--Relations with Africans

Afro-American art *(May Subd Geog)*
[N 6538.N5]
UF Art, Afro-American
--**African influences**
BT Africa--Civilization

Afro-American colonization
USE Afro-Americans--Colonization

Afro-American quilts *(May Subd Geog)*
UF Quilts, Afro-American
--**West African influences**
BT Africa, West--Civilization

Afro-Americans *(May Subd Geog)*
[E 185]
*Here are entered works on citizens of the United States
of black African descent. Works on blacks outside of the
United States are entered under Blacks--[place].*
UF African Americans
Afro-Americans--United States
Black Americans
Colored people (United States)
Negroes (United States)
BT Africans--United States
Blacks
NT Mulattoes
--**Colonization** *(May Subd Geog)*
[E 448]
UF Afro-American colonization
Colonization by Afro-Americans   *(Continued)*

UF = Used for; BT = Broader term; RT = Related term; SA = See also; NT = Narrower term

Afro-Americans
--Colonization   *(Continued)*
-- --Africa
  NT Back to Africa movement
--Relations with Africans
  UF African-Afro-American relations
    Africans--Relations with Afro-
Americans
    Afro-American-African relations
    Blacks--Africa--Relations with Afro-
Americans
--Ghana
  [DT 510.43.A37]
--United States
  USE Afro-Americans

Afro-Asian politics
  [DS 33.3]
  UF African-Asian politics
    Asian-African politics
  BT Africa--Politics and government
    Asia--Politics and government

Afroasiatic languages
  [PJ 991-PJ 995]
  Only the African languages are listed here.
  UF Erythraic languages
    Hamito-Semitic languages
    Semito-Hamitic languages
  RT Africa--Languages
    African languages
  NT Chadic languages
    Cushitic languages
    Hamitic languages
    Omotic languages
    Proto-Afroasiatic languages
    Semitic languages

Aga (African people)
  USE Kanuri (African people)

Agala (African people)
  USE Idoma (African people)

Agau language *(May Subd Geog)*
  [PJ 2425]
  UF Agaw language
  BT Cushitic languages
  RT Bilin language
    Quara language
  NT Kemant language

Agaw language
  USE Agau language

Agibba (African people)
  USE Murle (African people)

Agiryama (African people)
  USE Giryama (African people)

Agni (African people)
  USE Anyi (African people)

Agni language
  USE Anyi language

Agolok dialect
  USE Kagoro dialect

Agona (African people) *(May Subd Geog)*
  [DT 510.43.A]
  BT Ethnology--Ghana

Agrarian question
  USE Land tenure

Agricultural assistance *(May Subd Geog)*
  Here are entered works on international aid to
agriculture given to underdeveloped areas in the form of
technical assistance.
  UF Foreign aid to agriculture
--Africa
--Africa, Sub-Saharan

Agricultural assistance, Swiss *(May Subd Geog)*
  UF Swiss agricultural assistance
--Rwanda
  NT Projet pilote forestier

Agriculture *(May Subd Geog)*
  UF Agronomy
    Farming
    Husbandry
  RT Famines
  NT Arid regions agriculture
    Dry farming
    Farms
    Forests and forestry
--Africa
  [S 472.A35]
--Africa, West
  [S 472.W4]
--Sudan
  [S 473.S]

Agronomy
  USE Agriculture

Agucho River (Ethiopia) *(Not Subd Geog)*
  BT Rivers--Ethiopia

(May Subd Geog) = Place names may follow the heading

Ague
  USE Malaria

Aguro dialect
  USE Kagoro dialect

Agwolok dialect
  USE Kagoro dialect

Agwot dialect
  USE Kagoro dialect

Ahizi language *(May Subd Geog)*
  [PL 8046.A44]
  UF Aizi language
  BT Ivory Coast--Languages
      Lagoon languages

Ahmed Sékou Touré National Archives Building
(Monrovia, Liberia)
  [CD 2373]
  UF Centre National des Archives Ahmed
Sékou Touré (Monrovia, Liberia)
  BT Archive buildings--Liberia

AIDS (Disease) *(May Subd Geog)*
  [RA 644.A25]
  UF Acquired immune deficiency syndrome
      HIV disease
  BT Tropical medicine
  --Africa

Aikwe language
  USE Nharo language

Air rescue service
  USE Search and rescue operations

Airlift of Falashas, 1984-1985
  USE Falasha Rescue, 1984-1985

Aisan language
  USE Nharo language

Aizi language
  USE Ahizi language

Aja (African people) *(May Subd Geog)*
  [DT 541.45.A33 (Benin)]
  [DT 582.45.A34 (Togo)]
  UF Adja (African people)
  BT Ethnology--Benin
      Ethnology--Nigeria
      Ethnology--Togo
      Ewe (African people)
      Fon (African people)

Aja dialect *(May Subd Geog)*
  [PL 8164.Z9A4]
  UF Adja dialect
      Adya dialect
  BT Benin--Languages
      Ewe language
      Nigeria--Languages
      Togo--Languages

Aja language (Sudan) *(May Subd Geog)*
  [PL 8046.A]
  BT Bongo-Bagirmi languages
      Sudan--Languages

Ajalli (African people)
  USE Ujari (African people)

Ajawa language
  USE Yao language

Ajibba (African people)
  USE Murle (African people)

Ajjer (African people) *(May Subd Geog)*
  [DT 283.6.A44]
  UF Adjeur (African people)
      Asgar (African people)
      Azdjer (African people)
      Azjer (African people)
      Kel Azdjer (African people)
  BT Ethnology--Algeria
      Tuaregs

Ajukru (African people)
  USE Adyukru (African people)

Ajukru language
  USE Adyukru language

Aka (African people) *(May Subd Geog)*
  [DT 546.345.A35 (Central African Republic)]
  [DT 650.A38 (Zaire)]
  UF Asua (African people)
  BT Ethnology--Central African Republic
      Ethnology--Zaire
      Mbuti (African people)

Aka folk songs (Central African Republic)
  USE Folk songs, Aka (Central African Republic)

Aka language
  USE Akan language

UF = Used for; BT = Broader term; RT = Related term; SA = See also; NT = Narrower term

Aka language (Central African Republic) *(May Subd Geog)*
  [PL 8046.A59]
  BT Bantu languages
      Central African Republic--Languages
      Pygmies--Languages

Akagera National Park (Rwanda)
  USE Parc national de la Kagera (Rwanda)

Akagera River
  USE Kagera River

Akamba (African people)
  USE Kamba (African people)

Akan (African people) *(May Subd Geog)*
  [DT 510.43.A53 (Ghana)]
  UF Twi Fante (African people)
  BT Ethnology--Ghana
      Ethnology--Ivory Coast
  RT Fanti (African people)
  NT Ashanti (African people)
 --Funeral customs and rites
  UF Funeral rites and ceremonies, Akan
(African people)
 --Kings and rulers
  NT Stools--Ghana
 --Medicine
  BT Medicine, Primitive--Ghana
      Medicine, Primitive--Ivory Coast
 --Missions *(May Subd Geog)*
  [BV 3630.A4]
  UF Missions to Akan (African people)
 --Politics and government
 --Religion
  [BL 2480.A4]
 --Rites and ceremonies

Akan art
  USE Art, Akan

Akan drama *(May Subd Geog)*
  [PL 8046.A63]
  BT Akan literature
      Ghana--Drama
      Ivory Coast--Drama

Akan ethics
  USE Ethics, Akan

Akan folk songs
  USE Folk songs, Akan

Akan goldweights
  USE Goldweights, Akan

Akan imprints *(May Subd Geog)*
  [Z 7108.A45]
  UF Imprints, Akan

Akan language *(May Subd Geog)*
  [PL 8046.A63]
  *Here are entered works dealing collectively with the
dialect of the Fanti people and the dialects of the Akuapem,
Ashanti, and related peoples who accept the name Twi. Works
limited to the dialects of the latter groups are entered
under Twi language.*
  UF Aka language
      Twi-Fanti language
  BT Ghana--Languages
      Kwa languages
  NT Fanti language
      Twi language
 --Phonology

Akan literature *(May Subd Geog)*
  [PL 8046.A635-PL 8046.A638]
  BT Ghanaian literature
      Ivory Coast--Literatures
  NT Akan drama
      Akan poetry

Akan poetry *(May Subd Geog)*
  [PL 8046.A637]
  BT Akan literature
      Ghana--Poetry
      Ivory Coast--Poetry

Akan pottery
  USE Pottery, Akan

Akan proverbs
  USE Proverbs, Akan

Akapless language
  USE Abure language

Akare language
  USE Kare language

Akarimojong language
  USE Karamojong language

Akasele (Togolese and Ghanaian people)
  USE Bassari (Togolese and Ghanaian people)

Akasha Site (Sudan)
  USE Akashah Site (Sudan)

Akashah Site (Sudan) *(Not Subd Geog)*
  [DT 159.9.A35]
  UF Akasha Site (Sudan)

(May Subd Geog) = Place names may follow the heading

BT   Sudan--Antiquities

Akela (African people)
  USE Kela (African people)

Akeroa language
  USE Toposa language

Akikuyu (African people)
  USE Kikuyu (African people)

Akimbu (African people)
  USE Kimbu (African people)

Akoose dialect (Bakossi)
  USE Bakossi dialect

Akosombo Dam *(Not Subd Geog)*
  [TC 558.G62A4]
  BT   Dams--Ghana

Akposo (African people)
  USE Kposo (African people)

Akposo language
  USE Kposo language

Akposso (African people)
  USE Kposo (African people)

Akposso language
  USE Kposo language

Akpoto (African people)
  USE Idoma (African people)

Akra language
  USE Ga language

Aksum (Kingdom) *(Not Subd Geog)*
  [DT 390.A88]
  UF   Axum (Kingdom)
  BT   Ethiopia--History

Aku language
  USE Yoruba language

Aku language (Creole)
  USE Krio language

Akuapem language
  USE Twi language

Akwapim language
  USE Twi language

Akye (African people)
  USE Attie (African people)

Akye language
  USE Attie language

Ala (African people)
  USE Wala (African people)

Aladian (African people)
  USE Alagya (African people)

Aladian language *(May Subd Geog)*
  [PL 8046.A725]
  UF   Aladya language
       Aladyan language
       Alagia language
       Alagian language
       Alagya language
       Alladian language
       Alladyan language
  BT   Ivory Coast--Languages
       Lagoon languages

Aladya language
  USE Aladian language

Aladyan language
  USE Aladian language

Alagia language
  USE Aladian language

Alagian language
  USE Aladian language

Alagya (African people) *(May Subd Geog)*
  [DT 545.45.A]
  UF   Aladian (African people)
       Alladian (African people)
       Aragya (African people)
       Jack-Jack (African people)
  BT   Ethnology--Ivory Coast

Alagya language
  USE Aladian language

Alam El Halfa, Battle of, 1942
  USE Alam Halfa, Battle of, 1942

Alam Halfa, Battle of, 1942
  [D 766.9]
  UF   Alam El Halfa, Battle of, 1942
       Battle of Alam Halfa (Sudan), 1942
  BT   World War, 1939-1945--Campaigns--Sudan

UF = Used for; BT = Broader term; RT = Related term; SA = See also; NT = Narrower term

Alante (African people)
  USE Balanta (African people)

Alantika Mountains (Nigeria and Cameroon) *(Not Subd Geog)*
  UF Hossere-Alantika (Nigeria and
Cameroon)
      Monts Alantika (Nigeria and Cameroon)
  BT Mountains--Cameroon
      Mountains--Nigeria

Albany settlers (South Africa)
  USE British settlers of 1820 (South
Africa)

Albert Falls Public Resort (South Africa) *(Not Subd Geog)*
  BT Resorts--South Africa

Aldabra Island (Seychelles) *(Not Subd Geog)*
  [DT 469.S49A]
  BT Islands--Seychelles
      Seychelles

Alendu (African people)
  USE Lendu (African people)

Alexandra Nile River
  USE Kagera River

Alien labor *(May Subd Geog)*
  *Here are entered works on nationals of one country
working in another country.*
  UF Alien workers
      Foreign labor
      Foreign workers
      Guest workers
      Immigrant labor

Alien labor, African *(May Subd Geog)*
  UF African alien labor

Alien labor, Botswana *(May Subd Geog)*
  UF Botswana alien labor

Alien labor, Mozambican *(May Subd Geog)*
  UF Mozambican alien labor

Alien labor, Senegalese *(May Subd Geog)*
  UF Senegalese alien labor

Alien labor, Sudanese *(May Subd Geog)*
  UF Sudanese alien labor

Alien labor, Swazi *(May Subd Geog)*
  UF Swazi alien labor

Alien workers
  USE Alien labor

Alladian (African people)
  USE Alagya (African people)

Alladian language
  USE Aladian language

Alladyan language
  USE Aladian language

Almanacs
  UF Almanacs--Periodicals
      Annuals
      Facts, Miscellanous
      Miscellanous facts
  --Periodicals
  USE Almanacs

Almanacs, South African *(May Subd Geog)*
  [AY 1200-AY 1209]
  UF South African almanacs

Alomwe (African people)
  USE Lomwe (African people)

Aloro language
  USE Alur language

Altars, Fon *(May Subd Geog)*
  [NK 8289.6.D3 (Ironwork)]
  UF Fon altars

Alua language
  USE Alur language

Alulu language
  USE Alur language

Alunda (African people)
  USE Lunda, Northern (African people)

Alur (African people) *(May Subd Geog)*
  [DT 650.A48 (Zaire)]
  UF Luri (African people)
  BT Ethnology--Uganda
      Ethnology--Zaire
      Luo (African people)
      Nilo-Hamitic tribes

Alur language *(May Subd Geog)*
  [PL 8046.A73]
  UF Aloro language
      Alua language

(May Subd Geog) = Place names may follow the heading

UF   Alulu language
     Aluru language
     Dho Alur language
     Jo Alur language
     Lur language
     Luri language
BT   Nilotic languages
     Uganda--Languages
     Zaire--Languages

Aluru language
USE Alur language

Amaa (African people) *(May Subd Geog)*
[DT 155.2.A53]
BT   Ethnology--Sudan

Amabaca (African people)
USE Bhaca (African people)

Amadi language
USE Ma language

Amafengo (African people)
USE Fingo (African people)

Amafingo (African people)
USE Fingo (African people)

Amañarinya language
USE Amharic language

Amahlubi (African people)
USE Hlubi (African people)

Amampa (African people)
USE Sherbro (African people)

Amampa language
USE Sherbro language

Amanarinya (African people)
USE Amhara (African people)

Amanaya language
USE Nzima language

Amandebele (African people)
USE Ndebele (African people)

Amangbetu (African people)
USE Mangbetu (African people)

Amapondo (African people)
USE Pondo (African people)

Amaqaba (African people)
USE Qaba (African people)

Amaqwathi (African people)
USE Qaba (African people)

Amar (African people)
USE Hamar (African people)

Amar Koke (African people)
USE Hamar (African people)

Amarcocche (African people)
USE Hamar (African people)

Amarigna language
USE Amharic language

Amarinnya (African people)
USE Amhara (African people)

Amarinya (African people)
USE Amhara (African people)

Amarinya language
USE Amharic language

Amaawani (African people)
USE Swazi (African people)

Amatembu (African people)
USE Tembu (African people)

Amatola River (South Africa) *(Not Subd Geog)*
BT   Rivers--South Africa

Amaxosa (African people)
USE Xhosa (African people)

Amaya River (Kenya) *(Not Subd Geog)*
BT   Rivers--Kenya

Amazulu (African people)
USE Zulu (African people)

Amba (African people)
USE Baamba (African people)

Ambete (African people)
USE Mbete (African people)

Ambili language
USE Birri language

Ambo (Angolan and Namibian people)
USE Ovambo (African people)

UF = Used for; BT = Broader term; RT = Related term; SA = See also; NT = Narrower term

Ambo (Zambia) folk songs
  USE Folk songs, Ambo (Zambia)

Ambo (Zambian people) *(May Subd Geog)*
  [DT 963.42 : old class]
  [DT 3058.A63 : new class]
  UF Kambonsenga (Zambian people)
  BT Ethnology--Zambia
      Lala (African people)

Ambo dialect (Zambia) *(May Subd Geog)*
  [PL 8430.L3595A]
  BT Lala language
      Zambia--Languages

Ambo language (Southwest Africa and Angola)
  USE Kuanyama language

Amboseli Game Reserve (Kenya)
  USE Amboseli National Park (Kenya)

Amboseli National Park (Kenya) *(Not Subd Geog)*
  UF Amboseli Game Reserve (Kenya)
      Amboseli National Reserve (Kenya)
      Masai Amboseli Game Reserve (Kenya)
  BT National parks and reserves--Kenya

Amboseli National Reserve (Kenya)
  USE Amboseli National Park (Kenya)

Ambu dialect
  USE Annobon dialect

Ambundu (African people)
  USE Mbundu (African people)

Ambunu (African people)
  USE Bunda (African people)

Ambuun (African people)
  USE Bunda (African people)

American aborigines
  USE Indians of North America

American economic sanctions
  USE Economic sanctions, American

American Indians
  USE Indians of North America

Amhara (African people) *(May Subd Geog)*
  [DT 380.4.A43]
  UF Amanarinya (African people)
      Amarinnya (African people)

  UF Amarinya (African people)
      Amharinya (African people)
      Kuchumba (African people)
  BT Ethiopians
      Ethnology--Ethiopia

Amharic essays *(May Subd Geog)*
  [PJ 9268 (Collections)]
  BT Amharic literature

Amharic folk poetry
  USE Folk poetry, Amharic

Amharic language *(May Subd Geog)*
  [PJ 9201-PJ 9250]
  UF Abyssinian language
      Amaharinya language
      Amarigna language
      Amarinya language
      Amharinya language
      Ethiopian language
  BT Ethiopian languages
  --Names
  USE Names, Amharic

Amharic literature *(May Subd Geog)*
  [PJ 9260-PJ 9269]
  BT Ethiopian literature
  NT Amharic essays
      Amharic poetry

Amharic manuscripts
  USE Manuscripts, Amharic

Amharic names
  USE Names, Amharic

Amharic poetry *(May Subd Geog)*
  [PJ 9262 (History)]
  [PJ 9266 (Collections)]
  BT Amharic literature
  NT Folk poetry, Amharic

Amharic wit and humor *(May Subd Geog)*
  [PJ 9264 (History)]
  [PN 6222.E (Collections)]
  UF Wit and humor, Amharic

Amharinya (African people)
  USE Amhara (African people)

Amharinya language
  USE Amharic language

Ammar (African people)
  USE Hamar (African people)

(May Subd Geog) = Place names may follow the heading

Amput (African people)
  USE Mputu (African people)

Anambra River (Nigeria) *(Not Subd Geog)*
  BT Rivers--Nigeria

Anang (African people) *(May Subd Geog)*
  [DT 515.45.A52]
  UF Annang (African people)
  BT Ethnology--Nigeria
      Ibibio (African people)

Ananse (Legendary character)
  USE Anansi (Legendary character)

Anansi (Legendary character)
  UF Ananse (Legendary character)
      Annancy (Legendary character)
      Aunt Nancy (Legendary character)
      Brer Anansi (Legendary character)
      Gizo (Legendary character)
      Miss Nancy (Legendary character)
      Nanse (Legendary character)
      Nansi (Legendary character)
      Nanzi (Legendary character)
  BT Folklore--Africa, West
      Legends--Africa, West
      Spiders--Folklore
      Trickster--Africa, West

Ancient Roman Empire
  USE Rome

Andembu (African people)
  USE Ndembu (African people)

Ando (African people) *(May Subd Geog)*
  [DT 545.45.A53]
  UF Ano (African people)
      Anon (African people)
  BT Ethnology--Ivory Coast
  --Medicine
  BT Medicine, Primitive--Ivory Coast

Andone language
  USE Obolo language

Andoni language
  USE Obolo language

Andonni language
  USE Obolo language

Andorobo (African people)
  USE Dorobo (African people)

Androy (Madagascar : Region) *(Not Subd Geog)*
  [DT 469.M37A53]

Anga language (Ghana)
  USE Hanga language (Ghana)

Angas (African people) *(May Subd Geog)*
  [DT 515.45.A53]
  UF Karang (African people)
      Kerang (African people)
      Ngas (African people)
  BT Ethnology--Nigeria
  --Kinship

Angas language *(May Subd Geog)*
  [PL 8047]
  UF Angass language
      Karan language
      Karang language (Nigeria)
  BT Chadic languages
      Nigeria--Languages
  RT Hausa language
      Ron language

Angass language
  USE Angas language

Anglo (African people)
  USE Anlo (African people)

Anglo-Boer War, 1899-1902
  USE South African War, 1899-1902

Anglo-Egyptian Sudan
  USE Sudan

Anglo-Zulu War, 1879
  USE Zulu War, 1879

Angola *(Not Subd Geog)*
  [DT 611-DT 611.9 : old class]
  [DT 1251-DT 1465 : new class]
  UF Africa, Portuguese West
      People's Republic of Angola
      Portuguese West Africa
      West Africa, Portuguese
  --Civilization
  -- --Brazilian influences
  BT Brazil--Civilization
  -- --Portuguese influences
  BT Portugal--Civilization
  --Description and travel
  -- --1981-   *(Continued)*

UF = Used for; BT = Broader term; RT = Related term; SA = See also; NT = Narrower term

Angola   *(Continued)*
 --Economic conditions
  [HC 950]
 -- --1975-
 --Foreign relations *(May Subd Geog)*
 -- --To 1975
 -- --1975-
 --History
 -- --To 1482
 -- --1482-1648
 -- --1648-1885
 -- --1885-1961
   NT Bailundo War, Angola, 1902
 -- --Revolution, 1961-1975
   [DT 611.75 : old class]
   [DT 1398-DT 1405 : new class]
 -- --Civil War, 1975-
   [DT 611.8 : old class]
   [DT 1428 : new class]
   UF Civil war--Angola
 -- -- --Participation, Cuban
   BT Cubans--Angola
 -- --South African Invasion, 1975-1976
   UF South African Invasion of Angola,
1975-1976
   BT South Africa--History, Military
 -- --South African Incursions, 1978-
   UF South African Incursions into Angola,
1978-
   BT South Africa--History--1961-
 --Languages
   NT Chokwe language
       Diriku language
       Ganguela language
       Herero language
       Kimbundu language
       Kongo language
       Kuanyama language
       Kwangali language
       Lucazi language
       Mussele dialect
       Ndonga language
       Nyaneka language
       Ruund language
       Solongo dialect
       Umbundu language
       Vili language
       !Xu language
       Yaka language (Zaire and Angola)
       Zoombo dialect
 --Literatures
   USE Angolan literature
 --Massacre, 1961
   USE Massacres--Angola
 --Native races
   USE Indigenous peoples--Angola

 --Politics and government
 -- --1855-1961
 -- --1961-1975
 -- --1975-
   NT Zaire--History--Shaba Invasion, 1977
       Zaire--History--Shaba Uprising, 1978

Angola langauge
   USE Kimbundu language

Angolan literature *(May Subd Geog)*
   [PL 8014.A]
   UF Angola--Literatures
   NT Umbundu literature

Angolan literature (Portuguese) *(May Subd Geog)*
   [PQ 9920-PQ 9929]
   UF Portuguese literature--Angolan authors
   BT African literature (Portuguese)
   NT Angolan poetry (Portuguese)

Angolan poetry (Portuguese) *(May Subd Geog)*
   [PQ 9922 (History)]
   [PQ 9926-PQ 9926.5 (Collections)]
   UF Portuguese poetry--Angolan authors
   BT African poetry (Portuguese)
       Angolan literature (Portuguese)

Angoni (African people)
   USE Ngoni (African people)

Angónia Highlands (Mozambique) *(Not Subd Geog)*
   BT Mountains--Mozambique

Animism *(May Subd Geog)*
   BT Religion, Primitive
 --West Africa
   [BL 2465]

Ankobra River (Ghana) *(Not Subd Geog)*
   BT Rivers--Ghana

Anlo (African people) *(May Subd Geog)*
   [DT 582.45.A (Togo)]
   UF Anglo (African people)
   BT Ethnology--Ghana
       Ethnology--Togo
 --Rites and ceremonies
 --Religion
   [BL 2480.A5]

Annancy (Legendary character)
   USE Anansi (Legendary character)

Annang (African people)
   USE Anang (African people)

(May Subd Geog) = Place names may follow the heading

Annobon dialect *(May Subd Geog)*
　　[PM 7849.A5]
　　UF　Ambu dialect
　　BT　Creole dialects, Portuguese--
Equatorial Guinea
　　　　Equatorial Guinea--Languages

Annuals
　　USE　Almanacs

Ano (African people)
　　USE　Ando (African people)

Anon (African people)
　　USE　Ando (African people)

Antaimoro (Malagasy people)
　　USE　Taimoro (Malagaly people)

Antaisaka dialect *(May Subd Geog)*
　　[PL 5379]
　　UF　Antesaka dialect
　　BT　Malagasy language

Antaiva (Malagasy people)
　　USE　Bezanozano (Malagasy people)

Antakay (Malagasy people)
　　USE　Bezanozano (Malagasy people)

Antamorona (Malagasy people)
　　USE　Taimoro (Malagasy people)

Antamuro (Malagasy people)
　　USE　Taimoro (Malagasy people)

Antanala (Malagasy people)
　　USE　Tanala (Malagasy people)

Antanandro (Malagasy people)
　　USE　Antandroy (Malagasy people)

Antandroy (Malagasy people) *(May Subd Geog)*
　　[DT 469.M777A58]
　　UF　Antanandro (Malagasy people)
　　　　Tandroy (Malagasy people)
　　　　Tandruy (Malagasy people)
　　BT　Ethnology--Madagascar

Antandroy dialect *(May Subd Geog)*
　　[PL 5379]
　　BT　Malagasy language

Antandroy folk songs
　　USE　Folk songs, Antandroy

Antanka (Malagasy people)
　　USE　Bezanozano (Malagasy people)

Anteimoro (Malagasy people)
　　USE　Taimoro (Malagasy people)

Antemoro (Malagasy people)
　　USE　Taimoro (Malagasy people)

Antesaka dialect
　　USE　Antaisaka dialect

Anthropology *(May Subd Geog)*
　　[GN]
　　SA　*names of races, tribes, etc., e.g.* Black race;
Igbo (African people); *and subdivision* Race
relations *under names of countries, e.g.* South Africa--
Race relations
　　NT　Acculturation
　　　　Archaeology
　　　　Ethnology
　　　　Ethnopsychology
　　　　Language and languages
　　　　National characteristics
　　　　Race
　　　　Women

Anti-apartheid movements *(May Subd Geog)*
　　UF　Movements against apartheid
　　BT　Civil rights movements
　　RT　Apartheid
　--**South Africa**
　　[DT 737 : old class]
　　[DT 1757 : new class]
　　NT　South Africa--History--Soweto Uprising,
1976

Anti-colonialism
　　USE　Anti-imperialist movements
　　　　Colonies

Anti-imperialist movements *(May Subd Geog)*
　　Here are entered works discussing collectively
organizations and movements, whose stated purpose is to work
against what they regard as imperialism, i.e. the policy or
practice of a country extending power over other states or
areas of the world, often by annexing territory.
　　UF　Anti-colonialism
　　RT　National liberation movements
　--**Africa**
　--**Angola**
　--**Benin**

Antilles
　　USE　West Indies

UF = Used for; BT = Broader term; RT = Related term; SA = See also; NT = Narrower term

Antilles, French
  USE West Indies, French

Antilles, Greater
  USE West Indies

Antimerina (Malagasy people)
  USE Merina (Malagasy people)

Antiquities, Prehistoric
  USE Archaeology
       Man, Prehistoric

Antislavery
  USE Slavery

Anuak (African people) *(May Subd Geog)*
  [DT 155.2.A68]
  UF Anwak (African people)
      Anyuak (African people)
      Anywak (African people)
      Anywaq (African people)
      Dho Anywaa (African people)
      Jambo (African people)
      Nuro (African people)
      Yambo (African people)
  BT Ethnology--Sudan
      Nilotic tribes

Anuak language *(May Subd Geog)*
  [PL 8047.3.A57]
  UF Yambo language
  BT Ethiopia--Languages
      Nilotic languages
      Sudan--Languages

Anufo (African people)
  USE Chokossi (African people)

Anufo dialect *(May Subd Geog)*
  [PL 8047.3.A695]
  UF Chakosi dialect
      Chokosi dialect
  BT Kwa languages
      Togo--Languages

Anufo dialect (Ivory Coast)
  USE Brissa language

Anum dialect
  USE Gwa dialect (Ghana)

Anwak (African people)
  USE Anuak (African people)

Anyang (African people)
  USE Nyang (African people)

Anyang language *(May Subd Geog)*
  [PL 8024.1.A58]
  UF Banyangi language
      Dényá language
      Kenyang language
      Nyang language
  BT Cameroon--Languages
      Mamfe Bantu languages

Anyi (African people) *(May Subd Geog)*
  [DT 545.45.A58]
  UF Agni (African people)
  BT Ethnology--Ivory Coast

Anyi language *(May Subd Geog)*
  [PL 8047.3.A6]
  UF Agni language
  BT Kwa languages
      Ivory Coast--Languages
  NT Baoulé language
      Brissa language
      Sanvi dialect

Anyuak (African people)
  USE Anuak (African people)

Anywak (African people)
  USE Anuak (African people)

Anywaq (African people)
  USE Anuak (African people)

Aoudaghost (City) *(Not Subd Geog)*
  [DT 554.9.A68]
  UF Tegdaoust (Mauritania)
  BT Cities and towns, Ruined, extinct, etc.--
Mauritania
      Mauritania--Antiquities

Aowin language
  USE Brissa language

Apartheid *(May Subd Geog)*
  Here are entered works on the political, economic and
  social policies of the government of South Africa designed
  to keep racial groups in South Africa and Namibia separated
  UF Separate development (Race relations)
  BT Segregation
  RT Anti-apartheid movements
  --**Religious aspects**
  -- --**Buddhism [Christianity, etc.]**

(May Subd Geog) = Place names may follow the heading

--Namibia
  [DT 709 : old class]
  [DT 1556 : new class]
  UF Blacks--Namibia--Segregation
      Segegation--Namibia
--South Africa
  [DT 763 : old class]
  [DT 1757 : new class]
  UF Blacks--South Africa--Segregation
      Segregation--South Africa

Apende (African people)
  USE Pende (African people)

Apindji (African people)
  USE Mitsogho (African people)

Apindji language
  USE Tsogo language

Apono language
  USE Shira language

Applied arts
  USE Decorative arts

Ará Orun (Cult)
  USE Egúngún (Cult)

Arabic-Afrikaans dialect
  [PJ 6901.S68]
  UF Afrikaans-Arabic dialect
      Afrikaans language--Dialects--Arabic
      Arabic language--Dialects--South
Africa

Arabic Creole dialects
  USE Creole dialects, Arabic

Arabic language (May Subd Geog)
  --Dialects (May Subd Geog)
  -- --South Africa
    USE Arabic-Afrikaans dialect

Arabs (May Subd Geog)
  --Africa
    [DT 16.A]
  --Sudan
    [DT 155.2.A78]

Aragya (African people)
  USE Alagya (African people)

Ararge language
  USE Harari language

Arawa (African people)
  USE Mawri (African people)

Arbora language
  USE Arbore language

Arbore language (May Subd Geog)
  [PJ 2521]
  UF Abora language
      Erbore language
      Irbore language
  BT Cushitic languages

Arboretums (May Subd Geog)
  BT Forest reserves
  --Ivory Coast
    NT Parc National du Banco (Ivory Coast)

Archaeology (May Subd Geog)
  UF Antiquities, Prehistoric
      Archeology
      Paleoethnography
      Prehistoric antiquities
      Prehistory
      Ruins
  BT Anthropology
      History
  RT Stone age
  SA subdivision Antiquities under names of countries,
cities, etc., and under individual ethnic groups, e.g.
Ethiopia--Antiquities; Sao (Chad people)--
Antiquities
  NT Art, Primitive
      Man, Prehistoric

Archeology
  USE Archaeology

Architecture, Fang (May Subd Geog)
  [NA 1598]
  UF Fang architecture

Architecture, Gun (May Subd Geog)
  [NA 1599.D3]
  UF Gun architecture

Architecture, Hausa (May Subd Geog)
  [NA 1599.N5]
  UF Hausa architecture

Archive buildings (May Subd Geog)
  UF Buildings, Archive
  --Liberia
    NT Ahmed Sékou Touré National Archives
Building (Monrovia, Liberia)

UF = Used for; BT = Broader term; RT = Related term; SA = See also; NT = Narrower term

Argobba language *(May Subd Geog)*
  [PJ 9280]
  UF Argobbinya language
  BT Ethiopian languages

Argobbinya language
  USE Argobba language

Arguin Island (Mauritania) *(Not Subd Geog)*
  [DT 554.9.A73]
  UF Ile d'Arguin (Mauritania)
  BT Islands--Mauritania
      Mauritania

Ari (African people)
  USE Abidji (African people)

Ari language (Ivory Coast)
  USE Abidji language

Ariaal (African people) *(May Subd Geog)*
  [DT 433.545.A75]
  BT Ethnology--Kenya
  --Domestic animals

Arid regions *(May Subd Geog)*
  UF Arid zones
      Semiarid regions
  NT Deserts
  --Sudan
  [GB 618.88.S]
  NT Butana (Sudan)

Arid regions agriculture *(May Subd Geog)*
  UF Dryland farming
  BT Agriculture
  NT Dry farming
  --Africa
  [S 616.A44]
  --Africa, Sub-Saharan
  [S 616.A44]

Arid zones
  USE Arid regions

Aridization of land
  USE Desertification

Arimi (African people)
  USE Nyaturu (African people)

Arindrano (Madagascar : Region) *(Not Subd Geog)*
  [DT 469.M37A]

Arma (African people)
  USE Ruma (African people)

Art *(May Subd Geog)*
    Here are entered general works on the visual arts.
    Works on the arts in general, including the visual arts,
    literature and the performing arts are entered under Arts.
  UF Art, Visual
      Arts, Fine
      Arts, Visual
      Fine arts
      Visual arts
  BT Arts
  RT Aesthetics
  NT Africans in art
      Artists
      Blacks in art
      Decoration and ornament
      Decorative arts
      Folk art
      Portraits
      Prints
      Sculpture

Art, African *(May Subd Geog)*
  [N 7380]
  UF African art
  NT Art, Black
      Europeans in African art
  --Portuguese influences
  BT Portugal--Civilization

Art, Afro-American
  USE Afro-American art

Art, Akan *(May Subd Geog)*
  [N 7399.G52A]
  UF Akan art

Art, Ashanti *(May Subd Geog)*
  [N 7399.G52A]
  UF Ashanti art

Art, Bamun *(May Subd Geog)*
  [N 7399.C32B]
  UF Bamun art

Art, Benin *(May Subd Geog)*
  [N 7399.D3]
  UF Benin art

Art, Bijago *(May Subd Geog)*
  [N 7399.P62B]
  UF Bijago art

Art, Bini *(May Subd Geog)*
  [N 7399.N52B45]
  UF Bini art

(May Subd Geog) = Place names may follow the heading

Art, Black *(May Subd Geog)*
  [N 7391.65]
  UF Black art
  BT Art, African
--Zaire
  [N 7399.C6]

Art, Burkinabe *(May Subd Geog)*
  [N 7399.U6]
  UF Burkinabe art

Art, Cameroon *(May Subd Geog)*
  [N 7399.C3]
  UF Cameroon art

Art, Chokwe *(May Subd Coog)*
  [N 7399.A52C]
  UF Chokwe art

Art, Dan *(May Subd Geog)*
  [N 7399.I82D]
  UF Dan art

Art, Decorative
  USE Decoration and ornament

Art, Dogon *(May Subd Geog)*
  [N 7399.M22D]
  UF Dogon art

Art, East African
  [N 7397]
  UF East African art

Art, Ethiopian *(May Subd Geog)*
  [N 7386]
  UF Ethiopian art
  NT Illumination of books and manuscripts,
Ethiopian

Art, European
  UF European art
--African influences
  BT Africa--Civilization

Art, Fali *(May Subd Geog)*
  [N 7399.C32F]
  UF Fali art

Art, Fang *(May Subd Geog)*
  [N 7399.E682F]
  UF Fang art

Art, Folk
  USE Folk art

Art, Fon *(May Subd Geog)*
  [N 7399.D32F]
  UF Fon art

Art, French *(May Subd Geog)*
  UF French art
--African influences
  BT Africa--Civilization

Art, Gabon *(May Subd Geog)*
  [N 7399.G25]
  UF Gabon art

Art, Ghanaian *(May Subd Geog)*
  [N 7399.G5]
  UF Ghanaian art

Art, Hausa *(May Subd Geog)*
  [N 7399.N52H]
  UF Hausa art

Art, Hemba *(May Subd Geog)*
  [N 7399.C62H]
  UF Hemba art

Art, Hima *(May Subd Geog)*
  [N 7397.6.U]
  UF Hima art

Art, Igbo *(May Subd Geog)*
  [N7399.N52I]
  UF Igbo art

Art, Kenyan *(May Subd Geog)*
  [N 7397.6.K4]
  UF Kenyan art

Art, Kom *(May Subd Geog)*
  [N 7399.C32K]
  UF Kom art

Art, Kotoko *(May Subd Geog)*
  [N 7399.C32K]
  UF Kotoko art

Art, Liberian *(May Subd Geog)*
  [N 7399.L4]
  UF Liberian art

Art, LoWiili *(May Subd Geog)*
  [N 7399.U652L]
  UF LoWiili art

Art, Malagasy *(May Subd Geog)*
  [N 7397.6.M3]
  UF Malagasy art

UF = Used for; BT = Broader term; RT = Related term; SA = See also; NT = Narrower term

Art, Mambila *(May Subd Geog)*
[N 7399.N52M35]
UF Mambila art

Art, Mangbetu *(May Subd Geog)*
[N 7399.C62M]
UF Mangbetu art

Art, Mbuti *(May Subd Geog)*
[N 7399.C62M]
UF Mbuti art

Art, Mende *(May Subd Geog)*
[N 7399.S52M]
UF Mende art

Art, Mitsogho *(May Subd Geog)*
[N 7399.G252.M57]
UF Mitsogho art

Art, Namibian *(May Subd Geog)*
[N 7394.N3]
UF Namibian art

Art, Ndebele *(May Subd Geog)*
[N 7394.T732N]
UF Ndebele art

Art, Nigerian *(May Subd Geog)*
[N 7399.N5]
UF Nigerian art

Art, Nuba *(May Subd Geog)*
[N 7397.6.S732N]
UF Nuba art

Art, Peasant
USE Folk art

Art, Pende *(May Subd Geog)*
[N 7399.C62P]
UF Pende art

Art, Popular
USE Folk art

Art, Primitive *(May Subd Geog)*
UF Primitive art
BT Archaeology
     Ethnology
--Equatorial Guinea
[N 7399.E68]
--Mali
[N 7399.M3]
--Nigeria
[N 7399.N5]

--South Africa
-- --Transvaal
[N 7394.T73]

Art, Réunion *(May Subd Geog)*
[N 7399.5.R48]
UF Réunion art

Art, Rundi *(May Subd Geog)*
[N 7397.6.B82R]
UF Rundi art

Art, Sakalava *(May Subd Geog)*
[N 7397.6.M32S]
UF Sakalava art

Art, San *(May Subd Geog)*
[N 7391.7]
UF San art

Art, Sao *(May Subd Geog)*
[N 7399.C52S]
UF Sao art

Art, Senegalese *(May Subd Geog)*
[N 7399.S4]
UF Senegalese art

Art, Senufo *(May Subd Geog)*
[N 7399.I82S]
UF Senufo art

Art, Songe *(May Subd Geog)*
[N 7399.C62S]
UF Songe art

Art, South African *(May Subd Geog)*
[N 7392]
UF South African art

Art, Tabwa *(May Subd Geog)*
[N 7397.6.T32T]
UF Tabwa art

Art, Taveta *(May Subd Geog)*
[N 7397.6.K42T]
UF Taveta art

Art, Visual
USE Art

Art, Yoruba *(May Subd Geog)*
[N 7399.N52Y6]
UF Yoruba art

(May Subd Geog) = Place names may follow the heading

Art, Zairian (May Subd Geog)
  [N 7399.C6]
  UF Zairian art

Art, Zambian (May Subd Geog)
  [N 7396.6.Z3]
  UF Zambian art

Art, Zande (May Subd Geog)
  [N 7399.C62Z]
  UF Zande art

Art, Zimbabwean (May Subd Geog)
  [N 7396.6.R5]
  UF Zimbabwean art

Art, Zulu (May Subd Geog)
  [N 7396.Z]
  UF Zulu art

Art and race
  UF Race and art
  BT Ethnopsychology
      Race

Art industries and trade
  USE Decorative arts

Artificial lakes
  USE Reservoirs

Artificial weather control
  USE Weather control

Artists (May Subd Geog)
  BT Art
      Arts
  NT Actors
      Authors
      Musicians

Artists, Black (May Subd Geog)
  [N 8356.B55 (Art)]
  [NX 164.B55 (Arts)]
  UF Black artists
  --Africa
  --Africa, Sub-Saharan

Arts (May Subd Geog)
  Here are entered works on the arts in general,
including the visual arts, literature, and the
performing arts. General works on the visual arts are
entered under Art.
  UF Arts, Fine
      Fine arts

NT Art
    Artists
    Performing arts

Arts, African (May Subd Geog)
  [NX 587 (Africa)]
  [NX 588.75 (Sub-Saharan Africa)]
  UF African arts

Arts, Applied
  USE Decorative arts

Arts, Black (May Subd Geog)
  [NX 164.B55]
  UF Black arts
  --French influences
    BT France--Civilization

Arts, Brazilian (May Subd Geog)
  UF Brazilian arts
  --African influences
    BT Africa--Civilization

Arts, Congo (Brazzaville) (May Subd Geog)
  [NX 589.6.C7]
  UF Congo (Brazzaville) arts

Arts, Decorative
  USE Decoration and ornament
       Decorative arts

Arts, Fang (May Subd Geog)
  [NX 589.6.G252.F36]
  UF Fang arts

Arts, Fine
  USE Art
       Arts

Arts, French (May Subd Geog)
  UF French arts
  --African influences
    BT Africa--Civilization

Arts, Ghanaian (May Subd Geog)
  [NX 589.6.G5]
  UF Ghanaian arts

Arts, Igbo (May Subd Geog)
  [NX 589.6.N52I34]
  UF Igbo arts

Arts, Liberian (May Subd Geog)
  [NX 589.6.L5]
  UF Liberian arts

UF = Used for; BT = Broader term; RT = Related term; SA = See also; NT = Narrower term

Arts, Mende *(May Subd Geog)*
  [NX 589.6.S52M]
  UF Mende arts

Arts, Minor
  USE Decorative arts

Arts, Namibian *(May Subd Geog)*
  [NX 589.6.S6]
  UF Namibian arts

Arts, Primitive *(May Subd Geog)*
  UF Primitive arts
  BT Ethnology
 --**Gabon**
  [NX 589.6.G25]
 --**Sierra Leone**
  [NX 589.6.S5]

Arts, South African *(May Subd Geog)*
  [NX 589.8.S6]
  UF South African arts

Arts, Visual
  USE Art

Arts, Yoruba *(May Subd Geog)*
  [NX 589.6.N52Y]
  UF Yoruba arts

Arts, Zairian *(May Subd Geog)*
  [NX 589.8.C6]
  UF Zairian arts

Aruânqua River (Zambia and Mozambique)
  USE Luangwa River (Zambia and Mozambique)

Arund (African people)
  USE Lunda, Northern (African people)

Arusha (African people) *(May Subd Geog)*
  [DT 443.3.A]
  BT Ethnology--Kenya
      Ethnology--Tanzania
      Masai (African people)

Arusha law
  USE Law, Arusha

Asango language
  USE Shira language

Asante (Kingdom)
  USE Ashanti (Kingdom)

Asante (African people)
  USE Ashanti (African people)

Asante language
  USE Twi language

Asanti (African people)
  USE Ashanti (African people)

Asgar (African people)
  USE Ajjer (African people)

Ashango (African people)
  USE Shira (African people)

Ashango language
  USE Shira language

Ashante Twi (African people)
  USE Ashanti (African people)

Ashantee (African people)
  USE Ashanti (African people)

Ashanti (African people) *(May Subd Geog)*
  [DT 507]
  UF Achanti (African people)
      Asante (African people)
      Asanti (African people)
      Ashante Twi (African people)
      Ashantee (African people)
  BT Akan (African people)
      Ethnology--Ghana
 --**History**
  NT Ashanti (Kingdom)
 --**Kings and rulers**
  NT Stools--Ghana
 --**Religion**
  [BL 2480.A8]
 --**Wars**
  NT Ashanti War, 1822-1831
      Ashanti War, 1873-1874
      Ashanti War, 1900

Ashanti (Kingdom) *(Not Subd Geog)*
  [DT 507]
  UF Asante (Kingdom)
  BT Ashanti (African people)--History
      Ghana--History

Ashanti art
  USE Art, Ashanti

Ashanti decoration and ornament
  USE Decoration and ornament, Ashanti

(May Subd Geog) = Place names may follow the heading

Ashanti goldweights
USE Goldweights, Ashanti

Ashanti language
USE Twi language

Ashanti law
USE Law, Ashanti

Ashanti pottery
USE Pottery, Ashanti

Ashanti War, 1822-1831
[DT 507]
BT Ashanti (African people)--Wars
Ghana--History--To 1957

Ashanti War, 1873-1874
[DT 507]
BT Ashanti (African people--Wars
Ghana--History--To 1957
--Campaigns (May Subd Geog)
-- --Ghana
NT Kumasi (Ghana), Battle of, 1874

Ashanti War, 1900
[DT 507]
BT Ashanti (African people)--Wars
Ghana--History--To 1957

Ashanti women
USE Women, Ashanti

Ashanti wood carving
USE Wood-carving, Ashanti

Ashira language
USE Shira language

Ashogo (African people)
USE Mitsogho (African people)

Asia (Not Subd Geog)
--Civilization
-- --African influences
BT Africa--Civilization
--Politics and government
NT Afro-Asian politics

Asian-African politics
USE Afro-Asian politics

Asira language
USE Shira language

Assaorta-Saho language

USE Saho language

Astaboras River (Ethiopia and Sudan)
USE Atbara River (Ethiopia and Sudan)

Astrology, Malagasy
[BF 1714.M]
UF Malagasy astrology

Asu (African people)
USE Pare (African people)

Asu language (May Subd Geog)
[PL 8047.A77]
UF Athu language
Casu language
Chasu language
Chiasu language
CiAthu language
Pare language
BT Shambala languages
Tanzania--Languages

Asu proverbs
USE Proverbs, Asu

Asua (African people)
USE Aka (African people)

Aswanik language
USE Soninke language

Atbara River (Ethiopia and Sudan) (Not Subd Goog)
UF Astaboras River (Ethiopia and Sudan)
'Atbarah River (Ethiopia and Sudan)
Nahr 'Atbarah (Ethiopia and Sudan)
BT Rivers--Ethiopia
Rivers--Sudan

'Atbarah River (Ethiopia and Sudan)
USE Arbara River (Ethiopia and Sudan)

Atbay (Egypt and Sudan)
USE Red Sea Hills (Egypt and Sudan)

Atchi language
USE Attie language

Ateso (African people)
USE Teso (African people)

Ateso language
USE Teso language

Atharaka (African people)
USE Tharaka (African people)

UF = Used for; BT = Broader term; RT = Related term; SA = See also; NT = Narrower term

Athletes, Black *(May Subd Geog)*
   [GV 697.Al (Collective biography)]
   UF Black athletes

Athu language
   USE Asu language

Atie (African people)
   USE Attie (African people)

Atie language
   USE Attie language

Atisa language *(May Subd Geog)*
   [PL 8047.3.A8]
   UF Atissa language
       Epie language
   BT Kwa languages
       Nigeria--Languages
   --Glossaries, vocabularies, etc.

Atissa language
   USE Atisa language

Atlantic Coast (Africa) *(Not Subd Geog)*
   BT Coasts--Africa

Atlantic Coast (Angola) *(Not Subd Geog)*
   BT Coasts--Angola

Atlantic Coast (Benin) *(Not Subd Geog)*
   BT Coasts--Benin

Atlantic Coast (Cameroon) *(Not Subd Geog)*
   BT Coasts--Cameroon

Atlantic Coast (Congo) *(Not Subd Geog)*
   BT Coasts--Congo (Brazzaville)

Atlantic Coast (Gabon) *(Not Subd Geog)*
   BT Coasts--Gabon

Atlantic Coast (Ivory Coast) *(Not Subd Geog)*
   BT Coasts--Ivory Coast

Atlantic Coast (Liberia) *(Not Subd Geog)*
   BT Coasts--Liberia

Atlantic Coast (Namibia) *(Not Subd Geog)*
   BT Coasts--Namibia

Atlantic Coast (Togo) *(Not Subd Geog)*
   BT Coasts--Togo

Atlantic Coast (Zaire) *(Not Subd Geog)*
   BT Coasts--Zaire

Atlases
   UF Geographical atlases
       Geography--Atlases

Atlases, Botswana
   UF Botswana atlases

Atlases, Kenyan
   UF Kenyan atlases

Atlases, Nigerian
   UF Nigerian atlases

Atlases, Sotho
   UF Sotho atlases

Atlases, South African
   UF South African atlases

Atlases, Tanzanian
   UF Tanzanian atlases

Atlases, Zimbabwean
   UF Zimbabwean atlases

Atrocities *(May Subd Geog)*
   NT Massacres
   SA *subdivision* Atrocities *under names of wars, e.g.*
   South African War, 1899-1902--Atrocities

Atschoua (African people)
   USE Batwa (African people)

Atshe (African people)
   USE Attie (African people)

Atshe language
   USE Attie language

Attie (African people) *(May Subd Geog)*
   [DT 545.45.A]
   UF Akye (African people)
       Atie (African people)
       Atshe (African people)
       Kuroba (African people)
   BT Ethnology--Ivory Coast
   --Folklore
   [GR 351.82.A59]

Attie language *(May Subd Geog)*
   [PL 8047.3.A86]
   UF Akye language
       Atchi language
       Atie language
       Atshe language

(May Subd Geog) = Place names may follow the heading

UF Atye language
    Kurobu language
BT Ivory Coast--Languages
    Lagoon languages
--Tone
BT Tone (Phonetics)

Atuot (African people) *(May Subd Geog)*
[DT 155.2.A79]
BT Ethnology--Sudan
    Nilotic tribes
--Religion
[BL 2480.A88]

Atyap language
USE Katab language

Atye language
USE Attie language

Auen (African people)
USE !Kung (African people)

Aunt Nancy (Legendary character)
USE Anansi (Legendary character)

Aushi (African people)
USE Ushi (African people)

Australopithecus afarenis
[GN 283.4]
BT Fossil man--Ethiopia

Authors
UF Writers
BT Artists
RT Literature
SA *subdivision* Bio-bibliography *under special subjects, and under names of countries, cities, etc.*
NT Novelists
    Poets
    Women authors

Authors, African
UF African authors
RT African literature

Authors, Afrikaans *(May Subd Geog)*
UF Afrikaans authors
RT Afrikaans literature

Authors, Black *(May Subd Geog)*
[PN 490]
UF Black authors

Authors, Cameroon *(May Subd Geog)*
UF Cameroon authors

Authors, Congo (Brazzaville) *(May Subd Geog)*
UF Congo (Brazzaville) authors

Authors, Ethiopian *(May Subd Geog)*
UF Ethiopian authors

Authors, Ghanaian *(May Subd Geog)*
UF Ghanaian authors

Authors, Ivory Coast *(May Subd Geog)*
UF Ivory Coast authors

Authors, Kenyan *(May Subd Geog)*
UF Kenyan authors

Authors, Malagasy *(May Subd Geog)*
UF Malagasy authors

Authors, Mauritian *(May Subd Geog)*
UF Mauritian authors

Authors, Nigerian *(May Subd Geog)*
UF Nigerian authors

Authors, Senegalese *(May Subd Geog)*
UF Senegalese authors

Authors, South African *(May Subd Geog)*
UF South African authors
RT Novelists, South African

Authors, Women
USE Women authors

Authors, Xhosa *(May Subd Geog)*
UF Xhosa authors
RT Xhosa literature

Authors, Zairian *(May Subd Geog)*
UF Zairian authors

Authors, Zimbabwean *(May Subd Geog)*
UF Zimbabwean authors

Automatic data storage
USE Information storage and retrieval systems

Automatic information retrieval
USE Information storage and retrieval systems

Automation in documentation
USE Information storage and retrieval systems

UF = Used for; BT = Broader term; RT = Related term; SA = See also; NT = Narrower term

Autonomy and independence movements
  USE *subdivision* History--Autonomy and
  independence movements *under names of countries,*
  etc., e.g. Cabinda (Angola : Province)--
  History--Autonomy and independence movements.

Avak (African people)
  USE Bavêk (African people)

Avausi (African people)
  USE Ushi (African people)

Avekom (African people)
  USE Avikam (African people)

Avenue, The (Stellenbosch, South Africa) *(Not*
Subd Geog)
  UF Die Laan (Stellenbosch, South Africa)
      Laan, Die (Stellenbosch, South Africa)
      The Avenue (Stellenbosch, South
Africa)
  BT Streets--South Africa

Avenues
  USE Streets

Avikam (African people) *(May Subd Geog)*
  [DT 545.45.A86]
  UF Avekom (African people)
      Avikom (African people)
      Brignan (African people)
      Brinya (African people)
      Gbanda (African people)
      Kwaka (African people)
      Lahu (African people)
  BT Ethnology--Ivory Coast

Avikom (African people)
  USE Avikam (African people)

Avuk (African people)
  USE Bavêk (African people)

Avulsives
  USE Clicks (Phonetics)

Awash River (Ethiopia) *(Not Subd Geog)*
  UF Hawash River (Ethiopia)
  BT Rivers--Ethiopia

Aweer language
  USE Boni language

Aweera language
  USE Boni language

Awemba (African people)
  USE Bemba (African people)

Awisa (Zambian people)
  USE Bisa (Zambian people)

Axe, War of the (South Africa), 1847
  USE South Africa--History--Frontier Wars, 1811-
  1878

Axe routier transafricain
  USE Trans-African Highway

Axum (Kingdom)
  USE Aksum (Kingdom)

Ayan (Senegalese and Guinean people)
  USE Bassari (Senegalese and Guinean people)

Ayan language
  USE Bassari language

Ayaou (African people)
  USE Baoulé (African people)

Ayo (Game)
  [GV 1469.A96]
  UF Adjito
      Ayo J'odu
      Chuba
      Darra
      Iyagbe
      Jerin-Jerin
      Okwe
      Songo
      Wari
      Warri
  BT Games--Africa, Sub-Saharan
      Mancala (Game)

Ayo J'odu
  USE Ayo (Game)

Azande (African people)
  USE Zande (African people)

Azande language
  USE Zande language

Azdjer (African people)
  USE Ajjer (African people)

Azebo-Raya Revolt, Ethiopia, 1928-1930
  USE Ethiopia--History--Rebellion, 1928-1930

(May Subd Geog) = Place names may follow the heading

Azjer (African people)
USE Ajjer (African people)

B

Ba-katlha (African people)
USE Kgatla (African people)

Ba-Mbata (African people)
USE Mbata (African people)

Ba-Ushi (African people)
USE Ushi (African people)

Baakpe (African people)
USE Kwiri (African people)

Baakpe language
USE Kwiri language

Baamba (African people) *(May Subd Geog)*
[DT 433.245.B (Uganda)]
[DT 650.B (Zaire)]
UF Amba (African people)
BT Ethnology--Uganda
Ethnology--Zaire

Baatombu (African people)
USE Bariba (African people)

Baatonu (African people)
USE Bariba (African people)

Bab al-Mandab
USE Mandab, Strait of

'Bab el Mandeb
USE Mandab, Strait of

Babaála (African people)
USE Tagbana (African people)

Babemba (African people)
USE Bemba (African people)

Babembe (West African people)
USE Bembe (West African people)

Babenga (African people)
USE Babinga (African people)

Babinga (African people) *(May Subd Geog)*
[DT 571.B3 (Cameroon)]
[DT 546.345.B33 (Central African Republic)]
UF Babenga (African people)
UF Bambenga (African people)
Biaka (African people)
Mbinga (African people)
Yadinga (African people)
BT Ethnology--Cameroon
Ethnology--Central African Republic
Ethnology--Congo (Brazzaville)
Pygmies

Babira (African people)
USE Bira (African people)

Babisa (Zambian people)
USE Bisa (Zambian people)

Baboma (African people)
USE Boma (African people)

Babua (African people)
USE Ababua (African people)

Babunda (African people)
USE Bunda (African people)

Babundu (African people)
USE Bunda (African people)

Babungo language
USE Ngo language

Babuye (African people)
USE Hemba (African people)

Babwa (African people)
USE Ababua (African people)

Babwende (African people)
USE Bwende (African people)

Bacama (African people)
USE Bachama (African people)

Bace (African people)
USE Rukuba (African people)

Bacha (African people)
USE Kwegu (African people)

Bachama (African people) *(May Subd Geog)*
[DT 515.45.B]
UF Bacama (African people)
Bashama (African people)
Gboare (African people)
BT Ethnology--Nigeria
--Missions *(May Subd Geog)*
[BV 3630.B23]   *(Continued)*

UF = Used for; BT = Broader term; RT = Related term; SA = See also; NT = Narrower term

Bachama (African people)
--**Missions** *(Continued)*
 UF Missions to Bachama (African people)
--**Religion**
 [BL 2480.B22]

Bachapin (African people)
 USE Tlhaping (African people)

Bachiga (African people)
 USE Chiga (African people)

Bachilele (African people)
 USE Lele (African people)

Bachokwe (African people)
 USE Chokwe (African people)

Bachopi (African people)
 USE Chopi (African people)

Bachua (African people)
 USE Batwa (African people)

Back to Africa movement
 [DT 631 (Liberia)]
 BT Afro-Americans--Colonization--Africa

Bacwa (African people)
 USE Batwa (African people)

Baden (African people)
 USE Kunama (African people)

Baden language
 USE Kunama language

Badiaranke language
 USE Badyaranke language

Badin (African people)
 USE Kunama (African people)

Badukku (African people)
 USE Dukawa (African people)

Badyara language
 USE Badyaranke language

Badyaranké (African people) *(May Subd Geog)*
 [DT 549.45.B (Senegal)]
 BT Ethnology--Guinea
    Ethnology--Guinea-Bissau
    Ethnology--Senegal
    Tenda (African people)

Badyaranke language *(May Subd Geog)*
 [PL 8047.5.B33]
 UF Badiaranke language
    Badyara language
    Pajade language
    Pajadinca language
 BT Guinea--Languages
    Guinea-Bissau--Languages
    Niger-Congo languages
    Senegal--Languages

Baenya (African people)
 USE Genya (African people)

Bafang (Cameroon people)
 USE Fe'fe' (Cameroon people)

Bafang language
 USE Fe'fe' language

Bafeuk (African people)
 USE Bavĕk (African people)

Bafia (African people) *(May Subd Geog)*
 [DT 571.B32]
 UF Bapea (African people)
    Begpak (African people)
    Bekpak (African people)
    Fia (African people)
    Kpa (African people)
 BT Bantu-speaking peoples
    Ethnology--Cameroon

Bafia language *(May Subd Geog)*
 [PL 8047.5.B4]
 UF Kpa language
 BT Bantu languages
    Cameroon--Languages

Bafokeng (African people) *(May Subd Geog)*
 [DT 764.B : old class]
 [DT 1768.B35 : new class]
 BT Ethnology--South Africa
    Tswana (African people)

Bafokeng law
 USE Law, Bafokeng

Bafokeng women
 USE Women, Bafokeng

Bafuk (African people)
 USE Bavĕk (African people)

(May Subd Geog) = Place names may follow the heading

Bafut (African people) *(May Subd Geog)*
  [DT 571.B]
  UF Fut (African people)
  BT Ethnology--Cameroon

Bagamoyo (Tanzania). Magomeni
  USE Magomeni (Bagamoyo, Tanzania)

Baganda (African people)
  USE Ganda (African people)

Baganda ethics
  USE Ethics, Baganda

Baganda philosophy
  USE Philosophy, Baganda

Bagelli (African people)
  USE Bagyele (African people)

Bagelli language
  USE Bagyele language

Bagenya (African people)
  USE Genya (African people)

Bagesu (African people)
  USE Gisu (African people)

Baggara (African people) *(May Subd Geog)*
  [DT 155.2.B34]
  BT Ethnology--Sudan
  NT Hamar (African people)

Baghirmi (African people)
  USE Bagirmi (African people)

Bagielli language
  USE Bagyele language

Bagirmi (African people) *(May Subd Geog)*
  [DT 546.445.B34]
  UF Baghirmi (African people)
      Baguirmi (African people)
      Baguirmien (African people)
      Barma (African people)
      Masa Guelengdeng (African people)
      Mbara (African people)
  BT Ethnology--Chad

--**Marriage customs and rites**
  UF Marriage customs and rites, Bagirmi
(African people)
--**Rites and ceremonies**

Bagirmi language *(May Subd Geog)*
  [PL 8047.5.B47]
  UF Barma language
  BT Bongo-Bagirmi languages
      Chad--Languages

Bagishu (African people)
  USE Gisu (African people)

Bagiuni (African people)
  USE Bajun (African people)

Bagua (African people)
  USE Holoholo (African people)

Daguana (African people)
  USE Huana (African people)

Baguirmi (African people)
  USE Bagirmi (African people)

Baguirmien (African people)
  USE Bagirmi (African people)

Bagyele (African people) *(May Subd Geog)*
  [DT 571.B]
  UF Bagelli (African people)
      Dajeli (African people)
      Bako (African people)
      Bakola (African people)
      Bekoe (African people)
      Bogyel (African people)
      Bogyeli (African people)
  BT Ethnology--Cameroon
      Pygmies

Bagyele language *(May Subd Geog)*
  [PL 8047.6]
  UF Bagelli language
      Bagielli language
      Bajele language
      Bajeli language
      Bako language
      Bakola language
      Bayele language
      Bekoe language
      Bogyel language
      Bogyeli language
  BT Bantu languages
      Cameroon--Languages
      Pygmies--Languages

Bahanga (African people)
  USE Wanga (African people)

UF = Used for; BT = Broader term; RT = Related term; SA = See also; NT = Narrower term

Bahavu (African people)
  USE Havu (African people)

Bahema (African people)
  USE Hima (African people)

Bahemba (African people)
  USE Hemba (African people)

Bahia de Tungue (Mozambique)
  USE Tungue Bay (Mozambique)

Bahima (African people)
  USE Hima (African people)

Bahiro (African people)
  USE Bairo (African people)

Baholoholo (African people)
  USE Holoholo (African people)

Bahr al-Azraq (Ethiopia and Sudan)
  USE Blue Nile River (Ethiopia and Sudan)

Bahr al-Ghazal (Sudan : River) *(Not Subd Geog)*
  UF Bahr el Ghazal (Sudan : River)
      Gazelle River (Sudan)
      Ghazal, Bahr al- (Sudan : River)
      Ghazal River (Sudan)
  BT Rivers--Sudan

Bahr el Ghazal (Sudan : River)
  USE Bahr al-Ghazal (Sudan : River)

Bahr en Nil
  USE Nile River

Bahuana (African people)
  USE Huana (African people)

Bahuangana (African people)
  USE Huana (African people)

Bahuma (African people)
  USE Hima (African people)

Bahungana (African people)
  USE Huana (African people)

Bahusi (African people)
  USE Ushi (African people)

Bahutu (African people)
  USE Hutu (African people)

Bai (African people)

  USE Mbaï (African people)

Baía de Tungue (Mozambique)
  USE Tungue Bay (Mozambique)

Baía do Lobito (Angola)
  USE Lobito Bay (Angola)

Baila (African people)
  USE Ila (African people)

Bailundo War, Angola, 1902
  [DT 611.7 : old class]
  [DT 1392 : new class]
  BT Angola--History--1885-1961
      Mbundu (African people)--Wars

Baiot (African people)
  USE Bayot (African people)

Baiote (African people)
  USE Bayot (African people)

Bairo (African people) *(May Subd Geog)*
  [DT 433.245.B]
  UF Bahiro (African people)
      Bairu (African people)
      Wairu (African people)
      Whiro (African people)
      Wiro (African people)
  BT Ethnology--Uganda

Bairu (African people)
  USE Bairo (African people)

Baja (African people)
  USE Gbaya (African people)

Bajele language
  USE Bagyele language

Bajeli (African people)
  USE Bagyele (African people)

Bajeli language
  USE Bagyele language

Bajokwe (African people)
  USE Chokwe (African people)

Bajun (African people) *(May Subd Geog)*
  [DT 433.545.B (Kenya)]
  [DT 402.4.B (Somalia)]
  UF Bagiuni (African people)
  BT Ethnology--Kenya
      Ethnology--Somalia

(May Subd Geog) = Place names may follow the heading

BT Swahili-speaking peoples

Baka (West African people) *(May Subd Geog)*
[DT 571.B (Cameroon)]
UF Baka Bambuké (African people)
Bebayaga (African people)
Bebayaka (African people)
Bibaya (African people)
Bibayak (African people)
BT Ethnology--Cameroon
Ethnology--Central African Republic
Ethnology--Congo (Brazzaville)
Pgymies

Baka Bambuké (African people)
USE Baka (West African people)

Baka folk songs (Cameroon)
USE Folk songs, Baka (Cameroon)

Baka language *(May Subd Geog)*
[PL 8047.6.Z5B7]
UF Tara Baaka language
BT Bongo-Bagirmi languages
Sudan--Languages
Zaire--Languages

Baka language (Cameroon) *(May Subd Geog)*
[PL 8047.65]
UF Bihaya language
DT Cameroon--Languages
Niger-Congo languages
Pygmies--Languages

Bakahonde (African people)
USE Kaonde (African people)

Bakalahadi (African people)
USE Kgalagadi (African people)

Bakaonde (African people)
USE Kaonde (African people)

Bakare language
USE Kare language

Bakatla (African people)
USE Kgatla (African people)

Bakedi (African people)
USE Teso (African people)

Bakela (African people)
USE Kela (African people)

Bakele language

USE Kele language

Bakgalagadi (African people)
USE Kgalagadi (African people)

Bakgatla (African people)
USE Kgatla (African people)

Bakhaha (African people)
USE Kgaga (African people)

Bakhatla (African people)
USE Kgatla (African people)

Bakidi (African people)
USE Teso (African people)

Bakiga (African people)
USE Chiga (African people)

Bakiue (African people)
USE Batwa (African people)

Bako (African people)
USE Bagyele (African people)

Bako language
USE Bagyele language

Bakoko (Cameroon people)
USE Basa (Cameroon people)

Bakola (African people)
USE Bagyele (African people)

Bakola language
USE Bagyele language

Bakongo (African people)
USE Kongo (African people)

Bakosi (African people)
USE Kossi (African people)

Bakosi dialect
USE Bakossi dialect

Bakossi (African people)
USE Kossi (African people)

Bakossi dialect *(May Subd Geog)*
[PL 8506.M3695B3]
UF Akoose dialect (Bakossi)
Bakosi dialect
Koose dialect (Bakossi)
Nkosi dialect   *(Continued)*

UF = Used for; BT = Broader term; RT = Related term; SA = See also; NT = Narrower term

Bakossi dialect   *(Continued)*
  BT   Cameroon--Languages
     Mbo language (Cameroon)
 --**Phonology**

Bakota (African people)
  USE   Kota (African people)

Bakou language
  USE   Fe'fe' language

Bakpwe language
  USE   Kwiri language

Bakuba (African people)
  USE   Kuba (African people)

Bakuba language
  USE   Bushoong language

Bakulia (African people)
  USE   Kuria (African people)

Bakumbu (Zairian people)
  USE   Kumu (Zairian people)

Bakundu language *(May Subd Geog)*
  UF   Kundu language
     Lokundu language
  BT   Bantu languages
     Nigeria--Languages

Bakuria (African people)
  USE   Kuria (African people)

Bakwa (African people)
  USE   Batwa (African people)

Bakweri language
  USE   Kwiri language

Bakwese (African people)
  USE   Kwese (African people)

Bakwiri (African people)
  USE   Kwiri (African people)

Bakwiri language
  USE   Kwiri language

Bala (Musical instrument)
  USE   Balo

Balafo (Musical instrument)
  USE   Balo

Balafon (Musical instrument)
  USE   Balo

Balafou (Musical instrument)
  USE   Balo

Balala (African people)
  USE   Kgalagadi (African people)

Balala (African people)
  USE   Lala (African people)

Balali language
  USE   Teke language

Balambu language
  USE   Barambu language

Balanda (African people)
  USE   Balanta (African people)

Balanga (African people)
  USE   Balanta (African people)

Balanta (African people) *(May Subd Geog)*
  [DT 613.45.B34 (Guinea-Bissau)]
  UF   Alante (African people)
     Balanda (African people)
     Balanga (African people)
     Balante (African people)
     Belante (African people)
     Bolenta (African people)
     Brassa (African people)
     Bulanda (African people)
     Bulante (African people)
  BT   Ethnology--Guinea
     Ethnology--Guinea-Bissau
     Ethnology--Senegal

Balante (African people)
  USE   Balanta (African people)

Balante language *(May Subd Geog)*
  [PL 8047.8]
  UF   Balat language
     Bulanda language
     Fca language
  BT   Guinea--Languages
     Niger-Congo languages
     Senegal--Languages

Balaphon (Musical instrument)
  USE   Balo

Balat language
  USE   Balante language

(May Subd Geog) = Place names may follow the heading

Bale (African people)
  USE Lendu (African people)

Balega (African people)
  USE Lendu (African people)

Balega language
  USE Kilega language

Balegga (African people)
  USE Waregas

Balembe (East African people)
  USE Bembe (East African people)

Balendru (African people)
  USE Lendu (African people)

Balendu (African people)
  USE Lendu (African people)

Balenje (African people)
  USE Lenje (African people)

Balese (African people)
  USE Lese (African people)

Balese language (May Subd Geog)
  [PL 8048]
  UF Lese language
  BT Nilo-Saharan languages
     Zaire--Languages

Balcoging language
  USE Bamougoun-Bamenjou language

Bali (African people) (May Subd Geog)
  [DT 571.B33]
  UF Ban'i (African people)
     Banyonga (African people)
     Ngaaka (African people)
     Nyonga (African people)
  BT Ethnology--Cameroon

Balissi (African people)
  USE Lese (African people)

Ballads (May Subd Geog)
  BT Songs
  RT Folk songs

Ballads, Fang (May Subd Geog)
  [PL 8167.F38 (Words)]
  UF Fang ballads
  --Gabon

Ballads, Twi (May Subd Geog)
  [PL 8751.8 (Words)]
  UF Twi ballads
  --Ghana
  -- --Texts

Balo
  [ML 1048]
  UF Bala (Musical instrument)
     Balafo (Musical instrument)
     Balafon (Musical instrument)
     Balafou (Musical instrument)
     Balaphon (Musical instrument)
  BT Musical instruments--Africa, French-
  speaking West

Balojash (African people)
  USE Luchazi (African people)

Balolo (African people)
  USE Mongo (African people)

Balovale (African people)
  USE Luvale (African people)

Baluba (African people)
  USE Luba (African people)

Balunda (African people)
  USE Lunda, Northern (African people)
      Lunda, Southern (African people)

Baluyia (African people)
  USE Luyia (African people)

Bama (African people)
  USE Boma (African people)

Bamana (African people)
  USE Bambara (African people)

Bamana language
  USE Bambara language

Bamana language (Senufo)
  USE Mamara language

Bamangwato (African people)
  USE Ngwato (African people)

Bamba (African people)
  USE Mbete (African people)

Bamba language
  USE Mbete language

UF = Used for; BT = Broader term; RT = Related term; SA = See also; NT = Narrower term

Bambala (African people)
USE Mbala (African people)

Bambala language
USE Burji language

Bambara (African people) *(May Subd Geog)*
[DT 551.45.B35]
UF Bamana (African people)
Banmani (African people)
BT Ethnology--Mali
--Marriage customs and rites
UF Marriage customs and rites, Bambara
(African people)
--Medicine
BT Medicine, Primitive--Mali
--Religion
[BL 2480.B26]

Bambara folk songs
USE Folk songs, Bambara

Bambara Jihad, 1852-1863
[DT 532.3]
BT Africa, West--History--To 1884
Toucouleurs--History--19th century

Bambara language *(May Subd Geog)*
[PL 8049.B3]
UF Bamana language
BT Africa, West--Languages
Mandekan languages

Bambara language (Senufo)
USE Mamara language

Bambara proverbs
USE Proverbs, Bambara

Bambara riddles
USE Riddles, Bambara

Bambara sculpture
USE Sculpture, Bambara

Bambara women
USE Women, Bambara

Bambatha Rebellion, 1906
USE Zulu Rebellion, 1906

Bambenga (African people)
USE Babinga (African people)

Bambete (African people)
USE Mbete (African people)

Bambunda (African people)
USE Bunda (African people)

Bambute (African people)
USE Mbuti (African people)

Bameka language
USE Bamougoun-Bamenjou language

Bamekon (African people)
USE Kom (African people)

Bamendjou language
USE Bamougoun-Bamenjou language

Bamileke (African people) *(May Subd Geog)*
[DT 571.B34]
BT Ethnology--Cameroon
RT Bangwa (African people)
NT Bana (African people)
Bandja (African people)
Bandjoun (African people)
Fe'fe' (Cameroon people)
--Funeral customs and rites
UF Funeral customs and rites, Bamileke
(African people)
--Religion
[BL 2480.B27]
--Rites and customs

Bamileke folk literature
USE Folk literature, Bamileke

Bamileke folk songs
USE Folk songs, Bamileke

Bamileke-Jo language
USE Bandjoun language

Bamileke languages *(May Subd Geog)*
[PL 8049.B4]
UF Grafil languages
Grassfield languages
BT Benue-Congo languages
Cameroon--Languages
NT Bamougoun-Bamenjou language
Bandjoun language
Fe'fe' language
Medumba language

Bamileke law
USE Law, Bamileke

(May Subd Geog) = Place names may follow the heading

Bamitaba language
USE Mbomataba language

Bamongo language
USE Bushoong language
     Mongo language

Bamougoun-Bamenjou language *(May Subd Geog)*
[PL 8049.B]
UF Balessing language
    Bameka language
    Bamendjou language
    Bansoa language
    Mundju language
    Munju language
    Ngueba language
    Pamunguup language
BT Bamileke languages
    Cameroon--Languages

Bamoum (African people)
USE Bamun (African people)

Bamoun (African people)
USE Bamun (African people)

Bamputu (African people)
USE Mputu (African people)

Bamum (African people)
USE Bamun (African people)

Bamun (African people) *(May Subd Geog)*
[DT 571.B35]
UF Bamoun (African people)
    Bamoun (African people)
    Bamum (African people)
    Mom (African people)
    Mum (African people)
    Shupaman (African people)
BT Ethnology--Cameroon
--Medicine
BT Medicine, Primitive--Cameroon

Bamun art
USE Art, Bamun

Bamun language *(May Subd Geog)*
[PL 8050]
BT Benue-Congo languages
    Cameroon--Languages

Bamun proverbs
USE Proverbs, Bamun

Bana (African people) *(May Subd Geog)*
[DT 571.B36]
UF Ndeu (African people)
    Né (African people)
    Nee (African people)
BT Bamileke (African people)
    Ethnology--Cameroon

Bana language
USE Fe'fe' language

Banaa language
USE Masa language (Chadic)

Banana language (Masa)
USE Masa language (Chadic)

Banande (Zairian people)
USE Nande (Zairian people)

Banco National Park (Ivory Coast)
USE Parc National du Banco (Ivory Coast)

Band weaving, West African
USE West African strip weaving

Banda (African people) *(May Subd Geog)*
[DT 546.345.B]
UF Dar Banda (African people)
BT Ethnology--Central African Republic
NT Langbas (African people)

Banda language *(May Subd Geog)*
[PL 8051]
BT Banda languages
    Central African Republic--Languages
NT Linda dialect

Banda languages *(May Subd Geog)*
[PL 8052]
BT Central African Republic--Languages
    Niger-Congo languages
NT Banda language
    Gólo language

Bande language
USE Bedik language

Bandempo (African people)
USE Ndembu (African people)

Bandi (Liberian people)
USE Gbandi (Liberian people)

Bandi language
USE Gbandi language

UF = Used for; BT = Broader term; RT = Related term; SA = See also; NT = Narrower term

Bandja (African people) *(May Subd Geog)*
  [DT 571.B]
  UF Ndja (African people)
      Ndjë (African people)
  BT Bamileke (African people)
      Ethnology--Cameroon

Bandjoun (African people) *(May Subd Geog)*
  [DT 571.B365]
  UF Banjoum (African people)
      Banjoun (African people)
      Banjoun Baham (African people)
      Banjun (African people)
      Mahum (African people)
      Mandju (African people)
      Ngomahum (African people)
  BT Bamileke (African people)
      Bantu-speaking peoples
      Ethnology--Cameroon

Bandjoun language *(May Subd Geog)*
  [PL 8052.5]
  UF Bamileke-Jo language
      Ghomala language
  BT Bamileke languages
      Cameroon--Languages

Bandzabi (African people)
  USE Nzabi (African people)

Banen (African people) *(May Subd Geog)*
  [DT 571.B]
  BT Bantu-speaking peoples
      Ethnology--Cameroon
  NT Ndiki (African people)

Banen language *(May Subd Geog)*
  [PL 8053]
  UF Banend language
      Tunen language
  BT Bantu languages
      Cameroon--Languages
  NT Yambeta language

Banend language
  USE Banen language

Bangala language (Zaire)
  USE Lingala language

Bangalas *(May Subd Geog)*
  [DT 650.B]
  UF Wangala (African people)
  BT Ethnology--Zaire

Bangandu (African people)

USE Ngandu (African people)

Bangangte (African people)
  USE Ngangte (African people)

Bangante (African people)
  USE Ngangte (African people)

Bangobango language
  USE Bangubangu language

Bangongo (African people)
  USE Ngongo (African people)

Bangubangu language *(May Subd Geog)*
  [PL 8056.B25]
  UF Bangobango language
  BT Bantu languages
      Zaire--Languages

Banguella (African people)
  USE Ngangela (African people)

Bangwa (African people) *(May Subd Geog)*
  [DT 571.B]
  BT Ethnology--Cameroon
  RT Bamileke (African people)

Bangwaketse (African people)
  USE Ngwaketse (African people)

Bangweolo, Lake (Zambia)
  USE Bangweulu, Lake (Zambia)

Bangweulu, Lake (Zambia) *(Not Subd Geog)*
  UF Bangweolo, Lake (Zambia)
      Lake Bangweolo (Zambia)
      Lake Bangweulu (Zambia)
  BT Lakes--Zambia

Ban'i (African people)
  USE Bali (African people)

Baniabungu (African people)
  USE Bashi (African people)

Banjabi (African people)
  USE Nzabi (African people)

Banjal (African people) *(May Subd Geog)*
  [DT 549.45.B35]
  BT Diola (African people)
      Ethnology--Senegal

Banjal law
  USE Law, Banjal

(May Subd Geog) = Place names may follow the heading

Banjoum (African people)
USE Bandjoun (African people)

Banjoun (African people)
USE Bandjoun (African people)

Banjoun Baham (African people)
USE Bandjoun (African people)

Banjun (African people)
USE Bandjoun (African people)

Banks, Development
USE Development banks

Banmani (African people)
USE Bambara (African people)

Banna (African people)
USE Hamar (African people)

Banned persons (South Africa)
*Here are entered works on people who, under the
provisions of the South African Internal Security Act,
are unable to travel or to speak with anyone without
written permission from the authorities.*
UF Persons, Banned (South Africa)
BT Political prisoners--South Africa

Banoho (African people)
USE Tanga (African people)

Bansaw (African people)
USE Nso (African people)

Banso (African people)
USE Nso (African people)

Bansoa language
USE Bamougoun-Bamenjou language

Bantoetuislande (South Africa)
USE Homelands (South Africa)

Bantu courts
USE Courts, Bantu

Bantu decorative arts
USE Decorative arts, Bantu

Bantu folk literature
USE Folk literature, Bantu

Bantu folk songs
USE Folk songs, Bantu

Bantu Homelands (South Africa)
USE Homelands (South Africa)

Bantu languages *(May Subd Geog)*
[PL 8025]
BT Benue-Congo languages
NT Ababua language
Aduma language
Aka language (Central African Republic)
Bafia language
Bagyele language
Bakundu language
Banen language
Bangubangu language
Basa language
Bali language
Bemba language
Bembe language (Congo (Brazzaville))
Bembe language (Lake Tanganyika)
Benga language
Benge language
Bisa language
Bisio language
Bobangi language
Bolia language
Boma language
Bube language
Bushoong language
Chaga language
Chewa dialect
Chindau language
Chokwe language
Chopi language
Diriku language
Duala language
Ekoi languages
Embu language
Enya language
Ganda language
Ganguela language
Gisu language
Gogo language
Gunu language
Gusii language
Herero language
Holoholo language
Jita language
Kamba language
Kaonde language
Kare language
Kela language
Kele language
Kerebe language
Kete language
Kiga language
Kilega language   *(Continued)*

UF = Used for; BT = Broader term; RT = Related term; SA = See also; NT = Narrower term

Bantu languages *(Continued)*
  NT Kimbundu language
      Kinyarwanda language
      Kitabwa language
      Kombe language
      Kongo language
      Kuanyama language
      Kukwa language
      Kuria language
      Kwangali language
      Kwiri language
      Lala language
      Lamba language
      Lingala language
      Logooli language
      Lonkengo language
      Losengo language
      Luba-Katanga language
      Luba-Lulua language
      Lucazi language
      Lumbu language (Gabon)
      Lunda language
      Luyana language
      Luyia language
      Maka language (Cameroon)
      Makonde language
      Makua language
      Mambwe language
      Mbete language
      Mbinsa language
      Mbo language (Cameroon)
      Mbomotaba language
      Mbosi language
      Mbunda language (Zambia)
      Meru language
      Mituku language
      Mongo language
      Mpongwe language
      Mwera language
      Nande language
      Ndonga language
      Ndumbu language
      Ngombe languages
      Ngonde language
      Nguni languages
      Nika language
      Nilamba language
      Nkundu language
      Ntomba language
      Nyamwezi language
      Nyaneka language
      Nyanga language
      Nyanja language
      Nyankole language
      Nyankore-Kiga language

  NT Nyore language
      Nyoro language
      Nyoro-Tooro language
      Ombo language
      Orungu language
      Pangwa language
      Pogoro language
      Proto-Bantu language
      Punu language
      Ragoli language
      Ronga language
      Rundi language
      Ruund language
      Sagara language
      Sakata language
      Salampasu language
      Sanga language
      Sena language
      Senga language
      Shambala languages
      Shi language
      Shira language
      Shona language
      Soga language
      Songe language
      Sotho-Tswana languages
      Subiya language
      Sukuma language
      Swahili language
      Taita language
      Teke language
      Tembo language (Kivu, Zaire)
      Tete language
      Tetela language
      Tonga language (Inhambane)
      Tonga language (Nyasa)
      Tonga language (Zambesi)
      Tooro language
      Tsogo language
      Tsonga language
      Tswa language
      Tumbuka language
      Umbundu language
      Venda language
      Vili language
      Yanzi language
      Yao language
      Yaunde-Fang languages
      Yombe language
      Zanaki language
      Ziba language
  --Classification
  --Tone *(May Subd Geog)*
      [PL 8025.I]
  BT Tone (Phonetics)

(May Subd Geog) = Place names may follow the heading

Bantu languages, Grasslands
  USE Grasslands Bantu languages

Bantu languages, Mamfe
  USE Mamfe Bantu languages

Bantu law
  USE Law, Bantu

Bantu literature *(May Subd Geog)*
  [PL 8025.5 (History)]
  [PL 8025.6 (Collections)]
  BT African literature
  SA *names of literatures belonging to the Bantu*
group, e.g. Swahili literature
  NT Bantu poetry
      Folk literature, Bantu

Bantu philology
  [PL 8025]
  UF Philology, Bantu
  NT Soga philology

Bantu philosophy
  USE Philosophy, Bantu

Bantu poetry *(May Subd Geog)*
  [PL 8025.6 (History)]
  [PL 8025.7 (Collections)]
  BT African poetry
      Bantu literature

Bantu proverbs
  USE Proverbs, Bantu

Bantu songs
  USE Songs, Bantu

Bantu-speaking peoples *(May Subd Geog)*
  [DT 16.B2]
  UF Bantus
  BT Ethnology--Africa, Sub-Saharan
  NT Ababua (African people)
      Bafia (African people)
      Bandjoun (African people)
      Banen (African people)
      Basa (Cameroon people)
      Bemba (African people)
      Bembe (East African people)
      Bembe (West African people)
      Bena (African people)
      Beti (African people)
      Bira (African people)
      Bisa (Zambian people)
      Bisio (African people)
      Boma (African people)

  NT Bomvana (African people)
      Bubi (African people)
      Bulu (African people)
      Bunda (African people)
      Bwende (African people)
      Chaga (African people)
      Chewa (African people)
      Chiga (African people)
      Chokwe (African people)
      Chopi (African people)
      Dengese (African people)
      Duala (African people)
      Ekoi (African people)
      Ekonda (African people)
      Embu (African people)
      Evuzok (African people)
      Fingo (African people)
      Ganda (African people)
      Genya (African people)
      Ghoya (African people)
      Gisu (African people)
      Gogo (African people)
      Gusii (African people)
      Hanya (African people)
      Hehe (African people)
      Hemba (African people)
      Herero (African people)
      Hlaba (African people)
      Holoholo (African people)
      Huana (African people)
      Ila (African people)
      Kamba (African people)
      Kaonde (African people)
      Kavirondo (African people)
      Kerebe (African people)
      Kikuyu (African people)
      Kimbu (African people)
      Kongo (African people)
      Kossi (African people)
      Kuba (African people)
      Kukwa (African people)
      Kuria (African people)
      Kusu (African people)
      Kwiri (African people)
      Lala (African people)
      Lamba (African people)
      Lele (African people)
      Lobedu (African people)
      Lozi (African people)
      Luba (African people)
      Luenas (African people)
      Luguru (African people)
      Luvale (African people)
      Luyia (African people)
      Maka (African people)
      Makonde (African people)   *(Continued)*

UF = Used for; BT = Broader term; RT = Related term; SA = See also; NT = Narrower term

Bantu-speaking peoples *(Continued)*
  NT Makua (African people)
      Mamabolo (African people)
      Mambwe (African people)
      Matengo (African people)
      Mbala (African people)
      Mbandieru (African people)
      Mbata (African people)
      Mbati (Central African Republic
people)
      Mbete (African people)
      Mbosi (African people)
      Mbukushu (African people)
      Mbundu (African people)
      Meru (African people)
      Mongo (African people)
      Mpongwe (African people)
      Mwera (African people)
      Mwila (African people)
      Myene (African people)
      Nande (Zairian people)
      Ngandu (African people)
      Ngangela (African people)
      Ngangte (African people)
      Ngombe (African people)
      Ngonde (African people)
      Nguni (African people)
      Ngwato (African people)
      Nkundu (African people)
      Nyakyusa (African people)
      Nyamwezi (African people)
      Nyang (African people)
      Nyanga (African people)
      Nyanja (African people)
      Nyankole (African people)
      Nyaturu (African people)
      Nyoro (African people)
      Nzabi (African people)
      Ovambo (African people)
      Pangwa (African people)
      Pare (African people)
      Pedi (African people)
      Pende (African people)
      Phalaborwa (African people)
      Pogoro (African people)
      Pokomo (African people)
      Pondo (African people)
      Qaba (African people)
      Rangi (African people)
      Rundi (African people)
      Safwa (African people)
      Sakata (African people)
      Salampasu (African people)
      Sambyu (African people)
      Shambala (African people)
      Shira (African people)

  NT Shona (African people)
      Soga (African people)
      Songe (African people)
      Songola (African people)
      Sonjo (African people)
      Sotho (African people)
      Suba (African people)
      Suku (African people)
      Sukuma (African people)
      Swahili-speaking peoples
      Swazi (African people)
      Tanga (African people)
      Teke (African people)
      Tetela (African people)
      Tiriki (African people)
      Tonga (Zambesi people)
      Tooro (African people)
      Topoke (African people)
      Tsonga (African people)
      Tumbuka (African people)
      Venda (African people)
      Vili (African people)
      Wanga (African people)
      Yaka (African people)
      Yanzi (African people)
      Yao (African people)
      Yombe (African people)
      Zanaki (African people)
      Zigula (African people)
      Zinza (African people)
  --**Education** *(May Subd Geog)*
  -- --Art, [etc.]
  --**Food**
    BT Food
  --**Marriage customs and rites**
    UF Marriage customs and rites, Bantu
  --**Migrations**
    UF Mfecane
  --**Missions** *(May Subd Geog)*
    [BV 3630.B3]
    UF Missions to Bantus
  --**Music**
  --**Religion**
    [BL 2480.B3]
    UF Prayer (Bantu religion)
    NT Jamaa Movement

Bantus
  USE Bantu-speaking peoples
       Blacks--South Africa

Bantustans (South Africa)
  USE Homelands (South Africa)

Banunu (African people)
  USE Nunu (African people)

(May Subd Geog) = Place names may follow the heading

Banyabongo (African people)
  USE Bashi (African people)

Banyamwezi (African people)
  USE Nyamwezi (African people)

Banyang (African people)
  USE Nyang (African people)

Banyanga (African people)
  USE Nyanga (African people)

Banyangi language
  USE Anyang language

Banyankole (African people)
  USE Nyankole (African people)

Banyonga (African people)
  USE Bali (African people)

Banyoro (African people)
  USE Nyoro (African people)

Banzili (African people)
  USE Banziri (African people)

Banziri (African people) *(May Subd Geog)*
  [DT 546.345.B (Central African Republic)]
  UF Banzili (African people)
      Gbanzili (African people)
      Gbanziri (African people)
  BT Ethnology--Central African Republic
      Ethnology--Congo (Brazzaville)
      Ethnology--Zaire
  --Folklore

Baoulé (African people) *(May Subd Geog)*
  [DT 545.45.B36]
  UF Ayaou (African people)
      Baule (African people)
  BT Ethnology--Ivory Coast
  --Religion
  [BL 2480.B33]

Baoulé language *(May Subd Geog)*
  [PL 8056.B3]
  UF Baule language
      Poni language
  BT Anyi language
      Ivory Coast--Languages
  --Tone
  BT Tone (Phonetics)

Baoulé proverbs

  USE Proverbs, Baoulé

Baoulé sculpture
  USE Sculpture, Baoulé

Baousi (African people)
  USE Ushi (African people)

Baoussi (African people)
  USE Ushi (African people)

Bapea (African people)
  USE Bafia (African people)

Bapedi (African people)
  USE Pedi (African people)

Bapende (African people)
  USE Pende (African people)

Bapounou language
  USE Punu language

Baptists, Black *(May Subd Geog)*
  UF Black Baptists
  --Africa
  [BX 6320]
  --Liberia
  [BX 6322.L5]
  --South Africa
  [BX 6321]

Bapuku (African people)
  USE Tanga (African people)

Bara (Malagasy people) *(May Subd Geog)*
  [DT 469.M277B37]
  BT Ethnology--Madagascar

Bara dialect (Madagascar) *(May Subd Geog)*
  [PL 5379]
  BT Malagasy language

Barabaig (African people) *(May Subd Geog)*
  [DT 443.3.B37]
  UF Brariga (African people)
  BT Ethnology--Tanzania
      Nilo-Hamitic tribes

Barabaig women
  USE Women, Barabaig

Baraguku (African people)
  USE Baraguyu (African people)

UF = Used for; BT = Broader term; RT = Related term; SA = See also; NT = Narrower term

Baraguyu (African people) *(May Subd Geog)*
　[DT 443.3.B38]
　UF　Baraguku (African people)
　　　Ilparakuyo (African people)
　　　Paraguku (African people)
　　　Paraguyu (African people)
　BT　Ethnology--Tanzania
　　　Masai (African people)

Barambo language
　USE　Barambu language

Barambu language *(May Subd Geog)*
　[PL 8058]
　UF　Abarambo language
　　　Balambu language
　　　Barambo language
　BT　Zaire--Languages
　　　Zande languages

Barba (African people)
　USE　Bariba (African people)

Barea language
　USE　Baria language

Barega (African people)
　USE　Waregas

Bargu (African people)
　USE　Bariba (African people)

Bari language *(May Subd Geog)*
　[PL 8061]
　UF　Dzilio language
　BT　Nilo-Hamitic languages
　　　Sudan--Languages
　　　Uganda--Languages
　　　Zaire--Languages
　NT　Kakwa dialect
　　　Mandara language

Baria (African people) *(May Subd Geog)*
　[DT 393.5]
　BT　Ethnology--Ethiopia
　　　Nilo-Hamitic tribes

Baria language *(May Subd Geog)*
　[PL 8062]
　UF　Barea language
　　　Kolkotto language
　　　Mogoreb language
　　　Morda language
　　　Nara language
　　　Nere language
　BT　Ethiopia--Languages

　　　BT　Nilo-Hamitic languages

Bariba (African people) *(May Subd Geog)*
　[DT 541.45.B37 (Benin)]
　UF　Baatombu (African people)
　　　Baatonu (African people)
　　　Barba (African people)
　　　Bargu (African people)
　BT　Ethnology--Benin
　　　Ethnology--Nigeria
　--Medicine
　　BT　Medicine, Primitive--Benin
　　　Medicine, Primitive--Nigeria

Bariba women
　USE　Women, Bariba

Baribari (African people)
　USE　Kanuri (African people)

Baringo, Lake (Kenya) *(Not Subd Geog)*
　UF　Lake Baringo (Kenya)
　BT　Lakes--Kenya

Barma (African people)
　USE　Bagirmi (African people)

Barma language
　USE　Bagirmi language

Baroa (African people)
　USE　Batwa (African people)

Barolong (African people)
　USE　Rolong (African people)

Baron language
　USE　Ron language

Barotse (African people)
　USE　Lozi (African people)

Barotseland (Northern Rhodesia)
　USE　Western Province (Zambia)

Barotseland Protectorate
　USE　Western Province (Zambia)

Barotsi (African people)
　USE　Lozi (African people)

Barozi (African people)
　USE　Lozi (African people)

Barta (African people)
　USE　Berta (African people)

(May Subd Geog) = Place names may follow the heading

Baru language
  USE Loma language

Barundi (African people)
  USE Rundi (African people)

Barutse (African people)
  USE Lozi (African people)

Barwe (African people) *(May Subd Geog)*
  [DT 458.3.B (Mozambique : old class)]
  [DT 3328.B37 (Mozambique : new class)]
  [DT 962.42 (Zimbabwe : old class)]
  [DT 2913.B38 (Zimbabwe : new class)]
  UF Wabarwe (African people)
  BT Ethnology--Mozambique
      Ethnology--Zimbabwe
  NT Tangwena (African people)

Basa (Cameroon people) *(May Subd Geog)*
  [DT 571.B37]
  UF Bakoko (Cameroon people)
      Basaa (Cameroon people)
      Bassa (Cameroon people)
      Betjek (Cameroon people)
      Koko (Cameroon people)
      Mbene (Cameroon people)
      Mvele (Cameroon people)
      Mwelle (Cameroon people)
  BT Bantu-speaking peoples
      Ethnology--Cameroon
  --Religion
  [BL 2480.B337]

Basa (Liberian people)
  USE Bassa (Liberian people)

Basa language *(May Subd Geog)*
  [PL 8065]
  UF Basaa language
      Bassa language (Cameroon)
  BT Bantu languages
      Cameroon--Languages

Basa language (Liberia)
  USE Bassa language (Liberia)

Basa mythology
  USE Mythology, Basa

Basa women
  USE Women, Basa

Basaa (Cameroon people)
  USE Basa (Cameroon people)

Basaa language
  USE Basa language

Basaie (Togolese and Ghanaian people)
  USE Bassari (Togolese and Ghanaian people)

Basakata (African people)
  USE Sakata (African people)

Basanga (African people)
  USE Sanga (African people)

Basar (Senegalese and Guinean people)
  USE Bassari (Senegalese and Guinean people)

Basari (Senegalese and Guinean people)
  USE Bassari (Senegalese and Guinean people)

Basari (Togolese and Ghanaian people)
  USE Bassari (Togolese and Ghanaian people)

Basari du Bandemba language
  USE Bedik language

Basari language
  USE Bassari language

Basari language (Togo and Ghana)
  USE Tobote language

Basarwa (African people)
  USE San (African people)

Baseka (African people)
  USE Ekonda (African people)

Bashama (African people)
  USE Bachama (African people)

Bashi (African people) *(May Subd Geog)*
  [DT 650.B366]
  UF Baniabungu (African people)
      Banyabongo (African people)
      Wanyambungi (African people)
  BT Ethnology--Zaire

Bashi-Lele (African people)
  USE Lele (African people)

Bashilele (African people)
  USE Lele (African people)

Bashoobwa (African people)
  USE Shoowa (African people)

UF = Used for; BT = Broader term; RT = Related term; SA = See also; NT = Narrower term

Bashukulompo (African people)
  USE Ila (African people)

Basiba (African people)
  USE Haya (African people)

Basic Bantu language
  USE Fanakalo

Basins, Structural
  USE Basins (Geology)

Basins (Geology) *(May Subd Geog)*
  UF Basins, Structural
      Structural basins
  BT Landforms
  --Africa
  NT Chad Basin
  --Mali
  NT Taoudenni Basin (Mali)

Basonge (African people)
  USE Songe (African people)

Basotho (African people)
  USE Sotho (African people)

Bassa (Cameroon people)
  USE Basa (Cameroon people)

Bassa (Liberian people) *(May Subd Geog)*
  [DT 630.5.B]
  UF Basa (Liberian people)
      Gbasa (Liberian people)
  BT Ethnology--Liberia

Bassa language (Cameroon)
  USE Basa language

Bassa language (Liberia) *(May Subd Geog)*
  [PL 8066.B]
  UF Basa language (Liberia)
      Gbasa language
  BT Kru languages
      Liberia--Languages

Bassa-Nge (African people)
  USE Nupe (African people)

Bassanga (African people)
  USE Sanga (African people)

Bassari (Senegalese and Guinean people) *(May Subd Geog)*
  [DT 549.45.B37 (Senegal)]
  UF Ayan (Senegalese and Guinean people)

  UF Basar (Senegalese and Guinean people)
      Basari (Senegalese and Guinean people)
      Biyan (Senegalese and Guinean people)
      Onian (Senegalese and Guinean people)
      Wo (Senegalese and Guinean people)
  BT Ethnology--Guinea
      Ethnology--Senegal
      Tenda (African people)

Bassari (Togolese and Ghanaian people) *(May Subd Geog)*
  [DT 582.45.B37 (Togo)]
  UF Akasele (Togolese and Ghanaian people)
      Basaie (Togolese and Ghanaian people)
      Basari (Togolese and Ghanaian people)
      Cemba (Togolese and Ghanaian people)
      Chamba (Togolese and Ghanaian people)
      Djabe (Togolese and Ghanaian people)
      Djelib (Togolese and Ghanaian people)
      Ndjeli (Togolese and Ghanaian people)
      Tapoumbi (Togolese and Ghanaian people)
      Tchambe (Togolese and Ghanaian people)
      Tobote (Togolese and Ghanaian people)
  BT Ethnology--Ghana
      Ethnology--Togo
  --Industries

Bassari folk songs
  USE Folk songs, Bassari

Bassari language *(May Subd Geog)*
  [PL 8066.B3]
  UF Ayan language
      Basari language
      Biyan language
      Wo language
  BT Guinea--Languages
      Niger-Congo languages
      Senegal--Languages

Bassari language (Togo and Ghana)
  USE Tobote language

Bassin de Taoudenni (Mali)
  USE Taoudenni Basin (Mali)

Bassin Tchadien
  USE Chad Basin

Bassoa (African people)
  USE Batwa (African people)

Bassonge (African people)
  USE Songe (African people)

(May Subd Geog) = Place names may follow the heading

Bastaards
  USE Griquas

Bastaards (African people)
  USE Rehoboth Basters (African people)

Basters (African people)
  USE Rehoboth Basters (African people)

Basuku (African people)
  USE Suku (African people)

Basukuma (African people)
  USE Sukuma (African people)

Basuto (African people)
  USE Sotho (African people)

Basuto War, 1865-1866
  USE Sotho-Free State War, 1865-1866

Basutoland
  USE Lesotho

Batabwa (African people)
  USE Tabwa (African people)

Batahin (Arab people) (May Subd Geog)
  [DT 155.2.B]
  UF Bathan (Arab people)
  BT Ethnology--Sudan

Batambwa (African people)
  USE Tabwa (African people)

Batammaliba (African people)
  USE Somba (African people)

Batanga-Nda (African people)
  USE Tanga (African people)

Batchopi (African people)
  USE Chopi (African people)

Bateke (African people)
  USE Teke (African people)

Batende (African people)
  USE Kuria (African people)

Bateso (African people)
  USE Teso (African people)

Batetela (African people)
  USE Tetela (African people)

Bathan (Arab people)
  USE Batahin (Arab people)

Bati language (May Subd Geog)
  [PL 8067]
  BT Bantu languages
      Cameroon--Languages
--Texts

Bati proverbs
  USE Proverbs, Bati

Batjva (African people)
  USE Batwa (African people)

Batlapin (African people)
  USE Tlhaping (African people)

Batlokwa (African people)
  USE Tlokwa (African people)

Batloqua (African people)
  USE Tlokwa (African people)

Batoa (African people)
  USE Batwa (African people)

Batohwa (African people)
  USE Batwa (African people)

Batswa (African people)
  USE Batwa (African people)

Battas (African people) (May Subd Geog)
  [DT571.B]
  BT Ethnology--Cameroon

Battle of Adowa, 1896
  USE Adowa, Battle of, 1896

Battle of Alam Halfa (Sudan), 1942
  USE Alam Halfa, Battle of, 1942

Battle of Blood River (South Africa), 1838
  USE Blood River (South Africa), Battle of, 1838

Battle of Cheren (Ethiopia), 1941
  USE Cheren, Battle of, 1941

Battle of Dakar (Senegal), 1940
  USE Dakar, Battle of, 1940

Battle of Elandslaagte (South Africa), 1899
  USE Elandslaagte, South Africa, Battle of, 1899

UF = Used for; BT = Broader term; RT = Related term; SA = See also; NT = Narrower term

Battle of Imbabu (Ethiopia), 1882
  USE Imbabu, Ethiopia, Battle of, 1882

Battle of Isandlwana (South Africa), 1879
  USE Isandlwana (South Africa), Battle of,
1879

Battle of Kumasi (Ghana), 1874
  USE Kumasi (Ghana), Battle of, 1874

Battle of Magersfontein (South Africa), 1899
  USE Magersfontein, South Africa, Battle
of, 1899

Battle of Majuba Hill (South Africa), 1881
  USE Majuba Hill (South Africa), Battle of,
1881

Battle of Mak'edala (Ethiopia), 1868
  USE Mak'edala, Ethiopia, Battle of, 1868

Battle of Ndondakusuka (South Africa), 1856
  USE Ndondakusuka, Battle of, South Africa,
1856

Battle of Omdurman (Sudan), 1898
  USE Omdurman, Battle of, 1898

Battle of Rorke's Drift (South Africa), 1879
  USE Rorke's Drift (South Africa), Battle
of, 1878

Battle of Spioenkop (South Africa), 1900
  USE Spioenkop, Battle of, 1900

Battle of Stormberg (South Africa), 1899
  USE Stormberg, Battle of, 1899

Battle of Tungue Bay (Mozambique), 1887
  USE Tungue Bay (Mozambique), Battle of,
1887

Battle of Waima (Sierra Leone), 1893
  USE Waima (Sierra Leone), Battle of, 1893

Batua (African people)
  USE Batwa (African people)

Batumbuka (African people)
  USE Tumbuka (African people)

Batushi (African people)
  USE Ushi (African people)

Batutsi (African people)
  USE Tutsi (African people)

Batwa (African people) *(May Subd Geog)*
  [DT 450.65.B (Burundi)]
  [DT 450.25.B (Rwanda)]
  UF Abathwa (African people)
     Atschoua (African people)
     Bachua (African people)
     Bacwa (African people)
     Bakiue (African people)
     Bakwa (African people)
     Baroa (African people)
     Bassoa (African people)
     Batjva (African people)
     Batoa (African people)
     Batshwa (African people)
     Batswa (African people)
     Batua (African people)
     Bekoe (African people)
     Boroa (African people)
     Rutwa (African people)
     Twa (African people)
     Watshua (African people)
     Wattua (African people)
     Wotsschua (African people)
     Xegwe (African people)
     Xegwi (African people)
  BT Ethnology--Burundi
     Ethnology--Rwanda
     Ethnology--Zaire
     Pygmies
     Rundi (African people)

Bauchi languages, Southern
  USE Southern Bauchi languages

Bauchi Plateau (Nigeria)
  USE Jos Plateau (Nigeria)

Baule (African people)
  USE Baoulé (African people)

Baule language
  USE Baoulé language

Baushi (African people)
  USE Ushi (African people)

Bausi (African people)
  USE Ushi (African people)

Bavēk (African people) *(May Subd Geog)*
  [DT 571.B38]
  UF Avak (African people)
     Avuk (African people)

(May Subd Geog) = Place names may follow the heading

UF Bafeuk (African people)
    Bafuk (African people)
BT Ethnology--Cameroon

Bavenda (African people)
  USE Venda (African people)

Bavili (African people)
  USE Vili (African people)

Bavuma (African people) *(May Subd Geog)*
  [DT 433.245.B38]
  UF Buvuma (African people)
  BT Ethnology--Uganda

Bawenda (African people)
  USE Venda (African people)

Bawgott (African people)
  USE Suk (African people)

Baya (African people)
  USE Gbaya (African people)

Baya language
  USE Gbaya language

Baya Revolt, 1928-1931
  USE Kongo Wara, 1928-1931

Bayaka (African people)
  USE Yaka (African people)

Bayanzi (African people)
  USE Yanzi (African people)

Bayéké (African people)
  USE Yaka (African people)

Bayele language
  USE Bagyele language

Bayikpe (African people)
  USE Ewe (African people)

Bayombe (African people)
  USE Mayombe

Bayot (African people) *(May Subd Geog)*
  [DT 549.45.B39 (Senegal)]
  UF Baiot (African people)
      Baiote (African people)
      Bayotte (African people)
      Edii (African people)
      Ehing (African people)
      Essing (African people)

UF Kagere (African people)
BT Ethnology--Gambia
    Ethnology--Guinea-Bissau
    Ethnology--Senegal

Bayotte (African people)
  USE Bayot (African people)

Bays *(May Subd Geog)*
  UF Gulfs
  BT Coasts
  RT Inlets
  --**Africa, West**
    NT Benin, Bight of
        Guinea, Gulf of
  --**Angola**
    NT Lobito Bay (Angola)
  --**Cape Verde**
    NT Porto Grande (Cape Verde)
  --**Mozambique**
    NT Tunque Bay (Mozambique)
  --**South Africa**
    NT False Bay (Cape of Good Hope, South Africa)
        Kosi Bay (South Africa)
        Saldanha Bay (South Africa)

Bayuqu (African people)
  USE Mponqwe (African people)

Baza (African people)
  USE Kunama (African people)

Baza language
  UCB Kunama language

Bazela (African people)
  USE Zela (African people)

Bazen (African people)
  USE Kunama (African people)

Bazen language
  USE Kunama language

Bazezuru (African people)
  USE Zezuru (African people)

Baziba (African people)
  USE Haya (African people)

Bazimba (Malagasy people)
  USE Vazimbas

Bazin (African people)
  USE Kunama (African people)

UF = Used for; BT = Broader term; RT = Related term; SA = See also; NT = Narrower term

Bé Island (Madagascar)
  USE Nosy-Be Island (Madagascar)

Beadwork, Nguni *(May Subd Geog)*
  [NK 3650.5.S]
  UF Nguni beadwork

Beadwork, Xhosa *(May Subd Geog)*
  [NK 3650.5.S]
  UF Xhosa beadwork

Beadwork, Yoruba *(May Subd Geog)*
  [NK 3650.5.N64Y]
  UF Yoruba beadwork

Beauregard (Réunion) *(Not Subd Geog)*
  BT Dwellings--Réunion
      Plantations--Réunion

Beautiful, The
  USE Aesthetics

Beauty
  USE Aesthetics

Bebayaga (African people)
  USE Baka (West African people)

Bebayaka (African people)
  USE Baka (West African people)

Bechuana (African people)
  USE Tswana (African people)

Bechuana language
  USE Tswana language

Bechuanaland
  USE Botswana

Bedauye (African people)
  USE Beja (African people)

Bedauye language
  USE Beja language

Bedawie language
  USE Beja language

Bedawiye (African people)
  USE Beja (African people)

Bedawiye language
  USE Beja language

Bedawiyet (African people)

  USE Beja (African people)

Bedawiyet language
  USE Beja language

Bedawye language
  USE Beja language

Bedik (African people) *(May Subd Geog)*
  [DT 549.45.B]
  BT Ethnology--Senegal
      Tenda (African people)

Bedik language *(May Subd Geog)*
  [PL 8068.B39]
  UF Bande language
      Basari du Bandemba language
      Budik language
      Tandanke language
      Tenda language
      Tendanke language
  BT Niger-Congo languages
      Senegal--Languages

Bedja (African people)
  USE Beja (African people)

Bedja language
  USE Beja language

Beembe (East African people)
  USE Bembe (East African people)

Beembe (West African people)
  USE Bembe (West African people)

Beembe language (Congo (Brazzaville))
  USE Bembe language (Congo (Brazzaville))

Beembe language (Lake Tanganyika)
  USE Bembe language (Lake Tanganyika)

Beetjuans (African people)
  USE Tswana (African people)

Beetjuans language
  USE Tswana language

Bega (African people)
  USE Beja (African people)

Begia language
  USE Beja language

Begpak (African people)
  USE Bafia (African people)

(May Subd Geog) = Place names may follow the heading

Behosys *(May Subd Geog)*
  [DT 469.M277B]
  UF Beosis (Malagasy people)
      Kalios (Malagasy people)
  BT Ethnology--Madagascar

Beir (African people)
  USE Murle (African people)

Beir language
  USE Murle language

Beja (African people) *(May Subd Geog)*
  [DT 380.4.B45 (Ethiopia)]
  [DT 155.2.B44 (Sudan)]
  UF Bedauye (African people)
      Bedawiye (African people)
      Bedawiyet (African people)
      Bedja (African people)
      Bega (African people)
  BT Ethnology--Ethiopia
      Ethnology--Sudan

Beja language *(May Subd Geog)*
  [PJ 2451-PJ 2459]
  UF Bedauye language
      Bedawie language
      Bedawiye language
      Bedawiyet language
      Bedawye language
      Bedja language
      Begia language
      Beni-Aamir language
      Beni-Amer language
      Beni-Amir language
      Bishári dialect
      To-bedawie language
      Tu-bedawie language
  BT Cushitic languages
      Sudan--Languages

Bekoe (African people)
  USE Bagyele (African people)
      Batwa (African people)

Bekoe language
  USE Bagyele language

Bekom (African people)
  USE Kom (African people)

Bekpak (African people)
  USE Bafia (African people)

Bekwarra language *(May Subd Geog)*
  [PL 8068.B4]
  UF Bekworra language
      Bekworrah language
      Ebekwara language
      Yakoro language
  BT Benue-Congo languages
      Nigeria--Languages

Bekwiri language
  USE Kwiri language

Bekworra language
  USE Bekwarra language

Bekworrah language
  USE Bekworra language

Belanda language
  USE Bor language (Lwo)

Belante (African people)
  USE Balanta (African people)

Belen (African people)
  USE Bogos

Belgian Congo
  USE Zaire

Belgium *(Not Subd Geog)*
  --Colonies
      BT Colonies
  -- --Administration
      UF Belgium--Colonies--Politics and government
  -- --Boundaries *(May Subd Geog)*
  -- --Commerce *(May Subd Geog)*
  -- --Constitutional history
  -- --Constitutional law
  -- --Defenses
  -- --Description and travel
  -- --Discovery and exploration
  -- --Economic conditions
  -- --Economic policy
  -- --Emigration and immigration
  -- --Geography *(Not Subd Geog)*
  -- --History
  -- --Industries
  -- --Manufactures
  -- --Native races
      USE Indigenous peoples--Belgium--Colonies
  -- --Officials and employees
  -- --Politics and government
      USE Belgium--Colonies--Administration
  -- --Population
  -- --Public lands   *(Continued)*

UF = Used for; BT = Broader term; RT = Related term; SA = See also; NT = Narrower term

Belgium
--Colonies *(Continued)*
-- --Public works
-- --Race relations
-- --Religion
-- --Religious life and customs
-- --Rural conditions
-- --Social conditions
-- --Social life and customs
-- --Social policy
-- --Africa

Bemba (African people) *(May Subd Geog)*
  [DT 963.42 : old class]
  [DT 3058.B46 : new class]
  UF Awemba (African people)
      Babemba (African people)
      Wawemba (African people)
  BT Bantu-speaking peoples
      Ethnology--Zambia
  NT Ushi (African people)
--Missions *(May Subd Geog)*
  [BV 3630.B]
  UF Missions to Bemba (African people)
--Religion
  [BL 2480.B4]

Bemba hymns
  USE Hymns, Bemba

Bemba language *(May Subd Geog)*
  [PL 8069]
  UF Chibemba language
      Wemba language
  BT Bantu languages
      Zambia--Languages

Bemba literature *(May Subd Geog)*
  [PL 8069.5-PL 8069.9]
  BT Zambian literature
  NT Bemba poetry

Bemba poetry *(May Subd Geog)*
  [PL 8069.7 (Collections)]
  BT Bemba literature
      Zambian poetry

Bemba proverbs
  USE Proverbs, Bemba

Bembala language
  USE Burji language

Bembe (East African people) *(May Subd Geog)*
  UF Balembe (East African people)
      Beembe (East African people)

  UF Ebembe (East African people)
      Ibembe (East African people)
      Vabembe (East African people)
      Wabembe (East African people)
  BT Bantu-speaking peoples
      Ethnology--Burundi
      Ethnology--Tanzania
      Ethnology--Zaire

Bembe (West African people) *(May Subd Geog)*
  [DT 546.245.B44 (Congo (Brazzaville))]
  UF Babembe (West African people)
      Beembe (West African people)
  BT Bantu-speaking peoples
      Ethnology--Angola
      Ethnology--Congo (Brazzaville)
      Ethnology--Zaire

Bembe language (Congo (Brazzaville)) *(May Subd Geog)*
  [PL 8070.B45]
  UF Beembe language (Congo (Brazzaville))
      KiBeembe language
      KiBembe language
      Mbembe language (Congo (Brazzaville))
  BT Bantu languages
      Congo (Brazzaville)--Languages
      Kongo language

Bembe language (Lake Tanganyika) *(May Subd Geog)*
  [PL 8070.B]
  UF Beembe language (Lake Tanganyika)
      Ebembe language
      Ibembe language
  BT Bantu languages
      Burundi--Languages
      Tanzania--Languages
      Zaire--Languages

Bembe proverbs (Congo (Brazzaville))
  USE Proverbs, Bembe (Congo (Brazzaville))

Bembe riddles (Congo (Brazzaville))
  USE Riddles, Bembe (Congo (Brazzaville))

Bembola language
  USE Burji language

Bena (African people) *(May Subd Geog)*
  [DT 443.3.B45]
  UF Ekibena (African people)
      Wabena (African people)
  BT Bantu-speaking peoples
      Ethnology--Tanzania

Bena Lulua (African people)
  USE Lulua (African people)

(May Subd Geog) = Place names may follow the heading

Benda language
USE Venda language

Benga language *(May Subd Geog)*
[PL 8071-PL 8074]
BT Bantu languages
    Equatorial Guinea--Languages
    Gabon--Languages

Benge language *(May Subd Geog)*
[PL 8075.B4]
UF Libenge language
    Mobenge language
BT Bantu languages
    Zaire--Languages

Benguela language
USE Umbundu language

Benguella (African people)
USE Ngangela (African people)

Beni-Aamir language
USE Beja language

Beni-Amer language
USE Beja language

Beni Amer (African people) *(May Subd Geog)*
[DT 380.4.B (Ethiopia)
[DT 155.2.B (Sudan)
UF Beni Amir (African people)
BT Ethnology--Ethiopia
    Ethnology--Sudan

Beni Amir (African people)
USE Beni Amer (African people)

Beni-Amir language
USE Beja language

Benimukuni (African people)
USE Lenje (African people)

Benin *(Not Subd Geog)*
[DT 541-DT 541.9]
UF Dahomey
    People's Republic of Benin
    République Populaire du Bénin
--Drama
NT Yoruba drama
--Economic conditions
[HC 1010]
-- --1960-
--Fiction
NT Yoruba fiction

--Foreign relations *(May Subd Geog)*
-- --1960-
--History
-- --To 1894
[DT 541.65]
-- --Coup d'état, 1977
[DT 541.845]
BT Coups d'état--Benin
--Languages
NT Aja dialect
    Busa language
    Dendi dialect
    Dompago dialect
    Ewe language
    Fon dialect
    Gurma language
    Mina dialect
    Somba language
    Tofingbe dialect
    Yoruba language
    Zarma dialect
--Literatures
USE Benin literature
--Poetry
NT Fon poetry
    Yoruba poetry
--Politics and government
-- --To 1960
-- --1960-
--Social conditions
-- --1960-

Benin (Kingdom)
USE Benin (Nigeria)--History

Benin (Nigeria) *(Not Subd Geog)*
--History
[DT 515.65]
UF Benin (Kingdom)

Benin, Bight of *(Not Subd Geog)*
UF Bight of Benin
BT Bays--Africa, West

Benin art
USE Art, Benin

Benin language
USE Bini language

Benin literature *(May Subd Geog)*
[PL 8014.B]
UF Benin--Literatures
NT Fon literature
    Yoruba literature

UF = Used for; BT = Broader term; RT = Related term; SA = See also; NT = Narrower term

Benin literature (French) *(May Subd Geog)*
  [PQ 3988.5.B4 (History)]
  [PQ 3988.5.B42 (Collections)]
  UF French literature--Benin authors
  BT West African literature (French)
  NT Benin poetry (French)

Benin poetry (French) *(May Subd Geog)*
  [PQ 3988.5.B4 (History)]
  [PQ 3988.5.B42 (Collections)]
  UF French poetry--Benin authors
  BT Benin literature (French)
      West African poetry (French)

Benin proverbs
  USE Proverbs, Benin

Bénoué River (Cameroon and Nigeria)
  USE Benue River (Cameroon and Nigeria)

Benue-Congo languages *(May Subd Geog)*
  [PL 8026.B4]
  BT Niger-Congo languages
  NT Abua-Ogbia languages
      Bamileke languages
      Bamun language
      Bantu languages
      Bekwarra language
      Efik language
      Grasslands Bantu languages
      Ibibio language
      Jukunoid languages
      Kana language
      Mambila language
      Mamfe Bantu languages
      Mankon language
      Ngemba language (Cameroon)
      Ngo language
      Obolo language
      Plateau languages (Nigeria)
      Tikar language
      Tivi language
      Yakö language

Benue River (Cameroon and Nigeria) *(Not Subd Geog)*
  UF Bénoué River (Cameroon and Nigeria)
      Binue River (Cameroon and Nigeria)
  BT Rivers--Cameroon
      Rivers--Nigeria

Benue River Valley (Cameroon and Nigeria) *(Not Subd Geog)*
  BT Valleys--Cameroon
      Valleys--Nigeria

Beosis (Malagasy people)
  USE Behosys

Bequests
  USE Inheritance and succession

Berg River (South Africa) *(Not Subd Geog)*
  UF Bergrivier (South Africa)
  BT Rivers--South Africa

Bergdama (African people)
  USE Damara (African people)

Bergdamara (African people)
  USE Damara (African people)

Bergrivier (South Africa)
  USE Berg River (South Africa)

Beri (African people)
  USE Zaghawa (African people)

Beriberi (African people)
  USE Kanuri (African people)

Berom language
  USE Birom language

Berri (African people)
  USE Zaghawa (African people)

Berta (African people) *(May Subd Geog)*
  [DT 155.2.B (Sudan)]
  UF Barta (African people)
      Bertat (African people)
      Bertha (African people)
      Burta (African people)
  BT Ethnology--Ethiopia
      Ethnology--Sudan

Bertat (African people)
  USE Berta (African people)

Bertha (African people)
  USE Berta (African people)

Berti (African people) *(May Subd Geog)*
  [DT 155.2.B47]
  BT Ethnology--Sudan

Beshada (African people)
  USE Hamar (African people)

Beta Israel
  USE Falashas

(May Subd Geog) = Place names may follow the heading

Betammadibe language
    USE Somba language

Betammaribe language
    USE Somba language

Bété (African people) *(May Subd Geog)*
    [DT 545.45.B47]
    BT Ethnology--Ivory Coast

Bete language *(May Subd Geog)*
    [PL 8075.B57]
    UF Betegbo language
    BT Ivory Coast--Languages
        Kru languages
    NT Dida dialect
        Godye dialect
        Nyabwa language
        Wobe language
  --Names
    USE Names, Bete

Bete names
    USE Names, Bete

Betegbo language
    USE Bete language

Bethlehem Weather Modification Experiment
    [QC 928.74.S6]
    UF Weather Modification Experiment at
Bethlehem
    BT Meteorology--Research--South Africa
        Weather control--South Africa

Beti (African people) *(May Subd Geog)*
    [DT 571.B47]
    BT Bantu-speaking peoples
        Ethnology--Cameroon
    NT Eton (African people)
        Evuzok (African people)
  --Religion
    [BL 2480.B47]
  --Rites and ceremonies
    NT Abia (Rite)

Beti women
    USE Women, Beti

Beti language
    USE Ewondo language

Betjek (Cameroon people)
    USE Basa (Cameroon people)

Betsileo dialect *(May Subd Geog)*
    [PL 5379]
    BT Malagasy language

Betsileo wood-carving
    USE Wood-carving, Betsileo

Betsileos *(May Subd Geog)*
    [DT 469.M277B]
    BT Ethnology--Madagascar

Betsimaraka dialect
    USE Betsimisaraka dialect

Betsimisaraka *(May Subd Geog)*
    [DT 469.M277B]
    BT Ethnology--Madagascar
  --Religion
    [BL 2480.B49]

Betsimisaraka dialect *(May Subd Geog)*
    UF Betsimaraka dialect
    BT Malagasy language

Bezanozano (Malagasy people) *(May Subd Geog)*
    [DT 469.M277B]
    UF Antaiva (Malagasy people)
        Antakay (Malagasy people)
        Antanka (Malagasy people)
        Tankay (Malagasy people)
    BT Ethnology--Madagascar

Bhaca (African people) *(May Subd Geog)*
    [DT 764.B : old class]
    [DT 1768.B53 : new class]
    UF Amabaca (African people)
    BT Ethnology--South Africa
        Ngoni (African people)

Biafra
    USE Nigeria, Eastern

Biafran Conflict, 1967-1970
    USE Nigeria--History--Civil War, 1967-1970

Biaka (African people)
    USE Babinga (African people)

Bibaya (African people)
    USE Baka (West African people)

Bibaya language
    USE Baka language (Cameroon)

Bibayak (African people)
    USE Baka (West African people)

UF = Used for; BT = Broader term; RT = Related term; SA = See also; NT = Narrower term

Bible *(May Subd Geog)*
  UF Holy Scriptures
      Scriptures, Holy
  --Blacks
  USE Blacks in the Bible

Bibliography
  *For lists of titles about a particular country, see
  the name of the country with subdivision
  Bibliography, e.g. Uganda--Bibliography.*
  *For lists of titles published in a particular
  country, see the name of the country with subdivision
  Imprints, e.g. Zambia--Imprints.*
  *For lists of titles published in the language of a
  particular country without regard to place of
  publication, see phrase headings of the type Sotho
  imprints.*

Bidiya language
  USE Bidiyo language

Bidiyo language *(May Subd Geog)*
  [PL 8076.B35]
  UF Bidiya language
      Bidyo language
  BT Chad--Languages
      Chadic languages

Bidjogo (African people)
  USE Bijago (African people)

Bidyo language
  USE Bidiyo language

Bidyogo (African people)
  USE Bijago (African people)

Bight of Benin
  USE Benin, Bight of

Bijago (African people) *(May Subd Geog)*
  [DT 613.45.B]
  UF Bidjogo (African people)
      Bidyogo (African people)
      Bijogo (African people)
      Bijuga (African people)
      Bissago (African people)
      Budjago (African people)
      Bugago (African people)
  BT Ethnology--Guinea-Bissau

Bijago art
  USE Art, Bijago

Bijogo (African people)
  USE Bijago (African people)

Bijuga (African people)
  USE Bijago (African people)

Biko, Steve, 1946-1977, in motion pictures *(Not
Subd Geog)*
  [PN 1995.9.B]
  BT Motion pictures

Bikom (African people)
  USE Kom (African people)

Bilen language
  USE Bilin language

Bilin (African people)
  USE Bogos

Bilin language *(May Subd Geog)*
  [PJ 2430]
  UF Bilen language
  BT Cushitic languages
  RT Agau language

Bimbundu (African people)
  USE Mbundu (African people)

Bimoba language
  USE Moba language

Bini (African people) *(May Subd Geog)*
  [DT 515.45.B56]
  UF Edo (African people)
  BT Ethnology--Nigeria

Bini art
  USE Art, Bini

Bini bronzes
  USE Bronzes, Bini

Bini language *(May Subd Geog)*
  [PL 8077]
  UF Benin language
      Do language
      Edo language
  BT Kwa languages
      Nigeria--Languages

Bini textile fabrics
  USE Textile fabrics, Bini

Binja (African people)
  USE Songola (African people)

Binue River (Cameroon and Nigeria)
  USE Benue River (Cameroon and Nigeria)

(May Subd Geog) = Place names may follow the heading

Bioco (Equatorial Guinea)
  USE Fernando Po (Equatorial Guinea)

Biography
  USE *subdivision* Biography *under names of*
  countries, cities, etc., and under the names of ethnic
  groups, e.g. Ghana--Biography; Blacks--
  Biography.

Bioko (Equatorial Guinea)
  USE Fernando Po (Equatorial Guinea)

Biotu (African people)
  USE Isoko (African people)

Bira (African people) *(May Subd Geog)*
  [DT 650.B57 (Zaire)]
  UF Babira (African people)
  BT Bantu-speaking peoples
      Ethnology--Africa, Central
      Ethnology--Zaire

Biri language
  USE Birri language

Birifor (African people) *(May Subd Geog)*
  [DT 530.5.B (French West Africa)]
  [DT 510.43.B (Chana)]
  BT Ethnology--Burkina Faso
      Ethnology--Ghana
      Ethnology--Ivory Coast
 --Religion
  [BL 2480.B5]

Birom language *(May Subd Geog)*
  [PL 8078.B36]
  UF Berom language
      Bouroum language
      Burum language (Nigeria)
  BT Nigeria--Languages
      Plateau languages (Nigeria)

Birra (African people)
  USE Didinga (African people)

Birri language *(May Subd Geog)*
  [PL 8078.B37]
  UF Abiri language
      Ambili language
      Biri language
      Viri language
  BT Central African Republic--Languages
      Nilo-Saharan languages

Birth control *(May Subd Geog)*
  UF Family planning
      Planned parenthood
      Population control
  --Ghana
  NT Danfa Comprehensive Rural Health and Family
  Planning Project

Bisa (Burkinabe and Ghanaian people) *(May Subd Geog)*
  [DT 510.43.B (Ghana)]
  [DT 555.45.B57 (Burkina Faso)]
  UF Bissa (Burkinabe and Ghanaian people)
  BT Ethnology--Burkina Faso
      Ethnology--Ghana

Bisa (Zambian people) *(May Subd Geog)*
  [DT 963.42 : old class]
  [DT 3058.B58 : new class]
  UF Abisa (Zambian people)
      Awisa (Zambian people)
      Babisa (Zambian people)
      Muiza (Zambian people)
      Wisa (Zambian people)
  BT Bantu-speaking peoples
      Ethnology--Zambia

Bisa language *(May Subd Geog)*
  [PL 8078.B4]
  UF Wisa language
  DT Bantu languages
      Zambia--Languages

Bishari dialect
  USE Beja language

Bisio (African people) *(May Subd Geog)*
  [DT 620.45.B]
  UF Bisiwo (African people)
      Bujeba (African people)
      Mabea (African people)
      Mabi (African people)
  BT Bantu-speaking peoples
      Ethnology--Equatorial Guinea

Bisio language *(May Subd Geog)*
  [PL 8078.B5]
  UF Bujeba language
      Mabea language
  BT Bantu languages
      Equatorial Guinea--Languages

Bisiwo (African people)
  USE Bisio (African people)

UF = Used for; BT = Broader term; RT = Related term; SA = See also; NT = Narrower term

Bissa (Burkinabe and Ghanaian people)
  USE Bisa (Burkinabe and Ghanaian people)

Bissago (African people)
  USE Bijago (African people)

Biyan (Senegalese and Guinean people)
  USE Bassari (Senegalese and Guinean
people)

Biyan language
  USE Bassari language

Black actors
  USE Actors, Black

Black aesthetics
  USE Aesthetics, Black

Black Africa
  USE Africa, Sub-Saharan

Black Africans
  USE Blacks--Africa

Black American...
  USE *subject headings beginning with the words*
Afro-American

Black Americans
  USE Afro-Americans

Black art
  USE Art, Black

Black artists
  USE Artists, Black

Black arts
  USE Arts, Black

Black athletes
  USE Athletes, Black

Black authors
  USE Authors, Black

Black Baptists
  USE Baptists, Black

Black Bobo language
  USE Bobo Fing language

Black business enterprises *(May Subd Geog)*
  UF Business enterprises, Black
  BT Business enterprises

--**South Africa**
  [HD 2346.S632]

Black children
  USE Children, Black

Black Christians
  USE Christians, Black

Black college graduates
  USE College graduate, Black

Black college students
  USE College students, Black

Black college teachers
  USE College teachers, Black

Black colleges
  USE Universities and colleges, Black

Black communication
  USE Blacks--Communication

Black composers
  USE Composers, Black

Black drama
  USE Drama--Black authors

Black drama, African
  USE African drama

Black drama (English)
  USE English drama--Black authors

Black drama (French)
  USE French drama--Black authors

Black executives
  USE Executives, Black

Black families
  USE Families, Black

Black fiction
  USE Fiction--Black authors

Black fiction, African
  USE African fiction

Black fiction, Zimbabwean (English)
  USE Zimbabwean fiction (English)--Black authors

Black folk art
  USE Folk art, Black

(May Subd Geog) = Place names may follow the heading

Black hairdressing
  USE Hairdressing of Blacks

Black history
  USE Blacks--History

Black Homelands (South Africa)
  USE Homelands (South Africa)

Black-Jewish relations
  USE Blacks--Relations with Jews

Black libraries
  USE Libraries and Blacks

Black literature
  USE Literature--Black authors

Black literature, African
  USE African literature

Black literature (English)
  USE English literature--Black authors

Black literature (French)
  USE French literature--Black authors

Black literature (Portuguese)
  USE Portuguese literature--Black authors

Black literature, South African (English)
  USE South African literature (English)--
Black authors

Black militant organizations *(May Subd Geog)*
  UF Militant organizations, Black
  BT Black power

Black musicians
  USE Musicians, Black

Black nationalism *(May Subd Geog)*
  UF Black separatism
     Nationalism--Blacks
     Nationalism, Black
     Separatism, Black
  BT Blacks--Politics and government
     Blacks--Race identity
  RT Black power
  --Africa, West
  --Liberia

Black newspapers *(May Subd Geog)*
  UF Newspapers, Black
  BT Newspapers

Black painters
  USE Painters, Black

Black painting
  USE Painting, Black

Black poetry
  USE Poetry--Black authors

Black poetry, African
  USE African poetry

Black poetry (English)
  USE English poetry--Black authors

Black poetry (French)
  USE French poetry--Black authors

Black poetry (Portuguese)
  USE Portuguese poetry--Black authors

Black poetry, South African (English)
  USE South African poetry (English)--Black
authors

Black poets
  USE Poets, Black

Black police
  USE Police, Black

Black power *(May Subd Geog)*
  UF Power, Black
  RT Black nationalism
  NT Black militant organizations
  --Africa

Black prints
  USE Prints, Black

Black proverbs
  USE Proverbs, Black

Black race
  Here are entered theoretical works discussing the Black
  race from an anthropological point of view. Works on blacks
  as an element in the population are entered under Blacks.
  UF Negro race
  BT Race
  NT Blacks
  --Color
    UF Blacks--Color
    BT Color of man

Black sculpture
  USE Sculpture, Black

UF = Used for; BT = Broader term; RT = Related term; SA = See also; NT = Narrower term

Black separatism
  USE Black nationalism

Black soldiers
  USE Soldiers, Black

Black students
  USE Students, Black

Black studies
  USE Blacks--Study and teaching

Black teachers
  USE Teachers, Black

Black textile fabrics
  USE Textile fabrics, Black

Black theater *(May Subd Geog)*
  UF Theater, Black
  BT Theater
  NT Actors, Black
 --**Africa**
  [PN 2969-PN 3000]

Black theology
  [BT 82.7 (Christianity)]
  UF Theology, Black
  BT Blacks--Religion
      Theology

Black trade-unions
  USE Trade-unions, Black

Black universities and colleges
  USE Universities and colleges, Black

Black university graduates
  USE College graduates, Black

Black university students
  USE College students, Black

Black university teachers
  USE College teachers, Black

Black women
  USE Women, Black

Black women authors
  USE Women authors, Black

Black youth
  USE Youth, Black

Blacks *(May Subd Geog)*
  Here are entered works on blacks as an element in the
  population. Works on the black people of the United States
  are entered under the heading Afro-Americans.
  Theoretical works discussing the Black race from an
  anthropological point of view are entered under Black
  race.
  Works on black people in countries whose racial
  composition is predominantly black are assigned headings
  appropriate for the country as a whole without the use of
  the heading Blacks. The heading Blacks is assigned to
  works on such countries only if the work discusses blacks
  apart from other groups in the country.
  UF Negroes
  BT Black race
  SA *subdivision* Blacks *under individual wars, e.g.*
World War, 1939-1945--Blacks; *and headings beginning*
with the word Black
  NT Afro-Americans
      Libraries and Blacks
      Mulattoes
      Soldiers, Black
 --**Anthropometry**
  [GN 57.B]
 --**Attitudes**
 --**Children**
  USE Children, Black
 --**Civil rights** *(May Subd Geog)*
  NT Blacks--Politics and government
 --**Color**
  USE Black race--Color
 --**Communication**
  [P 94.5.B55]
  UF Black communication
 --**Cultural assimilation**
  BT Acculturation
 --**Dancing**
  [GV 1705 (Africa)]
  UF Dancing--Blacks
  BT Dancing
 --**Education** *(May Subd Geog)*
  [LC 2699-LC 2913 (for countries where Blacks
are not the controlling element of the
population)]
  [LA 1500-LA 2090 (Africa)]
  NT College students, Black
      Students, Black
      Universities and colleges, Black
 -- --**South Africa**
  [LC 2808.S7]
 --**Employment** *(May Subd Geog)*
 -- --**Law and legislation** *(May Subd Geog)*
 --**Families**
  USE Families, Black

                                        (Continued)

(May Subd Geog) = Place names may follow the heading

Blacks   *(Continued)*
--Funeral customs and rites
  UF Funeral rites and ceremonies, Black
--Hairdressing
 USE Hairdressing of Blacks
--History
  UF Black history
--Jewelry
  UF Jewelry, Black
--Languages
  BT African languages
--Missions *(May Subd Geog)*
  UF Missions to Blacks
--Music
  [ML 3760 (Africa)]
  NT Blacks Songs and music
--Politics and government
  BT Blacks--Civil rights
  NT Black nationalism
--Quotations
  [PN 6081.3]
  UF Quotations, Black
--Race identity
  [GN 645]
  UF Negritude
      Racial identity of Blacks
  BT Race awareness
      Ethnicity
  NT Black nationalism
--Relations with Jews
  UF Black-Jewish relations
      Jewish-Black relations
      Jews--Relations with Blacks
--Religion
  NT Black theology
      Muslims, Black
--Relocation
  UF Blacks--Resettlement
      Relocation of Blacks
      Removal of Blacks
      Resettlement of Blacks
  BT Race relations
      Segregation
-- --Religious aspects
-- -- --Buddhism, [Christianity, etc.]
--Resettlement
 USE Blacks--Relocation
--Segregation
  BT Blacks--Social conditions
      Segregation
--Social conditions
  NT Blacks--Segregation
--Songs and music
  [ML 3760 (Africa)]
  RT Blacks--Music

--Study and teaching *(May Subd Geog)*
  UF Black studies
--Africa
  UF Black Africans
-- --Relations with Afro-Americans
 USE Afro-Americans--Relations with Africans
--Africa, Southern
  [DT 737 : old class]
  [DT 1058.B53 : new class]
--Mauritius
  [DT 469.M445B55]
--Namibia
-- --Segregation
 USE Apartheid--Namibia
--Sierra Leone
  NT Creoles (Sierra Leone)
--South Africa
  [DT 764 : old class]
  [DT 1758 : new class]
  UF Bantus
-- --Politics and government
  NT African National Congress
-- --Segregation
 USE Apartheid--South Africa

Blacks and libraries
 USE Libraries and Blacks

Blacks as consumers *(May Subd Geog)*
  [HC 79.C6]
  UF Consumers, Black
--South Africa

Blacks in art
  [N 8232]
  BT Art

Blacks in literature
  [PN 56.3.B55]
  BT Literature

Blacks in medicine *(May Subd Geog)*
  [R 695]
  UF Medicine, Blacks in

Blacks in motion pictures
  [PN 1995.9.N4]
  *Here are entered works on the portrayal of Blacks in
  motion pictures. Works on all aspects of Black involvement
  in motion pictures are entered under Blacks in the
  motion picture industry. Works on specific aspects of
  Black involvement are entered under the particular subject,
  e.g. Actors, Black.*
  BT Motion pictures

UF = Used for; BT = Broader term; RT = Related term; SA = See also; NT = Narrower term

Blacks in television broadcasting *(May Subd Geog)*
  [PN 1992.8.A34]
  UF Blacks in the television industry
  BT Television broadcasting

Blacks in the Bible
  [BS 680.B48]
  UF Bible--Blacks

Blacks in the motion picture industry *(May Subd Geog)*
  [PN 1995.9.N4]
  Here are entered works on all aspects of Black involvement in motion pictures. Works on the portrayal of Blacks in motion pictures are entered under Blacks in motion pictures. Works on specific aspects of Black involvement are entered under the particular subject, e.g. Actors, Black.
  BT Motion picture industry

Blacks in the performing arts
  [PN 1590.B53]
  BT Performing arts
  NT Musicians, Black

Blacks in the press *(May Subd Geog)*
  BT Press

Blacks in the television industry
  USE Blacks in television broadcasting

Blood River (South Africa) *(Not Subd Geog)*
  BT Rivers--South Africa

Blood River (South Africa), Battle of, 1838
  [DT 777 : old class]
  [DT 2247.B56 : new class]
  UF Battle of Blood River (South Africa), 1838
  BT South Africa--History--Frontier Wars, 1811-1878

Blue Nile River (Ethiopia and Sudan) *(Not Subd Geog)*
  UF Abai River (Ethiopia and Sudan)
      Abay River (Ethiopia and Sudan)
      Abbai River (Ethiopia and Sudan)
      Bahr al-Azraq (Ethiopia and Sudan)
      Nile River, Blue (Ethiopia and Sudan)
  BT Rivers--Ethiopia
      Rivers--Sudan

Boa languages
  USE Bua languages

Boa Vista Island (Cape Verde) *(Not Subd Geog)*
  [DT 671.C29B]
  UF Sao Christovao Island (Cape Verde)
  BT Cape Verde
      Islands--Cape Verde

Bobangi language *(May Subd Geog)*
  [PL 8079]
  UF Bubangi language
      Dzamba language
      kiBangi language
      Lobobangi language
      Rebu language
  BT Bantu languages
      Congo (Brazzaville)--Languages
      Zaire--Languages

Bobe language
  USE Bube language

Bobo (African people) *(May Subd Geog)*
  [DT 555.45.B63]
  UF Bwa (African people)
      Bwawa (African people)
      Ma-da-re (African people)
  BT Ethnology--Burkina Faso
  --Funeral customs and rites
  UF Funeral rites and ceremonies, Bobo (African people)
  --Masks
  BT Masks--Burkina Faso
  --Religion
  [BL 2480.B64]
  --Rites and ceremonies

Bobo Fi language
  USE Bobo Fing language

Bobo Fign language
  USE Bobo Fing language

Bobo Fing language *(May Subd Geog)*
  [PL 8080.B58]
  UF Black Bobo language
      Bobo Fi language
      Bobo Fign language
      Bobo language
      Bulse language
      Finng language
  BT Burkina Faso--Languages
      Mali--Languages
      Mande languages

Bobo language
  USE Bobo Fing language
       Bwamu language

(May Subd Geog) = Place names may follow the heading

Bobo languages *(May Subd Geog)*
  [PL 8080]
  BT Burkina Faso--Languages
      Gur languages
      Mali--Languages
  NT Bwamu language

Bobo women
  USE Women, Bobo

Bobo Wule dialect, Western
  USE Boomu dialect

Bobo Wule language
  USE Bwamu language

Bobwa (African people)
  USE Ababua (African people)

Body-marking *(May Subd Geog)*
  UF Scarification
      Tribal marking
  BT Ethnology
      Manners and customs
  NT Tattooing
 --**Angola**
  [GN 655.A5]
 --**Nigeria**
  [GN 653]

Boer students
  USE Afrikaner students

Boer War, 1880-1881
  USE Transvaal (South Africa)--History--War
of 1880-1881

Boer War, 1899-1902
  USE South African War, 1899-1902

Boers
  USE Afrikaners

Bogos *(May Subd Geog)*
  [DT 380.4.B6]
  UF Belen (African people)
      Bilin (African people)
  BT Ethnology--Ethiopia

Bogyel (African people)
  USE Bagyele (African people)

Bogyel language
  USE Bagyele language

Bogyeli (African people)
  USE Bagyele (African people)

Bogyeli language
  USE Bagyele language

Boko language
  USE Busa language

Bokobaru language
  USE Busa language

Bokonya language
  USE Busa language

Bola language (Guinea-Bissau)
  USE Mankanya language

Boland (South Africa)

Bole (African people)
  USE Mbole (African people)

Bole languages
  USE Bolewa languages

Bole-Tangale languages
  USE Bolewa languages

Bolenta (African people)
  USE Balanta (African people)

Bolewa languages *(May Subd Geog)*
  [PL 8080.B63]
  UF Bole languages
      Bole-Tangale languages
  BT Chadic languages
      Nigeria--Languages
  NT Kanakuru language
      Pero language

Bolia language *(May Subd Geog)*
  [PL 8080.B64]
  UF Bulia language
  BT Bantu languages
      Zaire--Languages
  RT Ntomba language

Bolom language
  USE Northern Bullom language

Bolshevism
  USE Communism

UF = Used for; BT = Broader term; RT = Related term; SA = See also; NT = Narrower term

Boma (African people) *(May Subd Geog)*
　　[DT 650.B66]
　　UF　Baboma (African people)
　　　　Bama (African people)
　　　　Buma (African people)
　　　　Kiboma (African people)
　　　　Wabuma (African people)
　　BT　Bantu-speaking peoples
　　　　Ethnology--Zaire

Boma language *(May Subd Geog)*
　　[PL 8080.B65]
　　UF　Buma language
　　　　Kiboma language
　　BT　Bantu languages
　　　　Zaire--Languages

Boma mythology
　　USE　Mythology, Boma

Bomitaba language
　　USE　Mbomotaba language

Bomu dialect
　　USE　Boomu dialect

Bomvana (African people) *(May Subd Geog)*
　　[DT 764.B : old class]
　　[DT 1768.B : new class]
　　BT　Nguni (African people)
　　　　Ethnology--South Africa

Bon language
　　USE　Boni language

Bonde language
　　USE　Bondei language

Bondei language *(May Subd Geog)*
　　[PL 8080.B75]
　　UF　Bonde language
　　　　Boondei language
　　　　Kibondei language
　　BT　Shambala languages
　　　　Tanzania--Languages
　　NT　Zigula language

Bondelswarts (African people) *(May Subd Geog)*
　　[DT 709 : old class]
　　[DT 1558.B65 : new class]
　　UF　Bondelzwaarts (African people)
　　BT　Ethnology--Namibia
　　　　Khoikhoi (African people)

Bondelswarts Rebellion, 1922
　　[DT 714 : old class]

　　[DT 1630 : new class]
　　BT　Namibia--History--1915-1946

Bondelzwaarts (African people)
　　USE　Bondelswarts (African people)

Bongo (African people) *(May Subd Geog)*
　　[DT 155.2.B65]
　　UF　A-Bunga (African people)
　　　　Dor (African people)
　　　　Mundo (African people)
　　BT　Ethnology--Sudan

Bongo-Bagirmi languages *(May Subd Geog)*
　　[PL 8086.B12]
　　UF　Chari languages
　　BT　Africa, Central--Languages
　　　　Central Sudanic languages
　　NT　Aja language (Sudan)
　　　　Bagirmi language
　　　　Baka language
　　　　Bongo language
　　　　Kara language
　　　　Kresh language
　　　　Sara languages
　　　　Yulu language

Bongo language *(May Subd Geog)*
　　[PL 8085]
　　UF　Bungu language
　　　　Dor language
　　BT　Bongo-Bagirmi languages
　　　　Sudan--Languages

Boni language *(May Subd Geog)*
　　[PJ 2527]
　　UF　Aweer language
　　　　Aweera language
　　　　Bon language
　　　　Ogoda language
　　　　Sanye language
　　　　Waata language
　　　　Waboni language
　　　　Wasanye language
　　　　Wata language
　　　　Watabala language
　　BT　Cushitic languages
　　　　Kenya--Languages
　　　　Somalia--Languages

Bonkese (African people)
　　USE　Dengese (African people)

Bonkesse (African people)
　　USE　Dengese (African people)

(May Subd Geog) = Place names may follow the heading

Bonny dialect
USE Ibani dialect

Bonny River (Nigeria) *(Not Subd Geog)*
BT Rivers--Nigeria

Bono (African people)
USE Abron (African people)

Bono Manso Site (Ghana) *(Not Subd Geog)*
[DT 510.3]
BT Ghana--Antiquities

Boobe language
USE Bube language

Book awards
USE Literary prizes

Book prizes
USE Literary prizes

Books for children
USE Children's literature

Boombe language
USE Bube language

Boomu dialect *(May Subd Geog)*
UF Bobo Wule dialect, Western
Bomu dialect
Bore dialect
Western Bobo Wule dialect
DT Burkina Faso--Languages
Bwamu language
Mali--Languages

Boondei language
USE Bondei language

Bophuthatswana (South Africa)
[DT 944.B47 : old class]
[DT 2400.B66 : new class]
BT Homelands (South Africa)

Bor dialect (Dinka) *(May Subd Geog)*
[PL 8086.B]
BT Dinka language
Sudan--Languages

Bor language (Lwo) *(May Subd Geog)*
[PL 8086.B]
UF Belanda language
Dhe Bor language
Jo Bor language
Rodi language

BT Nilotic languages
Sudan--Languages

Boraha Island (Madagascar)
USE Sainte-Marie-de-Madagascar Island
(Madagascar)

Boran (African people) *(May Subd Geog)*
[DT 433.545.B67 (Kenya)]
UF Borani (African people)
BT Ethnology--Ethiopia
Ethnology--Kenya
Hamites
Oromo (African people)

Boran dialect *(May Subd Geog)*
[PJ 2475]
BT Kenya--Languages
Oromo language

Borani (African people)
USE Boran (African people)

Border War, 9th (South Africa), 1877-1878
USE Ngcayecibi, War of, South Africa, 1877-1878

Bore dialect
USE Boomu dialect

Bori (Cult)
[BL 2480.H3]
BT Cults--Nigeria
Hausa (African people)--Religion

Bornu (African people)
USE Kanuri (African people)

Bornu-Kanem Empire
USE Kanem-Bornu Empire

Bornu language
USE Kanuri language

Boro Oule language
USE Bwamu language

Boroa (African people)
USE Batwa (African people)

Bororo (African people) *(May Subd Geog)*
[DT 571.B67 (Cameroon)]
[DT 547.45.B67 (Niger)]
UF Mbororo (African people)
Wodaabe (African people)
BT Ethnology--Cameroon
Ethnology--Niger   *(Continued)*

UF = Used for; BT = Broader term; RT = Related term; SA = See also; NT = Narrower term

Bororo (African people)   *(Continued)*
  BT Ethnology--Sudan (Region)
      Fula (African people)
  --Missions *(May Subd Geog)*
    [BV 3630.B]
    UF Missions to Bororo (African people)

Bororo dialect (West Africa) *(May Subd Geog)*
  [PL 8086.B]
  UF Bororro dialect (West Africa)
      Borrroro dialect (West Africa)
  BT Cameroon--Languages
      Fula language
      Niger--Languages
      Nigeria--Languages

Bororo folk songs (West Africa)
  USE Folk songs, Bororo (West Africa)

Bororro dialect (West Africa)
  USE Bororo dialect (West Africa)

Borrroro dialect (West Africa)
  USE Bororo dialect (West Africa)

Bosquimana (African people)
  USE Kua (African people)

Bosquimano (African people)
  USE Kua (African people)

Bosso (African people)
  USE Bozo (African people)

Boteti River (Botswana) *(Not Subd Geog)*
  BT Rivers--Botswana

Botswana *(Not Subd Geog)*
  [DT 790-DT 803 : old class]
  [DT 2421-DT 2525 : new class]
  UF Bechuanaland
  --Description and travel
  -- --1981-
  --Economic conditions
    [HC 930]
  -- --1966
  --Fiction
    NT Sotho fiction
        Tonga fiction (Zambesi)
  --Foreign relations *(May Subd Geog)*
  -- --1961-
  --History
  -- --To 1966
  -- --1966-

--Languages
  NT G//ana language
      G/wi language
      Herero language
      Kgalagadi dialect
      Lilima language
      Mbukushu language
      Nharo language
      San languages
      Sotho language
      Subiya language
      Tonga language (Zambesi)
      Tswana language
      !Xo language
      !Xu language
--Literatures
  USE Botswana literature
--Poetry
  NT Tswana poetry
      Sotho poetry
--Politics and government
-- --To 1966
-- --1966-

Botswana alien labor
  USE Alien labor, Botswana

Botswana atlases
  USE Atlases, Botswana

Botswana children's stories (English)
  USE Children's stories, Botswana (English)

Botswana literature *(May Subd Geog)*
  [PL 8014.B67]
  UF Botswana--Literatures
  BT Southern African literature
  NT Sotha literature
      Tonga literature (Zambesi)

Boua languages
  USE Bua languages

Bouaka (African people)
  USE Ngbaka (African people)

Bouamou language
  USE Bwamu language

Boube language
  USE Bube language

Boudja (African people)
  USE Budja (African people)

(May Subd Geog) = Place names may follow the heading

Bouem language
  USE Lefana language

Bouende (African people)
  USE Bwende (African people)

Bouiti sect
  USE Bwiti sect

Bouity sect
  USE Bwiti sect

Boulevards
  USE Streets

Boulou language
  USE Bulu language

Boumpe (African people)
  USE Mende (African people)

Boumpe language
  USE Mende language

Bourbon (Island)
  USE Réunion

Bouroum language
  USE Birom language

Boussa language
  USE Busa language

Bouze language
  USE Loma language

Boya (African people)
  USE Longarim (African people)

Boyama Falls (Zaire)
  USE Stanley Falls (Zaire)

Bozo (African people) *(May Subd Geog)*
  [DT 547.45.B]
  UF Bosso (African people)
      Sorko (African people)
  BT Ethnology--Burkina Faso
      Ethnology--Mali
      Ethnology--Niger
      Mandingo (African people)

Bozo language *(May Subd Geog)*
  [PL 8087]
  UF Sorko language
      Sorogo language

BT Burkina Faso--Languages
    Mali--Languages
    Mande languages
    Niger--Languages

Brakna *(May Subd Geog)*
  [DT 530.5.B7 (French-speaking West Africa)]
  BT Ethnology--Mauritania
      Ethnology--Africa, French-speaking West

Brame language
  USE Mankanya language

Brariga (African people)
  USE Barabaig (African people)

Brassa (African people)
  USE Balanta (African people)

Brazil
  --Civilization
    NT Africa, West--Civilization--Brazilian
  influences
        Angola--Civilization--Brazilian influences
  -- --African influences
    BT Africa--Civilization

Brazilian arts
  USE Arts, Brazilian

Brer Anansi (Legendary character)
  USE Anansi (Legendary character)

Bridal customs
  USE Marriage customs and rites

Bride price *(May Subd Geog)*
  UF Lobolo
  BT Marriage
  --Africa, Southern
    [GN 656]
  --Chad
    [GN 652.C5]

Bride price (Dinka law)
  BT Law, Dinka

Brignan (African people)
  USE Avikam (African people)

Brinya (African people)
  USE Avikam (African people)

Brissa language *(May Subd Geog)*
  [PL 8089]
  UF Anufo dialect (Ivory Coast)   *(Continued)*

UF = Used for; BT = Broader term; RT = Related term; SA = See also; NT = Narrower term

Brissa language   *(Continued)*
  UF Aowin language
  BT Anyi language
      Ivory Coast--Languages

British *(May Subd Geog)*
  UF English
 --Kenya
  [DT 433.545.B74]
 --South Africa
  NT South Africa--English-Afrikaner
relations
 -- --History
 -- -- --19th century
  NT British settlers of 1820 (South
Africa)
 --Zimbabwe
  [DT 764.B7 : old class]
  [DT 2913.B85 : new class]

British settlers of 1820 (South Africa)
  [DT 844.5 : old class]
  [DT 1840 : new class]
  UF 1820 settlers (South Africa)
      Albany settlers (South Africa)
      Eighteen twenty settlers (South
Africa)
      Settlers of 1820 (South Africa)
  BT British--South Africa--History--19th
century
      Cape of Good Hope (South Africa)--
History--1795-1872
      Pioneers--South Africa

British Somaliland
  USE Somalia

Broken Hill skull
  USE Rhodesian man

Brong (African people)
  USE Abron (African people)

Bronzes *(May Subd Geog)*
  UF Statuettes
  BT Decoration and ornament
      Sculpture
 --Nigeria
  [NK 7989.6.N5]
  NT Bronzes, Bini
      Bronzes, Yoruba

Bronzes, Bini *(May Subd Geog)*
  [NK 7989.6.N5]
  UF Bini bronzes
  BT Bronzes--Nigeria

Bronzes, Yoruba *(May Subd Geog)*
  [NK 7989.6.N5]
  UF Yoruba bronzes
  BT Bronzes--Nigeria

Brooks
  USE Rivers

Bua languages *(May Subd Geog)*
  [PL 8090.B83]
  UF Boa languages
      Boua languages
  BT Adamawa languages
      Chad--Languages
  NT Kùlàál language
      Laal language
      Nielim language
 --Phonology

Bubangi language
  USE Bobangi language

Bube (African people)
  USE Bubi (African people)

Bube language *(May Subd Geog)*
  [PL 8091]
  UF Adeeyah language
      Adija language
      Adiyah language
      Bobe language
      Boobe language
      Boombe language
      Boube language
      Bubi language
      Ediya language
      Fernandian language
  BT Bantu languages
      Equatorial Guinea--Languages

Bubi (African people) *(May Subd Geog)*
  [DT 620.45.B]
  UF Adija (African people)
      Bube (African people)
      Ediye (African people)
  BT Bantu-speaking peoples
      Ethnology--Equatorial Guinea

Bubi language
  USE Bube language

Bubutubi (African people)
  USE Ewe (African people)

Budik language
  USE Bedik language

(May Subd Geog) = Place names may follow the heading

Budja (African people) *(May Subd Geog)*
[DT 650.B]
UF Boudja (African people)
    Bujia (African people)
BT Ethnology--Zaire

Budjago (African people)
USE Bijago (African people)

Buduma (African people) *(May Subd Geog)*
UF Yedina (African people)
BT Ethnology--Chad
    Ethnology--Niger
    Ethnology--Nigeria

Buem language
USE Lefana language

Buende (African people)
USE Bwende (African people)

Bugago (African people)
USE Bijago (African people)

Buildings, Archive
USE Archive buildings

Buildings, Public
USE Public buildings

Buile language
USE Buli language

Builsa (African people) *(May Subd Geog)*
[DT 510.43.B85 (Ghana)]
UF Bulea (African people)
    Buli (African people)
    Bulsa (African people)
    Kanjaga (African people)
BT Ethnology--Burkina Faso
    Ethnology--Ghana
    Gurunsi (African people)

Builsa language
USE Buli language

Buissi (African people) *(May Subd Geog)*
[DT 650.B84]
BT Ethnology--Zaire

Bujeba (African people)
USE Bisio (African people)

Bujeba language
USE Bisio language

Bujia (African people)
USE Budja (African people)

Bukanda (African people)
USE Lala (African people)

Bukuba language
USE Bushoong language

Bukusu (African people)
USE Kusu (African people)

Bukusu dialect *(May Subd Geog)*
[PL 8092.B87]
UF Kitosh dialect
    Lubukusu dialect
    UluBukusu dialect
BT Kenya--Languages
    Gisu language
    Uganda--Languages

Bulama language
USE Mankanya language

Bulanda (African people)
USE Balanta (African people)

Bulanda language
USE Balante language

Bulante (African people)
USE Balanta (African people)

Bulea (African people)
USE Builsa (African people)

Bulea language
USE Buli language

Bulem language
USE Northern Bullom language

Buli (African people)
USE Builsa (African people)

Buli language *(May Subd Geog)*
[PL 8092.B]
UF Buile language
    Builsa language
    Bulea language
    Bulugu language
    Guresha language
    Kandjaga language
    Kanjaga language
    Kanjago language   *(Continued)*

UF = Used for; BT = Broader term; RT = Related term; SA = See also; NT = Narrower term

Buli language *(Continued)*
  BT Burkina Faso--Languages
      Ghana--Languages
      Gur languages

Bulia language
  USE Bolia language

Bulin language
  USE Northern Bullom language

Bullin language
  USE Northern Bullom language

Bullom, Southern (African people)
  USE Sherbro (African people)

Bullom language
  USE Northern Bullom language

Bullom language, Northern
  USE Northern Bullom language

Bullom language, Southern
  USE Sherbro language

Bullum language
  USE Northern Bullom language

Bulom language
  USE Northern Bullom language

Bulsa (African people)
  USE Builsa (African people)

Bulse language
  USE Bobo Fing language

Bulu (African people) *(May Subd Geog)*
  [DT 571.B85]
  BT Bantu-speaking peoples
      Ethnology--Cameroon

Bulu language *(May Subd Geog)*
  [PL 8095]
  UF Boulou language
  BT Cameroon--Languages
      Yaunde-Fang languages

Buluba-Lulua language
  USE Luba-Lulua language

Bulugu language
  USE Buli language

Bum (African people)

USE Mbum (African people)

Buma (African people)
  USE Boma (African people)

Buma language
  USE Boma language

Bunda (African people) *(May Subd Geog)*
  [DT650.B]
  UF Ambunu (African people)
      Ambuun (African people)
      Babunda (African people)
      Babundu (African people)
      Bambunda (African people)
      Mbunu (African people)
  BT Bantu-speaking peoples
      Ethnology--Zaire

Bunda language
  USE Kimbundu language

Bunga Hill (Zambia)
  USE Bungua Hill (Zambia)

Bungu language
  USE Bongo language

Bungua Hill (Zambia) *(Not Subd Geog)*
  UF Bunga Hill (Zambia)
  BT Mountains--Zambia

Bunyoro (African people)
  USE Nyoro (African people)

Bunyoro-Kitara *(Not Subd Geog)*
  [DT 433.29.B33]
  BT Nyoro (African people)--History

Burama language
  USE Mankanya language

Burgerspond (Coin)
  [CJ 3948]
  BT Coins, South Africa
      Gold coins--South Africa

Burial laws *(May Subd Geog)*
  UF Law, Burial
      Mortuary law

Burial laws (Luo law) *(May Subd Geog)*
  BT Law, Luo

Buried cities
  USE Cities and towns, Ruined, extinct, etc.

(May Subd Geog) = Place names may follow the heading

Burji language *(May Subd Geog)*
  [PJ 2497]
  UF Bambala language
      Bembala language
      Bembola language
      Burjina language
      Burjinya language
  BT Cushitic languages
      Kenya--Languages

Burjina language
  USE Burji language

Burjinya language
  USE Burji language

Burkeneji (African people)
  USE Samburu (African people)

Burkeneji language
  USE Samburu language

Burkina Faso *(Not Subd Geog)*
  [DT 555-DT 555.9]
  UF Upper Volta
  --History
  -- --Coup d'état, 1987
    [DT 555.9]
    BT Coups d'état--Burkina Faso
  --Languages
    NT Bobo Fing language
        Bobo languages
        Boomu dialect
        Bozo language
        Buli language
        Bwamu language
        Dagari language
        Dogon language
        Dyan dialect
        Dyula language
        Gurma language
        Karaboro language
        Kasem language
        Kurumba language
        Kussassi language
        Lobi dialects
        Mooré language
        Mossi languages
        Nunuma dialect
        Samo language (West Africa)
        Sembla language
        Sisala language
        Tusia language
        Vige language
        Wule dialect

--Literatures
  USE Burkinabe literature

Burkinabe art
  USE Art, Burkinabe

Burkinabe literature *(May Subd Geog)*
  [PL 8014.B]
  UF Burkina Faso--Literatures
  BT West African literature
  NT Mooré language

Burkinabe literature (French) *(May Subd Geog)*
  [PQ 3988.5.B87 (History)]
  [PQ 3988.5.B872 (Collections)]
  UF French literature--Burkinabe authors
  BT West African literature (French)
  NT Burkinabe poetry (French)

Burkinabe poetry (French) *(May Subd Geog)*
  [PQ 3988.5.B87 (History)]
  [PQ 3988.5.B872 (Collections)]
  UF French poetry--Burkinabe authors
  BT Burkinabe literature (French)
      West African poetry (French)

Burta (African people)
  USE Berta (African people)

Buru language (Ghana and Ivory Coast)
  USE Mo language (Ghana and Ivory Coast)

Burum language (Nigeria)
  USE Birom language

Burundi *(Not Subd Geog)*
  [DT 450.5-DT 450.95]
  UF Burundi Kingdom
      Kindom of Burundi
      République du Burundi
      Ruanda-Urundi
      Urundi
  --Languages
    NT Bembe language (Lake Tanganyika)
        Kinyarwanda language
        Rundi language
  --Literatures
    NT Kinyarwanda literature
  --Religion
    [BL 2470.B94]
  --Religious life and customs
    NT Ukubandwa

Burundi Kingdom
  USE Burundi

UF = Used for; BT = Broader term; RT = Related term; SA = See also; NT = Narrower term

Burying-grounds
USE Cemeteries

Busa language *(May Subd Geog)*
[PL 8099]
UF   Boko language
Bokobaru language
Bokonya language
Boussa language
Busa-Boke language
Busagwe language
Busanchi language
Busawa language
Zugweya language
BT   Benin--Languages
Mande languages
Nigeria--Languages

Busa-Boke language
USE Busa language

Busagwe language
USE Busa language

Busanchi language
USE Busa language

Busawa language
USE Busa language

Bushman languages
USE San (African people)--Languages
San languages

Bushmen (African people)
USE San (African people)

Bushongo (African people)
USE Kuba (African people)

Bushong language
USE Bushoong language

Bushongo language
USE Bushoong language

Bushoong language *(May Subd Geog)*
[PL 8106]
UF   Bakuba language
Bamongo language
Bukuba language
Bushong language
Bushongo language
Busoong language
Ganga language
Kuba language

UF   Lukuba language
Mbala language (Kasai Occidental Region,
Zaire)
Mbale language
Shongo language
BT   Bantu languages
Zaire--Languages
RT   Mongo language
--**Grammar**

Business correspondence
USE Commercial correspondence

Business enterprises *(May Subd Geog)*
Here are entered works on business concerns as legal
entities, regardless of form of organization.
UF   Business organizations
Companies
Enterprises
Firms
Organizations, Business
NT   Black business enterprises

Business enterprises, Black
USE Black business enterprises

Business executives
USE Executives

Business letters
USE Commercial correspondence

Business organizations
USE Business enterprises

Busoong language
USE Bushoong language

Busy language
USE Loma language

Butana (Sudan) *(Not Subd Geog)*
BT   Arid regions--Sudan
Plains--Sudan

Bute language
USE Mbum language

Buvuma (African people)
USE Bavuma (African people)

Buye (African people)
USE Hemba (African people)

Buyenzi natural region (Burundi)
USE Buyenzi Region (Burundi)

(May Subd Geog) = Place names may follow the heading

Buyenzi Region (Burundi) *(Not Subd Geog)*
  UF Buyenzi natural region (Burundi)
      Région naturelle du Buyenzi (Burundi)
  BT Natural areas--Burundi

Buzela (African people)
  USE Zela (African people)

Buzi language
  USE Loma language

Bwa (African people)
  USE Bobo (African people)

Bwa language
  USE Bwamu language

Bwaba language
  USE Bwamu language

Bwaka (African people)
  USE Ngbaka (African people)

Bwamu language *(May Subd Geog)*
  UF Bobo language
      Bobo Wule language
      Boro Oule language
      Bouamou language
      Bwa language
      Bwaba language
      Nienege language
      Nyenege language
      Nyenyege language
      Oule language
      Pwe language
      Red Bobo language
  BT Bobo languages
      Burkina Faso--Languages
      Mali--Languages
  NT Boomu dialect

Bwanje River (Malawi) *(Not Subd Geog)*
  UF Bwanji River (Malawi)
  BT Rivers--Malawi

Bwanji River (Malawi)
  USE Bwanje River (Malawi)

Bwawa (African people)
  USE Bobo (African people)

Bweende (African people)
  USE Bwende (African people)

Bwem language
  USE Lefana language

Bwende (African people) *(May Subd Geog)*
  [DT 650.B]
  UF Babwende (African people)
      Bouende (African people)
      Buende (African people)
      Bweende (African people)
      Fiot (African people)
      Ngoy (African people)
  BT Bantu-speaking peoples
      Ethnology--Zaire

Bwine-Mukuni language
  USE Lenje language

Bwiti sect
  [BL 2465]
  UF Bouiti sect
      Bouity sect
      Mboeti sect
      Mbueti sect
  BT Fang (West African people)--Religion

C

C.E.A.O.
  USE Communanté économique de l'Afrique de
  l'Ouest

Cabinda (African people)
  USE Kongo (African people)

Cabinda (Angola : Province) *(Not Subd Geog)*
  [DT 611.9.C33 : old class]
  [DT 1450.C33 : new class]
  --History
  -- --Autonomy and independence movements

Cabo da Boa Esperança (South Africa : Cape)
  USE Cape of Good Hope (South Africa : Cape)

Cabo Tormentoso (South Africa : Cape)
  USE Cape of Good Hope (South Africa : Cape)

Cabrai (African people)
  USE Kabre (African people)

Cabrai dialect
  USE Kabre dialect

Cabrais dialect
  USE Kabre dialect

Caffa (African people)
  USE Kaffa (African people)

Caffina (African people)
  USE Kaffa (African people)

Cameroon *(Not Subd Geog)*
  [DT 561-DT 581]
  Here are entered works about the United Republic of
Cameroon, as well as works on the same territory when
know by other names such as Cameroons or the German
protectorate Kamerun.
  UF Africa, German West
     Cameroon, East
     Cameroons
     Cameroun
     East Cameroon
     Federal Republic of Cameroon
     German West Africa
     Kamerun
     United Republic of Cameroon
     West Africa, German
--**Antiquities**
  NT Houlouf Site (Cameroon)
--**Description and travel**
-- --**1981-**
--**Drama**
  USE Cameroon drama
--**Economic conditions**
  [HC 995]
-- --**To 1960**
-- --**1960-**
--**History**
-- --**Coup d'état, 1984**
  [DT 578]
  BT Coups d'état--Cameroon
--**Languages**
  NT Adamawa languages
     Anyang language
     Bafia language
     Bagyele language
     Baka language (Cameroon)
     Bakossi dialect
     Bamileke languages
     Bamougoun-Bamenjou language
     Bamun language
     Bandjoun language
     Banen language
     Basa language
     Bati language
     Bororo dialect (West Africa)
     Bulu language
     Daba language
     Duala language
     Ejagham language
     Ekoi languages
     Ewondo language
     Fali language
     Fang language

  NT Fe'fe' language
     Fula language
     Gbaya language
     Gisiga language
     Grasslands Bantu languages
     Gunu language
     Jukunoid languages
     Kamwe language
     Karang language (Cameroon)
     Kombe language
     Kotoko dialects
     Kuo language
     Kwiri languages
     Laamang language
     Lamé language (Cameroon)
     Limbun language
     Maka language (Cameroon)
     Mambila language
     Mamfe Bantu languages
     Mankon language
     Masa language (Chadic)
     Mbo language (Cameroon)
     Mbum language
     Medumba language
     Mofu-Gudur language
     Mumuye language
     Mundang language
     Musei language
     Ngemba language (Cameroon)
     Ngo language
     Nomaante language
     Paduko language
     Tikar language
     Tuburi language
     Uldeme language
     Yaayuwee dialect
     Yamba language (Cameroon and Nigeria)
     Yambeta language
     Yaunde-Fang languages
     Zulgo language
-- --**Alphabet**
--**Literatures**
  USE Cameroon literature
--**Poetry**
  NT Duala poetry
     Fang poetry
     Fula poetry
--**Politics and government**
-- --**To 1960**
-- --**1960-**
-- --**1960-1982**
-- --**1982-**
--**Social conditions**
-- --**1960-**

(May Subd Geog) = Place names may follow the heading

Cameroon, East
  USE Cameroon

Cameroon art
  USE Art, Cameroon

Cameroon authors
  USE Authors, Cameroon

Cameroon children's literature (English)
  USE Children's literature, Cameroon
(English)

Cameroon civics
  USE Civics, Cameroon

Cameroon cookery
  USE Cookery, Cameroon

Cameroon drama *(May Subd Geog)*
  [PL 8014.C3]
  UF Cameroon--Drama
  BT Cameroon literature

Cameroon fiction (English) *(May Subd Geog)*
  [PR 9372.4 (History)]
  [PR 9372.8 (Collections)]
  UF English fiction--Cameroon authors
  BT Cameroon literature (English)
     West African fiction (English)

Cameroon fiction (French) *(May Subd Geog)*
  [PQ 3988.5.C27 (History)]
  [PQ 3988.5.C272 (Collections)]
  UF French fiction--Cameroon authors
  BT Cameroon literature (French)
     West African fiction (French)

Cameroon literature *(May Subd Geog)*
  [PL 8014.C3]
  UF Cameroon--Literatures
  BT West African literature
  NT Cameroon drama
     Duala literature
     Fang literature
     Fula literature

Cameroon literature (English) *(May Subd Geog)*
  [PR 9372]
  UF English literature--Cameroon authors
  BT West African literature (English)
  NT Cameroon fiction (English)
     Children's literature, Cameroon
(English)
     Cameroon poetry (English)

Cameroon literature (French) *(May Subd Geog)*
  [PQ 3988.5.C27 (History)]
  [PQ 3088.5.C272 (Collections)]
  UF French literature--Cameroon authors
  BT West African literature (French)
  NT Cameroon fiction (French)
     Cameroon poetry (French)

Cameroon poetry (English) *(May Subd Geog)*
  [PR 9372.2 (History)]
  [PR 9372.6-PR 9372.65 (Collections)]
  UF English poetry--Cameroon authors
  BT Cameroon literature (English)
     West African poetry (English)

Cameroon poetry (French) *(May Subd Geog)*
  [PQ 3988.5.C27 (History)]
  [PQ 3988.5.C272 (Collections)]
  UF French poetry--Cameroon authors
  BT Cameroon literature (French)
     West African poetry (French)

Cameroon sculpture
  USE Sculpture, Cameroon

Cameroonians *(May Subd Geog)*
  BT Ethnology--Cameroon

Cameroons
  USE Cameroon

Cameroun
  USE Cameroon

Camma (African people)
  USE Nkomi (African people)

Campaign posters
  USE Political posters

Canal de Moçambique
  USE Mozambique Channel

Canal de Mozambique
  USE Mozambique Channel

Canals *(May Subd Geog)*
  --Sudan
     NT Jonglei Canal (Sudan)

Cangin languages *(May Subd Geog)*
  [PL 8108]
  BT Niger-Congo languages
     Senegal--Languages
  NT Falor language

UF = Used for; BT = Broader term; RT = Related term; SA = See also; NT = Narrower term

Cape Colony
  USE Cape of Good Hope (South Africa)

Cape coloured people
  USE Colored people (South Africa)

Cape Dutch language
  USE Afrikaans language

Cape Flats Nature Reserve (South Africa) *(Not Subd Geog)*
  BT National parks and reserves--South Africa

Cape Frontier War, 9th (South Africa), 1877-1878
  USE Ngcayecibi, War of, South Africa, 1877-1878

Cape of Good Hope (South Africa) *(Not Subd Geog)*
  [DT 821-DT 848 : old class]
  [DT 1991-DT 2054 : new class]
  UF Cape Colony
      Cape Province (South Africa)
      Kaapland (South Africa)
      Kapland (South Africa)
  --History
  -- --**To 1795**
  -- --**1795-1872**
    NT British settlers of 1820 (South Africa)
  --Politics and government
  -- --**To 1795**
  -- --**1795-1872**
  -- --**1872-1910**
  -- --**1910-**

Cape of Good Hope (South Africa : Cape) *(Not Subd Geog)*
  UF Cabo da Boa Esperança (South Africa : Cape)
      Cabo Tormentoso (South Africa : Cape)
      Cape of Storms (South Africa : Cape)
      Cape Peninsula (South Africa : Cape)
      Good Hope, Cape of (South Africa : Cape)
  BT Capes (Coasts)--South Africa
      Peninsulas--South Africa

Cape of Good Hope Nature Reserve (South Africa) *(Not Subd Geog)*
  BT National parks and reserves--South Africa
      Natural areas--South Africa

Cape of Storms (South Africa : Cape)

  USE Cape of Good Hope (South Africa : Cape)

Cape Peninsula (South Africa : Cape)
  USE Cape of Good Hope (South Africa : Cape)

Cape Province (South Africa)
  USE Cape of Good Hope (South Africa)

Cape Town (South Africa). District Six
  USE District Six (Cape Town, South Africa)

Cape Town (South Africa). Modderdam
  USE Modderdam (Cape Town, South Africa)

Cape Town (South Africa). Woodstock
  USE Woodstock (Cape Town, South Africa)

Cape Verde *(Not Subd Geog)*
  [DT 671.C2-DT 671.C29]
  UF Cape Verde Islands
      Republic of Cape Verde
  NT Boa Vista Island (Cape Verde)
      Sao Tiago Island (Cape Verde)
  --Economic conditions
  [HC 594]
  --History
  -- --**To 1975**
  --Politics and government
  -- --**To 1975**
  -- --**1975-**

Cape Verde Islands
  USE Cape Verde

Cape Verdean cookery
  USE Cookery, Cape Verdean

Cape Verdeans *(May Subd Geog)*
  BT Ethnology--Cape Verde

Capes (Coasts) *(May Subd Geog)*
  UF Headlands (Coasts)
      Heads (Coasts)
      Points (Coasts)
      Promontories (Coasts)
  BT Coasts
  --South Africa
    NT Cape of Good Hope (South Africa : Cape)

Career government service
  USE Civil service

Caribbean Area
  UF West Indies Region
  --Civilization
  -- --**African influences**

(**May Subd Geog**) = Place names may follow the heading

BT Africa--Civilization

Caribbean Islands
USE West Indies

Cassai River (Angola and Zaire)
USE Kasai River (Angola and Zaire)

Cassanga (African people)
USE Kasanga (African people)

Casu language
USE Asu language

Cataloging of African literature
[Z 695.1.A37]
UF African literature--Cataloging
BT Libraries--Special collections--Africa

Cataracts
USE Waterfalls

Catechisms, Zulu
[BV 510.Z8]
UF Zulu catechisms
BT Christianity--South Africa

Cathedral Peak (South Africa) (Not Subd Geog)
BT Drakensberg Mountains
Mountains--South Africa

Catholic Church (May Subd Geog)
--Zaire
[BX 1682.C6]
NT Gen Movement
Jamaa Movement

Cattle-Killing Movement (South Africa), 1856-
1857
USE South Africa--History--Xhosa Cattle-
Killing, 1856-1857

Cattle ranches
USE Ranches

Caverns
USE Caves

Caves (May Subd Geog)
UF Caverns
Grottos
Rock shelters
BT Landforms
--Lesotho
NT Sehonghong Rockshelter (Lesotho)

--Malawi
NT Chencherere II Rockshelter (Malawi)
--Mali
NT Fanfannyégèné I Site (Mali)
--South Africa
NT Nelson Bay Cave (South Africa)
--Sudan
NT Shaqadud Cave (Sudan)
--Zimbabwe
NT Diana's Vow Rock Shelter (Zimbabwe)

Cebaara Senoufo language
USE Senari language

Cedar Bergen (South Africa)
USE Cedar Mountains (South Africa)

Cedar Mountains (South Africa) (Not Subd Geog)
UF Cedar Bergen (South Africa)
Cedarberg (South Africa)
Ceder Bergen (South Africa)
Sederberge (South Africa)
BT Mountains--South Africa

Cedarberg (South Africa)
USE Cedar Mountains (South Africa)

Ceder Bergen (South Africa)
USE Cedar Mountains (South Africa)

Cemba (Togolese and Ghanaian people)
USE Bassari (Togolese and Ghanaian people)

Cemeteries (May Subd Geog)
UF Burying-grounds
Churchyards
Graves
Graveyards
--South Africa
NT Church Street Cemetery (Pretoria, South
Africa)

Cemual (African people)
USE Nandi (African people)

Census (Not Subd Geog)
[HA 4671-HA 4737 (Africa)
UF Census--Statistics
BT Population
SA subdivision Census or Census, [date] under
names of countries, cities, etc., and under ethnic groups
--Statistics
USE Census

Central Africa
USE Africa, Central

UF = Used for; BT = Broader term; RT = Related term; SA = See also; NT = Narrower term

Central African Empire
  USE Central African Republic

Central African Republic *(Not Subd Geog)*
  [DT 546.3-DT 546.39]
  UF Central African Empire
      Ubangi-Shari
      Ubangui-Chari
--History
-- --To 1960
  NT Kongo Wara, 1928-1931
-- --1960-
-- --Coup d'état, 1979
  [DT 546.384]
  BT Coups d'état--Central African Republic
--**Languages**
  NT Aka language (Central African
Republic)
      Banda language
      Banda languages
      Birri language
      Gabri language
      Gbaya language
      Kara language
      Kare language
      Linda dialect
      Majingai dialect
      Mbai language (Moissala)
      Mbum language
      Nancere language
      Ngama dialect
      Ngbaka ma'bo language
      Nzakara dialect
      Sango language
      Sara language
      Sara languages
      Yakoma language
      Yulu language
--Literatures
  USE Central African literature
--**Poetry**
  NT Nzakara poetry
--**Politics and government**
-- --1966-1979
-- --1979-

Central African literature *(May Subd Geog)*
  [PL 8014.C]
  *Here are entered works on the literatures of the
Central African Republic.*
  UF Central African Republic--Literatures
  NT Nzakara literature
      Ngbaka ma'bo literature

Central Ekoi language
  USE Ejagham language

Central Karroo (South Africa)
  USE Great Karroo (South Africa)

Central Sudanic languages *(May Subd Geog)*
  BT Africa, Central--Languages
      Nilo-Saharan languages
  NT Bongo-Bagirmi languages
      Kresh language
      Mangbetu language
      Moru language

Centre National des Archives Ahmed Sékou Touré
(Monrovia, Liberia)
  USE Ahmed Sékou Touré National Archives
Building (Monrovia, Liberia)

Ceramics (Art)
  USE Pottery

Ceremonies
  USE Manners and customs
       Rites and ceremonies

Cewa dialect
  USE Chewa dialect

Chad *(Not Subd Geog)*
  [DT 546.4-DT 546.49]
  UF Tchad
--**Antiquities**
  NT Mdaga Site (Chad)
--**Description and travel**
-- --1981-
--**History**
-- --1960-
-- --Civil War, 1965-
  [DT 546.48]
--**Languages**
  NT Adamawa languages
      Afade dialect
      Bagirmi language
      Bidiyo language
      Bua languages
      Dangaleat language
      Day language (Chad)
      Daza language
      Fur language
      Gabri language
      Gambai dialect
      Jongor language
      Kanuri language
      Karré language
      Kenga language
      Kera language
      Kotoko dialects
      Kùláál language

(May Subd Geog) = Place names may follow the heading

NT Kuo language
    Laal language
    Maba language
    Majingai dialect
    Masa language (Chadic)
    Mbai language (Moissala)
    Mbum language
    Mundang language
    Musei language
    Musgu language
    Nancere language
    Ngama dialect
    Nielim language
    Sango language
    Sara language
    Sara languages
    Teda language
    Tuburi language
    Tumak language
    Vulum dialect
--Politics and government
-- --1960-

Chad, Lake *(Not Subd Geog)*
   [DT 546.49.L34]
   UF Lac Tchad
       Lake Chad
       Tchad, Lake
   BT Lakes--Africa, West

Chad Basin *(Not Subd Geog)*
   UF Bassin Tchadien
   BT Basins (Geology)--Africa

Chadic languages
   [PL 8026.C53]
   BT Afroasiatic languages
   NT Angas language
       Bidiyo language
       Bolewa languages
       Daba language
       Dangaleat language
       Day language (Chad)
       Fali language
       Gabri language
       Gisiga language
       Glavda language
       Gude language
       Gwandara language
       Hausa language
       Jongor language
       Kamwe language
       Kera language
       Kotoko dialects
       Laamang language
       Lamé language (Cameroon)

NT Mandara language
    Margi language
    Masa language (Chadic)
    Mofu-Gudur language
    Musei language
    Musgu language
    Nancere language
    Ngizim language
    Paduko language
    Ron language
    Southern Bauchi languages
    Tera language
    Tuburi language
    Tumak language
    Uldeme language
    Yaghwatadaxa language
    Zulgo language

Chafukuma Hill (Zambia) *(Not Subd Geog)*
   BT Mountains--Zambia

Chaga (African people) *(May Subd Geog)*
   [DT 443.3.C]
   UF Chagga (African people)
       Dschagga (African people)
       Jagga (African people)
       Wachaga (African people)
       Wadschagga (African people)
   RT Bantu-speaking peoples
       Ethnology--Tanzania

Chaga language *(May Subd Geog)*
   [PL 8110.C1]
   UF Chagga language
       Djaga language
       Dschagga language
       Jagga language
       Tschagga language
   BT Bantu languages
       Tanzania--Languages

Chaga law
   USE Law, Chaga

Chagga (African people)
   USE Chaga (African people)

Chagga language
   USE Chaga language

Chainda (Lusaka, Zambia) *(Not Subd Geog)*
   UF Lusaka (Zambia). Chainda

Chakosi dialect
   USE Anufo dialect

UF = Used for; BT = Broader term; RT = Related term; SA = See also; NT = Narrower term

Chakossi (African people)
USE Chokossi (African people)

Chala language
USE Ron language

Chalbi Desert (Kenya) (Not Subd Geog)
BT Deserts--Kenya

Chamba (African people) (May Subd Geog)
[DT 474.6.C48 (West Africa)]
BT Ethnology--Africa, West
Ethnology--Cameroon
Ethnology--Nigeria

Chamba (Togolese and Ghanaian people)
USE Bassari (Togolese and Ghanaian people)

Chancellors (Prime ministers)
USE Prime ministers

Changana language
USE Tsonga language

Chapbooks
BT Folk literature
Periodicals

Chapbooks, Nigerian (May Subd Geog)
UF Nigerian chapbooks

Characteristics, National
USE National characteristics

Chari languages
USE Bongo-Bagirmi languages

Chasu language
USE Asu language

Chawama (Lusaka, Zambia) (Not Subd Geog)
UF Lusaka (Zambia). Chawama

Cheke language
USE Gude language

Chemin de fer Congo-océan
[TF 119.C75.C4]
BT Railroads--Congo (Brazzaville)

Chemin de fer du Bas-Congo au Katanga
[TF 119.Z3C]
BT Railroads--Zaire

Chencherere II Rockshelter (Malawi) (Not Subd Geog)
UF Mwana wa Chencherere Rockshelter (Malawi)
BT Caves--Malawi
Malawi--Antiquities

Cheren, Battle of, 1941
[D 766.84]
UF Battle of Cheren (Ethiopia), 1941
Keren, Battle of (Ethiopia), 1941
BT World War, 1939-1945--Campaigns--Ethiopia

Chewa (African people) (May Subd Geog)
[DT 864 : old class]
[DT 3192.C54 : new class]
UF Maravi (African people)
BT Bantu-speaking peoples
Ethnology--Malawi

Chewa dialect (May Subd Geog)
[PL 8110.C5]
UF Cewa dialect
Chichewa dialect
BT Bantu languages
Malawi--Languages
RT Nyanja language

Chewa imprints (May Subd Geog)
[Z 7108.C]
UF Imprints, Chewa

Chewa proverbs
USE Proverbs, Chewa

Cheykye (Arab people)
USE Shaikia (Arab people)

Chi (Igbo deity) (Not Subd Geog)
[BL 2480.I2]
BT Gods, Igbo
Religion, Primitive--Nigeria

Chi-chifundi dialect
USE Cifundi dialect

Chi-Tonga language (Nyasa)
USE Tonga language (Nyasa)

Chi-Tonga language (Zambesi)
USE Tonga language (Zambesi)

Chi-yao language
USE Yao language

Chiasu language
USE Asu language

(May Subd Geog) = Place names may follow the heading

Chibemba language
  USE Bemba language

Chichewa dialect
  USE Chewa dialect

Chifundi dialect
  USE Cifundi dialect

Chiga (African people) *(May Subd Geog)*
  [DT 433.245.C]
  UF Bachiga (African people)
      Bakiga (African people)
      Ciga (African people)
      Kiga (African people)
  BT Bantu-speaking peoples
      Ethnology--Uganda
 --Religion
  [BL 2480.C48]
  NT Nyabingi (African deity)

Chiga language
  USE Kiga language

Chigogo (African people)
  USE Gogo (African people)

Chigogo language
  USE Gogo language

Chihamba
  [BL 2480.N35]
  BT Ndembu (African people)--Rites and
 ceremonies
      Religion, Primitive--Zambia

Childhood
  USE Children

Children *(May Subd Geog)*
  Here are entered on people from birth through
twelve years of age.
  UF Childhood
 --Education
  USE Education
 --Recreation
  USE Games
 --Africa, West
  NT Yoruba (African people)--Children
 --Benin
  NT Yoruba (African people)--Children
 --Gambia
  NT Wolof (African people)--Children
 --Liberia
  NT Kpelle (African people)--Children

 --Mauritania
  NT Wolof (African people)--Children
 --Nigeria
  NT Ijo (African people)--Children
      Yoruba (African people)--Children
 --Senegal
  NT Wolof (African people)--Children
 --South Africa
  NT Shona (African people)--Children
 --Zaire
  NT Lele (African people)--Children
 --Zimbabwe
  NT Shona (African people)--Children

Children, Black *(May Subd Geog)*
  UF Black children
      Blacks--Children
 --South Africa
  [HQ 792.S6]

Children's books
  USE Children's literature

Children's drama
  USE Children's plays

Children's games
  USE Games

Children's literature *(May Subd Geog)*
  Here are entered collections of works published for
children. Collections of literary works or individual
literary works written by children under 15 years of age are
entered under Children's writings.
  UF Books for children
      Children's books
      Juvenile literature
  BT Literature
  NT Children's plays
      Children's poetry
      Children's stories

Children's literature, African
  UF African children's literature
  BT African literature

Children's literature, Afrikaans *(May Subd Geog)*
  UF Afrikaans children's literature
  BT Afrikaans literature

Children's literature, Cameroon (English) *(May Subd
Geog)*
  UF Cameroon children's literature (English)
  BT Cameroon literature (English)

UF = Used for; BT = Broader term; RT = Related term; SA = See also; NT = Narrower term

Children's literature, South African *(May Subd Geog)*
- UF   South African children's literature
- BT   South African literature

Children's plays
Here are entered *collections of plays for children and works on such plays.*
- UF   Children's drama
       Juvenile drama
       Juvenile plays
       Plays for children
       School plays
- BT   Children's literature
       Drama
       Theater
- RT   College and school drama

Children's plays, Afrikaans *(May Subd Geog)*
- UF   Afrikaans children's plays
- BT   Afrikaans drama

Children's poetry
- UF   Juvenile poetry
       Poetry for children
- BT   Children's literature
       Poetry
- NT   Lullabies
       Nursery rhymes

Children's poetry, Kenyan (English) *(May Subd Geog)*
- UF   Kenyan children's poetry (English)
- BT   Kenyan poetry (English)

Children's poetry, Sao Tomean *(May Subd Geog)*
- UF   Sao Tomean children's poetry
- BT   Sao Tomean poetry

Children's poetry, Swahili *(May Subd Geog)*
- UF   Swahili children's poetry
- BT   Swahili poetry

Children's poetry, Tsonga *(May Subd Geog)*
- UF   Tsonga children's poetry
- BT   Tsonga poetry

Children's poetry, Zimbabwean *(May Subd Geog)*
- UF   Zimbabwean children's poetry
- BT   Zimbabwean poetry

Children's poetry, Zulu *(May Subd Geog)*
- UF   Zulu children's poetry
- BT   Zulu poetry

Children's stories
- BT   Children's literature
       Fiction

Children's stories, African (French)
- UF   African children's stories, French
- BT   African fiction (French)

Children's stories, Afrikaans *(May Subd Geog)*
- UF   Afrikaans children's stories
- BT   Afrikaans fiction

Children's stories, Botswana (English) *(May Subd Geog)*
- UF   Botswana children's stories (English)

Children's stories, Ghanaian (English) *(May Subd Geog)*
- UF   Ghanaian children's stories (English)
- BT   Ghanaian literature (English)

Children's stories, Kenyan (English) *(May Subd Geog)*
- UF   Kenyan children's stories (English)
- BT   Kenyan fiction (English)

Children's stories, Mauritian (French) *(May Subd Geog)*
- UF   Mauritian children's stories, French
- BT   Mauritian fiction (French)

Children's stories, Mauritian (French Creole) *(May Subd Geog)*
- UF   Creole children's stories, Mauritian French
       French Creole children's stories, Mauritian
       Mauritian children's stories (French Creole)
- BT   Mauritian fiction (French Creole)

Children's stories, Ndebele (Zimbabwe) *(May Subd Geog)*
- [PZ 90.N44]
- UF   Ndebele children's stories (Zimbabwe)
- BT   Ndebele fiction (Zimbabwe)

Children's stories, Somali *(May Subd Geog)*
- [PZ 90.S57]
- UF   Somali children's stories
- BT   Somali fiction

Children's stories, Sotho *(May Subd Geog)*
- [PZ 90.S6]
- UF   Sotho children's stories
- BT   Sotho fiction

(May Subd Geog) = Place names may follow the heading

Children's stories, South African (English)
(May Subd Geog)
   UF South African children's stories
(English)
   BT South African fiction (English)

Children's stories, Swahili *(May Subd Geog)*
   [PZ 90.S94]
   UF Swahili children's stories
   BT Swahili fiction

Children's stories, Tonga (Zambesi) *(May Subd Geog)*
   [PZ 90.T54]
   UF Tonga children's stories (Zambesi)
   BT Tonga fiction (Zambesi)

Children's stories, Zambian (English) *(May Subd Geog)*
   UF Zambian children's stories (English)
   BT Zambian fiction (English)

Children's writings
Here are entered collections of literary works or
individual literary works written by children under 15
years of age. Collections of works published for
children are entered under Children's literature.
   NT School prose
        School verse

Children's writings, Ghanaian (English) *(May Subd Geog)*
   UF Ghanaian chidren's writing (English)
   BT Ghanaian literature (English)

Children's writings, South African (English)
(May Subd Geog)
   UF South African children's writings
(English)
   BT South African literature (English)

Children's writings, Zambian (English) *(May Subd Geog)*
   UF Zambian children's writings (English)
   BT Zambian literature (English)

Chilembwe Rebellion, 1915
   USE Malawi--History--Chilembwe Rebellion,
1915

Chills and fever
   USE Malaria

Chiluba language (Luba-Katanga)
   USE Luba-Katanga language

Chiluba language (Sanga)
   USE Sanga language

Chiluchazi (African people)
   USE Luchazi (African people)

Chiluwunda language
   USE Ruund language

Chimanyika (African people)
   USE Nika (African people)

Chimba dialect
   USE Himba dialect

Chimbunda language
   USE Mbunda language (Zambia)

Chimira (African people)
   USE Gimira (African people)

Chimurenga War (Zimbabwe), 1896-1897
   USE Zimbabwe--History--Ndebele Insurrection,
1896-1897

Chimurenga War (Zimbabwe), 1966-1980
   USE Zimbabwe--History--Chimurenga War, 1966-
1980

China language (Africa)
   USE Shona language

Chinaware
   USE Pottery

Chindau language *(May Subd Geog)*
   [PL 8110.C6]
   UF Cindau language
        Ndau language
        Sofala language
        Vandau language
   BT Bantu languages
        Zimbabwe--Languages

Chinyanja language
   USE Nyanja language

Chipembere Rebellion, 1965
   USE Malawi--History--1964-

Chire River (Malawi and Mozambique)
   USE Shire River (Malawi and Mozambique)

Chisalampsu language
   USE Salampasu language

UF = Used for; BT = Broader term; RT = Related term; SA = See also; NT = Narrower term

Chivowa Hill Site (Zimbabwe) *(Not Subd Geog)*
  [DT 962.3 : old class]
  [DT 3020.C45 : new class]
  BT Zimbabwe--Antiquities

Chobe National Park (Botswana) *(Not Subd Geog)*
  BT National parks and reserves--Botswana

Chokosi (African people)
  USE Chokossi (African people)

Chokosi dialect
  USE Anufo dialect

Chokossi (African people) *(May Subd Geog)*
  [DT 582.45.C]
  UF Anufo (African people)
      Chakossi (African people)
      Chokosi (African people)
      Tshokossi (African people)
      Tyokossi (African people)
  BT Ethnology--Togo
  --Religion
    [BL 2480.C49]

Chokossi law
  USE Law, Chokossi

Chokwe (African people) *(May Subd Geog)*
  [DT 611.45.C56 (Angola : old class)]
  [DT 1308.C67 (Angola : new class)]
  [DT 963.42 (Zambia : old class)]
  [DT 3058.C56 (Zambia : new class)]
  UF Bachokwe (African people)
      Bajokwe (African people)
      Cokwe (African people)
      Kioko (African people)
      Quioco (African people)
      Tchokwe (African people)
      Tshokwe (African people)
  BT Bantu-speaking peoples
      Ethnology--Angola
      Ethnology--Zaire
      Ethnology--Zambia
  --Religion
    [BL 2480.C5]

Chokwe art
  USE Art, Chokwe

Chokwe language *(May Subd Geog)*
  [PL 8113]
  UF Cibokwe language
      Ciokwe language
      Cokwe language
      Djok language

  UF Jok language
      Katchokue language
      Kioko language
      Kiokwe language
      Quioco language
      Shioko language
      Tschiokwe language
      Tshiboko language
      Tshokwe language
      Tutchokue language
  BT Angola--Languages
      Bantu languages
      Zaire--Languages
      Zambia--Languages

Chokwe sculpture
  USE Sculpture, Chokwe

Chokwe wood-carving
  USE Wood-carving, Chokwe

Chope (African people)
  USE Chopi (African people)

Chope language
  USE Chopi language

Chopi (African people) *(May Subd Geog)*
  [DT 458.3.C (Mozambique : old class)]
  [DT 3328.C67 (Mozambique : new class)]
  UF Bachopi (African people)
      Batchopi (African people)
      Chope (African people)
      Copi (African people)
      Lenge (African people)
      Muchopi (African people)
      Tchopi (African people)
      Tschopi (African people)
      Tshopi (African people)
      Vachopi (African people)
      Valenge (African people)
  BT Bantu-speaking peoples
      Ethnology--Mozambique
      Ethnology--South Africa

Chopi language *(May Subd Geog)*
  [PL 8115]
  UF Chope language
      Lenge language
      Shilenge language
      Silenge language
      Xilenge language
  BT Bantu languages
      Mozambique--Languages

(May Subd Geog) = Place names may follow the heading

Christian denominations
USE Christian sects

Christian missions
USE Missions

Christian sects *(May Subd Geog)*
UF Christian denominations
Denominations, Christian
Sects, Christian
--Africa
[BR 1359-BR 1470]
NT Zionist churches (Africa)
--Africa, West
[BR 1460-BR 1463]
--South Africa
[BR 1448-BR 1455]

Christian theology
USE Theology

Christianity *(May Subd Geog)*
BT Religions
NT Jews
Theology
--Missions
USE Missions
--Kenya
[BR 1443.K4]
--Rwanda
[BR 1443.R95]
--South Africa
NT Catechisms, Zulu
Zambia
[BR 1446.6-BR 1446.8]]

Christianity and other religions
BT Religions
--African
[BR 128.A16]

Christians, Black *(May Subd Geog)*
[BR 1702]
UF Black Christians

Chuana (African people)
USE Tswana (African people)

Chuana language
USE Tswana language

Chuba
USE Ayo (Game)

Church and race relations

USE Race relations--Religious aspects--
Christianity

Church Street Cemetery (Pretoria, South Africa)
(Not Subd Geog)
BT Cemeteries--South Africa

Churchyards
USE Cemeteries

Chute de Poubara (Gabon)
USE Poubara, Chute de (Gabon)

Chute Foulémé (Gabon)
USE Poubara, Chute de (Gabon)

Chutes de Poubara (Gabon)
USE Poubara, Chute de (Gabon)

Chwana language
USE Tswana language

Chwee language
USE Twi language

Chwi language
USE Twi language

Ci-Renje language
USE Lenje language

Ci-Tonga language
USE Tonga language (Zambezi)

Ci-venda language
USE Venda language

CiAthu language
USE Asu language

Cibokwe language
USE Chokwe language

Cifundi dialect *(May Subd Geog)*
[PL 8704.Z9G3]
UF Chi-chifundi dialect
Chifundi dialect
BT Kenya--Languages
Swahili language

Ciga (African people)
USE Chiga (African people)

Ciga language
USE Kiga language

UF = Used for; BT = Broader term; RT = Related term; SA = See also; NT = Narrower term

ciIkuhane language
  USE Subiya language

Ciina Mukuna (African people)
  USE Lenje (African people)

Cikuya language
  USE Kukwa language

Ciluba language
  USE Luba-Lulua language

Cimambwe language
  USE Mambwe language

Cimba (African people)
  USE Himba (African people)

Cimba dialect
  USE Himba dialect

Cindau language
  USE Chindau language

Cinema
  USE Motion pictures

Ciokwe language
  USE Chokwe language

Circumcision (May Subd Geog)
  [GN 484 (Ethnology)]
  BT Initiation rites
      Sex customs
  NT Clitoridectomy
      Infibulation
--Gabon
--Madagascar

ciSalampasu language
  USE Salampasu language

Ciskei (South Africa) (Not Subd Geog)
  [DT 846.C57 : old class]
  [DT 2400.C58 : new class]
  BT Homelands (South Africa)

Cities and towns, Ruined, extinct, etc. (May
Subd Geog)
  UF Abandoned cities
      Buried cities
      Deserted cities
      Extinct cities
      Ruined cities
--Guinea
  NT Niani (Guinea)

--Mauritania
  NT Aoudaghost (City)
--Sudan
  NT Meroe (Sudan)
      Napata (Ancient city)
--Zimbabwe
  NT Great Zimbabwe (City)

Civics, Cameroon
  [JQ 3529.A2]
  UF Cameroon civics

Civics, Senegalese
  [JQ 3396.A92]
  UF Senegalese civics

Civics, Zairian
  [JQ 3617.A2]
  UF Zairian civics

Civil disorders
  USE Riots

Civil liberation movements
  USE Civil rights movements

Civil procedure (Bantu law)
  BT Law, Bantu

Civil procedure (Tswana law)
  BT Law, Tswana

Civil rights movements (May Subd Geog)
  UF Civil liberation movements
      Liberation movements (Civil rights)
      Protest movements
  NT Anti-apartheid movements

Civil service (May Subd Geog)
  Here are entered works on career government service and
  the laws governing it.
  UF Career government service
      Government employees
      Government service
      Public employees
      Public service (Civil service)
  NT Strikes and lockouts--Civil service
--Ghana

Civil Service Strike, Ghana, 1978
  [HD 8004.2.G4]
  BT Strikes and lockouts--Civil service--Ghana

Civil war
  UF Rebellions
  BT Revolutions

(May Subd Geog) = Place names may follow the heading

NT Insurgency
--Angola
USE Angola--History--Civil War, 1975-
--Nigeria
USE Nigeria--History--Civil War, 1967-1970
--Rwanda
USE Rwanda--History--Civil War, 1959-1962
--Sudan
USE Sudan--History--Civil War, 1955-1972
--Zaire
USE Zaire--History--Civil War, 1960-1965
--Zululand (South Africa)
USE Zululand (South Africa)--History--
Civil War, 1879-1884

Civilization
For works on the civilization of a particular
place, see the name of the place with subdivision
Civilization, e.g., Angola--Civilization

Civilization, Greek
USE Greece--Civilization

Civilization, Jewish
USE Jews--Civilization

Civilization, Occidental
USE Civilization, Western

Civilization, Western
[CB 245]
UF Civilization, Occidental
Occidental civilization
Western civilization
NT Africa--Civilization--Western
influences
Africa, East--Civilization--Western
influences
Africa, West--Civilization--Western
influences
Ivory Coast--Civilization--Western
influences
Nigeria--Civilization--Western
influences
--African influences
BT Africa--Civilization

Clairwood (Durban, South Africa) *(Not Subd Geog)*
UF Durban (South Africa). Clairwood

Clans *(May Subd Geog)*
BT Family
RT Kinship
Tribes
--Cameroon
[DT 570]

Clay *(May Subd Geog)*
--Zambia
NT Kankomo Clay Deposit (Zambia)

Click languages, Non-Bantu
USE Khoisan languages

Clicks (Phonetics)
UF Avulsives
Language and languages--Clicks
NT African languages--Clicks
Khoisan languages--Clicks

Clitoridectomy *(May Subd Geog)*
BT Circumcision
--Law and legislation
--Sierra Leone
[GN 655.S5]
--Somalia
[GN 650.5.S65]

Cloth
USE Textile fabrics

Cloud modification
USE Weather control

Coana (African people)
USE Tswana (African people)

Coana language
USE Tswana language

Coast of Death (Namibia)
USE Skeleton Coast (Namibia)

Coasts *(May Subd Geog)*
BT Landforms
NT Bays
Capes (Coasts)
Estuaries
Inlets
--Africa
NT Atlantic Coast (Africa)
Indian Coast (Africa)
--Angola
NT Atlantic Coast (Angola)
--Benin
NT Atlantic Coast (Benin)
--Cameroon
NT Atlantic Coast (Cameroon)
--Congo (Brazzaville)
NT Atlantic Coast (Congo)
--Gabon
NT Atlantic Coast (Gabon)   *(Continued)*

UF = Used for; BT = Broader term; RT = Related term; SA = See also; NT = Narrower term

Coasts   *(Continued)*
  --Ivory Coast
    NT Atlantic Coast (Ivory Coast)
  --Kenya
    NT Indian Coast (Kenya)
  --Liberia
    NT Atlantic Coast (Liberia)
  --Namibia
    NT Atlantic Coast (Namibia)
        Skeleton Coast (Namibia)
  --South Africa
    NT Indian Coast (South Africa)
  --Tanzania
    NT Indian Coast (Tanzania)
  --Togo
    NT Atlantic Coast (Togo)
  --Zaire
    NT Atlantic Coast (Zaire)

Cocche (African people)
  USE Hamar (African people)

Cocoa trade *(May Subd Geog)*
  --Cameroon
    [HD 9200.C182]
  --Ghana
    [HD 9200.G62]

Coexistence
  USE *subdivision* Foreign relations *under names
  of countries, e.g.* Benin--Foreign relations

Coffee trade *(May Subd Geog)*
  --Africa, Sub-Saharan
    [HD 9199.A]
  --Angola
    [HD 9199.A52]

Coffino (African people)
  USE Kaffa (African people)

Coins, Ethiopian
  [CJ 3920-CJ 3939]
  UF Ethiopian coins

Coins, Gold
  USE Gold coins

Coins, South African
  [CJ 3940-CJ 3959]
  UF South African coins
  RT Gold coins--South Africa
  NT Burgerspond (Coin)
      Krugerrand (Coin)

Cokwe (African people)
  USE Chokwe (African people)

Cokwe language
  USE Chokwe language

Collective settlements *(May Subd Geog)*
  *Here are entered works on traditional, formally organized
  communal ventures, usually based on ideological, political
  on religious affiliation.*
  UF Communal settlements
      Communistic settlements
  BT Communism
      Socialism
  --Tanzania
    NT Ujamaa villages

College and school drama
  UF College drama
      College plays
      College theatricals
      Drama, Academic
      Plays, College
      School drama
      School plays
      School theatricals
      Theatricals, College
      University drama
  RT Children's plays

College and school drama, Kenyan (English) *(May
Subd Geog)*
  [PN 6120.A4]
  UF Kenyan college and school drama (English)
  BT Kenyan drama (English)

College and school drama, Swahili *(May Subd Geog)*
  [PL 8704.A2 (Collections)]
  UF Swahili college and school drama
  BT Swahili drama

College drama
  USE College and school drama

College graduates *(May Subd Geog)*
  *Here are entered works on college graduates as a socio-
  economic group.*
  UF Graduates, College
      University graduates

College graduates, Black *(May Subd Geog)*
  UF Black college graduates
      Black university graduates
  --South Africa
    [LB 2430.S6]

(May Subd Geog) = Place names may follow the heading

College life
USE College students

College plays
USE College and school drama

College poetry
USE College verse

College prose
UF Students' writings
BT School prose
Youths' writings

College prose, Ghanaian (English) *(May Subd Geog)*
[PR 9379.4 (History)]
[PR 9379.8 (Collections)]
UF Ghanaian college prose (English)
BT Ghanaian prose literature (English)

College students *(May Subd Geog)*
UF College life
Undergraduates
Universities and colleges--Students
University students
BT Students

College students, Black *(May Subd Geog)*
UF Black college students
Black university students
BT Blacks--Education
Students, Black
--South Africa
[LC 2808.S7]

College teachers *(May Subd Geog)*
UF Teachers, College
Teachers, University
University teachers
BT Teachers

College teachers, Black *(May Subd Geog)*
UF Black college teachers
Black university teachers
BT Teachers, Black

College theatricals
USE College and school drama

College verse
UF College poetry
Students' writings
BT Poetry
Youths' writings
RT School verse

College verse, Ghanaian (English) *(May Subd Geog)*
[PR 9379.2 (History)]
[PR 9379.6-PR 9379.65 (Collections)]
UF Ghanaian college verse (English)
BT Ghanaian poetry (English)

College verse, Nigerian (English) *(May Subd Geog)*
[PR 9387.2 (History)]
[PR 9387.6-PR 9387.65 (Collections)
UF Nigerian college verse (English)
BT Nigerian poetry (English)

College verse, Sierra Leone (English) *(May Subd Geog)*
[PR 9393.2 (History)]
[PR 9393.6-PR 9393.65 (Collections)]
UF Sierra Leone college verse (English)
BT Sierra Leone poetry (English)

Colleges
USE Universities and colleges

Colleges, Black
USE Universities and colleges, Black

Colo (African people)
USE Shilluk (African people)

Colombia
--Civilization
-- --African influences
BT Africa--Civilization

Colonial affairs
USE Colonies

Colonial research
USE Colonies--Research

Colonialism
USE Colonies

Colonies
[JV]
Works on the colonial period of individual regions or countries are entered under the name of the region or country with appropriate subdivision, e.g. Cameroon--Politics and government--To 1960.
Works on the influence of former colonial policies and structures on the existing institutions of former colonies are entered under the current name of the particular region or country with subdivision Colonial influence.
Topical subjects subdivided by place may also be subdivided further by Colonies, e.g. Education--Great Britain--Colonies. *(Continued)*

UF = Used for; BT = Broader term; RT = Related term; SA = See also; NT = Narrower term

Colonies   *(Continued)*
  UF Anti-colonialism
       Colonial affairs
       Colonialism
       Neocolonialism
       Nonselfgoverning territories
  NT Belgium--Colonies
       Decolonization
       Denmark--Colonies
       France--Colonies
       Germany--Colonies
       Great Britain--Colonies
       Greece--Colonies
       Netherlands--Colonies
       Portugal--Colonies
       Spain--Colonies
 --Research *(May Subd Geog)*
  UF Colonial research
 --Africa

Colonization by Afro-Americans
  USE Afro-Americans--Colonization

Colony and Protectorate of Kenya
  USE Kenya

Color of man
  [GN 197]
  UF Pigmentation
       Skin, Color of
       Skin pigmentation
  NT Black race--Color

Colored people (South Africa) *(May Subd Geog)*
  [DT 764.C6 : old class]
  [DT 1768.C65 : new class]
  Here are entered works on the mixed racial
population of South Africa.
  UF Cape coloured people
       Coloured persons (South Africa)
  BT Ethnology--South Africa
       Miscegenation
  NT Griquas
 --Relocation
  UF Relocation of Colored people (South
Africa)
       Removal of Colored people (South
Africa)
       Resettlement of Colored people (South
Africa)
  BT South Africa--Race relations

Colored people (United States)
  USE Afro-Americans

Coloured persons (South Africa)
  USE Colored people (South Africa)

Combinations of labor
  USE Strikes and lockouts

Comic literature
  USE Satire

Comic stories
  USE Humorous stories

Commerce
  For works on the trade, both foreign and domesitc, of
countries, cities, etc. see the name of the place with
subdivision Commerce, e.g., Senegal--Commerce.

Commercial correspondence
  UF Business correspondence
       Business letters
       Correspondence, Commercial

Commercial correspondence, Afrikaans
  [HF 5728.A36]
  UF Afrikaans commercial correspondence

Commi (African people)
  USE Nkomi (African people)

Common Monetary Area (Southern Africa)
  USE Rand area

Communal settlements
  USE Collective settlements

Communauté économique de l'Afrique de l'Ouest
  [HC 1005]
  A francophone subgroup within the Economic Community of
West African States.
  UF C.E.A.O.
       West African Economic Community
  BT Economic Community of West African States

Communication *(May Subd Geog)*
  Here are entered works on human communication, including
both the primary techniques of language, pictures, etc., and
the secondary techniques, such as the press and radio.
Works on the modern means of mass communication are entered
under Mass media.
  UF Mass communication
  SA *subdivision Communication under ethnic groups*
  NT Drum language
       Language and languages
       Mass media
       Popular culture
       Propaganda

--Government policy
  USE Communication policy
--Africa
  NT Crossroads Africa

Communication and state
  USE Communication policy

Communication policy *(May Subd Geog)*
  UF Communication--Government policy
    Communication and state
    State and communication
--Africa
  [P 95.82.A4]
  NT United Nations Transport and
Communications Decade in Africa, 1978-1988

Communism *(May Subd Geog)*
  Here are entered works on revolutionary ideologies
or movements inspired by Marx and advocating the
abolition of private property, dictatorship of the
proletariat, and gradual disappearance of the state.
Present day communist movements are characterized by
collective ownership of the means of production and
totalitarian, single party governments.
  UF Bolshevism
    Communist movements
    Leninism
    Maoism
    Marxism
  RT Socialism
  NT Collective settlements
--Africa, Sub-Saharan
  [HX 438.5]
--Tanzania
  [HX 448.5]

Communist movements
  USE Communism

Communistic settlements
  USE Collective settlements

Community songbooks, Afrikaner
  USE Songbooks, Afrikaner

Comoran language
  USE Comorian language

Comorian language *(May Subd Geog)*
  [PL 8116]
  UF Comoran language
    Comoro language
    Komoro language
  BT Comoros--Languages
    Swahili language

Comoro Islands
  USE Comoros

Comoro language
  USE Comorian language

Comoros *(Not Subd Geog)*
  [DT 469.C7]
  UF Comoro Islands
    Federal and Islamic Republic of the Comoros
    The Comoros
  BT Islands of the Indian Ocean
  NT Mayotte
--Economic conditions
  [HC 597]
--Languages
  [PL 8021.C6]
  NT Comorian language

Companies
  USE Business enterprises

Comparative religion
  USE Religions

Compensation for victims of crime
  USE Reparation

Composers *(May Subd Geog)*
  UF Music--Biography
    Songwriters
  BT Musicians

Composers, Black *(May Subd Geog)*
  [ML 390 (Collective biography)]
  [ML 410 (Individual biography)]
  UF Black composers

Computer-based information systems
  USE Information storage and retrieval systems

Concentration camps *(May Subd Geog)*
  UF Detention camps
    Internment camps
--South Africa
  [HV 8964.S]
  NT Irene Concentration Camp (South Africa)

Congo (African people)
  USE Kongo (African people)

Congo (Brazzaville) *(Not Subd Geog)*
  [DT 546.2-DT 546.29]
  UF Middle Congo
    The Congo   *(Continued)*

UF = Used for; BT = Broader term; RT = Related term; SA = See also; NT = Narrower term

Congo (Brazzaville)   *(Continued)*
--Description and travel
-- --1981-
--Economic conditions
   [HC 980]
--History
-- --To 1960
   NT Kongo Wara, 1928-1931
--Languages
   NT Bembe language (Congo (Brazzaville))
       Bobangi language
       Gbaya language
       Kituba language
       Kongo language
       Koongo dialect (Western Kongo)
       Kukwa language
       Laadi dialect
       Lingala language
       Ma language
       Mbete language
       Mbomotaba language
       Mbosi language
       Ndumu language
       Ngbandi language
       Punu language
       Sango language
       Teke language
       Yakoma language
--Literatures
   NT Mbosi literature
--Politics and government
-- --1960-

Congo (Brazzaville) arts
   USE Arts, Congo (Brazzaville)

Congo (Brazzaville) authors
   USE Authors, Congo (Brazzaville)

Congo (Brazzaville) literature (French)   *(May
Subd Geog)*
   [PQ 3988.5.C6 (History)]
   [PQ 3988.5.C62 (Collections)]
   UF French literature--Congo (Brazzaville)
authors
   BT African literature (French)
   NT Congo (Brazzaville) poetry (French)

Congo (Brazzaville) poetry (French)   *(May Subd
Geog)*
   [PQ 3988.5.C6 (History)]
   [PQ 3988.5.C62 (Collections)]
   UF French poetry--Congo (Brazzaville)
authors
   BT African poetry (French)

   BT Congo (Brazzaville) literature (French)

Congo (Brazzaville) proverbs
   USE Proverbs, Congo (Brazzaville)

Congo (Brazzaville) riddles
   USE Riddles, Congo (Brazzaville)

Congo (Democratic Republic)
   USE Zaire

Congo (Kingdom)
   USE Kongo Kingdom

Congo Crisis, 1960-1965
   USE Zaire--History--Civil War, 1960-1965

Congo Free State
   USE Zaire

Congo language
   USE Kongo language

Congo River   *(Not Subd Geog)*
   UF Rio Zaire
       Zaire River
   NT Stanley Falls (Zaire)
--Alluvial plain

Congo wit and humor, Pictorial
   [NC 1740.C]
   UF Wit and humor, Pictorial (Congo)

Coniagui (African people)
   USE Koniagui (African people)

Consumers, Black
   USE Blacks as consumers

Contact vernaculars
   USE Lingua francas
       Pidgin languages

Control of desertification
   USE Desertification--Control

Cookbooks
   USE Cookery

Cookery   *(May Subd Geog)*
   Here are entered works on the art of cooking, as well as
works which consist of collections of recipes. Works on the
cookery of special places are entered under Cookery
subdivided by the place. Works on the national cuisines and
styles of cooking are entered under headings of the type
Cookery, Malawi, which may be further subdivided to

(May Subd Geog) = Place names may follow the heading

designate regional styles.
UF Cookbooks
     Cooking
     Cuisine
     Food preparation

Cookery, African
[TX 725.A4]
UF African cookery

Cookery, Cameroon
[TX 725.C35]
UF Cameroon cookery

Cookery, Cape Verdean
[TX 725.C295]
UF Cape Verdean cookery

Cookery, Ethiopian
[TX 725.E84]
UF Ethiopian cookery

Cookery, Gambian
[TX 725.G25]
UF Gambian cookery

Cookery, Kenyan
[TX 725.K29]
UF Kenyan cookery

Cookery, Liberian
[TX 725.L7]
UF Liberian cookery

Cookery, Malagasy
[TX 725.M3]
UF Malagasy cookery

Cookery, Malawi
[TX 725.M32]
UF Malawi cookery

Cookery, Mauritian
[TX 725.M34]
UF Mauritian cookery

Cookery, Mozambican
[TX 725.M85]
UF Mozambican cookery

Cookery, Nigerian
[TX 725.N54]
UF Nigerian cookery

Cookery, Rwandan
[TX 725.R88]
UF Rwandan cookery

Cookery, Senegalese
[TX 725.S38]
UF Senegalese cookery

Cookery, Seychelles
[TX 725.S464]
UF Seychelles cookery

Cookery, South African
[TX 725.S6]
UF South African cookery

Cookery, Sudanese
[TX 725.S73]
UF Sudanese cookery

Cookery, Tanzanian
[TX 725.T295]
UF Tanzanian cookery

Cookery, West African
[TX 725.W47]
UF West African cookery

Cookery, Zairian
[TX 725.Z29]
UF Zairian cookery

Cookery, Zambian
[TX 725.Z]
UF Zambian cookery

Cookery, Zimbabwean
[TX 725.Z55]
UF Zimbabwean cookery

Cooking
USE Cookery

Copi (African people)
USE Chopi (African people)

Copper Miners' Strike, Zambia, 1935
[HD 5442.5.M72 1935]
BT Strikes and lockouts--Copper mining--Zambia

Copper Miners' Strike, Zambia, 1940
[HD 5442.5.M72 1940]
BT Strikes and lockouts--Copper mining--Zambia

UF = Used for; BT = Broader term; RT = Related term; SA = See also; NT = Narrower term

Coranna (African people)
  USE Korana (African people)

Coranna language
  USE Korana language

Coronation Safari
  USE East African Safari Rally

Corisco (Equatorial Guinea) *(Not Subd Geog)*
  UF Isla de Corisco (Equatorial Guinea)
  BT Islands--Equatorial Guinea
      Equatorial Guinea

Corporation executives
  USE Executives

Correspondence, Commercial
  USE Commercial correspondence

Côte d'Ivoire
  USE Ivory Coast

Cotocoli language
  USE Tem language

Coups d'état *(May Subd Geog)*
  *Here and with geographical subdivisions are entered
general and comprehensive works discussing coups d'état
collectively. Works on individual coups d'état are
entered under the name of the country with appropriate
historical subdivision, e.g. Sudan--History--Coup
d'état, 1985.*
  UF Political violence
  BT History
      Revolutions
 --Benin
  NT Benin--History--Coup d'état, 1977
 --Burkina Faso
  NT Burkina Faso--History--Coup d'état,
      1987
 --Cameroon
  NT Cameroon--History--Coup d'état, 1984
 --Central African Republic
  NT Central African Republic--History--
Coup d'état, 1979
 --Ethiopia
  NT Ethiopia--History--Coup d'état, 1960
 --Gambia
  NT Gambia--History--Coup d'état, 1981
 --Ghana
  NT Ghana--History--Coup d'état, 1966
      Ghana--History--Coup d'état, 1972
      Ghana--History--Coup d'état, 1979
      Ghana--History--Coup d'état, 1981
 --Guinea

  NT Guinea--History--Coup d'état, 1984
 --Guinea-Bissau
  NT Guinea-Bissau--History--Coup d'état, 1980
 --Liberia
  NT Liberia--History--Coup d'état, 1980
 --Mali
  NT Mali--History--Coup d'état, 1968
 --Nigeria
  NT Nigeria--History--Coup d'état, 1966
(January 15)
      Nigeria--History--Coup d'état, 1966 (July
29)
      Nigeria--History--Coup d'état, 1983
 --Senegal
  NT Senegal--History--Coup d'état, 1962
 --Seychelles
  NT Seychelles--History--Coup d'état, 1977
      Seychelles--History--Coup d'état, 1981
 --Sudan
  NT Sudan--History--Coup d'état, 1985

Courts, Bantu
  UF Bantu courts
  BT Law, Bantu

Courts, Sotho
  UF Sotho courts
  BT Law, Sotho

Cova (Shona-speaking people)
  USE Gova (Shona-speaking people)

Coverture
  USE Married women

Cradle songs
  USE Lullabies

Crau (African people)
  USE Kru (African people)

Creeks
  USE Rivers

Creole children's stories, Mauritian French
  USE Children's stories, Mauritian (French
Creole)

Creole dialects *(May Subd Geog)*
  [PM 7831-PM 7875]
  *Here are entered works discussing pidgin languages that
have become established as the native language of a speech
community. Works discussing auxiliary, sometimes mixed,
languages used among groups having no other language in
common are entered under the heading Lingua francas.
Works discussing lingua francas which are native to none of*

those using them and are characterized by a simplified grammar and often mixed vocabulary are entered under the heading Pidgin languages.
    UF Creole languages
        Creolized language
        Dialects
    BT Pidgin languages

Creole dialects, Arabic *(May Subd Geog)*
    [PJ 6901]
    UF Arabic creole dialects
  --Kenya
    NT Nubi language
  --Sudan
  -- --Southern Region
    [PJ 6901.S68]
  --Uganda
    NT Nubi language

Creole dialects, English *(May Subd Geog)*
    [PM 7871-PM 7874]
    UF English Creole languages
        Negro-English dialects
    NT Krio language

Creole dialects, French *(May Subd Geog)*
    [PM 7851-PM 7854]
    UF French Creole languages
  --Seychelles
    [PM 7854.S4]

Creole dialects, Portuguese *(May Subd Geog)*
    [PM 7846-PM 7849]
    UF Portuguese Creole languages
    NT Crioulo language
  --Equatorial Guinea
    NT Annobon dialect

Creole fiction, Mauritian French
    USE Mauritian fiction (French Creole)

Creole fiction, Réunion French
    USE Réunion fiction (French Creole)

Creole languages
    USE Creole dialects

Creole literature *(May Subd Geog)*
    [PM 7831-PM 7834]

Creole literature, Mauritian French
    USE Mauritian literature (French Creole)

Creole literature, Réunion French
    USE Réunion literature (French Creole)

Creole poetry, Réunion French
    USE Réunion poetry (French Creole)

Creole proverbs
    USE Proverbs, Creole

Creole riddles
    USE Riddles, Creole

Creole short stories, Réunion French
    USE Short stories, Réunion (French Creole)

Creoles (Sierra Leone)
    [DT 516.45.C73]
    UF Krio (African people)
    BT Blacks--Sierra Leone
        Ethnology--Sierra Leone

Creolized languages
    USE Creole dialects

Crime syndicates
    USE Organized crime

Criminal restitution
    USE Reparation

Crioulo language *(May Subd Geog)*
    [PM 7849.G8]
    BT Creole dialects, Portuguese
        Guinea-Bissau--Languages
        Senegal--Languages

Crobo (African people)
    USE Krobo (African people)

Crockery
    USE Pottery

Cross-cultural psychology
    USE Ethnopsychology

Cross River (Cameroon and Nigeria) *(Not Subd Geog)*
    BT Rivers--Cameroon
        Rivers--Nigeria

Cross River (Cameroon and Nigeria) African people
    USE Mbembe (Cross River African people)

Crossroads Africa
    UF Operation Crossroads Africa
    BT Communication--Africa

Cuana (African people)
    USE Tswana (African people)

UF = Used for; BT = Broader term; RT = Related term; SA = See also; NT = Narrower term

Cuana language
  USE Tswana language

Cuango River (Angola and Zaire)
  USE Kwango River (Angola and Zaire)

Cuanhama (African people)
  USE Kuanyama (African people)

Cuanhama language
  USE Kuanyama language

Cuba
 --Civilization
 -- --African influences
   BT Africa--Civilization

Cubango River
  USE Okavango River

Cubans *(May Subd Geog)*
 --Angola
   NT Angola--History--Civil War, 1975-
-Participation, Cuban

Cuisine
  USE Cookery

Cults *(May Subd Geog)*
  *Here are entered works on groups or movements whose
system of religious beliefs or practices differs
significantly from the major world religions and which
are often gathered around a specific deity or person.*
  *Works on the major world religions are entered under
Religions.*
   UF Religions, Modern
   BT Religions
   NT Nativistic movements
 --Congo (Brazzaville)
   NT Lemba (Cult)
 --Kenya
   NT Mumbo (Cult)
 --Nigeria
   NT Bori (Cult)
      Egúngún (Cult)
      Godianism (Cult)
      Ogboni (Cult)
      Owegbe Society
      Sopono (Cult)
 --Zaire
   NT Lemba (Cult)
      Vandists (Cult)

Cults, Messianic
  USE Nativistic movements

Cults, Prophetistic
  USE Nativistic movements

Cultural anthropology
  USE Ethnology

Culture, Popular
  USE Popular culture

Culture contact
  USE Acculturation

Cunama (African people)
  USE Kunama (African people)

Cunama language
  USE Kunama language

Cunene River (Angola and Namibia) *(Not Subd Geog)*
   UF Kunene River (Angola and Namibia)
      Rio Cunene (Angola and Namibia)
   BT Rivers--Angola
      Rivers--Namibia

Cushites *(May Subd Geog)*
  [DT 367.45.C86]
   BT Hamites
   NT Afar (African people)
      Gimira (African people)
      Konso (African people)
      Saho (African people)

Cushitic languages
  [PJ 2401-PJ 2413]
  *Here are entered works on the Cushitic languages of
Ethiopia. Works on the Semitic languages of Ethiopia are
entered under Ethiopian languages. General works on the
languages of Ethiopia are entered under Ethiopia--
Languages.*
   BT Afroasiatic languages
      Hamitic languages
   NT Afar language
      Agau language
      Arbore language
      Beja language
      Bilin language
      Boni language
      Burji language
      Cushitic languages, Southern
      Omotic languages
      Oromo language
      Proto-East-Cushitic language
      Quara language
      Rendile language
      Saho language

NT Sidamo languages
    Somali languages
    Werizoid languages

Cushitic languages, Southern *(May Subd Geog)*
    [PJ 2551]
    UF South Cushitic languages
        Southern Cushitic languages
    BT Cushitic languages
        Kenya--Languages
        Tanzania--Languages
    NT Dahalo language
        Iraqw language

Cushitic languages, West
    USE Omotic languages

Customary law *(May Subd Geog)*
    UF Customs (Law)
        Law, Customary
        Usage and custom (Law)
  --Africa, Eastern
    NT Law, Ngoni
  --Africa, West
    NT Law, Fula
  --Cameroon
    NT Law, Bamileke
  --Kenya
    NT Law, Kuria
  --Nigeria
    NT Law, Igbo
        Law, Jekri
  --South Africa
    NT Law, Shona
  --Tanzania
    NT Law, Chaga
        Law, Hehe
        Law, Kuria
  --Togo
    NT Law, Chokossi
  --Zaire
    NT Law, Yanzi
  --Zambia
    NT Law, Tonga
  --Zimbabwe
    NT Law, Shona

Customs, Social
    USE Manners and customs

Customs (Law)
    USE Customary law

Cwana language
    USE Tswana language

D

Daba (African people) *(May Subd Geog)*
    [DT 571.D33]
    BT Ethnology--Cameroon

Daba language *(May Subd Geog)*
    [PL 8117]
    UF Musgoy language
    BT Cameroon--Languages
        Chadic languages

Dabakala (African people)
    USE Dyula (African people)

Dabida dialect *(May Subd Geog)*
    [PL 8707.95.D3]
    UF Kidawida dialect
    BT Kenya--Languages
        Taita language

Dabossa language
    USE Toposa language

Dagaaba (African people)
    USE Dagari (African people)

Dagara language
    USE Dagari language

Dagari (African people) *(May Subd Geog)*
    [DT 555.45.D35 (Burkina Faso)]
    [DT 510.43.D33 (Ghana)]
    UF Dagaaba (African people)
        Dagati (African people)
        Lodagaa (African people)
    BT Ethnology--Burkina Faso
        Ethnology--Ghana
    NT Wala (African people)
  --Religion
    [BL 2480.D3]

Dagari language *(May Subd Geog)*
    [PL 8118.D35]
    UF Dagara language
        Dagati language
    BT Burkina Faso--Languages
        Ghana--Languages
        Mossi languages
    NT Wule dialect
  --Names
    USE Names, Dagari

Dagari mythology
    USE Mythology, Dagari

UF = Used for; BT = Broader term; RT = Related term; SA = See also; NT = Narrower term

Dagari names
    USE Names, Dagari

Dagati (African people)
    USE Dagari (African people)

Dagati language
    USE Dagari language

Dagbamba (African people)
    USE Dagomba (African people)

Dagbane language
    USE Dagomba language

Dagbani language
    USE Dagomba language

Dagomba (African people) *(May Subd Geog)*
    [DT 510.43.D34]
    UF Dagbamba (African people)
    BT Ethnology--Ghana
  --Kings and rulers

Dagomba language *(May Subd Geog)*
    [PL 8119]
    UF Dagbane language
        Dagbani language
    BT Ghana--Languages
        Mossi languages

Dahalo language *(May Subd Geog)*
    [PJ 2554]
    UF Sanye language (Dahalo)
    BT Cushitic languages, Southern
        Kenya--Languages

Dahoman language
    USE Fon dialect

Dahomans
    USE Fon (African people)

Dahomeans
    USE Fon (African people)

Dahomey
    USE Benin

Dahomey (African people)
    USE Fon (African people)

Dahomeyans
    USE Fon (African people)

Dai (African people)

    USE Day (African people)

Dai language (Chad)
    USE Day language (Chad)

Dairy farms *(May Subd Geog)*
  --Zambia
    NT Mpika Dairy Settlement Scheme (Zambia)

Dakar, Battle of, 1940
    [D 766.99]
    UF Battle of Dakar (Senegal), 1940
    BT Operation Menace
        World War, 1939-1945--Campaigns--Senegal

Dalebele (African people)
    USE Kulebele (African people)

Daleo (African people)
    USE Kulebele (African people)

Dama (African people)
    USE Murzu (African people)

Damara (African people) *(May Subd Geog)*
    [DT 709 : old class]
    [DT 1558.D : new class]
    UF Bergdama (African people)
        Bergdamara (African people)
        Hill Damara (African people)
    BT Ethnology--Namibia
        Khoikhoi (African people)
    RT Herero (African people)

Damaraland (Namibia : Region) *(Not Subd Geog)*
    [DT 720.D3 : old class]
    [DT 1670.D35 : new class]
    UF Herreroland (Namibia)

Damba (Dance drumming)
    [MT 655 (Instruction and study)]
    BT Dance music--Ghana
        Music, Islamic--Ghana

Dambos *(May Subd Geog)*
    BT Valleys--Africa

Dams *(May Subd Geog)*
  --Ghana
    NT Akosombo Dam
  --South Africa
    NT Grootdraai Dam (South Africa)
        Inanda Dam (South Africa)
        Zaaihoek Dam (South Africa)
  --Sudan
    NT Roseires Dam (Sudan)

(May Subd Geog) = Place names may follow the heading

--Tanzania
  NT Stiegler's Gorge Dam (Tanzania)
--Zambia
  NT Itezhi-Tezhi Dam (Zambia)

Dan (African people) (May Subd Geog)
  [DT 545.45.G47 (Ivory Coast)]
  [DT 630.5.G4 (Liberia)]
  UF Gere (Mande-speaking African people)
      Gio (African people)
      Guéré (Mande-speaking African people)
      Gyo (African people)
      Ngere (Mande-speaking African people)
      Nguéré (Mande-speaking African people)
      Yacouba (African people)
      Yakuba (African people)
  BT Ethnology--Ivory Coast
      Ethnology--Liberia
  --Funeral customs and rites
  UF Funeral rites and ceremonies, Dan
(African people)
  --Games
  --Masks
    BT Masks--Ivory Coast
        Masks--Liberia

Dan art
  USE Art, Dan

Dan language (May Subd Geog)
  [PL 8123]
  UF Gere language (Mande)
      Gio language
      Guere language (Mande)
      Mebe language
      Yabuba language
      Yacouba language
      Yakuba language
  BT Ivory Coast--Languages
      Liberia--Languages
      Southern Mande languages

Dan literature (May Subd Geog)
  [PL 8123.5-PL 8123.8]
  BT Ivory Coast--Literatures
      Liberian literature

Danagla (African people) (May Subd Geog)
  [DT 155.2.D36]
  UF Dongolawi (African people)
  BT Ethnology--Sudan
      Nubians

Danakil (African people)
  USE Afar (African people)

Danakil language
  USE Afar language

Dance
  USE Dancing

Dance music (May Subd Geog)
  [ML 3760 (History and criticism)]
  BT Dancing
  --Africa, West
    NT Gahu
        Highlife (Music)
  --Ghana
    NT Damba (Dance drumming)

Dancing (May Subd Geog)
  UF Dance
  NT Blacks--Dancing
      Dance music
      Folk dancing
  --Blacks
  USE Blacks--Dancing
  --Africa
    [GV 1705-GV 1713]
    NT Kalela (African dance)
  --Zambia
    [GV 1713.Z]
    NT Icila (African dance)

Danfa Comprehensive Rural Health and Family
Planning Project
  [RA 771.7]
  UF Danfa Project
  BT Birth control--Ghana
      Rural health--Ghana

Danfa Project
  USE Danfa Comprehensive Rural Health and Family
Planning Project

Dangagla dialect
  USE Dongola-Kenuz dialect

Dangaleat (African people) (May Subd Geog)
  [DT 546.445.D]
  BT Ethnology--Chad

Dangaleat language (May Subd Geog)
  [PL 8125]
  BT Chad--Languages
      Chadic languages

Dangme (African people)
  USE Adangme (African people)

UF = Used for; BT = Broader term; RT = Related term; SA = See also; NT = Narrower term

Dangme language
    USE Adangme language

Danish Settlements, Ghana, 1659-1850
    USE Ghana--History--Danish Settlements,
1659-1850

Dankali language
    USE Afar language

Dar-al-Kuti (Central African Republic) *(Not Subd Geog)*
    [DT 546.39.D]
    UF Dar-el-Kouti (Central African
Republic)

Dar Banda (African people)
    USE Banda (African people)

Dar-el-Kouti (Central African Republic)
    USE Dar-al-Kuti (Central African Republic)

Darasa language
    USE Gedeo language

Dari language (Chad)
    USE Day language (Chad)

Darra
    USE Ayo (Game)

Dasanek (African people)
    USE Dasanetch (African people)

Dasanetch (African people) *(May Subd Geog)*
    [DT 380.4.D3]
    UF Dasanek (African people)
        Dathanik (African people)
        Geleba (African people)
        Marille (African people)
    BT Ethnology--Ethiopia

Data storage and retrieval systems
    USE Information storage and retrieval
systems

Dathanik (African people)
    USE Dasanetch (African people)

Day (African people) *(May Subd Geog)*
    [DT 546.445.D]
    UF Dai (African people)
        Sara Dai (African people)
    BT Ethnology--Chad

Day language (Chad) *(May Subd Geog)*
    [PL 8126.D39]
    UF Dai language (Chad)
        Dari language (Chad)
        Sara Dai language
    BT Chad--Languages
        Chadic languages

Daza (African people) *(May Subd Geog)*
    [DT 346.D38 (Sahara)]
    UF Toubou (African people)
    BT Ethnology--Africa, West
        Ethnology--Sahara
    --Domestic animals

Daza language *(May Subd Geog)*
    [PL 8127]
    UF Dazza language
        Toubou language
        Tubu language
    BT Chad--Languages
        Niger--Languages
        Nilo-Saharan languages

Daza women
    USE Women, Daza

Dazza language
    USE Daza language

Dciriku language
    USE Diriku language

Death, Coast of (Namibia)
    USE Skeleton Coast (Namibia)

Decolonization *(May Subd Geog)*
    BT Colonies
    --Africa, Southern
        [DT 746 : old class]
        [DT 1177 : new class]

Decoration and ornament *(May Subd Geog)*
    UF Art, Decorative
        Arts, Decorative
        Decorative art
        Decorative design
        Design, Decorative
        Nature in ornament
        Ornament
        Painting, Decorative
    BT Art
        Decorative arts
    NT Bronzes

(May Subd Geog) = Place names may follow the heading

NT   Embroidery
    Ironwork
    Wood-carving

Decoration and ornament, Ashanti *(May Subd Geog)*
  [NK 1489.6.G5]
  UF   Ashanti decoration and ornament

Decoration and ornament, Hausa *(May Subd Geog)*
  [NK 1489.6.N5]
  UF   Hausa decoration and ornament

Decorative art
  USE   Decoration and ornament

Decorative arts *(May Subd Geog)*
  Here are entered comprehensive works on the various
art forms having some utilitarian as well as decorative
purpose. including furniture, woodwork, silverware,
glassware, ceramics, textiles, the decoration of
buildings, etc.
  UF   Applied arts
    Art industries and trade
    Arts, Applied
    Arts, Decorative
    Arts, Minor
    Minor arts
  RT   Art
  RT   Folk art
  NT   Decoration and ornament
    Textile fabrics

Decorative arts, Bantu *(May Subd Geog)*
  [NK 1088]
  UF   Bantu decorative arts

Decorative arts, Fula *(May Subd Geog)*
  [NK 1087.6.N5]
  UF   Fula decorative arts

Decorative design
  USE   Decoration and ornament

Deforo (African people)
  USE   Kurumba (African people)

Deforo language
  USE   Kurumba language

Deg language
  USE   Mo language (Ghana and Ivory Coast)

Degema language *(May Subd Geog)*
  BT   Kwa languages
    Nigeria--Languages

Degha language
  USE   Mo language (Ghana and Ivory Coast)

Dei language
  USE   Kissi language

Deido (African people)
  USE   Duala (African people)

Deities
  USE   Gods

Deltas *(May Subd Geog)*
  BT   Rivers
  --Botswana
    NT   Okavango River Delta (Botswana)
  --Ethiopia
    NT   Omo River Delta (Ethiopia and Kenya)
  --Kenya
    NT   Omo River Delta (Ethiopia and Kenya)
  --Madagascar
    NT   Morondava River Delta (Madagascar)
  --Mauritania
    NT   Senegal River Delta (Mauritania and
  Senegal)
  --Nigeria
    NT   Niger River Delta (Nigeria)
  --Senegal
    NT   Senegal River Delta (Mauritania and
  Senegal)

Dembo (African people)
  USE   Ndembu (African people)

Democracy *[subdivided by place]*
  USE   Representative government and
representation

Denca language
  USE   Dinka language

Dendi (African people) *(May Subd Geog)*
  [DT 551.45.D45 (Mali)]
  BT   Ethnology--Benin
    Ethnology--Mali
    Ethnology--Niger
    Ethnology--Nigeria
    Songhai (African people)

Dendi dialect *(May Subd Geog)*
  [PL 8685.95.D]
  BT   Benin--Languages
    Mali--Languages
    Niger--Languages
    Nigeria--Languages
    Songhai language

UF = Used for; BT = Broader term; RT = Related term; SA = See also; NT = Narrower term

Dengese (African people) *(May Subd Geog)*
  [DT 650.D44]
  UF Bonkese (African people)
      Bonkesse (African people)
      Ileo (African people)
      Ndengese (African people)
      Nkutu (African people)
  BT Bantu-speaking peoples
      Ethnology--Zaire

Denka language
  USE Dinka language

Denkawi (African people)
  USE Dinka (African people)

Denkyira (Kingdom) *(Not Subd Geog)*
  [DT 532.12]
  BT Ghana--History
      Ivory Coast--History

Denmark *(Not Subd Geog)*
 --Colonies
  BT Colonies
 -- --Africa
  NT Ghana--History--Danish Settlements,
1659-1850

Denominations, Christian
  USE Christian sects

Denominations, Religious
  USE Religions

Dente (African deity) *(Not Subd Geog)*
  [BL 2480.K]
  BT Gods, Krachi
      Krachi (African people)--Religion
      Religion, Primitive--Ghana
 --Cult

Dényá language
  USE Anyang language

Dependency
  USE *subdivision* Dependency on foreign
countries, or, Dependency on [place] *under names
of countries, regions, cities, etc.,* e.g. Africa,
Sub-Saharan--Dependency on foreign countries;
Africa, Sub-Saharan--Dependency on Great
Britain

Depression de la Lama (Benin)
  USE Lama Depression (Benin)

Dera language

USE Kanakuru language

Derasa language
  USE Gedeo language

Derasanya language
  USE Gedeo language

Derasinya language
  USE Gedeo language

Deresa language
  USE Gedeo language

Deru language
  USE Kanakuru language

Dervish Rebellion (Somalia), 1900-1920
  USE Maxamad Cabdulle Xasan's Rebellion, British
Somaliland, 1900-1920

Descent and distribution
  USE Inheritance and succession

Descents
  USE Inheritance and succession

Description and travel
  USE *subdivision* Description and travel *under the
names of countries and regions,* e.g. Namibia--
Description and travel

Desegregation
  USE Segregation

Desert enroachment control
  USE Desertification--Control

Deserted cities
  USE Cities and towns, Ruined, extinct,
etc.

Desertification *(May Subd Geog)*
  UF Aridization of land
      Desertization
  BT Deserts
 --Control *(May Subd Geog)*
  UF Control of desertification
      Desert enroachment control
 -- --Sudan
  [GB 618.88.S73]
 --Sudan
  [GB 618.88.S73]

Desertization
  USE Desertification

(May Subd Geog) = Place names may follow the heading

Deserto de Moçâmedes (Angola)
  USE Moçâmedes Desert (Angola)

Deserto de Massâmedes (Angola)
  USE Moçâmedes Desert (Angola)

Deserts *(May Subd Geog)*
  BT Arid regions
       Landforms
  NT Desertification
       Oases
--Africa
  NT Sahara
--Africa, Southern
  NT Kalahari Desert
--Angola
  NT Moçâmedes Desert (Angola)
--Botswana
  NT Kalahari Desert
--Kenya
  NT Chalbi Desert (Kenya)
--Namibia
  NT Namib Desert (Namibia)
--Niger
  NT Ténéré (Niger)

Design, Decorative
  UCD Decoration and ornament

Despots
  USE Dictators

Deutsch Ost-Afrika
  USE German East Africa

Detention camps
  USE Concentration camps

Detribalization
  [HN 773.5 (Africa)]
  BT Acculturation
       Tribes

Development, Economic
  USE *subdivision* Economic conditions *under*
names of countries, regions, cities, etc., e.g.,
Zimbabwe--Economic conditions

Development and women
  USE Women in development

Development banks *(May Subd Geog)*
  UF Banks, Development
--Law and legislation *(May Subd Geog)*
--Africa
  [HG 1976.A]

  NT African Development Bank
--Benin
  [HG 1976.B]

Development education
  USE Acculturation

Development projects, Forestry
  USE Forestry projects

Dhe Bor language
  USE Bor language (Lwo)

Dhe Lwo language
  USE Lwo language (Sudan)

Dhimba dialect
  USE Himba dialect

Dho Alur language
  USE Alur language

Dho Anywaa (African people)
  USE Anuak (African people)

Dho Luo (African people)
  USE Luo (African people)

Dho Luo language
  USE Luo language (Kenya and Tanzania)

Dhocolo (African people)
  USE Shilluk (African people)

Dholuo language
  USE Luo language (Kenya and Tanzania)

Di-kele language
  USE Kele language

Dialects
  USE Creole dialects

Dialonke (African people)
  USE Yalunka (African people)

Diamond mines and mining *(May Subd Geog)*
--Africa, West
  [HD 9677.A358]
--South Africa
  [HD 9677.S6]
--Zaire
  [HD 9677.Z]

Dian dialect
  USE Dyan dialect

UF = Used for; BT = Broader term; RT = Related term; SA = See also; NT = Narrower term

Diana's Vow Rock Shelter (Zimbabwe) *(Not Subd Geog)*
   [GN 865.Z55]
   BT Caves--Zimbabwe
       Zimbabwe--Antiquities

Diawara (African people) *(May Subd Geog)*
   [DT 155.2.D]
   UF Djawara (African people)
   BT Ethnology--Sudan (Region)

Dictators *(May Subd Geog)*
   UF Tyrants
       Despots
 --Biography
 --Wives
 --Africa, Sub-Saharan
   [DT 352.8]

Dictionaries, Picture
   USE Picture dictionaries

Dida (African people) *(May Subd Geog)*
   [DT 545.45.D]
   BT Ethnology--Ivory Coast

Dida dialect *(May Subd Geog)*
   [PL 8075.B5795.D52]
   UF Wawi dialect
   BT Bete language
       Ivory Coast--Languages

Didinga (African people) *(May Subd Geog)*
   [DT 155.2.D53]
   UF Birra (African people)
       Karoke (African people)
       Toi (African people)
   BT Ethnology--Sudan

Die Laan (Stellenbosch, South Africa)
   USE Avenue, The (Stellenbosch, South Africa)

Difaqane period, 1816-ca. 1840
   USE Africa, Southern--History--Mfecane period, 1816-ca. 1840

Digo (African people) *(May Subd Geog)*
   [DT 433.545.D54]
   UF Wadigo (African people)
   BT Ethnology--Kenya

Digo language *(May Subd Geog)*
   UF KiDigo language
   BT Kenya--Languages
       Nika language

Dique Island (Seychelles)
   USE La Dique Island (Seychelles)

Dinka (African people) *(May Subd Geog)*
   [DT 155.2.D56]
   UF Denkawi (African people)
       Jang (African people)
   BT Ethnology--Sudan
       Nilotic tribes
 --Marriage customs and rites
   UF Marriage customs and rites, Dinka (African people)
 --Religion
   [BL 2480.D5]
 --Rites and ceremonies

Dinka fables
   USE Fables, Dinka

Dinka folk songs
   USE Folk songs, Dinka

Dinka language *(May Subd Geog)*
   [PL 8131]
   UF Denca language
       Denka language
   BT Nilotic languages
       Sudan--Languages
   NT Bor dialect (Dinka)
       Padang dialect

Dinka law
   USE Law, Dinka

Diola (African people) *(May Subd Geog)*
   [DT 549.45.D56]
   UF Dya-ate (African people)
       Dyola (African people)
       Jola (African people)
       Kudamanta (African people)
       Kujamatak (African people)
       Yola (African people)
   BT Ethnology--Senegal
   NT Banjal (African people)
       Felup (African people)

Diola language *(May Subd Geog)*
   [PL 8134]
   UF Dyola language
       Yola language
   BT Gambia--Languages
       Guinea--Languages
       Niger-Congo languages
       Senegal--Languages

(May Subd Geog) = Place names may follow the heading

Dionkor language
  USE Jongor language

Dioula (African people)
  USE Dyula (African people)

Dioula language
  USE Dyula language

Dirico language
  USE Diriku language

Diriko language
  USE Diriku language

Diriku language *(May Subd Geog)*
  [PL 8135]
  UF Dciriku language
      Dirioo language
      Diriko language
      Gciriku language
      Mbogedu language
  BT Angola--Languages
      Bantu languages
      Namibia--Languages

Discrimination, Racial
  USE Race discrimination

Diseases, Tropical
  USE Tropical medicine

Disinvestment *(May Subd Geog)*
  UF Divestment
  BT Economic sanctions
  --South Africa
      [HF 1613.4 (Commercial policy)]
      [HG 5851 (Investments)]

District Six (Cape Town, South Africa) *(Not Subd Geog)*
  UF Cape Town (South Africa). District Six
      Zonnebloem (Cape Town, South Africa)

Ditamaba language
  USE Somba language

Ditammari language
  USE Somba language

Divestment
  USE Disinvestment

Divorce *(May Subd Geog)*
  BT Family

  BT Marriage

Divorce (Yoruba law)
  BT Law, Yoruba

Diwala (African people)
  USE Duala (African people)

Djabe (Togolese and Ghanaian people)
  USE Bassari (Togolese and Ghanaian people)

Djaga language
  USE Chaga language

Djakka (African people)
  USE Yaka (African people)

Djallonke (African people)
  USE Yalunka (African people)

Djawara (African people)
  USE Diawara (African people)

Djedji dialect
  USE Fon dialect

Djelib (Togolese and Ghanaian people)
  USE Bassari (Togolese and Ghanaian people)

Djerma (African people)
  USE Zarma (African people)

Djerma language
  USE Zarma language

Djibao language
  USE Lamé language (Cameroon)

Djibouti *(Not Subd Geog)*
  [DT 411-DT 411.9]
  UF French Somaliland
      French Territory of the Afars and Issas
      Somaliland, French
  --Anniversaries, etc.
  NT Independence Day (Djibouti)
  --Description and travel
  -- --1981-
  --Languages
  NT Afar language

Djimini (African people) *(May Subd Geog)*
  [DT 545.45.D]
  UF Dyimini (African people)
      Gimini (African people)
      Jimini (African people)
  BT Ethnology--Ivory Coast

UF = Used for; BT = Broader term; RT = Related term; SA = See also; NT = Narrower term

Djimini language *(May Subd Geog)*
  UF Dyimini language
      Gimini language
      Jimini language
  BT Gur languages
      Ivory Coast--Languages

Djo language
  USE Ijo language

Djok language
  USE Chokwe language

Djongor language
  USE Jongor language

Djonkor language
  USE Jongor language

Do language
  USE Bini language

Doayau (African people)
  USE Dowayo (African people)

Doayo (African people)
  USE Dowayo (African people)

Documents, Government
  USE Government documents

Dodos (African people)
  USE Dodoth (African people)

Dodosi (African people)
  USE Dodoth (African people)

Dodota (Ethiopia) *(Not Subd Geog)*

Dodoth (African people) *(May Subd Geog)*
  [DT 433.245.D63]
  UF Dodos (African people)
      Dodosi (African people)
      Dodotho (African people)
  BT Ethnology--Uganda
      Nilo-Hamitic tribes

Dodotho (African people)
  USE Dodoth (African people)

Dogo (African people)
  USE Dogon (African people)

Dogo language
  USE Dogon language

Dogom (African people)
  USE Dogon (African people)

Dogom language
  USE Dogon language

Dogon (African people) *(May Subd Geog)*
  [DT 530.5.D64 (French West Africa)]
  [DT 551.45.D64 (Mali)]
  UF Dogo (African people)
      Dogom (African people)
      Habbe (African people)
      Habe (African people)
      Kado (African people)
      Kibissi (African people)
      Tombo (African people)
  BT Ethnology--Africa, French-speaking West
      Ethnology--Burkina Faso
      Ethnology--Mali
 --**Masks**
  BT Masks--Mali
 --**Religion**
  [BL 2480.D6]

Dogon art
  USE Art, Dogon

Dogon language *(May Subd Geog)*
  [PL 8139]
  UF Dogo language
      Dogom language
      Habe language
      Tombo language
  BT Burkina Faso--Languages
      Gur languages
      Mali--Languages

Dogon philosophy
  USE Philosophy, Dogon

Dogon pottery
  USE Pottery, Dogon

Dogon women
  USE Women, Dogon

Doko language (Zaire) *(May Subd Geog)*
  [PL 8140.1]
  UF Doko Ngombe language
  BT Ngombe languages
      Zaire--Languages
 --**Grammar**

Doko Ngombe language
  USE Doko language (Zaire)

(May Subd Geog) = Place names may follow the heading

Dokwa (African people)
USE Tlokwa (African people)

Domestic relations (May Subd Geog)
UF Family--Law
Family law
BT Marriage
RT Family

Domestic relations (Bafokeng law) (May Subd Geog)
BT Law, Bafokeng

Domestic relations (Kgatla law) (May Subd Geog)
BT Law, Kgatla

Domestic relations (Kuria law) (May Subd Geog)
BT Law, Kuria

Domestic relations (Sotho law) (May Subd Geog)
BT Law, Sotho

Domestic relations (Tswana law) (May Subd Geog)
BT Law, Tswana

Domiciles
USE Dwellings

Dompago dialect (May Subd Geog)
BT Benin--Languages
Gur languages
Togo--Languages

Don (West African people)
USE Samo (West African people)

Dongalo-Kenuz dialect
USE Dongola-Kenuz dialect

Dongiro (African people)
USE Nyangatom (African people)

Dongo (African people)
USE Mbundu (African people)

Dongola dialect
USE Dongola-Kenuz dialect

Dongola-Kenuz dialect (May Subd Geog)
[PL 8574.Z9D6]
UF Dangagla dialect
Dongalo-Kenuz dialect
Dongola dialect
Dongolawi dialect
Kenuz dialect

UF Kenuzi dialect
Kenuzi-Dongola dialect
Kenzi dialect
Kunuzi dialect
Nile Nubian language
BT Nubian languages
Sudan--Languages

Dongolawi (African people)
USE Danagla (African people)

Dongolawi dialect
USE Dongola-Kenuz dialect

Donyanyo (African people)
USE Dowayo (African people)

Donyayo (African people)
USE Dowayo (African people)

Donyiro (African people)
USE Nyangatom (African people)

Doors (May Subd Geog)
--South Africa
NT Hyman Liberman Memorial Door (South African
National Gallery)

Dor (African people)
USE Dongo (African people)

Dor language
USE Bongo language

Dorobo (African people) (May Subd Geog)
[DT 429.5.D]
UF Andorobo (African people)
Ogiek (African people)
Torobo (African people)
Wandorobo (African people)
BT Ethnology--Africa, East
Nilo-Hamitic tribes

Dorsse (African people)
USE Dorze (African people)

Dorze (African people) (May Subd Geog)
[DT 380.4.D]
UF Dorsse (African people)
BT Ethnology--Ethiopia

Douala (Cameroon). New Bell
USE New Bell (Douala, Cameroon)

Douala (African people)
USE Duala (African people)

UF = Used for; BT = Broader term; RT = Related term; SA = See also; NT = Narrower term

Douma language
 USE Aduma language

Doumbou language
 USE Ndumu language

Dowayayo (African people)
 USE Dowayo (African people)

Dowayo (African people) *(May Subd Geog)*
 [DT 571.D68]
 UF Doayau (African people)
     Doayo (African people)
     Donyanyo (African people)
     Donyayo (African people)
     Dowayayo (African people)
     Doyayo (African people)
     Namchi (African people)
     Namshi (African people)
 BT Ethnology--Cameroon

Doyayo (African people)
 USE Dowayo (African people)

Dragon Mountains
 USE Drakensberg Mountains

Drakensberg Mountains *(Not Subd Geog)*
 [DT 878.D7 : old class]
 [DT 2400.D83 : new class]
 UF Dragon Mountains
     Drakensbergen
     Drakensburg Escarpment
     Drakensburg Mountains
     Kahlamba
     Kwathlamba
     Quathlamba
 BT Mountains--Lesotho
     Mountains--South Africa
     Mountains--Swaziland
 NT Cathedral Peak (South Africa)

Drakensbergen
 USE Drakensberg Mountains

Drakensburg Escarpment
 USE Drakensberg Mountains

Drakensburg Mountains
 USE Drakensberg Mountains

Drama
 Here are entered works on drama as a literary form.
 Works on drama as acted on the stage are entered under
 Theater.

 UF Plays
     Stage
 BT Literature
 SA Igbo drama, *and similar headings*
 NT Children's plays
     Folk-drama
     One-act plays
     Radio plays
     Religious drama
 --Black authors
 [PN 841 (History)]
 [PN 6119.7 (Collections)]
 UF Black drama

Drama, Academic
 USE College and school drama

Drama, African
 USE African drama

Drama, Folk
 USE Folk-drama

Drama, Primitive
 USE Folk-drama

Droughts *(May Subd Geog)*
 [QC 929.D8]
 UF Drouths
 BT Weather
 --Africa
 --Africa, Eastern

Drouths
 USE Droughts

Drum language
 [P 99.6 (Communication)]
 [ML 1035 (Music)]
 BT Communication

Dry farming *(May Subd Geog)*
 [SB 110]
 UF Dryland farming
     Farming, Dry
 BT Agriculture
     Arid regions agriculture
 --Africa, West

Dryland farming
 USE Arid regions agriculture
     Dry farming

Dschagga (African people)
 USE Chaga (African people)

(May Subd Geog) = Place names may follow the heading

Dschagga language
USE Chaga language

Duala (African people) *(May Subd Geog)*
[DT 571.D83]
UF Deido (African people)
Diwala (African people)
Douala (African people)
Dualla (African people)
Dwala (African people)
Dwalla (African people)
Dwela (African people)
BT Bantu-speaking peoples
Ethnology--Cameroon

Duala language *(May Subd Geog)*
[PL 8141]
UF Dualla language
BT Bantu languages
Cameroon--Languages

Duala literature *(May Subd Geog)*
[PL 8141.5-PL 8141.8]
BT Cameroon literature
NT Duala poetry

Duala poetry *(May Subd Geog)*
[PL 8141,7]
BT Cameroon--Poetry
Duala literature

Duala proverbs
USE Proverbs, Duala

Dualla (African people)
USE Duala (African people)

Dualla language
USE Duala language

Duka (African people)
USE Dukawa (African people)

Dukanchi (African people)
USE Dukawa (African people)

Dukawa (African people) *(May Subd Geog)*
[DT 515.45.D84]
UF Badukku (African people)
Duka (African people)
Dukanchi (African people)
Dukkawa (African people)
Hune (African people)
BT Ethnology--Nigeria

Dukkawa (African people)

USE Dukawa (African people)

Dullay languages
USE Werizoid languages

Duma language
USE Aduma language

Durban (South Africa). Clairwood
USE Clairwood (Durban, South Africa)

Dutch *(May Subd Geog)*
--South Africa
[DT 764.D8 : old class]
[DT 1768.D88 : new class]
NT Afrikaners

Dutch East Indies
USE Indonesia

Dutch language
--Dialects *(May Subd Geog)*
-- --South Africa
[PF 861-PF 884]
*Here are entered works on Dutch South African dialects
not conforming to Dutch as spoken or written in the
Netherlands. Works on the language spoken and written by
the descendants of the Dutch colonists in South Africa which
gradually evolved and differentiated from the Dutch South
African dialects of the earlier periods are entered under
Afrikaans language*

Dwala (African people)
USE Duala (African people)

Dwalla (African people)
USE Duala (African people)

Dwela (African people)
USE Duala (African people)

Dwellings *(May Subd Geog)*
*Here are entered works on the history and description of
human shelters. Works on the social and economic aspects of
housing are entered under Housing*
UF Domiciles
Homes
Houses
One-family houses
Residences
SA *subdivision* Dwellings *under classes of persons
and ethnic groups, e.g., Pygmies--Dwellings*
--Réunion
NT Beauregard (Réunion)
--South Africa
NT Groote Schuur (Cape Town, South Africa)

UF = Used for; BT = Broader term; RT = Related term; SA = See also; NT = Narrower term

Dya-ate (African people)
  USE Diola (African people)

Dyabarma (African people)
  USE Zarma (African people)

Dyakanke language
  USE Soninke language

Dyalonka (African people)
  USE Yalunka (African people)

Dyan dialect *(May Subd Geog)*
  [PL 8142.D]
  UF Dian dialect
  BT Burkina Faso--Languages
      Lobi dialects

Dyerma (African people)
  USE Zarma (African people)

Dyimini (African people)
  USE Djimini (African people)

Dyimini language
  USE Djimini language

Dyola (African people)
  USE Diola (African people)

Dyola language
  USE Diola language

Dyoula (African people)
  USE Dyula (African people)

Dyoura (African people)
  USE Dyula (African people)

Dyula (African people) *(May Subd Geog)*
  [DT 545.45.D85 (Ivory Coast)]
  UF Dabakala (African people)
      Dioula (African people)
      Dyoula (African people)
      Dyoura (African people)
  BT Ethnology--Burkina Faso
      Ethnology--Ivory Coast

Dyula language *(May Subd Geog)*
  [PL 8142.D94]
  UF Dioula language
      Jula language
  BT Burkina Faso--Languages
      Ivory Coast--Languages
      Mandekan languages

--Tone
  BT Tone (Phonetics)

Dyur language
  USE Lwo language (Sudan)

Dzalamo (African people)
  USE Zaramo (African people)

Dzamba language
  USE Bobangi language

Dzema language
  USE Maba language

Dzepao language
  USE Lamé language (Cameroon)

Dzilio language
  USE Bari language

Dzindza (African people)
  USE Zinza (African people)

Dzo language
  USE Ijo language

E

E.C.A.
  USE United Nations. Economic Commission for
Africa

E.C.O.W.A.S.
  USE Economic Community of West African States

Early man
  USE Fossil man

Earthenware
  USE Pottery

East Africa
  USE Africa, East

East Africa, Portuguese
  USE Mozambique

East Africa Federation *(Not Subd Geog)*
  [DT 421-DT 432.5]
  UF Federation of East Africa

East Africa Protectorate
  USE Kenya

(May Subd Geog) = Place names may follow the heading

East African art
  USE Art, East African

East African drama (English) *(May Subd Geog)*
  [PR 9343 (History)]
  [PR 9347 (Collections)]
  UF English drama--East African authors
  BT African drama (English)
      East African literature (English)
  NT Kenyan drama (English)

East African literature *(May Subd Geog)*
  [PL 8014.E22]
  UF Africa, East--Literatures
  BT African literature
  NT Kenyan literature
      Tanzanian literature
      Ugandan literature

East African literature (English) *(May Subd Geog)*
  [PR 9340-PR 9347.5]
  UF English literature--East African
authors
  BT African literature (English)
  NT East African drama (English)
      East African poetry (English)
      Kenyan literature (English)
      Tanzanian literature (English)
      Ugandan literature (English)

East African mythology
  USE Mythology, East African

East African poetry (English) *(May Subd Geog)*
  [PR 9342 (History)]
  [PR 9346 (Collections)]
  UF English poetry--East African authors
  BT African poetry (English)
      East African literature (English)
  NT Kenyan poetry (English)
      Tanzanian poetry (English)
      Ugandan poetry (English)

East African publications, Acquisition of
  USE Acquisition of East African
publications

East African Safari Rally
  [GV 1034.88.A34E37]
  UF Coronation Safari
      Safari Rally, East African

East Cameroon
  USE Cameroon

Eastern Africa
  USE Africa, Eastern

Eastern Fulani (African people)
  USE Fula (African people)

Eastern Galla dialect
  USE Qottu dialect

Eastern Nigeria
  USE Nigeria, Eastern

Ebekwara language
  USE Bekwarra language

Ebembe (East African people)
  USE Bembe (East African people)

Ebembe language
  USE Bembe language (Lake Tanganyika)

Ebira language
  USE Igbira language

Ebwe language
  USE Ewe language

Echira (African people)
  USE Shira (African people)

eciKerebe language
  USE Kerebe language

eciSubiya language
  USE Subiya language

Economic Commission for Africa (United Nations)
  USE United Nations. Economic Commission for
Africa

Economic Community of West African States
  [HC 1000]
  UF E.C.O.W.A.S.
  NT Communauté économique de l'Afrique de
l'Ouest

Economic development
  USE *subdivision* Economic conditions *under names of
countries, regions, cities, etc., e.g.* Benin--Economic
conditions

Economic policy
  USE *subdivision* Economic policy *under names of
countries, regions, cities, etc., e.g.* Kenya--Economic
policy

UF = Used for; BT = Broader term; RT = Related term; SA = See also; NT = Narrower term

Economic policy, Foreign
  USE *subdivision* Foreign economic relations
under names of countries, regions, cities, etc., e.g.
South Africa--Foreign economic relations

Economic sanctions *(May Subd Geog)*
  This heading is subdivided by the name of the
country against which economic sanctions are applied.
  UF Sanctions, Economic
  NT Disinvestment
--South Africa
  [HF 1413.5]

Economic sanctions, American *(May Subd Geog)*
  UF American economic sanctions
 --South Africa
  [HF 1613.4]

Economic theory
  USE Economics

Economics *(May Subd Geog)*
  [HB]
  Here and with geographical subdivisions are entered
works on the discipline of economics. Works on the
economic conditions of particular countries, regions,
cities, etc. are entered under the name of the place
subdivided by Economic conditions.
  UF Economic theory
      Political economy
  NT Markets
      Population
      Property
      Rand area

Ecuador
 --Civilization
 -- --African influences
  BT Africa--Civilization

Edii (African people)
  USE Bayot (African people)

Ediya language
  USE Bube language

Ediye (African people)
  USE Bubi (African people)

Edo (African people)
  USE Bini (African people)

Edo language
  USE Bini language

Education *(May Subd Geog)*
  [LA 1500-LA 2090 (Africa)]
  UF Children--Education
      Education of children
      Educational reform
      Human resource development
      Instruction
      Pedagogy
      Youth--Education
  NT Education, Rural
      Literacy
      Mathematics--Study and teaching
      Students
      Teachers
      Universities and colleges
 --Great Britain
 -- --Colonies
  [LA 669.5 (General)]
  UF Great Britain--Colonies--Education
 --Tanzania
  [LA 1840-LA 1844]

Education, Rural *(May Subd Geog)*
  UF Rural education
  BT Education
 --Botswana
  NT Laedza Batanani, Botswana

Education of children
  USE Education

Educational reform
  USE Education

Eenya (African people)
  USE Genya (African people)

Efe (African people) *(May Subd Geog)*
  [DT 650.E]
  UF Efeh (African people)
      Efet (African people)
  BT Ethnology--Zaire
      Mbuti (African people)

Efe language
  USE Ewe language

Efeh (African people)
  USE Efe (African people)

Efet (African people)
  USE Efe (African people)

Efik (African people) *(May Subd Geog)*
  [DT 515.45.E34]
  UF Riverain (African people)

(May Subd Geog) = Place names may follow the heading

BT Ethnology--Nigeria
--**Marriage customs and rites**
UF Marriage customs and rites, Efik
(African people)
--**Rites and ceremonies**

Efik folk literature
USE Folk literature, Efik

Efik language *(May Subd Geog)*
[PL 8147]
BT Benue-Congo languages
    Nigeria--Languages
RT Ibibio language
--**Tone**
BT Tone (Phonetics)

Efik proverbs
USE Proverbs, Efik

Egba (African people) *(May Subd Geog)*
[DT 515.45.E35]
BT Ethnology--Nigeria
    Yoruba (African people)

Egugu (Cult)
USE Egúngún (Cult)

Egúngún (Cult) *(May Subd Geog)*
[BL 2480.Y6]
UF Árá Orun (Cult)
    Egugu (Cult)
BT Cults--Nigeria
    Yoruba (African people)--Religion

Egypt
--**Civilization**
-- --**African influences**
BT Africa--Civilization

Ehing (African people)
USE Bayot (African people)

Ehwe (African people)
USE Ewe (African people)

Ehwe language
USE Ewe language

Eibe (African people)
USE Ewe (African people)

Eibe language
USE Ewe language

Eighteen twenty settlers (South Africa)
USE British settlers of 1820 (South Africa)

Ejagam language
USE Ejagham language

Ejagham language *(May Subd Geog)*
UF Central Ekoi language
    Ejagam language
    Ejaham language
    Ejam language
    Ekwe language
    Ezam language
BT Cameroon--Languages
    Ekoi languages

Ejaham language
USE Ejagham language

Ejam language
USE Ejagham language

Ejo language
USE Ijo language

Ekajuk language *(May Subd Geog)*
[PL 8150]
DT Ekoi languages
    Nigeria--Languages

Ekegusii language
USE Gusii language

Ekela (African people)
USE Kela (African people)

Ekele (African people)
USE Lokele (African people)

Ekibena (African people)
USE Bena (African people)

Ekihaya (African people)
USE Haya (African people)

ekiKerebe language
USE Kerebe language

ekiPangwa language
USE Pangwa language

Ekoi (African people) *(May Subd Geog)*
[DT 515.45.E (Nigeria)]
BT Bantu-speaking peoples
    Ethnology--Cameroon
    Ethnology--Nigeria

UF = Used for; BT = Broader term; RT = Related term; SA = See also; NT = Narrower term

Ekoi languages *(May Subd Geog)*
  [PL 8152]
  UF Ekoid languages
  BT Bantu languages
      Cameroon--Languages
      Nigeria--Languages
  NT Ejagham language
      Ekajuk language

Ekoid languages
  USE Ekoi languages

Ekonda (African people) *(May Subd Geog)*
  [DT 650.E45]
  UF Baseka (African people)
  BT Bantu-speaking peoples
      Ethnology--Zaire

Ekpeye language *(May Subd Geog)*
  [PL 8153.E33]
  BT Kwa languages
      Nigeria--Languages

Ekwe language
  USE Ejagham language

El-Afrihili (Artificial language)
  USE Afrihili (Artificial language)

Elandslaagte, South Africa, Battle of, 1899
  [DT 777 : old class]
  [DT 1908.E : new class]
  UF Battle of Elandslaagte (South Africa),
1899
  BT South African War, 1899-1902--
Campaigns--South Africa

Élé dialect
  USE Lele dialect

Elegbara, Esu (Legendary character)
  USE Esu (Legendary character)

Eleko dialect
  USE Leko dialect

Eleku dialect
  USE Leko dialect

Elgeyo (African people) *(May Subd Geog)*
  [DT 433.545.E]
  UF Keiyo (African people)
  BT Ethnology--Kenya
 --Religion
  [BL 2480.E45]

Elgume (African people)
  USE Turkana (African people)

Elgumi (African people)
  USE Teso (African people)

Emberre (African people)
  USE Mbere (African people)

Embroidery *(May Subd Geog)*
  BT Decoration and ornament
--Zaire
  [NK 9289.6.C6]
  NT Embroidery, Shoowa

Embroidery, Shoowa *(May Subd Geog)*
  [NK 9289.6.C6]
  UF Shoowa embroidery
  BT Embroidery--Zaire

Embu (African people) *(May Subd Geog)*
  [DT 433.545.E]
  UF Waembu (African people)
  BT Bantu-speaking peoples
      Ethnology--Kenya

Embu folk dancing
  USE Folk dancing, Embu

Embu folk songs
  USE Folk songs, Embu

Embu language *(May Subd Geog)*
  [PL 8153.E]
  BT Bantu languages
      Kenya--Languages

Emin Pasha Relief Expedition, 1887-1889
  [DT 363]
  BT Africa, Central--History--1884-1960
      Africa, East--History

Empires and kingdoms, Traditional
  SEE Adamawa (Emirate)
       Aksum (Kingdom)
       Ashanti (Kingdom)
       Benin (Nigeria)--History
       Bunyoro-Kitara
       Denkyira (Kingdom)
       Fula Empire
       Fuladu (Kingdom)
       Futa Jallon
       Ghana Empire
       Kaabu Empire
       Kanem-Bornu Empire
       Kongo Kingdom

(May Subd Geog) = Place names may follow the heading

SEE Mali Empire
     Niumi (Kingdom)
     Ouo Empire
     Songhai Empire
     Toucouleur Empire
     Yatenga (Kingdom)

Empoongwe (African people)
  USE Mpongwe (African people)

Ena language
  USE Enya language

Endo River (Kenya)
  USE Kerio River (Kenyo)

Engenni language *(May Subd Geog)*
  [PL 8154]
  BT Kwa languages
      Nigeria--Languages

English
  USE British

English Creole languages
  USE Creole dialects, English

English drama *(May Subd Geog)*
  BT English literature
  NT One-act plays, English
      Young adult drama, English
  --African authors
  USE African drama (English)
  --**Black authors**
  [PR 1246.B53 (Collections)]
  UF Black drama (English)
  --East African authors
  USE East African drama (English)
  --Kenyan authors
  USE Kenyan drama (English)
  --Malawi authors
  USE Malawi drama (English)
  --Nigerian authors
  USE Nigerian drama (English)
  --South African authors
  USE South African drama (English)
  --Zambian authors
  USE Zambian drama (English)
  --Zimbabwean authors
  USE Zimbabwean drama (English)

English essays *(May Subd Geog)*
  Here are entered collections of essays by several
  authors.
  BT English literature

  --South African authors
  USE South African essays (English)

English fiction *(May Subd Geog)*
  BT English literature
  NT Short stories, English
  --African authors
  USE African fiction (English)
  --Cameroon authors
  USE Cameroon fiction (English)
  --Ghanaian authors
  USE Ghanaian fiction (English)
  --Kenyan authors
  USE Kenyan fiction (English)
  --Liberian authors
  USE Liberian fiction (English)
  --Mauritian authors
  USE Mauritian fiction (English)
  --Nigerian authors
  USE Nigerian fiction (English)
  --South African authors
  USE South African fiction (English)
  --Southern African authors
  USE Southern African fiction (English)
  --Ugandan authors
  USE Ugandan fiction (English)
  --West African authors
  USE West African fiction (English)
  --Zambian authors
  USE Zambian fiction (English)
  --Zimbabwean authors
  USE Zimbabwean fiction (English)

English language *(May Subd Geog)*
  --Africa
  [PE 3401-PE 3452]
  UF African English

English literature *(May Subd Geog)*
  NT English drama
      English essays
      English fiction
      English poetry
      English prose literature
      Slaves' writings, English
  --African authors
  USE African literature (English)
  --**African influences**
  BT Africa--Civilization
  --**Black authors**
  [PR 1110.B5 (Collections)]
  UF Black literature (English)
  --Cameroon authors
  USE Cameroon literature (English)

(Continued)

UF = Used for; BT = Broader term; RT = Related term; SA = See also; NT = Narrower term

English literature *(Continued)*
--East African authors
 USE East African literature (English)
--Ghanaian authors
 USE Ghanaian literature (English)
--Kenyan authors
 USE Kenyan literature (English)
--Liberian authors
 USE Liberian literature (English)
--Malawi authors
 USE Malawi literature (English)
--Mauritian authors
 USE Mauritian literature (English)
--Nigerian authors
 USE Nigerian literature (English)
--Sierra Leone authors
 USE Sierra Leone literature (English)
--South African authors
 USE South African literature (English)
--Southern African authors
 USE Southern African literature (English)
--Sudanese authors
 USE Sudanese literature (English)
--Tanzanian authors
 USE Tanzanian literature (English)
--Ugandan authors
 USE Ugandan literature (English)
--West African authors
 USE West African literature (English)
--Zambian authors
 USE Zambian literature (English)
--Zimbabwean authors
 USE Zimbabwean literature (English)

English one-act plays
 USE One-act plays, English

English poetry *(May Subd Geog)*
 BT English literature
--African authors
 USE African poetry (English)
--**Black authors**
 [PR 1178.B (Collections)]
 UF Black poetry (English)
--Cameroon authors
 USE Cameroon poetry (English)
--East African authors
 USE East African poetry (English)
--Ghanaian authors
 USE Ghanaian poetry (English)
--Kenyan authors
 USE Kenyan poetry (English)
--Liberian authors
 USE Liberian poetry (English)
--Malawi authors
 USE Malawi poetry (English)

--Mauritian authors
 USE Mauritian poetry (English)
--Nigerian authors
 USE Nigerian poetry (English)
--Sierra Leone authors
 USE Sierra Leone poetry (English)
--South African authors
 USE South African poetry (English)
--Tanzanian authors
 USE Tanzanian poetry (English)
--Ugandan authors
 USE Ugandan poetry (English)
--West African authors
 USE West African poetry (English)
--Zambian authors
 USE Zambian poetry (English)
--Zimbabwean authors
 USE Zimbabwean poetry (English)

English prose literature *(May Subd Geog)*
 BT English literature
--African authors
 USE African prose literature (English)
--Ghanaian authors
 USE Ghanaian prose literature (English)
--South African authors
 USE South African prose literature (English)

English short stories
 USE Short stories, English

English slaves' writings
 USE Slaves' writings, English

English young adult drama
 USE Young adult drama, English

Entebbe Airport Raid, 1976
 [DS 119.7]
 UF Jonathan Operation, 1976
  Operation Jonathan, 1976
  Rescue of hijack victims at Entebbe
Airport, 1976
 BT Israel--Foreign relations--Uganda
  Uganda--Foreign relations--Israel

Enterprises
 USE Business enterprises

Enya (African people)
 USE Genya (African people)

Enya language *(May Subd Geog)*
 [PL 8156]
 UF Ena language
  Genya language

(May Subd Geog) = Place names may follow the heading

BT Bantu languages
    Zaire--Languages

Epic literature
  UF Literature, Epic
  BT Literature
  NT Epic poetry

Epic literature, African
  [PL 8010]
  UF African epic literature
  BT African literature

Epic poetry
  UF Heroic poetry
    Poetry, Epic
    Poetry, Heroic
  BT Epic literature
    Poetry

Epic poetry, African
  [PL 8010.4]
  UF African epic poetry
  BT African poetry

Epic poetry, Fula *(May Subd Geog)*
  [PL 8183.5 (History)]
  [PL 8184.A2 (Collections)]
  UF Fula epic poetry
  BT Fula poetry

Epic poetry, Kpelle *(May Subd Geog)*
  [PL 8411.5 (History)]
  [PL 8411.7 (Collections)]
  UF Kpelle epic poetry
  BT Kpelle poetry

Epic poetry, Swahili *(May Subd Geog)*
  [PL 8703.5 (History)]
  [PL 8703.4A2 (Collections)]
  UF Swahili epic poetry
  BT Swahili poetry

Epie language
  USE Atisa language

Equatorial Africa, French-speaking
  USE Africa, French-speaking Equatorial

Equatorial Guinea *(Not Subd Geog)*
  [DT 620-DT 620.9]
  UF Guinea, Spanish
    Spanish Guinea
  NT Corisco (Equatorial Guinea)
    Fernando Po (Equatorial Guinea)

--Languages
  NT Annobon dialect
    Benga language
    Bisio language
    Bube language
    Fang language
    Yaunde-Fang languages
--Literatures
  USE Equatorial Guinean literature
--Poetry
  NT Fang poetry
--Politics and government
  -- --1968-
  -- --1968-1979
  -- --1979-

Equatorial Guinean literature *(May Subd Geog)*
  [PL 8014.E]
  UF Equatorial Guinea--Literatures
  BT African literature
  NT Fang literature

Erbore language
  USE Arbore language

Eritrea (Ethiopia) *(Not Subd Geog)*
  [DT 391-DT 398]
  History
  -- --Autonomy and independence movements
  [DT 395.5]
  -- --Revolution, 1962-
--Politics and government
  -- --1890-1941
  -- --1941-1952
  -- --1952-1962
  -- --1962-

Eritrean national characteristics
  USE National characteristics, Eritrean

Erokh (African people)
  USE Iraqw (African people)

Erotic poetry, Senegalese (French)
  [PQ 3988.5.S38 (History)]
  [PQ 3988.5.S382 (Collections)]
  UF Senegalese erotic poetry (French)
  BT Senegalese poetry (French)

Erta'Ale Volcanic Range (Ethiopia)
  USE Ertale Volcano (Ethiopia)

Ertale Volcano (Ethiopia)
  UF Erta'Ale Volcanic Range (Ethiopia)
  BT Volcanos--Ethiopia

UF = Used for; BT = Broader term; RT = Related term; SA = See also; NT = Narrower term

Erythraic languages
  USE Afroasiatic languages

Eshu (Legendary character)
  USE Esu (Legendary character)

Eshu-Elegba (Legendary character)
  USE Esu (Legendary character)

Esira language
  USE Shira language

Essing (African people)
  USE Bayot (African people)

Esthetics
  USE Aesthetics

Estuaire du Gabon (Gabon)
  USE Gabon Estuary (Gabon)

Estuaries *(May Subd Geog)*
  BT Coasts
      Rivers
 --Gabon
  NT Gabon Estuary (Gabon)
 --Namibia
  NT Orange River Estuary (Namibia and
South Africa)
 --South Africa
  NT Great Brak River Estuary (South
Africa)
      Orange River Estuary (Namibia and
South Africa)

Esu (Legendary character)
  UF Elegbara, Esu (Legendary character)
      Eshu (Legendary character)
      Eshu-Elegba (Legendary character)
      Esu Elegbara (Legendary character)
  BT Folklore--Nigeria
      Legends--Nigeria
      Trickster--Nigeria

Esu Elegbara (Legendary character)
  USE Esu (Legendary character)

Etbai (Egypt and Sudan)
  USE Red Sea Hills (Egypt and Sudan)

Ethics *(May Subd Geog)*
  UF Ethology
      Moral philosophy
      Morality
      Morals

      UF Philosophy, Moral
          Science, Moral
      BT Philosophy

Ethics, Akan *(May Subd Geog)*
  [BJ 982.A38]
  UF Akan ethics

Ethics, Baganda *(May Subd Geog)*
  [BJ 982.B34]
  UF Baganda ethics
      Ethics, Ganda
      Ganda ethics

Ethics, Ganda
  USE Ethics, Baganda

Ethics, Zairian *(May Subd Geog)*
  [BJ 980]
  UF Zairian ethics

Ethiopia *(Not Subd Geog)*
  [DT 371-DT 398]
  UF Abyssinia
 --Antiquities
  NT Gotera Site (Ethiopia)
      Hadar Site (Ethiopia)
 --Description and travel
 -- --To 1900
 -- --1901-1945
 -- --1945-1980
 -- --1981-
 --Economic conditions
  [HC 845]
 -- --1974-
 --Foreign relations *(May Subd Geog)*
 -- --To 1889
 -- --1889-1974
 -- --1974-
 --History
  NT Aksum (Kingdom)
 -- --To 1490
 -- --1490-1889
  NT Abyssinian Expedition, 1867-1868
      Imbabu, Ethiopia, Battle of, 1882
 -- --19th century
 -- --1889-1974
  NT Italo-Ethiopian War, 1895-1896
      Italo-Ethiopian War, 1935-1936
 -- --Rebellion, 1928-1930
  UF Azebo-Raya Revolt, Ethiopia, 1928-1930
 -- --Coup d'état, 1960
  [DT 387.9]
  BT Coups d'état--Ethiopia

(May Subd Geog) = Place names may follow the heading

Ethiopia
--History   *(Continued)*
-- --1974-
  NT Somali-Ethiopian Conflict, 1977-1979
      Somali-Ethiopian Conflict, 1979-
-- --Revolution, 1974
  [DT 387.95]
--Languages
  Here are entered general works on the languages of
  Ethiopia. Works on the Semitic languages of Ethiopia
  are entered under Ethiopian languages. Works on
  the Cushitic languages of Ethiopia are entered under
  Cushitic languages.
  NT Anuak language
      Baria language
      Kunama language
      Murle language
      Nuer language
      Shilluk language
      Turkana language
      Uduk language
--Literatures
  USE Ethiopian literature
--Politics and government
-- --1889-1974
-- --1974-
--Social conditions
-- --1974-

Ethiopian art
  USE Art, Ethiopian

Ethiopian authors
  USE Authors, Ethiopian

Ethiopian coins
  USE Coins, Ethiopian

Ethiopian cookery
  USE Cookery, Ethiopian

Ethiopian folk songs
  USE Folk songs, Ethiopian

Ethiopian illumination of books and
manuscripts
  USE Illumination of books and manuscripts,
Ethiopian

Ethiopian-Italian War, 1895-1896
  USE Italo-Ethiopian War, 1895-1896

Ethiopian-Italian War, 1935-1936
  USE Italo-Ethiopian War, 1935-1936

Ethiopian Jews

  USE Falashas

Ethiopian language
  USE Amharic language

Ethiopian languages
  [PJ 8991-PJ 8999]
  Here are entered works on the Semitic languages of
  Ethiopia. Works on the Cushitic languages of Ethiopia are
  entered under Cushitic languages. General works on the
  languages of Ethiopia are entered under Ethiopia--
  Languages.
  BT Semitic languages, Southern Peripheral
  NT Amharic language
      Argobba language
      Ethiopic language
      Gafat language
      Gurage language
      Harari language
      Tigré language
      Tigrinya language

Ethiopian literature *(May Subd Geog)*
  [PL 8014.E8-PL 8014.E82]
  UF Ethiopia--Literatures
  BT African literature
  RT Ethiopic literature
  NT Amharic literature
      Ethiopian poetry

Ethiopian magic scrolls
  [ND 3285.7]
  UF Magic scrolls, Ethiopian
      Scrolls, Ethiopian magic
  BT Magic, Ethiopian

Ethiopian movement (South Africa)
  [BR 1450]
  BT Missions--South Africa
      Nativistic movements--South Africa
      South Africa--Church history
      South Africa--Race relations

Ethiopian painting
  USE Painting, Ethiopian

Ethiopian philosophy
  USE Philosophy, Ethiopian

Ethiopian poetry *(May Subd Geog)*
  [PL 8014.E8-PL 8014.E82]
  BT African poetry
      Ethiopian literature

Ethiopian political posters
  USE Political posters, Ethiopian

UF = Used for; BT = Broader term; RT = Related term; SA = See also; NT = Narrower term

Ethiopian-Somali Conflict, 1977-1979
  USE Somali-Ethiopian Conflict, 1977-1979

Ethiopian-Somali Conflict, 1979-
  USE Somali-Ethiopian Conflict, 1979-

Ethiopians *(May Subd Geog)*
  [DT 380]
  BT Ethnology--Ethiopia
  NT Amhara (African people)

Ethiopic language *(May Subd Geog)*
  [PJ 9001-PJ 9087]
  UF Geez language
  BT Ethiopian languages

Ethiopic literature *(May Subd Geog)*
  [PJ 9090-PJ 9101]
  RT Ethiopian literature
  NT Amharic literature

Ethiopic literature, Jewish
  USE Jewish literature, Ethiopic

Ethiopic manuscripts
  USE Manuscripts, Ethiopic

Ethiopic philology
  [PJ 9001-PJ 9101]
  UF Philology, Ethiopic

Ethnic group names
  USE Names, Ethnological

Ethnic medicine
  USE Folk medicine

Ethnic psychology
  USE Ethnopsychology

Ethnicity *(May Subd Geog)*
  *Here are entered works on the subjective sense of
belonging to an individual ethnic group.*
  BT Ethnology
      Race awareness
  SA *subdivision* Race identity *or* Ethnic
identity *under individual races or ethnic groups,*
e.g. Blacks--Race identity; Nyankole (African
people)--Ethnic identity
  NT Afrikaners--Ethnic identity
      Blacks--Race identity

Ethnic revivals
  USE Nativistic movements

Ethnography
  USE Ethnology

Ethnological names
  USE Names, Ethnological

Ethnology *(May Subd Geog)*
  *Here, with appropriate geographical subdivision, are
entered works on the discipline of ethnology, and works on
the origin, distribution, and characteristics of the
elements of the population of a particular region or
country.*
  UF Cultural anthropology
      Ethnography
      Races of man
      Social anthropology
  BT Anthropology
  SA *individual ethnic groups and peoples, e.g.* Tswana
(African people)
  NT Acculturation
      Art, Primitive
      Arts, Primitive
      Body-marking
      Ethnicity
      Ethnophilosophy
      Ethnopsychology
      Folklore
      Indigenous peoples
      Kinship
      Language and languages
      Man, Prehistoric
      Manners and customs
      Nativistic movements
      Race relations
      Religion, Primitive
      Tattooing
      Tribal government
      Whites
  --Names
   USE Names, Ethnological
  --Africa
    NT Africans
  --Africa, Central
    NT Abron (African people)
        Bira (African people)
        Mamvu (African people)
        Sonyo (African people)
        Zande (African people)
  --Africa, East
    NT Dorobo (African people)
        Kalenjin (African people)
        Kavirondo (African people)
        Luo (African people)
        Nilo-Hamitic tribes
        Tindiga (African people)
        Yao (African people)

(May Subd Geog) = Place names may follow the heading

--Africa, Eastern
  NT Makonde (African people)
      Ngoni (African people)
      One-leg resting position
      Swahili-speaking peoples
--Africa, French-speaking West
  NT Brakna
      Dogon (African people)
      Fang (West African people)
      Jaawambe (African people)
      Komo (Secret order)
      Koniaqui (African people)
      Pygmies
      Ruma (African people)
      Songhai (African people)
      Soninke (African people)
--Africa, Southern
  NT Khoikhoi (African people)
      Kua (African people)
      !Kung (African people)
      Naron (African people)
      Nguni (African people)
      Pedi (African people)
      San (African people)
--Africa, Sub-Saharan
  NT Bantu-speaking peoples
--Africa, West
  NT Abron (African people)
      Chamba (African people)
      Daza (African people)
      Ewe (African people)
      Fang (West African people)
      Fula (African people)
      Gbaya (African people)
      Kabre (African people)
      Kara (Gbayan people)
      Kru (African people)
      Mandingo (African people)
      Nyanga (African people)
      Tem (African people)
      Tenda (African people)
      Toma (African people)
      West Africans
      Yoruba (African people)
--Algeria
  NT Ajjer (African people)
--Angola
  NT Bembe (West African people)
      Chokwe (African people)
      Hanya (African people)
      Herero (African people)
      Himba (African people)
      Kongo (African people)
      Kuanyama (African people)
      Luchazi (African people)
      Luenas (African people)

  NT Lunda, Southern (African people)
      Mbundu (African people)
      Mwila (African people)
      Ndembu (African people)
      Ndonga (African people)
      Ngangela (African people)
      Ovambo (African people)
      Vili (African people)
      Yaka (African people)
--Benin
  NT Aja (African people)
      Bariba (African people)
      Dendi (African people)
      Ewe (African people)
      Fon (African people)
      Gun (African people)
      Gurma (African people)
      Mina (African people)
      Nyendo (African people)
      Somba (African people)
      Tofinnu (African people)
      Yoruba (African people)
      Zarma (African people)
--Botswana
  NT G/wi (African people)
      Herero (African people)
      Kgalagadi (African people)
      Kgatla (African people)
      Mbukushu (African people)
      Ngwaketse (African people)
      Ngwato (African people)
      Pedi (African people)
      Rolong (African people)
      San (African people)
      Sotho (African people)
      Tannekwe (African people)
      Tlhaping (African people)
      Tlokwa (African people)
      Tonga (Zambesi people)
      Tswana (African people)
--Burkina Faso
  NT Birifor (African people)
      Bisa (Burkinabe and Ghanaian people)
      Bobo (African people)
      Bozo (African people)
      Builsa (African people)
      Dagari (African people)
      Dogon (African people)
      Dyula (African people)
      Gouin (African people)
      Gurma (African people)
      Gurunsi (African people)
      Kurumba (African people)
      Lobi (African people)
      LoWiili (African people)
      Mossi (African people)   *(Continued)*

UF = Used for; BT = Broader term; RT = Related term; SA = See also; NT = Narrower term

Ethnology
--Burkina Faso *(Continued)*
  NT Samo (West African people)
      Sisala (African people)
      Tusia (African people)
      West Samo (African people)
--Burundi
  NT Batwa (African people)
      Bembe (East African people)
      Hutu (African people)
      Rundi (African people)
      Tutsi (African people)
--Cameroon
  NT Babinga (African people)
      Bafia (African people)
      Bafut (African people)
      Bagyele (African people)
      Baka (West African people)
      Bali (African people)
      Bamileke (African people)
      Bamun (African people)
      Bana (African people)
      Bandja (African people)
      Bandjoun (African people)
      Banen (African people)
      Bangwa (African people)
      Basa (Cameroon people)
      Battas (African people)
      Bavëk (African people)
      Beti (African people)
      Bororo (African people)
      Bulu (African people)
      Cameroonians
      Chamba (African people)
      Daba (African people)
      Dowayo (African people)
      Duala (African people)
      Ekoi (African people)
      Eton (African people)
      Evuzok (African people)
      Ewondo (African people)
      Fali (African people)
      Fe'fe' (Cameroon people)
      Fula (African people)
      Gemjek (African people)
      Guiziga (African people)
      Kamwe (African people)
      Kom (African people)
      Kossi (African people)
      Kotoko (African people)
      Kwiri (African people)
      Maka (African people)
      Mambila (African people)
      Masa (African people)
      Matakam (African people)
      Mbum (African people)

  NT Meta (African people)
      Mfumte (African people)
      Mouyeng (African people)
      Mukulehe (African people)
      Mumuye (African people)
      Mundang (African people)
      Ndiki (African people)
      Ngangte (African people)
      Ngemba (African people)
      Nso (African people)
      Nyang (African people)
      Paduko (African people)
      Pygmies
      Sao (Chad people)
      Suwa (Arab people)
      Tanga (African people)
      Tikar (African people)
      Uldeme (African people)
      We (African people)
      Yamba (African people)
      Zulgo (African people)
--Cape Verde
  NT Cape Verdeans
--Central African Republic
  NT Aka (African people)
      Babinga (African people)
      Baka (West African people)
      Banda (African people)
      Banziri (African people)
      Kara (Gbayan people)
      Langbas (African people)
      Mandjas
      Mbaï (African people)
      Mbati (Central African Republic people)
      Mbum (African people)
      Monjombo (African people)
      Ngandu (African people)
      Ngbaka (African people)
      Ngbaka-Ma'bo (African people)
      Nzakara (African people)
      Waregas
--Chad
  NT Bagirmi (African people)
      Buduma (African people)
      Dangaleat (African people)
      Day (African people)
      Gambaye (African people)
      Hadjerai (African people)
      Kanembu (African people)
      Kanuri (African people)
      Kera (African people)
      Kotoko (African people)
      Masa (African people)
      Mbaï (African people)
      Mbum (African people)
      Mundang (African people)

(May Subd Geog) = Place names may follow the heading

NT Nar (African people)
Sao (Chad people)
Sara (African people)
Zaghawa (African people)
--Congo (Brazzaville)
NT Babinga (African people)
Baka (West African people)
Banziri (African people)
Bembe (West African people)
Kota (African people)
Kukwa (African people)
Laadi (African people)
Mbete (African people)
Mbosi (African people)
Monjombo (African people)
Numu (African people)
Nzabi (African people)
Teke (African people)
--Djibouti
NT Afar (African people)
--Egypt
NT Kenuz (African people)
Kuku (African people)
--Equatorial Guinea
NT Bisio (African people)
Bubi (African people)
Fang (West African people)
--Ethiopia
NT Afar (African people)
Amhara (African people)
Baria (African people)
Beja (African people)
Beni Amer (African people)
Berta (African people)
Bogos
Boran (African people)
Dasanetch (African people)
Dorze (African people)
Ethiopians
Falashas
Gimira (African people)
Gonga (African people)
Gurage (African people)
Hadiya (African people)
Hamar (African people)
Harari (African people)
Kaffa (African people)
Kambata (African people)
Kemants
Konso (African people)
Kunama (African people)
Kwegu (African people)
Majangir (African people)
Male (African people)
Mensa (African people)
Murle (African people)

NT Murzu (African people)
Nilotic tribes
Nyangatom (African people)
Ochollo (African people)
Oromo (African people)
Saho (African people)
Shilluk (African people)
Sidamo (African people)
Tigrinya (African people)
Turkana (African people)
Uduk (African people)
--Gabon
NT Eviya (African people)
Fang (West African people)
Galwa (African people)
Kota (African people)
Mbete (African people)
Mitsogho (African people)
Mpongwe (African people)
Myene (African people)
Nkomi (African people)
Nzabi (African people)
Orungu (African people)
Shira (African people)
--Gambia
NT Bayot (African people)
Felup (African people)
Gambians
Mandjak (African people)
Serer (African people)
Wolof (African people)
--Ghana
NT Adangme (African people)
Agona (African people)
Akan (African people)
Anlo (African people)
Ashanti (African people)
Bassari (Togolese and Ghanaian people)
Birifor (African people)
Bisa (Burkinabe and Ghanaian people)
Builsa (African people)
Dagari (African people)
Dagomba (African people)
Ewe (African people)
Fanti (African people)
Ga (African people)
Ghanaians
Gonja (African people)
Kasena (African people)
Konkomba (African people)
Krachi (African people)
Krobo (African people)
Kuranko (African people)
Kwahu (African people)
Mamprusi (African people)
Mina (African people)   (Continued)

UF = Used for; BT = Broader term; RT = Related term; SA = See also; NT = Narrower term

Ethnology
--**Ghana** *(Continued)*
  NT Namnam (African people)
      Nzima (African people)
      Sisala (African people)
      Tallensi (African people)
      Twi (African people)
      Wala (African people)
--**Guinea**
  NT Badyaranké (African people)
      Balanta (African people)
      Bassari (Senegalese and Guinean
people)
      Kissi (African people)
      Koniagui (African people)
      Kono (African people)
      Kpelle (African people)
      Kuranko (African people)
      Limba (African people)
      Mano (African people)
      Nalu (African people)
      Tenda (African people)
      Yalunka (African people)
--**Guinea-Bissau**
  NT Badyaranké (African people)
      Balanta (African people)
      Bayot (African people)
      Bijago (African people)
      Kasanga (African people)
      Mandjak (African people)
      Nalu (African people)
      Tenda (African people)
--**Ivory Coast**
  NT Abidji (African people)
      Abron (African people)
      Adyukru (African people)
      Akan (African people)
      Alagya (African people)
      Ando (African people)
      Anyi (African people)
      Attie (African people)
      Avikam (African people)
      Baoulé (African people)
      Bété (African people)
      Birifor (African people)
      Dan (African people)
      Dida (African people)
      Djimini (African people)
      Dyula (African people)
      Gade (African people)
      Gagou (African people)
      Grebo (African people)
      Guro (African people)
      Kru (African people)
      Kulebele (African people)
      Lobi (African people)

  NT Minianka (African people)
      Senufo (African people)
      Tagbana (African people)
      Tura (African people)
      Vere (African people)
      Wobe (African people)
--**Kenya**
  NT Ariaal (African people)
      Arusha (African people)
      Bajun (African people)
      Boran (African people)
      Digo (African people)
      Elgeyo (African people)
      Embu (African people)
      Gabbra (African people)
      Giryama (African people)
      Gusii (African people)
      Ik (African people)
      Kalenjin (African people)
      Kamba (African people)
      Kavirondo (African people)
      Kikuyu (African people)
      Kipsigis (African people)
      Kuria (African people)
      Kusu (African people)
      Luo (African people)
      Luyia (African people)
      Marakwet (African people)
      Masai (African people)
      Mbere (African people)
      Meru (African people)
      Nandi (African people)
      Nika (African people)
      Njemps (African people)
      Oromo (African people)
      Pokomo (African people)
      Rendile (African people)
      Ribe (African people)
      Samburu (African people)
      Sapiny (African people)
      Suba (African people)
      Suk (African people)
      Swahili-speaking peoples
      Taita (African people)
      Taveta (African people)
      Teso (African people)
      Tharaka (African people)
      Tiriki (African people)
      Tugen (African people)
      Turkana (African people)
      Wanga (African people)
--**Lesotho**
  NT Khwakhwa (African people)
      Sotho (African people)
      Tlokwa (African people)

(May Subd Geog) = Place names may follow the heading

--Liberia
  NT Bassa (Liberian people)
      Dan (African people)
      Gbandi (Liberian people)
      Gola (African people)
      Grebo (African people)
      Jabo (African people)
      Kissi (African people)
      Kono (African people)
      Kpelle (African people)
      Kru (African people)
      Mano (African people)
      Mende (African people)
      Vai (African people)
      Wobe (African people)
--Madagascar
  NT Antandroy (Malagasy people)
      Bara (Malagasy people)
      Behosys
      Betsileos
      Betsimisaraka
      Bezanozano (Malagasy people)
      Mahafaly (Malagasy people)
      Menabe (Malagasy people)
      Merina (Malagasy people)
      Sakalava (Malagasy people)
      Taimoro (Malagasy people)
      Tanala (Malagasy people)
      Tsimihety (Malagasy people)
      Vazimbas
      Vezo (Malagasy people)
      Zafimaniry (Malagasy people)
--Malawi
  NT Chewa (African people)
      Lomwe (African people)
      Ngonde (African people)
      Ngoni (African people)
      Nyanja (African people)
      Phoka (African people)
      Tsonga (African people)
      Tumbuka (African people)
      Yao (African people)
      Yombe (African people)
--Mali
  NT Bambara (African people)
      Bozo (African people)
      Dendi (African people)
      Dogon (African people)
      Kulebele (African people)
      Minianka (African people)
      Samo (West African people)
      Senufo (African people)
      Songhai (African people)
--Mauritania
  NT Brakna
      Imragen (Berber tribe)

      NT Wolof (African people)
--Mauritius
  NT Mauritians
--Mozambique
  NT Barwe (African people)
      Chopi (African people)
      Lomwe (African people)
      Makonde (African people)
      Makua (African people)
      Mozambicans
      Nguni (African people)
      Nyanja (African people)
      Tawara (African people)
      Tonga (Mozambique people)
      Tsonga (African people)
      Yao (African people)
--Namibia
  NT Bondelswarts (African people)
      Damara (African people)
      Heikum (African people)
      Herero (African people)
      Himba (African people)
      Kuanyama (African people)
      Lobedu (African people)
      Mbandieru (African people)
      Mbukushu (African people)
      Nama (African people)
      Ndonga (African people)
      Ovambo (African people)
      Rehoboth Basters (African people)
      Sambyu (African people)
      San (African people)
--Niger
  NT Bororo (African people)
      Bozo (African people)
      Buduma (African people)
      Dendi (African people)
      Hausa (African people)
      Kanembu (African people)
      Kanuri (African people)
      Kurtey (African people)
      Manga (African people)
      Mawri (African people)
      Songhai (African people)
      Tuaregs
      Wogo (African people)
      Zarma (African people)
--Nigeria
  NT Abuan (African people)
      Aja (African people)
      Anang (African people)
      Angas (African people)
      Bachama (African people)
      Bariba (African people)
      Bini (African people)
      Buduma (African people)   *(Continued)*

UF = Used for; BT = Broader term; RT = Related term; SA = See also; NT = Narrower term

Ethnology
--**Nigeria** *(Continued)*
  NT Chamba (African people)
      Dendi (African people)
      Dukawa (African people)
      Efik (African people)
      Egba (African people)
      Ekoi (African people)
      Fon (African people)
      Gaanda (African people)
      Gade (African people)
      Gobir
      Gwari (African people)
      Hausa (African people)
      Ibibio (African people)
      Idoma (African people)
      Igala (African people)
      Igbo (African people)
      Igbona (African people)
      Ijo (African people)
      Isoko (African people)
      Jekri (African people)
      Jukun (African people)
      Kadara (African people)
      Kagoro (African people)
      Kamwe (African people)
      Kanembu (African people)
      Kanuri (African people)
      Koro (African people)
      Kotoko (African people)
      Mabo-Barkul (African people)
      Maguzawa (African people)
      Mambila (African people)
      Mbembe (Cross River African people)
      Mfumte (African people)
      Moba (African people)
      Mumuye (African people)
      Ngemba (African people)
      Ngwa (African people)
      Nigerians
      Nupe (African people)
      Oron (African people)
      Rukuba (African people)
      Sao (Chad people)
      Sobo (African people)
      Tivi (African people)
      Ubium (African people)
      Ujari (African people)
      Yamba (African people)
      Yebu (African people)
      Yoruba (African people)
      Zarma (African people)
--**Réunion**
  NT Réunion Islanders
--**Rwanda**
  NT Batwa (African people)

  NT Hutu (African people)
      Rundi (African people)
      Tutsi (African people)
--**Sahara**
  NT Daza (African people)
      Tibbu (African people)
      Tuaregs
--**Sao Tome and Principe**
  NT Sao Tomeans
--**Senegal**
  NT Badyaranké (African people)
      Balanta (African people)
      Banjal (African people)
      Bassari (Senegalese and Guinean people)
      Bayot (African people)
      Bedik (African people)
      Diola (African people)
      Felup (African people)
      Halpulaar (African people)
      Lebou (African people)
      Mandjak (African people)
      Senegalese
      Serer (African people)
      Soninke (African people)
      Tenda (African people)
      Toucouleurs
      Wolof (African people)
--**Sierra Leone**
  NT Creoles (Sierra Leone)
      Gola (African people)
      Kissi (African people)
      Kono (African people)
      Kuranko (African people)
      Limba (African people)
      Mende (African people)
      Sherbro (African people)
      Temne (African people)
      Vai (African people)
      Yalunka (African people)
--**Somalia**
  NT Bajun (African people)
      Rahanweyn (African people)
      Somalis
--**South Africa**
  NT Afrikaners
      Bafokeng (African people)
      Bhaca (African people)
      Bomvana (African people)
      Chopi (African people)
      Colored people (South Africa)
      Fingo (African people)
      Ghoya (African people)
      Griquas
      Hlubi (African people)
      Kgaga (African people)
      Kgatla (African people)

(May Subd Geog) = Place names may follow the heading

NT Khoikhoi (African people)
    Korana (African people)
    Lobedu (African people)
    Makhanyas (African people)
    Mamabolo (African people)
    Manala (African people)
    Nama (African people)
    Ndebele (African people)
    Nguni (African people)
    Pedi (African people)
    Phalaborwa (African people)
    Pondo (African people)
    Qaba (African people)
    Rehoboth Basters (African people)
    Rolong (African people)
    San (African people)
    Shona (African people)
    Sotho (African people)
    South Africans
    Tembu (African people)
    Tlhaping (African people)
    Tsonga (African people)
    Tswana (African people)
    Venda (African people)
    Xhosa (African people)
    Zulu (African people)
--Sudan
  NT Abdullab (Arab people)
      Acoli (African people)
      Amaa (African people)
      Anuak (African people)
      Atuot (African people)
      Baggara (African people)
      Batahin (Arab people)
      Beja (African people)
      Beni Amer (African people)
      Berta (African people)
      Berti (African people)
      Bongo (African people)
      Danagla (African people)
      Didinga (African people)
      Dinka (African people)
      Fungs
      Fur (African people)
      Hamar (African people)
      Hausa (African people)
      Ik (African people)
      Ja'aliyyin (Arab tribe)
      Kababish
      Koma (African people)
      Latuka (African people)
      Longarim (African people)
      Maban (African people)
      Mandari (African people)
      Murle (African people)
      Murzu (African people)

NT Nilotic tribes
    Nuba (African people)
    Nubians
    Nuer (African people)
    Nyangatom (African people)
    Rashayidah (Arab people)
    Rufa'a al-Hoi (African people)
    Shaikia (Arab people)
    Shatt (African people)
    Shilluk (African people)
    Sudanese
    Tepeth (African people)
    Uduk (African people)
    Zaghawa (African people)
    Zande (African people)
--Sudan (Region)
  NT Bororo (African people)
      Diawara (African people)
      Fula (African people)
      Kuku (African people)
      Toucouleurs
--Swaziland
  NT Swazi (African people)
--Tanzania
  NT Arusha (African people)
      Barabaig (African people)
      Baraguyu (African people)
      Bembe (East African people)
      Bena (African people)
      Chaga (African people)
      Fipa (African people)
      Ganda (African people)
      Gogo (African people)
      Haya (African people)
      Hehe (African people)
      Holoholo (African people)
      Iraqw (African people)
      Kaguru (African people)
      Kerebe (African people)
      Kilindi (African people)
      Kimbu (African people)
      Kuria (African people)
      Kwaya (African people)
      Losso (African people)
      Luguru (African people)
      Makonde (African people)
      Mangati (African people)
      Masai (African people)
      Matengo (African people)
      Meru (African people)
      Mwera (African people)
      Nandi (African people)
      Ndendeuli (African people)
      Ngonde (African people)
      Ngoni (African people)
      Ngulu (Tanzanian people)   *(Continued)*

UF = Used for; BT = Broader term; RT = Related term; SA = See also; NT = Narrower term

Ethnology
  --Tanzania *(Continued)*
    NT Nika (African people)
        Nyakyusa (African people)
        Nyamwezi (African people)
        Nyaturu (African people)
        Pangwa (African people)
        Pare (African people)
        Pogoro (African people)
        Rangi (African people)
        Safwa (African people)
        Sandawe (African people)
        Shambala (African people)
        Sonjo (African people)
        Sukuma (African people)
        Swahili-speaking peoples
        Tabwa (African people)
        Taita (African people)
        Tindiga (African people)
        Tutsi (African people)
        Yao (African people)
        Zanaki (African people)
        Zaramo (African people)
        Zigula (African people)
        Zinza (African people)
  --Togo
    NT Adangme (African people)
        Aja (African people)
        Anlo (African people)
        Bassari (Togolese and Ghanaian people)
        Chokossi (African people)
        Ewe (African people)
        Gouin (African people)
        Kabre (African people)
        Konkomba (African people)
        Kposo (African people)
        Mina (African people)
        Somba (African people)
        Tem (African people)
  --Uganda
    NT Acoli (African people)
        Alur (African people)
        Baamba (African people)
        Bairo (African people)
        Bavuma (African people)
        Chiga (African people)
        Dodoth (African people)
        Ganda (African people)
        Gisu (African people)
        Haya (African people)
        Hima (African people)
        Ik (African people)
        Jie (African people)
        Kalenjin (African people)
        Karamojong (African people)
        Labwor (African people)

    NT Lango (African people)
        Lugbara (African people)
        Luyia (African people)
        Mamvu (African people)
        Mbete (African people)
        Nandi (African people)
        Nilotic tribes
        Nyankole (African people)
        Nyoro (African people)
        Sapiny (African people)
        Soga (African people)
        Suk (African people)
        Tepeth (African people)
        Teso (African people)
        Tooro (African people)
  --Zaire
    NT Ababua (African people)
        Aka (African people)
        Alur (African people)
        Baamba (African people)
        Bangalas
        Banziri (African people)
        Bashi (African people)
        Batwa (African people)
        Bembe (East African people)
        Bembe (West African people)
        Bira (African people)
        Boma (African people)
        Budja (African people)
        Buissi (African people)
        Bunda (African people)
        Bwende (African people)
        Chokwe (African people)
        Dengese (African people)
        Efe (African people)
        Ekonda (African people)
        Foma (African people)
        Genya (African people)
        Havu (African people)
        Hemba (African people)
        Hima (African people)
        Holoholo (African people)
        Huana (African people)
        Kanyok (African people)
        Kasanga (African people)
        Kela (African people)
        Kongo (African people)
        Kota (African people)
        Kuba (African people)
        Kumu (Zairian people)
        Kwese (African people)
        Laadi (African people)
        Lala (African people)
        Lele (African people)
        Lendu (African people)
        Lese (African people)

(May Subd Geog) = Place names may follow the heading

NT Lokele (African people)
    Luba (African people)
    Lugbara (African people)
    Lulua (African people)
    Lunda, Northern (African people)
    Mangbetu (African people)
    Mamvu (African people)
    Matshaga (African people)
    Mayombe
    Mbala (African people)
    Mbata (African people)
    Mbole (African people)
    Mbuti (African people)
    Mongo (African people)
    Monjombo (African people)
    Mputu (African people)
    Nande (Zairian people)
    Ndembu (African people)
    Ngbaka (African people)
    Ngbaka-Ma'bo (African people)
    Ngombe (African people)
    Ngongo (African people)
    Nkundu (African people)
    Nyanga (African people)
    Ohendo (African people)
    Pende (African people)
    Pygmies
    Sakata (African people)
    Salampasu (African people)
    Sanga (African people)
    Shoowa (African people)
    Songe (African people)
    Songola (African people)
    Suku (African people)
    Sundi (African people)
    Tetela (African people)
    Topoke (African people)
    Vili (African people)
    Waregas
    Yaka (African people)
    Yanzi (African people)
    Zairians
    Zande (African people)
    Zela (African people)
--Zambia
NT Ambo (Zambian people)
    Bemba (African people)
    Bisa (Zambian people)
    Chokwe (African people)
    Fipa (African people)
    Gova (Shona-speaking people)
    Ila (African people)
    Kaonde (African people)
    Kwangwa (African people)
    Lala (African people)
    Lamba (African people)

NT Lenje (African people)
    Lozi (African people)
    Luchazi (African people)
    Lulua (African people)
    Lunda, Southern (African people)
    Luvale (African people)
    Mambwe (African people)
    Ndembu (African people)
    Ngangela (African people)
    Ngwato (African people)
    Nkoya (African people)
    Nyanja (African people)
    Sanga (African people)
    Tabwa (African people)
    Tonga (Zambesi people)
    Ungas
    Ushi (African people)
    Yombe (African people)
--Zimbabwe
NT Barwe (African people)
    Gova (Shona-speaking people)
    Hera (African people)
    Karanga (African people)
    Kgatla (African people)
    Ndebele (African people)
    Nika (African people)
    Pedi (African people)
    Shona (African people)
    Tangwena (African people)
    Tawara (African people)
    Tlhaping (African people)
    Tonga (Zambesi people)
    Tswana (African people)
    Zezuru (African people)
    Zimbabweans

Ethnomedicine
    USE Folk medicine
         Medicine, Primitive

Ethnophilosophy *(May Subd Geog)*
    UF   Folk philosophy
         Philosophy, Folk
         Philosophy, Primitive
         Primitive philosophy
    BT   Ethnology
         Philosophy
    --Africa, French-speaking West
    NT   Philosophy, Dogon
    --Africa, West
    NT   Philosophy, Yoruba
    --Benin
    NT   Philosophy, Yoruba
    --Burkina Faso
    NT   Philosophy, Gurma
         Philosophy, Lobi   *(Continued)*

UF = Used for; BT = Broader term; RT = Related term; SA = See also; NT = Narrower term

Ethnophilosophy   *(Continued)*
--**Cameroon**
  NT Philosophy, Fali
--**Kenya**
  NT Philosophy, Nika
--**Mali**
  NT Philosophy, Dogon
--**Nigeria**
  NT Philosophy, Igbo
      Philosophy, Yoruba
--**South Africa**
  NT Philosophy, Kgaga
      Philosophy, Zulu
--**Tanzania**
  NT Philosophy, Kaguru
      Philosophy, Nika
--**Uganda**
  NT Philosophy, Baganda
--**Zaire**
  NT Philosophy, Luba
      Philosophy, Yanzi
--**Zimbabwe**
  NT Philosophy, Karanga
      Philosophy, Nika

Ethnopsychology *(May Subd Geog)*
  UF Cross-cultural psychology
      Ethnic psychology
      Folk-psychology
      National psychology
      Psychological anthropology
      Psychology, Cross-cultural
      Psychology, Ethnic
      Psychology, Folk
      Psychology, National
      Psychology, Racial
      Race psychology
  BT Anthropology
      Ethnology
  SA *subdivision* Psychology *under names of racial*
or ethnic groups, e.g. Igbo (African people)--
Psychology
  RT National characteristics
  NT Art and race
      Music and race
      Race awareness
--**Africa**
  [GN 645]
--**Africa, Sub-Saharan**
  [GN 645]

Ethology
  USE Ethics

Eton (African people) *(May Subd Geog)*
  [DT 571.E86]
  UF Etum (African people)
      Toni (African people)
  BT Beti (African people)
      Ethnology--Cameroon
  NT Evuzok (African people)

Etosha Game Park (Namibia)
  USE Etosha National Park (Namibia)

Etosha National Park (Namibia) *(Not Subd Geog)*
  UF Etosha Game Park (Namibia)
  BT National parks and reserves--Namibia
      Parks--Namibia
      Wildlife refuges--Namibia

Etossio (African people)
  USE Teso (African people)

Etsako language *(May Subd Geog)*
  [PL 8159]
  UF Afenmai language
      Iyekhee language
      Kukuruku language
      Yekhee language
  BT Kwa languages
      Nigeria--Languages
--**Tone**
  BT Tone (Phonetics)

Etum (African people)
  USE Eton (African people)

Etymology
  USE *subdivision* Etymology *under particular languages*
or groups of cognate languages, e.g. Ganga language--
Etymology.

Eue language
  USE Ewe language

Eulogistic poetry
  USE Laudatory poetry

Europe
  UF Europe, Western
      Western Europe
--**Civilization**
  NT Painting, Ethiopian--European influences
-- --**African influences**
  BT Africa--Civilization

Europe, Western
  USE Europe

(May Subd Geog) = Place names may follow the heading

European art
  USE Art, European

European War, 1914-1918
  USE World War, 1914-1918

European War, 1939-1945
  USE World War, 1939-1945

Europeans in African art
  [N 7380]
  BT Art, African

Eve (African people)
  USE Ewe (African people)

Eve language
  USE Ewe language

Evhe (African people)
  USE Ewe (African people)

Eviya (African people) (May Subd Geog)
  [DT 546.145.E]
  UF Moviya (African people)
  BT Ethnology--Gabon

Evuzok (African people) (May Subd Geog)
  [DT 571.E94]
  BT Bantu-speaking peoples
      Beti (African people)
      Ethnology--Cameroon
      Eton (African people)
 --Medicine
  BT Medicine, Primitive--Cameroon

Ewe (African people) (May Subd Geog)
  [DT 510.43.E94 (Ghana)]
  [DT 582.45.E93 (Togo)]
  [DT 474.6.E83 (West Africa)]
  UF Bayikpe (African people)
      Bubutubi (African people)
      Ehwe (African people)
      Eibe (African people)
      Eve (African people)
      Evhe (African people)
      Krepe (African people)
      Krepi (African people)
  BT Ethnology--Africa, West
      Ethnology--Benin
      Ethnology--Ghana
      Ethnology--Togo
  NT Aja (African people)
      Fon (African people)
      Mina (African people)

--Marriage customs and rites
  UF Marriage customs and rites, Ewe (African
people)
--Religion
  [BL 2480.E96]
--Rites and ceremonies

Ewe imprints (May Subd Geog)
  [Z 7108.E85]
  UF Imprints, Ewe

Ewe language (May Subd Geog)
  [PL 8161-PL 8164]
  UF Ebwe language
      Efe language
      Ehwe language
      Eibe language
      Eue language
      Eve language
      Gbe language
      Krepe language
      Krepi language
      Popo language
  BT Africa, West--Languages
      Benin--languages
      Ghana--Languages
      Kwa languages
      Togo--Languages
  NT Aja dialect
      Fon dialect
      Mina dialect
      Tofingbe dialect

Ewe law
  USE Law, Ewe

Ewe literature (May Subd Geog)
  [PL 8163.5-PL 8164]
  BT Ghanaian literature
      Togolese literature
  NT Ewe poetry

Ewe poetry (May Subd Geog)
  [PL 8163.5-PL 8164]
  BT Ewe literature
      Ghana--Poetry
      Togo--Poetry

Ewe proverbs
  USE Proverbs, Ewe

Ewondo (African people) (May Subd Geog)
  [DT 571.E]
  UF Ewundu (African people)
      Jaunde (African people)
      Yaounde (African people)   (Continued)

Ewondo (African people)   *(Continued)*
  UF Yaunde (African people)
  BT Ethnology--Cameroon

Ewondo language *(May Subd Geog)*
  [PL 8165.E9]
  UF Beti language
      Jaunde language
      Yaunde language
  BT Cameroon--Languages
      Yaunde-Fang languages

Ewondo proverbs
  USE Proverbs, Ewondo

Ewundu (African people)
  USE Ewondo (African people)

Executives *(May Subd Geog)*
  UF Business executives
      Corporation executives
      Managers

Executives, Black *(May Subd Geog)*
  UF Black executives
  --South Africa
    [HD 38.25.S6]

Expeditions, Adventure
  USE Safaris

Extinct cities
  USE Cities and towns, Ruined, extinct,
etc.

Eyasi, Lake (Tanzania) *(Not Subd Geog)*
  UF Lake Eyasi (Tanzania)
      Lake Njarasa (Tanzania)
      Njarasa, Lake (Tanzania)
  BT Lakes--Tanzania

Eyo language
  USE Yoruba language

Ezaa language *(May Subd Geog)*
  [PL 8166]
  UF Ezza language
  BT Kwa languages
      Nigeria--Languages

Ezam language
  USE Ejagham language

Ezza language
  USE Ezaa language

F

Fa language (Bamileke)
  USE Fe'fe' language

Fables
  BT Fiction
      Legends
      Literature

Fables, African *(May Subd Geog)*
  UF African fables

Fables, Dinka *(May Subd Geog)*
  UF Dinka fables

Fables, Mozambican *(May Subd Geog)*
  UF Mozambican fables

Fables, Zairian *(May Subd Geog)*
  UF Zairian fables

Fabrics
  USE Textile fabrics

Facts, Miscellaneous
  USE Almanacs

Faculty (Education)
  USE Teachers

Fadicca language
  USE Mahas-Fiyadikka language

Fadicha language
  USE Mahas-Fiyadikka language

Fadija language
  USE Mahas-Fiyadikka language

Falasha Rescue, 1984-1985
  [DS 135.E75]
  UF Airlife of Falashas, 1984-1985
      Operation Moses, 1984-1985
  BT Search and rescue operations--Ethiopia
      Search and rescue operations--Sudan

Falasha Trial, Khartoum, Sudan, 1985
  BT Falashas

Falashas *(May Subd Geog)*
  [DS 135.E75]
  UF Beta Israel
      Ethiopian Jews
      Felashas

(May Subd Geog) = Place names may follow the heading

UF Fenjas
    Foggara
    House of Israel
    Israel, Beta
    Israel, House of
    Jews, Ethiopian
    Kaila
BT Ethnology--Ethiopia
    Jews
NT Falasha Trial, Khartoum, Sudan, 1985

Fali (African people) *(May Subd Geog)*
  [DT 571.F34]
BT Ethnology--Cameroon

Fali art
  USE Art, Fali

Fali language *(May Subd Geog)*
  UF Falli language
  BT Cameroon--Languages
      Chadic languages

Fali philosophy
  USE Philosophy, Fali

Falli language
  USE Fali language

Falls (Waterfalls)
  USE Waterfalls)

Falor language *(May Subd Geog)*
  UF Palor language
  BT Cangin language
      Senegal--Languages

False Bay (Cape of Good Hope, South Africa)
(Not Subd Geog)
  UF Valsbaai (Cape of Good Hope, South
Africa)
  RT Bays--South Africa

Families, Black *(May Subd Geog)*
  UF Black families
      Blacks--Families
  BT Family
  --Africa
  [HQ 691]

Family *(May Subd Geog)*
  UF Family relationships
  RT Domestic relations
      Kinship
      Marriage

NT Clans
    Divorce
    Families, Black
    Tribes
  --Law
  USE Domestic relations
  --**Africa**
  [HQ 691]

Family law
  USE Domestic relations

Family planning
  USE Birth control

Family relationships
  USE Family

Famines *(May Subd Geog)*
  RT Agriculture
      Food
  --**Africa, Sub-Saharan**
  [HC 800.Z9F3]
  --**Burkina Faso**
  [HC 547.U63]

Fan (Cameroon people)
  USE Fe'fe' (Cameroon people)

Fan (West African people)
  USE Fang (West African people)

Fan language (Bamileke)
  USE Fe'fe' language

Fan language (Bantu)
  USE Fang language

Fanagalo
  USE Fanakalo

Fanakalo
  [PM 7895.F3]
  UF Basic Bantu language
      Fanagalo
      Fanekalo
      Isi-Lololo
      Isi-Piki
      Kitchen Kaffir
      Pidgin Kaffir
  BT Lingua francas
      Xhosa language

Fanekalo
  USE Fanakalo

UF = Used for; BT = Broader term; RT = Related term; SA = See also; NT = Narrower term

Fanfannyégènè I Site (Mali) *(Not Subd Geog)*
  BT Caves--Mali
      Mali--Antiquities

Fang (Cameroon people)
  USE Fe'fe' (Cameroon people)

Fang (West African people) *(May Subd Geog)*
  [DT 620.45.F35 (Equatorial Guinea)]
  [DT 530.5.F34 (French-speaking West
Africa)]
  [DT 546.145.F34 (Gabon)]
  [DT 474.6.F35 (West Africa)]
  UF Fan (West African people)
      Mpangwe (West African people)
      Pahouin (West African people)
      Pahuin (West African people)
      Pamue (West African people)
      Pangwe (West African people)
  BT Ethnology--Africa, French-speaking
West
      Ethnology--Africa, West
      Ethnology--Equatorial Guinea
      Ethnology--Gabon
 --Religion
  [BL 2480.F3]
  NT Bwiti sect

Fang architecture
  USE Architecture, Fang

Fang art
  USE Art, Fang

Fang arts
  USE Arts, Fang

Fang ballads
  USE Ballads, Fang

Fang language *(May Subd Geog)*
  [PL 8167.F3]
  UF Fan language (Bantu)
      Fanwe language (Bantu)
      Pahouin language
      Pamue language
      Pangwe language
  BT Cameroon--Languages
      Equatorial Guinea--Languages
      Gabon--Languages
      Yaunde-Fang languages

Fang languages
  USE Yaunde-Fang languages

Fang literature *(May Subd Geog)*
  [PL 8167.F35-PL 8167.F38]
  BT Cameroon literature
      Equatorial Guinean literature
      Gabon literature
  NT Fang poetry

Fang poetry *(May Subd Geog)*
  [PL 8167.F37]
  BT Cameroon--Poetry
      Equatorial Guinea--Poetry
      Fang literature
      Gabon--Poetry

Fang songs
  USE Songs, Fang

Fante (African people)
  USE Fanti (African people)

Fante language
  USE Fanti language

Fanti (African people) *(May Subd Geog)*
  [DT 510.43.F35]
  UF Fante (African people)
      Mfantse (African people)
  BT Ethnology--Ghana
  RT Akan (African people)
  --Medicine
  BT Medicine, Primitive--Ghana
  --Music
  NT Konkoma

Fanti language *(May Subd Geog)*
  [PL 8167.F4]
  UF Fante language
      Fantsi language
  BT Ghana--Languages
      Akan language
  --Phonetic transcriptions

Fanti literature *(May Subd Geog)*
  [PL 8167.F45-PL 8167.F48]
  BT Ghanaian literature
  NT Fanti poetry

Fanti poetry *(May Subd Geog)*
  [PL 8167.F47]
  BT Fanti literature
      Ghana--Poetry

Fantsi language
  USE Fanti language

(May Subd Geog) = Place names may follow the heading

Fanwe language (Bamileke)
  USE Fe'fe' language

Fanwe language (Bantu)
  USE Fang language

Farming
  USE Agriculture

Farming, Dry
  USE Dry farming

Farms *(May Subd Geog)*
  BT Agriculture
  NT Plantations
      Ranches
      State farms
 --**Kenya**
  NT I.C.I.P.E. Farm (Kenya)
      Ithe-wa-Gathoni Farm (Kenya)
      Kelelwa Farm (Kenya)
      Tatton Farm (Kenya)

Fashoda Crisis, 1898
  [DT 156.6]
  BT Sudan--History--1862-1899

Fca language
  USE Balante language

Federal and Islamic Republic of the Comoros
  USE Comoros

Federal Republic of Cameroon
  USE Cameroon

Federation of East Africa
  USE East Africa Federation

Federation of Mali
  USE Mali (Federation)

Fe'e Fe'e (Cameroon people)
  USE Fe'fe' (Cameroon people)

Fe'e fe'e language
  USE Fe'fe' language

Fe'fe' (Cameroon people) *(May Subd Geog)*
  [DT 571.F43]
  UF Bafang (Cameroon people)
      Fan (Cameroon people)
      Fang (Cameroon people)
      Fe'e Fe'e (Cameroon people)
  BT Bamileke (African people)
      Ethnology--Cameroon

Fe'fe' language *(May Subd Geog)*
  [PL 8169]
  UF Bafang language
      Bakou language
      Bana language
      Fa language (Bamileke)
      Fan language (Bamileke)
      Fanwe language (Bamileke)
      Fe'e fe'e language
      Kuu language
      Nufi language
  BT Bamileke languages
      Cameroon--Languages

Felashas
  USE Falashas

Felata (African people)
  USE Fula (African people)

Fellani (African people)
  USE Fula (African people)

Feloup (African people)
  USE Felup (African people)

Felup (African people) *(May Subd Geog)*
  UF Feloup (African people)
      Felupe (African people)
      Floup (African people)
      Flup (African people)
      Fulup (African people)
      Huluf (African people)
      Karon (African people)
      Uluf (African people)
  BT Diola (African people)
      Ethnology--Gambia
      Ethnology--Senegal

Felupe (African people)
  USE Felup (African people)

Female gods
  USE Goddesses

Females, Human
  USE Women

Fenjas
  USE Falashas

Fer language
  USE Kara language

Ferlo (Senegal) *(Not Subd Geog)*

UF = Used for; BT = Broader term; RT = Related term; SA = See also; NT = Narrower term

Fernandian language
  USE Bube language

Fernando Po (Equatorial Guinea) *(Not Subd Geog)*
  [DT 620.9.F47]
  UF Bioco (Equatorial Guinea)
      Bioko (Equatorial Guinea)
      Fernando Póo (Equatorial Guinea)
      Isla de Bioco (Equatorial Guinea)
      Isla de Bioko (Equatorial Guinea)
      Macias Nguema (Equatorial Guinea)
  BT Equatorial Guinea
      Islands--Equatorial Guinea

Fernando Póo (Equatorial Guinea)
  USE Fernando Po (Equatorial Guinea)

Fero language
  USE Pero language

Feroge languages *(May Subd Geog)*
  [PL 8171]
  BT Niger-Congo languages
      Sudan--Languages

Fetishism *(May Subd Geog)*
  [GN 472]
  BT Religion, Primitive
 --**Africa, Sub-Saharan**

Feudal tenure
  USE Land tenure

Fia (African people)
  USE Bafia (African people)

Fiadicca language
  USE Mahas-Fiyadikka language

Fiadidja language
  USE Mahas-Fiyadikka language

Fiction
  UF Novellas (Short stories)
      Novels
      Stories
  BT Literature
  RT Novelists
  SA *headings for fiction qualified by linguistic,*
national, ethnic, or regional terms, e.g. Shona
fiction; West African fiction
  NT Children's stories
      Fables
      Humorous stories
      Legends
      Short stories

--**Black authors**
  [PN 841 (History)]
  [PN 6120.92.B45 (Collections)]
  UF Black fiction
      Fiction, Black

Fiction, Black
  USE Fiction--Black authors

Filiya language
  USE Pero language

Film industry (Motion pictures)
  USE Motion picture industry

Films
  USE Motion pictures

Fine arts
  USE Art
       Arts

Fingo (African people) *(May Subd Geog)*
  [DT 834 : old class]
  [DT 1768.F54 : new class]
  UF Amafengo (African people)
      Amafingo (African people)
      Fingu (African people)
      Mfengo (African people)
      Mfengu (African people)
  BT Bantu-speaking peoples
      Ethnology--South Africa
 --**Missions** *(May Subd Geog)*
  [BV 3630.F55]
  UF Missions to Fingo (African people)

Fingu (African people)
  USE Fingo (African people)

Finng language
  USE Bobo Fing language

Fiot (African people)
  USE Bwende (African people)

Fiote language
  USE Kituba language
       Kongo language
       Koongo dialect (Western Kongo)

Fipa (African people) *(May Subd Geog)*
  [DT 443.3.F56 (Tanzania)]
  [DT 963.42 (Zambia: old class)]
  [DT 3058.F56 (Zambia: new class)]
  UF Wafipa (African people)
  BT Ethnology--Tanzania

(May Subd Geog) = Place names may follow the heading

BT   Ethnology--Zambia

Fipa folk literature
  USE Folk literature, Fipa

Firms
  USE Business enterprises

First Chimurenga War (Zimbabwe), 1896-1897
  USE Zimbabwe--History--Ndebele
Insurrection, 1896-1897

First Street (Harare, Zimbabwe) *(Not Subd Geog)*
  UF   1st Street (Harare, Zimbabwe)
  BT   Streets--Zimbabwe

First World War
  USE World War, 1914-1918

Fiyadikka language
  USE Mahas-Fiyadikka language

Fiyadikkya language
  USE Mahas-Fiyadikka language

Fjort (African people)
  USE Kongo (African people)

Flat racing
  USE Horse racing

Fleuve Senegal
  USE Senegal River

Floodplains *(May Subd Geog)*
  *Works on the floodplains of individual rivers are
entered under the name of the river valley.*
  UF   River flood plains
  BT   Valleys
 --**Zambia**
  [GB 561-GB 568]
  NT   Kafue Flats (Zambia)

Floup (African people)
  USE Felup (African people)

Flup (African people)
  USE Felup (African people)

Fo dialect
  USE Fon dialect

Fogbe dialect
  USE Fon dialect

Foggara
  USE Falashas

Folk art *(May Subd Geog)*
  UF   Art, Folk
       Art, Peasant
       Art, Popular
       Peasant art
       Popular art
  BT   Art
  RT   Decorative arts
 --**Zambia**
  NT   Tusona

Folk art, Black *(May Subd Geog)*
  UF   Black folk art

Folk beliefs
  USE Folklore

Folk dancing *(May Subd Geog)*
  *Here are entered collections of miscellaneous folk
dances which include instructions for the dance.*
  UF   National dances
  BT   Dancing
  RT   Folk music

Folk dancing, Embu *(May Subd Geog)*
  [GV 1713.K]
  UF   Embu folk dancing

Folk dancing, Yoruba *(May Subd Geog)*
  [GV 1713.N]
  UF   Yoruba folk dancing

Folk-drama
  UF   Drama, Folk
       Drama, Primitive
       Folk-plays
  BT   Drama
       Folk literature

Folk-drama, Hausa *(May Subd Geog)*
  [PL 8233.8]
  UF   Hausa folk-drama
  BT   Hausa drama

Folk-drama, Igbo *(May Subd Geog)*
  [PL 8261.8]
  UF   Igbo folk-drama
  BT   Igbo drama

Folk festivals *(May Subd Geog)*
  BT   Folklore
 --**Botswana**
  NT   Laedza Batanani, Botswana

UF = Used for; BT = Broader term; RT = Related term; SA = See also; NT = Narrower term

Folk literature *(May Subd Geog)*
  UF Folk-tales
       Literature, Folk
       Literature, Primitive
       Oral literature
       Primitive literature
  BT Folklore
       Literature
  NT Chapbooks
       Folk-drama
       Folk poetry
       Folk songs
       Legends
       Nursery rhymes
       Proverbs
       Riddles

Folk literature, African *(May Subd Geog)*
  [GR 350]
  UF African folk literature
  BT African literature

Folk literature, Bamileke *(May Subd Geog)*
  [GR 351.2.B35]
  UF Bamileke folk literature

Folk literature, Bantu *(May Subd Geog)*
  [GR 350.2]
  UF Bantu folk literature
  BT Bantu literature

Folk literature, Efik *(May Subd Geog)*
  [GR 351.32.E]
  UF Efik folk literature

Folk literature, Fipa *(May Subd Geog)*
  [GR 356.72.F58]
  UF Fipa folk literature

Folk literature, Fula *(May Subd Geog)*
  [GR 350.32.F82]
  UF Fula folk literature
  BT Fula literature

Folk literature, Igbo *(May Subd Geog)*
  [GR 351.32.I]
  UF Igbo folk literature
  BT Igbo literature

Folk literature, Krio *(May Subd Geog)*
  [GR 352.32.K74]
  UF Krio folk literature
  BT Krio literature

Folk literature, Laadi *(May Subd Geog)*
  [GR 357.52.L33]
  UF Laadi folk literature

Folk literature, Luba *(May Subd Geog)*
  [GR 357.82.L82]
  UF Luba folk literature

Folk literature, Luyana *(May Subd Geog)*
  [GR 358.42.L]
  UF Luyana folk literature

Folk literature, Mandingo *(May Subd Geog)*
  [GR 350.32.M33]
  UF Mandingo folk literature
  BT Mandingo literature

Folk literature, Masai *(May Subd Geog)*
  [GR 356.42.M37]
  UF Masai folk literature
  BT Masai literature

Folk literature, Mbosi *(May Subd Geog)*
  [GR 357.52.M34]
  UF Mbosi folk literature
  BT Mbosi literature

Folk literature, Meru *(May Subd Geog)*
  [GR 355.62.M47]
  UF Meru folk literature
  BT Meru literature

Folk literature, Ndebele (Zimbabwe) *(May Subd Geog)*
  [GR 358.62.N34]
  UF Ndebele folk literature (Zimbabwe)
  BT Ndebele literature (Zimbabwe)

Folk literature, Ngonde *(May Subd Geog)*
  [GR 356.72.N47]
  UF Ngonde folk literature

Folk literature, Pular *(May Subd Geog)*
  [GR 352.72.P]
  UF Pular folk literature
  BT Pular literature

Folk literature, Sakata *(May Subd Geog)*
  [GR 357.82.S24]
  UF Sakata folk literature

Folk literature, Somali *(May Subd Geog)*
  [GR 356.3]
  UF Somali folk literature
  BT Somali literature

(May Subd Geog) = Place names may follow the heading

Folk literature, Sotho *(May Subd Geog)*
  [GR 359.52.S68]
  UF Sotho folk literature
  BT Sotho literature

Folk literature, Subiya *(May Subd Geog)*
  [GR 358.82.S (Botswana)]
  [GR 358.42.S (Zambia)]
  UF Subiya folk literature

Folk literature, Swahili *(May Subd Geog)*
  [GR 355.62.S93]
  UF Swahili folk literature
  BT Swahili literature

Folk literature, Tonga (Zambesi) *(May Subd Geog)*
  [GR 358.42.T66]
  UF Tonga folk literature (Zambesi)
  BT Tonga literature (Zambesi)

Folk literature, Umbundu *(May Subd Geog)*
  [GR 358.32.U]
  UF Umbundu folk literature
  BT Umbundu literature

Folk literature, Wolof *(May Subd Geog)*
  [GR 352.97.W64]
  UF Wolof folk literature
  RT Wolof literature

Folk-lore
  USE Folklore

Folk medicine *(May Subd Geog)*
  UF Ethnic medicine
      Ethnomedicine
      Medical folklore
      Medicine, Folk
  BT Folklore
  RT Medicine, Primitive
  NT Shamans
  --Africa

Folk music *(May Subd Geog)*
  BT Folklore
      Music
  RT Folk dancing
  NT Folk songs
  --Africa
    [M 1830-M 1838 (Music)]
    [ML 350-ML 350.5 (History and criticism)]

Folk philosophy
  USE Ethnophilosophy

Folk-plays
  USE Folk-drama

Folk poetry *(May Subd Geog)*
  UF Oral poetry
      Poetry, Folk
  BT Folk literature
      Folk songs
      Poetry
  NT Nursery rhymes

Folk poetry, African *(May Subd Geog)*
  [PL 8010.4]
  UF African folk poetry
  BT African poetry

Folk poetry, Amharic *(May Subd Geog)*
  [PR 9408.E83]
  UF Amharic folk poetry
  BT Amharic poetry

Folk poetry, Fula *(May Subd Geog)*
  [PL 8183.5 (History)]
  [PL 8184.A2 (Collections)]
  UF Fula folk poetry
  BT Fula poetry

Folk poetry, Igbo *(May Subd Geog)*
  [PL 8261.5 (History)]
  [PL 8261.8 (Collections)]
  UF Igbo folk poetry
  BT Igbo poetry

Folk poetry, Malagasy *(May Subd Geog)*
  [PL 5378.4 (History)]
  [PL 5378.8 (Collections)]
  UF Malagasy folk poetry
  BT Malagasy poetry

Folk poetry, Nigerian *(May Subd Geog)*
  [PL 8014.N6]
  UF Nigerian folk poetry
  BT Nigerian poetry

Folk poetry, Shona *(May Subd Geog)*
  [PL 8681.5 (History)]
  [PL 8681.8 (Collections)]
  UF Shona folk poetry
  BT Shona poetry

Folk poetry, Wolof *(May Subd Geog)*
  [PL 8785.5 (History)]
  [PL 8785.8 (Collections)]
  UF Wolof folk poetry
  BT Wolof poetry

UF = Used for; BT = Broader term; RT = Related term; SA = See also; NT = Narrower term

Folk poetry, Xhosa *(May Subd Geog)*
  [PL 8795.5 (History)]
  [PL 8795.8 (Collections)]
  UF   Xhosa folk poetry
  BT   Xhosa poetry

Folk poetry, Yoruba *(May Subd Geog)*
  [PL 8823.5 (History)]
  [PL 8824.A2 (Collections)]
  UF   Yoruba folk poetry
  BT   Yoruba poetry

Folk-psychology
  USE   Ethnopsychology

Folk songs *(May Subd Geog)*
  Here are entered collections of folk songs in
  various unrelated languages. Works in a single
  language or group of languages are entered under this
  heading with language qualifier, e.g. Folk songs,
  Fula.
  BT   Folk literature
       Folk music
       Music
       Songs
  RT   Ballads
  NT   Folk poetry

Folk songs, Acoli *(May Subd Geog)*
  [PL 8041 (Words)]
  [M 1831.A (Music)]
  UF   Acoli folk songs

Folk songs, Afrikaans *(May Subd Geog)*
  [PT 6545 (Words)]
  [M 1834 (Music)]
  UF   Afrikaans folk songs

Folk songs, Aka (Central African Republic)
(May Subd Geog)
  [PL 8046.A59 (Words)]
  [M 1831.A (Music)]
  UF   Aka folk songs (Central African
Republic)

Folk songs, Akan *(May Subd Geog)*
  [PL 8046.A63 (Words)]
  [M 1831.A (Music)]
  UF   Akan folk songs

Folk songs, Ambo (Zambia) *(May Subd Geog)*
  [PL 8430.L3595A4 (Words)]
  [M 1831.A (Music)]
  UF   Ambo (Zambia) folk songs

Folk songs, Antandroy *(May Subd Geog)*
  [PL 5379 (Words)]
  [M 1846.M (Music)]
  UF   Antandroy folk songs

Folk songs, Baka (Cameroon) *(May Subd Geog)*
  [PL 8047.65 (Words)]
  [M 1831.B (Music)]
  UF   Baka folk songs (Cameroon)

Folk songs, Bambara *(May Subd Geog)*
  [PL 8049.B3 (Words)]
  [M 1831.B (Music)]
  UF   Bambara folk songs

Folk songs, Bamileke *(May Subd Geog)*
  [PL 8049.B47 (Words)]
  [M 1831.B (Music)]
  UF   Bamileke folk songs

Folk songs, Bantu *(May Subd Geog)*
  [PL 8025 (Words)]
  [M 1831.B (Music)]
  UF   Bantu folk songs

Folk songs, Bassari *(May Subd Geog)*
  [PL 8066.B3 (Words)]
  [M 1831.B (Music)]
  UF   Bassari folk songs

Folk songs, Bororo (West Africa) *(May Subd Geog)*
  [PL 8086.B (Words)]
  [M 1831.B (Music)]
  UF   Bororo folk songs (West Africa)

Folk songs, Dinka *(May Subd Geog)*
  [PL 8131 (Words)]
  [M 1831.D (Music)]
  UF   Dinka folk songs

Folk songs, Embu *(May Subd Geog)*
  [PL 8153.E (Words)]
  [M 1831.E (Music)]
  UF   Embu folk songs

Folk songs, Ethiopian *(May Subd Geog)*
  [PJ 8999 (Words)]
  [M 1838.E (Music)]
  UF   Ethiopian folk songs

Folk songs, Fula *(May Subd Geog)*
  [PL 8183.5-PL 8184 (Words)]
  [M 1831.F (Music)]
  UF   Fula folk songs

(May Subd Geog) = Place names may follow the heading

Folk songs, Ga *(May Subd Geog)*
  [PL 8191 (Words)]
  [M 1831.G (Music)]
  UF Ga folk songs

Folk songs, Ganda *(May Subd Geog)*
  [PL 8201 (Words)]
  [M 1831.G (Music)]
  UF Ganda folk songs

Folk songs, Gbaya *(May Subd Geog)*
  [PL 8205 (Words)]
  [M 1831.G (Music)]
  UF Gbaya folk songs

Folk songs, Kamba *(May Subd Geog)*
  [PL 8351 (Words)]
  [M 1831.K (Collections)]
  UF Kamba folk songs

Folk songs, Karamojong *(May Subd Geog)*
  [PL 8373 (Words)]
  [M 1831.K (Music)]
  UF Karamojong folk songs

Folk songs, Kikuyu *(May Subd Geog)*
  [PL 8379 (Words)]
  [M 1831.K (Music)]
  UF Kikuyu folk songs

Folk songs, Kimbundu *(May Subd Geog)*
  [PL 8381 (Words)]
  [M 1831.K (Music)]
  UF Kimbundu folk songs

Folk songs, Kinyarwanda *(May Subd Geog)*
  [PL 8601 (Words)]
  [M 1831.K (Music)]
  UF Kinyarwanda folk songs

Folk songs, Kpelle *(May Subd Geog)*
  [PL 8411 (Words)]
  [M 1831.K (Music)]
  UF Kpelle folk songs

Folk songs, Lobi *(May Subd Geog)*
  [PL 8222.L (Words)]
  [M 1831.L (Music)]
  UF Lobi folk songs

Folk songs, Lunda *(May Subd Geog)*
  [PL 8465 (Words)]
  [M 1831.L (Music)]
  UF Lunda folk songs

Folk songs, Malagasy *(May Subd Geog)*
  [PL 5378.8 (Words)]
  [M 1846.M (Music)]
  UF Malagasy folk songs

Folk songs, Mandingo *(May Subd Geog)*
  [PL 8491 (Words)]
  [M 1831.M (Music)]
  UF Mandingo folk songs

Folk songs, Ngbaka ma'bo *(May Subd Geog)*
  [PL 8548 (Words)]
  [M 1831.N (Music)
  UF Ngbaka ma'bo folk songs

Folk songs, Nuer *(May Subd Geog)*
  [PL 8576.N4 (Words)]
  [M 1831.N (Music)]
  UF Nuer folk songs

Folk songs, Nzakara *(May Subd Geog)*
  [PL 8828.95.N (Words)]
  [M 1831.N95 (Music)]
  UF Nzakara folk songs

Folk songs, Punu *(Not Subd Geog)*
  [PL 8605 (Words)]
  [M 1831.P (Music)]
  UF Punu folk songs

Folk songs, Rundi *(May Subd Geog)*
  [PL 8611 (Words)]
  [M 1831.R (Music)]
  UF Rundi folk songs

Folk songs, Salampasu *(May Subd Geog)*
  [M 1831.S (Music)]
  UF Salampasu folk songs

Folk songs, Somali *(May Subd Geog)*
  [PJ 2534 (Words)]
  [M 1831.S (Music)]
  UF Somali folk songs

Folk songs, Teda *(May Subd Geog)*
  [PL 8724 (Words)]
  [M 1831.T (Music)]
  UF Teda folk songs

Folk songs, Teke *(May Subd Geog)*
  [PL 8725 (Words)]
  [M 1831.T (Music)]
  UF Teke folk songs

UF = Used for; BT = Broader term; RT = Related term; SA = See also; NT = Narrower term

Folk songs, Tsogo *(May Subd Geog)*
   [M 1831.T (Music)]
   UF Tsogo folk songs

Folk songs, Tsonga *(May Subd Geog)*
   [PL 8745 (Words)]
   [M 1831.T (Music)]
   UF Tsonga folk songs

Folk songs, Tswana *(May Subd Geog)*
   [PL 8747 (Words)]
   [M 1831.T (Music)]
   UF Tswana folk songs

Folk songs, Yoruba *(May Subd Geog)*
   [PL 8823.5-PL 8824 (Words)]
   [M 1831.Y (Music)]
   UF Yoruba folk songs

Folk songs, Zande *(May Subd Geog)*
   [PL 8825 (Words)]
   [M 1831.Z (Music)]
   UF Zande folk songs

Folk songs, Zarma *(May Subd Geog)*
   [PL 8685.95.Z3 (Words)]
   [M 1831.Z (Music)]
   UF Zarma folk songs

Folk-tales
   USE Folk literature
      Legends

Folklore *(May Subd Geog)*
   UF Folk beliefs
      Folk-lore
      Traditions
   BT Ethnology
      Manners and customs
      Religion, Primitive
   RT Mythology
      Oral tradition
   SA *subdivision* Folklore *under ethnic, national*
or occupational groups, e.g. Kera (African
people)--Folklore
   NT Folk festivals
      Folk literature
      Folk medicine
      Folk music
      Trickster
 --Africa, East
   NT Liyongo (Legendary character)
 --Africa, West
   NT Anansi (Legendary character)
 --Nigeria
   NT Esu (Legendary character)

--Zaire
   NT Kabundji (Legendary character)

Folkways
   USE Manners and customs

Folo (African people)
   USE Minianka (African people)

Foma (African people) *(May Subd Geog)*
   [DT 650.F]
   UF Fuma (African people)
      Lifoma (African people)
   BT Ethnology--Zaire

Fon (African people) *(May Subd Geog)*
   [DT 541.45.F65 (Benin)]
   UF Dahomans
      Dahomeans
      Dahomey (African people)
      Dahomeyans
   BT Ethnology--Benin
      Ethnology--Nigeria
      Ewe (African people)
   NT Aja (African people)
 --Religion
   [BL 2480.F65]

Fon altars
   USE Altars, Fon

Fon art
   USE Art, Fon

Fon dialect *(May Subd Geog)*
   [PL 8164.Z9F6]
   UF Dahoman language
      Djedji dialect
      Fo dialect
      Fogbe dialect
      Fongbe dialect
      Jeji dialect
   BT Benin--Languages
      Ewe language
      Nigeria--Languages
 --Etymology
   NT Gbè (The Fon word)
      Xó (The Fon word)

Fon ironwork
   USE Ironwork, Fon

Fon literature *(May Subd Geog)*
   [PL 8164.Z9F6]
   BT Benin literature
      Nigerian literature

(May Subd Geog) = Place names may follow the heading

NT Fon poetry

Fon poetry *(May Subd Geog)*
  [PL 8164.Z9F6]
  BT Benin--Poetry
      Fon literature
      Nigerian poetry

Fon proverbs
  USE Proverbs, Fon

Fongbe dialect
  USE Fon dialect

Food
  UF Foods
  RT Famines
  NT Bantu-speaking peoples--Food
      Igbo (African people)--Food
      Kikuyu (African people)--Food
      Nguni (African people)--Food
      Zande (African people)--Food

Food preparation
  USE Cookery

Foods
  USE Food

For (African people)
  USE Fur (African people)

Forawa (African people)
  USE Fur (African people)

Foreign aid to agriculture
  USE Agricultural assistance

Foreign economic policy
  USE *subdivision* Foreign economic relations
*under names of countries, cities, etc., e.g. South
Africa--Foreign economic relations*

Foreign labor
  USE Alien labor

Foreign relations
  USE *subdivision* Foreign relations *under names
of countries, e.g. Benin--Foreign relations*

Foreign students
  USE Students, Foreign

Foreign trade
  USE *name of place subdivided by Commerce and*

further subdivided by place, if appropriate, e.g.
Zimbabwe--Commerce--United States

Foreign workers
  USE Alien labor

Forest planting
  USE Forests and forestry

Forest preserves
  USE Forest reserves

Forest production
  USE Forests and forestry

Forest reserves *(May Subd Geog)*
  UF Forest preserves
      Forests, National
      Forests, State
      National forests
      Preserves, Forest
      Reserves, Forest
      State forests
  RT National parks and reserves
  NT Arboretums
  --Ivory Coast
    NT Parc National du Banco (Ivory Coast)
  --Kenya
    NT Kakamega Forest Reserve (Kenya)
  --Uganda
    NT Kibale Forest Reserve (Uganda)

Forestation
  USE Forest and forestry

Forestry development projects
  USE Forestry projects

Forestry industry
  USE Forests and forestry

Forestry projects *(May Subd Geog)*
  UF Development projects, Forestry
      Forestry development projects
      Projects, Forestry
  BT Forests and forestry
  --Kenya
  --Rwanda
    NT Projet pilote forestier
  --Zimbabwe

Forests, National
  USE Forest reserves

Forests, State
  USE Forest reserves

UF = Used for; BT = Broader term; RT = Related term; SA = See also; NT = Narrower term

Forests and forestry *(May Subd Geog)*
  UF Forest planting
      Forest production
      Forestation
      Forestry industry
      Woods (Forests)
  BT Agriculture
  NT Forestry projects
  --Kenya
  NT Nguruman Forest (Kenya)
  --Rwanda
  NT Gishwati (Rwanda)
  --Zaire
  NT Ituri Forest (Zaire)

Forêt de Gishwati (Rwanda)
  USE Gishwati (Rwanda)

Formations (Geology) *(May Subd Geog)*
  BT Geology
      Landforms
  --South Africa
  BT Goudini Formation (South Africa)
      Molteno Formation (South Africa)

Fossil man *(May Subd Geog)*
  UF Early man
      Hominidae, Fossil
      Hominids, Fossil
      Human paleontology
      Man, Fossil
  RT Man, Prehistoric
  --Ethiopia
  NT Australopithecus afarensis
  --Tanzania
  [GN 865.T33]
  --Zambia
  NT Rhodesian man

Foulah (African people)
  USE Fula (African people)

Foulbé (African people)
  USE Fula (African people)

Foulse language
  USE Kurumba language

Fournaise, Piton de la (Réunion) *(Not Subd Geog)*
  UF Piton de la Fournaise (Réunion)
  BT Mountains--Réunion
      Volcanoes--Runion

Fouta Djallon
  USE Futa Jallon

Fouta Djallon Range *(Not Subd Geog)*
  UF Fouta Djalon Range
      Fouta Jallon Range
      Futa Jallon Range
  BT Mountains--Africa, West

Fouta Djalon
  USE Futa Jallon

Fouta Djalon Range
  USE Fouta Djallon Range

Fouta Dyalon
  USE Futa Jallon

Fouta Jallon Range
  USE Fouta Djallon Range

Frafra language
  USE Nankanse language

France *(Not Subd Geog)*
  --Civilization
  NT Africa--Civilization--French influences
      Africa, West--Civilization--French influences
      Arts, Black--French influences
  -- --West African influences
  BT Africa, West--Civilization
  --Colonies
  BT Colonies
  -- --Administration
  UF France--Colonies--Politics and government
  -- --Boundaries *(May Subd Geog)*
  -- --Commerce *(May Subd Geog)*
  -- --Constitutional history
  -- --Constitutional law
  -- --Defenses
  -- --Description and travel
  -- --Discovery and exploration
  -- --Economic conditions
  -- --Economic policy
  -- --Emigration and immigration
  -- --Geography *(Not Subd Geog)*
  -- --History
  -- --Industries
  -- --Manufactures
  -- --Native races
  USE Indigenous peoples--France--Colonies
  -- --Officials and employees
  -- --Politics and government
  USE France--Colonies--Administration
  -- --Population
  -- --Public lands
  -- --Public works

(May Subd Geog) = Place names may follow the heading

-- --Race relations
-- --Religion
-- --Religious life and customs
-- --Rural conditions
-- --Social conditions
-- --Social life and customs
-- --Social policy
-- --Africa

Francophone West Africa
    USE Africa, French-speaking West

Free State-Sotho War, 1865-1866
    USE Sotho-Free State War, 1865-1866

Freedom Railway
    USE Tan-Zam Railway

Freehold
    USE Land tenure

French Antilles
    USE West Indies, French

French art
    USE Art, French

French arts
    USE Arts, French

French Creole children's stories, Mauritian
    USE Children's stories, Mauritian (French
Creole)

French Creole fiction, Mauritian
    USE Mauritian fiction (French Creole)

French Creole fiction, Réunion
    USE Réunion fiction (French Creole)

French Creole languages
    USE Creole dialects, French

French Creole literature, Mauritian
    USE Mauritian literature (French Creole)

French Creole literature, Réunion
    USE Réunion literature (French Creole)

French Creole poetry, Réunion
    USE Réunion poetry (French Creole)

French Creole short stories, Réunion
    USE Short stories, Réunion (French Creole)

French drama *(May Subd Geog)*
    BT French literature
  --African authors
    USE African drama (French)
  --Black authors
    [PQ 150.B (History)]
    [PQ 1109.5.B (Collections)]
    UF Black drama (French)
  --Senegalese authors
    USE Senegalese drama (French)

French Equatorial Africa
    USE Africa, French-speaking Equatorial

French fiction *(May Subd Geog)*
    BT French literature
    NT Short stories, French
  --African authors
    USE African fiction (French)
  --Cameroon authors
    USE Cameroon fiction (French)
  --Ivory Coast authors
    USE Ivory Coast fiction (French)
  --Mauritian authors
    USE Mauritian fiction (French)
  --Niger authors
    USE Niger fiction (French)
  --Réunion authors
    USE Réunion fiction (French)
    Senegalese authors
    USE Senegalese fiction (French)
  --West African authors
    USE West African fiction (French)

French Guinea
    USE Guinea

French Invasion of Madagascar, 1895
    USE Madagascar--History--French Invasion, 1895

French literature *(May Subd Geog)*
    NT French drama
         French fiction
         French poetry
  --African authors
    USE African literature (French)
  --Benin authors
    USE Benin literature (French)
  --Black authors
    [PQ 150.B (History)]
    [PQ 1109.5.B (Collections)]
    UF Black literature (French)
  --Burkinabe authors
    USE Burkinabe literature (French)
  --Cameroon authors
    USE Cameroon literature (French) *(Continued)*

UF = Used for; BT = Broader term; RT = Related term; SA = See also; NT = Narrower term

French literature   *(Continued)*
--Congo (Brazzaville) authors
 USE Congo (Brazzaville) literature
(French)
--Gabon authors
 USE Gabon literature (French)
--Guinean authors
 USE Guinean literature (French)
--Ivory Coast authors
 USE Ivory Coast literature (French)
--Malagasy authors
 USE Malagasy literature (French)
--Mauritian authors
 USE Mauritian literature (French)
--Niger authors
 USE Niger literature (French)
--Réunion authors
 USE Réunion literature (French)
--Senegalese authors
 USE Senegalese literature (French)
--Togolese authors
 USE Togolese literature (French)
--West African authors
 USE West African literature (French)
--Zairian authors
 USE Zairian literature (French)

French poetry *(May Subd Geog)*
 BT French literature
--African authors
 USE African poetry (French)
--Benin authors
 USE Benin poetry (French)
--**Black authors**
 [PQ 150.B (History)]
 [PQ 1109.5.B (Collections)]
 UF Black poetry (French)
--Burkinabe authors
 USE Burkinabe poetry (French)
--Cameroon authors
 USE Cameroon poetry (French)
--Congo (Brazzaville) authors
 USE Congo (Brazzaville) poetry (French)
--Gabon authors
 USE Gabon poetry (French)
--Guinean authors
 USE Guinean poetry (French)
--Malagasy authors
 USE Malagasy poetry (French)
--Mauritian authors
 USE Mauritian poetry (French)
--Niger authors
 USE Niger poetry (French)
--Réunion authors
 USE Réunion poetry (French)

--Senegalese authors
 USE Senegalese poetry (French)
--Togolese authors
 USE Togolese poetry (French)
--West African authors
 USE West African poetry (French)
--Zairian authors
 USE Zairian poetry (French)

French short stories
 USE Short stories, French

French Somaliland
 USE Djibouti

French-speaking Equatorial Africa
 USE Africa, French-speaking Equatorial

French-speaking West Africa
 USE Africa, French-speaking West

French Sudan
 USE Mali

French Territory of the Afars and Issas
 USE Djibouti

French West Africa
 USE Africa, French-speaking West

French West Indies
 USE West Indies, French

Frontier Wars (South Africa), 1811-1878
 USE South Africa--History--Frontier Wars, 1811-
1878

Frote (African people)
 USE Kongo (African people)

Ful (African people)
 USE Fula (African people)

Ful language
 USE Fula language

Fula (African people) *(May Subd Geog)*
 [DT 571.F84 (Cameroon)]
 UF Adamawa Fula (African people)
     Adamawa Fulani (African people)
     Eastern Fulani (African people)
     Felata (African people)
     Fellani (African people)
     Foulah (African people)
     Foulbé (African people)
     Ful (African people)

(May Subd Geog) = Place names may follow the heading

UF Fulah (African people)
    Fulani (African people)
    Fulbe (African people)
    Fulfede (African people)
    Fulfulde (African people)
    Futa (African people)
    Peul (African people)
    Peulh (African people)
BT Ethnology--Africa, West
    Ethnology--Cameroon
    Ethnology--Sudan (Region)
RT Toucouleurs
NT Bororo (African people)
--History
NT Adamawa (Emirate)
    Futa Jallon
-- --19th century
NT Fula Empire
    Sokoto Jihad, 1803-1830

Fula decorative arts
  USE Decorative arts, Fula

Fula Empire *(Not Subd Geog)*
  [DT 515.9.F8]
  UF Fulah Empire
    Fulani Empire
    Sokoto Caliphate
    Sokoto Empire
  BT Fula (African people)--History--19th
century

Fula epic poetry
  USE Epic poetry, Fula

Fula folk literature
  USE Folk literature, Fula

Fula folk poetry
  USE Folk poetry, Fula

Fula folk songs
  USE Folk songs, Fula

Fula Islamic poetry
  USE Islamic poetry, Fula

Fula language *(May Subd Geog)*
  [PL 8181-PL 8184]
  UF Adamawa dialect
    Ful language
    Fulah language
    Fulani language
    Fulbe language
    Fulde language
    Fulfulde language

UF Peul language
    Poul language
BT Africa, West--Languages
    Cameroon--Languages
    Niger-Congo languages
NT Bororo dialect (West Africa)
    Pular dialect

Fula law
  USE Law, Fula

Fula literature *(May Subd Geog)*
  [PL 8183.5 (History)]
  [PL 8184.A2 (Collections)]
  BT Cameroon literature
  NT Folk literature, Fula
    Fula poetry

Fula poetry *(May Subd Geog)*
  [PL 8183.5 (History)]
  [PL 8184.A2 (Collections)]
  BT Cameroon--Poetry
    Fula literature
  NT Epic poetry, Fula
    Folk poetry, Fula
    Islamic poetry, Fula

Fula proverbs
  USE Proverbs, Fula

Fula women
  USE Women, Fula

Puladu (Kingdom) *(Not Subd Geog)*
  [DT 532.128]
  NT Gambia--History
    Senegal--History--To 1960

Fulah (African people)
  USE Fula (African people)

Fulah Empire
  USE Fula Empire

Fulah language
  USE Fula language

Fulani (African people)
  USE Fula (African people)

Fulani Empire
  USE Fula Empire

Fulani Jihad, 1803-1830
  USE Sokoto Jihad, 1803-1830

UF = Used for; BT = Broader term; RT = Related term; SA = See also; NT = Narrower term

Fulani language
  USE Fula language

Fulbe (African people)
  USE Fula (African people)

Fulbe language
  USE Fula language

Fulde language
  USE Fula language

Fulfede (African people)
  USE Fula (African people)

Fulfulde (African people)
  USE Fula (African people)

Fulfulde language
  USE Fula language

Fulse (African people)
  USE Kurumba (African people)

Fulse language
  USE Kurumba language

Fuluka (African people)
  USE Kusu (African people)

Fulup (African people)
  USE Felup (African people)

Fuma (African people)
  USE Foma (African people)

Funeral rites and ceremonies *(May Subd Geog)*
  UF Funerals
      Graves
      Mortuary customs
  BT Manners and customs
      Rites and ceremonies
  SA *subdivision* Funeral customs and rites
under ethnic groups

Funeral rites and ceremonies, Acoli (African
people)
  USE Acoli (African people)--Funeral
customs and rites

Funeral rites and ceremonies, Akan (African
people)
  USE Akan (African people)--Funeral customs
and rites

Funeral rites and ceremonies, Bamileke (African
people)
  USE Bamileke (African people)--Funeral customs
and rites

Funeral rites and ceremonies, Black
  USE Blacks--Funeral customs and rites

Funeral rites and ceremonies, Bobo (African
people)
  USE Bobo (African people)--Funeral customs and
rites

Funeral rites and ceremonies, Dan (African people)
  USE Dan (African people)--Funeral customs and
rites

Funeral rites and ceremonies, Giryama (African
people)
  USE Giryana (African people)--Funeral customs
and rites

Funeral rites and ceremonies, Idoma (African
people)
  USE Idoma (African people)--Funeral customs and
rites

Funeral rites and ceremonies, Kongo (African
people)
  USE Kongo (African people)--Funeral customs and
rites

Funeral rites and ceremonies, Kumu (Zairian
people)
  USE Kumu (Zairian people)--Funeral customs and
rites

Funeral rites and ceremonies, Luyia (African
people)
  USE Luyia (African people)--Funeral customs and
rites

Funeral rites and ceremonies, Mahafaly (Malagasy
people)
  USE Mahafaly (Malagasy people)--Funeral customs
and rites

Funeral rites and ceremonies, Senufo (African
people)
  USE Senufo (African people)--Funeral customs
and rites

Funeral rites and ceremonies, Yaka (African
people)
  USE Yaka (African people)--Funeral customs and
rites

(May Subd Geog) = Place names may follow the heading

Funeral rites and ceremonies, Yoruba (African people)
USE Yoruba (African people)--Funeral customs and rites

Funerals
USE Funeral rites and ceremonies

Fungs *(May Subd Geog)*
[DT 155.2.F]
BT Ethnology--Sudan
--History
NT Sennar (Kingdom)

Fur (African people) *(May Subd Geog)*
[DT 155.2.F87]
UF For (African people)
Forawa (African people)
BT Ethnology--Sudan

Fur language *(May Subd Geog)*
[PL 8186]
BT Chad--Languages
Nilo-Saharan languages
Sudan--Languages

Fut (African people)
USE Bafut (African people)

Futa (African people)
USE Fula (African people)

Futa Jallon *(Not Subd Geog)*
[DT 532.13]
UF Fouta Djallon
Fouta Djalon
Fouta Dyalon
Futa Jalon
Kingdom of Fouta Jallon
BT Fula (African people)--History

Futa Jallon Range
USE Fouta Djallon Range

Futa Jalon
USE Futa Jallon

Futa Toro (African people)
USE Toucouleurs

Futankobe (African people)
USE Toucouleurs

G

G//ana-khwe language
USE G//ana language

G//ana language *(May Subd Geog)*
[PL 8104.Z9C5]
UF G//ana-khwe language
Gana language
//Ganakhoe language
Kanakhoe language
BT Botswana--Languages
Khoisan languages

G/wi (African people) *(May Subd Geog)*
[DT 797 : old class]
[DT 2458.G27 : new class]
UF Gewi (African people)
BT Ethnology--Botswana
San (African people)

G/wi-khwe language
USE G/wi language

G/wi language *(May Subd Geog)*
[PL 8104.Z9G]
UF G/wi-khwe language
/Guikhoe language
Gwi language
BT Botswana--Languages
Khoisan languages

Ga (African people) *(May Subd Geog)*
[DT 510.43.G3]
BT Ethnology--Ghana
--Religion
[BL 2480.G3]

Ga folk songs
USE Folk songs, Ga

Ga language *(May Subd Geog)*
[PL 8191]
UF Accra language
Acra language
Akra language
Incran language
BT Ghana--Languages
Kwa languages

Gaanda (African people) *(May Subd Geog)*
[DT 515.45.G32]
UF Gabin (African people)
Ganda (Nigerian people)
Kabin (African people) *(Continued)*

UF = Used for; BT = Broader term; RT = Related term; SA = See also; NT = Narrower term

Gaanda (African people) *(Continued)*
   UF Kanda (African people)
       Mokar (African people)
   BT Ethnology--Nigeria

Gaba (African people)
   USE Mbukushu (African people)

Gabbra (African people) *(May Subd Geog)*
   [DT 433.545.G32]
   UF Gabra (African people)
   BT Ethnology--Kenya
       Oromo (African people)

Gabere language
   USE Gabri language

Gaberi language
   USE Gabri language

Gabin (African people)
   USE Gaanda (African people)

Gabon *(Not Subd Geog)*
   [DT 546.1-DT 546.19]
   UF Gabonese Republic
       Gaboon
       Gabun
       République Gabonaise
 --Description and travel
 -- --1981-
 --Economic conditions
   [HC 975]
 -- --1960-
 --History
 -- --To 1839
 -- --1839-1960
 -- --1960-
 --Languages
   NT Aduma language
       Benga language
       Fang language
       Kele language
       Lumbu language
       Mbete language
       Mpongwe language
       Orungu language
       Punu language
       Shira language
       Tsogo language
       Yaunde-Fang languages
 --Literatures
 USE Gabon literature
 --Poetry
   NT Fang poetry
       Tsogo poetry

 --Politics and government
 -- --1960-

Gabon art
   USE Art, Gabon

Gabon Estuary (Gabon) *(Not Subd Geog)*
   UF Estuaire du Gabon (Gabon)
       Gabon River (Gabon)
   BT Estuaries--Gabon

Gabon literature *(May Subd Geog)*
   [PL 8014.G]
   UF Gabon--Literatures
   BT African literature
   NT Fang literature
       Tsogo literature

Gabon literature (French) *(May Subd Geog)*
   [PQ 3988.5.G3-PQ 3988.5.G32]
   UF French literature--Gabon authors
   BT African literature (French)
   NT Gabon poetry (French)

Gabon painting
   USE Painting, Gabon

Gabon poetry (French) *(May Subd Geog)*
   [PQ 3988.5.G3 (History)]
   [PQ 3988.5.G32 (Collections)]
   UF French poetry--Gabon authors
   BT African poetry (French)
       Gabon literature (French)

Gabon River (Gabon)
   USE Gabon Estuary (Gabon)

Gabon sculpture
   USE Sculpture, Gabon

Gabonese Republic
   USE Gabon

Gaboon
   USE Gabon

Gabra (African people)
   USE Gabbra (African people)

Gabri language *(May Subd Geog)*
   UF Gabere language
       Gaberi language
       Ngabre language
       Sara Ngabre language
       Tshere language
       Tshiri language

(May Subd Geog) = Place names may follow the heading

UF Tsiri language
BT Central African Republic--Languages
    Chad--Languages
    Chadic languages

Gabun
  USE Gabon

Gada River (Nigeria and Niger)
  USE Maradi River (Nigeria and Niger)

Gade (African people) *(May Subd Geog)*
  [DT 545.45.G33 (Ivory Coast)]
  UF Gadi (African people)
      Gede (African people)
      Code (African people)
      Kyedye (African people)
      Magwé (African people)
  BT Ethnology--Ivory Coast
      Ethnology--Nigeria

Gadi (African people)
  USE Gade (African people)

Gadyaga language
  USE Soninke language

Garat language *(May Subd Geog)*
  [PJ 9285]
  BT Ethiopian languages

Gagou (African people) *(May Subd Geog)*
  [DT 545.45.G34]
  UF Gban (African people)
      Kagou (African people)
  BT Ethnology--Ivory Coast

Gagou language
  USE Gagu language

Gagu language *(May Subd Geog)*
  [PL 8193]
  UF Gagou language
      Gban language
  BT Ivory Coast--Languages
      Kweni language
      Southern Mande languages

Gahu
  [MT 655 (Instruction and study)]
  BT Dance music--Africa, West

Gaika and Galeka, War of (South Africa),
1877-1878

  USE Ngcayecibi, War of, South Africa, 1877-1878

Gaingbe (African people)
  USE Mina (African people)

Gala (African people)
  USE Oromo (African people)

Galeka, War of (South Africa), 1877-1878
  USE Ngcayecibi, War of, South Africa, 1877-1878

Galla (African people)
  USE Oromo (African people)

Galla language
  USE Oromo language

Gallinya language
  USE Oromo language

Galloa (African people)
  USE Galwa (African people)

Galoa (African people)
  USE Galwa (African people)

Galwa (African people) *(May Subd Geog)*
  [DT 546.145.G34]
  UF Galloa (African people)
      Galoa (African people)
      Igulua (African people)
      Ngaloi (African people)
  BT Ethnology--Gabon
      Myene (African people)

Gamant language
  USE Kemant language

Gambai dialect *(May Subd Geog)*
  [PL 8197]
  UF Kabba Laka dialect
      Ngambai dialect
      Sara Gambai dialect
      Sara Ngambay dialect
  BT Chad--Languages
      Sara languages

Gambai proverbs
  USE Proverbs, Gambai

Gambaye (African people) *(May Subd Geog)*
  [DT 546.445.G]
  UF Ngambaye (African people)
  BT Ethnology--Chad

UF = Used for; BT = Broader term; RT = Related term; SA = See also; NT = Narrower term

Gambia *(Not Subd Geog)*
  [DT 509-DT 509.9]
  UF The Gambia
 --Economic conditions
  [HC 1070]
 -- --1965-
 --History
  NT Fuladu (Kingdom)
     Kaabu Empire
     Niumi (Kingdom)
 -- --**Coup d'état, 1981**
  [DT 509.8]
  BT Coups d'état--Gambia
 --Languages
  NT Diola language
     Mandjak language
     Pular dialect
     Serer language
     Wolof language
 --Literatures
 USE Gambian literature
 --Poetry
  NT Wolof poetry
 --Politics and government
 -- --1965-

Gambian cookery
 USE Cookery, Gambian

Gambian literature *(May Subd Geog)*
  [PL 8014.G]
  UF Gambia--Literatures
  BT West African literature
  NT Pular literature
     Wolof literature

Gambians *(May Subd Geog)*
  BT Ethnology--Gambia

Game-preserves
 USE Game reserves

Game reserves *(May Subd Geog)*
  UF Game-preserves
     Game sanctuaries
     Preserves, Game
     Reserves, Game
     Sanctuaries
  BT Natural areas
  RT National parks and reserves
     Wildlife refuges
 --Kenya
  NT Kora National Reserve (Kenya)
     Masai Mara Game Reserve (Kenya)
     Tsavo National Park (Kenya)

--South Africa
  NT Timbavati Game Reserve (South Africa)
--Tanzania
  NT Ngorongoro Game Control Area Reserve
(Tanzania)
     Selous Game Reserve (Tanzania)

Game sanctuaries
 USE Game reserves

Games *(May Subd Geog)*
  UF Children--Recreation
     Children's games
     Games for children
     Pastimes
  SA *subdivision* Games *under ethnic groups, e.g.,* Dan
(African people)--Games
 --Africa, Sub-Saharan
  NT Ayo (Game)
     Mancala (Game)
 --Uganda
  NT Omweso (Game)

Games for children
 USE Games

Gamsberg (South Africa) *(Not Subd Geog)*
  BT Mountains--South Africa

Gan (African people)
 USE Acoli (African people)

Gana language
 USE G//ana language

//Ganakhoe language
 USE G//ana language

Ganana River (Ethiopia and Somalia)
 USE Juba River (Ethiopia and Somalia)

Ganda (African people) *(May Subd Geog)*
  [DT 433.245.G35]
  UF Baganda (African people)
     Waganda (African people)
  BT Bantu-speaking peoples
     Ethnology--Tanzania
     Ethnology--Uganda

Ganda (Nigerian people)
 USE Gaanda (African people)

Ganda ethics
 USE Ethics, Baganda

(May Subd Geog) = Place names may follow the heading

Ganda fiction *(May Subd Geog)*
  [PL 8201.5 (History)]
  [PL 8201.6-PL 8201.8 (Collections)]
  BT Ganda literature
      Tanzania--Fiction
      Uganda--Fiction

Ganda folk songs
  USE Folk songs, Ganda

Ganda language *(May Subd Geog)*
  [PL 8201]
  UF Lu-ganda language
      Luganda language
  BT Bantu languages
      Tanzania--Languages
      Uganda--Languages
  --Etymology
  NT Obugezi (The Ganda word)

Ganda literature *(May Subd Geog)*
  [PL 8201.5 (History)]
  [PL 8201.6-PL 8201.8 (Collections)]
  BT Tanzanian literature
      Ugandan literature
  NT Ganda fiction

Ganda philosophy
  USE Philosophy, Baganda

Ganda proverbs
  USE Proverbs, Ganda

Gang language
  USE Acoli language

Ganga language
  USE Bushoong language

Ganguela language *(May Subd Geog)*
  [PL 8202]
  UF Ngangela language
  BT Angola--Languages
      Bantu languages

Ganguella (African people)
  USE Ngangela (African people)

Gaô Empire
  USE Songhai Empire

Garusi Site (Tanzania)
  USE Laetoli Site (Tanzania)

Gaya language
  USE Luo language (Kenya and Tanzania)

Gazelle River (Sudan)
  USE Bahr al-Ghazal (Sudan : River)

Gbagyi language *(May Subd Geog)*
  [PL 8203.G35]
  BT Kwa languages
      Nigeria--Languages

Gbaka (African people)
  USE Ngbaka (African people)

Gban (African people)
  USE Gagou (African people)

Gban language
  USE Gagu language

Gbanda (African people)
  USE Avikam (African people)

Gbande (Liberian people)
  USE Gbandi (Liberian people)

Gbandi (Liberian people) *(May Subd Geog)*
  [DT 630.5.G22]
  UF Bandi (Liberian people)
      Gbande (Liberian people)
      Gbassi (Liberian people)
  BT Ethnology--Liberia

Gbandi language *(May Subd Geog)*
  [PL 8204]
  UF Bandi language
  BT Liberia--Languages
      Mande languages

Gbandi language (Zaire)
  USE Ngbandi language

Gbanya (African people)
  USE Gonja (African people)

Gbanzili (African people)
  USE Banziri (African people)

Gbanziri (African people)
  USE Banziri (African people)

Gbari (African people)
  USE Gwari (African people)

Gbari language
  USE Gwari language

UF = Used for; BT = Broader term; RT = Related term; SA = See also; NT = Narrower term

Gbasa (Liberian people)
  USE Bassa (Liberian people)

Gbasa language
  USE Bassa language (Liberia)

Gbassi (Liberian people)
  USE Gbandi (Liberian people)

Gbaya (African people) *(May Subd Geog)*
  [DT 474.6.G32]
  UF Baja (African people)
      Baya (African people)
      Gbeya (African people)
      Igbaka (African people)
      Manja (African people)
  BT Ethnology--Africa, West
  NT Kara (Gbayan people)
      Ngbaka (African people)

Gbaya folk songs
  USE Folk songs, Gbaya

Gbaya language *(May Subd Geog)*
  [PL 8205]
  UF Baya language
      Gbea language
      Gbeya language
      Ngbaka Gbaya language
  BT Cameroon--Languages
      Central African Republic--Languages
      Congo (Brazzaville)--Languages
      Niger-Congo languages
  NT Yaayuwee dialect

Gbè (The Fon word)
  [PL 8164.Z9F6]
  BT Fon dialect--Etymology

Gbe language
  USE Ewe language

Gbea language
  USE Gbaya language

Gbeya (African people)
  USE Gbaya (African people)

Gbeya language
  USE Gbaya language

Gboare (African people)
  USE Bachama (African people)

Gcaleka, War of (South Africa), 1877-1878
  USE Ngcayccibi, War of, South Africa, 1877-1878

Gciriku language
  USE Diriku language

Gdebo language
  USE Grebo language

Ge (African people)
  USE Mina (African people)

Ge dialect
  USE Mina dialect

Geba River *(Not Subd Geog)*
  BT Rivers--Guinea
      Rivers--Guinea-Bissau
      Rivers--Senegal

Gebel 'Uweinat (Sudan)
  USE 'Uwaynat Mountain (Sudan)

Gede (African people)
  USE Gade (African people)

Gedebo language
  USE Grebo language

Gedeo language *(May Subd Geog)*
  [PL 2501]
  UF Darasa language
      Derasa language
      Derasanya language
      Derasinya language
      Deresa language
  BT Cushitic languages
      Sidamo languages

Geez language
  USE Ethiopic language

Geleba (African people)
  USE Dasanetch (African people)

Gemjek (African people) *(May Subd Geog)*
  [DT 571.G]
  BT Ethnology--Cameroon

Gen (African people)
  USE Mina (African people)

Gen dialect
  USE Mina dialect

(May Subd Geog) = Place names may follow the heading

Gen Movement *(May Subd Geog)*
  [BX 809.G45 (Catholic Church)]
  [BV 4487.G38 (General)]
  BT Catholic Church--Zaire
     Youth--Zaire--Religious life

Gendarmes
  USE Police

General Strike, Transvaal, South Africa, 1913
  [HD 5442]
  UF Transvaal (South Africa)--General
Strike, 1913
  BT Strikes and lockouts--South Africa

General Strike, Zanzibar, Zanzibar, 1948
  [HD 5441.3.Z9]
  UF Zanzibar (Zanzibar)--General Strike,
1948
  BT Strikes and lockouts--Tanzania

Gengbe dialect
  USE Mina dialect

Genya (African people) *(May Subd Geog)*
  [DT 650.G46]
  UF Baenya (African people)
     Bagenya (African people)
     Eenya (African people)
     Enya (African people)
     Ouénya (African people)
     Vouaghénia (African people)
     Wagenia (African people)
     Waggenia (African people)
     Wainya (African people)
     Wenya (African people)
  BT Bantu-speaking peoples
     Ethnology--Zaire

Genya language
  USE Enya language

Geographical atlases
  USE Atlases

Geography *(May Subd Geog)*
  Here and with geographical subdivisions are enterd
works on the discipline of geography. Comprehensive
geographical works about a place, including general
geography textbooks, are entered under headings of the
type [Place]--Geography. Works limited to
descriptive information including those derived from
travel narratives or intended to assist travelers are
entered under the name of the countries, etc. with the
subdivision Description and travel or

Description and travel--Guidebooks; or under names of
cities with the subdivision Description or Description-
-Guide-books.
  NT Military geography
  --Atlases
  USE Atlases

Geography, Military
  USE Military geography

Geology *(May Subd Geog)*
  UF Geoscience
  NT Formations (Geology)
     Rifts (Geology)
  --Africa
  [QE 320]
  --Mali
  [QE 331.M27]

George (Lusaka, Zambia) *(Not Subd Geog)*
  UF Lusaka (Zambia). George

Geoscience
  USE Geology

Gere (Kru-speaking African people)
  USE Wobe (African people)

Gere (Mande-speaking African people)
  USE Dan (African people)

Gere language (Kru)
  USE Wobo language

Gere language (Mande)
  USE Dan language

German East Africa *(Not Subd Geog)*
  [DT 436-DT 449]
  Here are entered works on the former German colony whose
territory corresponds to present-day Rwanda, Burundi, the
continental portion of Tanzania, and a small section of
Mozambique. Works on this territory for the period after
1919 when the colony ceased to exist are entered under one
or more of the names, as appropriate, of the countries now
occupying the territory.
  UF Africa, German East
     Deutsch Ost-Afrika

German Southwest Africa
  USE Namibia

German West Africa
  USE Cameroon

UF = Used for; BT = Broader term; RT = Related term; SA = See also; NT = Narrower term

Germany *(Not Subd Geog)*
--Colonies
  BT Colonies
-- --Administration
  UF Germany--Colonies--Politics and
government
-- --Boundaries *(May Subd Geog)*
-- --Commerce *(May Subd Geog)*
-- --Constitutional history
-- --Constitutional law
-- --Defenses
-- --Description and travel
-- --Discovery and exploration
-- --Economic conditions
-- --Economic policy
-- --Emigration and immigration
-- --Geography *(Not Subd Geog)*
-- --History
-- --Industries
-- --Manufactures
-- --Native races
  USE Indigenous peoples--Germany--Colonies
-- --Officials and employees
-- --Politics and government
  USE Germany--Colonies--Administration
-- --Population
-- --Public lands
-- --Public works
-- --Race relations
-- --Religion
-- --Religious life and customs
-- --Rural conditions
-- --Social conditions
-- --Social life and customs
-- --Social policy
-- --Africa

Gesinan (African people)
  USE Harari (African people)

Gesu (African people)
  USE Gisu (African people)

Gewi (African people)
  USE G/wi (African people)

Gezira (Sudan) *(Not Subd Geog)*

Ghana *(Not Subd Geog)*
  [DT 510-DT 512]
  UF Gold Coast
      Togoland (British)
--Antiquities
  NT Bono Manso Site (Ghana)
--Drama
  NT Akan drama

--Economic conditions
  [HC 1060]
-- --To 1957
-- --1957-1979
-- --1979-
--Foreign relations *(May Subd Geog)*
-- --1957-
--History
-- --To 1957
  NT Ashanti (Kingdom)
      Ashanti War, 1822-1831
      Ashanti War, 1873-1874
      Ashanti War, 1900
      Denkyira (Kingdom)
-- --Portuguese rule, 1469-1637
  UF Mina, Portuguese
      Portuguese Mina
-- --Danish Settlements, 1659-1850
  UF Danish Settlements, Ghana, 1659-1850
  BT Denmark--Colonies--Africa
-- --1957-
  [DT 512]
-- --Coup d'état, 1966
  BT Coups d'état--Ghana
-- --Coup d'état, 1972
  BT Coups d'état--Ghana
-- --Coup d'état, 1979
  BT Coups d'état--Ghana
-- --Coup d'état, 1981
  BT Coups d'état--Ghana
--Languages
  NT Adangme language
      Akan language
      Buli language
      Dagari language
      Dagomba language
      Ewe language
      Fanti language
      Ga language
      Gonja language
      Gwa dialect (Ghana)
      Hanga language (Ghana)
      Kasem language
      Konkomba language
      Kussassi language
      Lefana language
      Mampruli language
      Mina dialect
      Mo language (Ghana and Ivory Coast)
      Mossi languages
      Nankanse language
      Nchumburu language
      Nkunya language
      Nzima language
      Sisala language
      Tampulma language

(May Subd Geog) = Place names may follow the heading

NT Tobote language
     Twi language
     Vagala language
--Literatures
USE Ghanaian literature
--Poetry
NT Akan poetry
     Ewe poetry
     Fanti poetry
--Politics and government
-- --To 1957
-- --1957-1979
-- --1979-
-Social conditions
-- --17th century

Ghana Empire *(Not Subd Geog)*
  [DT 532.15]
  BT Africa, West--History--To 1884

Ghanaian art
  USE Art, Ghanaian

Ghanaian arts
  USE Arts, Ghanaian

Ghanaian authors
  USE Authors, Ghanaian

Ghanaian children's stories (English)
  USE Children's stories, Ghanaian (English)

Ghanaian children's writing (English)
  USE Children's writings, Ghanaian
(English)

Ghanaian college prose (English)
  USE College prose, Ghanaian (English)

Ghanaian college verse (English)
  USE College verse, Ghanaian (English)

Ghanaian fiction (English) *(May Subd Geog)*
  [PR 9379.4 (History)]
  [PR 9379.8 (Collections)]
  UF English fiction--Ghanaian authors
  BT Ghanaian literature (English)
     West African fiction (English)
  NT Short stories, Ghanaian (English)

Ghanaian literature *(May Subd Geog)*
  [PL 8014.G]
  UF Ghana--Literatures
  BT West African literature
  NT Akan literature
     Ewe literature

NT Fanti literature

Ghanaian literature (English) *(May Subd Geog)*
  [PR 9379]
  UF English literature--Ghanaian authors
  BT West African literature (English)
  NT Children's stories, Ghanaian (English)
     Children's writings, Ghanaian (English)
     Ghanaian fiction (English)
     Ghanaian poetry (English)
     Ghanaian prose literature (English)

Ghanaian newspapers *(May Subd Geog)*
  [PN 5499.G5]
  UF Newspapers, Ghanaian

Ghanaian periodicals *(May Subd Geog)*
  [PN 5499.G5]
  UF Periodicals, Ghanaian

Ghanaian poetry (English) *(May Subd Geog)*
  [PR 9379.2 (History)]
  [PR 9379.6-PR 9379.65 (Collections)]
  UF English poetry--Ghanaian authors
  BT Ghanaian literature (English)
     West African poetry (English)
  NT College verse, Ghanaian (English)
     Revolutionary poetry, Ghanaian (English)

Ghanaian prose literature (English) *(May Subd Geog)*
  [PR 9379.4 (History)]
  [PR 9379.8 (Collections)]
  UF English prose literature--Ghanaian authors
  BT Ghanaian literature (English)
  NT College prose, Ghanaian (English)

Ghanaian revolutionary poetry (English)
  USE Revolutionary poetry, Ghanaian (English)

Ghanaian short stories (English)
  USE Short stories, Ghanaian (English)

Ghanaian students *(May Subd Geog)*
  BT Students

Ghanaian wit and humor, Pictorial *(May Subd Geog)*
  [NC 1740.G]
  UF Wit and humor, Pictorial (Ghanaian)

Ghanaians *(May Subd Geog)*
  BT Ethnology--Ghana

Ghazal, Bahr al- (Sudan : River)
  USE Bahr al-Ghazal (Sudan : River)

UF = Used for; BT = Broader term; RT = Related term; SA = See also; NT = Narrower term

Ghazal River (Sudan)
USE Bahr al-Chazal (Sudan : River)

Ghomala language
USE Bandjoun language

Ghoya (African people) *(May Subd Geog)*
[DT 900 : old class]
[DT 1768.G56 : new class]
UF Kubung (African people)
Leghoya (African people)
BT Bantu-speaking peoples
Ethnology--South Africa

Gi-Tonga language
USE Tongo language (Inhambane)

Giaka (African people)
USE Yaka (African people)

Gibbe River (Ethiopia) *(Not Subd Geog)*
UF Gibe River (Ethiopia)
BT Rivers--Ethiopia

Gibe River (Ethiopia)
USE Gibbe River (Ethiopia)

Gien language
USE Tchien language

Gihi language
USE Kissi language

Gii language
USE Kissi language

Gikuyu (African people)
USE Kikuyu (African people)

Gikuyu language
USE Kikuyu language

Gikwezo language
USE Kwese language

Gimarra (African people)
USE Gimira (African people)

Gimbala (African people)
USE Mbala (African people)

Gimbala language
USE Mbala language (Bandundu region, Zaire)

Gimbunda language
USE Mbunda language (Zambia)

Gimini (African people)
USE Djimini (African people)

Gimini language
USE Djimini language

Gimira (African people) *(May Subd Geog)*
[DT 380.4.G35]
UF Chimira (African people)
Gimarra (African people)
BT Cushites
Ethnology--Ethiopia

Gio (African people)
USE Dan (African people)

Gio language
USE Dan language

Gipende language
USE Pende language

Giriama (African people)
USE Giryama (African people)

Giriama language
USE Giryama language

Giryama (African people) *(May Subd Geog)*
[DT 433.545.G55]
UF Agiryama (African people)
Giriama (African people)
Kigiriama (African people)
Wagiliama (African people)
BT Ethnology--Kenya
Nika (African people)
--Funeral customs and rites
UF Funeral rites and ceremonies, Giryama
(African people)
--Rites and ceremonies

Giryama language *(May Subd Geog)*
[PL 8207.G47]
UF Giriama language
Kigiryama language
BT Kenya--Languages
Nika language

Giryama sculpture
USE Sculpture, Giryama

(May Subd Geog) = Place names may follow the heading

Gishwati (Rwanda) *(Not Subd Geog)*
  UF Forêt de Gishwati (Rwanda)
      Massif forestier de Gishwati (Rwanda)
  BT Forests and forestry--Rwanda
      Mountains--Rwanda

Gisi language
  USE Kissi language

Gisiga language *(May Subd Geog)*
  [PL 8207.G5]
  UF Guissiga language
  BT Cameroon--Languages
      Chadic languages

Gisira (African people)
  USE Shira (African people)

Gisira language
  USE Shira language

Gisu (African people) *(May Subd Geog)*
  [DT 433.245.G57]
  UF Bagesu (African people)
      Bagishu (African people)
      Gesu (African people)
  BT Bantu-speaking peoples
      Ethnology--Uganda
      Kavirondo (African people)

Gisu language *(May Subd Geog)*
  [PL 8207.G55]
  UF Lugisu language
      Lumasaaba language
      Masaba language
  BT Bantu languages
      Uganda--Languages
  NT Bukusu dialect

Gitonga language
  USE Tonga language (Inhambane)

Giuba River (Ethiopia and Somalia)
  USE Juba River (Ethiopia and Somalia)

Giur language
  USE Lwo language (Sudan)

Gizi language
  USE Kissi language

Gizii (African people)
  USE Gusii (African people)

Gizima language
  USE Kissi language

Gizo (Legendary character)
  USE Anansi (Legendary character)

Glavda language *(May Subd Geog)*
  [PL 8207.G6]
  BT Chadic languages
      Mandara language
      Nigeria--Languages

Glebo (African people)
  USE Grebo (African people)

Glebo language
  USE Grebo language

Gmbwaga (African people)
  USE Ngbaka (African people)

Go dialect (Ivory Coast)
  USE Godye dialect

Goa (African people)
  USE Songola (African people)

Goba (Shona-speaking people)
  USE Gova (Shona-speaking people)

Goba language
  USE Mbukushu language

Gober (African people)
  USE Gobir

Gobir *(May Subd Geog)*
  [DT 515.45.G]
  UF Gober (African people)
      Gobirawa (African people)
  BT Ethnology--Nigeria
      Hausa (African people)

Gobirawa (African people)
  USE Gobir

God (African religion)
  [BL 2462.5]
  BT Africa--Religion

Goddesses *(May Subd Geog)*
  UF Female gods
  BT Gods

Goddesses, Yoruba *(Not Subd Geog)*
  [BL 2480.Y6]
  UF Yoruba goddesses
  NT Oya (Yoruba deity)

UF = Used for; BT = Broader term; RT = Related term; SA = See also; NT = Narrower term

Gode (African people)
  USE Gade (African people)

Godia dialect
  USE Godye dialect

Godianism (Cult) *(May Subd Geog)*
  [BL 2470.N5]
  BT Cults--Nigeria

Godié dialect
  USE Godye dialect

Gods
  UF Deities
  BT Religion, Primitive
  RT Mythology
      Religions
  NT Goddesses

Gods, African *(May Subd Geog)*
  [BL 2462.5-BL 2466]
  UF African gods
 --South Africa
  NT Mwari (Shona deity)
 --Uganda
  NT Nyabingi (African deity)
 --Zimbabwe
  NT Mwari (Shona deity)

Gods, Igbo *(May Subd Geog)*
  [BL 2480.I2]
  UF Igbo gods
  BT Igbo (African people)--Religion
  NT Chi (Igbo deity)

Gods, Krachi *(May Subd Geog)*
  [BL 2480.K]
  UF Krachi gods
  BT Krachi (African people)--Religion
  NT Dente (African deity)

Gods, Rundi *(May Subd Geog)*
  [BL 2480.R]
  UF Rundi gods
  BT Rundi (African people)--Religion
  NT Imana (Rundi deity)

Gods, Yoruba *(May Subd Geog)*
  [BL 2480.Y6]
  UF Yoruba gods
  BT Yoruba (African people)--Religion
  NT Ogun (Yoruba deity)

Gods, Zela *(May Subd Geog)*
  [BL 2480.Z]
  UF Zela gods
  BT Zela (African people)--Religion
  NT Yambe (Zela deity)

Godye dialect *(May Subd Geog)*
  [PL 8075.B5795.G6]
  UF Go dialect (Ivory Coast)
      Godia dialect
      Godié dialect
  BT Bete language
      Ivory Coast--Languages

Gogo (African people) *(May Subd Geog)*
  [DT 443.3.G]
  UF Chigogo (African people)
      Wagogo (African people)
  BT Bantu-speaking peoples
      Ethnology--Tanzania

Gogo language *(May Subd Geog)*
  [PL 8208]
  UF Chigogo language
  BT Bantu languages
      Tanzania--Languages

Gola (African people) *(May Subd Geog)*
  [DT 630.5.G6 (Liberia)]
  [DT 516.45.G (Sierra Leone)]
  BT Ethnology--Liberia
      Ethnology--Sierra Leone

Gola language *(May Subd Geog)*
  [PL 8211]
  UF Gora language
      Gura language
  BT Liberia--Languages
      Niger-Congo languages
      Sierra Leone--Languages

Gold Coast
  USE Ghana

Gold coins *(May Subd Geog)*
  UF Coins, Gold
 --South Africa
  [CJ 3948]
  RT Coins, South African
  NT Burgerspond (Coin)
      Krugerrand (Coin)

Gold discoveries
  USE Gold mines and mining

(May Subd Geog) = Place names may follow the heading

Gold mines and mining *(May Subd Geog)*
  UF Gold discoveries
       Gold rushes
 --**South Africa**
  [DT 745 : old class]
  NT Malmani gold fields

Gold rushes
  USE Gold mines and mining

Goldweights, Akan
  [NK 7889.6.G5]
  UF Akan goldweights
  NT Goldweights, Ashanti

Goldweights, Ashanti
  [NK 7889.A8]
  UF Ashanti goldweights
  BT Goldweights, Akan

Gole (African people)
  USE Zarma (African people)

Golfe de Tadjoura (Djibouti)
  USE Tadjoura, Gulf of (Djibouti)

Gólo language *(May Subd Geog)*
  BT Banda languages
       Sudan--Languages

Gomaro (African people)
  USE Kaffa (African people)

Gombe Stream National Park (Tanzania) *(Not Subd Geog)*
  UF Gombe Stream Reserve (Tanzania)
  BT National parks and reserves--Tanzania

Gombe Stream Reserve (Tanzania)
  USE Gombe Stream National Park (Tanzania)

Gonga (African people) *(May Subd Geog)*
  [DT 380.4.G66]
  BT Ethnology--Ethiopia

Gonja (African people) *(May Subd Geog)*
  [DT 510.43.G65]
  UF Gbanya (African people)
       Gonya (African people)
       Ngbanya (African people)
       Ngbanyito (African people)
  BT Ethnology--Ghana

Gonja language *(May Subd Geog)*
  [PL 8215]
  UF Guang language

  BT Ghana--Languages
       Kwa languages
  NT Nchumburu language
       Nkunya language

Gonja Region (Ghana) *(Not Subd Geog)*

Gonya (African people)
  USE Gonja (African people)

Good Hope, Cape of (South Africa : Cape)
  USE Cape of Good Hope (South Africa : Cape)

Goor languages
  USE Gur languages

Gora language
  USE Gola language

Gordon Relief Expedition, 1884-1885
  [DT 156.6]
  UF Khartoum Relief Expedition, 1884-1885
  BT Sudan--History--1862-1899

Gorges *(May Subd Geog)*
  UF Ravines
  BT Landforms
 --**Tanzania**
  NT Olduvai Gorge (Tanzania)

Gori language
  USE Laal language

Goro dialect
  USE Kagoro dialect

Gorona (African people)
  USE Korana (African people)

Gotera Site (Ethiopia) *(Not Subd Geog)*
  BT Ethiopia--Antiquities

Goudini Formation (South Africa) *(Not Subd Geog)*
  UF Goudini Sandstone Member (South Africa)
  BT Formations (Geology)--South Africa

Goudini Sandstone Member (South Africa)
  USE Goudini Formation (South Africa)

Gouin (African people) *(May Subd Geog)*
  [DT 555.45.G (Burkina Faso)]
  [DT 582.45.G68 (Togo)]
  UF Guen (African people)
       Guin (African people)
       Gwin (African people)
       Mbouin (African people)   *(Continued)*

UF = Used for; BT = Broader term; RT = Related term; SA = See also; NT = Narrower term

Gouin (African people) *(Continued)*
BT Ethnology--Burkina Faso
  Ethnology--Togo
  Senufo (African people)

Goulbin Maradi (Nigeria and Niger)
USE Maradi River (Nigeria and Niger)

Goum (African people)
USE Gun (African people)

Goun (African people)
USE Gun (African people)

Goura (Musical instrument)
[ML 544]
BT Musical instruments--Africa

Gouraghie (African people)
USE Gurage (African people)

Gourague language
USE Gurage language

Gourmantché (African people)
USE Gurma (African people)

Gourmantché language
USE Gurma language

Gouro (African people)
USE Guro (African people)

Gouro language
USE Kweni language

Gourounsi (African people)
USE Gurunsi (African people)

Gourounsi languages
USE Grusi languages

Gova (Shona-speaking people) *(May Subd Geog)*
[DT 963.42 (Zambia : old class)]
[DT 3058.G79 (Zambia : new class)]
[DT 962.42 (Zimbabwe : old class)]
[DT 2913.G68 (Zimbabwe : new class)]
UF Cova (Shona-speaking people)
  Goba (Shona-speaking people)
BT Ethnology--Zambia
  Ethnology--Zimbabwe
  Shona (African people)

Gova language
USE Mbukushu language

Government, Tribal
USE Tribal government

Government buildings
USE Public buildings

Government documents
USE Government publications

Government employee strikes
USE Strikes and lockouts--Civil service

Government employees
USE Civil service

Government publications *(May Subd Geog)*
UF Documents, Government
  Government documents
  Official publications
  Public documents
--Africa
[J 705-J 855]
--Africa, West
[J 741]
--Great Britain
-- --Colonies
UF Great Britain--Colonies--Government
publications

Government service
USE Civil service

Graduates, College
USE College graduates

Grafil languages
USE Bamileke languages

Grassfield languages
USE Bamileke languages

Grasshoppers
USE Locusts

Grasslands *(May Subd Geog)*
Here are entered works on the natural regions of the
world in which the characteristic plants are grasses and
forbs.
NT Savannas
--Africa, Southern
NT Veld

Grasslands Bantu languages *(May Subd Geog)*
[PL 8219]
UF Bantu languages, Grasslands
  Grasslands languages

(May Subd Geog) = Place names may follow the heading

UF   Plateau Bantoid languages
BT   Benue-Congo languages
     Cameroon--Languages
NT   Limbum language
     Yamba language (Cameroon and Nigeria)

Grasslands languages
  USE   Grasslands Bantu languages

Graves
  USE   Cemeteries
        Funeral rites and ceremonies

Graveyards
  USE   Cemeteries

Great Brak River (South Africa) *(Not Subd Geog)*
  UF   Groot-Brakrivier (South Africa)
       Grootbrakrivier (South Africa)
  BT   Rivers--South Africa

Great Brak River Estuary (South Africa) *(Not Subd Geog)*
  BT   Estuaries--South Africa

Great Britain *(Not Subd Geog)*
--Civilization
  NT   South Africa--Civilization--British influences
--Colonies
  BT   Colonies
-- --Administration
  UF   Great Britain--Colonies--Politics and government
-- --Boundaries *(May Subd Geog)*
-- --Commerce *(May Subd Geog)*
-- --Constitutional history
-- --Constitutional law
-- --Defenses
-- --Description and travel
-- --Discovery and exploration
-- --Economic conditions
-- --Economic policy
-- --Education
  USE   Education--Great Britain--Colonies
-- --Emigration and immigration
-- --Geography *(Not Subd Geog)*
-- --Government publications
  USE   Government publications--Great Britain--Colonies
-- --History
-- --Industries
-- --Manufactures
-- --Native races
  USE   Indigenous peoples--Great Britain--Colonies

-- --Officials and employees
-- --Politics and government
  USE   Great Britain--Colonies--Administration
-- --Population
-- --Public lands
-- --Public works
-- --Race relations
-- --Religion
-- --Religious life and customs
-- --Rural conditions
-- --Social conditions
-- --Social life and customs
-- --Social policy
-- --Africa

Great Karoo (South Africa)
  USE   Great Karroo (South Africa)

Great Karroo (South Africa) *(Not Subd Geog)*
  [DT 846.C73 : old class]
  [DT 2400.G84 : new class]
  UF   Central Karroo (South Africa)
       Great Karoo (South Africa)
       Groot Karroo (South Africa)
       Karoo, Great (South Africa)
       Karroo, Great (South Africa)
  BT   Plateaus--South Africa

Great Rift Valley *(Not Subd Geog)*
  UF   Rift Valley
  RT   Rifts (Geology)--Africa
       Valleys--Africa

Great Trek
  USE   South Africa--History--Great Trek, 1836-1840

Great Uhuru Railway
  USE   Tan-Zam Railway

Great Zimbabwe (City) *(Not Subd Geog)*
  [DT 962.9.Z5 : old class]
  [DT 3025.G84 : new class]
  UF   Zimbabwe, Great (City)
  BT   Cities and towns, Ruined, extinct, etc.--Zimbabwe
       Zimbabwe--Antiquities

Greater Antilles
  USE   West Indies

Grebo (African people) *(May Subd Geog)*
  [DT 545.45.G (Ivory Coast)]
  [DT 630.5.G6 (Liberia)]
  UF   Glebo (African people)
       Gweabo (African people)   *(Continued)*

UF = Used for; BT = Broader term; RT = Related term; SA = See also; NT = Narrower term

Grebo (African people)   *(Continued)*
    UF Krebo (African people)
    BT Ethnology--Ivory Coast
        Ethnology--Liberia
        Kru (African people)

Grebo language *(May Subd Geog)*
    [PL 8221]
    UF Gdebo language
        Gedebo language
        Glebo language
        Krebo language
    BT Kru languages
        Liberia--Languages

Grebo women
    USE Women, Grebo

Greece *(Not Subd Geog)*
  --Civilization
    UF Civilization, Greek
  -- --African influences
    BT Africa--Civilization
  --Colonies
    BT Colonies
  -- --Africa

Griots
    USE Storytellers

Griquas *(May Subd Geog)*
    [DT 764.G7 : old class]
    [DT 1768.G74 : new class]
    UF Bastaards
    BT Colored people (South Africa)
        Ethnology--South Africa
        Khoikhoi (African people)
        Miscegenation

Groot-Brakrivier (South Africa)
    USE Great Brak River (South Africa)

Groot Karroo (South Africa)
    USE Great Karroo (South Africa)

Grootbrakrivier (South Africa)
    USE Great Brak River (South Africa)

Grootdraai Dam (South Africa) *(Not Subd Geog)*
    UF Grootdraaidam (South Africa)
    BT Dams--South Africa

Grootdraaidam (South Africa)
    USE Grootdraai Dam (South Africa)

Groote Schuur (Cape Town, South Africa) *(Not Subd Geog)*
    BT Dwellings--South Africa
        Prime ministers--South Africa--Dwellings

Grottos
    USE Caves

Groups (Geology)
    USE Groups (Stratigraphy)

Groups (Stratigraphy) *(May Subd Geog)*
    UF Groups (Geology)
        Groups of formations (Stratigraphy)
        Megagroups (Stratigraphy)
        Stratigraphic groups
        Supergroups (Stratigraphy)
    BT Landforms
  --Africa, Southern
    NT Karroo Supergroup
  --South Africa
    NT West Rand Group (South Africa)

Groups of formations (Stratigraphy)
    USE Groups (Stratigraphy)

Gruinse (African people)
    USE Gurunsi (African people)

Grunshi (African people)
    USE Gurunsi (African people)

Grusi (African people)
    USE Gurunsi (African people)

Grusi languages *(May Subd Geog)*
    [PL 8223.G9]
    UF Gourounsi languages
        Grussi languages
        Gurumsi languages
        Gurunsi dialects
    BT Africa, West--Languages
        Gur languages
    NT Kasem language
        Mo language (Ghana and Ivory Coast)
        Sisala language
        Tampulma language
        Vagala language

Grussi (African people)
    USE Gurunsi (African people)

Grussi languages
    USE Grusi languages

(May Subd Geog) = Place names may follow the heading

Guang language
USE Gonja language

Gude language *(May Subd Geog)*
UF Cheke language
Mapodi language
Mapuda language
Shede language
BT Chadic languages
Nigeria--Languages

Gudela (African people)
USE Hadiya (African people)

Guen (African people)
USE Gouin (African people)

Guen dialect
USE Mina dialect

Guere (Kru-speaking African people)
USE Wobe (African people)

Guéré (Mande-speaking African people)
USE Dan (African people)

Guere language (Kru)
USE Wobe language

Guere language (Mande)
USE Dan language

Guerrillas *(May Subd Geog)*
UF Partisans
BT Insurgency
National liberation movements
--Africa, Portuguese-speaking
[DT 602]
--Africa, Southern
[DT 733]

Guerze (African people)
USE Kpelle (African people)

Guerzé language
USE Kpelle language

Guest workers
USE Alien labor

Guha (African people)
USE Holoholo (African people)

/Guikhoe language
USE G/wi language

Guin (African people)
USE Gouin (African people)

Guiné-Bissau
USE Guinea-Bissau

Guinea *(Not Subd Geog)*
[DT 543-DT 543.9]
UF French Guinea
Guinea, French
Guinée
--Antiquities
NT Niani (Guinea)
--Economic conditions
[HC 1030]
-- --1958-1984
-- --1984-
--Foreign relations *(May Subd Geog)*
-- --1958-
--History
-- --Portuguese Invasion, 1970
[DT 543.8]
UF Portuguese Invasion of Guinea, 1970
BT Guinea-Bissau--History, Military
-- --Coup d'état, 1984
[DT 543.825]
BT Coups d'état--Guinea
Languages
NT Badyaranke language
Balante language
Bassari language
Diola language
Kissi language
Kono language
Kpelle language
Limba language
Loko language
Loma language
Mandjak language
Mankanya language
Mano language
Susu language
--Literatures
USE Guinean literature
--Poetry
NT Kpelle poetry
--Politics and government
-- --To 1958
-- --1958-1984
-- --1984-

Guinea, French
USE Guinea

UF = Used for; BT = Broader term; RT = Related term; SA = See also; NT = Narrower term

Guinea, Gulf of *(Not Subd Geog)*
  UF Gulf of Guinea
  BT Bays--Africa, West

Guinea, Portuguese
  USE Guinea-Bissau

Guinea, Spanish
  USE Equatorial Guinea

Guinea-Bissau *(Not Subd Geog)*
  [DT 613-DT 613.9]
  UF Guinea, Portuguese
      Guiné-Bissau
      Guinée-Bissau
      Portuguese Guinea
 --**Economic conditions**
  [HC 1080]
 -- --**To 1974**
 -- --**1974-**
 --**History**
  NT Kaabu Empire
 -- --**Revolution, 1963-1974**
  [DT 613.78]
 -- --**Coup d'état, 1980**
  BT Coups d'état--Guinea-Bissau
 --**History, Military**
  NT Guinea--History--Portuguese Invasion, 1970
 --**Languages**
  NT Badyaranke language
      Crioulo language
 --**Politics and government**
 -- --**To 1974**
 -- --**1974-**

Guinea Current *(Not Subd Geog)*
  [GC 296.G8]

Guinean literature *(May Subd Geog)*
  [PL 8014.G]
  UF Guinea--Literatures
  BT West African literature
  NT Kpelle literature

Guinean literature (French) *(May Subd Geog)*
  [PQ 3988.5.G8 (History)]
  [PQ 3988.5.G82 (Collections)]
  UF French literature--Guinean authors
  BT West African literature (French)
  NT Guinean poetry (French)

Guinean poetry (French) *(May Subd Geog)*
  [PQ 3988.5.G8 (History)
  [PQ 3988.5.G82 (Collections)]
  UF French poetry--Guinean authors

  BT Guinean literature (French)
      West African poetry (French)
  NT Revolutionary poetry, Guinean (French)

Guinean revolutionary poetry (French)
  USE Revolutionary poetry, Guinean (French)

Guinée
  USE Guinea

Guinée-Bissau
  USE Guinea-Bissau

Guingbe (African people)
  USE Mina (African people)

Guissiga language
  USE Gisiga language

Guiziga (African people) *(May Subd Geog)*
  [DT 571.G]
  BT Ethnology--Cameroon

Gula language (Lake Iro, Chad)
  USE Kùláál language

Gulbin Maradi (Nigeria and Niger)
  USE Maradi River (Nigeria and Niger)

Guleo (African people)
  USE Kulebele (African people)

Gulf of Guniea
  USE Guinea, Gulf of

Gulf of Tadjoura (Djibouti)
  USE Tadjoura, Gulf of (Djibouti)

Gulf of Tajura (Djibouti)
  USE Tadjoura, Gulf of (Djibouti)

Gulfs
  USE Bays

Gulma (African people)
  USE Gurma (African people)

Gulmance language
  USE Gurma language

Gulmanceba (African people)
  USE Gurma (African people)

Gun (African people) *(May Subd Geog)*
  [DT 541.45.G85]
  UF Goum (African people)

(May Subd Geog) = Place names may follow the heading

UF Goun (African people)
BT Ethnology--Benin

Gun architecture
  USE Architecture, Gun

Gundo (African people)
  USE Nkundu (African people)

Gungu (African people)
  USE Nyoro (African people)

Gunu language *(May Subd Geog)*
  [PL 8221.6]
  UF Nugunu language
  RT Bantu languages
      Cameroon--Languages

Gur languages *(May Subd Geog)*
  [PL 8222]
  UF Goor languages
      Voltaic languages
  BT Niger-Congo languages
  NT Bobo languages
      Buli language
      Djimini language
      Dogon language
      Dompago dialect
      Grusi languages
      Gurma language
      Hanga language (Ghana)
      Karaboro language
      Konkomba language
      Kulango language
      Kurumba language
      Lele dialect
      Lobi dialects
      Lorhon language
      Mampruli language
      Mossi languages
      Nankanse language
      Senufo languages
      Somba language
      Tagbana language
      Tem language
      Tobote language
      Tusia language
      Vige language

Gura language
  USE Gola language

Gurage (African people) *(May Subd Geog)*
  [DT 380.4.G85]
  UF Gouraghie (African people)

UF Guraghe (African people)
    Guragie (African people)
    Guraque (African people)
BT Ethnology--Ethiopia

Gurage language *(May Subd Geog)*
  [PJ 9288]
  UF Gouraque language
  BT Ethiopian languages

Guraghe (African people)
  USE Gurage (African people)

Guragie (African people)
  USE Gurage (African people)

Guraque (African people)
  USE Gurage (African people)

Gurenne language
  USE Nankanse language

Guresha language
  USE Buli language

Gurma (African people) *(May Subd Geog)*
  [DT 541.45.G87 (Benin)]
  [DT 555.45.G85 (Burkina Faso)]
  UF Courmantché (African people)
      Gurma (African people)
      Gulmanceba (African people)
  BT Ethnology--Benin
      Ethnology--Burkina Faso

Gurma language *(May Subd Geog)*
  [PL 8223.G8]
  UF Gourmantché language
      Gulmance language
  BT Benin--Languages
      Burkina Faso--Languages
      Gur languages
  NT Moba language

Gurma philosophy
  USE Philosophy, Gurma

Guro (African people) *(May Subd Geog)*
  [DT 545.45.G87]
  UF Gouro (African people)
      Kweni (African people)
      Lo (African people)
  BT Ethnology--Ivory Coast

Guro language
  USE Kweni language

UF = Used for; BT = Broader term; RT = Related term; SA = See also; NT = Narrower term

Gurumsi (African people)
  USE Gurunsi (African people)

Gurumsi languages
  USE Grusi languages

Gurune language
  USE Nankanse language

Gurunga (African people)
  USE Gurunsi (African people)

Gurunsi (African people) *(May Subd Geog)*
  [DT 555.45.G87]
  UF Gourounsi (African people)
      Gruinse (African people)
      Grunshi (African people)
      Grusi (African people)
      Grussi (African people)
      Gurumsi (African people)
      Gurunga (African people)
  BT Ethnology--Burkina Faso
  NT Builsa (African people)

Gurunsi dialects
  USE Grusi languages

Gusii (African people) *(May Subd Geog)*
  [DT 433.545.G86]
  UF Gizii (African people)
      Kisii (African people)
      Kosova (African people)
  BT Bantu-speaking peoples
      Ethnology--Kenya

Gusii language *(May Subd Geog)*
  [PL 8224]
  UF Ekegusii language
      Guzii language
      Kisii language
  BT Bantu languages
      Kenya--Languages

Gusii women
  USE Women, Gusii

Guyuk dialect *(May Subd Geog)*
  [PL 8459.L5595G8]
  BT Longuda language
      Nigeria--Languages

Guzii language
  USE Gusii language

Gwa dialect (Ghana) *(May Subd Geog)*
  [PL 8215.95.G9]
  UF Anum dialect
  BT Ghana--Languages
      Kwa languages

Gwaka (African people)
  USE Ngbaka (African people)

Gwali language
  USE Gwari language

Gwamba language
  USE Tsonga language

Gwandara language *(May Subd Geog)*
  [PL 8226]
  UF Kwandara language
  BT Chadic languages
      Nigeria--Languages

Gwari (African people) *(May Subd Geog)*
  [DT 515.45.G83]
  UF Gbari (African people)
  BT Ethnology--Nigeria

Gwari language *(May Subd Geog)*
  [PL 8227]
  UF Gbari language
      Gwali language
  BT Kwa languages
      Nigeria--Languages

Gwazum language
  USE Ngizim language

Gwe language
  USE Sukuma language

Gweabo (African people)
  USE Grebo (African people)

Gweabo language
  USE Jabo language

Gwembe (Zambesi people)
  USE Tonga (Zambesi people)

Gwi language
  USE G/wi language

Gwin (African people)
  USE Gouin (African people)

Gworok dialect
  USE Kagoro dialect

(May Subd Geog) = Place names may follow the heading

Gxon language
USE !Xo language

Gyo (African people)
USE Dan (African people)

H

Haalpulaar (African people)
USE Halpulaar (African people)

Haalpulaar dialect
USE Pular dialect

Habbe (African people)
USE Dogon (African people)

Habe (African people)
USE Dogon (African people)

Habe language
USE Dogon language

Hadar Site (Ethiopia) *(Not Subd Geog)*
BT Ethiopia--Antiquities

Hadia (African people)
USE Hadiya (African people)

Hadiya (African people) *(May Subd Geog)*
[DT 380.4.H33]
UF Gudela (African people)
Hadia (African people)
BT Ethnology--Ethiopia

Hadjerai (African people) *(May Subd Geog)*
[DT 546.445.H]
BT Ethnology--Chad
--**Religion**
[BL 2480.H28]

Hadzapi (African people)
USE Tindiga (African people)

Hairdressing *(May Subd Geog)*
UF Hairstyling
Headdress
--**Africa**

Hairdressing of Blacks
[TT 975]
UF Afro (Hair style)
Black hairdressing
Blacks--Hairdressing

Hairstyling
USE Hairdressing

Haiti
--**Civilization**
-- --**African influences**
BT Africa--Civilization

Halpulaar (African people) *(May Subd Geog)*
[DT 549.45.H34]
UF Haalpulaar (African people)
BT Ethnology--Senegal

Hamar (African people) *(May Subd Geog)*
[DT 380.4.H36 (Ethiopia)]
UF Amar (African people)
Amar Koke (African people)
Amarcocche (African people)
Ammar (African people)
Banna (African people)
Beshada (African people)
Cocche (African people)
Hamer (African people)
Hamerkoke (African people)
Hammer (African people)
Humr (African people)
Koke (African people)
Nkamar (African people)
BT Daggara (African people)
Ethnology--Ethiopia
Ethnology--Sudan

Hambukushu (African people)
USE Mbukushu (African people)

Hamer (African people)
USE Hamar (African people)

Hamerkoke (African people)
USE Hamar (African people)

Hamites
BT Nilo-Hamitic tribes
NT Boran (African people)
Cushites
Somalis

Hamitic languages *(May Subd Geog)*
[PJ 2301-PJ 2551]
BT Afroasiatic languages
NT Cushitic languages
Nilo-Hamitic languages

Hamito-Semitic languages
USE Afroasiatic languages

UF = Used for; BT = Broader term; RT = Related term; SA = See also; NT = Narrower term

Hammer (African people)
  USE Hamar (African people)

Hand weaving *(May Subd Geog)*
  UF Weaving, Hand
  BT Weaving
--Africa, West
  NT West African strip weaving

Hanga dialect (Kenya) *(May Subd Geog)*
  [PL 8474.L895H]
  UF Kawanga dialect
      Luhanga dialect
      Oluhanga dialect
      Oluwanga dialect
      Wanga dialect
  BT Kenya--Languages
      Luyia language

Hanga language (Ghana) *(May Subd Geog)*
  [PL 8229]
  UF Anga language (Ghana)
  BT Ghana--languages
      Gur languages

Hanha (African people)
  USE Hanya (African people)

Hanya (African people) *(May Subd Geog)*
  [DT 611.45.H : old class]
  [DT 1308.H35 : new class]
  UF Hanha (African people)
      Muhanha (African people)
  BT Bantu-speaking peoples
      Ethnology--Angola

Harari (African people) *(May Subd Geog)*
  [DT 380.4.H]
  UF Gesinan (African people)
      Hararri (African people)
  BT Ethnology--Ethiopia

Harari language *(May Subd Geog)*
  [PJ 9293]
  UF Adari language
      Ararge language
      Harrarjie language
  BT Ethiopian languages

Hararri (African people)
  USE Harari (African people)

Harp-lute
  USE Kora (Musical instrument)

Harrarjie language
  USE Harari language

Haud (Ethiopia) *(Not Subd Geog)*

Hausa (African people) *(May Subd Geog)*
  [DT 547.45.H38 (Niger)]
  [DT 515.45.H38 (Nigeria)]
  [DT 155.2.H38 (Sudan)]
  UF Haussa (African people)
  BT Ethnology--Niger
      Ethnology--Nigeria
      Ethnology--Sudan
  NT Gobir
      Mawri (African people)
--Religion
  [BL 2480.H3]
  NT Bori (Cult)

Hausa architecture
  USE Architecture, Hausa

Hausa art
  USE Art, Hausa

Hausa decoration and ornament
  USE Decoration and ornament, Hausa

Hausa drama *(May Subd Geog)*
  [PL 8233.5-PL 8234]
  BT Hausa literature
      Nigerian drama
  NT Folk-drama, Hausa

Hausa folk-drama
  USE Folk-drama, Hausa

Hausa imprints *(May Subd Geog)*
  [Z 7108.H38]
  UF Imprints, Hausa

Hausa language *(May Subd Geog)*
  [PL 8231-PL 8234]
  UF Hawsa language
  BT Chadic languages
      Niger--Languages
      Nigeria--Languages
      Sudan--Languages
  RT Angas language
  NT Uwana language

Hausa literature *(May Subd Geog)*
  [PL 8233.5-PL 8234]
  BT Niger literature
      Nigerian literature
      Sudan--Literatures

(May Subd Geog) = Place names may follow the heading

NT Hausa drama
    Hausa poetry

Hausa love poetry
  USE Love poetry, Hausa

Hausa poetry *(May Subd Geog)*
  [PL 8233.5-PL 8234]
  BT Hausa literature
    Nigerian poetry
  NT Love poetry, Hausa

Hausa pottery
  USE Pottery, Hausa (African people)

Hausa women
  USE Women, Hausa

Haussa (African people)
  USE Hausa (African people)

Havu (African people) *(May Subd Geog)*
  [DT 650.H38]
  UF Bahavu (African people)
  BT Ethnology--Zaire

Hawash River (Ethiopia)
  USE Awash River (Ethiopia)

Hawsa language
  USE Hausa language

Haya (African people) *(May Subd Geog)*
  [DT 443.3.H (Tanzania)]
  [DT 433.245.H38 (Uganda)]
  UF Basiba (African people)
    Baziba (African people)
    Ekihaya (African people)
    Heia (African people)
    Kiziba (African people)
    Wahaya (African people)
    Wassiba (African people)
    Ziba (African people)
  BT Ethnology--Tanzania
    Ethnology--Uganda

Haya law
  USE Law, Haya

Haya language
  USE Ziba language

Headdress
  USE Hairdressing

Headlands (Coasts)

USE Capes (Coasts)

Heads (Coasts)
  USE Capes (Coasts)

Heads of households, Women
  USE Women heads of households

Health and race *(May Subd Geog)*
  UF Race and health
  BT Race

Hebrews
  USE Jews

Hehe (African people) *(May Subd Geog)*
  [DT 443.3.H]
  UF Wahehe (African people)
  BT Bantu-speaking peoples
    Ethnology--Tanzania

Hehe law
  USE Law, Hehe

Hei-kom (African people)
  USE Heikum (African people)

Heia (African people)
  USE Haya (African people)

Heikum (African people) *(May Subd Geog)*
  [DT 709 : old class]
  [DT 1558.H45 : new class]
  UF Hei-kom (African people)
  BT Ethnology--Namibia
    Khoikhoi (African people)
  --Religion
  [BL 2480.H37]

Heirs
  USE Inheritance and succession

Hema (African people)
  USE Hima (African people)

Hemba (African people) *(May Subd Geog)*
  [DT 650.H]
  UF Babuye (African people)
    Bahemba (African people)
    Buye (African people)
    Luba-Hemba (African people)
    Wabuyu (African people)
    Waruwa (African people)
  BT Bantu-speaking peoples
    Ethnology--Zaire
    Luba (African people)

UF = Used for; BT = Broader term; RT = Related term; SA = See also; NT = Narrower term

Hemba art
  USE Art, Hemba

Hemba sculpture
  USE Sculpture, Hemba

Hemba wood-carving
  USE Wood-carving, Hemba

Hera (African people) *(May Subd Geog)*
  [DT 962.42 : old class]
  [DT 2913.H : new class]
  UF Abahela (African people)
      Wahera (African people)
  BT Ethnology--Zimbabwe

Hereditary succession
  USE Inheritance and succession

Herero (African people) *(May Subd Geog)*
  [DT 611.45.H47 (Angola : old class)]
  [DT 1308.H48 (Angola : new class)]
  [DT 797 (Botswana : old class)]
  [DT 2458.H (Botswana : new class)]
  [DT 709 (Namibia : old class)]
  [DT 1558.H47 (Namibia : new class)]
  UF Herrero (African people)
      Ochiherero (African people)
      Ovaherero (African people)
  BT Bantu-speaking peoples
      Ethnology--Angola
      Ethnology--Botswana
      Ethnology--Namibia
  RT Damara (African people)
 --History
  NT Namibia--History--Herero Revolt, 1904-
1907
 --Religion
  [BL 2480.H4]

Herero language *(May Subd Geog)*
  [PL 8241]
  UF Otjiherero language
  BT Angola--Languages
      Bantu languages
      Botswana--Languages
      Namibia--Languages
  NT Himba dialect

Herero Revolt, Namibia, 1904-1907
  USE Namibia--History--Herero Revolt, 1904-
1907

Heroic poetry
  USE Epic poetry

Herrero (African people)
  USE Herero (African people)

Herreroland (Namibia)
  USE Damaraland (Namibia : Region)

Hertzogprys
  BT Afrikaans literature--Competitions--South
Africa
      Literary prizes--South Africa

Hi-life (Music)
  USE Highlife (Music)

High-life (Music)
  USE Highlife (Music)

High Veld (South Africa)
  USE Northern Karroo (South Africa)

High Veld Area (South Africa)
  USE Highveld Area (South Africa)

Highlands, Kenya (Kenya)
  USE Kenya Highlands (Kenya)

Highlife (Music) *(May Subd Geog)*
  UF Hi-life (Music)
      High-life (Music)
  BT Dance music--Africa, West
      Popular music--Africa, West

Highveld (South Africa)
  USE Northern Karroo (South Africa)

Highveld Area (South Africa) *(Not Subd Geog)*
  UF High Veld Area (South Africa)
      Hoëveldgebied (South Africa)

Highways
  USE Roads

Higi (African people)
  USE Kamwe (African people)

Higi language
  USE Kamwe language

Hiji (African people)
  USE Kamwe (African people)

Hill Damara (African people)
  USE Damara (African people)

Hill Suk (African people)
  USE Suk (African people)

(May Subd Geog) = Place names may follow the heading

Hillbrow (Johannesburg, South Africa) *(Not Subd Geog)*
UF Johannesburg (South Africa). Hillbrow

Hills
USE Mountains

Hima (African people) *(May Subd Geog)*
[DT 433.245.B35 (Uganda)]
[DT 650.H54 (Zaire)]
UF Bahema (African people)
    Bahima (African people)
    Bahuma (African people)
    Hema (African people)
    Huma (African people)
    Wahima (African people)
BT Ethnology--Uganda
    Ethnology--Zaire

Hima art
USE Art, Hima

Hima women
USE Women, Hima

Himba (African people) *(May Subd Geog)*
[DT 611.45.H47 (Angola : old class)]
[DT 1308.H56 (Angola : new class)]
[DT 709 (Namibia : old class)]
[DT 1558.H56 (Namibia : new class)]
UF Cimba (African people)
    Shimba (African people)
    Simba (African people)
    Tjimba (African people)
BT Bantu-speaking peoples
    Ethnology--Angola
    Ethnology--Namibia
--Marriage customs and rites
UF Marriage customs and rites, Himba (African people)
--Rites and ceremonies

Himba dialect *(May Subd Geog)*
UF Chimba dialect
    Cimba dialect
    Dhimba dialect
    Simba dialect
    Tjimba dialect
BT Herero language
    Namibia--Languages

Hissala language
USE Sisala language

History
SA *subdivision* History *under specific subjects,*

under *names of countries, states, cities, etc., and under the names of ethnic groups, e.g.* Lesotho--History; Fula (African people)--History
NT Archaeology
    Coups d'état
    Kings and rulers
    Massacres
    Revolutions
    Riots

HIV disease
USE AIDS (Disease)

Hlengwe (African people)
USE Tsonga (African people)

Hlubi (African people) *(May Subd Geog)*
[DT 872 : old class]
[DT 1768.H : new class]
UF Amahlubi (African people)
BT Ethnology--South Africa
    Nguni (African people)
--History
NT Langalibalele Rebellion, 1873

Hoe Handle, War of the, 1928-1931
USE Kongo Wara, 1928-1931

Hoëveldgebied (South Africa)
USE Highveld Area (South Africa)

Holidays *(May Subd Geog)*
UF Legal holidays
    National holidays
BT Manners and customs
--Djibouti
NT Independence Day (Djibouti)

Holoholo (African people) *(May Subd Geog)*
[DT 650.H (Zaire)]
UF Bagua (African people)
    Baholoholo (African people)
    Guha (African people)
    Horohoro (African people)
    Tombwa (African people)
    Tumbwe (African people)
    Vuahuha (African people)
BT Bantu-speaking peoples
    Ethnology--Tanzania
    Ethnology--Zaire

Holoholo language *(May Subd Geog)*
[PL 8247]
UF Horohoro language
BT Bantu languages   *(Continued)*

UF = Used for; BT = Broader term; RT = Related term; SA = See also; NT = Narrower term

Holoholo language   *(Continued)*
  BT Tanzania--Languages
    Zaire--Languages

Holy Scriptures
  USE Bible

Hombo language
  USE Ombo language

Hombolo Lake (Tanzania) *(Not Subd Geog)*
  UF Lake Hombolo (Tanzania)
  BT Lakes--Tanzania
    Reservoirs--Tanzania

Homelands (South Africa)
  [DT 763.6 : old class]
  [DT 1760 : new class]
  UF Bantoetuislande (South Africa)
    Bantu Homelands (South Africa)
    Bantustans (South Africa)
    Black Homelands (South Africa)
    South African Homelands (South Africa)
    Tuislande (South Africa)
  NT Bophuthatswana (South Africa)
    Ciskei (South Africa)
    Transkei (South Africa)
    Venda (South Africa)

Homes
  USE Dwellings

Hominidae, Fossil
  USE Fossil man

Hominids, Fossil
  USE Fossil man

Homo rhodesiensis
  USE Rhodesian man

Honoris Crux
  BT South Africa--Armed Forces--Medals,
badges, decorations, etc.

Horn of Africa
  USE Africa, Northeast

Horohoro (African people)
  USE Holoholo (African people)

Horohoro language
  USE Holoholo language

Horror tales, Mauritian (English) *(May Subd Geog)*
  [PR 9680.M33]
  UF Mauritian horror tales (English)
  BT Mauritian fiction (English)

Horse-racing *(May Subd Geog)*
  UF Flat racing
  --**South Africa**
  NT July Handicap (Horse Race)

Hossere-Alantika (Nigeria and Cameroon)
  USE Atlantika Mountains (Nigeria and Cameroon)

Hottentot (African people)
  USE Khoikhoi (African people)

Hottentot (Name)
  [DT 764.K45 : old class]
  [DT 1768.K56 : new class]
  BT Khoikhoi (African people)--Name

Hottentot language
  USE Khoikhoi language

Hottentots Holland Mountains (South Africa) *(Not Subd Geog)*
  UF Hottentots Hollandsberge (South Africa)
  BT Mountains--South Africa

Hottentots Hollandsberge (South Africa)
  USE Hottentots Holland Mountains (South Africa)

Houlouf Site (Cameroon) *(Not Subd Geog)*
  UF Tell Houlouf (Cameroon)
  BT Cameroon--Antiquities

House of Israel
  USE Falashas

Houses
  USE Dwellings

Hova (Malagasy people)
  USE Merina (Malagasy people)

Hova dialect
  USE Malagasy language

Hova rule, 1810-1885
  USE Madagascar--History--Hova rule, 1810-1885

!Hu language
  USE !Xu language

Hua-owani language
  USE !Xo language

(May Subd Geog) = Place names may follow the heading

Huana (African people) *(May Subd Geog)*
  [DT 650.H]
  UF Baguana (African people)
      Bahuana (African people)
      Bahuangana (African people)
      Bahungana (African people)
      Hungana (African people)
      Wangana (African people)
  BT Bantu-speaking peoples
      Ethnology--Zaire

Huana language
  USE Hungana language

Hulo (African people)
  USE Mende (African people)

Hulo language
  USE Mende language

Huluf (African people)
  USE Felup (African people)

Huma (African people)
  USE Hima (African people)

Huma language (Sudan)
  USE Topoga language

Human females
  USE Women

Human leopards
  USE Leopard men

Human paleontology
  USE Fossil man

Human remains (Archaeology)
  USE Man, Prehistoric

Human resource development
  USE Education

Humba (African people)
  USE Kuanyama (African people)

Humor
  USE Wit and humor

Humorous illustrations
  USE Wit and humor, Pictorial

Humorous stories
  UF Comic stories
  BT Fiction

  BT Wit and humor

Humorous stories, Shona *(May Subd Geog)*
  [PL 8681.6]
  UF Shona humorous stories
  BT Shona fiction
      Shona wit and humor

Humr (African people)
  USE Hamar (African people)

Hune (African people)
  USE Dukawa (African people)

Hungaan language
  USE Hungana language

Hungana (African people)
  USE Huana (African people)

Hungana language *(May Subd Geog)*
  UF Huana language
      Hungaan language
  BT Mbala language (Bandundu region, Zaire)
      Zaire--Languages

Hunyani River (Zimbabwe and Mozambique) *(Not Subd Geog)*
  UF Panhamo River (Zimbabwe and Mozambique)
      Rio Panhame (Zimbabwe and Mozambique)
  BT Rivers--Mozambique
      Rivers--Zimbabwe
  NT McIlwaine, Lake (Zimbabwe)

Huro (African people)
  USE Mende (African people)

Huro language
  USE Mende language

Husbandry
  USE Agriculture

Hutu (African people) *(May Subd Geog)*
  [DT 450.25.H (Burundi)]
  UF Bahutu (African people)
      Lera (African people)
      Ndara (African people)
      Ndoga (African people)
      Ndogo (African people)
      Shobyo (African people)
      Tshogo (African people)
      Urulera (African people)
  BT Ethnology--Burundi
      Ethnology--Rwanda
      Rundi (African people)

UF = Used for; BT = Broader term; RT = Related term; SA = See also; NT = Narrower term

Hybrid languages
  USE Pidgin languages

Hybridity of races
  USE Miscegenation

Hygiene, Tropical
  USE Tropical medicine

Hyman Liberman Memorial Door (South African National Gallery)
  UF Liberman Memorial Door (South African National Gallery)
  BT Doors--South Africa
       South African National Gallery

Hymns, African *(May Subd Geog)*
  [BV 459 (English)]
  UF African hymns

Hymns, Afrikaans *(May Subd Geog)*
  [BV 510.A]
  UF Afrikaans hymns

Hymns, Bemba *(May Subd Geog)*
  [BV 510.B]
  UF Bemba hymns

Hymns, Luo *(May Subd Geog)*
  [BV 510.L]
  UF Luo hymns

Hymns, Lwo (Sudan) *(May Subd Geog)*
  [BV 510.L]
  UF Lwo hymns (Sudan)

Hymns, Swahili *(May Subd Geog)*
  [BV 510.S]
  UF Swahili hymns

Hymns, Tsonga *(May Subd Geog)*
  [BV 510.T48]
  UF Tsonga hymns

Hymns, Tswana *(May Subd Geog)*
  [BV 510.T]
  UF Tswana hymns

Hymns, Xhosa *(May Subd Geog)*
  [BV 510.X]
  UF Xhosa hymns

Hymns, Zulu *(May Subd Geog)*
  [BV 510.Z8]
  UF Zulu hymns

I

I.C.I.P.E. Farm (Kenya) *(Not Subd Geog)*
  BT Farms--Kenya

I-hadja (African people)
  USE Kasanga (African people)

Iaka (African people)
  USE Yaka (African people)

Iaka language
  USE Yaka language

Ibani dialect *(May Subd Geog)*
  [PL 8276.95.I2]
  UF Bonny dialect
       Ubani dialect
  BT Ijo language
       Nigeria--Languages

Ibara (African people)
  USE Nupe (African people)

Ibembe (East African people)
  USE Bembe (East African people)

Ibembe language
  USE Bembe language (Lake Tanganyika)

Ibibio (African people) *(May Subd Geog)*
  [DT 515.45.I24]
  BT Ethnology--Nigeria
  NT Anang (African people)
       Ubium (African people)
  --Marriage customs and rites
  UF Marriage customs and rites, Ibibio (African people)
  --Rites and ceremonies

Ibibio language *(May Subd Geog)*
  BT Benue-Congo languages
       Nigeria--Languages
  RT Efik language

Ibo (African people)
  USE Igbo (African people)

Ibo language
  USE Igbo language

Ichilala (African people)
  USE Lala (African people)

(May Subd Geog) = Place names may follow the heading

Ichilamba (African people)
    USE Lamba (African people)

Icila (African dance)
    [GV 1713.Z]
    BT Dancing--Zambia

Idjwi Island (Zaire) *(Not Subd Geog)*
    UF Kwidjwi Island (Zaire)
    BT Islands--Zaire
        Zaire

Ido language
    USE Ijo language

Idoma (African people) *(May Subd Geog)*
    [DT 515.45.I25]
    UF Agala (African people)
        Akpoto (African people)
        Igumale (African people)
        Ochekwu (African people)
        Okwoga (African people)
        Oturkpo (African people)
    BT Ethnology--Nigeria
  --Funeral customs and rites
    UF Funeral rites and ceremonies, Idoma
(African people)
  --Rites and ceremonies

Idoma drama *(May Subd Geog)*
    [PL 8263.5-PL 8263.9]
    BT Idoma literature
        Nigerian drama

Idoma language *(May Subd Geog)*
    [PL 8263]
    UF Oturkpo dialect
    BT Kwa languages
        Nigeria--Languages

Idoma literature *(May Subd Geog)*
    [PL 8263.5-PL 8263.9]
    BT Nigerian literature
    NT Idoma drama

Idongiro (African people)
    USE Nyangatom (African people)

Idzcbu language
    USE Yebu language

Idzo language
    USE Ijo language

Igado (African people)
    USE Isoko (African people)

Igala (African people) *(May Subd Geog)*
    [DT 515.45.I32]
    UF Igara (African people)
    BT Ethnology--Nigeria

Igala wood-carving
    USE Wood-carving, Igala

Igara (African people)
    USE Igala (African people)

Igbaka (African people)
    USE Gbaya (African people)

Igbena (African people)
    USE Igbona (African people)

Igbira language *(May Subd Geog)*
    [PL 8273]
    UF Ebira language
    BT Kwa languages
        Nigeria--Languages

Igbo (African people) *(May Subd Geog)*
    [DT 515.45.I33]
    UF Ibo (African people)
    BT Ethnology--Nigeria
    NT Ngwa (African people)
        Ujari (African people)
  --Food
    BT Food
  --Missions *(May Subd Geog)*
    [BV 3630.I2]
    UF Missions to Igbo (African people)
  --Religion
    [BL 2480.I2]
    NT Gods, Igbo (African people)

Igbo art
    USE Art, Igbo

Igbo arts
    USE Arts, Igbo

Igbo drama *(May Subd Geog)*
    [PL 8261.5-PL 8261.9]
    BT Igbo literature
        Nigerian drama
    NT Folk-drama, Igbo
        Religious drama, Igbo

Igbo fiction *(May Subd Geog)*
    [PL 8261.5-PL 8261.9]
    BT Igbo literature
        Nigeria--Fiction
    NT Short stories, Igbo

UF = Used for; BT = Broader term; RT = Related term; SA = See also; NT = Narrower term

Igbo folk-drama
  USE Folk-drama, Igbo

Igbo folk literature
  USE Folk literature, Igbo

Igbo folk poetry
  USE Folk poetry, Igbo

Igbo gods
  USE Gods, Igbo

Igbo language *(May Subd Geog)*
  [PL 8261]
  UF Ibo language
  BT Kwa languages
      Nigeria--Languages
  NT Izi language
      Ngwa dialect

Igbo law
  USE Law, Igbo

Igbo literature *(May Subd Geog)*
  [PL 8261.5-PL 8261.9]
  BT Nigerian literature
  NT Folk literature, Igbo
      Igbo drama
      Igbo fiction
      Igbo poetry

Igbo mythology
  USE Mythology, Igbo

Igbo philology *(May Subd Geog)*
  [PL 8261]
  UF Philology, Igbo

Igbo philosophy
  USE Philosophy, Igbo

Igbo poetry *(May Subd Geog)*
  [PL 8261.5-PL 8261.9]
  BT Igbo literature
      Nigerian poetry
  NT Folk poetry, Igbo

Igbo proverbs
  USE Proverbs, Igbo

Igbo religious drama
  USE Religious drama, Igbo

Igbo short stories
  USE Short stories, Igbo

Igbo women
  USE Women, Igbo

Igbo wood-carving
  USE Wood-carving, Igbo

Igbomina (African people)
  USE Igbona (African people)

Igbona (African people) *(May Subd Geog)*
  [DT 515.45.I34]
  UF Igbena (African people)
      Igbomina (African people)
      Igboona (African people)
      Illa (African people)
  BT Ethnology--Nigeria
      Yoruba (African people)

Igboona (African people)
  USE Igbona (African people)

Igede language *(May Subd Geog)*
  BT Kwa languages
      Nigeria--Languages

Igulua (African people)
  USE Galwa (African people)

Igumale (African people)
  USE Idoma (African people)

Ijabu language
  USE Yebu language

Ijaw (African people)
  USE Ijo (African people)

Ijaw language
  USE Ijo language

Ijebu (African people)
  USE Yebu (African people)

Ijebu language
  USE Yebu language

Ijo (African people) *(May Subd Geog)*
  [DT 515.45.I35]
  UF Ijaw (African people)
      Kalabari (African people)
  BT Ethnology--Nigeria
  --Children
    BT Children--Nigeria
  --Youth
    BT Youth--Nigeria

(May Subd Geog) = Place names may follow the heading

Ijo language *(May Subd Geog)*
  [PL 8276]
  UF Djo language
      Dzo language
      Ejo language
      Ido language
      Idzo language
      Ijaw language
      Ijoh language
      Iyo language
      Izo language
      Izon language
      Ojo language
      Oru language
      Udzo language
      Uzo language
  BT Kwa languages
      Nigeria--Languages
  NT Ibani dialect
      Kalabari dialect
      Kolokuma dialect
      Nembe language
      Okrika dialect

Ijo sculpture
  USE Sculpture, Ijo

Ijoh language
  USE Ijo language

Ik (African people) *(May Subd Geog)*
  [DT 433.245.I37]
  UF Teuso (African people)
  BT Ethnology--Kenya
      Ethnology--Sudan
      Ethnology--Uganda

Ikela (African people)
  USE Kela (African people)

Ikeleve (African people)
  USE Kongo (African people)

Ikeleve language
  USE Kituba language

Iki-kukwe language
  USE Mwamba language

Iki-Zanaki language
  USE Zanaki language

Ikikuria (African people)
  USE Kuria (African people)

IkinyaRuanda language
  USE Kinyarwanda language

Ikinyi-Kiusa language
  USE Ngonde language

IkiZanaki language
  USE Zanaki language

Ikopa River (Madagascar) *(Not Subd Geog)*
  BT Rivers--Madagascar

Ikposo language
  USE Kposo language

Ikposso language
  USE Kposo language

Ikuhane language
  USE Subiya language

Ikumama (African people)
  USE Teso (African people)

Ikwahani language
  USE Subiya language

Ikwere language *(May Subd Geog)*
  UF Ikworro language
      Oratta-Ikwerri language
  BT Kwa languages
      Nigeria--Languages

Ikwere proverbs
  USE Proverbs, Ikwere

Ikwerre language
  USE Ikwere language

Ikwo language *(May Subd Geog)*
  [PL 8279]
  BT Kwa languages
      Nigeria--Languages

Ila (African people) *(May Subd Geog)*
  [DT 963.42 : old class]
  [DT 3058.I53 : new class]
  UF Baila (African people)
      Bashukulompo (African people)
      Mashukolumbwe (African people)
      Shukulumbwe (African people)
      Sukulumbwe (African people)
  BT Bantu-speaking peoples
      Ethnology--Zambia
  NT Lenje (African people)

UF = Used for; BT = Broader term; RT = Related term; SA = See also; NT = Narrower term

Ila language *(May Subd Geog)*
  [PL 8281]
  BT Tonga language (Zambesi)
      Zambia--Languages

Ila law
  USE Law, Ila

Ilali language
  USE Teke language

Ilamba language
  USE Nilamba language

Ile d'Arguin (Mauritania)
  USE Arguin Island (Mauritania)

Ile de France
  USE Mauritius

Ile Maurice
  USE Mauritius

Ile Mayotte
  USE Mayotte

Ile Sainte-Marie (Madagascar)
  USE Sainte-Marie-de-Madagascar Island
(Madagascar)

Ileo (African people)
  USE Dengese (African people)

Ilha de Moçambique (Mozambique)
  USE Mozambique Island (Mozambique)

iLiku dialect
  USE Leko dialect

Illa (African people)
  USE Igbona (African people)

Illiteracy
  USE Literacy

Illumination of books and manuscripts,
Ethiopian *(May Subd Geog)*
  [ND 3285.7]
  UF Ethiopian illumination of books and
manuscripts
  BT Art, Ethiopian

Illustrations, Humorous
  USE Wit and humor, Pictorial

Ilparakuyo (African people)

  USE Baraguyu (African people)

Ilumbu language
  USE Lumbu language (Gabon)

Imana (Rundi deity) *(Not Subd Geog)*
  [BL 2480.R]
  BT Gods, Rundi
      Religion, Primitive--Burundi
      Rundi (African people)--Religion

Imanan (Niger) *(Not Subd Geog)*
  UF Imannan (Niger)

Imannan (Niger)
  USE Imanan (Niger)

Imbabu, Ethiopia, Battle of, 1882
  [DT 386.7]
  UF Battle of Imbabu (Ethiopia), 1882
  BT Ethiopia--History--1490-1889

Imbuti (African people)
  USE Mbuti (African people)

Imerina (Malagasy people)
  USE Merina (Malagasy people)

Immigrant labor
  USE Alien labor

Imona (African people)
  USE Mbole (African people)

Imprints
    *For lists of titles **published in** a particular country*
    see the name of the country with subdivision Imprints,
    e.g. Zambia--Imprints.
    *For lists of titles **published in the language** of a*
    particular country without regard to place of publication,
    see phrase headings of the type Sotho imprints.
    *For lists of titles **about** a particular country, see the*
    name of the country with subdivision Bibliography, e.g.
    Uganda--Bibliography.

Imprints, Akan
  USE Akan imprints

Imprints, Chewa
  USE Chewa imprints

Imprints, Ewe
  USE Ewe imprints

Imprints, Hausa
  USE Hausa imprints

(May Subd Geog) = Place names may follow the heading

Imprints, Kongo
  USE Kongo imprints

Imprints, Nyanja
  USE Nyanja imprints

Imprints, Sotho
  USE Sotho imprints

Imprints, Swahili
  USE Swahili imprints

Imprints, Tsonga
  USE Tsonga imprints

Imprints, Tswana
  USE Tswana imprints

Imprints, Tumbuka
  USE Tumbuka imprints

Imprints, Xhosa
  USE Xhosa imprints

Imragen (Berber tribe) *(May Subd Geog)*
  [DT 554.45.I57]
  BT Ethnology--Mauritania

Inanda Dam (South Africa) *(Not Subd Geog)*
  UF Inandadam (South Africa)
  BT Dams--South Africa

Inandadam (South Africa)
  USE Inanda Dam (South Africa)

Incran language
  USE Ga language

Independence Day (Djibouti)
  [DT 411.8]
  BT Djibouti--Anniversaries, etc.
      Holidays--Djibouti

Independence movements
  USE *subdivision* History--Autonomy and
independence movements *under names of countries,*
etc. Cabinda (Angola : Province)--History--
Autonomy and independence movements.

India *(Not Subd Geog)*
  --Civilization
  NT Africa, Sub-Saharan--Civilization--
Indic influences
      Mauritius--Civilization--Indic
influences

  NT Meroe (Sudan)--Civilization--Indic
influences
      Réunion--Civilization--Indic influences

Indian Coast (Africa) *(Not Subd Geog)*
  BT Coasts--Africa

Indian Coast (Kenya) *(Not Subd Geog)*
  BT Coasts--Kenya

Indian Coast (South Africa) *(Not Subd Geog)*
  BT Coasts--South Africa

Indian Coast (Tanzania) *(Not Subd Geog)*
  BT Coasts--Tanzania

Indian Ocean Islands
  USE Islands of the Indian Ocean

Indians of North America *(May Subd Geog)*
  UF American aborigines
      American Indians
      Indians of North America--United States
      Indians of the United States
      Native Americans
      North American Indians
  --African influences
    BT Africa--Civilization
  --United States
    UON Indians of North America

Indians of the United States
  USE Indians of North America

Indigenous peoples *(May Subd Geog)*
  Here are entered works on the position in society and
relations with governing authorities of the aboriginal
inhabitants of colonial areas or modern states where the
aboriginal peoples are not in control of the government.
  UF Aborigines
      Native peoples
  BT Ethnology
  --Angola
  UF Angola--Native races
  --Belgium
  -- --Colonies
  UF Belgium--Colonies--Native races
  --France
  -- --Colonies
  UF France--Colonies--Native races
  -- Germany
  -- --Colonies
  UF Germany--Colonies--Native races
  --Great Britain   *(Continued)*

UF = Used for; BT = Broader term; RT = Related term; SA = See also; NT = Narrower term

Indigenous peoples
--**Great Britain**   *(Continued)*
-- --Colonies
 UF Great Britain--Colonies--Native races
--**Netherlands**
-- --Colonies
 UF Netherlands--Colonies--Native races
-- **Portugal**
-- --Colonies
 UF Portugal--Colonies--Native races
--**South Africa**
 UF South Africa--Native races
--**Spain**
-- --Colonies
 UF Spain--Colonies--Native races

Indonesia *(Not Subd Geog)*
 UF Dutch East Indies
--**Civilization**
 NT Africa, Sub-Saharan--Civilization--
Indonesian influences

Industrial Development Decade for Africa,
1980-1990 *(May Subd Geog)*
 UF United Nations Industrial Development
Decade for Africa, 1980-1990
 BT Africa--Industries

Industrial unions
 USE Trade-unions

Industry
 USE *subdivision* Industries *under the names of*
countries, cities, etc., e.g. Guinea-Bissau--
Industries.

Infibulation *(May Subd Geog)*
 [GN 481]
 BT Circumcision
     Sex customs
--**Africa**
--**Sierra Leone**
--**Somalia**
--**Sudan**

Information processing systems
 USE Information storage and retrieval
systems

Information storage and retrieval systems *(May*
Subd Geog)
 UF Automatic data storage
     Automatic information retrieval
     Automation in documentation
     Computer-based information systems
     Data storage and retrieval systems

 UF Information processing systems
     Machine data storage and retrieval
     Mechanized information storage and
retrieval systems
--**Africa**
 UF Africa--Information storage and retrieval
systems
 BT Africa--Bibliography
 NT PADIS (Information retrieval system)
--**Africa, West**
-- --Agriculture
 NT Moisture Utilization in Semi-Arid Tropics:
Summer Rainfall Agriculture Project

Ingassana language *(May Subd Geog)*
 [PL 8282.I55]
 UF Ingessana language
     Tabi language
 BT Nilo-Saharan languages
     Sudan--Languages

Ingessana language
 USE Ingassana language

Inhambane (Mozambique people)
 USE Tonga (Mozambique people)

Inheritance and succession *(May Subd Geog)*
 UF Bequests
     Descent and distribution
     Descents
     Heirs
     Hereditary succession
     Intestacy
     Intestate succession
     Law of succession
     Succession, Intestate
 BT Real property
 NT Land tenure

Inheritance and succession (Bafokeng law)
 BT Law, Bafokeng

Inheritance and succession (Kgatla law)
 BT Law, Kgatla

Inheritance and succession (Ngoni law)
 BT Law, Ngoni

Inheritance and succession (Tonga law)
 BT Law, Tonga

Initiation rites *(May Subd Geog)*
 BT Rites and ceremonies
 NT Circumcision
     Puberty rites

(May Subd Geog) = Place names may follow the heading

--Mythology
--Religious aspects
  BT Religion, Primitive
--Africa, Sub-Saharan
  [BL 2462.5 (Religion)]
  [GN 645 (Ethnology)]
--Benin
--Botswana

Inkundo (African people)
  USE Nkundu (African people)

Inlets *(May Subd Geog)*
  BT Coasts
  RT Bays
--Djibouti
  NT Tadjoura, Gulf of (Djibouti)

Inscriptions, Meroitic
  [PL 8512.M451]
  UF Meroitic inscriptions

Institution farms, State-owned
  USE State farms

Instruction
  USE Education

Instruments, Musical
  USE Musical instruments

Insurgency *(May Subd Geog)*
  UF Rebellions
  BT Civil war
    Revolutions
  NT Guerrillas
    Terrorism
--Africa
--Angola

Insurrection of Mamadou Lamine, 1885-1887
  USE Mamadou Lamine, Rebellion of, 1885-1887

Insurrections
  USE Revolutions

Integration, Racial
  USE Race relations

Intellectual life *(Not Subd Geog)*
  Here are entered general works on learning and scholarship, literature, the arts, etc. Works on literature, art, music, motion pictures, etc. produced for a mass audience are entered under Popular culture

  SA *subdivision* Intellectual life *under names of countries, cities, etc.; and under classes of persons and ethnic groups, e.g.* Kenya--Intellectual life

Intermittent fever
  USE Malaria

International Association of the Congo
  USE Zaire

International economic relations
  USE *subdivision* Foreign economic relations *further subdivided by place, if appropriate, e.g.* Mozambique--Foreign economic relations--South Africa

International relations
  USE *subdivision* Foreign relations *under names of countries, e.g.,* Zambia--Foreign relations

International students
  USE Students, Foreign

Internment camps
  USE Concentration camps

Intestacy
  USE Inheritance and succession

Intestate succession
  USE Inheritance and succession

Irakov (African people)
  USE Iraqw (African people)

Iramba language
  USE Nilamba language

Irangi (African people)
  USE Rangi (African people)

Iraqw (African people) *(May Subd Geog)*
  [DT 443.3.I]
  UF Erokh (African people)
    Irakov (African people)
    Mbulu (African people)
    Wambulu (African people)
  BT Ethnology--Tanzania
--Missions *(May Subd Geog)*
  [BV 3630.I]
  UF Missions to Iraqw (African people)

Iraqw language *(May Subd Geog)*
  [PJ 2556]
  BT Cushitic languages, Southern
    Tanzania--Languages

UF = Used for; BT = Broader term; RT = Related term; SA = See also; NT = Narrower term

Irbore language
  USE Arbore language

Ireland *(Not Subd Geog)*
 --Civilization
 -- --African influences
    BT Africa--Civilization

Irene Concentration Camp (South Africa) *(Not Subd Geog)*
    [HV 8964.S]
    BT Concentration camps--South Africa
        South African War, 1899-1902--
Concentration camps--South Africa

Irenge (African people)
  USE Murle (African people)

Ironwork *(May Subd Geog)*
    BT Decoration and ornament

Ironwork, Fon *(May Subd Geog)*
    [NK 8289.6.D3]
    UF Fon ironwork

Isala (African people)
  USE Sisala (African people)

Isandlwana (South Africa), Battle of, 1879
    [DT 777 : old class]
    [DT 1879.I83 : new class]
    UF Battle of Isandlwana (South Africa),
1879
    BT Zulu War, 1879--Campaigns

Isi-Lololo
  USE Fanakalo

Isi-Piki
  USE Fanakalo

IsiNdebele language
  USE Ndebele language (Zimbabwe)

Isiswazi (African people)
  USE Swazi (African people)

isiXhosa language
  USE Xhosa language

Isizulu (African people)
  USE Zulu (African people)

Isizulu language
  USE Zulu language

Isla de Bioco (Equatorial Guinea)
  USE Fernando Po (Equatorial Guinea)

Isla de Bioko (Equatorial Guinea)
  USE Fernando Po (Equatorial Guinea)

Isla de Corisco (Equatorial Guinea)
  USE Corisco (Equatorial Guinea)

Islam *(May Subd Geog)*
    Here are entered works on the religion of which
Muhammad is the prophet. Works on the community of
believers in Islam are entered under Muslims.
    UF Islamism
        Mohammedanism
        Muhammadanism
        Muslimism
        Mussulmanism
    BT Religions
    NT Muslims
 --Music
  USE Music, Islamic
 --Poetry
  USE Islamic poetry
 --**Africa, East**
    [BP 64.A4]
 --**Nigeria**
    [BP 64.N5]

Islam and music
  USE Music, Islamic

Islamic poetry *(May Subd Geog)*
    UF Islam--Poetry
        Muslim poetry
        Poetry, Islamic
        Poetry, Muslim

Islamic poetry, Fula *(May Subd Geog)*
    [PL 8183.5-PL 8184]
    UF Fula Islamic poetry
    BT Fula poetry

Islamism
  USE Islam

Islands *(May Subd Geog)*
    BT Landforms
 --**Cape Verde**
    NT Boa Vista Island (Cape Verde)
        Sao Tiago Island (Cape Verde)
 --Caribbean Area
  USE West Indies
 --**Equatorial Guinea**
    NT Corisco (Equatorial Guinea)
        Fernando Po (Equatorial Guinea)

(May Subd Geog) = Place names may follow the heading

--Indian Ocean
  USE Islands of the Indian Ocean
--Kenya
  NT Manda Island (Kenya)
--Madagascar
  NT Nosy-Be Island (Madagascar)
    Sainte-Marie-de-Madagascar Island
(Madagascar)
--Mauritania
  NT Arguin Island (Mauritania)
--Mauritius
  NT Rodrigues Island (Mauritius)
--Mozambique
  NT Mozambique Island (Mozambique)
--Seychelles
  NT Aldabra Island (Seychelles)
    La Digue Island (Seychelles)
    Praslin Island (Seychelles)
--South Africa
  NT Robben Island (South Africa)
--Zaire
  NT Idjwi Island (Zaire)

Islands of the Caribbean
  USE West Indies

Islands of the Indian Ocean
  UF Indian Ocean Islands
    Islands--Indian Ocean
  NT Comoros
    Mascarene Islands
    Seychelles

Isle de France
  USE Mauritius

Isogo (African people)
  USE Mitsogho (African people)

Isoko (African people) *(May Subd Geog)*
  [DT 515.45.I86]
  UF Biotu (African people)
    Igabo (African people)
  BT Ethnology--Nigeria
    Sobo (African people)

Isongo (Central African Republic people)
  USE Mbati (Central African Republic
people)

Israel *(Not Subd Geog)*
--Foreign relations *(May Subd Geog)*
-- --Uganda
  NT Entebbe Airport Raid, 1976

Israel, Beta

  USE Falashas

Israel, House of
  USE Falashas

Israelites
  USE Jews

Issala language
  USE Sisala language

Italian Somaliland
  USE Somalia

Italo-Ethiopian War, 1895-1896
  [DT 387.3]
  UF Abyssino-Italian War, 1895-1896
    Ethiopian-Italian War, 1895-1896
  RT Ethiopia--History--1889-1974
  NT Adowa, Battle of, 1896

Italo-Ethiopian War, 1935-1936
  [DT 387.8]
  UF Ethiopian-Italian War, 1935-1936
  BT Ethiopia--History--1889-1974
--Aerial operations
--Causes
--Diplomatic history
--Naval operations

Itawa (African people)
  USE Tabwa (African people)

Iteso (African people)
  USE Teso (African people)

Iteso language
  USE Teso language

Itesyo (African people)
  USE Teso (African people)

Itezhi-Tezhi Dam (Zambia) *(Not Subd Geog)*
  BT Dams--Zambia

Ithe-wa-Gathoni Farm (Kenya) *(Not Subd Geog)*
  BT Farms--Kenya

Itio language
  USE Teke language

Itsekiri (African people)
  USE Jekri (African people)

Ittu dialect
  USE Qottu dialect

UF = Used for; BT = Broader term; RT = Related term; SA = See also; NT = Narrower term

Ituri Forest *(Not Subd Geog)*
  BT Forests and forestry--Zaire

Ituri forest pygmies
  USE Mbuti (African people)

Ivory Coast *(Not Subd Geog)*
  [DT 545-DT 545.9]
  UF Côte d'Ivoire
      Republique of Ivory Coast
 --Civilization
 -- --Western influences
  BT Civilization, Western
 --Description and travel
 -- --1981-
 --Drama
  NT Akan drama
 --Economic conditions
  [HC 1025]
 -- --To 1960
 -- --1960-
 --History
  NT Denkyira (Kingdom)
 --Languages
  NT Abe language
      Abidji language
      Abure language
      Adyukru language
      Ahizi language
      Aladian language
      Anyi language
      Attie language
      Baoulé language
      Bete language
      Brissa language
      Dan language
      Dida dialect
      Djimini language
      Dyula language
      Gagu language
      Godye dialect
      Karaboro language
      Kru languages
      Kulango language
      Kweni language
      Lagoon languages
      Lobi dialects
      Lorhorn language
      Mamara language
      Mau dialect (Ivory Coast)
      Mo language (Ghana and Ivory Coast)
      Muana language
      Nyabwa language
      Sanvi dialect
      Senari language

  NT Senufo languages
      Southern Mande languages
      Tagbana language
      Téén dialect
      Tepo language
      Tura language
      Tyembara dialect
      Vige language
      Wobe language
 --Literatures
  NT Akan literature
      Dan literature
 --Poetry
  NT Akan poetry
 --Politics and government
 -- --To 1960
 -- --1960-
 --Social conditions
 -- --To 1960
 -- --1960-

Ivory Coast authors
  USE Authors, Ivory Coast

Ivory Coast fiction (French) *(May Subd Geog)*
  [PQ 3988.5.I9 (History)]
  [PQ 3988.5.I92 (Collections)]
  UF French fiction--Ivory Coast authors
  BT Ivory Coast literature (French)
      West African fiction (French)

Ivory Coast literature (French) *(May Subd Geog)*
  [PQ3988.5.I9 (History)]
  [PQ 3988.5.I92 (Collections)]
  UF French literature--Ivory Coast authors
  BT West African literature (French)
  NT Ivory Coast fiction (French)

Ivory Coast proverbs
  USE Proverbs, Ivory Coast

Iyagbe
  USE Ayo (Game)

iYans language
  USE Yanzi language

iYanzi language
  USE Yanzi language

Iyekhee language
  USE Etsako language

Iyo language
  USE Ijo language

(May Subd Geog) = Place names may follow the heading

Izi language *(May Subd Geog)*
  [PL 8286.I9]
  UF Izzi language
  BT Igbo language
      Kwa languages
      Nigeria--Languages

Izo language
  USE Ijo language

Izon language
  USE Ijo language

Izzi language
  USE Izi language

J

Ja'aliyin (Arab tribe)
  USE Ja'aliyyin (Arab tribe)

Ja'aliyyin (Arab tribe) *(May Subd Geog)*
  [DT 155.2.J33]
  UF Ja-aliyin (Arab tribe)
  BT Ethnology--Sudan

Jaawambe (African people) *(May Subd Geog)*
  [DT 530.5.J3]
  BT Ethnology--Africa, French-speaking
West

Jabal al-'Uwaynat (Sudan)
  USE 'Uwaynat Mountain

Jabal Marra (Sudan)
  USE Marra Mountains (Sudan)

Jabal Marrah (Sudan)
  USE Marra Mountains (Sudan)

Jabo (African people) *(May Subd Geog)*
  [DT 630.5.J]
  BT Ethnology--Liberia

Jabo language *(May Subd Geog)*
  [PL 8287]
  UF Gweabo language
  BT Kru languages
      Liberia--Languages

Jaca (African people)
  USE Yaka (African people)

Jack-Jack (African people)
  USE Alagya (African people)

Jagga (African people)
  USE Chaga (African people)

Jagga language
  USE Chaga language

Jakri (African people)
  USE Jekri (African people)

Jaloof language
  USE Wolof language

Jaluo (African people)
  USE Luo (African people)

Jamaa Movement
  [BL 2470.C6 (African religion)]
  [BX 1682.C6 (Catholic Church)]
  BT Bantu-speaking peoples--Religion
      Catholic Church--Zaire

Jamaica *(Not Subd Geog)*
  --Civilization
  -- --African influences
    [F 1874]
    BT Africa--Civilization

Jambo (African people)
  USE Anuak (African people)

Jameson's Raid, 1895-1896
  [DT 929 : old class]
  [DT 1889 : now class]
  BT South African War, 1899-1902
      Transvaal (South Africa)--History--1880-
1910

Jang (African people)
  USE Dinka (African people)

Jargons
  USE Pidgin languages

Jaunde (African people)
  USE Ewondo (African people)

Jaunde language
  USE Ewondo language

Jebel Marra (Sudan)
  USE Marra Mountains (Sudan)

Jebel Marrah (Sudan)
  USE Marra Mountains (Sudan)

UF = Used for; BT = Broader term; RT = Related term; SA = See also; NT = Narrower term

Jebel Oweinat (Sudan)
  USE 'Uwaynat Mountain (Sudan)

Jebel 'Uwaynat (Sudan)
  USE 'Uwaynat Mountain (Sudan)

Jebel 'Uweinat (Sudan)
  USE 'Uwaynat Mountain (Sudan)

Jeji dialect
  USE Fon dialect

Jekri (African people) *(May Subd Geog)*
  [DT 515.45.J44]
  UF Itsekiri (African people)
     Jakri (African people)
  BT Ethnology--Nigeria

Jekri law
  USE Law, Jekri

Jerin-Jerin
  USE Ayo (Game)

Jests
  USE Wit and humor

Jewelry, Black
  USE Blacks--Jewelry

Jewelry, Tuareg
  USE Tuaregs--Jewelry

Jewish-Black relations
  USE Blacks--Relations with Jews

Jewish literature (Ethiopic)
  UF Ethiopic literature, Jewish

Jews *(May Subd Geog)*
  UF Hebrews
     Israelites
  BT Christianity
  NT Falashas
     Kemants
 --Civilization
  UF Civilization, Jewish
  NT Africa--Civilization--Jewish
influences
 --Relations with Blacks
  USE Blacks--Relations with Jews

Jews, Ethiopian
  USE Falashas

Jibal an Nuban (Sudan)
  USE Nuba Mountains (Sudan)

Jie (African people) *(May Subd Geog)*
  [DT 433.245.J]
  BT Ethnology--Uganda
     Nilo-Hamitic tribes

Jimini (African people)
  USE Djimini (African people)

Jimini language
  USE Djimini language

Jinja (African people)
  USE Zinza (African people)

Jita language *(May Subd Geog)*
  [PL 8295]
  UF Kijita language
  BT Bantu languages
     Tanzania--Languages

Jo Alur language
  USE Alur language

Jo Bor language
  USE Bor language (Lwo)

Jo Luo (African people)
  USE Luo (African people)

Jo Luo language
  USE Luo language (Kenya and Tanzania)

Jo Lwo language
  USE Lwo language (Sudan)

Joca (African people)
  USE Yaka (African people)

Johannesburg (South Africa). Hillbrow
  USE Hillbrow (Johannesburg, South Africa)

Johannesburg (South Africa). Pageview
  USE Pageview (Johannesburg, South Africa)

Jok language
  USE Chokwe language

Jokes
  USE Wit and humor

Jola (African people)
  USE Diola (African people)

(May Subd Geog) = Place names may follow the heading

Jolof (African people)
USE Wolof (African people)

Jolof language
USE Wolof language

Jonathan Operation, 1976
USE Entebbe Airport Raid, 1976

Jonglei Canal (Sudan) *(Not Subd Geog)*
BT Canals--Sudan

Jongor language *(May Subd Geog)*
UF Dionkor language
Djongor language
Djonkor language
BT Chad--Languages
Chadic languages

Jos Plateau (Nigeria) *(Not Subd Geog)*
UF Bauchi Plateau (Nigeria)
BT Plateaus--Nigeria

Ju language (Benue-Congo)
USE Kaje language

Ju/wasi (African people)
USE !Kung (African people)

Juba River (Ethiopia and Somalia) *(Not Subd
Geog)*
UF Ganana River (Ethiopia and Somalia)
Giuba River (Ethiopia and Somalia)
BT Rivers--Ethiopia
Rivers--Somalia

Juju music *(May Subd Geog)*
[ML 3503.N6 (History and criticism)]
BT Popular music--Nigeria

Jukon language
USE Jukun language

Juku language
USE Jukun language

Jukun (African people) *(May Subd Geog)*
[DT 515.45.J83]
UF Kwararafa (African people)
BT Ethnology--Nigeria

Jukun language *(May Subd Geog)*
[PL 8301]
UF Jukon language
Juku language
Kurorofa language

BT Jukunoid languages
Nigeria--Languages

Jukunoid languages *(May Subd Geog)*
[PL 8302]
BT Benue-Congo languages
Cameroon--Languages
Nigeria--Languages
NT Jukun language

Jula language
USE Dyula language

July Handicap (Horse race)
[SF 357.J8]
UF Rothmans July Handicap (Horse race)
BT Horse-racing--South Africa

Jur language
USE Lwo language (Sudan)

Juvenile drama
USE Children's plays

Juvenile literature
USE Children's literature

Juvenile plays
USE Children's plays

Juvenile poetry
USE Children's poetry

K

Kaabu Empire *(Not Subd Geog)*
[DT 532.17]
BT Gambia--History
Guinea-Bissau--History

Kaapland (South Africa)
USE Cape of Good Hope (South Africa)

Kaapsedrifrivier (South Africa) *(Not Subd Geog)*
UF Klasies River (South Africa)
BT Rivers--South Africa

Kaapsedrifrivier Valley (South Africa) *(Not Subd
Geog)*
UF Klasies Valley (South Africa)
BT Valleys--South Africa

Kaarta (Mali) *(Not Subd Geog)*
UF Kaarta Massif (Mali)
Massif du Kaarta (Mali)
BT Plateaus--Mali

UF = Used for; BT = Broader term; RT = Related term; SA = See also; NT = Narrower term

Kaarta Massif (Mali)
USE Kaarta (Mali)

Kababish *(May Subd Geog)*
[DT 155.2.K32]
BT Ethnology--Sudan

Kabana River (Ethiopia)
BT Rivers--Ethiopia

Kabba Laka dialect
USE Gambai dialect

Kabiema dialect
USE Kabre dialect

Kabin (African people)
USE Gaanda (African people)

Kabiye (African people)
USE Kabre (African people)

Kabiye dialect
USE Kabre dialect

Kabre (African people) *(May Subd Geog)*
[DT 582.45.K33 (Togo)]
UF Cabrai (African people)
Kabiye (African people)
Kabure (African people)
Kabye (African people)
BT Ethnology--Africa, West
Ethnology--Togo

Kabre women
USE Women, Kabre

Kabre dialect *(May Subd Geog)*
[PL 8725.15.Z9K33]
UF Cabrai dialect
Cabrais dialect
Kabiema dialect
Kabiye dialect
Kabure dialect
Kabye dialect
BT Africa, West--Languages
Tem language
Togo--Languages

Kabundji (Legendary character)
BT Folklore--Zaire
Legends--Zaire

Kabure (African people)
USE Kabre (African people)

Kabure dialect
USE Kabre dialect

Kabye (African people)
USE Kabre (African people)

Kabye dialect
USE Kabre dialect

Kadara (African people) *(May Subd Geog)*
[DT 515.45.K33]
UF Adara (African people)
Kedara (African people)
BT Ethnology--Nigeria

Kado (African people)
USE Dogon (African people)

Kadumodi language
USE Krongo language

Kaduna Mafia *(May Subd Geog)*
[HV 6453.N63]
UF Mafia, Kaduna
BT Organized crime--Nigeria

Kaduna River (Nigeria) *(Not Subd Geog)*
BT Rivers--Nigeria

Kafa (African people)
USE Kaffa (African people)

Kaffa (African people) *(May Subd Geog)*
[DT 380.4.K]
UF Caffa (African people)
Caffina (African people)
Coffino (African people)
Gomaro (African people)
Kafa (African people)
Kafficho (African people)
Kafico (African people)
Kefa (African people)
Kefinya (African people)
BT Ethnology--Ethiopia

Kaffa language *(May Subd Geog)*
[PJ 2578]
BT Omotic languages

Kaffer language
USE Xhosa language

(May Subd Geog) = Place names may follow the heading

Kafficho (African people)
  USE Kaffa (African people)

Kaffir language
  USE Xhosa language

Kaffir Wars, 1811-1878
  USE South Africa--History--Frontier Wars,
1811-1878

Kaffirs (African people)
  USE Xhosa (African people)

Kafico (African people)
  USE Kaffa (African people)

Kafir language
  USE Xhosa language

Kafir Wars, 1811-1878
  USE South Africa--History--Frontier Wars,
1811-1878

Kafirs (African people)
  USE Xhosa (African people)
      Zulu (African people)

Kafu (African people)
  USE Sherbro (African people)

Kafue Flats (Zambia) (Not Subd Geog)
  BT Floodplains--Zambia
     Kafue River Valley (Zambia)

Kafue River (Zambia) (Not Subd Geog)
  BT Rivers--Zambia

Kafue River Valley (Zambia) (Not Subd Geog)
  BT Valleys--Zambia
  NT Kafue Flats (Zambia)

Kagera National Park (Rwanda)
  USE Parc national de la Kagera (Rwanda)

Kagera River (Not Subd Geog)
  UF Akagera River
     Alexandra Nile River
  BT Rivers--Africa, East

Kagere (African people)
  USE Bayot (African people)

Kagoro (African people) (May Subd Geog)
  [DT 515.45.K]
  BT Ethnology--Nigeria

--Missions (May Subd Geog)
  [BV 3630.K3]
  UF Missions to Kagoro (African people)

Kagoro dialect (May Subd Geog)
  [PL 8374.K3695K33]
  UF Agolok dialect
     Aguro dialect
     Agwolok dialect
     Agwot dialect
     Goro dialect
     Gworok dialect
  BT Katab language
     Nigeria--Languages

Kagou (African people)
  USE Gagou (African people)

Kaguru (African people) (May Subd Geog)
  [DT 433.3.K33]
  UF Wakaguru (African people)
  BT Ethnology--Tanzania
--Missions (May Subd Geog)
  [BV 3630.K32]
  UF Missions to Kaguru (African people)

Kaguru language (May Subd Geog)
  [PL 8341]
  BT Sagara language
     Tanzania--Languages

Kaguru philosophy
  USE Philosophy, Kaguru

Kahlamba
  USE Drakensberg Mountains

Kahonde (African people)
  USE Kaonde (African people)

Kaila
  USE Falashas

Kainji Lake (Nigeria)
  USE Kainji Resevoir (Nigeria)

Kainji Reservoir (Nigeria) (Not Subd Geog)
  UF Kainji Lake (Nigeria)
  BT Lakes--Nigeria
     Reservoirs--Nigeria

Kaje language (May Subd Geog)
  [PL 8345]
  UF Ju language (Benue-Congo)
  BT Nigeria--Languages
     Plateau languages (Nigeria)

UF = Used for; BT = Broader term; RT = Related term; SA = See also; NT = Narrower term

Kaka (African people)
  USE Mfumte (African people)
       Yamba (African people)

Kaka language (Grasslands Bantu)
  USE Yamba language (Cameroon and Nigeria)

Kakamega Forest Reserve (Kenya) *(Not Subd Geog)*
  BT Forest reserves--Kenya
      National parks and reserves--Kenya

Kakongo (African people)
  USE Kongo (African people)

Kakongo dialect
  USE Koongo dialect (Western Kongo)

Kakoongo dialect
  USE Koongo dialect (Western Kongo)

Kakua dialect
  USE Kakwa dialect

Kakwa dialect *(May Subd Geog)*
  [PL 8061.95.K]
  UF Kakua dialect
  BT Bari language
      Sudan--Languages
      Uganda--Languages
      Zaire--Languages

Kalabari (African people)
  USE Ijo (African people)

Kalabari dialect *(May Subd Geog)*
  [PL 8276.95.K3]
  BT Ijo language
      Nigeria--Languages

Kalahari Desert *(Not Subd Geog)*
  BT Deserts--Africa, Southern
      Deserts--Botswana

Kalanga (African people)
  USE Karanga (African people)

Kalebwe (African people)
  USE Lulua (African people)

Kalebwe language (Luba-Lulua)
  USE Luba-Lulua language

Kalebwe language (Songe)
  USE Songe language

Kalega (African people)
  USE Waregas

Kalela (African dance)
  [GV 1705]
  BT Dancing--Africa

Kalenjin (African people) *(May Subd Geog)*
  [DT 429.5.K35 (East Africa)]
  BT Ethnology--Africa, East
      Ethnology--Kenya
      Ethnology--Uganda

Kalenjin language *(May Subd Geog)*
  [PL 8349]
  BT Kenya--Languages
      Nandi languages
      Tanzania--Languages
      Uganda--Languages
  NT Nandi language
      Suk language
 --Tone
  BT Tone (Phonetics)

Kalenjin riddles
  USE Riddles, Kalenjin

Kaleri (African people)
  USE Mabo-Barkul (African people)

Kali (African people)
  USE Mbum (African people)

Kalibong (African people)
  USE Murzu (African people)

Kalimba (Musical instrument)
  USE Mbira

Kalios (Malagasy people)
  USE Behosys

Kalk Bay Mountains (South Africa) *(Not Subd Geog)*
  BT Mountains--South Africa

Kalunda (African people)
  USE Lunda, Northern (African people)

Kama language
  USE Karaboro language

Kamant language
  USE Kemant language

Kamasia (African people)
  USE Tugen (African people)

(May Subd Geog) = Place names may follow the heading

Kamasya (African people)
 USE Tugen (African people)

Kamba (African people) (May Subd Geog)
 [DT 433.545.K36]
 UF Akamba (African people)
    Wakamba (African people)
 BT Bantu-speaking peoples
    Ethnology--Kenya

Kamba folk songs
 USE Folk songs, Kamba

Kamba language (May Subd Geog)
 [PL 8351]
 UF Kikamba language
 BT Bantu languages
    Kenya--Languages
 NT Kikuyu language

Kamba law
 USE Law, Kamba

Kamba women
 USE Women, Kamba

Kambata (African people) (May Subd Geog)
 [DT 380.4.K34]
 BT Ethnology--Ethiopia

Kambilombilo State Farm (Zambia) (Not Subd Geog)
 BT State farms--Zambia

Kambonsenga (Zambian people)
 USE Ambo (Zambian people)

Kamerun
 USE Cameroon

Kamun (African people)
 USE Kamwe (African people)

Kamwe (African people) (May Subd Geog)
 [DT 515.45.K (Nigeria)]
 UF Higi (African people)
    Hiji (African people)
    Kamun (African people)
    Kapsiki (African people)
    Vacamwe (African people)
 BT Ethnology--Cameroon
    Ethnology--Nigeria
 --Missions (May Subd Geog)
 [BV 3630.K35]
 UF Missions to Kamwe (African people)

Kamwe language (May Subd Geog)
 UF Higi language
 BT Cameroon--Languages
    Chadic language
    Nigeria--Languages

Kana language (May Subd Geog)
 [PL 8357]
 UF Khana language
    Ogoni language
 BT Benue-Congo languages
    Nigeria--Languages

Kanakhoe language
 USE G//ana language

Kanakuru language (May Subd Geog)
 [PL 8358]
 UF Dera language
    Deru language
 BT Bolewa languages
    Nigeria--Languages

Kanda (African people)
 USE Gaanda (African people)

Kandjaga language
 USE Buli language

Kanem-Bornou (Empire)
 USE Kanem-Bornu Empire

Kanem-Bornu Empire
 UF Bornu-Kanem (Empire)
    Kanem-Bornou (Empire)
 BT Kanuri (African people)--History

Kanembu (African people) (May Subd Geog)
 [DT 546.445.K36 (Chad)]
 BT Ethnology--Chad
    Ethnology--Niger
    Ethnology--Nigeria

Kangable (African people)
 USE Tagbana (African people)

Kaniaka (African people)
 USE Kanyok (African people)

Kanjaga (African people)
 USE Builsa (African people)

Kanjaga language
 USE Buli language

UF = Used for; BT = Broader term; RT = Related term; SA = See also; NT = Narrower term

Kanjago language
  USE Buli language

Kankomo Clay Deposit (Zambia) *(Not Subd Geog)*
  UF Kankomo dambo (Zambia)
  BT Clay--Zambia

Kankomo dambo (Zambia)
  USE Kankomo Clay Deposit (Zambia)

Kanogo (Kiyovu, Rwanda) *(Not Subd Geog)*
  UF Kiyovu (Rwanda). Kanogo

Kanop language
  USE Mandjak language

Kanouri (African people)
  USE Kanuri (African people)

Kanoury (African people)
  USE Kanuri (African people)

Kanuri (African people) *(May Subd Geog)*
  [DT 515.45.K36 (Nigeria)]
  UF Aga (African people)
      Baribari (African people)
      Beriberi (African people)
      Bornu (African people)
      Kanouri (African people)
      Kanoury (African people)
  BT Ethnology--Chad
      Ethnology--Niger
      Ethnology--Nigeria
 --Education
 --History
  NT Kanem-Bornu Empire

Kanuri language *(May Subd Geog)*
  [PL 8361]
  UF Bornu language
  BT Chad--Languages
      Niger--Languages
      Nigeria--Languages
      Nilo-Saharan languages
  NT Teda language

Kanyika (African people)
  USE Kanyok (African people)

Kanyok (African people) *(May Subd Geog)*
  [DT 650.K33]
  UF Kaniaka (African people)
      Kanyika (African people)
      Kanyoka (African people)

  BT Ethnology--Zaire
      Luba (African people)

Kanyoka (African people)
  USE Kanyok (African people)

Kaokoveld Coast (Namibia)
  USE Skeleton Coast (Namibia)

Kaonde (African people) *(May Subd Geog)*
  [DT 963.42 : old class]
  [DT 3058.K36 : new class]
  UF Bakahonde (African people)
      Bakaonde (African people)
      Kahonde (African people)
      Kaunde (African people)
  BT Bantu-speaking peoples
      Ethnology--Zambia
      Luba (African people)

Kaonde language *(May Subd Geog)*
  [PL 8371]
  UF Luba-Kaonde language
  BT Bantu languages

Kaouar (Niger) *(Not Subd Geog)*
  UF Kawar (Niger)
  BT Oases--Niger

Kaoussan, Rebellion of, 1916-1918
  USE Senussite Rebellion, 1916-1918

Kapala language
  USE Kresh language

Kapland (South Africa)
  USE Cape of Good Hope (South Africa)

Kapsiki (African people)
  USE Kamwe (African people)

Kara (Gbayan people) *(May Subd Geog)*
  [DT 474.6.K (West Africa)]
  BT Ethnology--Africa, West
      Ethnology--Central African Republic
      Gbaya (African people)

Kara language *(May Subd Geog)*
  [PL 8372.5]
  UF Fer language
      Yama language
      Yamegi language
  BT Bongo-Bagirmi languages
      Central African Republic--Languages
      Sudan--Languages

(May Subd Geog) = Place names may follow the heading

Karaboro language *(May Subd Geog)*
  UF Kama language
      Karama language
      Koroma language
  BT Burkina Faso--Languages
      Gur languages
      Ivory Coast--Languages

Karama language
  USE Karaboro language

Karamojong (African people) *(May Subd Geog)*
  [DT 433.245.K35]
  UF Karimojong (African people)
  BT Ethnology--Uganda

Karamojong folk songs
  USE Folk songs, Karamojong

Karamojong language *(May Subd Geog)*
  [PL 8373]
  UF Akarimojong language
      Karimojong language
  BT Teso language
      Uganda--Languages

Karan language
  USE Angas language

Karang (African people)
  USE Angas (African people)

Karang language (Cameroon) *(May Subd Geog)*
  [PL 8374.K]
  BT Cameroon--Languages
      Niger-Congo languages

Karang language (Nigeria)
  USE Angas language

Karanga (African people) *(May Subd Geog)*
  [DT 962.42 : old class]
  [DT 2913.K38 : new class]
  UF Kalanga (African people)
      Wakaranga (African people)
  BT Ethnology--Zimbabwe
      Shona (African people)
  --Kings and rulers

Karanga philosophy
  USE Philosophy, Karanga

Kare (African people)
  USE Mbum (African people)

Kare language *(May Subd Geog)*
  [PL 8374.K33]
  UF Akare language
      Bakare language
      Kari language
  BT Bantu languages
      Central African Republic--Languages
      Zaire--Languages

Kare language (Sudan)
  USE Toposa language

Kari (African people)
  USE Mbum (African people)

Kari language
  USE Kare language

Karimojong (African people)
  USE Karamojong (African people)

Karimojong language
  USE Karamojong language

Karisimbi (Rwanda and Zaire) *(Not Subd Geog)*
  UF Karisimbi, Mount (Rwanda and Zaire)
      Karisimbra, Mount (Rwanda and Zaire)
      Mount Karisimbi (Rwanda and Zaire)
      Mount Karisimbra (Rwanda and Zaire)
  BT Mountains--Rwanda
      Mountains--Zaire
      Virunga
      Volcanoes--Rwanda
      Volcanoes--Zaire

Karisimbi, Mount (Rwanda and Zaire)
  USE Karisimbi (Rwanda and Zaire)

Karisimbra, Mount (Rwanda and Zaire)
  USE Karisimbi (Rwanda and Zaire)

Karoke (African people)
  USE Didinga (African people)

Karon (African people)
  USE Felup (African people)

Karoo, Great (South Africa)
  USE Great Karroo (South Africa)

Karoo, Northern (South Africa)
  USE Northern Karroo (South Africa)

Karoo, Upper (South Africa)
  USE Northern Karroo (South Africa)

UF = Used for; BT = Broader term; RT = Related term; SA = See also; NT = Narrower term

Karoo Supergroup
  USE Karroo Supergroup

Karre (African people)
  USE Mbum (African people)

Karré language *(May Subd Geog)*
  [PL 8374.K]
  BT Adamawa languages
      Chad--Languages

Karroo, Great (South Africa)
  USE Great Karroo (South Africa)

Karroo, Northern (South Africa)
  USE Northern Karroo (South Africa)

Karroo Beds
  USE Karroo Supergroup

Karroo Series
  USE Karroo Supergroup

Karroo Supergroup *(Not Subd Geog)*
  UF Karoo Supergroup
      Karroo Beds
      Karroo Series
      Karroo System
  BT Groups (Stratigraphy)--Africa,
Southern

Karroo System
  USE Karroo Supergroup

Kasai River (Angola and Zaire) *(Not Subd Geog)*
  UF Cassai River (Angola and Zaire)
      Kassai River (Angola and Zaire)
  BT Rivers--Angola
      Rivers--Zaire

Kasanga (African people) *(May Subd Geog)*
  [DT 650.K36 (Zaire)]
  UF Cassanga (African people)
      I-hadja (African people)
      Kasenga (African people)
      Kassanga (African people)
  BT Ethnology--Guinea-Bissau
      Ethnology--Zaire

Kasem language *(May Subd Geog)*
  [PL 8223.G995K34]
  UF Kasena dialect
      Kasene language
      Kason Bura language
      Kason Fra language
      Kassena language

  BT Burkina Faso--Languages
      Ghana--Languages
      Grusi languages
  NT Nunuma dialect

Kasena (African people) *(May Subd Geog)*
  [DT 510.43.K37]
  BT Ethnology--Ghana

Kasena dialect
  USE Kasem language

Kasene language
  USE Kasem language

Kasenga (African people)
  USE Kasanga (African people)

Kason Bura language
  USE Kasem language

Kason Fra language
  USE Kasem language

Kasona
  USE Tusona

Kassai River (Angola and Zaire)
  USE Kasai River (Angola and Zaire)

Kassanga (African people)
  USE Kasanga (African people)

Kassena language
  USE Kasem language

Katab language *(May Subd Geog)*
  [PL 8374.K36]
  UF Atyap language
      Tyap language
  BT Nigeria--Languages
      Plateau languages (Nigeria)
  NT Kagoro dialect

Katanga (Secessionist government, 1960-1963)
  USE Shaba (Zaire)

Katanga (Zaire)
  USE Shaba (Zaire)

Katanga language
  USE Luba-Katanga language

Katanganese Invasion (Zaire), 1977
  USE Zaire--History--Shaba Invasion, 1977

(May Subd Geog) = Place names may follow the heading

Katchokue language
USE Chokwe language

Katekelayi Hill (Zaire) *(Not Subd Geog)*
BT Mountains--Zaire

Katongo Site (Zaire) *(Not Subd Geog)*
BT Zaire--Antiquities

Kaunde (African people)
USE Kaonde (African people)

Kavirondo (African people) *(May Subd Geog)*
[DT 429.K (East Africa)]
[DT 433.545.K (Kenya)]
BT Bantu-speaking peoples
Ethnology--Africa, East
Ethnology--Kenya
NT Gisu (African people)

Kavirondo (Nilotic people)
USE Luo (African people)

Kavirondo language, Nilotic
USE Luo language (Kenya and Tanzania)

Kawanga dialect
USE Hanga dialect (Kenya)

Kawar (Niger)
USE Kaouar (Niger)

Kayumba (African people)
USE Luba (African people)

Kebadi (African people)
USE Zaghawa (African people)

Kebbi River (Nigeria)
USE Sokoto River (Nigeria)

Kebeirka (African people)
USE Uduk (African people)

Kedara (African people)
USE Kadara (African people)

Kedi (African people)
USE Teso (African people)

Kefa (African people)
USE Kaffa (African people)

Kefinya (African people)
USE Kaffa (African people)

Keiyo (African people)
USE Elgeyo (African people)

Kel Azdjer (African people)
USE Ajjer (African people)

Kela (African people) *(May Subd Geog)*
[DT 650.K39]
UF Ekela (African people)
Ikela (African people)
Lemba (African people)
Okela (African people)
BT Ethnology--Zaire

Kela language *(May Subd Geog)*
[PL 8376.K45]
UF Lemba language
Okela language
RT Bantu languages
Zaire--Languages

Kela women
USE Women, Kela

Kele (African people)
USE Lokele (African people)

Kele language *(May Subd Geog)*
[PL 8377]
UF Bakele language
Di-kele language
BT Bantu languages
Gabon--Languages

Kelelwa Farm (Kenya) *(Not Subd Geog)*
BT Farms--Kenya

Kemant language *(May Subd Geog)*
[PJ 2438]
UF Gamant language
Kamant language
Komant language
Qomant language
BT Agau language

Kemants *(May Subd Geog)*
[DT 380.4.K45]
BT Ethnology--Ethiopia
Jews

Kenga language *(May Subd Geog)*
[PL 8378.K3]
BT Chad--Languages
Sara languages

UF = Used for; BT = Broader term; RT = Related term; SA = See also; NT = Narrower term

Kenga proverbs
  USE Proverbs, Kenga

Kente cloth
  USE West African strip weaving

Kenu (African people)
  USE Kenuz (African people)

Kenuz (African people) *(May Subd Geog)*
  [DT 72.K]
  UF Kenu (African people)
      Mattokki (African people)
  BT Ethnology--Egypt

Kenuz dialect
  USE Dongola-Kenuz dialect

Kenuzi dialect
  USE Dongola-Kenuz dialect

Kenuzi-Dongola dialect
  USE Dongola-Kenuz dialect

Kenya *(Not Subd Geog)*
  [DT 433.5-DT 434]
  UF Colony and Protectorate of Kenya
      East Africa Protectorate
  NT Manda Island (Kenya)
 --**Antiquities**
  NT Lopoy Site (Kenya)
      Lothagam Site (Kenya)
      Mtongwe Site (Kenya)
 --**Description and travel**
 -- --1981-
 --**Economic conditions**
  [HC 865]
 -- --To 1963
 -- --1963-
 --**Fiction**
  NT Swahili fiction
 -- **History**
 -- --To 1895
  NT Mombasa (Kenya)--History--Uprising,
1631
 -- --To 1963
 -- --1895-1963
 -- --1963-
 --**Languages**
  NT Boni language
      Boran dialect
      Bukusu dialect
      Burji language
      Cifundi dialect
      Cushitic languages, Southern
      Dabida dialect

  NT Dahalo language
      Digo language
      Embu language
      Giryama language
      Gusii language
      Hanga dialect (Kenya)
      Kalenjin language
      Kamba language
      Kikuyu language
      Kipsikis dialect
      Kisa dialect
      Kuria language
      Kwafi language
      Logooli language
      Luo language (Kenya and Tanzania)
      Luyia language
      Masai language
      Meru language
      Nandi language
      Nandi languages
      Nika language
      Nubi language
      Nyore language
      Oromo language
      Ragoli language
      Rendile language
      Samburu language
      Shambala languages
      Somali languages
      Suk language
      Swahili language
      Taita language
      Taveta language
      Teso language
      Turkana language
 --**Literatures**
  USE Kenyan literature
 --**Poetry**
  NT Swahili poetry
 --**Politics and government**
 -- --To 1963
  NT Mau Mau
 -- --1963-1978
 -- --1978-
 -- **Social conditions**
 -- --1963-
 --**Social life and customs**
 -- --1895-1963

Kenya, Mount (Kenya) *(Not Subd Geog)*
  UF Kilinyaga (Kenya)
      Kirinyaga (Kenya)
      Mount Kenya (Kenya)
  BT Mountains--Kenya
      Volcanoes--Kenya

(May Subd Geog) = Place names may follow the heading

Kenya Highlands (Kenya) *(Not Subd Geog)*
  UF Highlands, Kenya (Kenya)
      White Highlands (Kenya)
  BT Mountains--Kenya
      Plateaus--Kenya

Kenyan art
  USE Art, Kenyan

Kenyan atlases
  USE Atlases, Kenyan

Kenyan authors
  USE Authors, Kenyan

Kenyan children's poetry (English)
  USE Children's poetry, Kenyan (English)

Kenyan children's stories (English)
  USE Children's stories, Kenyan (English)

Kenyan college and school drama (English)
  USE College and school drama, Kenyan
(English)

Kenyan cookery
  USE Cookery, Kenyan

Kenyan drama (English) *(May Subd Geog)*
  [PR 9381.3 (History)]
  [PR 9381.7 (Collections)]
  UF English drama--Kenyan authors
  BT East African drama (English)
      Kenyan literature (English)
  NT College and school drama, Kenyan
(English)
      Radio plays, Kenyan (English)

Kenyan fiction (English) *(May Subd Geog)*
  [PR 9381.4 (History)]
  [PR 9381.8 (Collections)]
  UF English fiction--Kenyan authors
  BT Kenyan literature (English)
  NT Children's stories, Kenyan (English)

Kenyan literature *(May Subd Geog)*
  [PL 8014.K]
  UF Kenya--Literatures
  BT East African literature
  NT Kenyan wit and humor
      Masai literature
      Meru literature
      Prisoners' writings, Kenyan
      Swahili literature

Kenyan literature (English) *(May Subd Geog)*
  [PR 9381]
  UF English literature--Kenyan authors
  BT East African literature (English)
  NT Kenyan drama (English)
      Kenyan fiction (English)
      Kenyan poetry (English)

Kenyan periodicals *(May Subd Geog)*
  [PN 5499.K4]
  UF Periodicals, Kenyan

Kenyan poetry (English) *(May Subd Geog)*
  [PR 9381.2 (History)]
  [PR 9381.6 (Collections)]
  UF English poetry--Kenyan authors
  BT East African poetry (English)
      Kenyan literature (English)
  NT Children's poetry, Kenyan (English)

Kenyan prisoners' writings
  USE Prisoners' writings, Kenyan

Kenyan radio plays (English)
  USE Radio plays, Kenyan (English)

Kenyan wit and humor *(May Subd Geog)*
  [PN 6222.K (Collections)]
  UF Wit and humor, Kenyan
  BT Kenyan literature

Kenyan wit and humor, Pictorial
  [NC 1740.K]
  UF Wit and humor, Pictorial (Kenyan)

Kenyang (African people)
  USE Nyang (African people)

Kenyang language
  USE Anyang language

Kenzi dialect
  USE Dongola-Kenuz dialect

Kera (African people) *(May Subd Geog)*
  [DT 546.445.K]
  BT Ethnology--Chad
  --Folklore
  [GR 355.52.K47]

Kera language *(May Subd Geog)*
  [PL 8378.K]
  BT Chad--Languages
      Chadic languages

UF = Used for; BT = Broader term; RT = Related term; SA = See also; NT = Narrower term

Kerang (African people)
  USE Angas (African people)

Kerebe (African people) *(May Subd Geog)*
  [DT 443.3.K47]
  BT Bantu-speaking peoples
       Ethnology--Tanzania

Kerebe language *(May Subd Geog)*
  [PL 8378.K37]
  UF eciKerebe language
       ekiKerebe language
       Kerewe language
  BT Bantu languages
       Tanzania--Languages

Keren, Battle of (Ethiopia), 1941
  USE Cheren, Battle of, 1941

Kerewe language
  USE Kerebe language

Kerio River (Kenya) *(Not Subd Geog)*
  UF Endo River (Kenya)
       Ndo River (Kenya)
  BT Rivers--Kenya

Kesem River (Ethiopia) *(Not Subd Geog)*
  UF Kessem River (Ethiopia)
  BT Rivers--Ethiopia

Kessem River (Ethiopia)
  USE Kesem River (Ethiopia)

Kesukuma language
  USE Sukuma language

Kete language *(May Subd Geog)*
  [PL 8378.K45]
  UF KiKete language
       LuKete language
  BT Bantu languages
       Zaire--Languages

Kgaga (African people) *(May Subd Geog)*
  [DT 764.K42 : old class]
  [DT 1768.K : new class]
  UF Bakhaha (African people)
       Khaha (African people)
       Kxaxa (African people)
  BT Ethnology--South Africa
       Sotho (African people)

Kgaga philosophy
  USE Philosophy, Kgaga

Kgalagadi (African people) *(May Subd Geog)*
  [DT 797 : old class]
  [DT 2458.K : new class]
  UF Bakalahadi (African people)
       Bakgalagadi (African people)
       Balala (African people)
  BT Ethnology--Botswana

Kgalagadi dialect *(May Subd Geog)*
  [PL 8747.95.K45]
  UF Khalahadi dialect
       Kxhalaxadi dialect
  BT Botswana--Languages
       Tswana language

Kgatla (African people) *(May Subd Geog)*
  [DT 797 (Botswana : old class]
  [DT 2458.K53 (Botswana : new class)]
  [DT 764.K (South Africa : old class)]
  [DT 1768.K53 (South Africa : new class)]
  [DT 962.42 (Zimbabwe : old class)]
  [DT 2913.K53 (Zimbabwe : new class)]
  UF Ba-Katlha (African people)
       Bakatla (African people)
       Bakgatla (African people)
       Bakhatla (African people)
  BT Ethnology--Botswana
       Ethnology--South Africa
       Ethnology--Zimbabwe
       Tswana (African people)
  --Missions *(May Subd Geog)*
  [BV 3630.K45]
  UF Missions to Kgatla (African people)

Kgatla law
  USE Law, Kgatla

Khaha (African people)
  USE Kgaga (African people)

Khalahadi dialect
  USE Kgalagadi dialect

Kham language *(May Subd Geog)*
  [PL 8378.K48]
  BT San languages
       South Africa--Languages

Khana language
  USE Kana language

Khartoum Relief Expedition, 1884-1885
  USE Gordon Relief Expedition, 1884-1885

(May Subd Geog) = Place names may follow the heading

Khoikhoi (African people) *(May Subd Geog)*
  [DT 764.K45 (South Africa : old class)]
  [DT 1768.K56 (South Africa : new class)]
  [DT 737 (Southern Africa : old class)]
  [DT 1058.K56 (Southern Africa : new
class)]
  UF Hottentot (African people)
  BT Ethnology--Africa, Southern
      Ethnology--South Africa
  NT Bondelswarts (African people)
      Damara (African people)
      Griquas
      Heikum (African people)
      Korana (African people)
      Nama (African people)
      Tannekwe (African people)
 --Anthropometry
 --Missions *(May Subd Geog)*
  [BV 3630.K47]
  UF Missions to Khoikhoi (African people)
 --Name
  NT Hottentot (Name)
 --Religion
  [BL 2480.K45]

Khoikhoi language *(May Subd Geog)*
  [PL 8251-PL 8254]
  UF Hottentot language
  BT Africa, Southern--Languages
      Khoisan languages
  NT Korana language
      Nama language
 --Names
 USE Names, Khoikhoi

Khoikhoi names
 USE Names, Khoikhoi

Khoisan languages *(May Subd Geog)*
  [PL 8026.K45]
  UF Click languages, Non-Bantu
  BT Africa, Southern--Languages
      African languages
  NT G//ana language
      G/wi language
      Khoikhoi language
      Nharo language
      San languages
      Sandawe language
 --Clicks
  BT Clicks (Phonetics)

Khora (African people)
 USE Korana (African people)

Khumi language (Sudan)
 USE Toposa language

!Khung (African people)
 USE !Kung (African people)

!Khung language
 USE !Xu language

Khwakhwa (African people) *(May Subd Geog)*
  [DT 786.5 : old class]
  [DT 2596.K : new class]
  BT Ethnology--Lesotho

Khwara language
 USE Quara language

Ki-Mtang'ata dialect
 USE Mtang'ata dialect

Ki-vili language
 USE Vili language

Ki-vumbu language
 USE Vili language

Kibale Forest Reserve (Uganda) *(Not Subd Geog)*
  BT Forest reserves--Uganda
      National parks and reserves--Uganda

kiBangi language
 USE Bobangi language

KiBeembe language
 USE Beembe language (Congo (Brazzaville))

KiBembe language
 USE Bembe language (Congo (Brazzaville))

Kibissi (African people)
 USE Dogon (African people)

Kiboma (African people)
 USE Boma (African people)

Kiboma language
 USE Boma language

Kibondei language
 USE Bondei language

Kibulamatadi language
 USE Kituba language

Kidawida dialect
 USE Dabida dialect

UF = Used for; BT = Broader term; RT = Related term; SA = See also; NT = Narrower term

KiDigo language
  USE Digo language

Kien language
  USE Tchien language

Kiga (African people)
  USE Chiga (African people)

Kiga language *(May Subd Geog)*
  [PL 8378.K]
  UF Chiga language
      Ciga language
      Lukiga language
      Rukiga language
  BT Bantu languages
      Uganda--Languages
  RT Nyankore-Kiga language

Kigiriama (African people)
  USE Giryama (African people)

Kigiryama language
  USE Giryama language

Kijita language
  USE Jita language

Kikamba language
  USE Kamba language

KiKete language
  USE Kete language

Kikongo language
  USE Kongo language

Kikongo ya Leta language
  USE Kituba language

Kikoria language
  USE Kuria language

Kikouria language
  USE Kuria language

Kikuria language
  USE Kuria language

Kikuyu (African people) *(May Subd Geog)*
  [DT 433.545.K55]
  UF Akikuyu (African people)
      Gikuyu (African people)
      Wakikuyu (African people)
  BT Bantu-speaking peoples
      Ethnology--Kenya

--**Food**
  BT Food
--**History**
  NT Mau Mau
--**Marriage customs and rites**
  UF Marriage customs and rites, Kikuyu (African
people)
--**Missions** *(May Subd Geog)*
  [BV 3630.K55]
  UF Missions to Kikuyu (African people)
--**Religion**
  [BL 2480.K54]
--**Rites and ceremonies**

Kikuyu folk songs
  USE Folk songs, Kikuyu

Kikuyu language *(May Subd Geog)*
  [PL 8379]
  UF Gikuyu language
  BT Kamba language
      Kenya--Languages

Kikuyu women
  USE Women, Kikuyu

Kikwango language
  USE Kituba language

KiKwese language
  USE Kwese language

Kilari dialect
  USE Laadi dialect

Kilega language *(May Subd Geog)*
  [PL 8380.K5]
  UF Balega language
      Lega language
  BT Bantu languages
      Zaire--Languages

Kileta (African people)
  USE Kongo (African people)

Kileta language
  USE Kituba language

Kili (African people)
  USE Lokele (African people)

Kilimandjaro, Mount (Tanzania)
  USE Kilimanjaro, Mount (Tanzania)

Kilimandscharo, Mount (Tanzania)
  USE Kilimanjaro, Mount (Tanzania)

(May Subd Geog) = Place names may follow the heading

Kilimanjaro, Mount (Tanzania) *(Not Subd Geog)*
   UF Kilimandjaro, Mount (Tanzania)
      Kilimandscharo, Mount (Tanzania)
      Mount Kilimanjaro (Tanzania)
   BT Mountains--Tanzania
      Volcanoes--Tanzania

Kilindi (African people) *(May Subd Geog)*
   [DT 443.3.K54]
   UF Wakilindi (African people)
   BT Ethnology--Tanzania

Kilinyaga (Kenya)
   USE Kenya, Mount (Kenya)

Kiluba language
   USE Luba-Katanga language

Kiluba-Sanga language
   USE Sanga language

Kimbala language
   USE Mbala language (Bandundu region, Zaire)

Kimberley (South Africa) *(Not Subd Geog)*
  --History
  -- --Siege, 1899-1900
   [DT 934.K5 : old class]
   [DT 1908.K56 : new class]
   BT South African War, 1899-1902

Kimbu (African people) *(May Subd Geog)*
   [DT 443.2.K]
   UF Akimbu (African people)
      Ukimbu (African people)
   BT Bantu-speaking peoples
      Ethnology--Tanzania

Kimbunda language
   USE Mbunda language (Zambia)

Kimbundu folk songs
   USE Folk songs, Kimbundu

Kimbundu language *(May Subd Geog)*
   [PL 8381]
   UF Angola language
      Bunda language
      Mbundu language
   BT Angola--Languages
      Bantu languages

Kimbundu proverbs
   USE Proverbs, Kimbundu

Kimegi language
   USE Sagara language

Kimeru language
   USE Meru language

Kindiga (African people)
   USE Tindiga (African people)

Kingala language
   USE Kituba language

Kingdom of Burundi
   USE Burundi

Kingdom of Fouta Diallon
   USE Futa Jallon

Kingdom of Kongo
   USE Kongo Kingdom

Kingdoms and empires, Traditional
   SEE Adamawa (Emirate)
      Aksum (Kingdom)
      Ashanti (Kingdom)
      Benin (Nigeria)--History
      Bunyoro-Kitara
      Denkyira (Kingdom)
      Fula Empire
      Fuladu (Kingdom)
      Futa Jallon
      Ghana Empire
      Kaabu Empire
      Kanem-Bornu Empire
      Kongo Kingdom
      Mali Empire
      Niumi (Kingdom)
      Oyo Empire
      Songhai Empire
      Toucouleur Empire
      Yatenga (Kingdom)

Kingeti (African people)
   USE Lendu (African people)

Kings and rulers *(Not Subd Geog)*
   UF Monarchs
      Royalty
      Rulers
      Sovereigns
   BT History
   SA *subdivisions* Kings and rulers *and* Queens *under names of countries, cities, etc., and under ethnic groups,* e.g., Karanga (African people)--Kings and rulers

UF = Used for; BT = Broader term; RT = Related term; SA = See also; NT = Narrower term

Kingwana language *(May Subd Geog)*
  [PL 8387]
  BT Swahili language
      Zaire--Languages

Kiniassa language
  USE Nyanja language

Kiniramba language
  USE Nilamba language

Kinship *(May Subd Geog)*
  [GN 480-GN 480.65]
  BT Ethnology
  RT Clans
      Family
      Tribes
 --Africa

Kintaandu dialect
  USE Ntaandu dialect

Kintandu dialect
  USE Ntaandu dialect

KiNubi language
  USE Nubi language

Kinyamwesi language
  USE Nyamwezi language

Kinyamwezi language
  USE Nyamwezi language

KiNyanga language
  USE Nyanga language

Kinyaruanda language
  USE Kinyarwanda language

Kinyarwanda folk songs
  USE Folk songs, Kinyarwanda

Kinyarwanda language *(May Subd Geog)*
  [PL 8608]
  UF IkinyaRuanda language
      Kinyaruanda language
      Nyaruanda language
      Orunyarwanda language
      Ruanda language
      Runyaruanda language
      Runyarwanda language
      Rwanda language
      Urunyaruanda language
      Urunyarwanda language
  BT Bantu languages

  BT Burundi--Languages
      Rwanda--Languages

Kinyarwanda literature *(May Subd Geog)*
  [PL 8608.5-PL 8608.9]
  UF Ruanda literature
  BT African literature
      Burundi--Literatures
      Rwanda--Literatures
  NT Kinyarwanda poetry

Kinyarwanda poetry *(May Subd Geog)*
  [PL 8608.5-PL 8608.9]
  UF Ruanda poetry
  BT African poetry
      Kinyarwanda literature

Kinyarwanda proverbs
  USE Proverbs, Kinyarwanda

Kinyarwanda riddles
  USE Riddles, Kinyarwanda

Kinyarwanda songs
  USE Songs, Kinyarwanda

Kinyarwanda wit and humor *(May Subd Geog)*
  [PL 8608 (History and major collections)]
  [PN 6222.R78 (Minor collections)]
  UF Wit and humor, Kinyarwanda

Kioko (African people)
  USE Chokwe (African people)

Kioko language
  USE Chokwe language

Kiokwe language
  USE Chokwe language

Kiombe (African people)
  USE Yombe (African people)

Kiombe language
  USE Yombe language

Kipende language
  USE Pende language

Kipimpi (Zairian mythology)
  [BL 2470.Z2]
  BT Mythology, Zairian

Kipsigis (African people) *(May Subd Geog)*
  [DT 433.545.K57]
  UF Kipsikis (African people)

       (May Subd Geog) = Place names may follow the heading

UF Lumbwa (African people)
    Sikisi (African people)
BT Ethnology--Kenya
    Nilo-Hamitic tribes

Kipsigis dialect
  USE Kipsikis dialect

Kipsigis law
  USE Law, Kipsigis

Kipsikis (African people)
  USE Kipsigis (African people)

Kipsikis dialect *(May Subd Geog)*
  [PL 8545.95.K]
  UF Kipsigis dialect
  BT Kenya--Languages
    Nandi language

Kira language
  USE Vagala language

Kirdiwat language
  USE Ngizim language

Kirimiro natural region (Burundi)
  USE Kirimiro Region (Burundi)

Kirimiro Region (Burundi) *(Not Subd Geog)*
  UF Kirimiro natural region (Burundi)
    Région du Kirimiro (Burundi)
    Région naturelle du Kirimiro (Burundi)
  BT Natural areas--Burundi

Kirinyaga (Kenya)
  USE Kenya, Mount (Kenya)

Kirundi language
  USE Rundi language

Kisa dialect *(May Subd Geog)*
  [PL 8474.L895K57]
  UF LuKisa dialect
    Lushisa dialect
    Olushisa dialect
  BT Kenya--Languages
    Luyia language
  --Transitivity
Kisakata language
  USE Sakata language

Kisantu dialect
  USE Ntaandu dialect

KiShambaa language
  USE Shambala language

Kishambala language
  USE Shambala language

Kisi language
  USE Kissi language

Kisii (African people)
  USE Gusii (African people)

Kisii language
  USE Gusii language

Kisogo language
  USE Kwafi language

Kisolongo dialect
  USE Solongo dialect

Kisonge language
  USE Songe language

Kissandaui language
  USE Sandawe language

Kissi (African people) *(May Subd Geog)*
  [DT 543.45.K (Guinea)]
  BT Ethnology--Guinea
    Ethnology--Liberia
    Ethnology--Sierra Leone

Kissi language *(May Subd Geog)*
  UF Dei language
    Gihi language
    Gii language
    Gisi language
    Gizi language
    Gizima language
    Kisi language
    Kissien language
  BT Guinea--Languages
    Liberia--Languages
    Niger-Congo languages
    Sierra Leone--Languages

Kissien language
  USE Kissi language

Kisuku language
  USE Suku language (Zaire)

Kiswahili language
  USE Swahili language

UF = Used for; BT = Broader term; RT = Related term; SA = See also; NT = Narrower term

Kitabwa language *(May Subd Geog)*
  [PL 8391]
  BT Bantu languages
      Zaire--Languages
      Zambia--Languages

Kitara (African people)
  USE Nyoro (African people)

KiTaveta language
  USE Taveta language

Kitchen Kaffir
  USE Fanakalo

Kiteke language
  USE Teke language

KiTembo language
  USE Tembo language (Kivu, Zaire)

Kitharaka (African people)
  USE Tharaka (African people)

Kitosh dialect
  USE Bukusu dialect

Kitswa language
  USE Tswa language

Kituba language *(May Subd Geog)*
  [PL 8404.Z9K5]
  UF Fiote language
      Ikeleve language
      Kibulamatadi language
      Kikongo ya Leta language
      Kikwango language
      Kileta language
      Kingala language
      Kizabave language
      Monokutuba language
      Munukutuba language
  BT Congo (Brazzaville)--Languages
      Kongo language
      Lingua francas
      Zaire--Languages

KiTubeta language
  USE Taveta language

Kiusa language
  USE Ngonde language

Kivili language
  USE Vili language

Kivu, Lake (Rwanda and Zaire) *(Not Subd Geog)*
  UF Lac Kivu (Rwanda and Zaire)
      Lake Kivu (Rwanda and Zaire)
  BT Lakes--Rwanda
      Lakes--Zaire

Kivumbu language
  USE Vili language

Kiyaka language
  USE Yaka language (Zaire and Angola)

KiYanzi language
  USE Yanzi language

Kiyombe language
  USE Yombe language

Kiyovu (Rwanda). Kanogo
  USE Kanogo (Kiyovu, Rwanda)

Kizabave language
  USE Kituba language

Kiziba (African people)
  USE Haya (African people)

Kizombo dialect
  USE Zoombo dialect

Kizoombo dialect
  USE Zoombo dialect

Klao language
  USE Kru language

Klasies River (South Africa)
  USE Kaapsedrifrivier (South Africa)

Klasies Valley (South Africa)
  USE Kaapsedrifrivier Valley (South Africa)

Kō language
  USE Yakö language

!Ko language (Botswana and Namibia)
  USE !Xo language

Koke (African people)
  USE Hamar (African people)

Koko (Cameroon people)
  USE Basa (Cameroon people)

Kolango language
  USE Kulango language

(May Subd Geog) = Place names may follow the heading

Kolanko (African people)
USE Kuranko (African people)

Kolkotto language
USE Baria language

Kolokuma dialect *(May Subd Geog)*
[PL 8276.95.K6]
UF Patani dialect (Nigeria)
BT Ijo language
Nigeria--Languages

Kololo language
USE Lozi language

Kolwezi (Zaire)--Massacre, 1978
USE Massacres--Zaire--Kolwezi

Kom (African people) *(May Subd Geog)*
[DT 571.K]
UF Damekon (African people)
Bekom (African people)
Bikom (African people)
Nkom (African people)
BT Ethnology--Cameroon

Kom art
USE Art, Kom

Koma (African people) *(May Subd Geog)*
[DT 155.2.K65]
BT Ethnology--Sudan

Komant language
USE Kemant language

Kombe language *(May Subd Geog)*
[PL 8396]
BT Bantu languages
Cameroon--Languages

Komo (Secret order)
[HS 326.Z6K]
BT Ethnology--Africa, French-speaking
West

Komo (Zairian people)
USE Kumu (Zairian people)

Komoro language
USE Comorian language

Konde (African people)
USE Makonde (African people)
Ngonde (African people)

Konde language
USE Makonde language
Ngonde language

Kongo (African people) *(May Subd Geog)*
[DT 611.45.K (Angola : old class)]
[DT 1308.K66 (Angola : new class)]
[DT 650.B33 (Zaire)]
UF Bakongo (African people)
Cabinda (African people)
Congo (African people)
Fjort (African people)
Frote (African people)
Ikeleve (African people)
Kakongo (African people)
Kileta (African people)
Nkongo (African people)
Wacongomani (African people)
DT Bantu-speaking peoples
Ethnology--Angola
Ethnology--Zaire
--Funeral customs and rites
UF Funeral rites and ceremonies, Kongo
(African people)
--History
NT Kongo Kingdom
--Medicine
BT Medicine, Primitive--Angola
Medicine, Primitive--Zaire
--Missions *(May Subd Geog)*
[BV 3630.B24]
UF Missions to Kongo (African people)
--Rites and ceremonies

Kongo imprints *(May Subd Geog)*
[Z 7108.K65]
UF Imprints, Kongo

Kongo Kingdom *(Not Subd Geog)*
[DT 654]
UF Congo (Kingdom)
Kingdom of Kongo
BT Kongo (African people)--History

Kongo language *(May Subd Geog)*
[PL 8401-PL 8404]
UF Congo language
Fiote language
Kikongo language
BT Angola--Languages
Bantu languages
Congo (Brazzaville)--Languages
Zaire--Languages
NT Bembe language (Congo (Brazzaville))
Kituba language

(Continued)

UF = Used for; BT = Broader term; RT = Related term; SA = See also; NT = Narrower term

Kongo language   *(Continued)*
  NT Koongo dialect (Western Kongo)
      Kwese language
      Laadi dialect
      Mbala language (Bandundu region,
Zaire)
      Ntaandu dialect
      Pende language
      Solongo dialect
      Suku language (Zaire)
      Yaka language (Zaire and Angola)
      Zoombo dialect

Kongo proverbs
  USE Proverbs, Kongo

Kongo sculpture
  USE Sculpture, Kongo

Kongo Wara, 1928-1931
  [DT 546.37]
  UF Baya Revolt, 1928-1931
      Hoe Handle, War of the, 1928-1931
      War of the Hoe Handle, 1928-1931
  BT Central African Republic--History--To
1960
      Congo (Brazzaville)--History--To 1960

Kongola (African people)
  USE Kusu (African people)

Koniagui (African people) *(May Subd Geog)*
  [DT 530.5.K64 (French West Africa)]
  UF Coniagui (African people)
  BT Ethnology--Africa, French-speaking
West
      Ethnology--Guinea

Konjo (Zairian people)
  USE Nande (Zairian people)

Konkoma
  [ML 3503.G4 (History)]
  BT Fanti (African people)--Music
      Popular music--Ghana

Konkomba (African people) *(May Subd Geog)*
  [DT 582.45.K (Togo)]
  BT Ethnology--Ghana
      Ethnology--Togo

Konkomba language *(May Subd Geog)*
  [PL 8405.K65]
  BT Ghana--Languages
      Gur languages
      Togo--Languages

Kono (African people) *(May Subd Geog)*
  [DT 516.45.K (Sierra Leone)]
  BT Ethnology--Guinea
      Ethnology--Liberia
      Ethnology--Sierra Leone
  --Religion
  [BL 2480.K6]

Kono language *(May Subd Geog)*
  [PL 8406]
  BT Guinea--Languages
      Liberia--Languages
      Sierra Leone--Languages
      Vai language

Konosara language
  USE Vagala language

Konosarola language
  USE Vagala language

Konso (African people) *(May Subd Geog)*
  [DT 380.4.K65]
  BT Cushites
      Ethnology--Ethiopia

Koon language
  USE !Xo language

Koongo dialect (Western Kongo) *(May Subd Geog)*
  UF Fiote language
      Kakongo dialect
      Kakoongo dialect
      Western Kongo dialect
  BT Congo (Brazzaville)--Languages
      Kongo language

Koosa (African people)
  USE Xhosa (African people)

Koose (African people)
  USE Kossi (African people)

Koose dialect (Bakossi)
  USE Bakossi dialect

Kora (Musical instrument)
  [ML 1015-ML 1018]
  UF Harp-lute
  BT Musical instruments--Africa

Kora language
  USE Korana language

(May Subd Geog) = Place names may follow the heading

Kora music
  [M 142.K595]
  BT Music--Africa

Kora National Reserve (Kenya) *(Not Subd Geog)*
  BT Game reserves--Kenya
    National parks and reserves--Kenya

Korana (African people) *(May Subd Geog)*
  [DT 764.K6 : old class]
  [DT 1768.K68 : new class]
  UF Coranna (African people)
    Gorona (African people)
    Khora (African people)
  BT Ethnology--South Africa
    Khoikhoi (African people)
--History
  NT Korana War, 1st, 1868-1870
    Korana War, 2nd, 1878-1879

Korana language *(May Subd Geog)*
  [PL 8407]
  UF Coranna language
    Kora language
  BT Khoikhoi language
    South Africa--Languages

Korana War, 1st, 1868-1870
  [DT 777 : old class]
  [DT 1837 : new class]
  UF Northern Border War, 1st (South
Africa), 1868-1870
    South Africa--History--Korana War,
1868-1870
  BT Korana (African people)--History
    South Africa--History--Frontier Wars,
1811-1878

Korana War, 2nd, 1878-1879
  [DT 777 : old class]
  [DT 1837 : new class]
  UF Northern Border War, 2nd (South
Africa), 1878-1879
    South Africa--History--Korana War,
1878-1879
  BT Korana (African people)--History
    South Africa--History--Frontier Wars,
1811-1878

Kordofanian languages *(May Subd Geog)*
  BT African languages
    Sudan--Languages
  NT Krongo language
    Moro language (Sudan)
    Tagoi language

Koria language
  USE Kuria language

Koro (African people) *(May Subd Geog)*
  [DT 515.45.K]
  UF Korofawa (African people)
  BT Ethnology--Nigeria

Koro Lafia language
  USE Migili language

Korofawa (African people)
  USE Koro (African people)

Koroma language
  USE Karaboro language

Koromfe language
  USE Kurumba language

Korongo language
  USE Krongo language

Kosi Bay (South Africa) *(May Subd Geog)*
  UF Kosibaai (South Africa)
  BT Bays--South Africa

Kosibaai (South Africa)
  USE Kosi Bay (South Africa)

Kosova (African people)
  USE Gusii (African people)

Kossa (African people)
  USE Mende (African people)

Kossa language
  USE Mende language

Kossi (African people) *(May Subd Geog)*
  [DT 571.K66]
  UF Bakosi (African people)
    Bakossi (African people)
    Koose (African people)
    Muamenam (African people)
    Nkosi (African people)
  BT Bantu-speaking peoples
    Ethnology--Cameroon

Kosso (African people)
  USE Mende (African people)

Kosso language
  USE Mende language

UF = Used for; BT = Broader term; RT = Related term; SA = See also; NT = Narrower term

Kota (African people) *(May Subd Geog)*
   [DT 650.K68 (Zaire)]
   UF Bakota (African people)
       Mahongwe (African people)
       Shake (African people)
   BT Ethnology--Congo (Brazzaville)
       Ethnology--Gabon
       Ethnology--Zaire

Kota reliquaries
   USE Reliquaries, Kota

Kota sculpture
   USE Sculpture, Kota

Kotoko (African people) *(May Subd Geog)*
   [DT 546.445.K (Chad)]
   BT Ethnology--Cameroon
       Ethnology--Chad
       Ethnology--Nigeria
   RT Sao (Chad people)
 --Antiquities

Kotoko art
   USE Art, Kotoko

Kotoko dialects *(May Subd Geog)*
   BT Cameroon--Languages
       Chad--Languages
       Chadic languages
       Nigeria--Languages
   NT Afade dialect

Kotokoli (African people)
   USE Tem (African people)

Kotokoli language
   USE Tem language

Koulango language
   USE Kulango language

Kourfey (African people)
   USE Kurtey (African people)

Kouroumba language
   USE Kurumba language

Kourtey (African people)
   USE Kurtey (African people)

Kpa (African people)
   USE Bafia (African people)

Kpa language
   USE Bafia language

Kpala language
   USE Kresh language

Kpara language
   USE Kresh language

Kpelego language
   USE Kulango language

Kpelle (African people) *(May Subd Geog)*
   [DT 630.5.K63 (Liberia)]
   UF Guerze (African people)
       Kpwélé (African people)
   BT Ethnology--Guinea
       Ethnology--Liberia
 --Children
   BT Children--Liberia
 --Marriage customs and rites
   UF Marriage customs and rites, Kpelle (African
people)
 --Missions *(May Subd Geog)*
   [BV 3630.K]
   UF Missions to Kpelle (African people)
 --Rites and ceremonies
 --Religion
   [BL 2480.K72]

Kpelle epic poetry
   USE Epic poetry, Kpelle

Kpelle folk songs
   USE Folk songs, Kpelle

Kpelle language *(May Subd Geog)*
   [PL 8411]
   UF Guerzé language
       Kpwélé language
   BT Guinea--Languages
       Liberia--Languages
       Mande languages

Kpelle literature *(May Subd Geog)*
   [PL 8411.5-PL 8411.9]
   BT Guinean literature
       Liberian literature
   NT Kpelle poetry

Kpelle poetry *(May Subd Geog)*
   [PL 8411.5-PL 8411.9]]
   BT Guinea--Poetry
       Kpelle literature
       Liberia--Poetry
   NT Epic poetry, Kpelle

Kposo (African people) *(May Subd Geog)*
[DT 582.45.K]
  UF Akposo (African people)
      Akposso (African people)
  BT Ethnology--Togo
 --Religion
  [BL 2480.K74]

Kposo language *(May Subd Geog)*
  [PL 8412.K66]
  UF Akposo language
      Akposso language
      Ikposo language
      Ikposso language
  BT Kwa languages
      Togo--Languages
 --Names
  USE Names, Kposo

Kposo names
  USE Names, Kposo

Kpwélé (African people)
  USE Kpelle (African people)

Kpwélé language
  USE Kpelle language

Krachi (African people) *(May Subd Geog)*
  [DT 510.43.K72]
  BT Ethnology--Ghana
 --Religion
  [BL 2480.K]
  NT Donte (African deity)
      Gods, Krachi

Krao (African people)
  USE Kru (African people)

Krao language
  USE Kru language

Krawi language
  USE Kru language

Krebo (African people)
  USE Grebo (African people)

Krebo language
  USE Grebo language

Kredj language
  USE Kresh language

Kreish language
  USE Kresh language

Krej language
  USE Kresh language

Krepe (African people)
  USE Ewe (African people)

Krepe language
  USE Ewe language

Krepi (African people)
  USE Ewe (African people)

Krepi language
  USE Ewe language

Kresh language *(May Subd Geog)*
  [PL 8413]
  UF Kapala language
      Kpala language
      Kpara language
      Kredj language
      Kreish language
      Krej language
  BT Central Sudanic languages
      Sudan--Languages

Krio (African people)
  USE Creoles (Sierra Leone)

Krio drama *(May Subd Geog)*
  [PM 7875.K735-PM 7875.K738]
  BT Krio literature
      Sierra Leone--Drama

Krio folk literature
  USE Folk literature, Krio

Krio language *(May Subd Geog)*
  [PM 7875.K73]
  UF Aku language (Creole)
  BT Creole dialects, English
      Sierra Leone--Languages

Krio literature *(May Subd Geog)*
  [PM 7875.K735-PM 7875.K739]
  BT Sierra Leone literature
  NT Folk literature, Krio
      Krio drama

Krio proverbs
  USE Proverbs, Krio

Krobo (African people) *(May Subd Geog)*
  [DT 510.43.K76]
  UF Crobo (African people)
  BT Ethnology--Ghana

UF = Used for; BT = Broader term; RT = Related term; SA = See also; NT = Narrower term

Krongo language *(May Subd Geog)*
  [PL 8414.K76]
  UF Kadumodi language
      Korongo language
      Kurungu language
  BT Kordofanian languages
      Sudan--Languages

Kroomen (African people)
  USE Kru (African people)

Krou (African people)
  USE Kru (African people)

Kroumen language
  USE Tepo language

Kru (African people) *(May Subd Geog)*
  [DT 545.K77 (Ivory Coast)]
  [DT 474.6.K78 (West Africa)]
  UF Crau (African people)
      Krao (African people)
      Kroomen (African people)
      Krou (African people)
      Krumen (African people)
  BT Ethnology--Africa, West
      Ethnology--Ivory Coast
      Ethnology--Liberia
  NT Grebo (African people)

Kru language *(May Subd Geog)*
  [PL 8415]
  UF Klao language
      Krao language
      Krawi language
  BT Kru languages
      Liberia--Languages

Kru languages *(May Subd Geog)*
  [PL 8416]
  BT Ivory Coast--Languages
      Kwa languages
      Liberia--Languages
  NT Bassa language (Liberia)
      Bete language
      Grebo language
      Jabo language
      Kru language
      Tchien language
      Tepo language

Kruger National Park (South Africa) *(Not Subd Geog)*
  UF Nasionale Kruger Wildtuin (South Africa)

  BT National parks and reserves--South Africa
      Parks--South Africa

Krugerrand (Coin) *(May Subd Geog)*
  [CJ 3948]
  BT Coins, South African
      Gold coins--South Africa

Krumen (African people)
  USE Kru (African people)

!Ku language
  USE !Xu language

Kua (African people) *(May Subd Geog)*
  [DT 1058.K83 : new class]
  UF Bosquimana (African people)
      Bosquimano (African people)
      Kuadam (African people)
  BT Ethnology--Africa, Southern
      !Kung (African people)

Kuadam (African people)
  USE Kua (African people)

Kuanyama (African people) *(May Subd Geog)*
  [DT 611.45.K (Angola : old class)]
  [DT 1308.K83 (Angola : new class)]
  [DT 709 (Namibia : old class)]
  [DT 1558.K83 (Namibia : new class)]
  UF Cuanhama (African people)
      Humba (African people)
      Kwanyama (African people)
      Oshikuanjame (African people)
      Osikuanyame (African people)
      Oswidonga (African people)
      Ovaguanyama (African people)
      Ovakuanyama (African people)
      Vakuanyama (African people)
  BT Ethnology--Angola
      Ethnology--Namibia
      Ovambo (African people)

Kuanyama language *(May Subd Geog)*
  [PL 8417]
  UF Ambo language (Southwest Africa and Angola)
      Cuanhama language
      Kwanyama language
      Ovambo language
  BT Angola--Languages
      Bantu languages
      Namibia--Languages

Kuanyama proverbs
  USE Proverbs, Kuanyama

(May Subd Geog) = Place names may follow the heading

Kuba (African people) *(May Subd Geog)*
  [DT 650.K83]
  UF Bakuba (African people)
      Bushongo (African people)
      Tukubba (African people)
  BT Bantu-speaking peoples
      Ethnology--Zaire
  NT Shoowa (African people)

Kuba language
  USE Bushoong language

Kubango River
  USE Okavango River

Kubung (African people)
  USE Ghoya (African people)

Kuce (African people)
  USE Rukuba (African people)

Kuchumba (African people)
  USE Amhara (African people)

Kudamata (African people)
  USE Diola (African people)

Kugho dialect
  USE Abua-Ogbia languages

Kuiseb River (Namibia) *(Not Subd Geog)*
  BT Rivers--Namibia

Kujamatak (African people)
  USE Diola (African people)

Kukuruku language
  USE Etsako language

Kuku (African people) *(May Subd Geog)*
  [DT 72.K8 (Egypt)]
  BT Ethnology--Egypt
      Ethnology--Sudan (Region)

Kukuya (African people)
  USE Kukwa (African people)

Kukuya language
  USE Kukwa language

Kukwa (African people) *(May Subd Geog)*
  [DT 546.245.K]
  UF Kukuya (African people)
  BT Bantu-speaking peoples
      Ethnology--Congo (Brazzaville)

Kukwa language *(May Subd Geog)*
  [PL 8418.K84]
  UF Cikuya language
      Kukuya language
  BT Bantu languages
      Congo (Brazzaville)--Languages

Kukwa proverbs
  USE Proverbs, Kukwa

Kùláál language *(May Subd Geog)*
  [PL 8419]
  UF Gula language (Lake Iro, Chad)
  BT Bua languages
      Chad--Languages

Kulal, Mount (Kenya) *(Not Subd Geog)*
  UF Mount Kulal (Kenya)
  BT Mountains--Kenya

Kulango language *(May Subd Geog)*
  UF Kolango language
      Koulango language
      Kpelego language
      Nabe language
      Nambai language
      Ngwala language
      Nkurange language
      Zazere language
  BT Gur languages
      Ivory Coast--Languages

Kulanko (African people)
  USE Kuranko (African people)

Kulebele (African people) *(May Subd Geog)*
  [DT 545.45.K (Ivory Coast)]
  UF Dalebele (African people)
      Daleo (African people)
      Guleo (African people)
  BT Ethnology--Ivory Coast
      Ethnology--Mali
      Senufo (African people)

Kuliak languages
  USE Teuso languages

Kumasi (Ghana), Battle of, 1874
  [DT 507]
  UF Battle of Kumasi (Ghana), 1874
  BT Ashanti War, 1873-1874--Campaigns--Ghana

Kumo (Zairian people)
  USE Kumu (Zairian people)

UF = Used for; BT = Broader term; RT = Related term; SA = See also; NT = Narrower term

Kumu (Zairian people) *(May Subd Geog)*
  [DT 650.K86]
  UF Bakumbu (Zairian people)
      Komo (Zairian people)
      Kumo (Zairian people)
      Kuumu (Zairian people)
      Wakumu (Zairian people)
  BT Ethnology--Zaire
--Funeral customs and rites
  UF Funeral rites and ceremonies, Kumu
(Zairian people)
--Rites and ceremonies

Kunama (African people) *(May Subd Geog)*
  [DT 393.5]
  UF Baden (African people)
      Badin (African people)
      Baza (African people)
      Bazen (African people)
      Bazin (African people)
      Cunama (African people)
  BT Ethnology--Ethiopia

Kunama language *(May Subd Geog)*
  [PL 8421]
  UF Baden language
      Baza language
      Bazan language
      Cunama language
  BT Ethiopia--Languages
      Nilo-Saharan languages
      Sudan--Languages

Kundu (African people)
  USE Nkundu (African people)

Kundu language
  USE Bakundu language

Kunene River (Angola and Namibia)
  USE Cunene River (Angola and Namibia)

!Kung (African people) *(May Subd Geog)*
  [DT 737 : old class]
  [DT 1058.K86 : new class]
  UF Auen (African people)
      Ju/wasi (African people)
      !Khung (African people)
      !Kuong (African people)
      Makaukau (African people)
      Qhung (African people)
      !Xu (African people)
      Zhu/twasi (African people)
  BT Ethnology--Africa, Southern
      San (African people)
  NT Kua (African people)

!Kung language
  USE !Xu language

Kunuzi dialect
  USE Dongola-Kenuz dialect

Kuo language *(May Subd Geog)*
  BT Cameroon--Languages
      Chad--Languages
      Niger-Congo languages

!Kuong (African people)
  USE !Kung (African people)

Kuranko (African people) *(May Subd Geog)*
  [DT 510.43.K87 (Ghana)]
  [DT 516.45.K85 (Sierra Leone)]
  UF Kolanko (African people)
      Kulanko (African people)
  BT Ethnology--Ghana
      Ethnology--Guinea
      Ethnology--Sierra Leone
      Mandingo (African people)

Kurfei (African people)
  USE Kurtey (African people)

Kuria (African people) *(May Subd Geog)*
  [DT 433.545.K87 (Kenya)]
  [DT 443.3.K87 (Tanzania)]
  UF Abakuria (African people)
      Bakulia (African people)
      Bakuria (African people)
      Batende (African people)
      Ikikuria (African people)
      Kurya (African people)
  BT Bantu-speaking peoples
      Ethnology--Kenya
      Ethnology--Tanzania

Kuria language *(May Subd Geog)*
  UF Kikoria language
      Kikouria language
      Kikuria language
      Koria language
      Kurya language
      Tende language
  BT Bantu languages
      Kenya--Languages
      Tanzania--Languages

Kuria law
  USE Law, Kuria

Kuria women
  USE Women, Kuria

(May Subd Geog) = Place names may follow the heading

Kuroba (African people)
USE Attie (African people)

Kurobu language
USE Attie language

Kurorofa language
USE Jukun language

Kursa language
USE Maba language

Kurtey (African people) *(May Subd Geog)*
[DT 547.45.K]
UF Kourfey (African people)
Kourtey (African people)
Kurfei (African people)
BT Ethnology--Niger

Kurumba (African people) *(May Subd Geog)*
[DT 555.45.K88]
UF Deforo (African people)
Fulse (African people)
Kurumbe (African people)
Lilse (African people)
Nioniosse (African people)
Nyonyosi (African people)
DT Ethnology--Burkina Faso

Kurumba language *(May Subd Geog)*
[PL 8422.K854]
UF Deforo language
Foulse language
Fulse language
Koromfe language
Kouroumba language
Kurumfe language
Lilse language
BT Burkina Faso--Languages
Gur languages

Kurumbe (African people)
USE Kurumba (African people)

Kurumfe language
USE Kurumba language

Kurungu language
USE Krongo language

Kurya (African people)
USE Kuria (African people)

Kurya language
USE Kuria language

Kusa language
USE Kussassi language

Kusae language
USE Kussassi language

Kusal language
USE Kussassi language

Kusasi language
USE Kussassi language

Kussassi language *(May Subd Geog)*
[PL 8423]
UF Kusa language
Kusae language
Kusal language
Kusasi language
DT Burkina Faso--Languages
Ghana--Languages
Mossi languages
--Phonology
--Syntax

Kusu (African people) *(May Subd Geog)*
[DT 433.545.B84]
UF Bukusu (African people)
Fuluka (African people)
Kongola (African people)
Kutsu (African people)
Lukutsu (African people)
BT Bantu-speaking peoples
Ethnology--Kenya

Kutsu (African people)
USE Kusu (African people)

Kuu language
USE Fe'fe' language

Kuumu (Zairian people)
USE Kumu (Zairian people)

Kuwe (African people)
USE We (African people)

Kwa languages *(May Subd Geog)*
[PL 8424]
BT Niger-Congo languages
NT Adangme language
Akan language
Anufo language
Anyi language
Atisa language
Bini language
Degema language   *(Continued)*

UF = Used for; BT = Broader term; RT = Related term; SA = See also; NT = Narrower term

Kwa languages   *(Continued)*
  NT Ekpeye language
      Engenni language
      Etsako language
      Ewe language
      Ezaa language
      Ga language
      Gbagyi language
      Gonja language
      Gwa dialect (Ghana)
      Gwari language
      Idoma language
      Igbira language
      Igbo language
      Igede language
      Ijo language
      Ikwere language
      Ikwo language
      Izi language
      Kposo language
      Kru languages
      Lagoon languages
      Lefana language
      Nupe language
      Nzima language
      Okpe language
      Yoruba language

Kwafi language *(May Subd Geog)*
  [PL 8425]
  UF Kisogo language
      Kwapi language
      Kwavi language
      Loygob language
      Loykop language
  BT Kenya--Languages
      Nilo-Hamitic languages
      Tanzania--Languages

Kwahu (African people) *(May Subd Geog)*
  [DT 510.43.K93]
  UF Okouahou (African people)
  BT Ethnology--Ghana

Kwaka (African people)
  USE Avikam (African people)

Kwandara language
  USE Gwandara language

Kwangali language *(May Subd Geog)*
  [PL 8427]
  UF Kwangari language
  BT Angola--Languages
      Bantu languages
      Namibia--Languages

Kwangari language
  USE Kwangali language

Kwango River (Angola and Zaire) *(Not Subd Geog)*
  UF Cuango River (Angola and Zaire)
  BT Rivers--Angola
      Rivers--Zaire

Kwangwa (African people) *(May Subd Geog)*
  [DT 963.42 : old class]
  [DT 3058.K93 : new class]
  UF Makwangwa (African people)
  BT Ethnology--Zambia
      Lozi (African people)

Kwanim pas (African people)
  USE Uduk (African people)

Kwanyama (African people)
  USE Kuanyama (African people)

Kwanyama language
  USE Kuanyama language

Kwapi language
  USE Kwafi language

Kwara language
  USE Quara language

Kwararafa (African people)
  USE Jukun (African people)

Kwathlamba
  USE Drakensberg Mountains

Kwavi language
  USE Kwafi language

Kwaya (African people) *(May Subd Geog)*
  [DT 443.3.K]
  BT Ethnology--Tanzania
  --Marriage customs and rites
  UF Marriage customs and rites, Kwaya (African people)
  --Rites and ceremonies

Kwedi language
  USE Kwiri language

Kwegi (African people)
  USE Kwegu (African people)

      (May Subd Geog) = Place names may follow the heading

Kwegu (African people) *(May Subd Geog)*
  [DT 380.4.K]
  UF Bacha (African people)
      Kwegi (African people)
      Menja (African people)
      Nyidi (African people)
      Yidi (African people)
  BT Ethnology--Ethiopia

Kweli (African people)
  USE Kwiri (African people)

Kweli language
  USE Kwiri language

Kwcni (African people)
  USE Guro (African people)

Kweni language *(May Subd Geog)*
  [PL 8429]
  UF Gouro language
      Guro language
  BT Ivory Coast--Languages
      Southern Mande languages
  NT Gagu language
      Tura language

Kwese (African people) *(May Subd Geog)*
  [DT 650.K]
  UF Bakwese (African people)
  BT Ethnology--Zaire

Kwese language *(May Subd Geog)*
  [PL 8430.K84]
  UF Gikwezo language
      KiKwese language
      Kwezo language
      Pindi language (Kwese)
      Ukwese language
  BT Kongo language
      Zaire--Languages

Kwezo language
  USE Kwese language

Kwidjwi Island (Zaire)
  USE Idjwi Island (Zaire)

Kwili (African people)
  USE Kwiri (African people)

Kwili language
  USE Kwiri language

Kwiri (African people) *(May Subd Geog)*
  [DT 571.B523]
  UF Baakpe (African people)
      Bakwiri (African people)
      Kweli (African people)
      Kwili (African people)
      Makpe (African people)
      Mokpe (African people)
  BT Bantu-speaking peoples
      Ethnology--Cameroon

Kwiri language *(May Subd Geog)*
  [PL 8430.K]
  UF Baakpe language
      Bakpwe language
      Bakweri language
      Bakwiri language
      Bekwiri language
      Kwedi language
      Kweli language
      Kwili language
      Mokpe language
      Mokpwe language
  BT Bantu languages
      Cameroon--Languages

Kwiri proverbs
  USE Proverbs, Kwiri

Kwottu dialect
  USE Qottu dialect

Kxaxa (African people)
  USE Kgaqa (African people)

Kxhalaxadi dialect
  USE Kgalagadi dialect

Kyaka (African people)
  USE Mbundu (African people)

Kyedye (African people)
  USE Gade (African people)

Kyopi (African people)
  USE Nyoro (African people)

L

La Digue Island (Seychelles) *(Not Subd Geog)*
  [DT 469.S49L]
  UF Digue Island (Seychelles)
  BT Islands--Seychelles
      Seychelles

UF = Used for; BT = Broader term; RT = Related term; SA = See also; NT = Narrower term

Laadi (African people) *(May Subd Geog)*
 [DT 546.245.L (Congo (Brazzaville))]
 UF Laali (African people)
     Lali (African people)
 BT Ethnology--Congo (Brazzaville)
     Ethnology--Zaire

Laadi dialect *(May Subd Geog)*
 [PL 8404.Z9L2]
 UF Kilari dialect
     Ladi dialect
     Lari dialect (Kongo)
 BT Congo (Brazzaville)--Languages
     Kongo language
     Zaire--Languages

Laadi folk literature
 USE Folk literature, Laadi

Laal language *(May Subd Geog)*
 [PL 8430.L318]
 UF Gori language
 BT Bua languages
     Chad--Languages

Laali (African people)
 USE Laadi (African people)

Laamang language *(May Subd Geog)*
 [PL 8430.L32]
 UF Lamang language
 BT Cameroon--Languages
     Chadic languages
     Nigeria--Languages

Laan, Die (Stellenbosch, South Africa)
 USE Avenue, The (Stellenbosch, South
Africa)

Laba (African people)
 USE Luba (African people)

Labor, Organized
 USE Trade-unions

Labor organizations
 USE Trade-unions

Labor unions
 USE Trade-unions

Labwor (African people) *(May Subd Geog)*
 [DT 433.245.L3]
 BT Ethnology--Uganda

Lac Kivu (Rwanda and Zaire)

USE Kivu, Lake (Rwanda and Zaire)

Lac Léopold II (Zaire)
 USE Mai-Ndombe, Lake (Zaire)

Lac Mai-Ndombe (Zaire)
 USE Mai-Ndombe, Lake (Zaire)

Lac Tanganika
 USE Tanganyika, Lake

Lac Tchad
 USE Chad, Lake

Ladi dialect
 USE Laadi dialect

Ladysmith (South Africa)
 --History
 -- --Siege, 1899-1900
     [DT 934.L2 : old class]
     [DT 1908.L34 : new class]
     BT South African War, 1899-1902

Laedza Batanani, Botswana
 [RA 440.5 (Health education)]
 BT Education, Rural--Botswana
     Folk festivals--Botswana

Laetoli Site (Tanzania) *(Not Subd Geog)*
 UF Garusi Site (Tanzania)
     Laetolil Site (Tanzania)
 BT Tanzania--Antiquities

Laetolil Site (Tanzania)
 USE Laetoli Site (Tanzania)

Lagoon languages *(May Subd Geog)*
 [PL 8430.L33]
 BT Ivory Coast--Languages
     Kwa languages
 NT Abe language
     Abidji language
     Abure language
     Adyukru language
     Ahizi language
     Aladian language
     Attie language

Lagoons *(May Subd Geog)*
 BT Lakes
 --Togo
 NT Togo, Lake (Togo)

Lagubi language
 USE Mambila language

(May Subd Geog) = Place names may follow the heading

Lahu (African people)
    USE Avikam (African people)

Lake Bangweolo (Zambia)
    USE Bangweulu, Lake (Zambia)

Lake Bangweulu (Zambia)
    USE Bangweulu, Lake (Zambia)

Lake Baringo (Kenya)
    USE Baringo, Lake (Kenya)

Lake Chad
    USE Chad, Lake

Lake Eyasi (Tanzania)
    USE Eyasi, Lake (Tanzania)

Lake Hombolo (Tanzania)
    USE Hombolo Lake (Tanzania)

Lake Kivu (Rwanda and Zaire)
    USE Kivu, Lake (Rwanda and Zaire)

Lake le Roux (South Africa)
    USE Le Roux, Lake (South Africa)

Lake Leopold II (Zaire)
    USE Mai-Ndombe, Lake (Zaire)

Lake Mai-Ndombe (Zaire)
    USE Mai-Ndombe, Lake (Zaire)

Lake Malawi
    USE Nyasa, Lake

Lake McIlwaine, Lake (Zimbabwe)
    USE McIlwaine, Lake (Zimbabwe)

Lake Moero (Zaire and Zambia)
    USE Mweru, Lake (Zaire and Zambia)

Lake Mweru (Zaire and Zambia)
    USE Mweru, Lake (Zaire and Zambia)

Lake Naivasha (Kenya)
    USE Naivasha, Lake (Kenya)

Lake Nasser (Egypt and Sudan)
    USE Nasser, Lake (Egypt and Sudan)

Lake Njarasa (Tanzania)
    USE Eyasi, Lake (Tanzania)

Lake Nuba (Egypt and Sudan)
    USE Nasser, Lake (Egypt and Sudan)

Lake Nubia (Egypt and Sudan)
    USE Nasser, Lake (Egypt and Sudan)

Lake Nyasa
    USE Nyasa, Lake

Lake Nyassa
    USE Nyasa, Lake

Lake Rudolf (Kenya and Ethiopia)
    USE Rudolf, Lake (Kenya and Ethiopia)

Lake Tana (Ethiopia)
    USE Tana, Lake (Ethiopia)

Lake Tanganyika
    USE Tanganyika, Lake

Lake Togo (Togo)
    USE Togo, Lake (Togo)

Lake Tsana (Ethiopia)
    USE Tana, Lake (Ethiopia)

Lake Turkana (Kenya and Ethiopia)
    USE Rudolf, Lake (Kenya and Ethiopia)

Lakes (May Subd Geog)
    NT Lagoons
    RT Reservoirs
--Africa, East
    NT Tanganyika, Lake
--Africa, West
    NT Chad, Lake
--Ethiopia
    NT Rudolf, Lake (Kenya and Ethiopia)
        Tana, Lake (Ethiopia)
--Kenya
    NT Baringo, Lake (Kenya)
        Naivasha, Lake (Kenya)
        Rudolf, Lake (Kenya and Ethiopia)
--Malawi
    NT Nyasa, Lake
--Mozambique
    NT Nyasa, Lake
--Nigeria
    NT Kainji Reservoir (Nigeria)
--Rwanda
    NT Kivu, Lake (Rwanda and Zaire)
--South Africa
    NT Le Roux, Lake (South Africa)
--Sudan
    NT Nasser, Lake (Egypt and Sudan)
--Tanzania
    NT Eyasi, Lake (Tanzania)   (Continued)

UF = Used for; BT = Broader term; RT = Related term; SA = See also; NT = Narrower term

Lakes
 --Tanzania   *(Continued)*
  NT Hombolo Lake (Tanzania)
      Nyasa, Lake
 --Zaire
  NT Kivu, Lake (Rwanda and Zaire)
      Mai-Ndombe, Lake (Zaire)
      Mweru, Lake (Zaire and Zambia)
 --Zambia
  NT Bangweulu, Lake (Zambia)
      Mweru, Lake (Zaire and Zambia)
 --Zimbabwe
  NT McIlwaine, Lake (Zimbabwe)

Lala (African people) *(May Subd Geog)*
  [DT 963.42 (Zambia : old class)]
  [DT 3058.L35 (Zambia : new class)]
  UF Balala (African people)
      Bukanda (African people)
      Ichilala (African people)
      Walala (African people)
  BT Bantu-speaking peoples
      Ethnology--Zaire
      Ethnology--Zambia
  NT Ambo (Zambian people)

Lala language *(May Subd Geog)*
  [PL 8430.L35]
  BT Bantu languages
      Zaire--Languages
      Zambia--Languages
  NT Ambo dialect (Zambia)

Lali (African people)
  USE Laadi (African people)

Lali language
  USE Teke language

Lama Depression (Benin) *(Not Subd Geog)*
  UF Depression de la Lama (Benin)
      Lama Marsh (Benin)
  BT Marshes--Benin

Lama Marsh (Benin)
  USE Lama Depression (Benin)

Lamang language
  USE Laamang language

Lamba (African people) *(May Subd Geog)*
  [DT 955 : old class]
  [DT 3058.L36 : new class]
  UF Ichilamba (African people)
  BT Bantu-speaking peoples
      Ethnology--Zambia

 --Missions *(May Subd Geog)*
  [BV 3630.L]
  UF Missions to Lamba (African people)

Lamba language *(May Subd Geog)*
  [PL 8431]
  BT Bantu languages
      Zambia--Languages

Lamé language (Cameroon) *(May Subd Geog)*
  [PL 8433]
  UF Djibao language
      Dzepao language
  BT Cameroon--Languages
      Chadic languages

Lamnso (African people)
  USE Nso (African people)

Lamso (African people)
  USE Nso (African people)

Lamto (Ivory Coast) *(Not Subd Geog)*
  BT Savannas--Ivory Coast

Land forms
  USE Landforms

Land question
  USE Land tenure

Land tenure *(May Subd Geog)*
  UF Agrarian question
      Feudal tenure
      Freehold
      Land question
      Tenure of land
  BT Inheritance and succession
      Real property
  SA *subdivision* Land tenure *under ethnic groups, e.g.*
Mbere (African people)--Land tenure

Land tenure (Igbo law) *(May Subd Geog)*
  BT Law, Igbo

Land tenure (Jekri law) *(May Subd Geog)*
  BT Law, Jekri

Land tenure (Kipsigis law) *(May Subd Geog)*
  BT Law, Kipsigis

Land tenure (Yoruba law) *(May Subd Geog)*
  BT Law, Yoruba

Landforms *(May Subd Geog)*
  UF Land forms

(May Subd Geog) = Place names may follow the heading

NT Basins (Geology)
    Caves
    Coasts
    Deserts
    Formations (Geology)
    Gorges
    Groups (Stratigraphy)
    Islands
    Marshes
    Mountains
    Peninsulas
    Plains
    Rifts (Geology)
    Rivers
    Straights
    Valleys
    Volcanoes

Landim language
  USE Ronga language

Landogo language
  USE Loko language

Langalibalele Rebellion, 1873
  [DT 875 : old class]
  [DT 2257 : new class]
  DT Hlubi (African people)--History
      Natal (South Africa)--History--1843-
1893

Lang'ata Region (Kenya) (Not Subd Geog)

Langbas (African people) (May Subd Geog)
  [DT 546.345.L]
  UF Langbase (African people)
      Langbwasse (African people)
      Languassi (African people)
      Langwasi (African people)
  BT Banda (African people)
      Ethnology--Central African Republic

Langbase (African people)
  USE Langbas (African people)

Langbwasse (African people)
  USE Langbas (African people)

Langi (African people)
  USE Rangi (African people)

Lango (African people) (May Subd Geog)
  [DT 433.245.L]
  BT Ethnology--Uganda
      Luo (African people)

Lango language (May Subd Geog)
  [PL 8437]
  BT Latuka language
      Uganda--Languages

Lango women
  USE Women, Lango

Language and languages
  Here are entered works on language in general, works on
  the origin and history of language, and surveys of
  languages.
  BT Anthropology
      Communication
      Ethnology
      Philology
  SA individual languages and groups of languages, e.g.
  Wolof language; Gur languages; and subdivision
  Languages under names of countries, cities, etc., and
  under ethnic groups, e.g. Zaire--Languages
  NT Afrihili (Artificial language)
      Lingua francas
      Literature
      Racism in language
  --Clicks
    USE Clicks (Phonetics)
  --Tone
    USE Tone (Phonetics)

Language and racism
  USE Racism in language

Languassi (African people)
  USE Langbas (African people)

Langwasi (African people)
  USE Langbas (African people)

Lari dialect (Kongo)
  USE Laadi dialect

Lari language
  USE Teke language

Latin America (Not Subd Geog)
  UF Spanish America
  --Civilization
  -- --African influences
    BT Africa--Civilization

Latooka (African people)
  USE Latuka (African people)

Latouka language
  USE Latuka language

UF = Used for; BT = Broader term; RT = Related term; SA = See also; NT = Narrower term

Latuka (African people) *(May Subd Geog)*
   [DT 155.2.L37]
   UF Latooka (African people)
       Latuko (African people)
       Lotuka (African people)
       Lotuko (African people)
   BT Ethnology--Sudan
       Nilo-Hamitic tribes

Latuka language *(May Subd Geog)*
   [PL 8441]
   UF Latouka language
       Lotuho language
       Lotuko language
   BT Nilo-Hamitic languages
       Sudan--Languages
   NT Lango language

Latuko (African people)
   USE Latuka (African people)

Laudatory poetry
   UF Eulogistic poetry
       Poetry, Laudatory
       Praise poems
   BT Poetry

Laudatory poetry, African
   [PL 8010.4]
   UF African laudatory poetry
   BT African poetry

Laudatory poetry, Tswana *(May Subd Geog)*
   [PL 8747.7 (Collections)]
   UF Tswana laudatory poetry
   BT Tswana poetry

Law, Arusha
   UF Arusha law

Law, Ashanti
   UF Ashanti law
   NT Real property (Ashanti law)

Law, Bafokeng
   UF Bafokeng law
   NT Domestic relations (Bafokeng law)
       Inheritance and succession (Bafokeng
law)

Law, Bamileke
   UF Bamileke law
   BT Customary law--Cameroon

Law, Banjal
   UF Banjal law

Law, Bantu
   UF Bantu law
   NT Civil procedure (Bantu law)
       Courts, Bantu

Law, Burial
   USE Burial laws

Law, Chaga
   UF Chaga law
   BT Customary law--Tanzania

Law, Chokossi
   UF Chokossi law
   BT Customary law--Togo

Law, Customary
   USE Customary law

Law, Dinka
   UF Dinka law
   NT Bride price (Dinka law)

Law, Ewe
   UF Ewe law
   NT Property (Ewe law)

Law, Fula
   UF Fula law
   BT Customary law--Africa, West

Law, Haya
   UF Haya law

Law, Hehe
   UF Hehe law
   BT Customary law--Tanzania

Law, Igbo
   UF Igbo law
   BT Customary law--Nigeria
   NT Land tenure (Igbo law)
       Marriage (Igbo law)
       Property (Igbo law)

Law, Ila
   UF Ila law
   NT Married women (Ila law)

Law, Jekri
   UF Jekri law
   BT Customary law--Nigeria
   NT Land tenure (Jekri law)

Law, Kamba
   UF Kamba law

(May Subd Geog) = Place names may follow the heading

Law, Kgatla
 UF Kgatla law
 BT Law, Tswana
 NT Domestic relations (Kgatla law)
     Inheritance and succession (Kgatla
law)

Law, Kipsigis
 UF Kipsigis law
 NT Land tenure (Kipsigis law)

Law, Kuria
 UF Kuria law
 BT Customary law--Kenya
     Customary law--Tanzania
 NT Domestic relations (Kuria law)

Law, Lozi
 UF Lozi law

Law, Luo
 UF Luo law
 NT Burial laws (Luo law)
     Marriage (Luo law)

Law, Mossi
 UF Mossi law

Law, Nandi
 UF Nandi law

Law, Ngoni
 UF Ngoni law
 BT Customary law--Africa, Eastern
 NT Inheritance and succession (Ngoni law)
     Property (Ngoni law)

Law, Nuer
 UF Nuer law

Law, Sapiny
 USE Law, Sebei

Law, Sebei
 UF Law, Sapiny
     Sapiny law
     Sebei law

Law, Shona
 UF Shona law
 BT Customary law--South Africa
     Customary law--Zimbabwe

Law, Sotho
 UF Sotho law
 NT Courts, Sotho

 NT Domestic relations (Sotho law)

Law, Sukuma
 UF Sukuma law

Law, Tivi
 UF Tivi law

Law, Tonga
 UF Tonga law
 BT Customary law--Zambia
 NT Inheritance and succession (Tonga law)

Law, Tswana
 UF Tswana law
 NT Civil procedure (Tswana law)
     Domestic relations (Tswana law)
     Law, Kgatla

Law, Venda
 UF Venda law

Law, Yanzi
 UF Yanzi law
 BT Customary law--Zaire
 NT Adultery (Yanzi law)
     Reparation (Yanzi law)

Law, Yoruba
 UF Yoruba law
 NT Divorce (Yoruba law)
     Land tenure (Yoruba law)
     Marriage (Yoruba law)

Law, Zande
 UF Zande law

Law enforcement officers
 USE Police

Law of succession
 USE Inheritance and succession

Le Roux, Lake (South Africa) *(Not Subd Geog)*
 UF Lake le Roux (South Africa)
 BT Lakes--South Africa
     Reservoirs--South Africa

Lebou (African people) *(May Subd Geog)*
 [DT 549.45.L42]
 BT Ethnology--Senegal
     Wolof (African people)

Lebou dialect *(May Subd Geog)*
 BT Senegal--Languages
     Wolof language

UF = Used for; BT = Broader term; RT = Related term; SA = See also; NT = Narrower term

Lebou women
USE Women, Lebou

Lefana language *(May Subd Geog)*
  [PL 8447]
  UF Bouem language
      Buem language
      Bwem language
      Lelemi language
  BT Ghana--Languages
      Kwa languages

Lega language
USE Kilega language

Legal holidays
USE Holidays

Legends *(May Subd Geog)*
  UF Folk-tales
      Traditions
  BT Fiction
      Folk literature
  NT Fables
      Mythology
 --Africa, East
  NT Liyongo (Legendary character)
 --Africa, West
  NT Anansi (Legendary character)
 --Nigeria
  NT Esu (Legendary character)
 --Zaire
  NT Kabundji (Legendary character)

Leghoya (African people)
USE Ghoya (African people)

Leigh Ranch (Zimbabwe) *(Not Subd Geog)*
  BT Ranches--Zimbabwe

Leke language
USE Mbomotabe language

Leko dialect *(May Subd Geog)*
  [PL 8459.L6695.L6]
  UF Eleko dialect
      Eleku dialect
      iLiku dialect
      loLeku dialect
  BT Losengo language
      Zaire--Languages

Lela dialect
USE Lele dialect

Lele (African people) *(May Subd Geog)*
  [DT 650.L38]
  UF Bachilele (African people)
      Bashi-Lele (African people)
      Bashilele (African people)
      Lyela (African people)
  BT Bantu-speaking peoples
      Ethnology--Zaire
 --Children
  BT Children--Zaire

Lele dialect *(May Subd Geog)*
  [PL 8452]
  UF Elé dialect
      Lela dialect
      Lere dialect
      Lyele dialect
  BT Gur languages
      Zaire--Languages

Lelemi language
USE Lefana language

Lemba (African people)
USE Kela (African people)

Lemba (Cult)
  [BL 2470.C6]
  BT Cults--Congo (Brazzaville)
      Cults--Zaire

Lemba language
USE Kela language

Lendu (African people) *(May Subd Geog)*
  [DT 650.L]
  UF Alendu (African people)
      Bale (African people)
      Balega (African people)
      Balendru (African people)
      Balendu (African people)
      Kingeti (African people)
      Walega (African people)
      Walendu (African people)
  BT Ethnology--Zaire

Lenge (African people)
USE Chopi (African people)

Lenge language
USE Chopi language

Leninism
USE Communism

(May Subd Geog) = Place names may follow the heading

Lenje (African people) *(May Subd Geog)*
  [DT 963.42 : old class]
  [DT 3058.L46 : new class]
  UF Balenje (African people)
      Benimukuni (African people)
      Ciina Mukuna (African people)
  BT Ethnology--Zambia
      Ila (African people)

Lenje language *(May Subd Geog)*
  [PL 8453]
  UF Bwine-Mukuni language
      Ci-Renje language
  BT Tonga language (Zambesi)
      Zambia--Languages

Leopard men
  [GN 655.S5 (Sierra Leone)]
  UF Human leopards
      Leopard societies
      Wereleopards
      Werleopards

Leopard societies
  USE Leopard men

Leopold II, Lake (Zaire)
  USE Mai-Ndombe, Lake (Zaire)

Lera (African people)
  USE Hutu (African people)

Lere dialect
  USE Lele dialect

Lesa (African people)
  USE Lese (African people)

Lese (African people) *(May Subd Geog)*
  [DT 650.B34]
  UF Balese (African people)
      Balissi (African people)
      Lesa (African people)
      Lesse (African people)
      Lissi (African people)
      Walese (African people)
      Walisi (African people)
  BT Ethnology--Zaire
      Mamvu (African people)

Lese language
  USE Balese language

Lesotho *(Not Subd Geog)*
  [DT 781-DT 803 : old class]
  [DT 2541-DT 2686 : new class]

    UF Basutoland
--Antiquities
  NT Sehonghong Rockshelter (Lesotho)
--Economic conditions
  [HC 920]
-- --To 1966
-- --1966-
--Fiction
  NT Sotho fiction
--History
-- --To 1966
  NT Sotho-Free State War, 1865-1866
-- --1966-
--Languages
  NT Sotho language
--Literatures
  NT Sotho literature
--Poetry
  NT Sotho poetry
--Politics and government
-- --To 1966
-- --1966-
--Social conditions
-- --1966-

Lesse (African people)
  USE Lese (African people)

Lexical tone (Phonetics)
  USE Tone (Phonetics)

Libenge language
  USE Bengo language

Liberation movements (Civil rights)
  USE Civil rights movements

Liberation movements, National
  USE National liberation movements

Liberia *(Not Subd Geog)*
  [DT 621-DT 637]
--Civilization
-- --American influences
  BT United States--Civilization
--Description and travel
-- --1981-
--Economic conditions
  [HC 1075]
-- --1971-1980
-- --1980-
--History
-- --To 1847
-- --1847-1944
-- --1944-1971
-- --1971-1980   *(Continued)*

UF = Used for; BT = Broader term; RT = Related term; SA = See also; NT = Narrower term

Liberia
--History *(Continued)*
-- --Coup d'état, 1980
 [DT 636.5]
  BT Coups d'état--Liberia
-- --1980-
--Languages
 NT Bassa language (Liberia)
  Dan language
  Gbandi language
  Gola language
  Grebo language
  Jabo language
  Kissi language
  Kono language
  Kpelle language
  Kru language
  Kru languages
  Loma language
  Mano language
  Mende language
  Southern Mande languages
  Tchien language
  Vai language
  Wobe language
--Literatures
 USE Liberian literature
--Poetry
 NT Kpelle poetry
--Politics and government
-- --To 1944
-- --1944-1971
-- --1971-1980
-- --1980-
--Social conditions
-- --1971-1980
-- --1980-

Liberian art
 USE Art, Liberian

Liberian arts
 USE Arts, Liberian

Liberian cookery
 USE Cookery, Liberian

Liberian fiction (English) *(May Subd Geog)*
 [PR 9384.4 (History)]
 [PR 9384.8 (Collections)]
 UF English fiction--Liberian authors
 BT Liberian literature (English)
  West African fiction (English)
 NT Short stories, Liberian (English)

Liberian literature *(May Subd Geog)*
 [PL 8014.L]
 UF Liberia--Literatures
 BT West African literature
 NT Dan literature
  Kpelle literature

Liberian literature (English) *(May Subd Geog)*
 [PR 9384]
 UF English fiction--Liberian authors
 BT West African literature (English)
 NT Liberian fiction (English)
  Liberian poetry (English)

Liberian poetry (English) *(May Subd Geog)*
 [PR 9384.2 (History)]
 [PR 9384.6-PR 9384.65 (Collections)]
 UF English poetry--Liberian authors
 BT Liberian literature (English)
  West African poetry (English)

Liberian short stories (English)
 USE Short stories, Liberian (English)

Liberman Memorial Door (South African National
Gallery)
 USE Hyman Liberman Memorial Door (South African
National Gallery)

Libraries *(May Subd Geog)*
 NT Acquisition of African publications
  Acquisition of East African publications
  Acquisition of West African publications
 --Special collections--Africa
 [Z 688.A54]
 NT Cataloging of African literature
 --Africa
 [Z 665.2.A]

Libraries, Black
 USE Libraries and Blacks

Libraries and Blacks *(May Subd Geog)*
 [Z 711.9 (Reference service)]
 UF Black libraries
  Blacks and libraries
  Libraries, Black
  Library services to Blacks
 BT Blacks
--South Africa
 [Z 857.S7]

Library services to Blacks
 USE Libraries and Blacks

(May Subd Geog) = Place names may follow the heading

Libtako (Burkina Faso)
  USE Liptako (Burkina Faso)

Lifaqane period, 1816-ca. 1840
  USE Africa, Southern--History--Mfecane
period, 1816-ca. 1840

Lifoma (African people)
  USE Foma (African people)

Likelo (African people)
  USE Lokele (African people)

Likile (African people)
  USE Lokele (African people)

Likembe (Musical instrument)
  USE Mbira

Lilima language *(May Subd Geog)*
  [PL 8454]
  BT Botswana--Languages
      Shona language
      Zimbabwe--Languages

Lilse (African people)
  USE Kurumba (African people)

Lilse language
  USE Kurumba language

Lima (African people)
  USE Nyaturu (African people)

Limba (African people) *(May Subd Geog)*
  [DT 543.45.L (Guinea)]
  [DT 516.L (Sierra Leone)]
  BT Ethnology--Guinea
      Ethnology--Sierra Leone

Limba language *(May Subd Geog)*
  [PL 8455]
  BT Guinea--Languages
      Niger-Congo languages
      Sierra Leone--Languages

Limbom language
  USE Limbum language

Limbum language *(May Subd Geog)*
  UF Limbom language
      Llimbumi language
      Ndzungle language
      Ndzungli language
      Njungene language
      Nsugni language

  UF Nsungali language
      Nsungli language
      Nsungni language
      Wimbum language
      Zungle language
  BT Cameroon--Languages
      Grasslands Bantu languages

Limi (African people)
  USE Nyaturu (African people)

Limuria
  USE Mascarene Islands

Linda dialect *(May Subd Geog)*
  [PL 8051.Z9L56]
  BT Banda language
      Central African Republic--Languages

Lingala language *(May Subd Geog)*
  [PL 8456]
  UF Bangala language (Zaire)
      Mangala language (Zaire)
      Ngala language (Zaire)
  BT Bantu languages
      Congo (Brazzaville)--Languages
      Lingua francas
      Zaire--Languages

Lingala proverbs
  USE Proverbs, Lingala

Lingala songs
  USE Songs, Lingala

LiNgombe language
  USE Ngombe language

Lingua francas *(May Subd Geog)*
  [PM 7801-PM 7895]
  Here are entered works discussing auxiliary, sometimes
  mixed, languages used among groups having no other language
  in common. Works discussing lingua francas which are native
  to none of those using them and are characterized by a
  simplified grammar and often mixed vocabulary are entered
  under the heading Pidgin languages. Works discussing
  pidgin languages that have become established as the native
  language of a speech community are entered under the heading
  Creole dialects.
  UF Contact vernaculars
      Trade languages
      Vehicular languages
  BT Language and languages
  NT Fanakalo
      Kituba language
      Lingala language   *(Continued)*

UF = Used for; BT = Broader term; RT = Related term; SA = See also; NT = Narrower term

Lingua francas   *(Continued)*
  NT Pidgin languages
     Sango language

Liptako (Burkina Faso) *(Not Subd Geog)*
  UF Libtako (Burkina Faso)

Lisango language
  USE Shira language

Lisira language
  USE Shira language

Lisongo (Central African Republic people)
  USE Mbati (Central African Republic
people)

Lissi (African people)
  USE Lese (African people)

Lissongo (Central African Republic people)
  USE Mbati (Central African Republic
people)

Literacy *(May Subd Geog)*
  UF Illiteracy
  BT Education
 --Africa
  [LC 158]
 --Zimbabwe
  [LC 158.Z55]

Literary awards
  USE Literary prizes

Literary prizes *(May Subd Geog)*
  UF Book awards
     Book prizes
     Literary awards
     Literature--Awards
     Literature--Prizes
 --South Africa
  NT Hertzogprys

Literature
  UF World literature
  BT Language and languages
     Philology
  RT Authors
  SA *headings of the type [language] literature,*
e.g. Swahili literature; and headings of the type
[country] literature, e.g., Angolan literature or
names of countries followed by the subdivision
Literatures, *e.g.,* Lesotho--Literatures
  NT Africa in literature
     Africans in literature

  NT Afrikaans in literature
     Blacks in literature
     Children's literature
     Drama
     Epic literature
     Fables
     Fiction
     Folk literature
     Poetry
     Prisoners' writings
     Protest literature
     Race awareness in literature
     Racism in literature
     Revolutionary literature
     Satire
     Slavery and slaves in literature
     Slaves' writings
     Soldiers' writings
     Wit and humor
     Women, Black, in literature
     Youths' writings
 --Black authors
  [PN 841 (History)]
  [PN 6068 (Collections)]
  UF Black literature
  SA *subdivision* Black authors *under headings for*
individual literatures and genres, e.g. English poetry--
Black authors; Drama--Black authors
  NT Negritude (Literary movement)
 --Awards
  USE Literary prizes
 --Prizes
  USE Literary prizes

Literature, Comic
  USE Satire

Literature, Epic
  USE Epic literature

Literature, Folk
  USE Folk literature

Literature, Primitive
  USE Folk literature

Literature, Protest
  USE Protest literature

Literature, Revolutionary
  USE Revolutionary literature

Liyongo (Legendary character)
  BT Folklore--Africa, East
     Legends--Africa, East

(May Subd Geog) = Place names may follow the heading

Llimbumi language
USE Limbum language

Llogole language
USE Logooli language

Lo (African people)
USE Guro (African people)

Loango (African people)
USE Vili (African people)

Loangwa River (Zambia and Mozambique)
USE Luangwa River (Zambia and Mozambique)

Lobatse (Botswana). Peleng
USE Pelend (Lobatse, Botswana)

Lobaye (African people)
USE Ngbaka (African people)

Lobedu (African people) *(May Subd Geog)*
[DT 920 : (South Africa : old class)]
[DT 2322 (South Africa : new class)]
UF Lovedu (African people)
Lubedu (African people)
BT Bantu-speaking peoples
Ethnology Namibia
Ethnology--South Africa

Lobi (African people) *(May Subd Geog)*
[DT 555.45.L63 (Burkina Faso)]
UF Lobiri (African people)
Miwi (African people)
BT Ethnology--Burkina Faso
Ethnology--Ivory Coast
NT LoWiili (African people)

Lobi dialects *(May Subd Geog)*
[PL 8222.L]
BT Burkina Faso--Languages
Gur languages
Ivory Coast--Languages
NT Dyan dialect

Lobi folk songs
USE Folk songs, Lobi

Lobi philosophy
USE Philosophy, Lobi

Lobi sculpture
USE Sculpture, Lobi

Lobiri (African people)
USE Lobi (African people)

Lobito Bay (Angola) *(Not Subd Geog)*
UF Baía do Lobito (Angola)
BT Bays--Angola

Lobobangi language
USE Bobangi language

Lobolo
USE Bride price

Lockouts
USE Strikes and lockouts

Locusts *(May Subd Geog)*
UF Grasshoppers
--Control *(May Subd Geog)*
-- --Research *(May Subd Geog)*
-- -- --Burkina Faso
NT Programme de recherches interdisciplinaire
français sur les acridiens du Sahel
-- -- --Niger
NT Programme de recherches interdisciplinaire
français sur les acridiens du Sahel

Lodagaa (African people)
USE Dagari (African people)

Logbara (African people)
USE Lugbara (African people)

Logbara language *(May Subd Geog)*
[PL 8458]
UF Logbware language
Lugbara language
Luguaret language
Lugware language
BT Nilo-Saharan languages
Uganda--Languages

Logbware language
USE Logbara language

Loghoma language
USE Lorhon language

Loghon language
USE Lorhon language

Logoma language
USE Lorhon language

Logooli language *(May Subd Geog)*
[PL 8459.L3]
UF Llogole language
Lougouli language   *(Continued)*

UF = Used for; BT = Broader term; RT = Related term; SA = See also; NT = Narrower term

Logooli language   *(Continued)*
  UF Lugooli language
      Lulogooli language
      Luragoli language
  BT Bantu languages
      Kenya--Languages

Lokele (African people) *(May Subd Geog)*
  [DT 650.L]
  UF Ekele (African people)
      Kele (African people)
      Kili (African people)
      Likelo (African people)
      Likile (African people)
      Yakusu (African people)
  BT Ethnology--Zaire

Loko language *(May Subd Geog)*
  [PL 8459.L]
  UF Landogo language
  BT Guinea--Languages
      Mande languages
      Sierra Leone--Languages

Lokop language
  USE Samburu language

Lokundu language
  USE Bakundu language

loLeku dialect
  USE Leko dialect

Lolo (Bantu language)
  USE Mongo language

Loma language *(May Subd Geog)*
  [PL 8459.L52]
  UF Baru language
      Bouze language
      Busy language
      Buzi language
      Lorma language
      Toma language
  BT Guinea--Languages
      Liberia--Languages
      Mande languages

Lomongo (Bantu language)
  USE Mongo language

Lomwe (African people) *(May Subd Geog)*
  [DT 864 (Malawi : old class)]
  [DT 3192.L66 (Malawi : new class)]
  [DT 458.L (Mozambique : old class)]
  [DT 3328.L66 (Mozambique : new class)]

  UF Acilowe (African people)
      Alomwe (African people)
      Nguru (African people)
      Walomwe (African people)
  BT Ethnology--Malawi
      Ethnology--Mozambique

Longandu (African people)
  USE Ngandu (African people)

Longarim (African people) *(May Subd Geog)*
  [DT 155.2.L]
  UF Boya (African people)
  BT Ethnology--Sudan
      Murle (African people)

Longuda language *(May Subd Geog)*
  [PL 8459.L55]
  UF Nunguda language
  BT Adamawa languages
      Nigeria--Languages
  NT Guyuk dialect

Lonkengo language *(May Subd Geog)*
  [PL 8459.L6]
  UF Nkengo language
  BT Bantu languages
      Zaire--Languages

Lonkundu language
  USE Nkundu language

Loombo language
  USE Ombo language

Lopoy Site (Kenya) *(Not Subd Geog)*
  [GN 776.42.K : old class]
  [DT 434.L : new class]
  BT Kenya--Antiquities

Lorhon language *(May Subd Geog)*
  [PL 8459.L]
  UF Loghoma language
      Loghon language
      Logoma language
      Loron language
  BT Gur languages
      Ivory Coast--Languages
  NT Téén dialect

Lorma language
  USE Loma language

Loron language
  USE Lorhon language

(May Subd Geog) = Place names may follow the heading

Losengo language *(May Subd Geog)*
[PL 8459.L66]
UF Lusengo language
BT Bantu languages
     Zaire--Languages
NT Leko dialect

Losso (African people) *(May Subd Geog)*
[DT 443.3.L]
BT Ethnology--Tanzania

Lothagam Site (Kenya) *(Not Subd Geog)*
[GN 776.42.K : old class]
[DT 434.L : new class]
BT Kenya--Antiquities

Lotuho language
USE Latuka language

Lotuka (African people)
USE Latuka (African people)

Lotuko (African people)
USE Latuka (African people)

Lotuko language
USE Latuka language

Lougouli language
USE Logooli language

Lovale (African people)
USE Luvale (African people)

Love poetry
UF Poetry, Love
BT Poetry

Love poetry, Hausa *(May Subd Geog)*
[PL 8234.A2]
UF Hausa love poetry
BT Hausa poetry

Lovedu (African people)
USE Lobedu (African people)

LoWiili (African people) *(May Subd Geog)*
[DT 555.45.L68]
UF Oulé (African people)
BT Ethnology--Burkina Faso
     Lobi (African people)

LoWiili art
USE Art, LoWiili

Loyalists, Afrikaner
USE Afrikaner loyalists

Loygob language
USE Kwafi language

Loykop language
USE Kwafi language

Lozi (African people) *(May Subd Geog)*
[DT 963.42 : old class]
[DT 3058.L69 : new class]
UF Barotse (African people)
     Barotsi (African people)
     Barozi (African people)
     Barutse (African people)
     Marotse (African people)
     Rotse (African people)
     Rozi (African people)
BT Bantu-speaking peoples
     Ethnology--Zambia
NT Kwangwa (African people)
--**Missions** *(May Subd Geog)*
[BV 3630.L6]
UF Missions to Lozi (African people)

Lozi language *(May Subd Geog)*
[PL 8460]
UF Kololo language
     Sikololo language
     Silozi language
BT Sotho-Tswana languages

Lozi law
USE Law, Lozi

Lu-ganda language
USE Ganda language

Lu-wumbu language
USE Vili language

Lua language
USE Nielim language

Luango language
USE Yombe language

Luangwa River (Zambia and Mozambique) *(Not Subd Geog)*
UF Aruângua River (Zambia and Mozambique)
     Loangwa River (Zambia and Mozambique)
     Rio Aruângua (Zambia and Mozambique)
BT Rivers--Mozambique
     Rivers--Zambia

UF = Used for; BT = Broader term; RT = Related term; SA = See also; NT = Narrower term

Luapula River (Zambia and Zaire) *(Not Subd Geog)*
  BT Rivers--Zaire
      Rivers--Zambia

Luba (African people) *(May Subd Geog)*
  [DT 650.L8]
  UF Baluba (African people)
      Kayumba (African people)
      Laba (African people)
      Luba Shaba (African people)
      Luba Shakandi (African people)
      Mulongo (African people)
      Nkondja (African people)
      Nkulu (African people)
      Tumba (African people)
      Turruba (African people)
      Waluba (African people)
  BT Bantu-speaking peoples
      Ethnology--Zaire
  NT Hemba (African people)
      Kanyok (African people)
      Kaonde (African people)
      Lulua (African people)
      Sanga (African people)
      Songe (African people)

Luba folk literature
  USE Folk literature, Luba

Luba-Hemba (African people)
  USE Hemba (African people)

Luba-Kaonde language
  USE Kaonde language

Luba-Katanga language *(May Subd Geog)*
  [PL 8461]
  UF Chiluba language (Luba-Katanga)
      Katanga language
      Kiluba language
      Tshiluba language (Luba-Katanga)
  BT Bantu languages
      Zaire--Languages

Luba language, Northeastern
  USE Songe language

Luba language, Southern
  USE Sanga language

Luba language, Western
  USE Luba-Lulua language

Luba-Lulua (African people)
  USE Lulua (African people)

Luba-Lulua language *(May Subd Geog)*
  [PL 8461.2]
  UF Buluba-Lulua language
      Ciluba language
      Kalebwe language (Luba-Lulua)
      Luba language, Western
      Lulua language
      Luva language
      Tshiluba language (Luba-Lulua)
      Western Luba language
  BT Bantu languages
      Zaire--Languages

Luba-Lulua proverbs
  USE Proverbs, Luba-Lulua

Luba-Lulua riddles
  USE Riddles, Luba-Lulua

Luba philosophy
  USE Philosophy, Luba

Luba-Sanga language
  USE Sanga language

Luba Shaba (African people)
  USE Luba (African people)

Luba Shakandi (African people)
  USE Luba (African people)

Lubedu (African people)
  USE Lobedu (African people)

Lubukusu dialect
  USE Bukusu dialect

Lucazi (African people)
  USE Luchazi (African people)

Lucazi language *(May Subd Geog)*
  UF Luchazi language
      Lujazi language
      Ponda language
  BT Angola--Languages
      Bantu languages
      Zambia--Languages

Luchazi (African people) *(May Subd Geog)*
  [DT 3058.L83 (Zambia : new class)]
  UF Balojash (African people)
      Chiluchazi (African people)
      Lucazi (African people)
      Lujash (African people)
      Lujazi (African people)
      Luksage (African people)

(May Subd Geog) = Place names may follow the heading

UF Lutshase (African people)
    Luxage (African people)
    Mulochazi (African people)
    Ponda (African people)
    VaLuchazi (African people)
    Waluchazi (African people)
BT Ethnology--Angola
    Ethnology--Zambia

Luchazi language
  USE Lucazi language

Luenas (African people) *(May Subd Geog)*
  [DT 611.45.L : old class]
  [DT 1308.L84 : new class]
  UF Lwenas (African people)
  BT Bantu-speaking peoples
      Ethnology--Angola

Luganda language
  USE Ganda language

Lugbara (African people) *(May Subd Geog)*
  [DT 433.245.L (Uganda)]
  [DT 650.L (Zaire)]
  UF Logbara (African people)
      Ma'di (African people)
  RT Ethnology--Uganda
      Ethnology--Zaire
 --**Medicine**
  BT Medicine, Primitive--Uganda
      Medicine, Primitive--Zaire
 --**Religion**
  [BL 2480.L76]

Lugbara language
  USE Logbara language

Lugisu language
  USE Gisu language

Lugooli language
  USE Logooli language

Luguaret language
  USE Logbara language

Luguru (African people) *(May Subd Geog)*
  [DT 443.2.L]
  UF Ruguru (African people)
  BT Bantu-speaking peoples
      Ethnology--Tanzania

Lugware language
  USE Logbara language

Luhanga dialect
  USE Hanga dialect (Kenya)

Luhya (African people)
  USE Luyia (African people)

Luhya language
  USE Luyia language

Lujash (African people)
  USE Luchazi (African people)

Lujazi (African people)
  USE Luchazi (African people)

Lujazi language
  USE Lucazi language

LuKete language
  USE Kete language

Lukiqa language
  USE Kiga language

LuKisa dialect
  USE Kisa dialect

Luko language
  USE Yakö language

Luksage (African people)
  USE Luchazi (African people)

Lukuba language
  USE Bushoong language

Lukulu River (Zambia) *(Not Subd Geog)*
  BT Rivers--Zambia

Lukutsu (African people)
  USE Kusu (African people)

Lullabies
  UF Cradle songs
      Slumber songs
  BT Children's poetry
      Nursery rhymes
      Songs

Lullabies, Mongo *(May Subd Geog)*
  [PL 8518.8]
  UF Mongo lullabies

Lulogooli language
  USE Logooli language

UF = Used for; BT = Broader term; RT = Related term; SA = See also; NT = Narrower term

Lulua (African people) *(May Subd Geog)*
  [DT 650.L83 (Zaire)]
  UF Bena Lulua (African people)
      Kalebwe (African people)
      Luba-Lulua (African people)
      Luluwa (African people)
      Luva (African people)
      Western Luba (African people)
  BT Ethnology--Zaire
      Ethnology--Zambia
      Luba (African people)

Lulua language
  USE Luba-Lulua language

Luluhya language
  USE Luyia language

Luluwa (African people)
  USE Lulua (African people)

Luluyia language
  USE Luyia language

Lumasaaba language
  USE Gisu language

Lumbu language (Gabon) *(May Subd Geog)*
  UF Ilumbu language
  BT Bantu languages
      Gabon--Languages

Lumbwa (African people)
  USE Kipsigis (African people)

Lunda, Northern (African people) *(May Subd Geog)*
  [DT 650.L86]
  UF Alunda (African people)
      Arund (African people)
      Balunda (African people)
      Kalunda (African people)
      Northern Lunda (African people)
      Valunda (African people)
  BT Ethnology--Zaire

Lunda, Southern (African people) *(May Subd Geog)*
  [DT 611.45.L (Angola : old class)]
  [DT 1308.L86 (Angola: new class)]
  [DT 963.42 (Zambia : old class)]
  [DT 3058.L (Zambia : new class)]
  UF Balunda (African people)
      Southern Lunda (African people)
  BT Ethnology--Angola
      Ethnology--Zambia
  RT Ndembu (African people)

--Missions *(May Subd Geog)*
  [BV 3630.L]
  UF Missions to Southern Lunda (African people)

Lunda folk songs
  USE Folk songs, Lunda

Lunda language *(May Subd Geog)*
  [PL 8465]
  BT Bantu languages
  NT Luvale language

Lunda language, Northern
  USE Ruund language

Lunkundu language
  USE Nkundu language

Lunyaneka language
  USE Nyaneka language

Lunyankole language
  USE Nyankole language

Lunyore language
  USE Nyore language

Lunyoro language
  USE Nyoro language

Luo (African people) *(May Subd Geog)*
  [DT 433.545.L85 (Kenya)]
  UF Dho Luo (African people)
      Jaluo (African people)
      Jo Luo (African people)
      Kavirondo (Nilotic people)
      Nyifwa (African people)
  BT Ethnology--Africa, East
      Ethnology--Kenya
      Nilotic tribes
  NT Acoli (African people)
      Alur (African people)
      Lango (African people)
      Maban (African people)
      Shilluk (African people)
--Religion
  [BL 2480.L8]

Luo hymns
  USE Hymns, Luo

Luo language (Kenya and Tanzania) *(May Subd Geog)*
  [PL 8375]
  UF Dho Luo language
      Dholuo language
      Gaya language

(May Subd Geog) = Place names may follow the heading

UF Jo Luo language
    Kavirondo language, Nilotic
    Nife language
    Nilotic Kavirindo language
    Nyife language
    Wagaya language
BT Kenya--Languages
    Nilotic languages
    Tanzania--Languages

Luo language (Sudan)
  USE Lwo language (Sudan)

Luo law
  USE Law, Luo

Lur language
  USE Alur language

Luragoli language
  USE Logooli language

Luri (African people)
  USE Alur (African people)

Luri language
  USE Alur language

Lusaka (Zambia). Chainda
  USE Chainda (Lusaka, Zambia)

Lusaka (Zambia). Chawama
  USE Chawama (Lusaka, Zambia)

Lusaka (Zambia). George
  USE George (Lusaka, Zambia)

Lusalo
  [GT 2789.L8]
  BT Marriage customs and rites--Zaire

Lusengo language
  USE Losengo language

Lushisa dialect
  USE Kisa dialect

Lusiba language
  USE Ziba language

Lusoga language
  USE Soga language

Lusonge language
  USE Songe language

Lusophone Africa
  USE Africa, Portuguese-speaking

Lutoro language
  USE Tooro language

Lutshase (African people)
  USE Luchazi (African people)

Luunda language
  USE Ruund language

Luva (African people)
  USE Lulua (African people)

Luva language
  USE Luba-Lulua language

Luvale (African people) *(May Subd Geog)*
  [DT 963.42 : old class]
  [DT 3058.L89 : new class]
  UF Balovale (African people)
    Lovale (African people)
  BT Bantu-speaking peoples
    Ethnology--Zambia

Luvale language *(May Subd Geog)*
  [PL 8473]
  BT Lunda language
    Zambia--Languages

Luwumbu language
  USE Vili language

Luwunda language
  USE Ruund language

Luxage (African people)
  USE Luchazi (African people)

Luyana folk literature
  USE Folk literature, Luyana

Luyana language *(May Subd Geog)*
  [PL 8474.L78]
  UF Luyi language
    SiLuyana language
  BT Bantu languages
    Zambia--Languages
  NT Mbukushu language

Luyi language
  USE Luyana language

UF = Used for; BT = Broader term; RT = Related term; SA = See also; NT = Narrower term

Luyia (African people) *(May Subd Geog)*
  [DT 433.545.L88 (Kenya)]
  UF Abaluyia (African people)
      Baluyia (African people)
      Luhya (African people)
  BT Bantu-speaking peoples
      Ethnology--Kenya
      Ethnology--Uganda
 --Funeral customs and rites
  UF Funeral rites and ceremonies, Luyia
(African people)
 --Rites and ceremonies

Luyia language *(May Subd Geog)*
  [PL 8474.L8]
  UF Luhya language
      Luluhya language
      Luluyia language
      Oluluyia language
  BT Bantu languages
      Kenya--Languages
      Uganda--Languages
  NT Hanga dialect (Kenya)
      Kisa dialect

Luyia proverbs
  USE Proverbs, Luyia

Lwenas (African people)
  USE Luenas (African people)

Lwo hymns (Sudan)
  USE Hymns, Lwo (Sudan)

Lwo language
  USE Acoli language

Lwo language (Sudan) *(May Subd Geog)*
  [PL 8474.L]
  UF Dhe Lwo language
      Dyur language
      Giur language
      Jo Lwo language
      Jur language
      Luo language (Sudan)
  BT Nilotic languages
      Sudan--Languages

Lyela (African people)
  USE Lele (African people)

Lyele dialect
  USE Lele dialect

M

Ma-da-re (African people)
  USE Bobo (African people)

Ma language *(May Subd Geog)*
  [PL 8474.M3]
  UF Amadi language
      Madi language
      Madyo language
  BT Congo (Brazzaville)--Languages
      Niger-Congo languages

Ma-wi language
  USE Mano language

Maa language
  USE Mano language

Maa language (Kenya and Tanzania)
  USE Masai language

Maale (African people)
  USE Male (African people)

Maasai (African people)
  USE Masai (African people)

Maasai language
  USE Masai language

Maba language *(May Subd Geog)*
  [PL 8475]
  UF Dzema language
      Kursa language
  BT Chad--Languages
      Nilo-Saharan languages
      Sudan--Languages

Mabaan language
  USE Maban language

Maban (African people) *(May Subd Geog)*
  [DT 155.2.M]
  UF Meban (African people)
  BT Ethnology--Sudan
      Luo (African people)

Maban language *(May Subd Geog)*
  [PL 8477]
  UF Mabaan language
      Meban language
  BT Nilotic languages
      Sudan--Languages

(May Subd Geog) = Place names may follow the heading

Mabea (African people)
  USE Bisio (African people)

Mabea language
  USE Bisio language

Mabi (African people)
  USE Bisio (African people)

Mabiha language
  USE Makonde language

Mabinza language
  USE Mbinsa language

Mabo (African people)
  USE Mabo-Barkul (African people)

Mabo-Barkul (African people) *(May Subd Geog)*
  [DT 515.45.K34]
  UF Kaleri (African people)
      Mabo (African people)
      Mada (African people)
  BT Ethnology--Nigeria

Machar Marshes (Sudan) *(Not Subd Geog)*
  UF Machar Swamp (Sudan)
  DT Marshes--Sudan

Machar Swamp (Sudan)
  USE Machar Marshes (Sudan)

Machine data storage and retrieval
  USE Information storage and retrieval
systems

Machine-readable Catalog System
  USE MARC System

Macias Nguema (Equatorial Guinea)
  USE Fernando Po (Equatorial Guinea)

Maconde language
  USE Makonde language

Macua (African people)
  USE Makua (African people)

Macua language
  USE Makua language

Mad Mullah Rebellion (Somalia), 1900-1920
  USE Maxamad Cabdulle Xasan's Rebellion,
British Somaliland, 1900-1920

Mada (African people)
  USE Mabo-Barkul (African people)
       Paduko (African people)

Madagascan...
  USE *subject headings beginning with the word* Malagasy

Madagascar *(Not Subd Geog)*
  [DT 469.M21-DT 469.M38]
  UF Malagasy Republic
  NT Nosy-Be Island (Madagascar)
      Sainte-Marie-de-Madagascar Island
(Madagascar)
  --Description and travel
  -- --1981-
  --Economic conditions
   [HC 895]
  --History
  -- --To 1810
  -- --Hova rule, 1810-1885
     UF Hova rule, 1810-1885
  -- --1885-1960
  -- --French Invasion, 1895
     UF French Invasion of Madagascar, 1895
  -- --Menalamba Rebellion, 1895-1899
     UF Menalamba Rebellion (Madagascar), 1895-1899
         Red Shawls Rebellion (Madagascar), 1895-
1899
  -- --Revolution, 1947
  --Languages
     NT Malagasy language
  --Literatures
     USE Malagasy literature
  --Politics and government
  -- --1947-1960
  -- --1960-

Ma'di (African people)
  USE Lugbara (African people)

Madi language
  USE Ma language

Ma'di language (Uganda and Sudan) *(May Subd Geog)*
  [PL 8479.1]
  UF Madi-ti language (Uganda and Sudan)
  BT Nilo-Saharan languages
      Sudan--Languages
      Uganda--Languages

Madi-ti language (Uganda and Sudan)
  USE Ma'di language (Uganda and Sudan)

Madjinngay dialect
  USE Majingai dialect

UF = Used for; BT = Broader term; RT = Related term; SA = See also; NT = Narrower term

Madyo language
    USE Ma language

Mafa (African people)
    USE Matakam (African people)

Mafia, Kaduna
    USE Kaduna Mafia

Mafeking (South Africa)
    USE Mafikeng (South Africa)

Mafikeng (South Africa)
    UF Mafeking (South Africa)
  --History
  -- --Siege, 1899-1900
    [DT 934.M2 : old class]
    [DT 1908.M34 : new class]
    BT South African War, 1899-1902

Maga language
    USE Tumak language

Magazines
    USE Periodicals

Magdala Campaign, 1867-1868
    USE Abyssinian Expedition, 1867-1868

Magersfontein, South Africa, Battle of, 1899
    [DT 934.M22 : old class]
    [DT 1908.M35 : new class]
    UF Battle of Magersfontein (South
Africa), 1899
    BT South African War, 1899-1902--
Campaigns--South Africa

Magic, Ethiopian
    [BF 1622.E8]
    NT Ethiopian magic scrolls

Magic scrolls, Ethiopian
    USE Ethiopian magic scrolls

Magomeni (Bagamoyo, Tanzania) *(Not Subd Geog)*
    UF Bagamoyo (Tanzania). Magomeni

Magong language
    USE !Xo language

Maguzawa (African people) *(May Subd Geog)*
    [DT 515.45.M33]
    BT Ethnology--Nigeria

Magwé (African people)
    USE Gade (African people)

Mah (African people)
    USE Mano (African people)

Mah language
    USE Mano language

Mahafalay (Malagasy people)
    USE Mahafaly (Malagasy people)

Mahafaly (Malagasy people) *(May Subd Geog)*
    [DT 469.M277M34]
    UF Mahafalay (Malagasy people)
    BT Ethnology--Madagascar
  --Funeral customs and rites
    UF Funeral rites and ceremonies, Mahafaly
(Malagasy people)
  --Rites and ceremonies

Mahali Mountains (Tanzania) *(Not Subd Geog)*
    UF Mahari Mountains (Tanzania)
    BT Mountains--Tanzania

Mahari Mountains (Tanzania)
    USE Mahali Mountains (Tanzania)

Mahas-Fiadicca language
    USE Mahas-Fiyadikka language

Mahas-Fiadidja language
    USE Mahas-Fiyadikka language

Mahas-Fiyadikka language *(May Subd Geog)*
    [PL 8574.Z9H3]
    UF Fadicca language
        Fadicha language
        Fadija language
        Fiadicca language
        Fiadidja language
        Fiyadikka language
        Fiyadikkya language
        Mahas-Fiadicca language
        Mahas-Fiadidja language
        Nile Nubian language
        Nobiin language
    BT Nubian languages
        Sudan--Languages

Mahongwe (African people)
    USE Kota (African people)

Mahoré
    USE Mayotte

Mahou dialect
    USE Mau dialect (Ivory Coast)

(May Subd Geog) = Place names may follow the heading

Mahu dialect
  USE Mau dialect (Ivory Coast)

Mahum (African people)
  USE Bandjoun (African people)

Mai-Ndombe, Lake (Zaire) *(Not Subd Geog)*
  UF Lac Léopold II (Zaire)
      Lac Mai-Ndombe (Zaire)
      Lake Leopold II (Zaire)
      Lake Mai-Ndombe (Zaire)
      Leopold II, Lake (Zaire)
      Maindombe, Lake (Zaire)
  BT Lakes--Zaire

Maindombe, Lake (Zaire)
  USE Mai-Ndombe, Lake (Zaire)

Majangir (African people) *(May Subd Geog)*
  [DT 380.4.M3]
  UF Masongo (African people)
      Tama (African people)
      Ujang (African people)
  BT Ethnology--Ethiopia

Maji Maji Uprising, 1905-1907
  [DT 447]
  RT Tanganyika--History

Majingai dialect *(May Subd Geog)*
  [PL 8482.M79]
  UF Madjinngay dialect
      Midjinngay dialect
      Modjinngay dialect
      Moggingain dialect
      Sar dialect
      Sara-Majingai dialect
  BT Central African Republic--Languages
      Chad--Languages
      Sara language

Majingai-Ngama language
  USE Sara language

Majingai proverbs
  USE Proverbs, Majingai

Majuba Hill (South Africa), Battle of, 1881
  [DT 928 : old class]
  [DT 2359.M36 : new class]
  UF Battle of Majuba Hill (South Africa),
1881
  BT Transvaal (South Africa)--History--War
of 1880-1881

Maka (African people) *(May Subd Geog)*
  [DT 571.M35]
  UF Makie (African people)
  BT Bantu-speaking peoples
      Ethnology--Cameroon

Maka language (Cameroon) *(May Subd Geog)*
  [PL 8482.M]
  UF Makaa language
      Mekaa language
  BT Bantu languages
      Cameroon--Languages

Makaa language
  USE Maka language (Cameroon)

Makaukau (African people)
  USE !Kung (African people)

Mak'edala, Ethiopia, Battle of, 1868
  [DT 386.3]
  UF Battle of Mak'edala (Ethiopia), 1868
  BT Abyssinian Expedition, 1867-1868

Makhanyas (African people) *(May Subd Geog)*
  [DT 764.M : old class]
  [DT 1768.M : new class]
  BT Ethnology--South Africa

Makhuwa (African people)
  USE Makua (African people)

Makie (African people)
  USE Maka (African people)

Makonde (African people) *(May Subd Geog)*
  [DT 458.3.M (Mozambique : old class)]
  [DT 3328.M35 (Mozambique : new class)]
  [DT 443.3.M34 (Tanzania)
  UF Konge (African people)
  BT Bantu-speaking peoples
      Ethnology--Africa, Eastern
      Ethnology--Mozambique
      Ethnology--Tanzania

Makonde language *(May Subd Geog)*
  [PL 8482.M8]
  UF Konge language
      Mabiha language
      Maconde language
      Mavia language
  BT Africa, Eastern--Languages
      Bantu languages
      Mozambique--Languages
      Tanzania--Languages

UF = Used for; BT = Broader term; RT = Related term; SA = See also; NT = Narrower term

Makonde sculpture
    USE Sculpture, Makonde

Makpe (African people)
    USE Kwiri (African people)

Makua (African people) *(May Subd Geog)*
    [DT 458.3.M35 : old class]
    [DT 3328.M36 : new class]
    UF Macua (African people)
        Makhuwa (African people)
        Makwa (African people)
        Wakua (African people)
        Wamakua (African people)
    BT Bantu-speaking peoples
        Ethnology--Mozambique

Makua language *(May Subd Geog)*
    [PL 8483]
    UF Macua language
    BT Bantu languages
        Mozambique--Languages

Makua proverbs
    USE Proverbs, Makua

Makwa (African people)
    USE Makua (African people)

Makwangwa (African people)
    USE Kwangwa (African people)

Malagasy art
    USE Art, Malagasy

Malagasy astrology
    USE Astrology, Malagasy

Malagasy authors
    USE Authors, Malagasy

Malagasy cookery
    USE Cookery, Malagasy

Malagasy fiction *(May Subd Geog)*
    [PL 5378.4 (History)]
    [PL 5378.8 (Collections)]
    BT Malagasy literature

Malagasy folk poetry
    USE Folk poetry, Malagasy

Malagasy folk songs
    USE Folk songs, Malagasy

Malagasy language *(May Subd Geog)*
    [PL 5371-PL 5379]
    UF Hova dialect
        Malgache language
        Merina dialect
    BT Madagascar--Languages
    NT Antaisaka dialect
        Antandroy dialect
        Bara dialect (Madagascar)
        Betsileo dialect
        Betsimisaraka dialect
        Sakalava dialect
        Tsimihety dialect
    --Dialects *(May Subd Geog)*

Malagasy literature *(May Subd Geog)*
    [PL 5378]
    UF Madagascar--Literatures
    NT Malagasy fiction
        Malagasy poetry

Malagasy literature (French) *(May Subd Geog)*
    [PQ 3988.5.M28 (History)]
    [PQ 3988.5.M282 (Collections)]
    UF French literature--Malagasy authors
    NT Malagasy poetry (French)

Malagasy national characteristics
    USE National characteristics, Malagasy

Malagasy orations
    USE Speeches, addresses, etc., Malagasy

Malagasy periodicals *(May Subd Geog)*
    [PN 5499.M]
    UF Periodicals, Malagasy

Malagasy philosophy
    USE Philosophy, Malagasy

Malagasy poetry *(May Subd Geog)*
    [PL 5378.2 (History)]
    [PL 5378.6 (Collections)]
    BT Malagasy literature
    NT Folk poetry, Malagasy

Malagasy poetry (French) *(May Subd Geog)*
    [PQ 3988.5.M28 (History)]
    [PL 3988.5.M282 (Collections)]
    UF French poetry--Malagasy authors
    BT Malagasy literature (French)

Malagasy pottery
    USE Pottery, Malagasy

(May Subd Geog) = Place names may follow the heading

Malagasy proverbs
    USE Proverbs, Malagasy

Malagasy Republic
    USE Madagascar

Malagasy songs
    USE Songs, Malagasy

Malagasy speeches
    USE Speeches, addresses, etc., Malagasy

Malaria *(May Subd Geog)*
    UF Ague
        Chills and fever
        Intermittent fever
    BT Tropical medicine
--Africa, West
    [RC 165.W47]

Malawi *(Not Subd Geog)*
    [DT 857-DT 865 : old class]
    [DT 3161-DT 3257 : new class]
    UF Nyasaland
--Antiquities
    NT Chencherere II Rockshelter (Malawi)
--Description and travel
-- --1981-
--Economic conditions
    [HC 935]
--Foreign relations *(May Subd Geog)*
-- --1964-
--History
-- --To 1891
-- --1891-1953
-- --Chilembwe Rebellion, 1915
    [DT 862 : old class]
    [DT 3225 : new class]
    UF Chilembwe Rebellion, 1915
-- --1953-1964
-- --1964-
    UF Chipembere Rebellion, 1965
--Languages
    NT Chewa dialect
        Ngonde language
        Nyanja language
        Senga language
        Tonga language (Nyasa)
        Tsonga language
        Tumbuka language
        Yao language
        Yombe language
--Literatures
    USE Malawi literature
--Poetry
    NT Tsonga poetry

--Politics and government
-- --1964-

Malawi, Lake
    USE Nyasa, Lake

Malawi cookery
    USE Cookery, Malawi

Malawi drama (English) *(May Subd Geog)*
    [PR 9385.3 (History)]
    [PR 9385.7 (Collections)]
    UF English drama--Malawi authors
    BT Malawi literature (English)

Malawi literature *(May Subd Geog)*
    [PL 8014.M32]
    UF Malawi--Literatures
    BT Southern African literature
    NT Nyanja literature

Malawi literature (English) *(May Subd Geog)*
    [PR 9385]
    UF English literature--Malawi authors
    BT Southern African literature (English)
    NT Malawi drama (English)
        Malawi poetry (English)

Malawi poetry (English) *(May Subd Geog)*
    [PR 9385.2 (History)]
    [PR 9385.6-PR 9385.65 (Collections)]
    UF English poetry--Malawi authors
    BT Malawi literature (English)

Malawi Railways
    [HE 3432.Z8M34]
    BT Railroads--Malawi

Male (African people) *(May Subd Geog)*
    [DT 380.4.M32]
    UF Maale (African people)
    BT Ethnology--Ethiopia

Malgache language
    USE Malagasy language

Mali *(Not Subd Geog)*
    [DT 551-DT 551.9]
    UF French Sudan
        Sudan, French
        Sudanese Republic
--Antiquities
    NT Fanfannyégèné I Site (Mali)
--Description and travel
-- --1981-   *(Continued)*

UF = Used for; BT = Broader term; RT = Related term; SA = See also; NT = Narrower term

Mali   *(Continued)*
--Economic conditions
  [HC 1035]
--History
  NT Mamadou Lamine, Rebellion of, 1885-
1887
-- --Coup d'état, 1968
  [DT 551.8]
  BT Coups d'état--Mali
--Languages
  NT Bobo Fing language
      Bobo languages
      Boomu dialect
      Bozo language
      Bwamu language
      Dendi dialect
      Dogon language
      Mamara language
      Samo language (West Africa)
      Sembla language
      Senari language
      Senufo languages
      Tuwunro dialect
--Politics and government
-- --1968-1991
-- --1991-

Mali (Federation) *(Not Subd Geog)*
  [DT 551.8-DT 551.82]
  Here are entered works for the period 1959-1960.
  UF Federation of Mali

Mali (Guinea)
  USE Niani (Guinea)

Mali Empire *(Not Subd Geog)*
  [DT 532.2]
  UF Malinke Empire
      Mandinga Empire
  BT Mandingo (African people)--History

Malinka language
  USE Mandingo language

Malinke (African people)
  USE Mandingo (African people)

Malinke Empire
  USE Mali Empire

Malinke language
  USE Mandingo language

Malmani gold fields
  [DT 745 : old class]
  BT Gold mines and mining--South Africa

Mamabolo (African people) *(May Subd Geog)*
  [DT 764.M : old class]
  [DT 1768.M36 : new class]
  BT Bantu-speaking peoples
      Ethnology--South Africa

Mamadou Lamine, Rebellion of, 1885-1887
  [DT 551.65]
  UF Insurrection of Mamadou Lamine, 1885-1887
      Rebellion of Mamadou Lamine, 1885-1887
  BT Mali--History
      Senegambia--History
      Soninke (African people)--History

Mamara language *(May Subd Geog)*
  [PL 8484.M23]
  UF Bamana language (Senufo)
      Bambara language (Senufo)
      Mamara Senoufo language
      Mamara Senufo language
      Mambar language
      Mianka language
      Minianka language
      Minyanka language
      Nanergue language
      Sendege language
  BT Ivory Coast--Languages
      Mali--Languages
      Senufo languages

Mamara proverbs
  USE Proverbs, Minianka

Mamara Senoufo language
  USE Mamara language

Mamara Senufo language
  USE Mamara language

Mambar language
  USE Mamara language

Mambere (African people)
  USE Mambila (African people)

Mambere language
  USE Mambila language

Mambetto (African people)
  USE Mangbetu (African people)

Mambila (African people) *(May Subd Geog)*
  [DT 515.45.M35 (Nigeria)]
  UF Mambere (African people)
  BT Ethnology--Cameroon
      Ethnology--Nigeria

(May Subd Geog) = Place names may follow the heading

Mambila art
  USE Art, Mambila

Mambila language *(May Subd Geog)*
  [PL 8484.M25]
  UF Lagubi language
      Mambere language
      Nor language
      Tagbo language
      Tongbo language
      Torbi language
  BT Benue-Congo languages
      Cameroon--Languages
      Nigeria--Languages

Mambukush (African people)
  USE Mbukushu (African people)

Mambukush language
  USE Mbukushu language

Mambuti (African people)
  USE Mbuti (African people)

Mambwe (African people) *(May Subd Geog)*
  [DT 963.42 : old class]
  [DT 3058.M35 : new class]
  BT Bantu-speaking peoples
      Ethnology--Zambia

Mambwe language *(May Subd Geog)*
  [PL 8484.M3]
  UF Cimambwe language
  BT Bantu languages
      Zambia--Languages

Mamfe Bantu languages *(May Subd Geog)*
  [PL 8484.M]
  UF Bantu languages, Mamfe
  BT Benue-Congo languages
      Cameroon--Languages
  NT Anyang language

Mampa (African people)
  USE Sherbro (African people)

Mampa language
  USE Sherbro language

Mampruli language *(May Subd Geog)*
  [PL 8485]
  UF Mamprusi language
  BT Gur languages
      Ghana--Languages

Mampruli proverbs

  USE Proverbs, Mampruli

Mamprusi (African people) *(May Subd Geog)*
  [DT 510.43.M35]
  BT Ethnology--Ghana
  --Kings and rulers

Mamprusi language
  USE Mampruli language

Mampua (African people)
  USE Sherbro (African people)

Mampukush (African people)
  USE Mbukushu (African people)

Mampukush language
  USE Mbukushu language

Mampwa (African people)
  USE Sherbro (African people)

Mampwa language
  USE Sherbro language

Mamvu (African people) *(May Subd Geog)*
  [DT 650.M (Zaire)]
  UF Mangutu (African people)
      Momfu (African people)
      Momvou (African people)
      Monfou (African people)
      Mumvu (African people)
      Mvuba (African people)
  BT Ethnology--Africa, Central
      Ethnology--Uganda
      Ethnology--Zaire
  NT Lese (African people)

Mamvu language *(May Subd Geog)*
  [PL 8487]
  UF Momvu language
      Monvu language
  BT Nilo-Saharan languages
      Uganda--Languages
      Zaire--Languages

Man, Fossil
  USE Fossil man

Man, Prehistoric *(May Subd Geog)*
  UF Antiquities, Prehistoric
      Human remains (Archaeology)
      Paleoanthropology
      Paleoethnography
      Prehistoric antiquities   *(Continued)*

UF = Used for; BT = Broader term; RT = Related term; SA = See also; NT = Narrower term

Man, Prehistoric   *(Continued)*
  UF Prehistoric man
      Prehistory
      Skeletal remains
  BT Archaeology
      Ethnology
  RT Fossil man
 --Africa, East
  [GN 865.E2]
 --Kenya
  [GN 865.K4]
 --Tanzania
  [GN 865.T33]

Man-made lakes
  USE Reservoirs

Managers
  USE Executives

Manala (African people) *(May Subd Geog)*
  [DT 764.M : old class]
  [DT 1768.M : new class]
  BT Ethnology--South Africa
      Ndebele (African people)
 --Religion
  [BL 2480.M25]

Mancagne language
  USE Mankanya language

Mancala (Game)
  [GV 1469.M35]
  BT Games--Africa, Sub-Saharan
  NT Ayo (Game)

Mancanha language
  USE Mankanya language

Manda Island (Kenya) *(Not Subd Geog)*
  [DT 434.M35]
  BT Islands--Kenya
      Kenya

Mandab, Strait of *(Not Subd Geog)*
  UF Bab al-Mandab
      'Bab el Mandeb
      Mandeb, Bab el
      Strait of Mandab
  BT Straits--Africa

Mandago language
  USE Mandjak language

Mandara language *(May Subd Geog)*
  [PL 8489]
  UF Wandala language
  BT Bari language
      Chadic languages
      Nigeria--Languages
  NT Glavda language

Mandara Mountains (Cameroon and Nigeria) *(Not Subd Geog)*
  UF Monts Mandara (Cameroon and Nigeria)
  BT Mountains--Cameroon
      Mountains--Nigeria

Mandari (African people) *(May Subd Geog)*
  [DT 155.2.M36]
  UF Wandala (African people)
  BT Ethnology--Sudan
 --Religion
  [BL 2480.M28]

Mandé (African people)
  USE Mandingo (African people)

Mande language
  USE Mandingo language

Mande languages *(May Subd Geog)*
  [PL 8490.M35]
  BT Africa, West--Languages
      Niger-Congo languages
  NT Bobo Fing language
      Bozo language
      Busa language
      Gbandi language
      Kpelle language
      Loko language
      Loma language
      Mandekan languages
      Mende language
      Samo language (West Africa)
      Sembla language
      Soninke language
      Southern Mande languages
      Susu language
      Vai language

Mande languages, Southern
  USE Southern Mande languages

Mandeb, Bab el
  USE Mandab, Strait of

Mandeka language
  USE Mandingo language

(May Subd Geog) = Place names may follow the heading

Mandekan languages *(May Subd Geog)*
  [PL 8490.M36]
  BT Africa, West--Languages
      Mande languages
  NT Bambara language
      Dyula language
      Mandingo language

Mandenga language
  USE Mandingo language

Manding (African people)
  USE Mandingo (African people)

Manding language
  USE Mandingo language

Mandinga Empire
  USE Mali Empire

Mandingi language
  USE Northern Bullom language

Mandingo (African people) *(May Subd Geog)*
  [DT 509.M34 (Gambia)]
  [DT 543.45.M34 (Guinea)]
  [DT 613.45.M36 (Guinea-Bissau)]
  [DT 551.45.M36 (Mali)]
  [DT 474.6.M36 (West Africa)]
  UF Malinke (African people)
      Mandé (African people)
      Manding (African people)
      Mandinque (African people)
      Mandinka (African people)
      Mandino (African people)
      Maninkaalu (African people)
      Soce (African people)
      Sosse (African people)
  BT Ethnology--Africa, West
  NT Bozo (African people)
      Kuranko (African people)
  --History
  NT Mali Empire
      Niumi (Kingdom)

Mandingo folk literature
  USE Folk literature, Mandingo

Mandingo folk songs
  USE Folk songs, Mandingo

Mandingo language *(May Subd Geog)*
  [PL 8491]
  UF Malinka language
      Malinke language
      Mande language

  UF Mandeka language
      Mandenga language
      Manding language
      Mandingue language
      Mandika language
      Manenka language
      Maninka language
      Maniyaka language
      Meninka language
  BT Africa, West--Languages
      Mandekan languages
  NT Mau dialect (Ivory Coast)

Mandingo literature *(May Subd Geog)*
  [PL 8491.5-PL 8491.9]
  BT West African literature
  NT Folk literature, Mandingo
      Mandingo poetry

Mandingo poetry *(May Subd Geog)*
  [PL 8491.7]
  BT Mandingo literature
      West African poetry

Mandingo proverbs
  USE Proverbs, Mandingo

Mandingo sculpture
  USE Sculpture, Mandingo

Mandingo terra-cotta sculpture
  USE Terra-cotta sculpture, Mandingo

Mandingo women
  USE Women, Mandingo

Mandingue (African people)
  USE Mandingo (African people)

Mandingue language
  USE Mandingo language

Mandinka (African people)
  USE Mandingo (African people)

Mandinka language
  USE Mandingo language

Mandino (African people)
  USE Mandingo (African people)

Mandjack (African people)
  USE Mandjak (African people)

Mandjack language
  USE Mandjak language

UF = Used for; BT = Broader term; RT = Related term; SA = See also; NT = Narrower term

Mandjak (African people) *(May Subd Geog)*
  [DT 549.45.M (Senegal)]
  UF Mandjack (African people)
      Mandyak (African people)
      Mandyako (African people)
      Manjaco (African people)
      Manjago (African people)
      Manjaku (African people)
  BT Ethnology--Gambia
      Ethnology--Guinea-Bissau
      Ethnology--Senegal

Mandjak language *(May Subd Geog)*
  [PL 8493]
  UF Kanop language
      Mandago language
      Mandjack language
      Manjacos language
  BT Gambia--Languages
      Guinea--Languages
      Niger-Congo languages
      Senegal--Languages

Mandjas *(May Subd Geog)*
  [DT 546.345.M]
  UF Manjas (African people)
      Manza (African people)
  BT Ethnology--Central African Republic
  --Folklore
  [GR 357.42.M36]

Mandju (African people)
  USE Bandjoun (African people)

Mandyak (African people)
  USE Mandjak (African people)

Mandyako (African people)
  USE Mandjak (African people)

Manenka language
  USE Mandingo language

Manga (African people) *(May Subd Geog)*
  [DT 547.45.M2]
  UF Mangawa (African people)
  BT Ethnology--Niger

Manga women
  USE Women, Manga

Mangala language (Zaire)
  USE Lingala language

Manganja (African people)
  USE Nyanja (African people)

Mang'anja language
  USE Nyanja language

Mangati (African people) *(May Subd Geog)*
  [DT 443.3.M]
  UF Tatoga (African people)
  BT Ethnology--Tanzania

Mangawa (African people)
  USE Manga (African people)

Mangbettu (African people)
  USE Mangbetu (African people)

Mangbetu (African people) *(May Subd Geog)*
  [DT 650.M64]
  UF Amangbetu (African people)
      Mambetto (African people)
      Mangbettu (African people)
      Mombuttu (African people)
      Monbattu (African people)
      Monbuttu (African people)
      Namangbetu (African people)
  BT Ethnology--Zaire

Mangbetu art
  USE Art, Mangbetu

Mangbetu language *(May Subd Geog)*
  [PL 8495]
  UF Monbuttu language
  BT Central Sudanic languages
      Zaire--Languages

Mangbua (African people)
  USE Ababua (African people)

Mangoni (African people)
  USE Ngoni (African people)

Mangoro River (Madagascar) *(Not Subd Geog)*
  BT Rivers--Madagascar

Mangutu (African people)
  USE Mamvu (African people)

Mani (Guinea)
  USE Niani (Guinea)

Maninka language
  USE Mandingo language

Maninkaalu (African people)
  USE Mandingo (African people)

(May Subd Geog) = Place names may follow the heading

Maniyaka language
  USE Mandingo language

Manja (African people)
  USE Gbaya (African people)

Manjaco (African people)
  USE Mandjak (African people)

Manjacos language
  USE Mandjak language

Manjago (African people)
  USE Mandjak (African people)

Manjaku (African people)
  USE Mandjak (African people)

Manjas (African people)
  USE Mandjas

Mankanya language *(May Subd Geog)*
  [PL 8496.M33]
  UF Bola language (Guinea-Bissau)
     Brame language
     Bulama language
     Burama language
     Mancagne language
     Mancanha language
  BT Guinea--Languages
     Niger-Congo languages

Mankon language *(May Subd Geog)*
  [PL 8496.M35]
  BT Benue-Congo languages
     Cameroon--Languages

Mankoya (African people)
  USE Nkoya (African people)

Manners and customs *(Not Subd Geog)*
  Here are entered general works on folkways,
customs, ceremonies, festivals, popular traditions,
etc., treated collectively.
  UF Ceremonies
     Customs, Social
     Folkways
     Social customs
     Social life and customs
     Traditions
     Usages
  BT Ethnology
  RT Rites and ceremonies
  SA subdivision Social life and customs under
names of countries, cities, etc. and under ethnic

groups, e.g. Kenya--Social life and customs; Kwiri
(African people)--Social life and customs
  NT Body-marking
     Folklore
     Funeral rites and ceremonies
     Holidays
     Marriage customs and rites
     Sex customs
     Tattooing

Mano (African people) *(May Subd Geog)*
  [DT 630.5.M35 (Liberia)]
  UF Mah (African people)
  BT Ethnology--Guinea
     Ethnology--Liberia

Mano language *(May Subd Geog)*
  [PL 8496.M37]
  UF Ma-wi language
     Maa language
     Mah language
     Manon language
     Mia language
  BT Guinea--Languages
     Liberia--Languages
     Southern Mande languages

Manon language
  USE Mano language

Manuscripts, Abyssinian
  USE Manuscripts, Ethiopic

Manuscripts, Amharic *(May Subd Geog)*
  UF Amharic manuscripts

Manuscripts, Ethiopic *(May Subd Geog)*
  UF Abyssinian manuscripts
     Ethiopic manuscripts
     Manuscripts, Abyssinian

Manyanga (African people)
  USE Sundi (African people)

Manyika (African people)
  USE Nika (African people)

Manza (African people)
  USE Mandjas

Maoism
  USE Communism

Maou dialect
  USE Mau dialect (Ivory Coast)

UF = Used for; BT = Broader term; RT = Related term; SA = See also; NT = Narrower term

Mapodi language
  USE Gude language

Mapuda language
  USE Gude language

Mapungubwe Site (South Africa) *(Not Subd Geog)*
  BT South Africa--Antiquities

Maputaland (South Africa) *(Not Subd Geog)*
  [DT 878.T6 : old class]
  [DT 2400.T66 : new class]
  UF Tongaland (South Africa)

Maradi River (Nigeria and Niger) *(Not Subd Geog)*
  UF Gada River (Nigeria and Niger)
      Goulbin Maradi (Nigeria and Niger)
      Gulbin Maradi (Nigeria and Niger)
  BT Rivers--Niger
      Rivers--Nigeria

Maragwet (African people)
  USE Marakwet (African people)

Marakwet (African people) *(May Subd Geog)*
  [DT 433.545.M32]
  UF Maragwet (African people)
      Markweta (African people)
  BT Ethnology--Kenya
      Nilo-Hamitic tribes

Maravi (African people)
  USE Chewa (African people)

MARC Project
  USE MARC System

MARC System *(May Subd Geog)*
  UF Machine-readable Catalog System
      MARC Project
      Project MARC
  --South Africa
  [Z 699.4.M2]
  UF SAMARC System

Marghi language
  USE Margi language

Margi language *(May Subd Geog)*
  [PL 8497]
  UF Marghi language
  BT Chadic languages
      Nigeria--Languages

Marico River (South Africa and Botswana) *(Not Subd Geog)*
  BT Rivers--Botswana
      Rivers--South Africa

Marille (African people)
  USE Dasanetch (African people)

Maritu (African people)
  USE Murzu (African people)

Maritz's Rebellion, 1914-1915
  USE South Africa--History--Rebellion, 1914-1915

Marka language
  USE Soninke language

Markets *(May Subd Geog)*
  BT Economics
  --Africa, West
  [HF 5475.W4]

Markweta (African people)
  USE Marakwet (African people)

Marotse (African people)
  USE Lozi (African people)

Marovoay Plain (Madagascar) *(Not Subd Geog)*
  UF Plaine de Marovoay (Madagascar)
  BT Plains--Madagascar

Marra, Jabal (Sudan)
  USE Marra Mountains (Sudan)

Marra Mountains (Sudan) *(Not Subd Geog)*
  UF Jabal Marra (Sudan)
      Jabal Marrah (Sudan)
      Jebel Marra (Sudan)
      Jebel Marrah (Sudan)
      Marra, Jabal (Sudan)
      Marrah, Jabal (Sudan)
      Marrah Mountains (Sudan)
  BT Mountains--Sudan

Marrah, Jabal (Sudan)
  USE Marra Mountains (Sudan)

Marrah Mountains (Sudan)
  USE Marra Mountains (Sudan)

Marriage *(May Subd Geog)*
  UF Matrimony
      Wedlock
  RT Family

(May Subd Geog) = Place names may follow the heading

NT Bride price
    Divorce
    Domestic relations
    Married women

Marriage (Igbo law)
  BT Law, Igbo

Marriage (Luo law)
  BT Law, Luo

Marriage (Yoruba law)
  BT Law, Yoruba

Marriage customs and rites *(May Subd Geog)*
  UF Bridal customs
  BT Manners and customs
    Rites and ceremonies
  SA *subdivision* Marriage customs and rites
under ethnic groups, e.g. Swazi (African people)--
Marriage customs and rites
  --Zaire
  NT Lusalo

Marriage customs and rites, Bagirmi (African
people)
  USE Bagirmi (African people)--Marriage
customs and rites

Marriage customs and rites, Bambara (African
people)
  USE Bambara (African people)--Marriage
customs and rites

Marriage customs and rites, Bantu
  USE Bantu-speaking peoples--Marriage
customs and rites

Marriage customs and rites, Dinka (African
people)
  USE Dinka (African people)--Marriage
customs and rites

Marriage customs and rites, Efik (African
people)
  USE Efik (African people)--Marriage
customs and rites

Marriage customs and rites, Ewe (African
people)
  USE Ewe (African people)--Marriage customs
and rites

Marriage customs and rites, Himba (African
people)

  USE Himba (African people)--Marriage customs
and rites

Marriage customs and rites, Ibibio (African
people)
  USE Ibibio (African people)--Marriage customs
and rites

Marriage customs and rites, Kikuyu (African
people)
  USE Kikuyu (African people)--Marriage customs
and rites

Marriage customs and rites, Kpelle (African
people)
  USE Kpelle (African people)--Marriage customs
and rites

Marriage customs and rites, Kwaya (African people)
  USE Kwaya (African people)--Marriage customs
and rites

Marriage customs and rites, Mossi (African people)
  USE Mossi (African people)--Marriage customs
and rites

Marriage customs and rites, Ndonga (African
people)
  USE Ndonga (African people)--Marriage customs
and rites

Marriage customs and rites, Swazi (African people)
  USE Swazi (African people)--Marriage customs
and rites

Marriage customs and rites, Yoruba (African
people)
  USE Yoruba (African people)--Marriage customs
and rites

Marriage customs and rites, Zande (African people)
  USE Zande (African people)--Marriage customs
and rites

Married women *(May Subd Geog)*
  *Here are entered works on the legal status of women
during marriage, especially on the effect of marriage on the
legal capacity.*
  UF Coverture
  BT Marriage
    Women

Married women (Ila law)
  BT Law, Ila

UF = Used for; BT = Broader term; RT = Related term; SA = See also; NT = Narrower term

Marshes *(May Subd Geog)*
  BT Landforms
 --**Benin**
  NT Lama Depression (Benin)
 --**Sudan**
  NT Machar Marshes (Sudan)

Marxism
  USE Communism
      Socialism

Masa (African people) *(May Subd Geog)*
  [DT 546.445.M3 (Chad)]
  UF Massa (African people)
  BT Ethnology--Cameroon
      Ethnology--Chad

Masa Guelengdeng (African people)
  USE Bagirmi (African people)

Masa language (Chadic) *(May Subd Geog)*
  [PL 8499]
  UF Banaa language
      Banana language (Masa)
      Masana language
      Massa language
      Walai language
  BT Cameroon--Languages
      Chad--Languages
      Chadic languages

Masaba language
  USE Gisu language

Masai (African people) *(May Subd Geog)*
  [DT 433.545.M33 (Kenya)]
  [DT 443.3.M37 (Tanzania)]
  UF Maasai (African people)
      Massai (African people)
  BT Ethnology--Kenya
      Ethnology--Tanzania
      Nilo-Hamitic tribes
  NT Arusha (African people)
      Baraguyu (African people)
      Samburu (African people)
 --**Missions** *(May Subd Geog)*
  [BV 3630.M3]
  UF Missions to Masai (African people)

Masai Amboseli Game Reserve (Kenya)
  USE Amboseli National Park (Kenya)

Masai folk literature
  USE Folk literature, Masai

Masai language *(May Subd Geog)*
  [PL 8501]
  UF Maa language (Kenya and Tanzania)
      Maasai language
  BT Kenya--Languages
      Nilo-Hamitic languages
      Tanzania--Languages
  RT Samburu language

Masai literature *(May Subd Geog)*
  [PL 8501.5-PL 8501.9]
  BT Kenyan literature
      Tanzanian literature
  NT Folk literature, Masai

Masai Mara Game Reserve (Kenya) *(Not Subd Geog)*
  BT Game reserves--Kenya
      National parks and reserves--Kenya

Masai women
  USE Women, Masai

Masana language
  USE Masa language (Chadic)

Masango language
  USE Shira language

Mascarene Islands *(Not Subd Geog)*
  [DT 469.M39]
  UF Limuria
  BT Islands of the Indian Ocean
  NT Mauritius
      Réunion
 --**Literatures**
  USE Mascarene literature

Mascarene literature *(May Subd Geog)*
  [PN 849.M]
  UF Mascarene Islands--Literatures
  NT Mauritian literature
      Mauritian literature (English)
      Mauritian literature (French)
      Mauritian literature (French Creole)
      Réunion literature (French)
      Réunion literature (French Creole)

Mashi language
  USE Shi language

Mashona (African people)
  USE Shona (African people)

Mashukolumbwe (African people)
  USE Ila (African people)

(May Subd Geog) = Place names may follow the heading

Masks *(May Subd Geog)*
  BT Theater
 --Burkina Faso
  NT Bobo (African people)--Masks
 --Ivory Coast
  NT Dan (African people)--Masks
 --Liberia
  NT Dan (African people)--Masks
 --Mali
  NT Dogon (African people)--Masks
 --Zaire
  NT Pende (African people)--Masks

Masks (Sculpture) *(May Subd Geog)*
  [NB 1310]
  BT Sculpture
 --Africa
 --Nigeria

Masongo (African people)
  USE Majangir (African people)

Mass communication
  USE Communication
      Mass media

Mass culture
  USE Popular culture

Mass media *(May Subd Geog)*
  Here are entered works on the modern means of mass
communication. Works on human communication, including
both the primary techniques of language, pictures, etc.
and the secondary techniques, such as the press and
radio, are entered under Communication.
  UF Mass communication
  BT Communication
  NT Africa in mass media
      Mass media and race relations
      Newspapers
      Periodicals
      Television broadcasting
      Zaire in mass media

Mass media and race relations *(May Subd Geog)*
  UF Race relations and mass media
  BT Mass media
      Race relations

Massa (African people)
  USE Masa (African people)

Massa language
  USE Masa language (Chadic)

Massacres *(May Subd Geog)*
  BT Atrocities
      History
 --Angola
  UF Angola--Massacre, 1961
 --South Africa
 -- --Sharpeville
  [DT 944.S5 : old class]
  [DT 1941 : new class]
  UF Sharpeville Massacre, 1960
      South Africa--History--Sharpeville
      Massacre, 1960
 --Zaire
 -- --Kolwezi
  [DT 658.Z5]
  UF Kolwezi (Zaire)--Massacre, 1978
 -- --Katekelayi Hill
 -- --Luamuela
 --Zimbabwe
  NT Shangani River Massacre, 1893

Massai (African people)
  USE Masai (African people)

Massawarat es Sufra Site (Sudan)
  USE Musawwarat al-Sufrah Site (Sudan)

Massif du Kaarta (Mali)
  USE Kaarta (Mali)

Massif du Ruwenzori (Uganda and Zaire)
  USE Ruwenzori Mountains (Uganda and Zaire)

Massif forestier de Gishwati (Rwanda)
  USE Gishwati (Rwanda)

Matabele (African people)
  USE Ndebele (African people)

Matabele War, 1893
  [DT 958 : old class]
  [DT 2699 : new class]
  UF Ndebele War, 1893
      Zimbabwe--History--Ndebele War, 1893
  BT Ndebele (African people)--History
  NT Shangani River Massacre, 1893

Matabele War (Zimbabwe), 1896-1897
  USE Zimbabwe--History--Ndebele Insurrection,
1896-1897

Matakam (African people) *(May Subd Geog)*
  [DT 571.M]
  UF Mafa (African people)
  BT Ethnology--Cameroon

UF = Used for; BT = Broader term; RT = Related term; SA = See also; NT = Narrower term

Matawara (African people)
  USE Tawara (African people)

Matengo (African people) *(May Subd Geog)*
  [DT 443.3.M]
  UF Wamatengo (African people)
  BT Bantu-speaking peoples
      Ethnology--Tanzania

Mathematics *(May Subd Geog)*
  BT Education
 --Study and teaching *(May Subd Geog)*
 -- --Africa, Sub-Saharan
  [QA 14.A4]
  NT African Mathematics Program

Matopo Hills (Zimbabwe) *(Not Subd Geog)*
  [DT 962.9.M38 : old class]
  [DT 3020.M39 : new class]
  UF Matopos (Zimbabwe)
      Matoppo Hills (Zimbabwe)
  BT Mountains--Zimbabwe

Matopos (Zimbabwe)
  USE Matopo Hills (Zimbabwe)

Matoppo Hills (Zimbabwe)
  USE Matopo Hills (Zimbabwe)

Matrimony
  USE Marriage

Matshaqa (African people) *(May Subd Geog)*
  [DT 650.M]
  BT Ethnology--Zaire

Mattokki (African people)
  USE Kenuz (African people)

Matya (West African people)
  USE Samo (West African people)

Matye (West African people)
  USE Samo (West African people)

Mau dialect (Ivory Coast) *(May Subd Geog)*
  [PL 8491.95.I9]
  UF Mahou dialect
      Mahu dialect
      Maou dialect
      Mauka dialect
      Maukakan dialect
  BT Ivory Coast--Languages
      Mandingo language

Mau Mau
  [DT 433.577]
  BT Kenya--Politics and government--To 1963
      Kikuyu (African people)--History

Mauka dialect
  USE Mau dialect (Ivory Coast)

Maukakan dialect
  USE Mau dialect (Ivory Coast)

Mauri (African people)
  USE Mawri (African people)

Maurice
  USE Mauritius

Mauritania *(Not Subd Geog)*
  [DT 554-DT 554.9]
  NT Arguin Island (Mauritiana)
  --Antiquities
  NT Aoudaghost (City)
  --Economic conditions
  [HC 1050]
  -- --1960-
  -- Languages
  NT Pular dialect
      Wolof language
  --Literatures
  USE Mauritanian literature
  --Poetry
  NT Wolof poetry
  --Politics and government
  -- --1960-
  --Social conditions
  -- --1960-

Mauritanian literature *(May Subd Geog)*
  [PL 8014.M]
  UF Mauritania--Literatures
  BT West African literature
  NT Pular literature
      Wolof literature

Mauritian authors
  USE Authors, Mauritian

Mauritian children's stories (French)
  USE Children's stories, Mauritian (French)

Mauritian children's stories (French Creole)
  USE Children's stories, Mauritian (French
Creole)

Mauritian cookery
  USE Cookery, Mauritian

(May Subd Geog) = Place names may follow the heading

Mauritian fiction (English) *(May Subd Geog)*
[PR 9680.M3-PR 9680.M33]
UF English fiction--Mauritian authors
BT Mauritian literature (English)
NT Horror tales, Mauritian (English)

Mauritian fiction (French) *(May Subd Geog)*
[PQ 3988.5.M3 (History)]
[PQ 3988.5.M32 (Collections)]
UF French fiction--Mauritian authors
BT Mauritian literature (French)
NT Children's stories, Mauritian (French)

Mauritian fiction (French Creole) *(May Subd Geog)*
[PM 7854.M]
UF Creole fiction, Mauritian French
     French Creole fiction, Mauritian
BT Mauritian literature (French Creole)
NT Children's stories, Mauritian (French Creole)

Mauritian horror tales (English)
 USE Horror tales, Mauritian (English)

Mauritian literature *(May Subd Geog)*
[PN 849.M38-PN 849.M382]
UF Mauritius--Literatures
BT Mascarene literature

Mauritian literature (English) *(May Subd Geog)*
[PR 9680.M3-PR 9680.M33]
UF English literature--Mauritian authors
BT Mascarene literature
NT Mauritian fiction (English)
     Mauritian poetry (English)

Mauritian literature (French) *(May Subd Geog)*
[PQ 3988.5.M3 (History)]
[PQ 3988.5.M32 (Collections)]
UF French literature--Mauritian authors
BT Mascarene literature
NT Mauritian fiction (French)
     Mauritian poetry (French)

Mauritian literature (French Creole) *(May Subd Geog)*
[PM 7854.M]
UF Creole literature, Mauritian French
     French Creole literature, Mauritian
BT Mascarene literature
NT Mauritian fiction (French Creole)

Mauritian newspapers *(May Subd Geog)*
[PN 5499.M]
UF Newspapers, Mauritian

Mauritian painting
 USE Painting, Mauritian

Mauritian poetry (English) *(May Subd Geog)*
[PR 9680.M3-PR 9680.M33]
UF English poetry--Mauritian authors
BT Mauritian literature (English)

Mauritian poetry (French) *(May Subd Geog)*
[PQ 3988.5.M3 (History)]
[PQ 3988.5.M32 (Collections)]
UF French poetry--Mauritian authors
BT Mauritian literature (French)

Mauritians *(May Subd Geog)*
BT Ethnology--Mauritius

Mauritius *(Not Subd Geog)*
[DT 469.M4-DT 469.M495]
UF Ile de France
     Ile Maurice
     Isle de France
     Maurice
BT Mascarene Islands
NT Rodrigues Island (Mauritius)
--Civilization
-- --Indic influences
    BT India--Civilization
--Description and travel
-- --1981-
--Economic conditions
   [HC 597.5]
--History
-- --To 1810
--Literatures
   USE Mauritian literature
--Politics and government
-- --To 1968
-- --1968-

Mavia language
 USE Makonde language

Mawri (African people) *(May Subd Geog)*
[DT 547.45.M38]
UF Arawa (African people)
     Mauri (African people)
BT Ethnology--Niger
     Hausa (African people)

Mawri women
 USE Women, Mawri

UF = Used for; BT = Broader term; RT = Related term; SA = See also; NT = Narrower term

Maxamad Cabdulle Xasan's Rebellion, British Somaliland, 1900-1920
   [DT 404-DT 404.3]
   UF Dervish Rebellion (Somalia), 1900-1920
       Mad Mullah Rebellion (Somalia), 1900-1920
   BT Somalia--History

May-may (African people)
   USE Rahanweyn (African people)

Maya (West African people)
   USE Samo (West African people)

Mayaka (African people)
   USE Yaka (African people)

Mayombe *(May Subd Geog)*
   [DT 650.M38]
   UF Bayombe (African people)
   BT Ethnology--Zaire

Mayotte *(Not Subd Geog)*
   [DT 469.M497]
   UF Ile Mayotte
       Mahoré
   BT Comoros

Mazega (Ethiopia) *(Not Subd Geog)*
   BT Plains--Ethiopia

Mba-tivi (African people)
   USE Tivi (African people)

Mbacca (African people)
   USE Ngbaka (African people)

Mbai (African people) *(May Subd Geog)*
   [DT 546.345.M (Central African Republic)]
   [DT 546.445.M (Chad)]
   UF Bai (African people)
   BT Ethnology--Central African Republic
       Ethnology--Chad

Mbai language (Moissala) *(May Subd Geog)*
   [PL 8648.4]
   UF Mbay language (Moissala)
       Moissala Mbai language
       Sara Mbai language (Moissala)
   BT Central African Republic--Languages
       Chad--Languages
       Sara languages

Mbai proverbs (Moissala)
   USE Proverbs, Mbai (Moissala)

Mbaka (African people)
   USE Ngbaka (African people)

Mbala (African people) *(May Subd Geog)*
   [DT 650.M42]
   UF Bambala (African people)
       Gimbala (African people)
       Rumbala (African people)
   BT Bantu-speaking peoples
       Ethnology--Zaire
  --Religion
   [BL 2480.M33]

Mbala language (Bandundu region, Zaire) *(May Subd Geog)*
   [PL 8403]
   UF Gimbala language
       Kimbala language
       Mumbala language
       Rumbala language
   BT Kongo language
       Zaire--Languages
   NT Hungana language

Mbala language (Kasai Occidental Region, Zaire)
   USE Bushoong language

Mbale language
   USE Bushoong language

Mbam language
   USE Mbum language

Mbanderu (African people)
   USE Mbandieru (African people)

Mbandieru (African people) *(May Subd Geog)*
   [DT 709 : old class]
   [DT 1558.M33 : new class]
   UF Mbanderu (African people)
       Mbandyeru (African people)
       Ovambadyeru (African people)
       Ovambanderu (African people)
   BT Bantu-speaking peoples
       Ethnology--Namibia

Mbandyeru (African people)
   USE Mbandieru (African people)

Mbara (African people)
   USE Bagirmi (African people)

Mbata (African people) *(May Subd Geog)*
   [DT 650.M]
   UF Ba-Mbata (African people)
   BT Bantu-speaking peoples

(May Subd Geog) = Place names may follow the heading

BT Ethnology--Zaire
--**Missions** *(May Subd Geog)*
[BV 3630.M35]
UF Missions to Mbata (African people)

Mbati (Central African Republic people) *(May Subd Geog)*
[DT 546.345.M]
UF Isongo (Central African Republic people)
Lisongo (Central African Republic people)
Lissongo (Central African Republic people)
Songo (Central African Republic people)
BT Bantu-speaking peoples
Ethnology--Central African Republic

Mbati language
USE Ngbandi language

Mbay language (Moissala)
USE Mbai language (Moissala)

Mbede (African people)
USE Mbete (African people)

Mbede language
USE Mboto language

Mbeere (African people)
USE Mbere (African people)

Mbem (African people)
USE Mfumte (African people)
Yamba (African people)

Mbem language
USE Yamba language (Cameroon and Nigeria)

Mbembe (Cross River African people) *(May Subd Geog)*
[DT 515.45.M]
UF Cross River (Cameroon and Nigeria)
African people
Mbenbe (Cross River African people)
BT Ethnology--Nigeria

Mbembe language (Congo (Brazzaville))
USE Bembe language (Congo (Brazzaville))

Mbembe sculpture
USE Sculpture, Mbembe

Mbembe wood-carving
USE Wood-carving, Mbembe

Mbenbe (Cross River African people)
USE Mbembe (Cross River African people)

Mbene (Cameroon people)
USE Basa (Cameroon people)

Mbere (African people) *(May Subd Geog)*
[DT 433.545.M34]
UF Emberre (African people)
Mbeere (African people)
BT Ethnology--Kenya
--**Land tenure**

Mbete (African people) *(May Subd Geog)*
[DT 546.245.M (Congo (Brazzaville))]
[DT 545.145.M (Gabon)]
UF Ambete (African people)
Bamba (African people)
Bambete (African people)
Mbede (African people)
Obamba (African people)
Umbete (African people)
BT Bantu-speaking peoples
Ethnology--Congo (Brazzaville)
Ethnology--Gabon
Ethnology--Uganda

Mbete language *(May Subd Geog)*
UF Bamba language
Mbede language
Obamba language
BT Bantu languages
Congo (Brazzaville)--Languages
Gabon--Languages
Uganda--Languages

Mbete reliquaries
USE Reliquaries, Mbete

Mbete sculpture
USE Sculpture, Mbete

Mbiem (African people)
USE Yanzi (African people)

Mbila (Musical instrument)
USE Mbira

Mbinga (African people)
USE Babinga (African people)

UF = Used for; BT = Broader term; RT = Related term; SA = See also; NT = Narrower term

Mbinsa language *(May Subd Geog)*
  [PL 8504]
  UF Mabinza language
  BT Bantu languages
      Zaire--Languages

Mbira
  [ML 1015-ML 1018]
  UF African hand piano
      Kalimba (Musical instrument)
      Likembe (Musical instrument)
      Mbila (Musical instrument)
  BT Musical instruments--Africa
      Sanza

Mbira music
  [M 142.M3]
  BT Music--Africa

Mbita Point (Kenya) *(Not Subd Geog)*
  BT Peninsulas--Kenya

Mbo language (Cameroon) *(May Subd Geog)*
  [PL 8506.M36]
  BT Bantu languages
      Cameroon--Languages
  NT Bakossi dialect

Mbochi (African people)
  USE Mbosi (African people)

Mboeti sect
  USE Bwiti sect

Mbogedu language
  USE Diriku language

Mbole (African people) *(May Subd Geog)*
  [DT 650.M46]
  UF Bole (African people)
      Imona (African people)
  BT Ethnology--Zaire
      Mongo (African people)

Mbomotaba language *(May Subd Geog)*
  [PL 8026.M33]
  UF Bamitaba language
      Bomitaba language
      Leke language
      Mitaba language
  BT Bantu languages
      Congo (Brazzaville)--Languages

Mbororo (African people)
  USE Bororo (African people)

Mboshi language
  USE Mbosi language

Mbosi (African people) *(May Subd Geog)*
  [DT 546.245.M]
  UF Mbochi (African people)
      Ombosi (African people)
  BT Bantu-speaking peoples
      Ethnology--Congo (Brazzaville)

Mbosi folk literature
  USE Folk literature, Mbosi

Mbosi language *(May Subd Geog)*
  [PL 8506.M]
  UF Mboshi language
  BT Bantu languages
      Congo (Brazzaville)--Languages

Mbosi literature *(May Subd Geog)*
  [PL 8506.M]
  BT Congo (Brazzaville)--Literatures
  NT Folk literature, Mbosi

Mbouin (African people)
  USE Gouin (African people)

Mboum (African people)
  USE Mbum (African people)

Mbuera (African people)
  USE Mwera (African people)

Mbueti sect
  USE Bwiti sect

Mbukuhu (African people)
  USE Mbukushu (African people)

Mbukuhu language
  USE Mbukushu language

Mbukushu (African people) *(May Subd Geog)*
  [DT 797 (Botswana : old class)]
  [DT 2458.M (Botswana : new class)]
  UF Gaba (African people)
      Hambukushu (African people)
      Mambukush (African people)
      Mampukush (African people)
      Mbukuhu (African people)
      Mucusso (African people)
  BT Bantu-speaking peoples
      Ethnology--Botswana
      Ethnology--Namibia

(May Subd Geog) = Place names may follow the heading

Mbukushu language *(May Subd Geog)*
  [PL 8507]
  UF Goba language
       Gova language
       Mambukush language
       Mampukush language
       Mbukuhu language
       Mpukusu language
  BT Botswana--Languages
       Luyana language
       Namibia--Languages

Mbulu (African people)
  USE Iraqw (African people)

Mbum (African people) *(May Subd Geog)*
  [DT 546.345.M38 (Central African
Republic)]
  UF Bum (African people)
       Kali (African people)
       Kare (African people)
       Kari (African people)
       Karre (African people)
       Mboum (African people)
       Pana (African people)
       Pani (African people)
  BT Ethnology--Cameroon
       Ethnology--Central African Republic
       Ethnology--Chad

Mbum language *(May Subd Geog)*
  [PL 8508]
  UF Bute language
       Mbam language
       Vouté language
       Vute language
  BT Adamawa languages
       Cameroon--Languages
       Central African Republic--Languages
       Chad--Languages

Mbunda language (Zambia) *(May Subd Geog)*
  [PL 8509.M]
  UF Chimbunda language
       Gimbunda language
       Kimbunda language
       Mbuunda language
  BT Bantu languages
       Zambia--Languages

Mbundu (African people) *(May Subd Geog)*
  [DT 611.45.O84 : old class]
  [DT 1308.M38 : new class]
  UF Ambundu (African people)
       Bimbundu (African people)
       Dongo (African people)

      UF Kyaka (African people)
         Mbundu Banquella (African people)
         Mbuni (African people)
         Nano (African people)
         N'Bundo (African people)
         Nbundu (African people)
         Ndongo (African people)
         Ovimbali (African people)
         Ovimbundu (African people)
         Umbundu (African people)
         Vakuanano (African people)
      BT Bantu-speaking peoples
         Ethnology--Angola
  --Religion
    [BL 2480.M35]
  --Wars
    NT Bailundo War, Angola, 1902

Mbundu Banquella (African people)
  USE Mbundu (African people)

Mbundu language
  USE Kimbundu language

Mbundu language (Benguela District, Angola)
  USE Umbundu language

Mbuni (African people)
  USE Mbundu (African people)

Mbunu (African people)
  USE Bunda (African people)

Mbuti (African people) *(May Subd Geog)*
  [DT 650.B36]
  UF Bambute (African people)
       Imbuti (African people)
       Ituri forest pygmies
       Mambuti (African people)
       Wambouti (African people)
  BT Ethnology--Zaire
       Pygmies
  NT Aka (African people)
       Efe (African people)

Mbuti art
  USE Art, Mbuti

Mbuunda language
  USE Mbunda language (Zambia)

McIlwaine, Lake (Zimbabwe) *(Not Subd Geog)*
  UF Lake McIlwaine (Zimbabwe)
  BT Hunyani River (Zimbabwe and Mozambique)
       Lakes--Zimbabwe
       Reservoirs--Zimbabwe

UF = Used for; BT = Broader term; RT = Related term; SA = See also; NT = Narrower term

Ndaga Site (Chad) *(Not Subd Geog)*
  [DT 546.49.M]
  UF Midigui Site (Chad)
  BT Chad--Antiquities

Meban (African people)
  USE Maban (African people)

Meban language
  USE Maban language

Mebe language
  USE Dan language

Mechanized information storage and retrieval
systems
  USE Information storage and retrieval
systems

Medical assistance, Scandinavian *(May Subd Geog)*
  --Tanzania
  NT Nordic Tanganyika Project

Medical folklore
  USE Folk medicine

Medicine, Blacks in
  USE Blacks in medicine

Medicine, Folk
  USE Folk medicine

Medicine, Primitive *(May Subd Geog)*
  UF Ethnomedicine
      Primitive medicine
  RT Folk medicine
  SA *subdivision* Medicine *under ethnic groups*
  NT Shamans
  --Africa, West
  NT Yoruba (African people)--Medicine
  --Angola
  NT Kongo (African people)--Medicine
  --Benin
  NT Bariba (African people)--Medicine
      Yoruba (African people)--Medicine
  --Botswana
  NT Sotho (African people)--Medicine
  --Cameroon
  NT Bamun (African people)--Medicine
      Evuzok (African people)--Medicine
  --Ghana
  NT Akan (African people)--Medicine
      Fanti (African people)--Medicine
  --Ivory Coast
  NT Akan (African people)--Medicine
      Ando (African people)--Medicine

  --Kenya
  NT Samburu (African people)--Medicine
  --Lesotho
  NT Sotho (African people)--Medicine
  --Mali
  NT Bambara (African people)--Medicine
  --Nigeria
  NT Bariba (African people)--Medicine
      Yoruba (African people)--Medicine
  --South Africa
  NT Shona (African people)--Medicine
      Sotho (African people)--Medicine
      Zulu (African people)--Medicine
  --Swaziland
  NT Swazi (African people)--Medicine
  --Uganda
  NT Lugbara (African people)--Medicine
  --Zaire
  NT Kongo (African people)--Medicine
      Lugbara (African people)--Medicine
  --Zimbabwe
  NT Shona (African people)--Medicine

Medicine, Tropical
  USE Tropical medicine

Medicine-man
  USE Shamans

Medicine men
  USE Shamans

Medicine women
  USE Shamans

Medumba language *(May Subd Geog)*
  [PL 8510.M42]
  BT Bamileke languages
      Cameroon--Languages

Medumba proverbs
  USE Proverbs, Medumba

Megagroups (Stratigraphy)
  USE Groups (Stratigraphy)

Megi language
  USE Sagara language

Megili language
  USE Migili language

Megimba (African people)
  USE Ngemba (African people)

(May Subd Geog) = Place names may follow the heading

Megimba language
  USE Ngemba language (Cameroon)

Mekaa language
  USE Maka language (Cameroon)

Mélikhouré River (Forécariah, Guinea) *(Not Subd Geog)*
  UF Mellacorée River (Forécariah, Guinea)
      Rivière Mellacorée (Forécariah, Guinea)
  BT Rivers--Guinea

Mellacorée River (Forécariah, Guinea)
  USE Mélikhouré River (Forécariah, Guinea)

Mema Plain (Mali) *(Not Subd Geog)*
  BT Plains--Mali

Men weavers *(May Subd Geog)*
  BT Weaving
--**Africa, West**
  RT West African strip weaving

Menabe (Malagasy people) *(May Subd Geog)*
  [DT 469.M277M]
  BT Ethnology--Madagascar
      Sakalava (Malagasy people)

Menace, Operation
  USE Operation Menace

Menalamba Rebellion (Madagascar), 1895-1899
  USE Madagascar--History--Menalamba Rebellion, 1895-1899

Mende (African people) *(May Subd Geog)*
  [DT 516.45.M45 (Sierra Leone)]
  UF Boumpe (African people)
      Hulo (African people)
      Huro (African people)
      Kossa (African people)
      Kosso (African people)
      Mendi (African people)
  BT Ethnology--Liberia
      Ethnology--Sierra Leone
--**Religion**
  [BL 2480.M4]

Mende art
  USE Art, Mende

Mende arts
  USE Arts, Mende

Mende language *(May Subd Geog)*
  [PL 8511]
  UF Boumpe language
      Hulo language
      Huro language
      Kossa language
      Kosso language
      Mendi language
  BT Mande languages
      Liberia--Languages
      Sierra Leone--Languages

Mendi (African people)
  USE Mende (African people)

Mendi language
  USE Mende language

Menemo (African people)
  USE Meta (African people)

Meninka language
  USE Mandingo language

Menja (African people)
  USE Kwegu (African people)

Mensa (African people) *(May Subd Geog)*
  [DT 393.5 (Eritrea)]
  BT Ethnology--Ethiopia

Merdu (African people)
  USE Murzu (African people)

Merida (African people)
  USE Zaghawa (African people)

Merina (Malagasy people) *(May Subd Geog)*
  [DT 469.M277M47]
  UF Antimerina (Malagasy people)
      Hova (Malagasy people)
      Imerina (Malagasy people)
      Ovah (Malagasy people)
  BT Ethnology--Madagascar

Merina dialect
  USE Malagasy language

Meritu (African people)
  USE Murzu (African people)

Mero language
  USE Meru language

UF = Used for; BT = Broader term; RT = Related term; SA = See also; NT = Narrower term

Meroe (Sudan) *(Not Subd Geog)*
  [DT 159.9.M47]
  UF Merowe (Sudan)
  BT Cities and towns, Ruined, extinct,
etc.--Sudan
      Sudan--Antiquities
 --Civilization
 -- --Indic influences
  BT India--Civilization

Meroitic inscriptions
  USE Inscriptions, Meroitic

Meroitic language *(May Subd Geog)*
  [PL 8512.M45]
  BT Nilo-Saharan languages
      Sudan--Languages

Merowe (Sudan)
  USE Meroe (Sudan)

Meru (African people) *(May Subd Geog)*
  [DT 433.545.M47 (Kenya)]
  UF Mwere (African people)
      Wameru (African people)
  BT Bantu-speaking peoples
      Ethnology--Kenya
      Ethnology--Tanzania
 --Religion
  [BL 2480.M43]

Meru folk literature
  USE Folk literature, Meru

Meru language *(May Subd Geog)*
  [PL 8513]
  UF Kimeru language
      Mero language
  BT Bantu languages
      Kenya--Languages
      Tanzania--Languages

Meru literature *(May Subd Geog)*
  [PL 8513.5-PL 8513.9]
  BT Kenyan literature
      Tanzanian literature
  NT Folk literature, Meru

Messianic cults
  USE Nativistic movements

Meta (African people) *(May Subd Geog)*
  [DT 571.M47]
  UF Menemo (African people)
  BT Ethnology--Cameroon

Meteorological research
  USE Meteorology--Research

Meteorology *(May Subd Geog)*
  NT Weather
      Weather control
 --Research *(May Subd Geog)*
  UF Meteorological research
      Weather--Research
      Weather research
  NT West African Monsoon Experiment
 -- --South Africa
  NT Bethlehem Weather Modification Experiment

Mfantse (African people)
  USE Fanti (African people)

Mfecane
  USE Bantu-speaking peoples--Migrations

Mfecane period, 1816-ca. 1840
  USE Africa, Southern--History--Mfecane period,
1816-ca. 1840

Mfengo (African people)
  USE Fingo (African people)

Mfengu (African people)
  USE Fingo (African people)

Mfumbiro
  USE Virunga

Mfumte (African people) *(May Subd Geog)*
  [DT 571.M (Cameroon)]
  [DT 515.45.M (Nigeria)]
  UF Kaka (African people)
      Mbem (African people)
  BT Ethnology--Cameroon
      Ethnology--Nigeria
      Tikar (African people)

Mgeni River (South Africa) *(Not Subd Geog)*
  UF Umgeni River (South Africa)
  BT Rivers--South Africa

Mia language
  USE Mano language

Mianka (African people)
  USE Minianka (African people)

Mianka language
  USE Mamara language

(May Subd Geog) = Place names may follow the heading

Michi (African people)
USE Tivi (African people)

Middle Congo
USE Congo (Brazzaville)

Midigui Site (Chad)
USE Mdaga Site (Chad)

Midjinngay dialect
USE Majingai dialect

Migili language *(May Subd Geog)*
[PL 8515.M53]
UF Koro Lafia language
Megili language
BT Plateau languages (Nigeria)
Nigeria--Languages

Mijikenda (African people)
USE Nika (African people)

Mikgware Hills (Botswana)
USE Mokgware Hills (Botswana)

Militant organizations, Black
USE Black militant organizations

Military geography *(May Subd Geog)*
UF Geography, Military
BT Geography
SA *subdivision* Strategic aspects *under names
of regions, countries, cities, etc*
NT Africa--Strategic aspects
Africa, Northeast--Strategic aspects
Africa, Sub-Saharan--Strategic aspects

Military life
USE Soldiers

Military personnel
USE Soldiers

Mina, Portuguese
USE Ghana--History--Portuguese rule, 1469-
1637

Mina (African people) *(May Subd Geog)*
[DT 582.45.M55 (Togo)]
UF Gaingbe (African people)
Ge (African people)
Gen (African people)
Guingbe (African people)
Popo (African people)
BT Ethnology--Benin
Ethnology--Ghana

BT Ethnology--Togo
Ewe (African people)

Mina dialect *(May Subd Geog)*
[PL 8164.Z9M5]
UF Ge dialect
Gen dialect
Gengbe dialect
Guen dialect
BT Benin--Languages
Ewe language
Ghana--Languages
Togo--Languages

Mina proverbs
USE Proverbs, Mina

Minduumo language
USE Ndumu language

Minianka (African people) *(May Subd Geog)*
[DT 551.45.M55 (Mali)]
UF Folo (African people)
Mianka (African people)
Minya (African people)
Minyanka (African people)
BT Ethnology--Ivory Coast
Ethnology--Mali
Senufo (African people)

Minianka language
USE Mamara language

Minianka proverbs
USE Proverbs, Minianka

Minor arts
USE Decorative arts

Minya (African people)
USE Minianka (African people)

Minyanka (African people)
USE Minianka (African people)

Minyanka language
USE Mamara language

Miscegenation *(May Subd Geog)*
[GN 254 (Ethnology)]
Here are entered works on marriage or sexual relations
between persons of different races and on the resulting
mixture or hybridity of races.
UF Hybridity of races
Racial amalgamation
Racial crossing   *(Continued)*

UF = Used for; BT = Broader term; RT = Related term; SA = See also; NT = Narrower term

Miscegenation   *(Continued)*
    BT   Race relations
    NT   Colored people (South Africa)
         Griquas
         Mulattoes
  --**Law and legislation** *(May Subd Geog)*

Miscellaneous facts
    USE Almanacs

Miss Nancy (Legendary character)
    USE Anansi (Legendary character)

Missions *(May Subd Geog)*
    Here are entered general works on the activities
and programs of missionaries and works on Christian
missions.
    UF   Christian missions
         Christianity--Missions
         Missions, Foreign
    SA   *subdivision* Missions *under ethnic groups*
  --**African influences**
    BT   Africa--Civilization
  --**South Africa**
    NT   Ethiopian movement (South Africa)

Missions, Foreign
    USE Missions

Missions to Akan (African people)
    USE Akan (African people)--Missions

Missions to Bachama (African people)
    USE Bachama (African people)--Missions

Missions to Bantus
    USE Bantu-speaking peoples--Missions

Missions to Bemba (African people)
    USE Bemba (African people)--Missions

Missions to Blacks
    USE Blacks--Missions

Missions to Bororo (African people)
    USE Bororo (African people)--Missions

Missions to Fingo (African people)
    USE Fingo (African people)--Missions

Missions to Igbo (African people)
    USE Igbo (African people)--Missions

Missions to Iraqw (African people)
    USE Iraqw (African people)--Missions

Missions to Kagoro (African people)
    USE Kagoro (African people)--Missions

Missions to Kaguru (African people)
    USE Kaguru (African people)--Missions

Missions to Kamwe (African people)
    USE Kamwe (African people)--Missions

Missions to Kgatla (African people)
    USE Kgatla (African people)--Missions

Missions to Khoikhoi (African people)
    USE Khoikhoi (African people)--Missions

Missions to Kikuyu (African people)
    USE Kikuyu (African people)--Missions

Missions to Kongo (African people)
    USE Kongo (African people)--Missions

Missions to Kpelle (African people)
    USE Kpelle (African people)--Missions

Missions to Lamba (African people)
    USE Lamba (African people)--Missions

Missions to Lozi (African people)
    USE Lozi (African people)--Missions

Missions to Masai (African people)
    USE Masai (African people)--Missions

Missions to Mbata (African people)
    USE Mbata (African people)--Missions

Missions to Mongo (African people)
    USE Mongo (African people)--Missions

Missions to Ngoni (African people)
    USE Ngoni (African people)--Missions

Missions to Ngwato (African people)
    USE Ngwato (African people)--Missions

Missions to Oromo (African people)
    USE Oromo (African people)--Missions

Missions to Pygmies
    USE Pygmies--Missions

Missions to Shona (African people)
    USE Shona (African people)--Missions

Missions to Southern Lunda (African people)
    USE Lunda, Southern (African people)--Missions

(May Subd Geog) = Place names may follow the heading

Missions to Xhosa (African people)
USE Xhosa (African people)--Missions

Missions to Yaka (African people)
USE Yaka (African people)--Missions

Missions to Yoruba (African people)
USE Yoruba (African people)--Missions

Missions to Zulu (African people)
USE Zulu (African people)--Missions

Mitaba language
USE Mbomotaba language

Mitsogho (African people) (May Subd Geog)
[DT 546.145.M]
UF Apindji (African people)
Ashogo (African people)
Isogo (African people)
Shogo (African people)
Tsogho (African people)
BT Ethnology--Gabon

Mitsogho art
USE Art, Mitsogho

Mitsogo language
USE Tsogo language

Mituku language (May Subd Geog)
[PL 8515.M56]
RT Bantu languages
Zaire--Languages

Miwa (African people)
USE Lobi (African people)

Njillem language
USE Nielim language

Mkata Plain, North (Tanzania)
USE North Mkata Plain (Tanzania)

Mkwaja Ranch (Tanzania) (Not Subd Geog)
BT Ranches--Tanzania

Mmani language
USE Northern Bullom language

Mmfo language
USE Mo language (Ghana and Ivory Coast)

Mo language (Ghana and Ivory Coast) (May Subd
Geog)
[PL 8515.M62]

UF Buru language (Ghana and Ivory Coast)
Deg language
Degha language
Mmfo language
BT Ghana--Languages
Grusi languages
Ivory Coast--Languages

Moa language
USE Moba language

Moaaga (African people)
USE Mossi (African people)

Moaaga languages
USE Mossi languages

Moba (African people) (May Subd Geog)
[DT 515.45.M62]
UF Mwaba (African people)
BT Ethnology--Nigeria
--Religion
[BL 2480.M63]

Moba language (May Subd Geog)
[PL 8516]
UF Bimoba language
Moa language
BT Gurma language
Nigeria--Languages

Moba proverbs
USE Proverbs, Moba

Mobenge language
USE Benge language

Moca language
USE Mocha language

Moçambique
USE Mozambique

Moçambique Channel
USE Mozambique Channel

Moçâmedes Desert (Angola) (Not Subd Geog)
UF Deserto de Moçâmedes (Angola)
Deserto de Mossâmedes (Angola)
Mossâmedes Desert (Angola)
BT Deserts--Angola

Mocha language (May Subd Geog)
[PJ 2586]
UF Moca language
BT Omotic languages

UF = Used for; BT = Broader term; RT = Related term; SA = See also; NT = Narrower term

Modderdam (Cape Town, South Africa) *(Not Subd Geog)*
  UF Cape Town (South Africa). Modderdam

Modjinngay dialect
  USE Majingai dialect

Moero, Lake (Zaire and Zambia)
  USE Mweru, Lake (Zaire and Zambia)

Mofu-Gudur language *(May Subd Geog)*
  [PL 8517]
  UF Mofu language
  BT Cameroon--Languages
      Chadic languages

Mofu language
  USE Mofu-Gudur language

Moggingain dialect
  USE Majingai dialect

Mogimba (African people)
  USE Ngemba (African people)

Mogimba language
  USE Ngemba language (Cameroon)

Mogoreb language
  USE Baria language

Mohammedanism
  USE Islam

Mohammedans
  USE Muslims

Moisi languages
  USE Mossi languages

Moissala Mbai language
  USE Mbai language (Moissala)

Moisture Utilization in Semi-Arid Tropics: Summer Rainfall Agriculture Project
  [SB 110]
  UF Summer Rainfall Agriculture Project
  BT Information storage and retrieval
systems--Africa, West--Agriculture

Mokar (African people)
  USE Gaanda (African people)

Mokgware Hills (Botswana) *(Not Subd Geog)*
  UF Mikgware Hills (Botswana)
  BT Mountains--Botswana

Mokpe (African people)
  USE Kwiri (African people)

Mokpe language
  USE Kwiri language

Mokpwe language
  USE Kwiri language

Mole (African people)
  USE Mossi (African people)

Mole language
  USE Mooré language

Mole languages
  USE Mossi languages

Molteno Formation (South Africa) *(Not Subd Geog)*
  BT Formations (Geology)--South Africa

Mom (African people)
  USE Bamun (African people)

Mombasa (Kenya) *(Not Subd Geog)*
  --History
  -- --Uprising, 1631
    [DT 433.565]
    BT Kenya--History--To 1895

Mombasa (Kenya). Old Town
  USE Old Town (Mombasa, Kenya)

Mombuttu (African people)
  USE Mangbetu (African people)

Momfu (African people)
  USE Mamve (African people)

Momvou (African people)
  USE Mamvu (African people)

Momvu language
  USE Mamvu language

Monarchs
  USE Kings and rulers

Monbattu (African people)
  USE Mangbetu (African people)

Monbuttu (African people)
  USE Mangbetu (African people)

Monbuttu language
  USE Mangbetu language

(May Subd Geog) = Place names may follow the heading

Monfou (African people)
  USE Mamvu (African people)

Mongandu (African people)
  USE Ngandu (African people)

Mongo (African people) *(May Subd Geog)*
  [DT 650.M65]
  UF Balolo (African people)
  BT Bantu-speaking peoples
      Ethnology--Zaire
  NT Mbole (African people)
 --Missions *(May Subd Geog)*
  [BV 3630.M64]
  UF Missions to Mongo (African people)

Mongo language *(May Subd Geog)*
  [PL 8518]
  UF Bamongo language
      Lolo (Bantu language)
      Lomongo (Bantu language)
  BT Bantu languages
      Zaire--Languages
  RT Bushoong language

Mongo lullabies
  USE Lullabies, Mongo

Mongo poetry *(May Subd Geog)*
  [PL 8518.7]
  BT Zaire--Poetry

Mongwandi language
  USE Ngbandi language

Monjombo (African people) *(May Subd Geog)*
  [DT 546.345.M65 (Central African
Republic)]
  UF Monzombo (African people)
  BT Ethnology--Central African Republic
      Ethnology--Congo (Brazzaville)
      Ethnology--Zaire

Monokutuba language
  USE Kituba language

Monomotapa Empire *(Not Subd Geog)*
  [DT 995.M7 : old class]
  [DT 1113 : new class]
  UF Munhumutapa Empire
      Mwanamutapa Empire
      Mwene Mutapa Empire
      Mwenemutapa Empire
  BT Shona (African people)--History

Monts Atlantika (Nigeria and Cameroon)

  USE Alantika Mountains (Nigeria and Cameroon)

Monts Mandara (Cameroon and Nigeria)
  USE Mandara Mountains (Cameroon and Nigeria)

Monvu language
  USE Mamvu language

Monzombo (African people)
  USE Monjombo (African people)

Moon, Mountains of the (Uganda and Zaire)
  USE Ruwenzori Mountains (Uganda and Zaire)

Mooré (African people)
  USE Mossi (African people)

Mooré language *(May Subd Geog)*
  [PL 8521]
  UF Mole language
      Moré language
      Moshi language
      Mossi language
  BT Burkina Faso--Languages
      Mossi languages

Mooré literature *(May Subd Geog)*
  [PL 8521.5-PL 8521.9]
  BT Burkinabe literature

Moors
  USE Muslims

Moose (African people)
  USE Mossi (African people)

Moral philosophy
  USE Ethics

Morality
  USE Ethics

Morals
  USE Ethics

Morda language
  USE Baria language

Moré (African people)
  USE Mossi (African people)

Moré language
  USE Mooré language

More languages
  USE Mossi languages

UF = Used for; BT = Broader term; RT = Related term; SA = See also; NT = Narrower term

Moré proverbs
USE Proverbs, Moré

Moro language (Sudan) *(May Subd Geog)*
BT Kordofanian languages
Sudan--Languages

Morondava River (Madagascar) *(Not Subd Geog)*
BT Rivers--Madagascar

Morondava River Delta (Madagascar)
BT Deltas--Madagascar

Mortality and race *(May Subd Geog)*
UF Race and motality
BT Race

Mortuary customs
USE Funeral rites and ceremonies

Mortuary law
USE Burial laws

Moru language *(May Subd Geog)*
[PL 8523]
BT Central Sudanic languages
Sudan--Languages

Moshi (African people)
USE Mossi (African people)

Moshi language
USE Mooré language

Moshi languages
USE Mossi languages

Mosi (African people)
USE Mossi (African people)

Moslems
USE Muslims

Mossâmedes Desert (Angola)
USE Moçâmedes Desert (Angola)

Mossé (African people)
USE Mossi (African people)

Mossi (African people) *(May Subd Geog)*
[DT 555.45.M67 (Burkina Faso)]
UF Moaaga (African people)
Mole (African people)
Mooré (African people)
Moose (African people)
Moré (African people)

UF Moshi (African people)
Mosi (African people)
Mosse (African people)
BT Ethnology--Burkina Faso
--History
NT Yatenga (Kingdom)
--Marriage customs and rites
UF Marriage customs and rites, Mossi (African people)
--Religion
[BL 2480.M67]
--Rites and ceremonies

Mossi language
USE Mooré language

Mossi languages *(May Subd Geog)*
[PL 8521]
UF Moaaga languages
Moisi languages
Mole languages
More languages
Moshi languages
BT Burkina Faso--Languages
Ghana--Languages
Gur languages
NT Dagari language
Dagomba language
Kussassi language
Mooré language

Mossi law
USE Law, Mossi

Mossi proverbs
USE Proverbs, Mossi

Motion picture industry *(May Subd Geog)*
UF Film industry (Motion picture)
Moving picture industry
NT Blacks in the motion picture industry

Motion pictures *(May Subd Geog)*
UF Cinema
Films
Movies
Moving-pictures
NT Africa, Sub-Saharan, in motion pictures
Africa in motion pictures
Biko, Steve, 1946-1977, in motion pictures
Blacks in motion pictures
Racism in motion pictures
South Africa in motion pictures

Moundan (African people)
USE Mundang (African people)

(May Subd Geog) = Place names may follow the heading

Moundan language
USE Mundang language

Moundang (African people)
USE Mundang (African people)

Moundang language
USE Mundang language

Mount Karisimbi (Rwanda and Zaire)
USE Karisimbi (Rwanda and Zaire)

Mount Karisimbra (Rwanda and Zaire)
USE Karisimbi (Rwanda and Zaire)

Mount Kenya (Kenya)
USE Kenya, Mount (Kenya)

Mount Kilimanjaro (Tanzania)
USE Kilimanjaro, Mount (Tanzania)

Mount Kulal (Kenya)
USE Kulal, Mount (Kenya)

Mount Paarl (South Africa)
USE Paarl, Mount (South Africa)

Mountains (May Subd Geog)
UF Hills
Peaks
Ranges, Mountain
Ridges, Mountain
BT Landforms
NT Plateaus
--Africa, West
NT Fouta Djallon Range
--Botswana
NT Mokgware Hills (Botswana)
--Cameroon
NT Alantika Mountains (Nigeria and Cameroon)
Mandara Mountains (Cameroon and Nigeria)
--Chad
NT Tibesti Mountains
--Ethiopia
NT Simen Mountains (Ethiopia)
--Kenya
NT Kenya, Mount (Kenya)
Kenya Highlands (Kenya)
Kulal, Mount (Kenya)
Taita Hills (Kenya)
--Lesotho
NT Drakensberg Mountains
--Mali
NT Sarnyéré (Mali)

--Mozambique
NT Angónia Highlands (Mozambique)
--Niger
NT Tibesti Mountains
--Nigeria
NT Atlantika Mountains (Nigeria and Cameroon)
Mandara Mountains (Cameroon and Nigeria)
--Réunion
NT Fournaise, Piton de la (Réunion)
--Rwanda
NT Gishwati (Rwanda)
Karisimbi (Rwanda and Zaire)
Virunga
--South Africa
NT Cathedral Peak (South Africa)
Cedar Mountains (South Africa)
Drakensberg Mountains
Gamsberg (South Africa)
Hottentots Holland Mountains (South Africa)
Kalk Bay Mountains (South Africa)
Paarl, Mount (South Africa)
Stormberg Range (South Africa)
Table Mountain (Cape of Good Hope, South Africa)
Table Mountain (Natal, South Africa)
--Sudan
NT Marra Mountains (Sudan)
Nuba Mountains (Sudan)
Red Sea Hills (Egypt and Sudan)
'Uwaynat Mountain (Sudan)
--Swaziland
NT Drakensberg Mountains
--Tanzania
NT Kilimanjaro, Mount (Tanzania)
Mahali Mountains (Tanzania)
Nguru Mountains (Tanzania)
Southern Highlands (Tanzania)
Uluguru Mountains (Tanzania)
--Uganda
NT Ruwenzori Mountains (Uganda and Zaire)
Virunga
--Zaire
NT Karisimbi (Rwanda and Zaire)
Katekelayi Hill (Zaire)
Nyamlagira (Zaire)
Ruwenzori Mountains (Uganda and Zaire)
Virunga
--Zambia
NT Bunqua Hill (Zambia)
Chafukuma Hill (Zambia)
--Zimbabwe
NT Matopo Hills (Zimbabwe)

Mountains of the Moon (Uganda and Zaire)
USE Ruwenzori Mountains (Uganda and Zaire)

UF = Used for; BT = Broader term; RT = Related term; SA = See also; NT = Narrower term

Mouyeng (African people) *(May Subd Geog)*
  [DT 571.M]
  BT Ethnology--Cameroon

Movements against apartheid
  USE Anti-apartheid movements

Movies
  USE Motion pictures

Moving-picture industry
  USE Motion picture industry

Moving-pictures
  USE Motion pictures

Moviya (African people)
  USE Eviya (African people)

Moye (African people)
  USE Nunu (African people)

Mozambican alien labor
  USE Alien labor, Mozambican

Mozambican cookery
  USE Cookery, Mozambican

Mozambican fables
  USE Fables, Mozambican

Mozambican literature *(May Subd Geog)*
  [PL 8014.M]
  UF Mozambique--Literatures
  BT Southern African literature
  NT Nyanja literature

Mozambican literature (Portuguese) *(May Subd Geog)*
  [PQ 9930-PQ 9939]
  UF Portuguese literature--Mozambican authors
  BT African literature (Portuguese)
  NT Mozambican poetry (Portuguese)

Mozambican periodicals *(May Subd Geog)*
  [PN 5499.M]
  UF Periodicals, Mozambican

Mozambican poetry (Portuguese) *(May Subd Geog)*
  [PQ 9932 (History)]
  [PQ 9936.5 (Collections)]
  UF Portuguese poetry--Mozambican authors
  BT African poetry (Portuguese)
      Mozambican literature (Portuguese)

  NT Political poetry, Mozambican (Portuguese)

Mozambican political poetry (Portuguese)
  USE Political poetry, Mozambican (Portuguese)

Mozambican political posters
  USE Political posters, Mozambican

Mozambican sculpture
  USE Sculpture, Mozambican

Mozambicans *(May Subd Geog)*
  NT Ethnology--Mozambique

Mozambique *(Not Subd Geog)*
  [DT 451-DT 463 : old class]
  [DT 3291-DT 3415 : new class]
  UF Africa, Portuguese East
      East Africa, Portuguese
      Moçambique
      People's Republic of Mozambique
  NT Mozambique Island (Mozambique)
--**Antiquities**
  NT University Campus Site (Maputo, Mozambique)
--**Description and travel**
-- --1981-
--**Economic conditions**
  [HC 890]
-- --To 1975
-- --1975-
--**History**
-- --To 1505
-- --1505-1698
-- --1698-1891
-- --1891-1975
-- --**War of 1894-1895**
-- --**Revolution, 1964-1974**
  [DT 463-DT463.3 : old class]
-- --1975-
--**Languages**
  NT Chopi language
      Makonde language
      Makua language
      Nguni languages
      Nyanja language
      Ronga language
      Sena language
      Tonga language (Inhambane)
      Tsonga language
      Tswa language
      Yao language
--**Literatures**
  USE Mozambican literature
--**Poetry**
  NT Tsonga poetry

(May Subd Geog) = Place names may follow the heading

--Politics and government
-- --To 1975
-- --1975-
--Social conditions
-- --To 1975
-- --1975-

Mozambique Channel (Not Subd Geog)
  UF Canal de Moçambique
      Canal de Mozambique
      Moçambique Channel
  BT Straits--Madagascar
      Straits--Mozambique

Mozambique Island (Mozambique) (Not Subd Geog)
  [DT 465.M8]
  UF Ilha de Moçambique (Mozambique)
      Muipiti (Mozambique)
  BT Islands--Mozambique
      Mozambique

Mpangwe (West African people)
  USE Fang (West African people)

Mpika Dairy Settlement Scheme (Zambia)
  [S 599.5.Z32M75]
  BT Dairy farms--Zambia
      Ranches--Zambia

Mpondo (African people)
  USE Pondo (African people)

Mponqwe (African people) (May Subd Geog)
  [DT 546.145.M66]
  UF Bayugu (African people)
      Empoongwe (African people)
      Mpungwe (African people)
      Npongwe (African people)
      Pongo (African people)
  BT Bantu-speaking peoples
      Ethnology--Gabon
      Myene (African people)
  NT Nkomi (African people)

Mpongwe language (May Subd Geog)
  [PL 8531]
  UF Pongwe language
  BT Bantu languages
      Gabon--Languages

Mpukusu language
  USE Mbukushu language

Mpungwe (African people)
  USE Mpongwe (African people)

Mpur dialect (May Subd Geog)
  [PL 8532.M]
  UF Mputu dialect
  BT Yanzi language
      Zaire--Languages

Mputu (African people) (May Subd Geog)
  [DT 650.M]
  UF Amput (African people)
      Bamputu (African people)
  BT Ethnology--Zaire

Mputu dialect
  USE Mpur dialect

Mtang'ata dialect (May Subd Geog)
  [PL 8704.Z9M76]
  UF Ki-Mtang'ata dialect
      Mtanjata dialect
  BT Swahili language
      Tanzania--Languages

Mtanjata dialect
  USE Mtang'ata dialect

Mtongwe Site (Kenya) (Not Subd Geog)
  BT Kenya--Antiquities

Muamenam (African people)
  USE Kossi (African people)

Muana language (May Subd Geog)
  [PL 8532.M85]
  BT African languages
      Ivory Coast--Languages

Muatiamvua language
  USE Ruund language

Muchopi (African people)
  USE Chopi (African people)

Mucusso (African people)
  USE Mbukushu (African people)

Muera (African people)
  USE Mwera (African people)

Mufumbiro
  USE Virunga

Muhammadanism
  USE Islam

Muhammadans
  USE Muslims

UF = Used for; BT = Broader term; RT = Related term; SA = See also; NT = Narrower term

Muhanha (African people)
  USE Hanya (African people)

Muila (African people)
  USE Mwila (African people)

Muipiti (Mozambique)
  USE Mozambique Island (Mozambique)

Muiza (Zambian people)
  USE Bisa (Zambian people)

Mukulehe (African people) *(May Subd Geog)*
  [DT 571.M]
  BT Ethnology--Cameroon

Mulattoes *(May Subd Geog)*
  UF Octoroons
      Quadroons
  BT Afro-Americans
      Blacks
      Miscegenation
 --Senegambia
  [DT 474.5]

Mulochazi (African people)
  USE Luchazi (African people)

Mulongo (African people)
  USE Luba (African people)

Mulwi dialect
  USE Vulum dialect

Mum (African people)
  USE Bamun (African people)

Mumbala language
  USE Mbala language (Bandundu region,
Zaire)

Mumbo (Cult) *(May Subd Geog)*
  [BL 2470.K4]
  BT Cults--Kenya

Mumuye (African people) *(May Subd Geog)*
  [DT 515.45.M (Nigeria)]
  BT Ethnology--Cameroon
      Ethnology--Nigeria
 --Folklore
  [GR 351.32.M85]

Mumuye language *(May Subd Geog)*
  [PL 8532.M73]
  BT Adamawa languages
      Cameroon--Languages

BT Nigeria--Languages

Mumvu (African people)
  USE Mamvu (African people)

Mun (African people)
  USE Murzu (African people)

Mundang (African people) *(May Subd Geog)*
  [DT 546.445.M85 (Chad)]
  UF Moundan (African people)
      Moundang (African people)
  BT Ethnology--Cameroon
      Ethnology--Chad
 --Kings and rulers

Mundang language *(May Subd Geog)*
  [PL 8532.M]
  UF Moundan language
      Moundang language
  BT Adamawa languages
      Cameroon--Languages
      Chad--Languages

Mundju language
  USE Bamougoun-Bamenjou language

Mundo (African people)
  USE Bongo (African people)

Mundu language *(May Subd Geog)*
  [PL 8532.M]
  BT Niger-Congo languages
      Sudan--Languages
      Zaire--Languages

Munhumutapa Empire
  USE Monomotapa Empire

Munju language
  USE Bamougoun-Bamenjou language

Munshi (African people)
  USE Tivi (African people)

Munsi (African people)
  USE Tivi (African people)

Munukutuba language
  USE Kituba language

Murle (African people) *(May Subd Geog)*
  [DT 155.2.M87 (Sudan)]
  UF Agibba (African people)
      Ajibba (African people)
      Beir (African people)

(May Subd Geog) = Place names may follow the heading

UF   Irenge (African people)
    Murule (African people)
BT   Ethnology--Ethiopia
    Ethnology--Sudan
NT   Longarim (African people)

Murle language *(May Subd Geog)*
  [PL 8532.M8]
UF   Beir language
BT   Ethiopia--Languages
    Nilo-Saharan languages
    Sudan--Languages

Mursi (African people)
  USE Murzu (African people)

Murule (African people)
  USE Murle (African people)

Muruta (African people)
  USE Murzu (African people)

Murzi (African people)
  USE Murzu (African people)

Murzu (African people) *(May Subd Geog)*
  [DT 380.4.M85 (Ethiopia)]
UF   Dama (African people)
    Kalibong (African people)
    Maritu (African people)
    Merdu (African people)
    Meritu (African people)
    Mun (African people)
    Mursi (African people)
    Muruta (African people)
    Murzi (African people)
    Ngalibong (African people)
BT   Ethnology--Ethiopia
    Ethnology--Sudan

Musalmans
  USE Muslims

Musanga (African people)
  USE Sanga (African people)

Musawarat Site (Sudan)
  USE Musawwarat al-Sufrah Site (Sudan)

Musawwarat al-Sufrah Site (Sudan) *(Not Subd Geog)*
  [DT 159.9.M]
UF   Massawarat es Sufra Site (Sudan)
    Musawarat Site (Sudan)
    Musawwarat es Sufra Site (Sudan)
    Musawwaret el-Sufra Site (Sudan)

BT   Sudan--Antiquities

Musawwarrat es Sufra Site (Sudan)
  USE Musawwarat al-Sufrah Site (Sudan)

Musawwaret el-Sufra Site (Sudan)
  USE Musawwarat al-Sufrah Site (Sudan)

Musei language *(May Subd Geog)*
  [PL 8633]
UF   Musey language
BT   Cameroon--Languages
    Chad--Languages
    Chadic languages

Museku language
  USE Musgu language

Mussele dialect
  USE Mussele dialect

Musey language
  USE Musei language

Musgoy language
  USE Daba language

Musgu language *(May Subd Geog)*
  [PL 8535]
UF   Museku language
    Musuk language
    Muzuk language
BT   Chad--Languages
    Chadic languages
NT   Vulum dialect

Music *(May Subd Geog)*
  SA   *subdivision* Songs and music *under ethnic groups;*
and subdivision Music *under ethnic groups for music of the*
group
  NT   Folk music
    Folk songs
    Popular music
    Songs
 --Biography
  USE Composers
    Musicians
 --Africa
  [ML 350-ML 350.5]
  NT   Kora music
    Mbira music

Music, Islamic *(May Subd Geog)*
  UF   Islam--Music
    Islam and music
    Music, Muslim   *(Continued)*

UF = Used for; BT = Broader term; RT = Related term; SA = See also; NT = Narrower term

Music, Islamic   *(Continued)*
  UF Muslim music
      Muslims--Music
 --Ghana
  NT Damba (Dance drumming)

Music, Muslim
  USE Music, Islamic

Music, Popular
  USE Popular music

Music and race
  UF Race and music
  BT Ethnopsychology
      Race

Musical instruments *(May Subd Geog)*
  UF Instruments, Musical
 --Africa
  NT Goura (Musical instrument)
      Kora (Musical instrument)
      Mbira
      Sanza
 --Africa, French-speaking West
  NT Balo
 --Kenya
  NT Zumari

Musicians *(May Subd Geog)*
  UF Music--Biography
  BT Artists
  NT Composers

Musicians, Black
  [ML 128.B45 (Bibliography)]
  [ML 385 (General biography)]
  UF Black musicians
  BT Blacks in the performing arts
 --Africa
 --Kenya

Muslim music
  USE Music, Islamic

Muslim poetry
  USE Islamic poetry

Muslimism
  USE Islam

Muslims *(May Subd Geog)*
  Here are entered works on the community of
believers in Islam. Works on the religion of which
Muhammad is the prophet are entered under Islam.
  UF Mohammedans

  UF Moors
      Moslems
      Muhammadans
      Musalmans
      Mussulmen
  BT Islam
 --Music
  USE Music, Islamic
 --Burundi
  [DT 450.65.M67]
 --Ethiopia
  [DT 380.4.M87]
 --Mauritania
  [DT 554.45.M84]
 --Réunion
  [DT 469.R39M87]
 --Zaire
  [DT 650.M97]

Muslims, Black
  [BP 62.N4]
  Here are entered works on persons of the Black race who
are Muslims.
  BT Blacks--Religion

Mussele dialect *(May Subd Geog)*
  [PL 8755.95.M]
  UF Musele dialect
  BT Angola--Languages
      Umbundu language

Musserongo dialect
  USE Solongo dialect

Mussulmanism
  USE Islam

Mussulmen
  USE Muslims

Musuk language
  USE Musgu language

Muzela (African people)
  USE Zela (African people)

Muzuk language
  USE Musgu language

Mvele (Cameroon people)
  USE Basa (Cameroon people)

Mvuba (African people)
  USE Mamvu (African people)

(May Subd Geog) = Place names may follow the heading

Mwaba (African people)
    USE Moba (African people)

Mwamba language *(May Subd Geog)*
    [PL 8538]
    UF Iki-kukwe language
        Swciri language
        Wanda language
    BT Ngonde language
        Tanzania--Languages

Mwana wa Chencherere Rockshelter (Malawi)
    USE Chencherere II Rockshelter (Malawi)

Mwanabantu (African people)
    USE Safwa (African people)

Mwanamutapa Empire
    USE Monomotapa Empire

Mwari (Shona deity) *(Not Subd Geog)*
    [BL 2480.M3]
    BT Gods, African--South Africa
        Gods, African--Zimbabwe
        Shona (African people)--Religion
        Religion, Primitive--South Africa
        Religion, Primitive--Zimbabwe

Mwela (African people)
    USE Mwera (African people)

Mwelle (Cameroon people)
    USE Basa (Cameroon people)

Mwene Mutapa Empire
    USE Monomotapa Empire

Mwenemutapa Empire
    USE Monomotapa Empire

Mwera (African people) *(May Subd Geog)*
    [DT 443.3.M]
    UF Mbuera (African people)
        Muera (African people)
        Mwela (African people)
        Wamwera (African people)
    BT Bantu-speaking peoples
        Ethnology--Tanzania

Mwera language *(May Subd Geog)*
    [PL 8539]
    BT Bantu languages
        Tanzania--Languages

Mwere (African people)
    USE Meru (African people)

Mweru, Lake (Zaire and Zambia) *(Not Subd Geog)*
    UF Lake Moero (Zaire and Zambia)
        Lake Mweru (Zaire and Zambia)
        Moero, Lake (Zaire and Zambia)
    BT Lakes--Zaire
        Lakes--Zambia

Mwila (African people) *(May Subd Geog)*
    [DT 611.45.M : old class]
    [DT 1308.M85 : new class]
    UF Muila (African people)
    BT Bantu-speaking peoples
        Ethnology--Angola

Mwindo (Nyanga folk epic)
    [PL 8592.N439M9]
    BT Nyanga (African people)--Folklore

Myagatwa (African people)
    USE Zaramo (African people)

Myene (African people) *(May Subd Geog)*
    [DT 546.145.M93]
    UF Ngwemyene (African people)
        Omyene (African people)
    BT Bantu-speaking peoples
        Ethnology--Gabon
    NT Galwa (African people)
        Mpongwe (African people)
        Orungu (African people)

Mythology
    RT Legends
        Religions
    RT Folklore
        Gods
    NT Religion, Primitive

Mythology, African
    [BL 2400]
    UF African mythology

Mythology, Basa (Cameroon people) *(May Subd Geog)*
    [BL 2480.B337]
    UF Basa mythology

Mythology, Boma *(May Subd Geog)*
    [BL 2480.B]
    UF Boma mythology

Mythology, Dagari *(May Subd Geog)*
    [BL 2430.D3]
    UF Dagari mythology

UF = Used for; BT = Broader term; RT = Related term; SA = See also; NT = Narrower term

Mythology, Dogon *(May Subd Geog)*
[BL 2480.D]
UF Dogon mythology

Mythology, East African
[BL 2464]
UF East African mythology

Mythology, Igbo *(May Subd Geog)*
[BL 2480.I2]
UF Igbo mythology

Mythology, Sub-Saharan African
[BL 2462.5]
UF Africa, Sub-Saharan mythology

Mythology, West African
[BL 2465]
UF West African mythology

Mythology, Yaka *(May Subd Geog)*
[BL 2480.Y32]
UF Yaka mythology

Mythology, Zairian *(May Subd Geog)*
[BL 2470.C6]
UF Zairian mythology
NT Kipimpi (Zairian mythology)

N

Nabdam (African people)
USE Namnam (African people)

Nabe language
USE Kulango language

Nago language
USE Yoruba language

Nahr al-Rahad (Ethiopia and Sudan)
USE Rahad River (Ethiopia and Sudan)

Nahr an Nil
USE Nile River

Nahr ar-Rahad (Ethiopia and Sudan)
USE Rahad River (Ethiopia and Sudan)

Nahr 'Atbarah (Ethiopia and Sudan)
USE Atbara River (Ethiopia and Sudan)

Nahr er-Rahad (Ethiopia and Sudan)
USE Rahad River (Ethiopia and Sudan)

Nairobi National Park (Kenya) *(Not Subd Geog)*
BT National parks and reserves--Kenya
Parks--Kenya

Naivasha, Lake (Kenya) *(Not Subd Geog)*
UF Lake Naivasha (Kenya)
BT Lakes--Kenya

Nakambala Sugar Estates (Zambia) *(Not Subd Geog)*
BT Plantations--Zambia

Nalou (African people)
USE Nalu (African people)

Nalu (African people) *(May Subd Geog)*
[DT 543.45.N (Guinea)]
[DT 613.45.N (Guinea-Bissau)]
UF Nalou (African people)
BT Ethnology--Guinea
Ethnology--Guinea-Bissau

Nama (African people) *(May Subd Geog)*
[DT 709 (Namibia : old class)]
[DT 1558.N36 (Namibia : new class)]
[DT 764.N (South Africa : old class)]
[DT 1768.N37 (South Africa : new class)]
UF Namaqua (African people)
BT Ethnology--Namibia
Ethnology--South Africa
Khoikhoi (African people)

Nama language *(May Subd Geog)*
[PL 8541]
BT Khoikhoi language
Namibia--Languages
South Africa--Languages
--Tone
BT Tone (Phonetics)

Namangbetu (African people)
USE Mangbetu (African people)

Namaqua (African people)
USE Nama (African people)

Nambai language
USE Kulango language

Namchi (African people)
USE Dowayo (African people)

Names, African *(May Subd Geog)*
[DT 15]
UF African languages--Names
African names
BT African languages--Etymology--Names

(May Subd Geog) = Place names may follow the heading

Names, Amharic *(May Subd Geog)*
  [DT 380.4.A43]
  UF Amharic language--Names
     Amharic names

Names, Bete *(May Subd Geog)*
  [DT 545.45.B47]
  UF Bete language--Names
     Bete names

Names, Dagari *(May Subd Geog)*
  [DT 510.44.D33 (Ghana)]
  UF Dagari language--Names
     Dagari names

Names, Ethnic
  USE Names, Ethnological

Names, Ethnological *(May Subd Geog)*
  UF Ethnic group names
     Ethnological names
     Ethnology--Names
     Names, Ethnic
     Names of peoples
     Tribal names
  --Cameroon
    [GN 655.C3]
  --Ivory Coast
    [GN 655.I9]

Names, Khoikhoi *(May Subd Geog)*
  [DT 764.K45 (South Africa : old class)]
  [DT 1768.K56 (South Africa : new class)]
  [DT 737 (Southern Africa : old class)]
  [DT 1058.K56 (Southern Africa : new
class)]
  UF Khoikhoi language--Names
     Khoikhoi names

Names, Kposo *(May Subd Geog)*
  [DT 582.45.K]
  UF Kposo language--Names
     Kposo names

Names, Shona *(May Subd Geog)*
  [DT 962.42 : old class]
  [DT 2913.S : new class]
  UF Shona language--Names
     Shona names

Names, Yanzi *(May Subd Geog)*
  [DT 650.Y3 (Zaire)]
  UF Yanzi language--Names
     Yanzi names

Names of peoples
  USE Names, Ethnological

Namib Desert (Namibia) *(Not Subd Geog)*
  BT Deserts--Namibia

Namibia *(Not Subd Geog)*
  [DT 701-DT 720 : old class]
  [DT 1501-DT 1685 : new class]
  UF Africa, German Southwest
     Africa, Southwest
     German Southwest Africa
     South-West Africa
     Southwest Africa
  --Description and travel
  -- --1981-
  --Economic conditions
  [HC 940]
  --History
  -- --To 1884
  -- --1884-1915
  -- --Herero Revolt, 1904-1907
  [DT 714 : old class]
  [DT 1618 : new class]
  UF Herero Revolt, Namibia, 1904-1907
  BT Herero (African people)--History
  -- --1915-1946
    NT Bondelswarts Rebellion, 1922
      Rehoboth Bastors Rebellion, 1925
  -- --1946-1990
  -- --1990-
  --Languages
    NT Diriku language
      Herero language
      Himba dialect
      Kuanyama language
      Kwangali language
      Mbukushu language
      Nama language
      Ndonga language
      San languages
      !Xo language
      !Xu language
  --Politics and government
  -- --1884-1915
  -- --1915-1946
  -- --1946-1990
  -- --1990-

Namibian art
  USE Art, Namibian

Namibian arts
  USE Arts, Namibian

UF = Used for; BT = Broader term; RT = Related term; SA = See also; NT = Narrower term

Namibian students *(May Subd Geog)*
  BT Students
  --Foreign countries
  BT Students, Foreign

Namnam (African people) *(May Subd Geog)*
  [DT 510.43.N]
  UF Nabdam (African people)
  BT Ethnology--Ghana

Namshi (African people)
  USE Dowayo (African people)

Namwezi language
  USE Nyamwezi language

Nancere language *(May Subd Geog)*
  UF Nanchere language
      Nantcere language
      Nantjere language
  BT Central African Republic--Languages
      Chad--Languages
      Chadic languages

Nanchere language
  USE Nancere language

Nande (Zairian people) *(May Subd Geog)*
  [DT 650.N34]
  UF Banande (Zairian people)
      Konjo (Zairian people)
      Nandi (Zairian people)
      Ndande (Zairian people)
      Ndgandi (Zairian people)
      Wahondjo (Zairian people)
      Wanande (Zairian people)
  BT Bantu-speaking peoples
      Ethnology--Zaire

Nande language *(May Subd Geog)*
  [PL 8544]
  BT Bantu languages
      Zaire--Languages

Nandi (African people) *(May Subd Geog)*
  [DT 433.545.N34 (Kenya)]
  UF Cemual (African people)
  BT Ethnology--Kenya
      Ethnology--Tanzania
      Ethnology--Uganda
      Nilo-Hamitic tribes

Nandi (Zairian people)
  USE Nande (Zairian people)

Nandi language *(May Subd Geog)*
  [PL 8545]
  BT Kalenjin language
      Kenya--Languages
      Nandi languages
  NT Kipsikis dialect

Nandi languages *(May Subd Geog)*
  [PL 8545.97]
  UF Nandi-Suk languages
      Southern Nilotic languages
  BT Kenya--Languages
      Nilo-Hamitic languages
      Tanzania--Languages
      Uganda--Languages
  NT Kalenjin language
      Nandi language

Nandi law
  USE Law, Nandi

Nandi-Suk languages
  USE Nandi languages

Nanerge Sembla (West African people)
  USE Samo (West African people)

Nanergue language
  USE Mamara language

Nangerge Sembla language
  USE Samo language (West Africa)

Nani (Guinea)
  USE Niani (Guinea)

Nankanse language *(May Subd Geog)*
  [PL 8546]
  UF Frafra language
      Gurenne language
      Gurune language
  BT Ghana--Languages
      Gur languages

Nano (African people)
  USE Mbundu (African people)

Nanse (Legendary character)
  USE Anansi (Legendary character)

Nansi (Legendary character)
  USE Anansi (Legendary character)

Nantcere language
  USE Nancere language

(May Subd Geog) = Place names may follow the heading

Nantjere language
USE Nancere language

Nanzi (Legendary character)
USE Anansi (Legendary character)

Napata (Ancient city) *(Not Subd Geog)*
[DT 159.9.N]
BT Cities and towns, Ruined, extinct,
etc.--Sudan
Sudan--Antiquities

Napier Expedition, 1867-1868
USE Abyssinian Expedition, 1867-1868

Nar (African people) *(May Subd Geog)*
[DT 546.445.N35]
UF Sara Nar (African people)
BT Ethnology--Chad
Sara (African people)

Nara language
USE Baria language

Naro (African people)
USE Naron (African people)

Naro language
USE Nharo language

Naron (African people) *(May Subd Geog)*
[DT 797 (Botswana : old class)]
[DT 2458.N (Botswana : new class)]
[DT 709 (Namibia : old class)]
[DT 1558.N (Namibia : new class)]
[DT 764.B8 (South Africa : old class)]
[DT 1768.N38 (South Africa : new class)]
UF Naro (African people)
Nharo (African people)
Nhauru (African people)
Nhaurun (African people)
BT Ethnology--Africa, Southern
San (African people)

Narrow band weaving, West African
USE West African strip weaving

Nasionale Kruger Wildtuin (South Africa)
USE Kruger National Park (South Africa)

Nasser, Lake (Egypt and Sudan) *(Not Subd Geog)*
UF Lake Nasser (Egypt and Sudan)
Lake Nuba (Egypt and Sudan)
Lake Nubia (Egypt and Sudan)
Nuba, Lake (Egypt and Sudan)
Nubia, Lake (Egypt and Sudan)

BT Lakes--Sudan
Reservoirs--Sudan

Natal (South Africa) *(Not Subd Geog)*
[DT 866-DT 880 : old class]
[DT 2181-DT 2278 : new class]
--History
-- --To 1843
-- --1843-1893
NT Langalibalele Rebellion, 1873
-- --1893-1910
NT Zulu Rebellion, 1906
-- --1910-
--Politics and government
-- --1843-1893
-- --1910-

Nath language
USE Nuer language

National characteristics
UF Characteristics, National
National images
National psychology
Psychology, National
BT Anthropology
Nationalism
RT Ethnopsychology

National characteristics, African
[DT 352.4]
UF African national characteristics

National characteristics, Eritrean
[DT 393.4]
UF Eritrean national characteristics

National characteristics, Malagasy
[DT 469.M274]
UF Malagasy national characteristics

National characteristics, Nigerian
[DT 515.4]
UF Nigerian national characteristics

National characteristics, South African
[DT 736 : old class]
[DT 1755 : new class]
UF South African national characteristics

National characteristics, Sudanese
[DT 154.9]
UF Sudanese national characteristics

National consciousness
USE Nationalism

UF = Used for; BT = Broader term; RT = Related term; SA = See also; NT = Narrower term

National dances
USE Folk dancing

National forests
USE Forest reserves

National holidays
USE Holidays

National images
USE National characteristics

National liberation movements *(May Subd Geog)*
  Here are entered works dealing with minority or
  other groups in armed rebellion against a colonial
  government, or against a national government charged
  with corruption or foreign domination. In general,
  this heading is applicable only to the post World War
  II period.
  UF Liberation movements, National
  BT Nationalism
     Revolutions
  RT Anti-imperialist movements
  NT Guerrillas
 --**Africa, Southern**
  [DT 746 : old class]
  [DT 1177 : new class]

National parks and reserves *(May Subd Geog)*
  UF National reserves
     Parks, National
     Reserves, National
  BT Parks
  RT Forest reserves
     Game reserves
     Natural areas
  SA *names of parks*
 --**Botswana**
  NT Chobe National Park (Botswana)
 --**Central African Republic**
  NT Parc national de Saint-Floris (Central
African Republic)
 --**Ethiopia**
  NT Simen Mountains National Park
(Ethiopia)
 --**Ivory Coast**
  NT Parc National du Banco (Ivory Coast)
 --**Kenya**
  NT Amboseli National Park (Kenya)
     Kakamega Forest Reserve (Kenya)
     Kora National Reserve (Kenya)
     Masai Mara Game Reserve (Kenya)
     Nairobi National Park (Kenya)
     Tsavo National Park (Kenya)
 --**Namibia**
  NT Etosha National Park (Namibia)

 --**Rwanda**
  NT Parc national de la Kagera (Rwanda)
 --**South Africa**
  NT Cape Flats Nature Reserve (South Africa)
     Cape of Good Hope Nature Reserve (South
Africa)
     Kruger National Park (South Africa)
 --**Tanzania**
  NT Gombe Stream National Park (Tanzania)
     Ngorongoro Game Control Area Reserve
(Tanzania)
     Selous Game Reserve (Tanzania)
     Serengeti National Park (Tanzania)
 --**Uganda**
  NT Kibale Forest Reserve (Uganda)
 --**Zaire**
  NT Parc National des Virunga (Zaire)

National psychology
  USE Ethnopsychology
     National characteristics

National reserves
  USE National parks and reserves

Nationalism *(May Subd Geog)*
  UF National consciousness
  NT National characteristics
     National liberation movements
     Nativistic movements
 --**Blacks**
  USE Black nationalism

Nationalism, Black
  USE Black nationalism

Native Americans
  USE Indians of North America

Native peoples
  USE Indigenous peoples

Nativistic movements *(May Subd Geog)*
  UF Cults, Messianic
     Cults, Prophetistic
     Ethnic revivals
     Messianic cults
     Prophetistic movements
     Revivals, Ethnic
     Sects, Nativistic
  BT Cults
     Ethnology
     Nationalism
     Religion, Primitive
 --**South Africa**
  NT Ethiopian movement (South Africa)

(May Subd Geog) = Place names may follow the heading

Natural areas *(May Subd Geog)*
  UF Nature reserves
  RT National parks and reserves
  NT Game reserves
      Wildlife refuges
 --Burundi
  NT Buyenzi Region (Burundi)
      Kirimiro Region (Burundi)
--South Africa
  NT Cape of Good Hope Nature Reserve
(South Africa)

Nature in ornament
  USE Decoration and ornament

Nature reserves
  USE Natural areas

N'Bundo (African people)
  USE Mbundu (African people)

Nbundu (African people)
  USE Mbundu (African people)

Nchimburu language
  USE Nchumburu language

Nchumburu language *(May Subd Geog)*
  [PL 8547.N25]
  UF Nchimburu language
  BT Ghana--Languages
      Gonja language

Ndande (Zairian people)
  USE Nande (Zairian people)

Ndara (African people)
  USE Hutu (African people)

Ndau language
  USE Chindau language

Ndebele (African people) *(May Subd Geog)*
  [DT 962 (Zimbabwe : old class)]
  [DT 2913.N44 (Zimbabwe : new class)]
  UF Amandebele (African people)
      Matabele (African people)
      Rhodesian Ndebele (African people)
      Tabele (African people)
      Tebele (African people)
  BT Ethnology--South Africa
      Ethnology--Zimbabwe
      Nguni (African people)
      Zulu (African people)
  NT Manala (African people)

--History
  NT Matabele War, 1893
      Zimbabwe--History--Ndebele Insurrection,
1896-1897
--Religion
  [BL 2480.N33]

Ndebele art
  USE Art, Ndebele

Ndebele children's stories (Zimbabwe)
  USE Children's stories, Ndebele (Zimbabwe)

Ndebele fiction (Zimbabwe) *(May Subd Geog)*
  [PL 8547.N28]
  BT Ndebele literature (Zimbabwe)
      Zimbabwean fiction
  NT Children's stories, Ndebele (Zimbabwe)

Ndebele folk literature (Zimbabwe)
  USE Folk literature, Ndebele (Zimbabwe)

Ndebele Insurrection (Zimbabwe), 1896-1897
  USE Zimbabwe--History--Ndebele Insurrection,
1896-1897

Ndebele language (South Africa) *(May Subd Geog)*
  UF Ndebele-Sotho language
      Ndzundza language
      Nrebele language (South Africa)
      Transvaal Ndebele language
  BT Northern Sotho language
      South Africa--Languages
      Zulu language

Ndebele language (Zimbabwe) *(May Subd Geog)*
  [PL 8547.N28]
  UF IsiNdebele language
      Nrebele language (Zimbabwe)
      Sindebele language
      Tabele language
      Tebele language
  BT Zimbabwe--Languages
      Zulu language

Ndebele literature (Zimbabwe) *(May Subd Geog)*
  [PL 8547.N285-PL 8547.N289]
  BT Zimbabwean literature
  NT Folk literature, Ndebele (Zimbabwe)
      Ndebele fiction (Zimbabwe)
      Ndebele poetry (Zimbabwe)
      Ndebele prose literature (Zimbabwe)

Ndebele nursery rhymes (Zimbabwe)
  USE Nursery rhymes, Ndebele (Zimbabwe)

UF = Used for; BT = Broader term; RT = Related term; SA = See also; NT = Narrower term

Ndebele poetry (Zimbabwe) *(May Subd Geog)*
  [PL 8547.N287]
  BT Ndebele literature (Zimbabwe)
      Zimbabwean poetry
  NT Nursery rhymes, Ndebele (Zimbabwe)

Ndebele prose literature (Zimbabwe) *(May Subd Geog)*
  [PL 8547.N286]
  BT African prose literature
      Ndebele literature (Zimbabwe)
  NT School prose, Ndebele (Zimbabwe)

Ndebele proverbs (Zimbabwe)
  USE Proverbs, Ndebele (Zimbabwe)

Ndebele school prose (Zimbabwe)
  USE School prose, Ndebele (Zimbabwe)

Ndebele songs (Zimbabwe)
  USE Songs, Ndebele (Zimbabwe)

Ndebele-Sotho language
  USE Ndebele language (South Africa)

Ndebele War, 1893
  USE Matabele War, 1893

Ndembu (African people) *(May Subd Geog)*
  [DT 963.42 (Zambia : old class)]
  [DT 3058.N44 (Zambia : new class)]
  UF Andembu (African people)
      Bandempo (African people)
      Dembo (African people)
  BT Ethnology--Angola
      Ethnology--Zaire
      Ethnology--Zambia
  RT Lunda, Southern (African people)
  --Religion
  [BL 2480.N35]
  --Rites and ceremonies
  NT Chihamba

Ndendeuli (African people) *(May Subd Geog)*
  [DT 443.3.N43]
  BT Ethnology--Tanzania

Ndengese (African people)
  USE Dengese (African people)

Ndeu (African people)
  USE Bana (African people)

Ndgandi (Zairian people)
  USE Nande (Zairian people)

Ndiki (African people) *(May Subd Geog)*
  [DT 571.N]
  BT Banen (African people)
      Ethnology--Cameroon

Ndja (African people)
  USE Bandja (African people)

Ndjë (African people)
  USE Bandja (African people)

Ndjeli (Togolese and Ghanaian people)
  USE Bassari (Togolese and Ghanaian people)

Ndo River (Kenya)
  USE Kerio River (Kenya)

Ndoga (African people)
  USE Hutu (African people)

Ndogo (African people)
  USE Hutu (African people)

Ndogo-Sere languages *(May Subd Geog)*
  [PL 8547.N3]
  BT Niger-Congo languages
      Sudan--Languages

Ndondakusuka, Battle of, South Africa, 1856
  [DT 878.Z9 : old class]
  [DT 2400.Z85 : new class]
  UF Battle of Ndondakusuka (South Africa), 1856
  BT Zululand (South Africa)--History--To 1879

Ndonga (African people) *(May Subd Geog)*
  [DT 611.42 (Angola : old class)]
  [DT 1308.N56 (Angola : new class)]
  [DT 709 (Namibia : old class)]
  [DT 1558.N46 (Namibia : new class)]
  UF Ondonga (African people)
  BT Ethnology--Angola
      Ethnology--Namibia
      Ovambo (African people)
  --Marriage customs and rites
  UF Marriage customs and rites, Ndonga (African
people)
  --Rites and ceremonies

Ndonga language *(May Subd Geog)*
  [PL 8547.N4]
  UF Oshindonga language
      Oshiwambo language
      Ovambo language
  BT Angola--Languages
      Bantu languages
      Namibia--Languages

(May Subd Geog) = Place names may follow the heading

Ndongo (African people)
  USE Mbundu (African people)

Ndore language
  USE Tuburi language

Ndumbo language
  USE Ndumu language

Ndumu language *(May Subd Geog)*
  [PL 8547.N5]
  UF Doumbou language
     Minduumo language
     Ndumbo language
     Ondoumbo language
  BT Bantu languages
     Congo (Brazzaville)--Languages

Ndzubuqa (African people)
  USE Ngangte (African people)

Ndzundza language
  USE Ndebele language (South Africa)

Ndzungle language
  USE Limbum language

Ndzungli language
  USE Limbum language

Né (African people)
  USE Bana (African people)

Neé (African people)
  USE Bana (African people)

Negrillos
  [DT 16.P8]
  UF Nigrillos
  BT Pygmies

Negritude
  USE Blacks--Race identity

Negritude (Literary movement) *(May Subd Geog)*
  [PQ 3897 (French literature)]
  [PQ 9034.B53 (Portuguese literature)]
  BT Literature--Black authors

Negro-English dialects
  USE Creole dialects, English

Negro race
  USE Black race

Negroes

  USE Blacks

Negroes (United States)
  USE Afro-Americans

Nelson Bay Cave (South Africa) *(Not Subd Geog)*
  BT Caves--South Africa
     South Africa--Antiquities

Nembe language *(May Subd Geog)*
  [PL 8548]
  UF Nimbi language
  BT Ijo language
     Nigeria--Languages

Nembe songs
  USE Songs, Nembe

Neocolonialism
  USE Colonies

Neolithic period *(May Subd Geog)*
  UF New Stone age
  BT Stone age
  --Kenya
     [GN 776.42.K4]

Nere language
  USE Baria language

Netherlands *(Not Subd Geog)*
  --Colonies
     BT Colonies
  -- --Administration
     UF Netherlands--Colonies--Politics and
government
  -- --Boundaries *(May Subd Geog)*
  -- --Commerce *(May Subd Geog)*
  -- --Constitutional history
  -- --Constitutional law
  -- --Defenses
  -- --Description and travel
  -- --Discovery and exploration
  -- --Economic conditions
  -- --Economic policy
  -- --Emigration and immigration
  -- --Geography *(Not Subd Geog)*
  -- --History
  -- --Industries
  -- --Manufactures
  -- --Native races
     USE Indigenous peoples--Netherlands--Colonies
  -- --Officials and employees
  -- --Politics and government
     USE Netherlands--Colonies--Administration
                                        (Continued)

UF = Used for; BT = Broader term; RT = Related term; SA = See also; NT = Narrower term

Netherlands
--Colonies   (Continued)
-- --Population
-- --Public lands
-- --Public works
-- --Race relations
-- --Religion
-- --Religious life and customs
-- --Rural conditions
-- --Social conditions
-- --Social life and customs
-- --Social policy
-- --Africa

New Bell (Douala, Cameroon) (Not Subd Geog)
   [DT 581.N]
   UF Douala (Cameroon). New Bell

New Stone age
   USE Neolithic period

Newspapers (Not Subd Geog)
   Here are entered works on the newspapers of the
world. Works on newspapers in a specific language, or
in a specific country or larger area, are entered under
the adjectivial form of the language or area, e.g.
Afrikaans newspapers; Nigerian newspapers.
   BT Mass media
   RT Periodicals
        Press
   NT Black newspapers

Newspapers, African
   USE African newspapers

Newspapers, Afrikaans
   USE Afrikaans newspapers

Newspapers, Black
   USE Black newspapers

Newspapers, Ghanaian
   USE Ghanaian newspapers

Newspapers, Mauritian
   USE Mauritian newspapers

Newspapers, Nigerian
   USE Nigerian newspapers

Newspapers, South African
   USE South African newspapers

Newspapers, Southern African
   USE Southern African newspapers

Newspapers, Tanzanian
   USE Tanzanian newspapers

Newspapers, Togolese
   USE Togolese newspapers

Newspapers, Zambian
   USE Zambian newspapers

Newspapers, Zimbabwean
   USE Zimbabwean newspapers

Ngaaka (African people)
   USE Bali (African people)

Ngabre language
   USE Gabri language

Ngala language (Zaire)
   USE Lingala language

Ngalibong (African people)
   USE Murzu (African people)

Ngaloi (African people)
   USE Galwa (African people)

Ngam dialect
   USE Ngama dialect

Ngama dialect (May Subd Geog)
   [PL 8644.95.N45]
   UF Ngam dialect
        Sara Ngama dialect
   BT Central African Republic--Languages
        Chad--Languages
        Sara language

Ngambai dialect
   USE Gambai dialect

Ngambaye (African people)
   USE Gambaye (African people)

Ngando (African people)
   USE Ngandu (African people)

Ngandou (African people)
   USE Ngandu (African people)

Ngandu (African people) (May Subd Geog)
   [DT 546.345.N]
   UF Bangandu (African people)
        Longandu (African people)
        Mongandu (African people)
        Ngando (African people)

(May Subd Geog) = Place names may follow the heading

UF Ngandou (African people)
BT Bantu-speaking peoples
    Ethnology--Central African Republic

Ng'anga language
  USE Nyanja language

Ngangela (African people) *(May Subd Geog)*
    [DT 611.45.N (Angola : old class)]
    [DT 1308.N53 (Angola : new class)]
    [DT 963.42 (Zambia : old class)]
    [DT 3058.N53 (Zambia : new class)]
    UF Banguella (African people)
        Benguella (African people)
        Ganguella (African people)
        Va Nyangela (African people)
    BT Bantu-speaking peoples
        Ethnology--Angola
        Ethnology--Zambia

Ngangela language
  USE Ganguela language

Ngangte (African people) *(May Subd Geog)*
    [DT 571.N]
    UF Bangangte (African people)
        Bangante (African people)
        Ndzubuya (African people)
        Ngoteng (African people)
        Njuboga (African people)
    BT Bantu-speaking peoples
        Ethnology--Cameroon

Ngas (African people)
  USE Angas (African people)

Ngazam language
  USE Ngizim language

Ngbaka (African people) *(May Subd Geog)*
    [DT 546.345.N44 (Central African
Republic)]
    [DT 650.N45 (Zaire)]
    UF Bouaka (African people)
        Bwaka (African people)
        Gbaka (African people)
        Gmbwaga (African people)
        Gwaka (African people)
        Lobaye (African people)
        Mbacca (African people)
        Mbaka (African people)
    BT Ethnology--Central African Republic
        Ethnology--Zaire
        Gbaya (African people)
    NT Ngbaka-Ma'bo (African people)

Ngbaka Gbaya language
  USE Gbaya language

Ngbaka limba language
  USE Ngbaka ma'bo language

Ngbaka-Ma'bo (African people) *(May Subd Geog)*
    [DT 546.345.N]
    BT Ethnology--Central African Republic
        Ethnology--Zaire
        Ngbaka (African people)
  --Religion
    [BL 2480.N45]

Ngbaka ma'bo folk songs
  USE Folk songs, Ngbaka ma'bo

Ngbaka ma'bo language *(May Subd Geog)*
    [PL 8548.5]
    UF Ngbaka limba language
    BT Central African Republic--Languages
        Niger-Congo languages
        Zaire--Languages

Ngbaka ma'bo literature *(May Subd Geog)*
    [PL 8548.55-PL 8548.59]
    BT Central African literature
        Zaire--Literatures

Ngbandi language *(May Subd Geog)*
    UF Gbandi language (Zaire)
        Mbati language
        Mongwandi language
    BT Congo (Brazzaville)--Languages
        Niger-Congo languages
    RT Yakoma language
    NT Sango language

Ngbanya (African people)
  USE Gonja (African people)

Ngbanyito (African people)
  USE Gonja (African people)

Ngcaycibi, War of (South Africa), 1877-1878
  USE Ngcayecibi, War of, South Africa, 1877-1878

Ngcayecibi, War of, South Africa, 1877-1878
    [DT 1874 : new class]
    UF Border War, 9th (South Africa), 1877-1878
        Cape Frontier War, 9th (South Africa),
1877-1878
        Gaika and Galeka, War of (South Africa),
1877-1878
        Galeka, War of (South Africa), 1877-1878
                                    (Continued)

UF = Used for; BT = Broader term; RT = Related term; SA = See also; NT = Narrower term

Ngcayecibi, War of, South Africa, 1877-1878
  (Continued)
  UF Gcaleka, War of (South Africa), 1877-
1878
      Ngcaycibi, War of (South Africa),
1877-1878
      Ngika and Gcaleka, War of (South
Africa), 1877-1878
      South Africa--History--War of
Ngcayecibi, 1877-1878
      War of Ngcayecibi (South Africa),
1877-1878
  BT South Africa--History--Frontier Wars,
1811-1878

Ngemba (African people) *(May Subd Geog)*
  [DT 515.45.N (Nigeria)]
  [DT 571.N (Cameroon)]
  UF Megimba (African people)
      Mogimba (African people)
      Ngomba (African people)
      Widerkum (African people)
  BT Ethnology--Cameroon
      Ethnology--Nigeria

Ngemba language (Cameroon) *(May Subd Geog)*
  [PL 8548.65]
  UF Megimba language
      Mogimba language
      Ngomba language
      Nguemba language
      Ngyemboon language
  BT Benue-Congo languages
      Cameroon--Languages

Ngere (Kru-speaking African people)
  USE Wobe (African people)

Ngere (Mande-speaking African people)
  USE Dan (African people)

Ngezzim language
  USE Ngizim language

Ngiaka (African people)
  USE Yaka (African people)

Ngika and Gcaleka, War of (South Africa),
1877-1878
  USE Ngcayecibi, War of, South Africa,
1877-1878

Ngizim language *(May Subd Geog)*
  [PL 8548.67]
  UF Gwazum language
      Kirdiwat language

  UF Ngazam language
      Ngezzim language
      Ngodjin language
      Nugzum language
      Walu language
  BT Chadic languages
      Nigeria--Languages

Ngo language *(May Subd Geog)*
  [PL 8548.68]
  UF Babungo language
  BT Benue-Congo languages
      Cameroon--Languages

Ngodjin language
  USE Ngizim language

Ngomahum (African people)
  USE Bandjoun (African people)

Ngomba (African people)
  USE Ngemba (African people)

Ngomba language
  USE Ngemba language (Cameroon)

Ngombe (African people) *(May Subd Geog)*
  [DT 650.N48]
  BT Bantu-speaking peoples
      Ethnology--Zaire

Ngombe language *(May Subd Geog)*
  [PL 8548.7]
  UF LiNgombe language
  BT Ngombe languages
      Zaire--Languages

Ngombe languages *(May Subd Geog)*
  BT Africa, West--Languages
      Bantu languages
  NT Doko language (Zaire)
      Ngombe language

Ngonde (African people) *(May Subd Geog)*
  [DT 864 (Malawi : old class)]
  [DT 3192.N56 (Malawi : new class)]
  UF Konde (African people)
      Nkhonde (African people)
      Nkonde (African people)
      Wangonde (African people)
  BT Bantu-speaking peoples
      Ethnology--Malawi
      Ethnology--Tanzania
  RT Nyakyusa (African people)

(May Subd Geog) = Place names may follow the heading

Ngonde folk literature
 USE Folk literature, Ngonde

Ngonde language *(May Subd Geog)*
 [PL 8549]
 UF Ikinyi-Kiusa language
     Kiusa language
     Konde language
     Nkonde language
     Nyakyusa language
 BT Bantu languages
     Malawi--Languages
     Tanzania--Languages
 NT Mwamba language

Ngongo (African people) *(May Subd Geog)*
 [DT 650.N]
 UF Bangongo (African people)
 BT Ethnology--Zaire

Ngoni (African people) *(May Subd Geog)*
 [DT 864 (Malawi : old class)]
 [DT 3192.N44 (Malawi : new class)]
 [DT 443.3.N54 (Tanzania)]
 UF Angoni (African people)
     Mangoni (African people)
     Wangoni (African people)
 DT Ethnology--Africa, Eastern
     Ethnology--Malawi
     Ethnology--Tanzania
     Nguni (African people)
 NT Bhaca (African people)
 --Migrations
 --Missions *(May Subd Geog)*
 [BV 3630.N]
 UF Missions to Ngoni (African people)

Ngoni law
 USE Law, Ngoni

Ngono River (Tanzania) *(Not Subd Geog)*
 BT Rivers--Tanzania

Ngorongoro Conservation Area (Tanzania)
 USE Ngorongoro Game Control Area Reserve
(Tanzania)

**Ngorongoro Game Control Area Reserve
(Tanzania)** *(Not Subd Geog)*
 UF Ngorongoro Conservation Area
(Tanzania)
 BT Game reserves--Tanzania
     National parks and reserves--Tanzania

Ngoteng (African people)
 USE Ngangte (African people)

Ngoy (African people)
 USE Bwende (African people)

Ngueba language
 USE Bamougoun-Bamenjou language

Nguemba language
 USE Ngemba language (Cameroon)

Nguere (Kru-speaking African people)
 USE Wobe (African people)

Nguéré (Mande-speaking African people)
 USE Dan (African people)

Ngulu (Tanzanian people) *(May Subd Geog)*
 [DT 443.3.N58]
 UF Nguru (Tanzanian people)
 BT Ethnology--Tanzania

Nguni (African people) *(May Subd Geog)*
 [DT 458.3.N (Mozambique : old class)]
 [DT 3328.N58 (Mozambique : new class)]
 [DT 764.N34 (South Africa : old class)]
 [DT 1508.N58 (Southern Africa : new class)]
 BT Bantu-speaking peoples
     Ethnology--African, Southern
     Ethnology--Mozambique
     Ethnology--South Africa
 NT Bomvana (African people)
     Hlubi (African people)
     Ndebele (African people)
     Ngoni (African people)
     Swazi (African people)
     Tembu (African people)
     Xhosa (African people)
     Zulu (African people)
 --Food
 BT Food

Nguni beadwork
 USE Beadwork, Nguni

Nguni languages *(May Subd Geog)*
 [PL 8550.N44]
 BT Africa, Southern--Languages
     Bantu languages
     Mozambique--Languages
     South Africa--Languages
 NT Swazi language
     Xhosa language
     Zulu language
 --Tone
 BT Tone (Phonetics)

UF = Used for; BT = Broader term; RT = Related term; SA = See also; NT = Narrower term

Nguru (African people)
USE Lomwe (African people)

Nguru (Tanzanian people)
USE Ngulu (Tanzanian people)

Nguru Mountains (Tanzania) *(Not Subd Geog)*
BT Mountains--Tanzania

Nguruman Forest (Kenya) *(Not Subd Geog)*
BT Forests and forestry--Kenya

Ngwa (African people) *(May Subd Geog)*
[DT 515.45.N48]
BT Ethnology--Nigeria
Igbo (African people)

Ngwa dialect *(May Subd Geog)*
[PL 8261.95.N48]
BT Igbo language
Nigeria--Languages

Ngwaketse (African people) *(May Subd Geog)*
[DT 799.N48 : old class]
[DT 2458.N : new class]
UF Bangwaketse (African people)
BT Ethnology--Botswana

Ngwala language
USE Kulango language

Ngwato (African people) *(May Subd Geog)*
[DT 797 (Botswana : old class)]
[DT 2458.N45 (Botswana : new class)]
UF Bamangwato (African people)
Ngwatu (African people)
BT Bantu-speaking peoples
Ethnology--Botswana
Ethnology--Zambia
--**Missions** *(May Subd Geog)*
[BV 3630.B25]
UF Missions to Ngwato (African people)

Ngwatu (African people)
USE Ngwato (African people)

Ngwemyene (African people)
USE Myene (African people)

Ngyemboon language
USE Ngemba language (Cameroon)

Nharo (African people)
USE Naron (African people)

Nharo language *(May Subd Geog)*
[PL 8550.N49]
UF Aikwe language
Aisan language
Naro language
Nhauru language
BT Botswana--Languages
Khoisan languages

Nhauru (African people)
USE Naron (African people)

Nhauru language
USE Nharo language

Nhaurun (African people)
USE Naron (African people)

Niabua language
USE Nyabwa language

Niam-Niam (African people)
USE Zande (African people)

Niani (Guinea) *(Not Subd Geog)*
UF Mali (Guinea)
Mani (Guinea)
Nani (Guinea)
Nianimadougou (Guinea)
Yani (Guinea)
BT Cities and towns, Ruined, extinct, etc.--
Guinea
Guinea--Antiquities

Nianimadougou (Guinea)
USE Niani (Guinea)

Niassa, Lake
USE Nyasa, Lake

Niaturu (African people)
USE Nyaturu (African people)

Nibulu dialect
USE Nunuma dialect

Nielim language *(May Subd Geog)*
[PL 8550.N53]
UF Lua language
Mjillem language
Niellim language
Nyilem language
BT Bua languages
Chad--Languages

(May Subd Geog) = Place names may follow the heading

Niellim language
  USE Nielim language

Niende (African people)
  USE Nyende (African people)

Nienegue language
  USE Bwamu language

Nife language
  USE Luo language (Kenya and Tanzania)

Niger *(Not Subd Geog)*
  [DT 547-DT 547.9]
 --Description and travel
 -- --1981-
 --Economic conditions
  [HC 1020]
 --History
 -- --To 1960
  NT Senussite Rebellion, 1916-1918
 --Languages
  NT Bororo dialect (West Africa)
      Bozo language
      Daza language
      Dendi dialect
      Hausa language
      Kanuri language
      Zarma dialect
 -- --Terms and phrases
 --Literatures
  USE Niger literature
 --Politics and government
 -- --1960-

Niger-Congo languages *(May Subd Geog)*
  BT Africa--Languages
      African languages
  NT Adamawa languages
      Badyaranke language
      Baka language (Cameroon)
      Balante language
      Banda languages
      Bassari language
      Bedik language
      Benue-Congo languages
      Cangin languages
      Diola language
      Feroge languages
      Fula language
      Gbaya language
      Gola language
      Gur languages
      Karang language (Cameroon)
      Kissi language
      Kuo language

  NT Kwa languages
      Limba language
      Ma language
      Mande languages
      Mandjak language
      Mankanya language
      Mundu language
      Ndogo-Sere languages
      Ngbaka ma'bo language
      Ngbandi language
      Nomaante language
      Northern Bullom language
      Serer language
      Shebro language
      Timne language
      Wolof language
      Yakoma language
      Zande language

Niger fiction (French) *(May Subd Geog)*
  [PQ 3988.5.N5 (History)]
  [PQ 3988.5.N52 (Collections)]
  UF French fiction--Niger authors
  BT Niger literature (French)
      West African fiction (French)
  NT Short stories, Niger (French)

Niger literature *(May Subd Geog)*
  [PL 8014.N]
  UF Niger--Literatures
  BT West African literature
  NT Hausa literature

Niger literature (French) *(May Subd Geog)*
  [PQ 3988.5.N5 (History)]
  [PQ 3988.5.N52 (Collections)]
  UF French literature--Niger authors
  BT West African literature (French)
  NT Niger fiction (French)
      Niger poetry (French)

Niger poetry (French) *(May Subd Geog)*
  [PQ 3988.5.N5 (History)]
  [PQ 3988.5.N52 (Collections)]
  UF French poetry--Niger authors
  BT Niger literature (French)
      West African poetry (French)

Niger River *(Not Subd Geog)*
  [DT 360]
  UF River Niger
  BT Rivers--Africa, West

Niger River Delta (Nigeria) *(Not Subd Geog)*
  BT Deltas--Nigeria

UF = Used for; BT = Broader term; RT = Related term; SA = See also; NT = Narrower term

Niger River Valley *(Not Subd Geog)*
  BT Valleys--Africa, West

Niger short stories (French)
  USE Short stories, Niger (French)

Nigeria *(Not Subd Geog)*
  [DT 515-DT 515.9]
--Civilization
-- --Western influences
  BT Civilization, Western
--Drama
  USE Nigerian drama
--Description and travel
-- --1981-
--Economic conditions
  [HC 1055]
-- --To 1960
-- --1960-
-- --1970-
--Fiction
  NT Igbo fiction
      Yoruba fiction
--Foreign relations *(May Subd Geog)*
-- --1960-
--History
-- --To 1851
-- --1851-1899
-- --1900-1960
  NT Senussite Rebellion, 1916-1918
-- --1960-
-- --Coup d'état, 1966 (January 15)
  BT Coups d'état--Nigeria
-- --Coup d'état, 1966 (July 29)
  BT Coups d'état--Nigeria
-- --Civil War, 1967-1970
  [DT 515.836]
  UF Biafran Conflict, 1967-1970
      Civil War--Nigeria
-- -- --Causes
-- -- --Charities
  USE Nigeria--History--Civil War, 1967-
1970--War work
-- -- --Civilian relief
  NT Nigeria--History--Civil War, 1967-
1970--War work
-- -- --Destruction and pillage
-- -- --Foreign public opinion
-- -- --Personal narratives
-- -- --Pictorial works
-- -- --Social work
  USE Nigeria--History--Civil War, 1967-
1970--War work
-- -- --War work
  UF Nigeria--History--Civil War, 1967-
1970--Charities

  UF Nigeria--History--Civil War, 1967-1970--
Social work
  BT Nigeria--History--Civil War, 1967-1970--
Civilian relief
-- -- -- --Red Cross
-- --Coup d'état, 1983
  BT Coups d'état--Nigeria
--Languages
  NT Abua language
      Abua-Ogbia languages
      Adamawa languages
      Aja dialect
      Angas language
      Atisa language
      Bakundu language
      Bekwarra language
      Bini language
      Birom language
      Bolewa languages
      Bororo dialect (West Africa)
      Busa language
      Degema language
      Dendi dialect
      Efik language
      Ekajuk language
      Ekoi languages
      Ekpeye language
      Engenni language
      Etsako language
      Ezaa language
      Fon dialect
      Gbagyi language
      Glavda language
      Gude language
      Guyuk dialect
      Gwandara language
      Gwari language
      Hausa language
      Ibani dialect
      Ibibio language
      Idoma language
      Igbira language
      Igbo language
      Igede language
      Ijo language
      Ikwere language
      Ikwo language
      Izi language
      Jukun language
      Jukunoid languages
      Kagoro dialect
      Kaje language
      Kalabari dialect
      Kamwe language
      Kana language
      Kanakuru language

(May Subd Geog) = Place names may follow the heading

NT Kanuri language
    Katab language
    Kolokuma dialect
    Kotoko dialects
    Laamang language
    Longuda language
    Mambila language
    Mandara language
    Margi language
    Migili language
    Moba language
    Mumuye language
    Nembe language
    Ngizim language
    Ngwa dialect
    Nupe language
    Obolo language
    Odual language
    Okpe language
    Okrika dialect
    Pero language
    Plateau languages (Nigeria)
    Ron language
    Southern Bauchi languages
    Teda language
    Tera language
    Tivi language
    Vaghwatadaxa language
    Yakö language
    Yamba language (Cameroon and Nigeria)
    Yebu language
    Yoruba language
    Zarma dialect
  --Literatures
  USE Nigerian literature
  --Poetry
  USE Nigerian poetry
  --Politics and government
  -- --To 1960
  -- --1960-
  -- --1960-1975
  -- --1975-1979
  -- --1979-1983
  -- --1984-
  --Religion
  --Social conditions
  -- --1960-

Nigeria, Eastern (Not Subd Geog)
  [DT 515.9.E3]
  UF Biafra
      Eastern Nigeria

Nigeria, Northern (Not Subd Geog)
  [DT 515.9.N5]
  UF Northern Nigeria (Region)

Nigerian art
  USE Art, Nigerian

Nigerian atlases
  USE Atlases, Nigerian

Nigerian authors
  USE Authors, Nigerian

Nigerian chapbooks
  USE Chapbooks, Nigerian

Nigerian college verse (English)
  USE College verse, Nigerian (English)

Nigerian cookery
  USE Cookery, Nigerian

Nigerian drama (May Subd Geog)
  [PL 8014.N]
  UF Nigeria--Drama
  BT Nigerian literature
  NT Hausa drama
      Idoma drama
      Igbo drama
      Yoruba drama

Nigerian drama (English) (May Subd Geog)
  [PR 9387.3 (History)]
  [PR 9387.7 (Collections)]
  UF English drama--Nigerian authors
  BT Nigerian literature (English)
  --20th century

Nigerian fiction (English) (May Subd Geog)
  [PR 9387.4 (History)]
  [PR 9387.8 (Collections)]
  UF English fiction--Nigerian authors
  BT Nigerian literature (English)
      West African fiction (English)
  NT Short stories, Nigerian (English)

Nigerian folk poetry
  USE Folk poetry, Nigerian

Nigerian literature (May Subd Geog)
  [PL 8014.N]
  UF Nigeria--Literatures
  BT West African literature
  NT Fon literature
      Hausa literature
      Idoma literature
      Igbo literature
      Nigerian drama
      Nigerian poetry
      Yoruba literature

UF = Used for; BT = Broader term; RT = Related term; SA = See also; NT = Narrower term

Nigerian literature (English) *(May Subd Geog)*
  [PR 9387]
  UF English literature--Nigerian authors
  BT West African literature (English)
  NT Nigerian drama (English)
      Nigerian fiction (English)
      Nigerian poetry (English)
      Nigerian wit and humor (English)

Nigerian national characteristics
  USE National characteristics, Nigerian

Nigerian newspapers *(May Subd Geog)*
  [PN 5499.N5]
  UF Newspapers, Nigerian

Nigerian periodicals *(May Subd Geog)*
  [PN 5499.N5]
  UF Periodicals, Nigerian

Nigerian poetry *(May Subd Geog)*
  [PL 8014.N]
  UF Nigeria--Poetry
  BT Nigerian literature
      West African poetry
  NT Folk poetry, Nigerian
      Fon poetry
      Hausa poetry
      Igbo poetry
      Yoruba poetry

Nigerian poetry (English) *(May Subd Geog)*
  [PR 9387.2 (History)]
  [PR 9387.6-PR 9387.65 (Collections)]
  UF English poetry--Nigerian authors
  BT Nigerian literature (English)
      West African poetry (English)]
  NT College verse, Nigerian (English)
      Revolutionary poetry, Nigerian
(English)

Nigerian poets
  USE Poets, Nigerian

Nigerian revolutionary poetry (English)
  USE Revolutionary poetry, Nigerian
(English)

Nigerian satire (English)
  USE Satire, Nigerian (English)

Nigerian sculpture
  USE Sculpture, Nigerian

Nigerian short stories (English)
  USE Short stories, Nigerian (English)

Nigerian soldiers' writings (English)
  USE Soldiers' writings, Nigerian (English)

Nigerian terra-cotta sculpture
  USE Terra-cotta sculpture, Nigerian

Nigerian wit and humor *(May Subd Geog)*
  [PN 6222.N6 (Collections)]
  UF Wit and humor, Nigerian

Nigerian wit and humor (English) *(May Subd Geog)*
  UF Wit and humor, Nigerian (English)
  BT Nigerian literature (English)

Nigerian wit and humor, Pictorial *(May Subd Geog)*
  [NC 1740.N]
  UF Wit and humor, Pictorial (Nigerian)

Nigerians *(May Subd Geog)*
  BT Ethnology--Nigeria
  --Zaire
    NT Zaire--History--Civil War, 1960-1965--
Participation, Nigerian

Nigrillos
  USE Negrillos

Nika (African people) *(May Subd Geog)*
  [DT 433.545.N55 (Kenya)]
  UF Chimanyika (African people)
      Manyika (African people)
      Mijikenda (African people)
      Nyika (African people)
      Wanika (African people)
      Wanyika (African people)
  BT Ethnology--Kenya
      Ethnology--Tanzania
      Ethnology--Zimbabwe
      Shona (African people)
  NT Giryama (African people)
      Ribe (African people)

Nika language *(May Subd Geog)*
  [PL 8551]
  BT Bantu languages
      Kenya--Languages
      Tanzania--Languages
      Zimbabwe--Languages
  NT Digo language
      Giryama language

Nika philosophy
  USE Philosophy, Nika

Nil River
  USE Nile River

(May Subd Geog) = Place names may follow the heading

Nilamba language *(May Subd Geog)*
[PL 8555]
UF Ilamba language
    Iramba language
    Kiniramba language
    Nilyamba language
    Niramba language
BT Bantu languages
    Tanzania--Languages

Nile Nubian language
USE Dongola-Kenuz dialect
     Mahas-Fiyadikka language

Nile River *(Not Subd Geog)*
[DT 115-DT 117]
UF Bahr en Nil
    Nahr an Nil
    Nil River
    Nilus River
BT Rivers--Africa
--**Barrages**
--**Regulation**
--**Religious aspects**

Nile River, Blue (Ethiopia and Sudan)
USE Blue Nile River (Ethiopia and Sudan)

Nilo-Hamitic languages
[PL 8026.N47]
BT Africa, Eastern--Languages
    Hamitic languages
    Nilotic languages
NT Bari language
    Baria language
    Kwafi language
    Latuka language
    Masai language
    Nandi languages
    Samburu language
    Teso language
    Toposa language
    Turkana language

Nilo-Hamitic tribes
BT Ethnology--Africa, East
NT Alur (African people)
    Barabaig (African people)
    Baria (African people)
    Dodoth (African people)
    Dorobo (African people)
    Hamites
    Jie (African people)
    Kipsigis (African people)
    Latuka (African people)

NT Marakwet (African people)
    Masai (African people)
    Nandi (African people)
    Sandawe (African people)
    Sapiny (African people)
    Suk (African people)
    Teso (African people)
    Turkana (African people)

Nilo-Saharan languages
[PL 8026.N49]
BT Africa--Languages
    African languages
NT Balese language
    Birri language
    Central Sudanic languages
    Daza language
    Fur language
    Ingassana language
    Kanuri language
    Kunama language
    Logbara language
    Maba language
    Ma'di language (Uganda and Sudan)
    Mamvu language
    Meroitic language
    Murle language
    Nilotic languages
    Nubian languages
    Songhai language
    Teuso languages
    Uduk language

Nilotes
USE Nilotic tribes

Nilotic Kavirondo language
USE Luo language (Kenya and Tanzania)

Nilotic languages
[PL 8026.N5]
BT Africa, Eastern--Languages
    Nilo-Saharan languages
NT Acoli language
    Alur language
    Anuak language
    Bor language (Lwo)
    Dinka language
    Luo language (Kenya and Tanzania)
    Lwo language (Sudan)
    Maban language
    Nilo-Hamitic languages
    Nuer language
    Päri language (Sudan)
    Shilluk language

UF = Used for; BT = Broader term; RT = Related term; SA = See also; NT = Narrower term

Nilotic position
  USE One-leg resting position

Nilotic tribes
  [DT 380.4.N54 (Ethiopia)]
  [DT 155.2.N55 (Sudan)]
  UF Nilotes
  BT Ethnology--Ethiopia
      Ethnology--Sudan
      Ethnology--Uganda
  NT Anuak (African people)
      Atuot (African people)
      Dinka (African people)
      Luo (African people)
      Nuer (African people)
 --Religion
  [BL 2480.N46]

Nilus River
  USE Nile River

Nilyamba language
  USE Nilamba language

Nimbi language
  USE Nembe language

Ninisi (West African people)
  USE Samo (West African people)

Ninisi language
  USE Samo language (West Africa)

Nioniosse (African people)
  USE Kurumba (African people)

Niramba language
  USE Nilamba language

Nirere dialect *(May Subd Geog)*
  UF Abri dialect (Sudan)
  BT Sudan--Languages

Niumi (Kingdom) *(Not Subd Geog)*
  [DT 532.23]
  BT Gambia--History
      Mandingo (African people)--History
      Senegal--History

Njarasa, Lake (Tanzania)
  USE Eyasi, Lake (Tanzania)

Njassa See
  USE Nyasa, Lake

Njavi (African people)
  USE Nzabi (African people)

Njawi (African people)
  USE Nzabi (African people)

Njemps (African people) *(May Subd Geog)*
  [DT 433.545.N]
  UF Njempsian (African people)
      Tiamus (African people)
  BT Ethnology--Kenya

Njempsian (African people)
  USE Njemps (African people)

Njuboga (African people)
  USE Ngangte (African people)

Njungene language
  USE Limbum language

Nkamar (African people)
  USE Hamar (African people)

Nkâmi (African people)
  USE Nkomi (African people)

Nkengo language
  USE Lonkengo language

Nkhonde (African people)
  USE Ngonde (African people)

Nkole (African people)
  USE Nyankole (African people)

Nkole language
  USE Nyankole language

Nkom (African people)
  USE Kom (African people)

Nkomi (African people) *(May Subd Geog)*
  [DT 546.145.N56]
  UF Camma (African people)
      Commi (African people)
      Nkâmi (African people)
  BT Ethnology--Gabon
      Mpongwe (African people)

Nkonde (African people)
  USE Ngonde (African people)

Nkonde language
  USE Ngonde language

(May Subd Geog) = Place names may follow the heading

Nkondja (African people)
  USE Luba (African people)

Nkongo (African people)
  USE Kongo (African people)

Nkonya language
  USE Nkunya language

Nkore-Kiga language
  USE Nyankore-Kiga language

Nkore language
  USE Nyankole language

Nkosi (African people)
  USE Kossi (African people)

Nkosi dialect
  USE Bakossi dialect

Nkoya (African people) *(May Subd Geog)*
  [DT 963 : old class]
  [DT 3058.N56 : new class]
  UF Mankoya (African people)
      Shinkoya (African people)
  BT Ethnology--Zambia

Nkulu (African people)
  USE Luba (African people)

Nkundo (African people)
  USE Nkundu (African people)

Nkundo language
  USE Nkundu language

Nkundu (African people) *(May Subd Geog)*
  [DT 650.N58]
  UF Gundo (African people)
      Inkundo (African people)
      Kundu (African people)
      Nkundo (African people)
  BT Bantu-speaking peoples
      Ethnology--Zaire
  --Folklore
  [GR 357.82.N57]

Nkundu language *(May Subd Geog)*
  [PL 8467]
  UF Lonkundu language
      Lunkundu language
      Nkundo language
  BT Bantu languages
      Zaire--Languages

Nkunya language *(May Subd Geog)*
  [PL 8563]
  UF Nkonya language
  BT Ghana--Languages
      Gonja language

Nkurange language
  USE Kulango language

Nkutu (African people)
  USE Dengese (African people)

Nkutuk language
  USE Samburu language

Nkwaleni River (South Africa)
  USE Nkwalini River (South Africa)

Nkwalini River (South Africa) *(Not Subd Geog)*
  UF Nkwaleni River (South Africa)
  BT Rivers--South Africa

Nobiin language
  USE Mahas-Fiyadikka language

Noho (African people)
  USE Tanqa (African people)

Nok terra-cotta sculpture
  USE Terra-cotta sculpture, Nok

Nomaante language *(May Subd Geog)*
  DT Cameroon--Languages
      Niger-Congo languages

Nonselfgoverning territories
  USE Colonies

Nope language
  USE Nupe language

Nor language
  USE Mambila language

Nordic Tanganyika Project
  BT Medical assistance, Scandinavian--Tanzania
      Technical assistance, Scandinavian--
Tanzania

North American Indians
  USE Indians of North America

North Mkata Plain (Tanzania) *(Not Subd Geog)*
  UF Mkata Plain, North (Tanzania)
  BT Plains--Tanzania

UF = Used for; BT = Broader term; RT = Related term; SA = See also; NT = Narrower term

Northeast Africa
  USE Africa, Northeast

Northeastern Luba language
  USE Songe language

Northern Border War, 1st (South Africa),
1868-1870
  USE Korana War, 1st, 1868-1870

Northern Border War, 2nd (South Africa),
1878-1879
  USE Korana War, 2nd, 1878-1879

Northern Bullom language *(May Subd Geog)*
  [PL 8093]
  UF Bolom language
      Bulem language
      Bulin language
      Bullin language
      Bullom language
      Bullom language, Northern
      Bullum language
      Bulom language
      Mandingi language
      Mmani language
  BT Niger-Congo languages
      Sierra Leone--Languages

Northern Karoo (South Africa)
  USE Northern Karroo (South Africa)

Northern Karroo (South Africa) *(Not Subd Geog)*
  UF High Veld (South Africa)
      Highveld (South Africa)
      Karoo, Northern (South Africa)
      Karoo, Upper (South Africa)
      Karroo, Northern (South Africa)
      Northern Karoo (South Africa)
      Upper Karoo (South Africa)
  BT Plateaus--South Africa

Northern Lunda (African people)
  USE Lunda, Northern (African people)

Northern Lunda language
  USE Ruund language

Northern Nigeria (Region)
  USE Nigeria, Northern

Northern Rhodesia
  USE Zambia

Northern Sotho (African people)
  USE Pedi (African people)

Northern Sotho language *(May Subd Geog)*
  [PL 8690]
  UF Pedi language
      Sepedi language
      Sotho language, Northern
      Transvaal Sotho language
  BT Sotho-Tswana languages
  NT Ndebele language (South Africa)

Northern Sotho philology
  [PL 8690]
  UF Philology, Northern Sotho

Northwest Africa
  USE Africa, Northwest

Nosibe (Madagascar)
  USE Nosy-Be Island (Madagascar)

Nossi-Bé (Madagascar)
  USE Nosy-Be Island (Madagascar)

Nosy-Be Island (Madagascar) *(Not Subd Geog)*
  [DT 469.M37N67]
  UF Bé Island (Madacasgar)
      Nosibe (Madagascar)
      Nossi-Bé (Madagascar)
  BT Islands--Madagascar
      Madagascar

Nosy Boraha (Madacascar)
  USE Sainte-Marie-de Madagascar Island
(Madagascar)

Nouni dialect
  USE Nunuma dialect

Novelists
  BT Authors
  RT Fiction

Novelists, South African *(May Subd Geog)*
  UF South African novelists
  RT Authors, South African

Novellas (Short novels)
  USE Fiction

Novels
  USE Fiction

Npongwe (African people)
  USE Mpongwe (African people)

Nrebele language (South Africa)
  USE Ndebele language (South Africa)

(May Subd Geog) = Place names may follow the heading

Nrebele language (Zimbabwe)
  USE Ndebele language (Zimbabwe)

Nsaw (African people)
  USE Nso (African people)

Nsenga language
  USE Senga language

Nsima language
  USE Nzima language

Nso (African people) *(May Subd Geog)*
  [DT 571.N74]
  UF Bansaw (African people)
      Banso (African people)
      Lamnso (African people)
      Lamso (African people)
      Nsaw (African people)
  BT Ethnology--Cameroon

Nsugni language
  USE Limbum language

Nsundi (African people)
  USE Sundi (African people)

Noungali language
  USE Limbum language

Nsungli language
  USE Limbum language

Nsungni language
  USE Limbum language

Ntaandu dialect *(May Subd Geog)*
  UF Kintaandu dialect
      Kintandu dialect
      Kisantu dialect
      Ntandu dialect
      Santu dialect
  BT Kongo language
      Zaire--Languages

Ntandu dialect
  USE Ntaandu dialect

Ntomba language *(May Subd Geog)*
  [PL 8568]
  UF Ntumba language
      Tomba language
  BT Bantu language
      Zaire--Languages
  RT Bolia language

Ntondozi (Swaziland) *(Not Subd Geog)*

Ntumba language
  USE Ntomba language

Nuba (African people) *(May Subd Geog)*
  [DT 155.2.N82]
  BT Ethnology--Sudan

Nuba, Lake (Egypt and Sudan)
  USE Nasser, Lake (Egypt and Sudan)

Nuba art
  USE Art, Nuba

Nuba languages
  USE Nubian languages

Nuba Mountains (Sudan) *(Not Subd Geog)*
  UF Jibal an Nubah (Sudan)
      Nubah, Jibal an (Sudan)
  BT Mountains--Sudan

Nubah, Jibal an (Sudan)
  USE Nuba Mountains (Sudan)

Nubi language *(May Subd Geog)*
  [PM 7895.N83]
  UF Kinubi language
  BT Creole dialects, Arabic--Kenya
      Creole dialects, Arabic--Uganda
      Kenya--Languages
      Uganda--Languages

Nubia *(Not Subd Geog)*
  [DT 159.6.N83]
  --Antiquities

Nubia, Lake (Egypt and Sudan)
  USE Nasser, Lake (Egypt and Sudan)

Nubian language
  USE Nubian languages

Nubian languages *(May Subd Geog)*
  [PL 8571-PL 8574]
  UF Nuba languages
      Nubian language
  BT Nilo-Saharan languages
      Sudan--Languages
  NT Dongola-Kenuz dialect
      Mahas-Fiyadikka language

Nubian pottery
  USE Pottery, Nubian

UF = Used for; BT = Broader term; RT = Related term; SA = See also; NT = Narrower term

Nubians *(May Subd Geog)*
  [DT 159.6.N83]
  BT Ethnology--Sudan
  NT Danagla (African people)
 --**Ethnic identity**

Nuer (African people) *(May Subd Geog)*
  [DT 155.2.N85]
  BT Ethnology--Sudan
      Nilotic tribes
 --**Religion**
  [BL 2480.N7]

Nuer folk songs
  USE Folk songs, Nuer

Nuer language *(May Subd Geog)*
  [PL 8576.N4]
  UF Abigar language
      Nath language
  BT Ethiopia--Languages
      Nilotic languages
      Sudan--Languages

Nuer law
  USE Law, Nuer

Nuer women
  USE Women, Nuer

Nufawa (African people)
  USE Nupe (African people)

Nufi language
  USE Fe'fe' language

Nugunu language
  USE Gunu language

Nugzum language
  USE Ngizim language

Nuna dialect (Burkina Faso)
  USE Nunuma dialect

Nunguda language
  USE Longuda language

Nunu (African people) *(May Subd Geog)*
  [DT 546.245.N86]
  UF Banunu (African people)
      Moye (African people)
  BT Ethnology--Congo (Brazzaville)

Nunuma dialect *(May Subd Geog)*
  [PL 8576.N47]
  UF Nibulu dialect
      Nouni dialect
      Nuna dialect (Burkina Faso)
      Nuruma dialect
  BT Burkina Faso--Languages
      Kasem language

Nupe (African people) *(May Subd Geog)*
  [DT 515.45.N86]
  UF Bassa-Nge (African people)
      Ibara (African people)
      Nufawa (African people)
      Nupeci (African people)
      Nupecidji (African people)
      Nupenchi (African people)
      Nupencizi (African people)
  BT Ethnology--Nigeria
 --**Religion**
  [BL 2480.N8]

Nupe language *(May Subd Geog)*
  [PL 8577]
  UF Nope language
  BT Kwa languages
      Nigeria--Languages

Nupeci (African people)
  USE Nupe (African people)

Nupecidji (African people)
  USE Nupe (African people)

Nupenchi (African people)
  USE Nupe (African people)

Nupencizi (African people)
  USE Nupe (African people)

Nuro (African people)
  USE Anuak (African people)

Nursery rhymes
  UF Poetry for children
  BT Children's poetry
      Folk literature
      Folk poetry
      Poetry
  NT Lullabies

Nursery rhymes, Ndebele (Zimbabwe) *(May Subd Geog)*
  UF Ndebele nursery rhymes (Zimbabwe)
  BT Ndebele poetry (Zimbabwe)

(May Subd Geog) = Place names may follow the heading

Nuruma dialect
  USE Nunuma dialect

Nuy River (South Africa) *(Not Subd Geog)*
  BT Rivers--South Africa

Nyabingi (African deity) *(Not Subd Geog)*
  [BL 2480.C48]
  BT Chiga (African people)--Religion
      Gods, African--Uganda
      Religion, Primitive--Uganda

Nyabungu language
  USE Shi language

Nyabwa language *(May Subd Geog)*
  [PL 8579]
  UF Niabua language
  BT Bete language
      Ivory Coast--Languages

Nyai language
  USE Tete language

Nyakyusa (African people) *(May Subd Geog)*
  [DT 443.3.N92]
  UF Sokile (African people)
  BT Bantu-speaking peoples
      Ethnology--Tanzania
  RT Ngonde (African people)

Nyakyusa language
  USE Ngonde language

Nyam-Nyam (African people)
  USE Zande (African people)

Nyam-Nyam language
  USE Zande language

Nyamlagira (Zaire) *(Not Subd Geog)*
  UF Nyamuragira (Zaire)
  BT Mountains--Zaire
      Virunga
      Volcanoes--Zaire

Nyamuragira (Zaire)
  USE Nyamlagira (Zaire)

Nyamwesi language
  USE Nyamwezi language

Nyamwezi (African people) *(May Subd Geog)*
  [DT 443.3.N93]
  UF Banyamwezi (African people)
      Wanyamwezi (African people)

  BT Bantu-speaking peoples
      Ethnology--Tanzania

Nyamwezi language *(May Subd Geog)*
  [PL 8591]
  UF Kinyamwesi language
      Kinyamwezi language
      Namwezi language
      Nyamwesi language
  BT Bantu languages
      Tanzania--Languages

Nyandja language
  USE Nyanja language

Nyaneka language *(May Subd Geog)*
  [PL 8592.N3]
  UF Lunyaneka language
      Olunyaneka language
  BT Angola--Languages
      Bantu languages

Nyang (African people) *(May Subd Geog)*
  [DT 571.N]
  UF Anyang (African people)
      Banyang (African people)
      Kenyang (African people)
      Nyangi (African people)
  DT Bantu-speaking peoples
      Ethnology--Cameroon

Nyang language
  USE Anyang language

Nyanga (African people) *(May Subd Geog)*
  [DT 474.6.N (West Africa)]
  [DT 650.N (Zaire)]
  UF Banyanga (African people)
      Wanyanga (African people)
  BT Bantu-speaking peoples
      Ethnology--Africa, West
      Ethnology--Zaire
  --Folklore
  NT Mwindo (Nyanga folk epic)

Nyanga language *(May Subd Geog)*
  [PL 8592.N43]
  UF KiNyanga language
  BT Bantu languages
      Zaire--Languages

Nyangatom (African people) *(May Subd Geog)*
  [DT 380.4.N92 (Ethiopia)]
  UF Dongiro (African people)
      Donyiro (African people)
      Idongiro (African people)   *(Continued)*

UF = Used for; BT = Broader term; RT = Related term; SA = See also; NT = Narrower term

Nyangatom (African people) *(Continued)*
  UF Toposa (African people)
  BT Ethnology--Ethiopia
      Ethnology--Sudan

Nyangi (African people)
  USE Nyang (African people)

Nyanja (African people) *(May Subd Geog)*
  [DT 864 (Malawi : old class)]
  [DT 3192.N83 (Malawi : new class)]
  [DT 963.42 (Zambia : old class)]
  [DT 3058.N93 (Zambia: new class)]
  UF Manganja (African people)
  BT Bantu-speaking peoples
      Ethnology--Malawi
      Ethnology--Mozambique
      Ethnology--Zambia

Nyanja imprints *(May Subd Geog)*
  [Z 7108.N93]
  UF Imprints, Nyanja

Nyanja language *(May Subd Geog)*
  [PL 8593]
  UF Chinyanja language
      Kiniassa language
      Mang'anja language
      Ng'anga language
      Nyandja language
      Nyassa language
  BT Bantu languages
      Malawi--Languages
      Mozambique--Languages
      Zambia--Languages
  RT Chewa dialect
      Sena language
      Tete language
      Tumbuka language

Nyanja literature *(May Subd Geog)*
  [PL 8593.5-PL 8593.9]
  BT Malawi literature
      Mozambican literature
      Zambian literature

Nyankole (African people) *(May Subd Geog)*
  [DT 433.245.N9]
  UF Banyankole (African people)
      Nkole (African people)
      Runyankole (African people)
      Ulunyankole (African people)
      Ulunyankore (African people)
  BT Bantu-speaking peoples
      Ethnology--Uganda
 --**Ethnic identity**

Nyankole language *(May Subd Geog)*
  [PL 8594.N3]
  UF Lunyankole language
      Nkole language
      Nkore language
      Nyankore language
      Runyankore language
  BT Bantu languages
      Uganda--Languages
  RT Nyankore-Kiga language

Nyankole literature *(May Subd Geog)*
  [PL 8594.N35-PL 8594.N39]
  BT Ugandan literature
  NT Nyankole poetry

Nyankole poetry *(May Subd Geog)*
  [PL 8594.N35-PL 8594.N39]
  BT Nyankole literature
      Uganda--Poetry

Nyankore-Kiga language *(May Subd Geog)*
  [PL 8594.N45]
  UF Nkore-Kiga language
      Runyankore-Rukiga language
  BT Bantu languages
      Uganda--Languages
  RT Kiga language
      Nyankole language

Nyankore language
  USE Nyankole language

Nyaruanda language
  USE Kinyarwanda language

Nyasa, Lake *(Not Subd Geog)*
  UF Lake Malawi
      Lake Nyasa
      Lake Nyassa
      Malawi, Lake
      Niassa, Lake
      Njassa See
      Nyassa, Lake
  BT Lakes--Malawi
      Lakes--Mozambique
      Lakes--Tanzania

Nyasa (African people)
  USE Tumbuka (African people)

Nyasaland
  USE Malawi

Nyassa, Lake
  USE Nyasa, Lake

           (May Subd Geog) = Place names may follow the heading

Nyassa language
  USE Nyanja language

Nyaturu (African people) *(May Subd Geog)*
  [DT 443.2.N]
  UF Arimi (African people)
      Lima (African people)
      Limi (African people)
      Niaturu (African people)
      Remi (African people)
      Rimi (African people)
      Taturu (African people)
      Turu (African people)
      Wanyaturu (African people)
  BT Bantu-speaking peoples
      Ethnology--Tanzania

Nyende (African people) *(May Subd Geog)*
  [DT 541.45.N]
  UF Niende (African people)
  BT Ethnology--Benin

Nyenege language
  USE Bwamu language

Nyenyege language
  USE Bwamu language

Nyidi (African people)
  USE Kwegu (African people)

Nyife language
  USE Luo language (Kenya and Tanzania)

Nyifwa (African people)
  USE Luo (African people)

Nyika (African people)
  USE Nika (African people)

Nyilem language
  USE Nielim language

Nyole language
  USE Nyore language

Nyonga (African people)
  USE Bali (African people)

Nyonyosi (African people)
  USE Kurumba (African people)

Nyore language *(May Subd Geog)*
  [PL 8594.N]
  UF Lunyore language
      Nyole language

UF Olunyore language
BT Bantu languages
    Kenya--Languages

Nyoro (African people) *(May Subd Geog)*
  [DT 443.245.N]
  UF Banyoro (African people)
      Bunyoro (African people)
      Gungu (African people)
      Kitara (African people)
      Kyopi (African people)
      Runyoro (African people)
  BT Bantu-speaking peoples
      Ethnology--Uganda
  --History
  NT Bunyoro-Kitara

Nyoro language *(May Subd Geog)*
  [PL 8595]
  UF Lunyoro language
      Urunyoro language
  BT Bantu languages
      Uganda--Languages
  RT Nyoro-Tooro language

Nyoro-Tooro language *(May Subd Geog)*
  [PL 8596.N9]
  UF Runyoro-Rutooro language
  BT Bantu languages
      Uganda--Languages
  RT Nyoro language
      Tooro language

Nyungwe language
  USE Tete language

Nzabi (African people) *(May Subd Geog)*
  [DT 546.145.N93 (Gabon)]
  UF Bandzabi (African people)
      Banjabi (African people)
      Njavi (African people)
      Njawi (African people)
      Nzebi (African people)
  BT Bantu-speaking peoples
      Ethnology--Congo (Brazzaville)
      Ethnology--Gabon

Nzakara (African people) *(May Subd Geog)*
  [DT 546.345.N]
  BT Ethnology--Central African Republic

Nzakara dialect *(May Subd Geog)*
  [PL 8828.95.N]
  UF Sakara dialect
  BT Central African Republic--Languages
      Zande language

UF = Used for; BT = Broader term; RT = Related term; SA = See also; NT = Narrower term

Nzakara folk songs
  USE Folk songs, Nzakara

Nzakara literature *(May Subd Geog)*
  [PL 8828.95.N]
  BT Central African literature
  NT Nzakara poetry

Nzakara poetry *(May Subd Geog)*
  [PL 8828.95.N]
  BT Central African Republic--Poetry
      Nzakara literature

Nzebi (African people)
  USE Nzabi (African people)

Nzema (African people)
  USE Nzima (African people)

Nzema language
  USE Nzima language

Nzima (African people) *(May Subd Geog)*
  [DT 510.43.N95]
  UF Nzema (African people)
      Zema (African people)
  BT Ethnology--Ghana
--**Religion**
  [BL 2480.N9]

Nzima language *(May Subd Geog)*
  [PL 8597]
  UF Amanaya language
      Nsima language
      Nzema language
      Zema language
      Zimba language
  BT Ghana--Languages
      Kwa languages

Nzombo dialect
  USE Zoombo dialect

Nzoombo dialect
  USE Zoombo dialect

O

O.A.U.
  USE Organization of African Unity

Oases *(May Subd Geog)*
  BT Deserts
--**Niger**
  NT Kaouar (Niger)

Obamba (African people)
  USE Mbete (African people)

Obamba language
  USE Mbete language

Obolo language *(May Subd Geog)*
  [PL 8598.027]
  UF Andone language
      Andoni language
      Andonni language
  BT Benue-Congo languages
      Nigeria--Languages

Obugezi (The Ganda word)
  [PL 8201.3]
  BT Ganda language--Etymology

Occidental civilization
  USE Civilization, Western

Occupations and race
  UF Race and occupations
  BT Race

Ochekwu (African people)
  USE Idoma (African people)

Ochiherero (African people)
  USE Herero (African people)

Ochollo (African people) *(May Subd Geog)*
  [DT 380.4.025]
  BT Ethnology--Ethiopia

Octoroons
  USE Mulattoes

Odschi language
  USE Twi language

Odual language *(May Subd Geog)*
  [PL 8598.029]
  UF Saka language (Nigeria)
  BT Abua-Ogbia languages
      Nigeria--Languages

Official publications
  USE Government publications

Ogaden (Ethiopia) *(Not Subd Geog)*
  [DT 390.033]

Ogbia dialect
  USE Abua-Ogbia languages

(May Subd Geog) = Place names may follow the heading

Ogboni (Cult)
[BL 2480.Y6]
BT Cults--Nigeria
Yoruba (African people)--Religion

Ogiek (African people)
USE Dorobo (African people)

Ogoda language
USE Boni language

Ogoni language
USE Kana language

Ogooué River (Gabon) *(Not Subd Geog)*
UF Ogowe River (Gabon)
BT Rivers--Gabon
NT Poubara, Chute de (Gabon)

Ogowe River (Gabon)
USE Ogooué River (Gabon)

Ogun (Yoruba deity) *(Not Subd Geog)*
[BL 2480.Y6]
BT Gods, Yoruba
Religion, Primitive--Nigeria

Ohendo (African people) *(May Subd Geog)*
[DT 650.0]
BT Ethnology--Zaire

Oil-painting
USE Painting

Oji language
USE Twi language

Ojo language
USE Ijo language

Okavango River *(Not Subd Geog)*
UF Cubango River
Kubango River
Okovanggo River
Rio Cubango
BT Rivers--Angola
Rivers--Botswana
Rivers--Namibia

Okavango River Delta (Botswana) *(Not Subd Geog)*
BT Deltas--Botswana

Okela (African people)
USE Kela (African people)

Okela language
USE Kela language

Okouahou (African people)
USE Kwahu (African people)

Okovanggo River
USE Okavango River

Okpe language *(May Subd Geog)*
[PL 8598.O357]
BT Kwa languages
Nigeria--Languages
--Vowel harmony

Okrika dialect *(May Subd Geog)*
[PL 8276.95.O4]
BT Ijo language
Nigeria Languages

Okwe
USE Ayo (Game)

Okwogo (African people)
USE Idoma (African people)

Old Town (Mombasa, Kenya) *(Not Subd Geog)*
UF Mombasa (Kenya). Old Town

Olduvai Gorge (Tanzania) *(Not Subd Geog)*
UF Olduwai Gorge (Tanzania)
BT Gorges--Tanzania

Olduwai Gorge (Tanzania)
USE Olduvai Gorge (Tanzania)

Oluhanga dialect
USE Hanga dialect (Kenya)

Oluluyia language
USE Luyia language

Olunyaneka language
USE Nyaneka language

Olunyore language
USE Nyore language

Olushisa dialect
USE Kisa dialect

Oluwanga dialect
USE Hanga dialect (Kenya)

Ombeke (African people)
USE Orungu (African people)

UF = Used for; BT = Broader term; RT = Related term; SA = See also; NT = Narrower term

Ombo language *(May Subd Geog)*
  [PL 8598.04]
  UF Hombo language
      Loombo language
      Songola language
  BT Bantu languages
      Zaire--Languages

Ombosi (African people)
  USE Mbosi (African people)

Omdurman, Battle of, 1898
  [DT 156.5]
  UF Battle of Omdurman (Sudan), 1898
  BT Sudan--History--1862-1899

Omo Botego (Ethiopia and Kenya)
  USE Omo River (Ethiopia and Kenya)

Omo River (Ethiopia and Kenya) *(Not Subd Geog)*
  UF Omo Botego (Ethiopia and Kenya)
      Omo Wenz (Ethiopia and Kenya)
  BT Rivers--Ethiopia
      Rivers--Kenya

Omo River Delta (Ethiopia and Kenya) *(Not Subd Geog)*
  BT Deltas--Ethiopia
      Deltas--Kenya

Omo River Valley (Ethiopia and Kenya) *(Not Subd Geog)*
  UF Vallée de l'Omo (Ethiopia and Kenya)
  BT Valleys--Ethiopia
      Valleys--Kenya

Omo Wenz (Ethiopia and Kenya)
  USE Omo River (Ethiopia and Kenya)

Omotic languages
  [PJ 2561-PJ 2594]
  UF Cushitic languages, West
      West Cushitic languages
  BT Afroasiatic languages
      Cushitic languages
  NT Kaffa language
      Mocha language
      Walamo language

Omweso (Game)
  [GV 1469.04]
  BT Games--Uganda

Omyene (African people)
  USE Myene (African people)

Ondonga (African people)
  USE Ndonga (African people)

Ondoumbo language
  USE Ndumu language

One-act plays
  UF Plays, One-act
      Short plays
  BT Drama

One-act plays, English *(May Subd Geog)*
  UF English one-act plays
  BT English drama
  --South African authors
  USE One-act plays, South African (English)

One-act plays, Shona *(May Subd Geog)*
  [PL 8681.5-PL 8681.9]
  UF Shona one-act plays
  BT Shona drama

One-act plays, South African (English) *(May Subd Geog)*
  [PR 9361.2-PR 9361.7 (History)]
  [PR 9366.7.05 (Collections)]
  UF One-act plays, English--South African authors
      South African one-act plays (English)
  NT South African drama (English)

One-family houses
  USE Dwellings

One-leg resting position
  UF Nilotic position
      Standing on one foot
  BT Ethnology--Africa, Eastern

One party systems *(May Subd Geog)*
  UF Single party systems
  --Africa
      [JQ 1879.A795]

Onian (Senegalese and Guinean people)
  USE Bassari (Senegalese and Guinean people)

Operation Crossroads Africa
  USE Crossroads Africa

Operation Jonathan, 1976
  USE Entebbe Airport Raid, 1976

(May Subd Geog) = Place names may follow the heading

Operation Menace
[D 766.99]
UF Menace, Operation
BT World War, 1939-1945--Campaigns--
Africa, French-speaking West
NT Dakar, Battle of, 1940

Operation Moses, 1984-1985
USE Falasha Rescue, 1984-1985

Oral literature
USE Folk literature

Oral poetry
USE Folk poetry

Oral tradition *(May Subd Geog)*
UF Tradition, Oral
RT Folklore
    Storytellers
--**Africa**
[DT 19]

Orange Free State (South Africa) *(Not Subd Geog)*
[DT 891-DT 909 : old class)]
[DT 2075-DT 2145 : new class]
--**Description and travel**
-- --To 1854
-- **History**
-- --To 1854
-- --1854-1900
NT Sotho-Free State War, 1865-1866

Orange River *(Not Subd Geog)*
UF Oranjerivier
DT Rivers--Lesotho
    Rivers--Namibia
    Rivers--South Africa

**Orange River Estuary (Namibia and South
Africa)** *(Not Subd Geog)*
BT Estuaries--Namibia
    Estuaries--South Africa

Orange River Project
[TC 519.S6]
BT Water resources development--South
Africa

Oranjerivier
USE Orange River

Oratta-Ikwerri language
USE Ikwere language

Organization of African Unity
[DT 1.0752]
UF O.A.U.
RT Pan-Africanism

Organizations, Business
USE Business enterprises

Organizations, Labor
USE Trade-unions

Organized crime *(May Subd Geog)*
UF Crime syndicates
--**Nigeria**
[HV 6453.N63]
NT Kaduna Mafia

Organized labor
USE Trade-unions

Orig dialect (Sudan) *(May Subd Geog)*
[PL 8706.T349507]
BT Sudan--Languages
    Tagoi language

Orma (African people)
USE Oromo (African people)

Ornament
USE Decoration and ornament

Oro (African people)
USE Oron (African people)

Oro Ukpaban (African people)
USE Oron (African people)

Oromo (African people) *(May Subd Geog)*
[DT 390.G2 (Ethiopia)]
UF Gala (African people)
    Galla (African people)
    Orma (African people)
BT Ethnology--Ethiopia
    Ethnology--Kenya
NT Boran (African people)
    Gabbra (African people)
--**Missions** *(May Subd Geog)*
[BV 3630.G3]
UF Missions to Oromo (African people)

Oromo language *(May Subd Geog)*
[PJ 2471-PJ 2479]
UF Afan language
    Galla language
    Gallinya language

(Continued)

UF = Used for; BT = Broader term; RT = Related term; SA = See also; NT = Narrower term

Oromo language   *(Continued)*
  BT Cushitic languages
      Kenya--Languages
  NT Boran dialect
      Qottu dialect

Oron (African people) *(May Subd Geog)*
  [DT 515.45.O74]
  UF Oro (African people)
      Oro Ukpaban (African people)
  BT Ethnology--Nigeria

Oru language
  USE Ijo language

Orungu (African people) *(May Subd Geog)*
  [DT 546.145.O]
  UF Ombeke (African people)
  BT Ethnology--Gabon
      Myene (African people)

Orungu language *(May Subd Geog)*
  [PL 8598.08]
  UF Sekiani language
      Shekiani language
  BT Bantu languages
      Gabon--Languages

Orunyarwanda language
  USE Kinyarwanda language

Oshikuanjame (African people)
  USE Kuanyama (African people)

Oshindonga language
  USE Ndonga language

Oshiwambo language
  USE Ndonga language

Osikuanyame (African people)
  USE Kuanyama (African people)

Oswidonga (African people)
  USE Kuanyama (African people)

Otetela (African people)
  USE Tetela (African people)

Otetela language
  USE Tetela language

Othan (African people)
  USE Uduk (African people)

Otji language
  USE Twi language

Otjiherero language
  USE Herero language

Oturkpo (African people)
  USE Idoma (African people)

Oturkpo dialect
  USE Idoma language

Ouala (African people)
  USE Wala (African people)

Ouénya (African people)
  USE Genya (African people)

Oulaf (African people)
  USE Wolof (African people)

Ouldémé (African people)
  USE Uldeme (African people)

Ouldémé language
  USE Uldeme language

Oulé (African people)
  USE LoWiili (African people)

Oule language
  USE Bwamu language

Ouobé (African people)
  USE Wobe (African people)

Ouobe language
  USE Wobe language

Ouolof language
  USE Wolof language

Ovaguanyama (African people)
  USE Kuanyama (African people)

Ovah (Malagasy people)
  USE Merina (Malagasy people)

Ovaherero (African people)
  USE Herero (African people)

Ovakuanyama (African people)
  USE Kuanyama (African people)

Ovambadyeru (African people)
  USE Mbandieru (African people)

(May Subd Geog) = Place names may follow the heading

Ovambanderu (African people)
  USE Mbandieru (African people)

Ovambo (African people) *(May Subd Geog)*
  [DT 611.45.0 (Angola : old class)]
  [DT 1308.083 (Angola : new class)]
  [DT 709.5.093 (Namibia : old class)]
  [DT 1558.083 (Namibia : new class)]
  UF Ambo (Angolan and Namibian people)
      Ovampo (African people)
  BT Bantu-speaking peoples
      Ethnology--Angola
      Ethnology--Namibia
  NT Kuanyama (African people)
      Ndonga (African people)
  --Material culture
  --Religion
      [BL 2480.077]

Ovambo language
  USE Kuanyama language
      Ndonga language

Ovampo (African people)
  USE Ovambo (African people)

Overberg (South Africa) *(Not Subd Geog)*

Ovimbali (African people)
  USE Mbundu (African people)

Ovimbundu (African people)
  USE Mbundu (African people)

Owegbe (Cult)
  USE Owegbe Society

Owegbe Society
  [BL 2480.08]
  UF Owegbe (Cult)
  BT Cults--Nigeria

Ownership
  USE Property

Ownership of slaves
  USE Slavery

Oya (Yoruba deity) *(Not Subd Geog)*
  [BL 2480.Y6]
  BT Goddesses, Yoruba

Oyo Empire *(Not Subd Geog)*
  [DT 515.45.Y67]
  BT Yoruba (African people)--History

P

Paarl, Mount (South Africa) *(Not Subd Geog)*
  UF Mount Paarl (South Africa)
      Paarlberg (South Africa)
  BT Mountains--South Africa

Paarlberg (South Africa)
  USE Paarl, Mount (South Africa)

Padang dialect *(May Subd Geog)*
  BT Dinka language
      Sudan--Languages

PADIS (Information retrieval system)
  [Z 699.4.P2]
  UF Pan-African Documentation and Information
System for Social and Economic Development
(Information retrieval system)
  BT Information storage and retrieval systems--
Africa

Padogo (African people)
  USE Paduko (African people)

Padogo language
  USE Paduko language

Padoko language
  USE Paduko language

Padokwa (African people)
  USE Paduko (African people)

Padokwa language
  USE Paduko language

Paduko (African people) *(May Subd Geog)*
  [DT 571.P]
  UF Mada (African people)
      Padogo (African people)
      Padokwa (African people)
      Podogo (African people)
      Podoko (African people)
      Podokwo (African people)
  BT Ethnology--Cameroon

Paduko language *(May Subd Geog)*
  [PL 8599.P]
  UF Padogo language
      Padoko language
      Padokwa language
      Podogo language
      Podoko language
      Podokwo language
  BT Cameroon--Languages   *(Continued)*

UF = Used for; BT = Broader term; RT = Related term; SA = See also; NT = Narrower term

Paduko language   *(Continued)*
  BT   Chadic languages

Pageview (Johannesburg, South Africa) *(Not Subd Geog)*
  UF   Johannesburg (South Africa). Pageview

Pahouin (West African people)
  USE   Fang (West African people)

Pahouin language
  USE   Fang language

Pahuin (West African people)
  USE   Fang (West African people)

Painters, Black *(May Subd Geog)*
  UF   Black painters

Painting *(May Subd Geog)*
  UF   Oil-painting
         Paintings
  NT   Watercolor painting

Painting, Black *(May Subd Geog)*
  UF   Black painting

Painting, Decorative
  USE   Decoration and ornament

Painting, Ethiopian *(May Subd Geog)*
  [ND 1086]
  UF   Ethiopian painting
--**European influences**
  BT   Europe--Civilization

Painting, Gabon *(May Subd Geog)*
  [ND 1099.G25]
  UF   Gabon painting

Painting, Mauritian *(May Subd Geog)*
  [ND 1099.5.M38]
  UF   Mauritian painting

Painting, South African *(May Subd Geog)*
  [ND 1092]
  UF   South African painting

Paintings
  USE   Painting

Pajade language
  USE   Badyaranke language

Pajadinca language
  USE   Badyaranke language

Payot (African people)
  USE   Suk (African people)

Paleoanthropology
  USE   Man, Prehistoric

Paleoethnography
  USE   Archaeology
         Man, Prehistoric

Palor language
  USE   Falor language

Pamue (West African people)
  USE   Fang (West African people)

Pamue language
  USE   Fang language

Pamunguup language
  USE   Bamougoun-Bamenjou language

Pan-African Documentation and Information System for Social and Economic Development (Information retrieval system)
  USE   PADIS (Information retrieval system)

Pan-Africanism
  UF   African relations
  BT   Africa--Politics and government
  RT   African cooperation
         Organization of African Unity

Pana (African people)
  USE   Mbum (African people)

Pangwa (African people) *(May Subd Geog)*
  [DT 443.3.W36]
  UF   Wanena (African people)
         Wapangwa (African people)
  BT   Bantu-speaking peoples
         Ethnology--Tanzania

Pangwa language *(May Subd Geog)*
  [PL 8599.P33]
  UF   ekiPangwa language
  BT   Bantu languages
         Tanzania--Languages

Pangwe (West African people)
  USE   Fang (West African people)

Pangwe language
  USE   Fang language

(May Subd Geog) = Place names may follow the heading

Panhame River (Zimbabwe and Mozambique)
USE Hunyani River (Zimbabwe and Mozambique)

Pani (African people)
USE Mbum (African people)

Paraguku (African people)
USE Baraguyu (African people)

Paraguyu (African people)
USE Baraguyu (African people)

Parc National Albert (Zaire)
USE Parc National des Virunga (Zaire)

Parc national de l'Akagera (Rwanda)
USE Parc national de la Kagera (Rwanda)

Parc national de la Kagera (Rwanda) (Not Subd Geog)
UF Akagera National Park (Rwanda)
Kagera National Park (Rwanda)
Parc national de l'Akagera (Rwanda)
BT National parks and reserves--Rwanda

Parc national de Saint-Floris (Central African Republic) (Not Subd Geog)
UF Parc national Saint-Floris (Central African Republic)
Saint Floris National Park (Central African Republic)
St. Floris National Park (Central African Republic)
BT National Parks and reserves--Central African Republic

Parc National des Virunga (Zaire) (Not Subd Geog)
UF Parc National Albert (Zaire)
Virunga, Parc National des (Zaire)
BT National parks and reserves--Zaire

Parc National du Banco (Ivory Coast) (Not Subd Geog)
UF Banco National Park (Ivory Coast)
BT Arboretums--Ivory Coast
Forest reserves--Ivory Coast
National parks and reserves--Ivory Coast
Parks--Ivory Coast

Parc national Saint Floris (Central African Republic)
USE Parc national de Saint-Floris (Central African Republic)

Pare (African people) (May Subd Geog)
[DT 443.3.P37]
UF Asu (African people)
Wapare (African people)
BT Bantu-speaking peoples
Ethnology--Tanzania

Pare language
USE Asu language

Pāri language (Sudan) (May Subd Geog)
[PL 8599.P35]
BT Nilotic languages
Sudan--Languages

Parks (May Subd Geog)
UF State parks
NT National parks and reserves
Ivory Coast
NT Parc National du Banco (Ivory Coast)
--Kenya
NT Nairobi National Park (Kenya)
Tsavo National Park (Kenya)
--Namibia
NT Etosha National Park (Namibia)
--South Africa
NT Kruger National Park (South Africa)

Parks, National
USE National parks and reserves

Parliamentary government
USE Representative government and representation

Partisans
USE Guerrillas

Pastimes
USE Games

Patani dialect (Nigeria)
USE Kolokuma dialect

Paxala language
USE Vagala language

Peaks
USE Mountains

Peasant art
USE Folk art

Pedagogy
USE Education

UF = Used for; BT = Broader term; RT = Related term; SA = See also; NT = Narrower term

Pedi (African people) *(May Subd Geog)*
  [DT 797 (Botswana : old class)]
  [DT 2458.P44 (Botswana : new class)]
  [DT 764.P4 (South Africa : old class)]
  [DT 1768.P44 (South Africa : new class)]
  [DT 962.42 (Zimbabwe : old class)]
  [DT 2913.P44 (Zimbabwe : new class)]
  UF Bapedi (African people)
      Northern Sotho (African people)
      Peli (African people)
      Sepedi (African people)
      Sotho, Northern (African people)
      Transvaal Sotho (African people)
  BT Bantu-speaking peoples
      Ethnology--Africa, Southern
      Ethnology--Botswana
      Ethnology--South Africa
      Ethnology--Zimbabwe
      Sotho (African people)

Pedi language
  USE Northern Sotho language

Peleng (Lobatse, Botswana) *(Not Subd Geog)*
  UF Lobatse (Botswana). Peleng

Peli (African people)
  USE Pedi (African people)

Pende (African people) *(May Subd Geog)*
  [DT 650.P46]
  UF Apende (African people)
      Bapende (African people)
      Pindi (African people)
      Tupende (African people)
  BT Bantu-speaking peoples
      Ethnology--Zaire
 --Masks
  BT Masks--Zaire

Pende art
  USE Art, Pende

Pende language *(May Subd Geog)*
  [PL 8403]
  UF Gipende language
      Kipende language
      Pindi language (Pende)
      Pinji language
  BT Kongo language
      Zaire--Languages

Peninsulas *(May Subd Geog)*
  BT Landforms
 --Kenya
  NT Mbita Point (Kenya)

 --South Africa
  NT Cape of Good Hope (South Africa : Cape)

People's Republic of Angola
  USE Angola

People's Republic of Benin
  USE Benin

People's Republic of Mozambique
  USE Mozambique

Performing arts *(May Subd Geog)*
  UF Show business
  BT Arts
  NT Blacks in the performing arts
      Theater

Periodicals
  Here are entered works on the periodicals of the world.
  Works on periodicals in a specific language, or in a
  specific country or larger area, are entered under the
  adjectival form of the language or area, e.g. Afrikaans
  periodicals; Nigerian periodicals
  UF Magazines
  BT Mass media
  RT Newspapers
      Press
  NT Chapbooks

Periodicals, African
  USE African periodicals

Periodicals, Afrikaans
  USE Afrikaans periodicals

Periodicals, Ghanaian
  USE Ghanaian periodicals

Periodicals, Kenyan
  USE Kenyan periodicals

Periodicals, Malagasy
  USE Malagasy periodicals

Periodicals, Mozambican
  USE Mozambican periodicals

Periodicals, Nigerian
  USE Nigerian periodicals

Periodicals, South African
  USE South African periodicals

Periodicals, Southern African
  USE Southern African periodicals

Periodicals, Tanzanian
  USE Tanzanian periodicals

Periodicals, Togolese
  USE Togolese periodicals

Periodicals, Zairian
  USE Zairian periodicals

Periodicals, Zambian
  USE Zambian periodicals

Periodicals, Zimbabwean
  USE Zimbabwean periodicals

Poro language *(May Subd Geog)*
  [PL 8599.P47]
  UF Fero language
      Filiya language
      Pipero language
  BT Bolewa languages
      Nigeria--Languages

Persons, Banned (South Africa)
  USE Banned persons (South Africa)

Petaga (Burkina Faso)
  USE Pétéga (Burkina Faso)

Pétéga (Burkina Faso) *(Not Subd Geog)*
  UF Petaga (Burkina Faso)

Peul (African people)
  USE Fula (African people)

Peul language
  USE Fula language

Peulh (African people)
  USE Fula (African people)

Phalaborwa (African people) *(May Subd Geog)*
  [DT 764.P : old class]
  [DT 1768.P53 : new class]
  BT Bantu-speaking peoples
      Ethnology--South Africa

Philology
  *Here are entered general works on language and
  literature treated together.*
    SA *specific branches of philology and literature,
  e.g. Soga philology; Somali literature*
    NT Language and languages
        Literature

Philology, African
  USE African philology

Philology, Afrikaans
  USE Afrikaans philology

Philology, Bantu
  USE Bantu philology

Philology, Ethiopic
  USE Ethiopic philology

Philology, Igbo
  USE Igbo philology

Philology, Northern Sotho
  USE Northern Sotho philology

Philology, Sogo
  USE Sogo philology

Philology, Somali
  USE Somali philology

Philology, Swahili
  USE Swahili philology

Philology, Yoruba
  USE Yoruba philology

Philology, Zairian
  USE Zairian philology

Philosophy *(May Subd Geog)*
  NT Ethics
      Ethnophilosophy

Philosophy, African
  [B 5300-B 5320]
  UF African philosophy

Philosophy, Baganda
  [DT 433.245.G35]
  UF Baganda philosophy
      Ganda philosophy
      Philosophy, Ganda
  BT Ethnophilosophy--Uganda

Philosophy, Bantu
  [DT 16.B2]
  UF Bantu philosophy

Philosophy, Dogon
  [DT 551.45.D64 (Mali)]
  [DT 530.5.D64 (West Africa)]
  UF Dogon philosophy   *(Continued)*

UF = Used for; BT = Broader term; RT = Related term; SA = See also; NT = Narrower term

Philosophy, Dogon   *(Continued)*
   BT Ethnophilosophy--Africa, French-
speaking West
       Ethnophilosophy--Mali

Philosophy, Ethiopian
   [B 5404-B 5409]
   UF Ethiopian philosophy

Philosophy, Fali
   [DT 571.F34]
   UF Fali philosophy
   BT Ethnophilosophy--Cameroon

Philosophy, Folk
   USE Ethnophilosophy

Philosophy, Ganda
   USE Philosophy, Baganda

Philosophy, Gurma
   [DT 555.45.G85]
   UF Gurma philosophy
   BT Ethnophilosophy--Burkina Faso

Philosophy, Igbo
   [DT 515.45.I33]
   UF Igbo philosophy
   BT Ethnophilosophy--Nigeria

Philosophy, Kaguru
   [DT 433.3.K33]
   UF Kaguru philosophy
   BT Ethnophilosophy--Tanzania

Philosophy, Karanga
   [DT 962.42 : old class]
   [DT 2913.K38 : new class]
   UF Karanga philosophy
   BT Ethnophilosophy--Zimbabwe

Philosophy, Kgaga
   [DT 764.K42 : old class]
   [DT 1768.K : new class]
   UF Kgaga philosophy
   BT Ethnophilosophy--South Africa

Philosophy, Lobi
   [DT 555.45.L63]
   UF Lobi philosophy
   BT Ethnophilosophy--Burkina Faso

Philosophy, Luba
   [DT 650.L8]
   UF Luba philosophy
   BT Ethnophilosophy--Zaire

Philosophy, Malagasy
   [B 5460-B 5464]
   UF Malagasy philosophy

Philosophy, Moral
   USE Ethics

Philosophy, Nika
   [DT 433.545.N55 (Kenya)]
   UF Nika philosophy
   BT Ethnophilosophy--Kenya
       Ethnophilosophy--Tanzania
       Ethnophilosophjy--Zimbabwe

Philosophy, Primitive
   USE Ethnophilosophy

Philosophy, Yanzi
   [DT 650.Y3]
   UF Yanzi philosophy
   BT Ethnophilosophy--Zaire

Philosophy, Yoruba
   [DT 515.45.Y67 (Nigeria)]
   [DT 474.6.Y67 (West Africa)]
   UF Yoruba philosophy
   BT Ethnophilosophy--Africa, West
       Ethnophilosophy--Benin
       Ethnophilosophy--Nigeria

Philosophy, Zambian
   [B 5449.Z33]
   UF Zambian philosophy

Philosophy, Zulu
   [DT 878.Z9 : old class]
   [DT 1768.Z95 : new class]
   UF Zulu philosophy
   BT Ethnophilosophy--South Africa

Phoka (African people) *(May Subd Geog)*
   [DT 864 : old class]
   [DT 3192.P : new class]
   UF Poka (African people)
   BT Ethnology--Malawi
       Tumbuka (African people)

Pictorial wit and humor
   USE Wit and humor, Pictorial

Picture dictionaries
   UF Dictionaries, Picture
       Word books

(May Subd Geog) = Place names may follow the heading

Picture dictionaries, Tswana *(May Subd Geog)*
  [PL 8747.4]
  UF Tswana picture dictionaries
      Tswana language--Dictionaries

Pictures, Humorous
  USE Wit and humor, Pictorial

Pidgeon English
  USE Pidgin English

Pidgeon languages
  USE Pidgin languages

Pidgin English *(May Subd Geog)*
  [PM 7891]
  UF Pidgeon English
      Pigeon English
  BT Pidgin languages
--**Cameroon**
  [PM 7891.Z9C3]
--**Nigeria**
  [PM 7891.Z9N6]

Pidgin Kaffir
  USE Fanakalo

Pidgin languages *(May Subd Geog)*
  [PM 7801-PM 7895]
  Here are entered works discussing lingua francas
which are native to none of those using them and are
characterized by a simplified grammar and often mixed
vocabulary. Works discussing auxiliary, sometimes
mixed, languages used among groups having no other
languages in common are entered under the heading
Lingua francas. Works discussing pidgin languages
that have become established as the native languages of
a speech community are entered under the heading
Creole dialects.
  UF Contact vernaculars
      Hybrid languages
      Jargons
      Pidgeon languages
      Pigeon languages
  BT Lingua francas
  NT Creole dialects
      Pidgin English

Pigeon English
  USE Pidgin English

Pigeon languages
  USE Pidgin languages

Pigmentation
  USE Color of man

Pigmies
  USE Pygmies

Pilote forestier, Projet
  USE Projet pilote forestier

Pindi (African people)
  USE Pende (African people)

Pindi language (Kwese)
  USE Kwese language

Pindi language (Pende)
  USE Pende language

Pinji language
  USE Pende language

Pioneers *(May Subd Geog)*
--**South Africa**
  NT British settlers of 1820 (South Africa)

Pipero language
  USE Pero language

Piton de la Fournaise (Réunion)
  USE Fournaise, Piton de la (Réunion)

Plaine de Marovoay (Madagascar)
  USE Marovoay Plain (Madagascar)

Plains *(May Subd Geog)*
  BT Landforms
  NT Savannas
--**Ethiopia**
  NT Mazega (Ethiopia)
--**Ghana**
  NT Accra Plains (Ghana)
--**Madagascar**
  NT Marovoay Plain (Madagascar)
--**Mali**
  NT Mema Plain (Mali)
--**Niger**
  NT Ténéré (Niger)
--**South Africa**
  NT Richtersveld (South Africa)
--**Sudan**
  NT Butana (Sudan)
--**Tanzania**
  NT North Mkata Plain (Tanzania)
      Serengeti Plain (Tanzania)

Plains Suk (African people)
  USE Suk (African people)

UF = Used for; BT = Broader term; RT = Related term; SA = See also; NT = Narrower term

Planned parenthood
  USE Birth control

Plantations *(May Subd Geog)*
  BT Farms
 --Réunion
  NT Beauregard (Réunion)
 --Zambia
  NT Nakambala Sugar Estates (Zambia)

Plateau Bantoid languages
  USE Grasslands Bantu languages

Plateau Benue-Congo languages
  USE Plateau languages (Nigeria)

Plateau languages (Nigeria) *(May Subd Geog)*
  [PL 8600.P55]
  UF Plateau Benue-Congo languages
  BT Benue-Congo languages
      Nigeria--Languages
  NT Birom language
      Kaje language
      Katab language
      Migili language

Plateau Tongo (Zambesi people)
  USE Tonga (Zambesi people)

Plateaus *(May Subd Geog)*
  UF Tablelands
  BT Mountains
 --Kenya
  NT Kenya Highlands (Kenya)
 --Mali
  NT Kaarta (Mali)
 --Nigeria
  NT Jos Plateau (Nigeria)
 --South Africa
  NT Great Karroo (South Africa)
      Northern Karroo (South Africa)
 --Tanzania
  NT Southern Highlands (Tanzania)

Plays
  USE Drama

Plays, College
  USE College and school drama

Plays, One-act
  USE One-act plays

Plays for children
  USE Children's plays

Podogo (African people)
  USE Paduko (African people)

Podogo language
  USE Paduko language

Podoko (African people)
  USE Paduko (African people)

Podoko language
  USE Paduko language

Podokwo (African people)
  USE Paduko (African people)

Padokwo language
  USE Paduko language

Poems
  USE Poetry

Poetry
  UF Poems
  BT Literature
  SA *headings for poetry qualified by linguistic,
national or regional terms, e.g. Igbo poetry; Zambian
poetry; West African poetry*
  NT Children's poetry
      College verse
      Epic poetry
      Folk poetry
      Laudatory poetry
      Love poetry
      Nursery rhymes
      Political poetry
      Songs
 --Black authors
  [PN 1025]
  UF Black poetry

Poetry, Epic
  USE Epic poetry

Poetry, Folk
  USE Folk poetry

Poetry, Heroic
  USE Epic poetry

Poetry, Islamic
  USE Islamic poetry

Poetry, Laudatory
  USE Laudatory poetry

(May Subd Geog) = Place names may follow the heading

Poetry, Love
USE Love poetry

Poetry, Muslim
USE Islamic poetry

Poetry, Political
USE Political poetry

Poetry, Protest
USE Protest poetry

Poetry, Revolutionary
USE Revolutionary poetry

Poetry for children
USE Children's poetry
Nursery rhymes

Poets
BT Authors

Poets, Black (May Subd Geog)
UF Black poets

Poets, Nigerian (May Subd Geog)
UF Nigerian poets

Poets, South African (May Subd Geog)
UF South African poets

Poets, Zairian (May Subd Geog)
UF Zairian poets

Poets, Zimbabwean (May Subd Geog)
UF Zimbabwean poets

Pogoro (African people) (May Subd Geog)
[DT 443.3.P]
UF Wapogoro (African people)
BT Bantu-speaking peoples
Ethnology--Tanzania

Pogoro language (May Subd Geog)
[PL 8601]
BT Bantu languages
Tanzania--Languages

Points (Coasts)
USE Capes (Coasts)

Poka (African people)
USE Phoka (African people)

Pokomo (African people) (May Subd Geog)
[DT 433.545.P65]
UF Wapokomo (African people)
BT Bantu-speaking peoples
Ethnology--Kenya

Pokot (African people)
USE Suk (African people)

Pokot language
USE Suk language

Police (May Subd Geog)
UF Gendarmes
Law enforcement officers

Police, Black (May Subd Geog)
UF Black police
--South Africa
[HV 8272]

Political behavior
USE subdivision Politics and government under the
names of countries, cities, etc., and under ethnic groups,
e.g., Mauritiana--Politics and government; Akan
(African people)--Politics and government

Political culture (May Subd Geog)
Africa
-- --American influences
BT United States--Civilization

Political economy
USE Economics

Political poetry
UF Poetry, Political
BT Poetry
NT Revolutionary poetry

Political poetry, Mozambican (Portuguese) (May Subd
Geog)
[PQ 9936-PQ 9936.5 (Collections)]
UF Mozambican political poetry (Portuguese)
BT Mozambican poetry (Portuguese)

Political posters
UF Campaign posters
Posters, Political

Political posters, African (May Subd Geog)
UF African political posters

Political posters, Ethiopian (May Subd Geog)
UF Ethiopian political posters

UF = Used for; BT = Broader term; RT = Related term; SA = See also; NT = Narrower term

Political posters, Mozambican *(May Subd Geog)*
UF Mozambican political posters

Political prisoners *(May Subd Geog)*
UF Prisoners, Political
Prisoners of conscience
--South Africa
[HV 9850.5]
NT Banned persons (South Africa)

Political representation
USE Representative government and
representation

Political systems
SEE Communism
One party systems
Representative government and
representation
Socialism

Political violence
USE Coups d'état
Revolutions
Riots
Terrorism

Ponda (African people)
USE Luchazi (African people)

Ponda language
USE Lucazi language

Pondo (African people) *(May Subd Geog)*
[DT 764.P6 : old class]
[DT 1768.P66 : new class]
UF Amapondo (African people)
Mpondo (African people)
BT Bantu-speaking peoples
Ethnology--South Africa

Pondoland (South Africa) *(Not Subd Geog)*
[DT 846.P6 : old class]
[DT 2400.P66 : new class]

Pongo (African people)
USE Mpongwe (African people)

Pongwe language
USE Mpongwe language

Poni language
USE Baoulé language

Popo (African people)
USE Mina (African people)

Popo language
USE Ewe language

Popular art
USE Folk art

Popular arts
USE Popular culture

Popular culture *(Not Subd Geog)*
Here are entered works on literature, art, music,
motion pictures, etc. produced for a mass audience.
UF Culture, Popular
Mass culture
Popular arts
BT Communication
SA subdivision Popular culture under names of
regions, countries, cities, etc., e.g. Africa, West--
Popular culture

Popular music *(May Subd Geog)*
Here are entered works on popular vocal music and
collections containing both popular instrumental and vocal
music.
UF Music, Popular
Popular songs
Popular vocal music
Songs, Popular
Vocal music, Popular
BT Music
Songs
--To 1901
--1901-1910
--1911-1920
--1921-1930
--1931-1940
--1941-1950
--1951-1960
--1961-1970
--1971-1980
--1981-1990
--1991-
--Africa, West
NT Highlife (Music)
--Ghana
[ML 3503.G4]
NT Konkoma
--Great Britain
-- --African influences
[ML 3492]
BT Africa--Civilization
--Nigeria
[ML 3503.N]
NT Juju music

(May Subd Geog) = Place names may follow the heading

Popular songs
  USE Popular music

Popular vocal music
  USE Popular music

Population *(Not Subd Geog)*
  UF Populations, Human
  BT Economics
  SA *subdivision* Population *under names of
countries, cities, etc., e.g. Equatorial Guinea--
Population
  NT Census

Population control
  USE Birth control

Populations, Human
  USE Population

Porto Grande (Cape Verde) *(Not Subd Geog)*
  UF Pôrto-Grande de Sao Vicente (Cape
Verde)
  BT Bays--Cape Verde

Pôrto-Grande de Sao Vicente (Cape Verde)
  USE Porto Grande (Cape Verde)

Portrait sculpture *(May Subd Geog)*
  BT Sculpture

Portrait sculpture, African *(May Subd Geog)*
  [NB 1305.A]
  UF African portrait sculpture
      Sculpture, African portrait

Portraits *(May Subd Geog)*
  BT Art

Portraits, African *(May Subd Geog)*
  [N 7615.2-N 7615.3]
  UF African portraits

Portugal *(Not Subd Geog)*
 --Civilization
  NT Africa--Civilization--Portuguese
influences
      Angola--Civilization--Portuguese
influences
      Art, African--Portuguese influences
 --Colonies
  BT Colonies
 -- --Administration
  UF Portugal--Colonies--Politics and
government

-- --**Boundaries** *(May Subd Geog)*
-- --**Commerce** *(May Subd Geog)*
-- --**Constitutional history**
-- --**Constitutional law**
-- --**Defenses**
-- --**Description and travel**
-- --**Discovery and exploration**
-- --**Economic conditions**
-- --**Economic policy**
-- --**Emigration and immigration**
-- --**Geography** *(Not Subd Geog)*
-- --**History**
-- --**Industries**
-- --**Manufactures**
-- --**Native races**
  USE Indigenous peoples--Portugal--Colonies
-- --**Officials and employees**
-- --**Politics and government**
  USE Portugal--Colonies--Administration
-- --**Population**
-- --**Public lands**
-- --**Public works**
-- --**Race relations**
-- --**Religion**
-- --**Religious life and customs**
-- --**Rural conditions**
-- --**Social conditions**
-- --**Social life and customs**
   --**Social policy**
-- --**Africa**

Portuguese Africa
  USE Africa, Portuguese-speaking

Portuguese Creole languages
  USE Creole dialects, Portuguese

Portuguese fiction *(May Subd Geog)*
  BT Portuguese literature
 --African authors
  USE African fiction (Portuguese)

Portuguese Guinea
  USE Guinea-Bissau

Portuguese Invasion of Guinea, 1970
  USE Guinea--History--Portuguese Invasion, 1970

Portuguese literature *(May Subd Geog)*
  NT Portuguese fiction
      Portuguese poetry
 --African authors
  USE African literature (Portuguese)
 --Angolan authors
  USE Angolan literature (Portuguese)
                                          (Continued)

UF = Used for; BT = Broader term; RT = Related term; SA = See also; NT = Narrower term

Portuguese literature *(Continued)*
--Black authors
  [PQ 9034.B53 (History)]
  UF Black literature (Portuguese)
--Mozambican authors
  USE Mozambican literature (Portuguese)
--Sao Tomean authors
  USE Sao Tomean literature

Portuguese Mina
  USE Ghana--History--Portuguese rule, 1469-
1637

Portuguese poetry *(May Subd Geog)*
  BT Portuguese literature
--African authors
  USE African poetry (Portuguese)
--Angolan authors
  USE Angolan poetry (Portuguese)
--Black authors
  [PQ 9034.B53 (History)]
  UF Black poetry (Portuguese)
--Mozambican authors
  USE Mozambican poetry (Portuguese)
--Sao Tomean authors
  USE Sao Tomean poetry

Portuguese-speaking Africa
  USE Africa, Portuguese-speaking

Portuguese West Africa
  USE Angola

Posters, Political
  USE Political posters

Pottery *(May Subd Geog)*
  UF Ceramics (Art)
      Chinaware
      Crockery
      Earthenware

Pottery, African *(May Subd Geog)*
  [NK 3700-NK 4695]
  UF African pottery

Pottery, Akan *(May Subd Geog)*
  [NK 4177.6.G52A]
  UF Akan pottery

Pottery, Ashanti *(May Subd Geog)*
  [NK 4177.6.G52A]
  UF Ashanti pottery

Pottery, Dogon *(May Subd Geog)*
  [NK 4177.6.M32D]
  UF Dogon pottery

Pottery, Hausa *(May Subd Geog)*
  [NK 4177.6.N52H]
  UF Hausa pottery

Pottery, Malagasay *(May Subd Geog)*
  [NK 4176.9.M3]
  UF Malagasy pottery

Pottery, Nubian *(May Subd Geog)*
  [NK 4174.75]
  UF Nubian pottery

Pottery, Primitive *(May Subd Geog)*
  UF Primitive pottery
  --Ghana
  [NK 4177.6.G5]

Pottery, Sao *(May Subd Geog)*
  [NK 4177.6.C52S]
  UF Sao pottery

Pottery, South African *(May Subd Geog)*
  [NK 4178.6.S6]
  UF South African pottery

Poubara, Chute de (Gabon) *(Not Subd Geog)*
  UF Chute de Poubara (Gabon)
      Chute Foulémé (Gabon)
      Chutes de Poubara (Gabon)
      Poubara Foulémé (Gabon)
  BT Ogooué River (Gabon)
      Waterfalls-Gabon

Poubara Foulémé (Gabon)
  USE Poubara, Chute de (Gabon)

Poul language
  USE Fula language

Poular dialect
  USE Pular dialect

Pounou language
  USE Punu language

Power, Black
  USE Black power

Praise poems
  USE Laudatory poetry

(May Subd Geog) = Place names may follow the heading

Praslin Island (Seychelles) *(Not Subd Geog)*
  [DT 469.S49P]
  BT Islands--Seychelles
      Seychelles

Prayer (Bantu religion)
  USE Bantu-speaking peoples--Religion

Prehistoric antiquities
  USE Archaeology
      Man, Prehistoric

Prehistoric man
  USE Man, Prehistoric

Prehistory
  USE Archaeology
      Man, Prehistoric

Premiers
  USE Prime ministers

Preserves, Forest
  USE Forest reserves

Preserves, Game
  USE Game reserves

Press *(May Subd Geog)*
  RT Newspapers
      Periodicals
  NT Blacks in the press
      Race relations and the press
      Racism in the press
      Segregation and the press

Press and race relations
  USE Race relations and the press

Press and segregation
  USE Segregation and the press

Prime ministers *(May Subd Geog)*
  UF Chancellors (Prime ministers)
      Premiers
 --South Africa
 -- --Dwellings
  NT Groote Schuur (Cape Town, South
Africa)

Primitive art
  USE Art, Primitive

Primitive arts
  USE Arts, Primitive

Primitive literature
  USE Folk literature

Primitive medicine
  USE Medicine, Primitive

Primitive philosophy
  USE Ethnophilosophy

Primitive pottery
  USE Pottery, Primitive

Primitive religion
  USE Religion, Primitive

Primitive sculpture
  USE Sculpture, Primitive

Prints *(May Subd Geog)*
  BT Art

Prints, Black *(May Subd Geog)*
  UF Black prints
 --South Africa
  [NE 788.6.S6]

Prints, South African *(May Subd Geog)*
  [NE 788.6.S6]
  UF South African prints

Prisoners, Political
  USE Political prisoners

Prisoners of conscience
  USE Political prisoners

Prisoners' writings *(May Subd Geog)*
  BT Literature

Prisoners' writings, Kenyan *(May Subd Geog)*
  UF Kenyan prisoners' writings
  BT Kenyan literature

Prisons and race relations *(May Subd Geog)*
  UF Race relations and prisons
  BT Race relations

Programme de recherches interdisciplinaire
français sur les acridiens du Sahel
  [SB 945.L7]
  BT Locusts--Control--Research--Burkina Faso
      Locusts--Control--Research--Niger

Project MARC
  USE MARC System

UF = Used for; BT = Broader term; RT = Related term; SA = See also; NT = Narrower term

Projects, Forestry
USE Forestry projects

Projet pilote forestier
[SD 242.R95]
UF Pilote forestier, Projet
BT Agricultural assistance, Swiss--Rwanda
Forestry projects--Rwanda

Promontories (Coasts)
USE Capes (Coasts)

Propaganda
BT Communication

Propaganda, South African *(May Subd Geog)*
UF South African propaganda

Propaganda, Zimbabwean *(May Subd Geog)*
UF Zimbabwean propaganda

Property *(May Subd Geog)*
UF Ownership
BT Economics
NT Real property

Property, Real
USE Real property

Property (Ewe law)
BT Law, Ewe

Property (Igbo law)
BT Law, Igbo

Property (Ngoni law)
BT Law, Ngoni

Prophetistic movements
USE Nativistic movements

Protest literature *(May Subd Geog)*
UF Literature, Protest
BT Literature
NT Protest poetry

Protest literature, African (English) *(May Subd Geog)*
[PR 9340-PR 9348]
UF African protest literature (English)
BT African literature (English)
NT Protest literature, South African
(English)

Protest literature, South African (English) *(May Subd Geog)*
[PR 9355.5.P (History)]
[PR 9364.52.P (Collections)]
UF South African protest literature (English)
BT Protest literature, African (English)
South African literature (English)
NT Protest poetry, South African (English)

Protest movements
USE Civil rights movements

Protest poetry *(May Subd Geog)*
UF Poetry, Protest
BT Protest literature
Revolutionary poetry

Protest poetry, South African (English) *(May Subd Geog)*
[PR 9360.9.P (History)]
[PR 9365.85.P76 (Collections)]
UF South Africa protest poetry (English)
BT Protest literature, South African (English)
South Africa poetry (English)

Protest poetry, Xhosa *(May Subd Geog)*
[PL 8795.5 (History)]
[PL 8795.7 (Collections)]
UF Xhosa protest poetry
BT Xhosa poetry

Proto-Afroasiatic language
[PJ 991-PJ 995]
BT Afroasiatic languages

Proto-Bantu language
[PL 8025]
BT Bantu languages

Proto-East-Cushitic language
[PJ 2463]
BT Cushitic languages

Proverbs
UF Adages
Sayings
BT Folk literature

Proverbs, Abidji *(May Subd Geog)*
[PN 6519.A24]
UF Abidji proverbs

Proverbs, African *(May Subd Geog)*
[PN 6519.A6]
UF African proverbs
Proverbs, Black--Africa

(May Subd Geog) = Place names may follow the heading

Proverbs, Akan *(May Subd Geog)*
  [PN 6519.A625]
  UF Akan proverbs

Proverbs, Asu *(May Subd Geog)*
  [PN 6519.A87]
  UF Asu proverbs

Proverbs, Bambara *(May Subd Geog)*
  [PN 6519.B3]
  UF Bambara proverbs

Proverbs, Bamum *(May Subd Geog)*
  [PN 6519.B33]
  UF Bamum proverbs

Proverbs, Bantu *(May Subd Geog)*
  [PN 6519.B33]
  UF Bantu proverbs

Proverbs, Baoulé *(May Subd Geog)*
  [PN 6519.B34]
  UF Baoulé proverbs

Proverbs, Bati *(May Subd Geog)*
  [PN 6519.B375]
  UF Bati proverbs

Proverbs, Bemba *(May Subd Geog)*
  [PN 6519.B4]
  UF Bemba proverbs

Proverbs, Bembe (Congo (Brazzaville)) *(May Subd Geog)*
  [PN 6519.B]
  UF Bembe proverbs (Congo (Brazzaville))

Proverbs, Benin *(May Subd Geog)*
  [PN 6519.B]
  UF Benin proverbs

Proverbs, Black *(May Subd Geog)*
  [PN 6519.B]
  UF Black proverbs
 --Africa
  USE Proverbs, African

Proverbs, Chewa *(May Subd Geog)*
  [PN 6519.C47]
  UF Chewa proverbs

Proverbs, Congo (Brazzaville) *(May Subd Geog)*
  [PN 6519.C62]
  UF Congo (Brazzaville) proverbs

Proverbs, Creole *(May Subd Geog)*
  [PN 6519.C8]
  UF Creole proverbs
 --Réunion

Proverbs, Duala *(May Subd Geog)*
  [PN 6519.D8]
  UF Duala proverbs

Proverbs, Efik *(May Subd Geog)*
  [PN 6519.E33]
  UF Efik proverbs

Proverbs, Ewe *(May Subd Geog)*
  [PN 6519.E9]
  UF Ewe proverbs

Proverbs, Ewondo *(May Subd Geog)*
  [PN 6519.E96]
  UF Ewondo proverbs

Proverbs, Fon *(May Subd Geog)*
  [PN 6519.F]
  UF Fon proverbs

Proverbs, Fula *(May Subd Geog)*
  [PN 6519.F8]
  UF Fula proverbs

Proverbs, Gambai *(May Subd Geog)*
  [PN 6519.G23]
  UF Gambai proverbs

Proverbs, Ganda *(May Subd Geog)*
  [PN 6519.G25]
  UF Ganda proverbs

Proverbs, Igbo *(May Subd Geog)*
  [PN 6519.I33]
  UF Igbo proverbs

Proverbs, Ikwere *(May Subd Geog)*
  [PN 6519.I35]
  UF Ikwere proverbs

Proverbs, Ivory Coast *(May Subd Geog)*
  [PN 6519.I85]
  UF Ivory Coast proverbs

Proverbs, Kenga *(May Subd Geog)*
  [PN 6519.K44]
  UF Kenga proverbs

Proverbs, Kimbundu *(May Subd Geog)*
  [PN 6519.K55]
  UF Kimbundu proverbs

UF = Used for; BT = Broader term; RT = Related term; SA = See also; NT = Narrower term

Proverbs, Kinyarwanda *(May Subd Geog)*
  [PN 6519.R8]
  UF Kinyarwanda proverbs

Proverbs, Kongo *(May Subd Geog)*
  [PN 6519.K59]
  UF Kongo proverbs

Proverbs, Krio *(May Subd Geog)*
  [PN 6519.K75]
  UF Krio proverbs

Proverbs, Kuanyama *(May Subd Geog)*
  [PN 6519.K8]
  UF Kuanyana proverbs

Proverbs, Kukwa *(May Subd Geog)*
  [PN 6519.K83]
  UF Kukwa proverbs

Proverbs, Kwiri *(May Subd Geog)*
  [PN 6519.K]
  UF Kwiri proverbs

Proverbs, Lingala *(May Subd Geog)*
  [PN 6519.L]
  UF Lingala proverbs

Proverbs, Luba-Lulua *(May Subd Geog)*
  [PN 6519.L]
  UF Luba-Lulua proverbs

Proverbs, Luyia *(May Subd Geog)*
  [PN 6519.L]
  UF Luyia proverbs

Proverbs, Majingai *(May Subd Geog)*
  [PN 6519.M22]
  UF Majingai proverbs

Proverbs, Makua *(May Subd Geog)*
  [PN 6519.M23]
  UF Makua proverbs

Proverbs, Malagasy *(May Subd Geog)*
  [PN 6519.M24]
  UF Malagasy proverbs

Mamara proverbs
  USE Proverbs, Minianka

Proverbs, Mampruli *(May Subd Geog)*
  [PN 6519.M29]
  UF Mampruli proverbs

Proverbs, Mandingo *(May Subd Geog)*
  [PN 6519.M316]
  UF Mandingo proverbs

Proverbs, Mbai (Moissala) *(May Subd Geog)*
  [PN 6519.M39]
  UF Mbai proverbs (Moissala)

Proverbs, Medumba *(May Subd Geog)*
  [PN 6519.M44]
  UF Medumba proverbs

Proverbs, Mina *(May Subd Geog)*
  [PN 6519.M54]
  UF Mina proverbs

Proverbs, Minianka *(May Subd Geog)*
  [PN 6519.M55]
  UF Mamara proverbs
      Minianka proverbs
      Proverbs, Mamara

Proverbs, Moba *(May Subd Geog)*
  [PN 6519.M57]
  UF Moba proverbs

Proverbs, Moré *(May Subd Geog)*
  [PN 6519.M64]
  UF Moré proverbs

Proverbs, Mossi *(May Subd Geog)*
  [PN 6519.M]
  UF Mossi proverbs

Proverbs, Ndebele (Zimbabwe) *(May Subd Geog)*
  [PN 6519.N38]
  UF Ndebele proverbs (Zimbabwe)

Proverbs, Rundi *(May Subd Geog)*
  [PN 6519.R84]
  UF Rundi proverbs

Proverbs, Serer *(May Subd Geog)*
  [PN 6519.S38]
  UF Serer proverbs

Proverbs, Shona *(May Subd Geog)*
  [PN 6519.S45]
  UF Shona proverbs

Proverbs, Somali *(May Subd Geog)*
  [PN 6519.S58]
  UF Somali proverbs

(May Subd Geog) = Place names may follow the heading

Proverbs, Sukuma *(May Subd Geog)*
  [PN 6519.S]
  UF Sukuma proverbs

Proverbs, Swahili *(May Subd Geog)*
  [PN 6519.S9]
  UF Swahili proverbs

Proverbs, Tetela *(May Subd Geog)*
  [PN 6519.T]
  UF Tetela proverbs

Proverbs, Tigrinya *(May Subd Geog)*
  [PN 6519.T]
  UF Tigrinya proverbs

Proverbs, Tobote *(May Subd Geog)*
  [PN 6519.T58]
  UF Tobote proverbs

Proverbs, Twi *(May Subd Geog)*
  [PN 6519.T]
  UF Twi proverbs

Proverbs, Umbundu *(May Subd Geog)*
  [PN 6519.U52]
  UF Umbundu proverbs

Proverbs, Wobe *(May Subd Geog)*
  [PN 6519.W62]
  UF Wobe proverbs

Proverbs, Yaka (Zaire and Angola) *(May Subd Geog)*
  [PN 6519.Y19]
  UF Yaka proverbs (Zaire and Angola)

Proverbs, Yoruba *(May Subd Geog)*
  [PN 6519.Y6]
  UF Yoruba proverbs

Psychological anthropology
  USE Ethnopsychology

Psychology, Cross-cultural
  USE Ethnopsychology

Psychology, Ethnic
  USE Ethnopsychology

Psychology, Folk
  USE Ethnopsychology

Psychology, National
  USE Ethnopsychology
      National characteristics

Psychology, Racial
  USE Ethnopsychology

Puberty rites *(May Subd Geog)*
  BT Initiation rites
      Rites and ceremonies
      Sex customs
 --Ghana
 --Zambia

Public buildings *(May Subd Geog)*
  UF Buildings, Public
      Government buildings
 --Nigeria
  NT Republic Building (Lagos, Nigeria)

Public documents
  USE Government publications

Public employee strikes
  USE Strikes and lockouts--Civil service

Public employees
  USE Civil service

Public health, Tropical
  USE Tropical medicine

Public sector strikes
  USE Strikes and lockouts--Civil service

Public service (Civil service)
  USE Civil service

Public worker strikes
  USE Strikes and lockouts--Civil service

Puku (African people)
  USE Tanga (African people)

Pulaar dialect
  USE Pular dialect

Pular dialect *(May Subd Geog)*
  [PL 8184.Z9P85]
  UF Haalpulaar dialect
      Poular dialect
      Pulaar dialect
  BT Fula language
      Gambia--Languages
      Mauritania--Languages
      Senegal--Languages

Pular folk literature
  USE Folk literature, Pular

UF = Used for; BT = Broader term; RT = Related term; SA = See also; NT = Narrower term

Pular literature *(May Subd Geog)*
  [PL 8184.Z9P85]
  BT Gambian literature
      Mauritanian literature
      Senegalese literature
  NT Folk literature, Pular

Punt Region *(Not Subd Geog)*
  BT Africa, Eastern--History

Punu folk songs
  USE Folk songs, Punu

Punu language *(May Subd Geog)*
  [PL 8605]
  UF Bapounou language
      Pounou language
      Yaka language
  BT Bantu languages
      Congo (Brazzaville)--Languages
      Gabon--Languages

Pwe language
  USE Bwamu language

Pygmies
  [DT 16.P8 (General)]
  [DT 571.P93 (Cameroon)]
  [DT 530.5.P94 (French West Africa)]
  [DT 650.P94 (Zaire)]
  UF Pigmies
  BT Ethnology--Africa, French-speaking
West
      Ethnology--Cameroon
      Ethnology--Zaire
  NT Babinga (African people)
      Bagyele (African people)
      Baka (West African people)
      Batwa (African people)
      Mbuti (African people)
      Negrillos
  --Anthropometry
  --Languages
    NT Aka language (Central African
Republic)
      Bagyele language
      Baka language (Cameroon)
  --Missions *(May Subd Geog)*
    [BV 3630.P]
    UF Missions to Pygmies

                Q

Qaba (African people) *(May Subd Geog)*
  [DT 834 : old class]

  [DT 1768.Q : new class]
  UF Amaqaba (African people)
      Amaqwathi (African people)
      Qwathi (African people)
  BT Bantu-speaking peoples
      Ethnology--South Africa

Qhung (African people)
  USE !Kung (African people)

Qomant language
  USE Kemant language

Qottu dialect *(May Subd Geog)*
  [PJ 2478]
  UF Eastern Galla dialect
      Ittu dialect
      Kwottu dialect
      Quottu dialect
      Qwottu dialect
  BT Oromo language

Quadroons
  USE Mulattoes

Quara language *(May Subd Geog)*
  [PJ 2439]
  UF Khwara language
      Kwara language
      Qwara language
  BT Cushitic languages
  RT Agau language

Quathlamba
  USE Drakensberg Mountains

Qué (African people)
  USE We (African people)

Quilts, Afro-American
  USE Afro-American quilts

Quioco (African people)
  USE Chokwe (African people)

Quioco language
  USE Chokwe language

Qung language
  USE !Xu language

Quotations, Afrikaans *(May Subd Geog)*
  [PN 6095.A35]
  UF Afrikaans quotations
  BT Afrikaans literature

(May Subd Geog) = Place names may follow the heading

Quotations, Black
  USE Blacks--Quotations

Quottu dialect
  USE Qottu dialect

Qwara language
  USE Quara language

Qwathi (African people)
  USE Qaba (African people)

Qwottu dialect
  USE Qottu dialect

R

Race
  [CB 195-CB 281 (Civilization)]
  [GN (Anthropology)]
  [HT 1501-HT 1595 (Sociology)]
  BT Anthropology
  NT Art and race
      Black race
      Health and race
      Mortality and race
      Music and race
      Occupations and race
  --Religious aspects
    [BL 65.R3]
    UF Race and religion
       Religion and race
  -- --Baptists, [Catholic Church, etc.]
      Buddhism, [Christianity, etc.]
  -- --Christianity
    [BT 734]
    UF Race (Theology)

Race (Theology)
  USE Race--Religious aspects--Christianity

Race and art
  USE Art and race

Race and health
  USE Health and race

Race and mortality
  USE Mortality and race

Race and music
  USE Music and race

Race and occupations
  USE Occupations and race

Race and religion
  USE Race--Religious aspects

Race awareness (May Subd Geog)
  [BF 724.R3 (Youth)]
  BT Ethnopsychology
  NT Blacks--Race identity
      Ethnicity
      Race awareness in children
      Race discrimination--Psychological aspects
      Racism

Race awareness in children (May Subd Geog)
  [BF 723.R3]
  BT Race awareness

Race awareness in literature
  [PN 56.R]
  BT Literature

Race discrimination (May Subd Geog)
  Here are entered works which are limited to overt
  discriminatory behavior directed against racial or ethnic
  groups. Works on racism as an attitude as well as works on
  both attitude and overt discriminatory behavior directed
  against racial or ethnic groups are entered under Racism.
  Works on discrimination directed against a particular group
  are entered under the name of the group with subdivision
  Social conditions or similar subdivisions, e.g. Civil
  rights.
    UF Discimination, Racial
       Racial discrimination
    DT Race relations
       Racism
    NT Segregation
  --Psychological aspects
    BT Race awareness
  --Religious aspects
  -- --Buddhism, [Christianity, etc.]

Race prejudice
  USE Racism

Race problems
  USE Race relations

Race psychology
  USE Ethnopsychology

Race question
  USE Race relations

Race relations (Not Subd Geog)
  [GN 496-GN 498 (Ethnology)]
  [HT 1501-HT 1595 (Sociology)]
  UF Integration, Racial   (Continued)

UF = Used for; BT = Broader term; RT = Related term; SA = See also; NT = Narrower term

Race relations   *(Continued)*
  UF   Race problems
         Race question
         Relations, Race
  BT   Ethnology
  RT   Racism
  SA   *subdivision* Race relations *under names of*
countries, cities, etc. and individual races and ethnic
groups with pertinent topical subdivision, e.g. South
Africa--Race relations; Blacks--Relations
with Jews; Blacks--Civil rights
  NT   Blacks--Relocation
         Mass media and race relations
         Miscegenation
         Prisons and race relations
         Race discrimination
         Social service and race relations
  --Religious aspects
  -- --Baptists [Catholic Church, etc.]
  -- --Buddhism [Christianity, etc.]
  -- --Christianity
  UF   Church and race relations
         Race relations and the Church
  --Botswana
  [DT 797 : old class]
  [DT 2456 : new class]
  --South Africa
  [DT 763 : old class]
  [DT 1756 : new class]

Race relations and mass media
  USE   Mass media and race relations

Race relations and prisons
  USE   Prisons and race relations

Race relations and social service
  USE   Social service and race relations

Race relations and the Church
  USE   Race relations--Religious aspects--
Christianity

Race relations and the press *(May Subd Geog)*
  UF   Press and race relations
  BT   Press

Race riots
  USE   Riots

Races of man
  USE   Ethnology

Racial amalgamation
  USE   Miscegenation

Racial crossing
  USE   Miscegenation

Racial discrimination
  USE   Race discrimination

Racial identity of Blacks
  USE   Blacks--Race identity

Racism *(May Subd Geog)*
         Here are entered works on racism *as an attitude as well*
as works on both attitude and overt discriminatory behavior
directed against racial or ethnic groups. Works which are
limited to overt discriminatory behavior *directed against*
racial or ethnic groups are entered under Race
discrimination. Works on racism directed against a
particular group are entered under the name of the group
with subdivision Social conditions, *or similar*
subdivision, e.g. Civil rights.
  UF   Race prejudice
  BT   Race awareness
  RT   Race relations
  NT   Race discrimination
  --Religious aspects
  -- --Buddhism [Christianity, etc.]

Racism and language
  USE   Racism in language

Racism in language
  [P 120.R32]
  UF   Language and racism
         Racism and language
         Racist language
  BT   Language and languages

Racism in literature
  [PN 56.R18]
  BT   Literature

Racism in motion pictures
  [PN 1995.9.R]
  BT   Motion pictures

Racism in the press *(May Subd Geog)*
  BT   Press

Racist language
  USE   Racism in language

Raconteurs
  USE   Storytellers

Radio drama
  USE   Radio plays

(May Subd Geog) = Place names may follow the heading

Radio plays *(May Subd Geog)*
  UF Radio drama
  BT Drama

Radio plays, African (English) *(Not Subd Geog)*
  [PR 9343 (History)]
  [PR 9347 (Collections)]
  UF African radio plays (English)
  BT African drama (English)

Radio plays, African (French) *(Not Subd Geog)*
  [PQ 3983 (History)]
  [PQ 3987 (Collections)]
  UF African radio plays (French)
  BT African drama (French)

Radio plays, Afrikaans *(May Subd Geog)*
  [PT 6575]
  UF Afrikaans radio plays
  BT Afrikaans drama

Radio plays, Kenyan (English) *(May Subd Geog)*
  [PR 9381.3 (History)]
  [PR 9381.7 (Collections)]
  UF Kenyan radio plays (English)
  BT Kenyan drama (English)

Radio plays, Swahili *(May Subd Geog)*
  [PL 8704]
  UF Swahili radio plays
  BT Swahili drama

Raqoli language *(May Subd Geog)*
  [PL 8607.R]
  BT Bantu languages
      Kenya--Languages

Rahad River (Ethiopia and Sudan) *(Not Subd Geog)*
  UF Nahr al-Rahad (Ethiopia and Sudan)
      Nahr ar-Rahad (Ethiopia and Sudan)
      Nahr er-Rahad (Ethiopia and Sudan)
  BT Rivers--Ethiopia
      Rivers--Sudan

Rahanwein (African people)
  USE Rahanweyn (African people)

Rahanweyn (African people) *(May Subd Geog)*
  [DT 402.4.R35]
  UF May-may (African people)
      Rahanwein (African people)
      Rahanwin (African people)
      Rahanwiyyin (African people)
  BT Ethnology--Somalia

Rahanwin (African people)
  USE Rahanweyn (African people)

Rahanwiyyin (African people)
  USE Rahanweyn (African people)

Railroads *(May Subd Geog)*
  BT Transportation
  --Africa, East
    NT Tan-Zam Railway
  --Congo (Brazzaville)
    NT Chemin de fer Congo-océan
  --Malawi
    NT Malawi Railways
  --Tanzania
    NT Tan-Zam Railway
  --Zaire
    NT Chemin de fer du Bas-Congo au Katanga
  --Zambia
    NT Tan-Zam Railway
  --Zimbabwe

Ranches *(May Subd Geog)*
  UF Cattle ranches
  BT Farms
  --Tanzania
    NT Mkwaja Ranch (Tanzania)
  --Zambia
    NT Mpika Dairy Settlement Scheme (Zambia)
  --Zimbabwe
    NT Leigh Ranch (Zimbabwe)

Rand area *(May Subd Geog)*
  UF Common Monetary Area (Southern Africa)
      Rand Monetary Area
      Rand Zone
  BT Economics

Rand Monetary Area
  USE Rand area

Rand Zone
  USE Rand area

Randile (African people)
  USE Rendile (African people)

Randile language
  USE Rendile language

Ranges, Mountain
  USE Mountains

Rangi (African people) *(May Subd Geog)*
  [DT 443.R35]
  UF Irangi (African people)   *(Continued)*

UF = Used for; BT = Broader term; RT = Related term; SA = See also; NT = Narrower term

Rangi (African people)   *(Continued)*
  UF Langi (African people)
      Warangi (African people)
  BT Bantu-speaking peoples
      Ethnology--Tanzania

Rashaida (Arab people)
  USE Rashayidah (Arab people)

Rashayidah (Arab people) *(May Subd Geog)*
  [DT 155.2.R37]
  UF Rashaida (Arab people)
  BT Ethnology--Sudan

Ravines
  USE Gorges

Real estate
  USE Real property

Real estate law
  USE Real property

Real property *(May Subd Geog)*
  Here are entered works on real property in the
legal sense, i.e. the law of immovable property, works
on real estate in general, and, with geographical
subdivision, surveys of property in particular places.
  UF Property, Real
      Real estate
      Real estate law
      Realty
  BT Property
  NT Inheritance and succession
      Land tenure

Real property (Ashanti law)
  BT Law, Ashanti

Realty
  USE Real property

Rebellion of Kaoussan, 1916-1918
  USE Senussite Rebellion, 1916-1918

Rebellion of Mamadou Lamine, 1885-1887
  USE Mamadou Lamine, Rebellion of, 1885-
1887

Rebellions
  USE Civil war
      Insurgency
      Revolutions

Rebu language
  USE Bobangi language

Red Bobo language
  USE Bwamu language

Red Sea Hills (Egypt and Sudan) *(Not Subd Geog)*
  UF Atbay (Egypt and Sudan)
      Etbai (Egypt and Sudan)
  BT Mountains--Sudan

Red Shawls Rebellion (Madagascar), 1895-1899
  USE Madagascar--History--Menalamba Rebellion,
1895-1899

Refuges, Wildlife
  USE Wildlife refuges

Rega (African people)
  USE Waregas

Région du Kirimiro (Burundi)
  USE Kirimiro Region (Burundi)

Région naturelle du Buyenzi (Burundi)
  USE Buyenzi Region (Burundi)

Région naturelle du Kirimiro (Burundi)
  USE Kirimiro Region (Burundi)

Rehoboth Bastards (African people)
  USE Rehoboth Basters (African people)

Rehoboth Basters (African people) *(May Subd Geog)*
  [DT 737 (Namibia : old class)]
  [DT 1558.R45 (Namibia : new class)]
  [DT 764.R (South Africa : old class)]
  [DT 1768.R45 (South Africa : new class)]
  UF Bastaards (African people)
      Basters (African people)
      Rehoboth Bastards (African people)
      Rehobothers (African people)
  BT **Ethnology--Namibia**
      Ethnology--South Africa
 --History
  NT Rehoboth Basters Rebellion, 1925

Rehoboth Basters Rebellion, 1925
  [DT 714 : old class]
  [DT 1632 : new class]
  BT Namibia--History--1915-1946
      Rehoboth Basters (African people)--History

Rehobothers (African people)
  USE Rehoboth Basters (African people)

Relations, Race
  USE Race relations

(May Subd Geog) = Place names may follow the heading

Relics and reliquaries, Kota
  USE Reliquaries, Kota

Relics and reliquaries, Mbete
  USE Reliquaries, Mbete

Religion
  USE *subdivision* Religion under *the names of*
countries, cities, etc., and under ethnic groups, e.g.,
Nigeria--Religion; Fang (West African
people)--Religion

Religion, Comparative
  USE Religions

Religion, Primitive *(May Subd Geog)*
  UF Primitive religion
  BT Ethnology
      Mythology
  SA *subdivision* Religion under *individual ethnic*
groups, e.g. Birifor (African people)--Religion
  NT Animism
      Fetishism
      Folklore
      Gods
      Initiation rites--Religious aspects
      Nativistic movements
--Burundi
  NT Imana (Rundi deity)
--Ghana
  NT Dente (African deity)
--Nigeria
  NT Chi (Igbo deity)
      Ogun (Yoruba deity)
--South Africa
  NT Mwari (Shona deity)
--Uganda
  NT Nyabingi (African deity)
--Zaire
  NT Yambe (Zela deity)
--Zambia
  NT Chihamba
--Zimbabwe
  NT Mwari (Shona deity)

Religion and race
  USE Race--Religious aspects

Religions
  Here are entered works on the major world
religions. Works on groups or movements whose system
of religious beliefs or practices differs significantly
from the major world religions and which are often
gathered around a specific deity or person are entered
under Cults.

  UF Comparative religion
      Denominations, Religious
      Religion, Comparative
      Religions, Comparative
      Religious denominations
  RT Gods
  NT Christianity
      Christianity and other religions
      Cults
      Islam
      Mythology
  --African influences

Religions, Comparative
  USE Religions

Religions, Modern
  USE Cults

Religious ceremonies
  USE Rites and ceremonies

Religious denominations
  USE Religions

Religious drama
  BT Drama

Religious drama, Igbo *(May Subd Geog)*
  [PL 8261.5]
  UF Igbo religious drama
  BT Igbo drama

Religious rites
  USE Rites and ceremonies

Reliquaries, Kota *(May Subd Geog)*
  [NB 1099.G252K (Sculpture)]
  UF Kota reliquaries
      Relics and reliquaries, Kota

Reliquaries, Mbete *(May Subd Geog)*
  [NB 1099.G252M (Sculpture)]
  UF Mbete reliquaries
      Relics and reliquaries, Mbete

Relocation of Blacks
  USE Blacks--Relocation

Relocation of Colored people (South Africa)
  USE Colored people (South Africa)--Relocation

Remi (African people)
  USE Nyaturu (African people)

UF = Used for; BT = Broader term; RT = Related term; SA = See also; NT = Narrower term

Removal of Blacks
  USE Blacks--Relocation

Removal of Colored people (South Africa)
  USE Colored people (South Africa)--
Relocation

Rendile (African people) *(May Subd Geog)*
  [DT 433.545.R45]
  UF Randile (African people)
      Rendili (African people)
      Rendille (African people)
  BT Ethnology--Kenya

Rendile language *(May Subd Geog)*
  [PJ 2529]
  UF Randile language
  BT Cushitic languages
      Kenya--Languages
      Somali languages

Rendile women
  USE Women, Rendile

Rendili (African people)
  USE Rendile (African people)

Rendille (African people)
  USE Rendile (African people)

Reparation *(May Subd Geog)*
  UF Compensation for victims of crime
      Criminal restitution
      Restitution (Criminal procedure)
      Restitution for victims of crime

Reparation (Yanzi law)
  BT Law, Yanzi

Reportage literature, South African (English)
(May Subd Geog)
  UF South African reportage literature
(English)
  BT South African prose literature
(English)

Representative government and representation
(May Subd Geog)
  UF Democracy [subdivided by place]
      Parliamentary government
      Political representation
      Self-government
 --Africa, Sub-Saharan
  [JQ 1879.A15]

Republic Building (Lagos, Nigeria)
  BT Public buildings--Nigeria

Republic of Cape Verde
  USE Cape Verde

Republic of Ivory Coast
  USE Ivory Coast

Republic of Rwanda
  USE Rwanda

Republic of South Africa
  USE South Africa

République du Burundi
  USE Burundi

République Gabonaise
  USE Gabon

République Populaire du Bénin
  USE Benin

République Rwandaise
  USE Rwanda

Rescue of hijack victims at Entebbe Airport, 1976
  USE Entebbe Airport Raid, 1976

Reserves, Forest
  USE Forest reserves

Reserves, Game
  USE Game reserves

Reserves, National
  USE National parks and reserves

Reservoirs *(May Subd Geog)*
  UF Artificial lakes
      Man-made lakes
  RT Lakes
 --**Nigeria**
  NT Kainji Reservoir (Nigeria)
 --**South Africa**
  NT Le Roux, Lake (South Africa)
 --**Sudan**
  NT Nasser, Lake (Egypt and Sudan)
 --**Tanzania**
  NT Hombolo Lake (Tanzania)
 --**Zimbabwe**
  NT McIlwaine, Lake (Zimbabwe)

Resettlement of Blacks
  USE Blacks--Relocation

(May Subd Geog) = Place names may follow the heading

Resettlement of Colored people (South Africa)
 USE Colored people (South Africa)--
Relocation

Residences
 USE Dwellings

Resorts *(May Subd Geog)*
 --South Africa
   NT Albert Falls Public Resort (South
Africa)

Restitution (Criminal procedure)
 USE Reparation

Restitution for victims of crimes
 USE Reparation

Réunion *(Not. Subd Geog)*
 [DT 469.R3-DT 469.R5]
 UF Bourbon (Island)
 BT Mascarene Islands
 --Civilization
 -- --Indic influences
   BT India--Civilization
 --Description and travel
 -- --1981-
   Economic conditions
   [HC 598]
 --History
 -- --To 1764
 -- --1764-1946
 -- --1946-

Réunion art
 USE Art, Réunion

Réunion fiction (French) *(May Subd Geog)*
 [PQ 3988.5.R4 (History)]
 [PQ 3988.5.R42 (Collections)]
 UF French fiction--Réunion authors
 BT Réunion literature (French)
 NT Short stories, Réunion (French)

Réunion fiction (French Creole) *(May Subd Geog)*
 [PM 7854.R4]
 UF Creole fiction, Réunion French
     French Creole fiction, Réunion
 BT Réunion literature (French Creole)
 NT Short stories, Réunion (French Creole)

Réunion Islanders *(May Subd Geog)*
 UF Réunionnais
 BT Ethnology--Réunion

Réunion literature (French) *(May Subd Geog)*
 [PQ 3988.5.R4 (History)]
 [PQ 3988.5.R42 (Collections)]
 UF French literature--Réunion authors
 BT Mascarene literature
 NT Réunion fiction (French)
     Réunion poetry (French)

Réunion literature (French Creole) *(May Subd Geog)*
 [PM 7854.R4]
 UF Creole literature, Réunion French
     French Creole literature, Réunion
 BT Mascarene literature
 NT Réunion fiction (French Creole)
     Réunion poetry (French Creole)

Réunion poetry (French) *(May Subd Geog)*
 [PQ 3988.5.R4 (History)]
 [PQ 3988.5.R42 (Collections)]
 UF French poetry--Réunion authors
 BT Réunion literature (French)

Réunion poetry (French Creole) *(May Subd Geog)*
 [PM 7854.R4]
 UF Creole poetry, Réunion French
     French Creole poetry, Réunion
 BT Réunion literature (French Creole)

Réunion short stories (French)
 USE Short stories, Réunion (French)

Réunion short stories (French Creole)
 USE Short stories, Réunion (French Creole)

Réunion wit and humor, Pictorial
 [NC 1740.R]
 UF Wit and humor, Pictorial (Réunion)

Réunionnais
 USE Réunion Islanders

Revivals, Ethnic
 USE Nativistic movements

Revolutionary literature *(May Subd Geog)*
 UF Literature, Revolutionary
 BT Literature
     Revolutions
 NT Revolutionary poetry

Revolutionary literature, African (Portuguese)
(May Subd Geog)
 [PQ 9900-PQ 9908]
 UF African revolutionary literature
(Portuguese)   *(Continued)*

UF = Used for; BT = Broader term; RT = Related term; SA = See also; NT = Narrower term

Revolutionary literature, African (Portuguese) *(Continued)*
BT African literature (Portuguese)
NT Revolutionary poetry, African (Portuguese)

Revolutionary poetry *(May Subd Geog)*
UF Poetry, Revolutionary
BT Political poetry
Revolutionary literature
Revolutions
NT Protest poetry

Revolutionary poetry, African (Portuguese) *(May Subd Geog)*
[PQ 9902 (History)]
[PQ 9906-PQ 9906.5 (Collections)]
UF African revolutionary poetry (Portuguese)
BT African poetry (Portuguese)
Revolutionary literature, African (Portuguese)

Revolutionary poetry, Ghanaian (English) *(May Subd Geog)*
[PR 9379.2 (History)]
[PR 9379.6-PR 9379.65 (Collections)]
UF Ghanaian revolutionary poetry (English)
BT Ghanaian poetry (English)

Revolutionary poetry, Guinean (French) *(May Subd Geog)*
[PQ 3988.5.G8 (History)]
[PQ 3988.5.G82 (Collections)]
UF Guinean revolutionary poetry (French)
BT Guinean poetry (French)

Revolutionary poetry, Nigerian (English) *(May Subd Geog)*
[PR 9387.2 (History)]
[PR 9387.6-PR 9387.66 (Collections)]
UF Nigerian revolutionary poetry (English)
BT Nigerian poetry (English)

Revolutionary poetry, Somali *(May Subd Geog)*
[PJ 2533.5-PJ 2534]
UF Somali revolutionary poetry
BT Somali poetry

Revolutionary poetry, South African (English) *(May Subd Geog)*
[PR 9360.9 (History)]
[PR 9365.85.R47 (Collections)]

UF South African revolutionary poetry (English)
BT South African poetry (English)

Revolutionary poetry, Zimbabwean (English) *(May Subd Geog)*
[PR 9390.2 (History)]
[PR 9390.6-PR 9390.65 (Collections)]
UF Zimbabwean revolutionary poetry (English)
BT Zimbabwean poetry (English)

Revolutions *(May Subd Geog)*
UF Insurrections
Political violence
Rebellions
BT History
SA *subdivision* History--Revolution [date] *under names of places, e.g.,* Angola--History--Revolution, 1961-1975
NT Civil war
Coups d'état
Insurgency
National liberation movements
Revolutionary literature
Revolutionary poetry
--Africa
-- --History
-- -- --20th century
[DT 30.5]

Rhodesia *(Not Subd Geog)*
[DT 946-DT 963 : old class]
[DT 2862 : new class]
Here are entered works limited in subject coverage to the historical, political, or cultural aspects of the two former British colonies of Northern and Southern Rhodesia combined for the pre-1953 period. Works dealing with these same aspects of the Federation of Rhodesia and Nyasaland for the 1953-1963 period are entered under Rhodesia and Nyasaland. All works covering the same area for which these limitations do not apply are entered under the name or names of the current jurisdictions, Zambia and/or Zimbabwe.
--Languages

Rhodesia, Northern
USE Zambia

Rhodesia, Southern
USE Zimbabwe

Rhodesia and Nyasaland *(Not Subd Geog)*
[DT 856 : old class]
[DT 2864 : new class]
Here are entered works limited in subject coverage to the historical, political, or cultural aspects of the

(May Subd Geog) = Place names may follow the heading

*Federation of Rhodesia and Nyasaland for the 1953-1963
period. Works dealing with these same aspects of the
two former British colonies of Northern and Southern
Rhodesia combined for the pre-1953 period are entered
under* Rhodesia. *All works covering the same area for
which these limitations do not apply are entered under
the name or names of the current jurisdictions,*
Zambia, Zimbabwe *and/or* Malawi.

Rhodesian man
  [GN 285]
  UF Broken Hill skull
      Homo rhodesiensis
  BT Fossil man--Zambia

Rhodesian Ndebele (African people)
  USE Ndebele (African people)

Rhodesian War (Zimbabwe), 1966-1980
  USE Zimbabwe--History--Chimurenga War,
1966-1980

Ribe (African people) *(May Subd Geog)*
  [DT 433.545.R]
  UF Waribe (African people)
  BT Ethnology--Kenya
      Nika (African people)

Richtersveld (South Africa) *(Not Subd Geog)*
  BT Plains--South Africa

Riddles
  BT Folk literature
      Wit and humor

Riddles, Bambara *(May Subd Geog)*
  [PN 6377.B35]
  UF Bambara riddles

Riddles, Bembe (Congo (Brazzaville)) *(May Subd
Geog)*
  [PN 6377.B]
  UF Bembe riddles (Congo (Brazzaville))

Riddles, Congo (Brazzaville)) *(May Subd Geog)*
  [PN 6377.C]
  UF Congo (Brazzaville) riddles

Riddles, Creole *(May Subd Geog)*
  UF Creole riddles
  --Mauritius

Riddles, Kalenjin *(May Subd Geog)*
  [PN 6377.K28]
  UF Kalenjin riddles

Riddles, Kinyarwanda *(May Subd Geog)*
  [PN 6377.R8]
  UF Kinyarwanda riddles

Riddles, Luba-Lulua *(May Subd Geog)*
  [PN 6377.L8]
  UF Luba-Lulua riddles

Riddles, Serer *(May Subd Geog)*
  [PN 6377.S]
  UF Serer riddles

Riddles, Swahili *(May Subd Geog)*
  [PN 6377.S]
  UF Swahili riddles

Riddles, Umbundu *(May Subd Geog)*
  [PN 6377.U]
  UF Umbundu riddles

Ridges, Mountain
  USE Mountains

Rift Valley
  USE Great Rift Valley

Rifts (Geology) *(May Subd Geog)*
  BT Geology
      Landforms
  --Africa
  NT Great Rift Valley

Rimi (African people)
  USE Nyaturu (African people)

Rio Aruângua (Zambia and Mozambique)
  USE Luangwa River (Zambia and Mozambique)

Rio Cubango
  USE Okavango River

Rio Cunene (Angola and Namibia)
  USE Cunene River (Angola and Namibia)

Rio Panhame (Zimbabwe and Mozambique)
  USE Hunyani River (Zimbabwe and Mozambique)

Rio Save (Zimbabwe and Mozambique)
  USE Save River (Zimbabwe and Mozambique)

Rio Umbeluzi (Swaziland and Mozambique)
  USE Umbeluzi River (Swaziland and Mozambique)

Rio Zaire
  USE Congo River

UF = Used for; BT = Broader term; RT = Related term; SA = See also; NT = Narrower term

Rio Zambeze
  USE Zambezi River

Rio Zambezi
  USE Zambezi River

Riots *(May Subd Geog)*
  UF Civil disorders
     Political violence
     Race riots
  BT History
 --South Africa
  NT South Africa--History--Soweto
Uprising, 1976

Rites and ceremonies *(May Subd Geog)*
  UF Ceremonies
     Religious ceremonies
     Religious rites
     Rites of passage
     Traditions
  RT Manners and customs
  SA *subdivision* Rites and ceremonies *under*
ethnic groups, e.g. Kikuyu (African people)--
Rites and ceremonies
  NT Funeral rites and ceremonies
     Initiation rites
     Marriage customs and rites
     Puberty rites
 --Burundi
  NT Ukubandwa
 --Cameroon
  NT Abia (Rite)
 --Zambia
  NT Tusona

Rites of passage
  USE Rites and ceremonies

River flood plains
  USE Floodplains

River Niger
  USE Niger River

River valleys
  USE Valleys

Riverain (African people)
  USE Efik (African people)

Rivers *(May Subd Geog)*
  UF Brooks
     Creeks
     Runs (Rivers)
     Streams

  BT Landforms
  NT Deltas
     Estuaries
     Waterfalls
--Africa
  NT Nile River
--Africa, East
  NT Kagera River
--Africa, Southern
  NT Zambezi River
--Africa, West
  NT Niger River
--Angola
  NT Cunene River (Angola and Namibia)
     Kasai River (Angola and Zaire)
     Kwango River (Angola and Zaire)
     Okavango River
--Botswana
  NT Boteti River (Botswana)
     Marico River (South Africa and Botswana)
     Okavango River
--Burundi
  NT Ruzizi River
--Cameroon
  NT Benue River (Cameroon and Nigeria)
     Cross River (Cameroon and Nigeria)
--Ethiopia
  NT Agucho River (Ethiopia)
     Atbara River (Ethiopia and Sudan)
     Awash River (Ethiopia)
     Blue Nile River (Ethiopia and Sudan)
     Gibbe River (Ethiopia)
     Juba River (Ethiopia and Somalia)
     Kabana River (Ethiopia)
     Kesem River (Ethiopia)
     Omo River (Ethiopia and Kenya)
     Rahad River (Ethiopia and Sudan)
     Shebeli River (Ethiopia and Somalia)
--Gabon
  NT Ogooué River (Gabon)
--Ghana
  NT Ankobra River (Ghana)
     Volta River (Ghana)
--Guinea
  NT Geba River
     Mélikhouré River (Forécariah, Guinea)
--Guinea-Bissau
  NT Geba River
--Kenya
  NT Amaya River (Kenya)
     Kerio River (Kenya)
     Omo River (Ethiopia and Kenya)
--Lesotho
  NT Orange River
--Madagascar
  NT Ikopa River (Madagascar)

(May Subd Geog) = Place names may follow the heading

NT Mangoro River (Madagascar)
    Morondava River (Madagascar)
    Sahatorendrika River (Antananarivo,
Madagascar)
    Tsiribihina River (Madagascar)
--Malawi
NT Bwanje River (Malawi)
    Shire River (Malawi and Mozambique)
--Mali
NT Senegal River
--Mauritania
NT Senegal River
--Mozambique
NT Hunyani River (Zimbabwe and
Mozambique)
    Luangwa River (Zambia and Mozambique)
    Save River (Zimbabwe and Mozambique)
    Shire River (Malawi and Mozambique)
    Umbeluzi River (Swaziland and
Mozambique)
--Namibia
NT Cunene River (Angola and Namibia)
    Kuiseb River (Namibia)
    Okavango River
    Orange River
    Tumas River (Namibia)
--Niger
NT Maradi River (Nigeria and Niger)
--Nigeria
NT Anambra River (Nigeria)
    Benue River (Cameroon and Nigeria)
    Bonny River (Nigeria)
    Cross River (Cameroon and Nigeria)
    Kaduna River (Nigeria)
    Maradi River (Nigeria and Niger)
    Sokoto River (Nigeria)
--Rwanda
NT Ruzizi River
--Senegal
NT Geba River
    Senegal River
--Somalia
NT Juba River (Ethiopia and Somalia)
    Shebeli River (Ethiopia and Somalia)
--South Africa
NT Amatola River (South Africa)
    Berg River (South Africa)
    Blood River (South Africa)
    Great Brak River (South Africa)
    Kaapsedrifrivier (South Africa)
    Marico River (South Africa and
Botswana)
    Mgeni River (South Africa)
    Nkwalini River (South Africa)
    Nuy River (South Africa)
    Orange River

NT Sak River (South Africa)
    Seacow River (South Africa)
--Sudan
NT Atbara River (Ethiopia and Sudan)
    Bahr al-Ghazal (Sudan : River)
    Blue Nile River (Ethiopia and Sudan)
    Rahad River (Ethiopia and Sudan)
--Swaziland
NT Umbeluzi River (Swaziland and Mozambique)
--Tanzania
NT Ngono River (Tanzania)
    Rufiji River (Tanzania)
    Wama River (Tanzania)
--Uganda
NT Semliki River (Zaire and Uganda)
--Zaire
NT Kasai River (Angola and Zaire)
    Kwango River (Angola and Zaire)
    Luapula River (Zambia and Zaire)
    Ruzizi River
    Semliki River (Zaire and Uganda)
--Zambia
NT Kafue River (Zambia)
    Luangwa River (Zambia and Mozambique)
    Luapula River (Zambia and Zaire)
    Lukulu River (Zambia)
--Zimbabwe
NT Hunyani River (Zimbabwe and Mozambique)
    Sanyati River (Zimbabwe)
    Save River (Zimbabwe and Mozambique)

Rivière Mellacorée (Forécariah, Guinea)
    USE Mélikhouré River (Forécariah, Guinea)

Roads (May Subd Geog)
    UF Highways
        Thoroughfares
    BT Transportation
    NT Streets
--Africa
    NT Trans-African Highway
--Kenya
    [HE 367.K43]

Robben Island (South Africa) (Not Subd Geog)
    [DT 846.R6 : old class]
    [DT 2400.R : new class]
    UF Robbeneiland (South Africa)
    BT Islands--South Africa
        South Africa

Robbeneiland (South Africa)
    USE Robben Island (South Africa)

Rock shelters
    USE Caves

UF = Used for; BT = Broader term; RT = Related term; SA = See also; NT = Narrower term

Rodi language
USE Bor language (Lwo)

Rodrigues Island (Mauritius) *(Not Subd Geog)*
[DT 469.M492]
UF Rodriguez Island (Mauritius)
BT Islands--Mauritius
Mauritius

Rodriguez Island (Mauritius)
USE Rodrigues Island (Mauritius)

Rolon (African people)
USE Rolong (African people)

Rolong (African people) *(May Subd Geog)*
[DT 797 (Botswana : old class)]
[DT 2458.R75 (Botswana : new class)]
[DT 764.R65 (South Africa : old class]
[DT 1768.R65 (South Africa : new class)]
UF Barolong (African people)
Rolon (African people)
BT Ethnology--Botswana
Ethnology--South Africa

Roman Empire
USE Rome

Rome *(Not Subd Geog)*
UF Ancient Roman Empire
Roman Empire
--Civilization
-- --African influences
BT Africa--Civilization

Ron language *(May Subd Geog)*
[PL 8607.R6]
UF Baron language
Chala language
Rone language
Run language
BT Chadic languages
Nigeria--Languages
RT Angas language

Rone language
USE Ron language

Ronga (African people)
USE Tsonga (African people)

Ronga language *(May Subd Geog)*
[PL 8607.R73]
UF Landim language
Shironga language
Xironga language

BT Bantu languages
Mozambique--Languages
South Africa--Languages
RT Tsonga language
Tswa language

Rorke's Drift (South Africa), Battle of, 1879
[DT 777 : old class]
[DT 1879.R68 : new class]
UF Battle of Rorke's Drift (South Africa),
1879
BT Zulu War, 1879--Campaigns

Roseires Dam (Sudan)
BT Dams--Sudan

Rothmans July Handicap (Horse race)
USE July Handicap (Horse race)

Rotse (African people)
USE Lozi (African people)

Royalty
USE Kings and rulers

Rozi (African people)
USE Lozi (African people)

Ruanda
USE Rwanda

Ruanda...
USE *subject headings beginning with the word*
Kinyarwanda

Ruanda language
USE Kinyarwanda language

Ruanda literature
USE Kinyarwanda literature

Ruanda poetry
USE Kinyarwanda poetry

Ruanda-Urundi
USE Burundi
Rwanda

Rudolf, Lake (Kenya and Ethiopia) *(Not Subd Geog)*
UF Lake Rudolf (Kenya and Ethiopia)
Lake Turkana (Kenya and Ethiopia)
Turkana, Lake (Kenya and Ethiopia)
BT Lakes--Ethiopia
Lakes--Kenya

(May Subd Geog) = Place names may follow the heading

Rufa'a al-Hoi (African people) *(May Subd Geog)*
  [DT 155.2.R83]
  UF Abu Rof (African people)
  BT Ethnology--Sudan

Rufiji River (Tanzania) *(Not Subd Geog)*
  BT Rivers--Tanzania

Ruguru (African people)
  USE Luguru (African people)

Ruhaya language
  USE Ziba language

Ruined cities
  USE Cities and towns, Ruined, extinct,
etc.

Ruins
  USE Archaeology
      subdivision Antiquities *under names of*
countries, cities, etc.; and names of individual ruins

Rukiga language
  USE Kiga language

Rukuba (African people) *(May Subd Geog)*
  [DT 515.45.R84]
  UF Bace (African people)
      Kuco (African people)
  BT Ethnology--Nigeria

Rulers
  USE Kings and rulers

Ruma (African people) *(May Subd Geog)*
  [DT 530.5.R]
  UF Arma (African people)
  BT Ethnology--Africa, French-speaking
West

Rumbala (African people)
  USE Mbala (African people)

Rumbala language
  USE Mbala language (Bandundu region,
Zaire)

Run language
  USE Ron language

Rundi (African people) *(May Subd Geog)*
  [DT 450.65.R86 (Burundi)]
  UF Barundi (African people)
      Warundi (African people)

  BT Bantu-speaking peoples
      Ethnology--Burundi
      Ethnology--Rwanda
  NT Batwa (African people)
      Hutu (African people)
      Tutsi (African people)
  --Religion
    [BL 2480.R]
    NT Gods, Rundi
        Imana (Rundi deity)

Rundi art
  USE Art, Rundi

Rundi folk songs
  USE Folk songs, Rundi

Rundi gods
  USE Gods, Rundi

Rundi language *(May Subd Geog)*
  [PL 8611]
  UF Kirundi language
  BT Bantu languages
      Burundi--Languages
      Rwanda--Languages

Rundi proverbs
  USE Proverbs, Rundi

Rundi wit and humor *(May Subd Geog)*
  [PL 8611 (History and major collections)]
  [PN 6222 (Minor collections)]
  UF Wit and humor, Rundi

Rungu (African people)
  USE Tabwa (African people)

Runs (Rivers)
  USE Rivers

Runyankole (African people)
  USE Nyankole (African people)

Runyankore language
  USE Nyankole language

Runyankore-Rukiga language
  USE Nyankore-Kiga language

Runyaruanda language
  USE Kinyarwanda language

Runyarwanda language
  USE Kinyarwanda language

UF = Used for; BT = Broader term; RT = Related term; SA = See also; NT = Narrower term

Runyoro (African people)
  USE Nyoro (African people)

Runyoro-Rutooro language
  USE Nyoro-Tooro language

Rural education
  USE Education, Rural

Rural health *(May Subd Geog)*
  UF Rural public health
  --Ghana
  NT Danfa Comprehensive Rural Health and
Family Planning Project

Rural public health
  USE Rural health

Rusizi River
  USE Ruzizi River

Rutwa (African people)
  USE Batwa (African people)

Ruund language *(May Subd Geog)*
  UF Chiluwunda language
      Lunda language, Northern
      Luunda language
      Luwunda language
      Muatiamvua language
      Northern Lunda language
      Uruund language
  BT Angola--Languages
      Bantu languages
      Zaire--Languages

Ruwenzori Mountains (Uganda and Zaire) *(Not Subd Geog)*
  [DT 361-DT 363.3]
  UF Massif du Ruwenzori (Uganda and Zaire)
      Moon, Mountains of the (Uganda and Zaire)
      Mountains of the Moon (Uganda and Zaire)
      Ruwenzori Range (Uganda and Zaire)
      Rwenzori Mountains (Uganda and Zaire)
  BT Mountains--Uganda
      Mountains--Zaire

Ruwenzori Range (Uganda and Zaire)
  USE Ruwenzori Mountains (Uganda and Zaire)

Ruzizi River *(Not Subd Geog)*
  UF Rusizi River
  BT Rivers--Burundi
      Rivers--Rwanda

  BT Rivers--Zaire

Rwanda *(Not Subd Geog)*
  [DT 450-DT 450.49]
  UF Republic of Rwanda
      République Rwandaise
      Ruanda
      Ruanda-Urundi
  --Economic conditions
  [HC 875]
  --History
  -- --Civil War, 1959-1962
  [DT 450.43]
  UF Civil war--Rwanda
  --Languages
  NT Kinyarwanda language
      Rundi language
  --Literatures
  NT Kinyarwanda literature

Rwanda language
  USE Kinyarwanda language

Rwanda cookery
  USE Cookery, Rwandan

Rwenzori Mountains (Uganda and Zaire)
  USE Ruwenzori Mountains (Uganda and Zaire)

S

Sa (African people)
  USE Teke (African people)

Sabaot (African people)
  USE Sapiny (African people)

Sabei (African people)
  USE Sapiny (African people)

Sabi River (Zimbabwe and Mozambique)
  USE Save River (Zimbabwe and Mozambique)

Sadama (African people)
  USE Sidamo (African people)

Sadaminya (African people)
  USE Sidamo (African people)

Safari Rally, East African
  USE East African Safari Rally

Safaris *(May Subd Geog)*
  [G 516]
  UF Expeditions, Adventure
      Tours, Adventure

(May Subd Geog) = Place names may follow the heading

Safwa (African people) *(May Subd Geog)*
  [DT 443.3.S]
  UF Mwanabantu (African people)
  BT Bantu-speaking peoples
      Ethnology--Tanzania

Sagalla dialect
  USE Taita language

Sagara language *(May Subd Geog)*
  [PL 8625]
  UF Kimegi language
      Megi language
  BT Bantu languages
      Tanzania--Languages
  NT Kaguru language

Sahara *(Not Subd Geog)*
  UF Sahara Desert
  BT Deserts--Africa
  NT Ténéré (Niger)

Sahara Desert
  USE Sahara

Sahatorendrika River (Antananarivo,
Madagascar) *(Not Subd Geog)*
  RT Rivers--Madagascar

Sahel *(Not Subd Geog)*
  [DT 521-DT 533]
  Here are entered works on the region of West
  Africa which extends from northern Senegal and southern
  Mauritania generally easterly to South Central Chad.
  --Economic conditions
    [HC 1002]

Saho (African people) *(May Subd Geog)*
  [DT 380.4.S]
  BT Cushites
      Ethnology--Ethiopia

Saho language *(May Subd Geog)*
  [PJ 2465]
  UF Assaorta-Saho language
  BT Cushitic languages
  RT Afar language

Saint Floris National Park (Central African
Republic)
  USE Parc national de Saint-Floris (Central
African Republic)

Saint Helena *(Not Subd Geog)*
  [DT 671.S2]
  UF St. Helena

  --Economic conditions
    [HC 594.5]

Saint Marie Island (Madagascar)
  USE Sainte-Marie-de-Madagascar Island
  (Madagascar)

Sainte-Marie-de-Madagascar Island (Madagascar)
(Not Subd Geog)
  UF Boraha Island (Madagascar)
      Ile Sainte-Marie (Madagascar)
      Nosy Boraha (Madagascar)
      Saint Marie Island (Madagascar)
      Sainte-Marie Island (Madagascar)
  BT Islands--Madagascar
      Madagascar

Sainte-Marie Island (Madagascar)
  USE Sainte-Marie-de-Madagascar Island
  (Madagascar)

Sak River (South Africa) *(Not Subd Geog)*
  UF Zak River (South Africa)
  BT Rivers--South Africa

Saka language (Nigeria)
  USE Odual language

Sakalava (Malagasy people) *(May Subd Geog)*
  [DT 469.M277S355]
  BT Ethnology--Madagascar
  NT Menabe (Malagasy people)

Sakalava art
  USE Art, Sakalava

Sakalava dialect *(May Subd Geog)*
  [PL 5379]
  BT Malagasy language

Sakalava wood-carving
  USE Wood-carving, Sakalava

Sakara dialect
  USE Nzakara dialect

Sakata (African people) *(May Subd Geog)*
  [DT 650.B365]
  UF Basakata (African people)
  BT Bantu-speaking peoples
      Ethnology--Zaire
  --Folklore
    [GR 357.82.S24]

Sakata folk literature
  USE Folk literature, Sakata

UF = Used for; BT = Broader term; RT = Related term; SA = See also; NT = Narrower term

Sakata language *(May Subd Geog)*
  [PL 8627]
  UF Kisakata language
  BT Bantu languages
       Zaire--Languages

sala-Mpasu language
  USE Salampasu language

Salampasu (African people) *(May Subd Geog)*
  [DT 650.S]
  BT Bantu-speaking peoples
       Ethnology--Zaire

Salampasu folk songs
  USE Folk songs, Salampusu

Salampasu language *(May Subd Geog)*
  UF Chisalampasu language
       ciSalampasu language
       sala-Mpasu language
       tshi-sala-Mpasu language
  BT Bantu languages
       Zaire--Languages

Saldanha Bay (South Africa) *(Not Subd Geog)*
  UF Saldanhabaai (South Africa)
  BT Bays--South Africa

Saldanhabaai (South Africa)
  USE Saldanha Bay (South Africa)

Sam languages
  USE Somali languages

Samajo language
  USE Samo language (West Africa)

SAMARC System
  USE MARC System--South Africa

Sambaa (African people)
  USE Shambala (African people)

Sambaa language
  USE Shambala language

Sambala (African people)
  USE Shambala (African people)

Sambála language
  USE Shambala language

Sambara (African people)
  USE Shambala (African people)

Sambára language
  USE Shambala language

Sambio (African people)
  USE Sambyu (African people)

Sambur (African people)
  USE Samburu (African people)

Sambur language
  USE Samburu language

Samburu (African people) *(May Subd Geog)*
  [DT 433.545.S26]
  UF Burkeneji (African people)
       Sambur (African people)
       Sampur (African people)
  BT Ethnology--Kenya
       Masai (African people)
  --Medicine
  BT Medicine, Primitive--Kenya

Samburu language *(May Subd Geog)*
  UF Burkeneji language
       Lokop language
       Nkutuk language
       Sambur language
       Sampur language
  BT Kenya--Languages
       Nilo-Hamitic languages
  RT Masai language

Sambyu (African people) *(May Subd Geog)*
  [DT 709 : old class]
  [DT 1558.S36 : new class]
  UF Sambio (African people)
       Shambiu (African people)
  BT Bantu-speaking peoples
       Ethnology--Namibia

Samo (West African people) *(May Subd Geog)*
  [DT 555.45.S (Burkina Faso)]
  [DT 551.45.S (Mali)]
  UF Don (West African people)
       Matya (West African people)
       Matye (West African people)
       Maya (West African people)
       Nanerge Sembla (West African people)
       Ninisi (West African people)
       Samogho (West African people)
       Samojo (West African people)
       Samorho (West African people)
       Samoxo (West African people)
       San (West African people)
       Sanan (West African people)
       Sane (West African people)

Sambára language
  USE Shambala language

(May Subd Geog) = Place names may follow the heading

UF Saneno (West African people)
      Sano Nanerge (West African people)
      Sanu (West African people)
      Semou (West African people)
      Semu (West African people)
BT Ethnology--Burkina Faso
      Ethnology--Mali

Samo language (West Africa) *(May Subd Geog)*
UF Nangerge Sembla language
      Ninisi language
      Samajo language
      Samogho language
      Samojo language
      Samorho language
      Samoxo language
      Sano language
      Sanu language
      Semou language
      Semu language
BT Burkina Faso--Languages
      Mali--Languages
      Mande languages
RT Sembla language

Samogho (West African people)
   USE Samo (West African people)

Samogho language
   USE Samo language (West Africa)

Samojo (West African people)
   USE Samo (West African people)

Samojo language
   USE Samo language (West Africa)

Samorho (West African people)
   USE Samo (West African people)

Samorho language
   USE Samo language (West Africa)

Samoxo (West African people)
   USE Samo (West African people)

Samoxo language
   USE Samo language (West Africa)

Sampur (African people)
   USE Samburu (African people)

Sampur language
   USE Samburu language

Samwi dialect

USE Sanvi dialect

San (African people) *(May Subd Geog)*
   [DT 797 (Botswana : old class)]
   [DT 2458.S26 (Botswana : new class)]
   [DT 709 (Namibia : old class)]
   [DT 1558.S38 (Namibia : new class)]
   [DT 764.B8 (South Africa : old class)]
   [DT 1768.S36 (South Africa : new class)]
   [DT 737 (Southern Africa : old class)]
   [DT 1058.S36 (Southern Africa : new class)]
UF Basarwa (African people)
      Bushmen (African people)
BT Ethnology--Africa, Southern
      Ethnology--Botswana
      Ethnology--Namibia
      Ethnology--South Africa
NT G/wi (African people)
      !Kung (African people)
      Naron (African people)
      Tannekwe (African people)
--Anthropometry
   [GN 57.S26]
--Languages
   Here are entered works on all languages of the San
people, including the group known as "Central Bushman"
languages. Works on the Northern and Southern groups of the
Khoisan languages spoken by the San are entered under
San languages.
   UF Bushman languages
--Psychology
--Religion
   [BL 2480.624]

San (West African people)
   USE Samo (West African people)

San art
   USE Art, San

San languages
   [PL 8101-PL 8104]
   Here are entered works on the Northern and Southern
groups of the Khoisan languages spoken by the San people.
Works on all languages of the San people, including the
group known as "Central Bushman" languages , are entered
under San (African people)--Languages.
UF Bushman languages
BT Africa, Southern--Languages
      Botswana--Languages
      Khoisan languages
      Namibia--Languages
      South Africa--Languages
NT Kham language
      !Xo language
      !Xu language

UF = Used for; BT = Broader term; RT = Related term; SA = See also; NT = Narrower term

Sanakki (African people)
  USE Zanaki (African people)

Sanan (West African people)
  USE Samo (West African people)

Sanctions, Economic
  USE Economic sanctions

Sanctuaries, Game
  USE Game reserves

Sanctuaries, Wildlife
  USE Wildlife refuges

Sandaui (African people)
  USE Sandawe (African people)

Sandawe (African people) *(May Subd Geog)*
  [DT 443.3.S]
  UF Sandaui (African people)
      Sandawi (African people)
      Sandwe (African people)
      Wassandaui (African people)
  BT Ethnology--Tanzania
      Nilo-Hamitic tribes

Sandawe language *(May Subd Geog)*
  [PL 8631]
  UF Kissandaui language
      Wassandaui language
  BT Khoisan languages
      Tanzania--Languages

Sandawi (African people)
  USE Sandawe (African people)

Sandwe (African people)
  USE Sandawe (African people)

Sane (West African people)
  USE Samo (West African people)

Saneno (West African people)
  USE Samo (West African people)

Sanga (African people) *(May Subd Geog)*
  [DT 650.S25 (Zaire)]
  UF Basanga (African people)
      Bassanga (African people)
      Musanga (African people)
  BT Ethnology--Zaire
      Ethnology--Zambia
      Luba (African people)

Sanga language *(May Subd Geog)*
  UF Chiluba language (Sanga)
      Kiluba-Sanga language
      Luba language, Southern
      Luba-Sanga language
      Southern Luba language
  BT Bantu languages
      Zaire--Languages
      Zambia--Languages

Sanga Site (Zaire) *(Not Subd Geog)*
  [GN 780.42.Z27 : old class]
  [DT 648 : new class]
  BT Zaire--Antiquities

Sango language *(May Subd Geog)*
  [PL 8641]
  BT Central African Republic--Languages
      Chad--Languages
      Congo (Brazzaville)--Languages
      Lingua francas
      Ngbandi language
  RT Yakoma language

Sanitation, Tropical
  USE Tropical medicine

Sano language
  USE Samo language (West Africa)

Sano Nanerge (West African people)
  USE Samo (West African people)

Sansa (Musical instrument)
  USE Sanza

San Tiago Island (Cape Verde)
  USE Sao Tiago Island (Cape Verde)

Santiago Island (Cape Verde)
  USE Sao Tiago Island (Cape Verde)

Santomenses
  USE Sao Tomeans

Santu dialect
  USE Ntaandu dialect

Sanu (West African people)
  USE Samo (West African people)

Sanu language
  USE Samo language (West Africa)

(May Subd Geog) = Place names may follow the heading

Sanvi dialect *(May Subd Geog)*
[PL 8047.3.A695S]
UF Afema dialect
Samwi dialect
Sanwi dialect
BT Anyi language
Ivory Coast--Languages
--Phonemics

Sanwi dialect
USE Sanvi dialect

Sanyati River (Zimbabwe) *(Not Subd Geog)*
BT Rivers--Zimbabwe

Sanye language
USE Boni language

Sanye language (Dahalo)
USE Dahalo language

Sanza
[ML 1015.S35 (History and criticism)]
UF Sansa (Musical instrument)
Zanza (Musical instrument)
BT Musical instruments--Africa
NT Mbira

Sao (Chad people) *(May Subd Geog)*
[DT 546.445.S25 (Chad)]
UF So (Chad people)
BT Ethnology--Cameroon
Ethnology--Chad
Ethnology--Nigeria
RT Kotoko (African people)
--Antiquities

Sao art
USE Art, Sao

Sao Christovao Island (Cape Verde)
USE Boa Vista Island (Cape Verde)

Sao pottery
USE Pottery, Sao

Sao Tiage Island (Cape Verde) *(Not Subd Geog)*
UF San Tiago Island (Cape Verde)
Santiago Island (Cape Verde)
BT Cape Verde
Islands--Cape Verde

Sao Tome and Principe *(Not Subd Geog)*
[DT 615-DT 615.9]
--Economic conditions
[HC 965]

--Literatures
NT Sao Tomean literature

Sao Tomean children's poetry
USE Children's poetry, Sao Tomean

Sao Tomean literature *(May Subd Geog)*
[PQ 9948-PQ 9948.9]
UF Portuguese literature--Sao Tomean authors
BT Sao Tome and Principe--Literatures
NT Sao Tomean poetry

Sao Tomean poetry *(May Subd Geog)*
[PQ 9948.2 (History)]
[PQ 9948.6-PQ 9948.65 (Collections)]
UF Portuguese poetry--Sao Tomean authors
BT Sao Tomean literature
NT Children's poetry, Sao Tomean

Sao Tomeans *(May Subd Geog)*
UF Santomenses
BT Ethnology--Sao Tome and Principe

Sapiny (African people) *(May Subd Geog)*
[DT 433.245.S24 (Uganda)]
UF Sabaot (African people)
Sabei (African people)
Saviny (African people)
Sebei (African people)
BT Ethnology--Kenya
Ethnology--Uganda
Nilo-Hamitic tribes

Sapiny law
USE Law, Sebei

Sar dialect
USE Majingai dialect

Sara (African people) *(May Subd Geog)*
[DT 546.445.S27]
BT Ethnology--Chad
NT Nar (African people)
--Religion
[BL 2480.S25]

Sara Dai (African people)
USE Day (African people)

Sara Dai language
USE Day language (Chad)

Sara Gambai dialect
USE Gambai dialect

UF = Used for; BT = Broader term; RT = Related term; SA = See also; NT = Narrower term

Sara language *(May Subd Geog)*
  UF Majingai-Ngama language
  BT Central African Republic--Languages
      Chad--Languages
      Sara languages
  NT Majingai dialect
      Ngama dialect

Sara languages *(May Subd Geog)*
  [PL 8645]
  BT Bongo-Bagirimi languages
      Central African Republic--Languages
      Chad--Languages
  NT Gambai dialect
      Kenga language
      Mbai language (Moissala)
      Sara language

Sara-Majingai dialect
  USE Majingai dialect

Sara Mbai language (Moissala)
  USE Mbai language (Moissala)

Sara Nar (African people)
  USE Nar (African people)

Sara Ngabre language
  USE Gabri language

Sara Ngama dialect
  USE Ngama dialect

Sara Ngambay dialect
  USE Gambai dialect

Sara Toumak language
  USE Tumak language

Saraka (African people)
  USE Tharaka (African people)

Sarakole language
  USE Soninke language

Sarakolle language
  USE Soninke language

Saramo (African people)
  USE Zaramo (African people)

Sarawule language
  USE Soninke language

Sarnyéré (Mali) *(Not Subd Geog)*
  BT Mountains--Mali

Satire
  UF Comic literature
      Literature, Comic
  BT Literature
      Wit and humor

Satire, Afrikaans *(May Subd Geog)*
  [PT 6530 (History and criticism)]
  [PT 6575 (Collections)]
  UF Afrikaans satire
  BT Afrikaans wit and humor

Satire, Nigerian (English) *(May Subd Geog)*
  [PR 9387.4]
  UF Nigerian satire (English)

Savannas *(May Subd Geog)*
  BT Grasslands
      Plains
 --Ivory Coast
  NT Lamto (Ivory Coast)

Save River (Zimbabwe and Mozambique) *(Not Subd Geog)*
  UF Rio Save (Zimbabwe and Mozambique)
      Sabi River (Zimbabwe and Mozambique)
  BT Rivers--Mozambique
      Rivers--Zimbabwe

Saviny (African people)
  USE Sapiny (African people)

Sawmill workers *(May Subd Geog)*
 --Cameroon
  [HD 8039.S32C]

Sayings
  USE Proverbs

Scandinavian technical assistance
  USE Technical assistance, Scandinavian

Scarification
  USE Body-marking

School drama
  USE College and school drama

School life
  USE Students

School plays
  USE Children's plays
      College and school drama

(May Subd Geog) = Place names may follow the heading

School prose
  UF Students' writings
  BT Children's writings
      Youths' writings
  NT College prose

School prose, Ndebele (Zimbabwe) (May Subd Geog)
  [PL 8547.N285-PL 8547.N289]
  UF Ndebele school prose (Zimbabwe)
  BT Ndebele prose literature (Zimbabwe)

School prose, Tanzanian (May Subd Geog)
  [PL 8014.T342]
  UF Tanzanian school prose
  BT Tanzanian prose literature

School songbooks, African
  UF African school songbooks

School songbooks, Afrikaner (May Subd Geog)
  [M 1990-M 1994]
  UF Afrikaner school songbooks
  BT Songbooks, Afrikaner

School songbooks, Zulu (May Subd Geog)
  UF Zulu school songbooks

School theatricals
  USE College and school drama

School verse
  UF Students' writings
  BT Children's writings
      Youths' writings
  RT College verse

School verse, Tanzanian (May Subd Geog)
  [PL 8014.T342]
  UF Tanzanian school verse
  BT Tanzanian poetry

Science, Moral
  USE Ethics

Scriptures, Holy
  USE Bible

Scrolls, Ethiopian magic
  USE Ethiopian magic scrolls

Sculpture (May Subd Geog)
  UF Stonework, Decorative
  BT Art
  NT Bronzes
      Masks (Sculpture)
      Portrait sculpture

  NT Terra-cotta sculpture
      Wood-carving

Sculpture, African (May Subd Geog)
  [NB 1080]
  UF African sculpture

Sculpture, African portrait
  USE Portrait sculpture, African

Sculpture, Bambara (May Subd Geog)
  [NB 1099.M32B35]
  UF Bambara sculpture

Sculpture, Baoulé (May Subd Geog)
  [NB 1099.I82.B]
  UF Baoulé sculpture

Sculpture, Black (May Subd Geog)
  UF Black sculpture
  --Africa, Sub-Saharan
    [NB 1091.65]
  --Mozambique
    [NB 1097.6.M6]
  --Sudan
    [NB 1097.6.S73]

Sculpture, Cameroon (May Subd Geog)
  [NB 1099.C3]
  UF Cameroon sculpture

Sculpture, Chokwe (May Subd Geog)
  [NB 1099.A63C]
  UF Chokwe sculpture

Sculpture, Gabon (May Subd Geog)
  [NB 1099.G25]
  UF Gabon sculpture

Sculpture, Giryama (May Subd Geog)
  [NB 1097.6.K42G]
  UF Giryama sculpture

Sculpture, Hemba (May Subd Geog)
  [NB 1099.C62H]
  UF Hemba sculpture

Sculpture, Ijo (May Subd Geog)
  [NB 1099.N52I]
  UF Ijo sculpture

Sculpture, Kongo (May Subd Geog)
  [NB 1099.C62K]
  UF Kongo sculpture

UF = Used for; BT = Broader term; RT = Related term; SA = See also; NT = Narrower term

Sculpture, Kota *(May Subd Geog)*
  [NB 1099.G252K]
  UF Kota sculpture

Sculpture, Lobi *(May Subd Geog)*
  [NB 1099.U62L]
  UF Lobi sculpture

Sculpture, Makonde *(May Subd Geog)*
  [NB 1097.6.M62M]
  UF Makonde sculpture

Sculpture, Mandingo *(May Subd Geog)*
  [NB 1098]
  UF Mandingo sculpture

Sculpture, Mbembe *(May Subd Geog)*
  [NB 1099.N52M]
  UF Mbembe sculpture

Sculpture, Mbete *(May Subd Geog)*
  [NB 1099.G252M]
  UF Mbete sculpture

Sculpture, Mozambican *(May Subd Geog)*
  [NB 1097.6.M6]
  UF Mozambican sculpture

Sculpture, Nigerian *(May Subd Geog)*
  [NB 1099.N5]
  UF Nigerian sculpture

Sculpture, Primitive *(May Subd Geog)*
  UF Primitive sculpture
 --Cameroon
  [NB 1225.C17]

Sculpture, Senufo *(May Subd Geog)*
  [ND 1099.I82S]
  UF Senufo sculpture

Sculpture, Shona *(May Subd Geog)*
  [NB 1096.S]
  UF Shona sculpture

Sculpture, South African *(May Subd Geog)*
  [NB 1092-NB 1096]
  UF South African sculpture

Sculpture, Yoruba *(May Subd Geog)*
  [NB 1099.N52Y]
  UF Yoruba sculpture

Sculpture, Zairian *(May Subd Geog)*
  [NB 1099.C6]
  UF Zairian sculpture

Sculpture, Zande *(May Subd Geog)*
  [NB 1091.65]
  UF Zande sculpture

Seacow River (South Africa) *(Not Subd Geog)*
  UF Seekoei River (South Africa)
      Zeekoe River (South Africa)
  BT Rivers--South Africa

Search and rescue operations *(May Subd Geog)*
  UF Air rescue service
 --Ethiopia
  NT Falasha Rescue, 1984-1985
 --Sudan
  NT Falasha Rescue, 1984-1984

Sebei (African people)
  USE Sapiny (African people)

Sebei law
  USE Law, Sebei

Sebungwe Region (Zimbabwe) *(Not Subd Geog)*
  [DT 962.9.S : old class]
  [DT 3020.S : new class]

Sechuana language
  USE Tswana language

Secoana language
  USE Tswana language

Second Basuto War, 1865-1866
  USE Sotho-Free State War, 1865-1866

Second Chimurenga War (Zimbabwe), 1966-1980
  USE Zimbabwe--History--Chimurenga War, 1966-
1980

Second Free State-Sotho War, 1865-1866
  USE Sotho-Free State War, 1865-1866

Second Sotho-Free State War, 1865-1866
  USE Sotho-Free State War, 1865-1866

Second World War
  USE World War, 1939-1945

Sects, Christian
  USE Christian sects

Sects, Nativistic
  USE Nativistic movements

Secwana language
  USE Tswana language

(May Subd Geog) = Place names may follow the heading

Sederberge (South Africa)
USE Cedar Mountains (South Africa)

Seekoei River (South Africa)
USE Seacow River (South Africa)

Segregation *(May Subd Geog)*
UF Desegregation
BT Race discrimination
NT Apartheid
Blacks--Relocation
Blacks--Segregation
--Law and legislation *(May Subd Geog)*
--Religious aspects
--Namibia
UOE Apartheid--Namibia
--South Africa
USE Apartheid--South Africa

Segregation and the press
UF Press and segregation
BT Press

Sehonghong Rockshelter (Lesotho) *(Not Subd Geog)*
BT Caves--Lesotho
Lesotho--Antiquities

Sekiani language
USE Orungu language

Self-government
USE Representative government and
representation

Selous Game Reserve (Tanzania) *(Not Subd Geog)*
BT Game reserves--Tanzania
National parks and reserves--Tanzania

Sembila language
USE Sembla language

Sembla language *(May Subd Geog)*
[PL 8653]
UF Sembila language
Southern Samo language
BT Burkina Faso--Languages
Mali--Languages
Mande languages
RT Samo language (West Africa)

Semiarid regions
USE Arid regions

Semien Mountains (Ethiopia)
USE Simen Mountains (Ethiopia)

Semitic languages
[PJ 3001-PJ 9278]
BT Afroasiatic languages
NT Semitic languages, Southern Peripheral

Semitic languages, Southeast
USE Semitic languages, Southern Peripheral

Semitic languages, Southern Peripheral *(May Subd Geog)*
[PJ 5901-PJ 5909]
UF Semitic languages, Southeast
BT Semitic languages
NT Ethiopian languages

Semito-Hamitic languages
USE Afroasiatic languages

Semliki River (Zaire and Uganda) *(Not Subd Geog)*
BT Rivers--Uganda
Rivers--Zaire

Semou (West African people)
USE Samo (West African people)

Semou language
USE Samo language (West Africa)

Semu (West African people)
USE Samo (West African people)

Semu language
USE Samo language (West Africa)

Sena language *(May Subd Geog)*
[PL 8655]
UF Senna language
BT Bantu languages
Mozambique--Languages
RT Nyanja language
Tete language

Senadi language
USE Senari language

Senari language *(May Subd Geog)*
[PL 8658]
UF Cebaara Senoufo language
Senadi language
Senufo language
Syenere language
BT Ivory Coast--Languages
Mali--Languages
Senufo languages
NT Tyembara dialect

UF = Used for; BT = Broader term; RT = Related term; SA = See also; NT = Narrower term

Sendege language
  USE Mamara language

Senegal *(Not Subd Geog)*
  [DT 549-DT 549.9]
 --Civilization
 -- --Dravidian influences
 --Description and travel
 -- --1981-
 --Economic conditions
  [HC 1045]
 --History
 -- --To 1960
  NT Fuladu (Kingdom)
      Niumi (Kingdom)
 -- --1960-
 -- --Coup d'état, 1962
  [DT 549.8]
  BT Coups d'état--Senegal
 --Languages
  NT Badyaranke language
      Balante language
      Bassari language
      Bedik language
      Cangin languages
      Crioulo language
      Diola language
      Falor language
      Lebou dialect
      Mandjak language
      Pular dialect
      Serer language
      Soninke language
      Wolof language
 --Literatures
  USE Senegalese literature
 --Poetry
  NT Wolof poetry
 --Politics and government
 -- --To 1960
 -- --1960-

Senegal River *(Not Subd Geog)*
  UF Fleuve Senegal
      Senegal River, Mali-Senegal
  BT Rivers--Mali
      Rivers--Mauritania
      Rivers--Senegal

Senegal River, Mali-Senegal
  USE Senegal River

Senegal River Delta (Mauritania and Senegal)
(Not Subd Geog)
  BT Deltas--Mauritania
      Deltas--Senegal

Senegalese *(May Subd Geog)*
  BT Ethnology--Senegal

Senegalese alien labor
  USE Alien labor, Senegal

Senegalese art
  USE Art, Senegalese

Senegalese authors
  USE Authors, Senegalese

Senegalese civics
  USE Civics, Senegalese

Senegalese cookery
  USE Cookery, Senegalese

Senegalese drama (French) *(May Subd Geog)*
  [PQ 3988.5.S38 (History)]
  [PQ 3988.5.S382 (Collections)]
  UF French drama--Senegalese authors
  BT Senegalese literature (French)

Senegalese erotic poetry (French)
  USE Erotic poetry, Senegalese (French)

Senegalese fiction (French) *(May Subd Geog)*
  [PQ 3988.5.S38 (History)]
  [PQ 3988.5.S382 (Collections)]
  UF French fiction--Senegalese authors
  BT Senegalese literature (French)
      West African fiction (French)

Senegalese literature *(May Subd Geog)*
  [PL 8014.S]
  UF Senegal--Literatures
  BT West African literature
  NT Pular literature
      Wolof literature

Senegalese literature (French) *(May Subd Geog)*
  [PQ 3988.5.S38 (History)]
  [PQ 3988.5.S382 (Collections)]
  UF French literature--Senegalese authors
  BT West African literature (French)
  NT Senegalese drama (French)
      Senegalese fiction (French)
      Senegalese poetry (French)

Senegalese poetry (French) *(May Subd Geog)*
  [PQ 3988.5.S38 (History)]
  [PQ 3988.5.S382 (Collections)]
  UF French poetry--Senegalese authors
  BT Senegalese literature (French)

(May Subd Geog) = Place names may follow the heading

BT   West African poetry (French)
NT   Erotic poetry, Senegalese (French)

Senegalese students *(May Subd Geog)*
BT   Students
--**Foreign countries**
BT   Students, Foreign

Senegambia *(Not Subd Geog)*
[DT 532.25]
--**History**
NT   Mamadou Lamine, Rebellion of, 1885-1887

Senga language *(May Subd Geog)*
[PL 8656]
UF   Nsenga language
BT   Bantu languages
     Malawi--Languages

Senna language
USE   Sena language

Sennar (Kingdom)
[DT 159.6.S46]
BT   Fungs--History

Senoufo (African people)
USE   Senufo (African people)

Senoufo languages
USE   Senufo languages

Senufo (African people) *(May Subd Geog)*
[DT 545.45.S44 (Ivory Coast)]
[DT 551.45.S (Mali)]
UF   Senoufo (African people)
     Siena (African people)
     Syena (African people)
BT   Ethnology--Ivory Coast
     Ethnology--Mali
NT   Gouin (African people)
     Kulebele (African people)
     Minianka (African people)
     Tagbana (African people)
--**Funeral customs and rites**
UF   Funeral rites and ceremonies, Senufo
(African people)
--**Religion**
[BL 2480.S44]
--**Rites and ceremonies**

Senufo art
USE   Art, Senufo

Senufo language

USE   Senari language

Senufo languages *(May Subd Geog)*
[PL 8658]
UF   Senoufo languages
BT   Gur languages
     Ivory Coast--Languages
     Mali--Languages
NT   Mamara language
     Senari language

Senufo sculpture
USE   Sculpture, Senufo

Senufo textile fabrics
USE   Textile fabrics, Senufo

Senussite Rebellion, 1916-1918
[DT 547.75]
UF   Kaoussan, Rebellion of, 1916-1918
     Rebellion of Kaoussan, 1916-1918
BT   Niger--History--To 1960
     Nigeria--History--1900-1960
     Tuaregs--History
     World War, 1914-1918--Campaigns--Africa

Separate development (Race relations)
USE   Apartheid

Separatism, Black
USE   Black nationalism

Separatist movements
USE   *subdivision* History--Autonomy and
independence movements *under names of regions,
countries, etc, e.g.,* Eritrea (Ethiopia)--History--
Autonomy and independence movements

Sepedi (African people)
USE   Pedi (African people)

Sepedi language
USE   Northern Sotho language

Seqiti War, 1865-1866
USE   Sotho-Free State War, 1865-1866

Serahuli language
USE   Soninke language

Serengeti National Park (Tanzania) *(Not Subd Geog)*
BT   National parks and reserves--Tanzania

Serengeti Plain (Tanzania) *(Not Subd Geog)*
UF   Serengetti Plains (Tanzania)
BT   Plains--Tanzania

UF = Used for; BT = Broader term; RT = Related term; SA = See also; NT = Narrower term

Senergetti Plains (Tanzania)
  USE Serengeti Plain (Tanzania)

Serer (African people) *(May Subd Geog)*
  [DT 549.45.S47 (Senegal)]
  BT Ethnology--Gambia
      Ethnology--Senegal

Serer language *(May Subd Geog)*
  [PL 8662]
  BT Gambia--Languages
      Niger-Congo languages
      Senegal--Languages

Serer proverbs
  USE Proverbs, Serer

Serer riddles
  USE Riddles, Serer

Servicemen, Military
  USE Soldiers

Sesotho language
  USE Sotho language

Sesuto language
  USE Sotho language

Setswana language
  USE Tswana language

Settlements, Squatter
  USE Squatter settlements

Settlers of 1820 (South Africa)
  USE British settlers of 1820 (South
Africa)

Sex customs *(May Subd Geog)*
  BT Manners and customs
  SA *subdivision* Sexual behavior *under ethnic*
groups
  NT Circumcision
      Infibulation
      Puberty rites

Seychelles *(Not Subd Geog)*
  [DT 469.S4-DT 469.S49]
  BT Islands of the Indian Ocean
  NT Aldabra Island (Seychelles)
      La Digue Island (Seychelles)
      Praslin Island (Seychelles)
 --Description and travel
 -- --1981-

--Economic conditions
  [HC 596.5]
-- --1976-
--History
-- --Coup d'état, 1977
  [DT 469.S48]
  BT Coups d'état--Seychelles
-- --Coup d'état, 1981
  BT Coups d'état--Seychelles
--Politics and government
-- --To 1976
-- --1976-
--Social conditions
-- --1976

Seychelles cookery
  USE Cookery, Seychelles

Shaba (Zaire)
  [DT 665.K3]
  UF Katanga (Secessionist government, 1960-
1963)
      Katanga (Zaire)
 --History
  NT Zaire--History--Shaba Invasion, 1977

Shaba Invasion (Zaire), 1977
  USE Zaire--History--Shaba Invasion, 1977

Shaba Uprising (Zaire), 1978
  USE Zaire--History--Shaba Uprising, 1978

Shaba War (Zaire), 1977
  USE Zaire--History--Shaba Invasion, 1977

Shack towns
  USE Squatter settlements

Shaikia (Arab people) *(May Subd Geog)*
  [DT 155.2.S45]
  UF Cheykye (Arab people)
      Shaikieh (Arab people)
      Shaiqiya (Arab people)
      Sheygyeh (Arab people)
  BT Ethnology--Sudan

Shaikieh (Arab people)
  USE Shaikia (Arab people)

Shaiqiya (Arab people)
  USE Shaikia (Arab people)

Shake (African people)
  USE Kota (African people)

(May Subd Geog) = Place names may follow the heading

Shamans *(May Subd Geog)*
  [GN 475.8]
  UF Medicine-man
      Medicine men
      Medicine women
  BT Folk medicine
      ·Medicine, Primitive
 --Africa
 --Cameroon

Shambaa (African people)
  USE Shambala (African people)

Shambaa languages
  USE Shambala languages

Shambala (African people) *(May Subd Geog)*
  [DT 443.3.S45]
  UF Sambaa (African people)
      Sambala (African people)
      Sambara (African people)
      Shambaa (African people)
      Washambala (African people)
      Washambara (African people)
  BT Bantu-speaking peoples
      Ethnology--Tanzania

Chambala language *(May Subd Geog)*
  [PL 8666]
  UF KiChambaa language
      Kishambala language
      Sambaa language
      Sambála language
      Sambára language
  BT Shambala languages
      Tanzania--Languages

Shambala languages *(May Subd Geog)*
  UF Shambaa languages
  BT Bantu languages
      Kenya--Languages
      Tanzania--Languages
  NT Asu language
      Bondei language
      Shambala language
      Taveta language

Shambiu (African people)
  USE Sambyu (African people)

Shangaan (African people)
  USE Tsonga (African people)

Shangaan language
  USE Tsonga language

Shangana (African people)
  USE Tsonga (African people)

Shangani River Massacre, 1893
  [DT 958 : old class]
  [DT 2966 : new class]
  BT Massacres--Zimbabwe
      Matabele War, 1893

Shantytowns
  USE Squatter settlements

Shaqadud Cave (Sudan) *(Not Subd Geog)*
  BT Caves--Sudan
      Sudan--Antiquities

Sharoka (African people)
  USE Tharaka (African people)

Sharpeville Massacre, 1960
  USE Massacres--South Africa--Sharpeville

Shatt (African people) *(May Subd Geog)*
  [DT 155.2.S]
  BT Ethnology--Sudan

Shebele River (Ethiopia and Somalia)
  USE Shebeli River (Ethiopia and Somalia)

Shebeli River (Ethiopia and Somalia) *(Not Subd Geog)*
  UF Shebele River (Ethiopia and Somalia)
      Shebelle River (Ethiopia and Somalia)
      Shebelli River (Ethiopia and Somalia)
      Uebi Scebeli River (Ethiopia and Somalia)
      Webi River (Ethiopia and Somalia)
      Webi Shebeli River (Ethiopia and Somalia)
  BT Rivers--Ethiopia
      Rivers--Somalia

Shebelle River (Ethiopia and Somalia)
  USE Shebeli River (Ethiopia and Somalia)

Shebelli River (Ethiopia and Somalia)
  USE Shebeli River (Ethiopia and Somalia)

Shede language
  USE Gude language

Sheetswa language
  USE Tswa language

Shekiani language
  USE Orungu language

Shengwe (Mozambique people)
  USE Tonga (Mozambique people)

UF = Used for; BT = Broader term; RT = Related term; SA = See also; NT = Narrower term

Sherbro (African people) *(May Subd Geog)*
  [DT 516.45.S]
  UF Amampa (African people)
      Bullom, Southern (African people)
      Kafu (African people)
      Mampa (African people)
      Mampua (African people)
      Mampwa (African people)
      Shiba (African people)
      Southern Bullom (African people)
  BT Ethnology--Sierra Leone
  --Religion
  [BL 2470.S55]

Sherbro language *(May Subd Geog)*
  [PL 8668]
  UF Amampa language
      Bullom language, Southern
      Mampa language
      Mampwa language
      Shiba language
      Southern Bullom language
  BT Niger-Congo languages
      Sierra Leone--Languages

Sheygyeh (Arab people)
  USE Shaikia (Arab people)

Shi language *(May Subd Geog)*
  [PL 8670]
  UF Mashi language
      Nyabungu language
  BT Bantu languages
      Zaire--Languages

Shiba (African people)
  USE Sherbro (African people)

Shiba language
  USE Sherbro language

Shilenge language
  USE Chopi language

Shilluk (African people) *(May Subd Geog)*
  [DT 155.2.S46 (Sudan)]
  UF Colo (African people)
      Dhocolo (African people)
      Sholo (African people)
  BT Ethnology--Ethiopia
      Ethnology--Sudan
      Luo (African people)
  --Intelligence levels

Shilluk language *(May Subd Geog)*
  [PL 8671]
  BT Ethiopia--Languages
      Nilotic languages
      Sudan--Languages

Shimba (African people)
  USE Himba (African people)

Shinkoya (African people)
  USE Nkoya (African people)

Shioke language
  USE Chokwe language

Shira (African people) *(May Subd Geog)*
  [DT 546.145.S55]
  UF Ashango (African people)
      Echira (African people)
      Gisira (African people)
      Sira (African people)
  BT Bantu-speaking peoples
      Ethnology--Gabon

Shira language *(May Subd Geog)*
  [PL 8675]
  UF Apono language
      Asango language
      Ashango language
      Ashira language
      Asira language
      Esira language
      Gisira language
      Lisango language
      Lisira language
      Masango language
  BT Bantu languages
      Gabon--Languages

Shire River (Malawi and Mozambique) *(Not Subd Geog)*
  UF Chire River (Malawi and Mozambique)
      Tchiri River (Malawi and Mozambique)
  BT Rivers--Malawi
      Rivers--Mozambique

Shironga language
  USE Ronga language

Shitsonga language
  USE Tsonga language

Shitswa language
  USE Tswa language

Shoba (African people)
  USE Shoowa (African people)

(May Subd Geog) = Place names may follow the heading

Shobwa (African people)
  USE Shoowa (African people)

Shobyo (African people)
  USE Hutu (African people)

Shogo (African people)
  USE Mitsogho (African people)

Sholo (African people)
  USE Shilluk (African people)

Shona (African people) *(May Subd Geog)*
  [DT 962.42 (Zimbabwe : old class)]
  [DT 2913.S (Zimbabwe : new class)]
  UF Mashona (African people)
  BT Bantu-speaking peoples
      Ethnology--South Africa
      Ethnology--Zimbabwe
  NT Gova (Shona-speaking people)
      Karanga (African people)
      Nika (African people)
      Tawara (African people)
      Zezuru (African people)
 --Children
  BT Children--South Africa
      Children--Zimbabwe
 --History
  NT Monomotapa Empire
 -- --19th century
  NT Zimbabwe--History--Ndebele
Insurrection, 1896-1897
 --Medicine
  BT Medicine, Primitive--South Africa
      Medicine, Primitive--Zimbabwe
 --Missions *(May Subd Geog)*
  [BV 3630.M32]
  UF Missions to Shona (African people)
 --Religion
  NT Mwari (Shona deity)

Shona drama *(May Subd Geog)*
  [PL 8681.5-PL 8681.9]
  BT Shona literature
      South African drama
      Zimbabwean drama
  NT One-act plays, Shona

Shona fiction *(May Subd Geog)*
  [PL 8681.5-PL 8681.9]
  BT Shona literature
      South African fiction
      Zimbabwean fiction
  NT Humorous stories, Shona
      Short stories, Shona

Shona folk poetry
  USE Folk poetry, Shona

Shona humorous stories
  USE Humorous stories, Shona

Shona language *(May Subd Geog)*
  [PL 8681]
  UF China language (Africa)
      Zezuru language
  BT Bantu languages
      South Africa--Languages
      Zimbabwe--Languages
  NT Lilima language
 --Names
  USE Names, Shona
 --Tone
  BT Tone (Phonetics)

Shona law
  USE Law, Shona

Shona literature *(May Subd Geog)*
  [PL 8681.5-PL 8681.9]
  BT South African literature
      Zimbabwean literature
  NT Shona drama
      Shona fiction
      Shona poetry

Shona names
  USE Names, Shona

Shona one-act plays
  USE One-act plays, Shona

Shona poetry *(May Subd Geog)*
  [PL 8681.5 (History)]
  [PL 8681.7 (Collections)]
  BT Shona literature
      South African poetry
      Zimbabwean poetry
  NT Folk poetry, Shona

Shona proverbs
  USE Proverbs, Shona

Shona sculpture
  USE Sculpture, Shona

Shona short stories
  USE Short stories, Shona

Shona songs
  USE Songs, Shona

UF = Used for; BT = Broader term; RT = Related term; SA = See also; NT = Narrower term

Shona wit and humor *(May Subd Geog)*
  [PL 8681 (History and major collections)]
  [PN 6222.S (Minor collections)]
  UF Wit and humor, Shona
  NT Humorous stories, Shona

Shongo language
  USE Bushoong language

Shoowa (African people) *(May Subd Geog)*
  [DT 650.S]
  UF Bashoobwa (African people)
      Shoba (African people)
      Shobwa (African people)
      Tshobwa (African people)
  BT Ethnology--Zaire
      Kuba (African people)

Shoowa embroidery
  USE Embroidery, Shoowa

Short plays
  USE One-act plays

Short stories
  UF Stories, Short
  BT Fiction

Short stories, African (English) *(Not Subd Geog)*
  [PR 9344 (History)]
  [PR 9348 (Collections)]
  UF African short stories (English)
      Short stories, English--African
authors
  BT African fiction (English)

Short stories, African (French) *(Not Subd Geog)*
  [PQ 3984 (History)]
  [PQ 3988 (Collections)]
  UF African short stories (French)
      Short stories, French--African authors
  BT African fiction (French)

Short stories, English *(May Subd Geog)*
  UF English short stories
  BT English fiction
 --African authors
  USE Short stories, African (English)
 --Ghanaian authors
  USE Short stories, Ghanaian (English)
 --Liberian authors
  USE Short stories, Liberian (English)
 --Nigerian authors
  USE Short stories, Nigerian (English)
 --South African authors
  USE Short stories, South African (English)

--Southern African authors
 USE Short stories, Southern African (English)
--Ugandan authors
 USE Short stories, Ugandan (English)
--West African authors
 USE Short stories, West African (English)

Short stories, French *(May Subd Geog)*
  UF French short stories
  BT French fiction
--African authors
 USE Short stories, African (French)
--Niger authors
 USE Short stories, Niger (French)
--Réunion authors
 USE Short stories, Réunion (French)
--West African authors
 USE Short stories, West African (French)

Short stories, Ghanaian (English) *(May Subd Geog)*
  [PR 9379.4 (History)]
  [PR 9379.8 (Collections)]
  UF Ghanaian short stories (English)
      Short stories, English--Ghanaian authors
  BT Ghanaian fiction (English)

Short stories, Igbo *(May Subd Geog)*
  [PL 8261.5-PL 8261.9]
  UF Igbo short stories
  BT Igbo fiction

Short stories, Liberian (English) *(May Subd Geog)*
  [PR 9384.4 (History)]
  [PR 9384.8 (Collections)]
  UF Liberian short stories (English)
      Short stories, English--Liberian authors
  BT Liberian fiction (English)

Short stories, Niger (French) *(May Subd Geog)*
  [PQ 3988.5.N5 (History)]
  [PQ 2988.5.N52 (Collections)]
  UF Niger short stories (French)
      Short stories, French--Niger authors
  BT Niger fiction (French)

Short stories, Nigerian (English) *(May Subd Geog)*
  [PR 9387.4 (History)]
  [PR 9387.8 (Collections)]
  UF Nigerian short stories (English)
      Short stories, English--Nigerian authors
  BT Nigerian fiction (English)

Short stories, Réunion (French) *(May Subd Geog)*
  [PQ 3988.5.R4 (History)]
  [PQ 3988.5.R42 (Collections)]
  UF Réunion short stories (French)

(May Subd Geog) = Place names may follow the heading

UF   Short stories, French--Réunion authors
BT   Réunion fiction (French)

Short stories, Réunion (French Creole) *(May Subd Geog)*
  [PM 7854.R4]
  UF   Creole short stories, Réunion French
       French Creole short stories, Réunion
       Réunion short stories (French Creole)
  BT   Réunion fiction (French Creole)

Short stories, Shona *(May Subd Geog)*
  [PL 8681.5-PL 8681.9]
  UF   Shona short stories
  BT   Shona fiction

Short stories, South African *(May Subd Geog)*
  [PR 8014.S6 (History)]
  [PR 8014.S62 (Collections)]
  UF   South African short stories
  BT   South African fiction

Short stories, South African (English) *(May Subd Geog)*
  [PR 9363.7 (History)]
  [PR 9367.32 (Collections)]
  UF   Short stories, English--South African
authors
       South African short stories (English)
  BT   South African fiction (English)

Short stories, Southern African
  [PL 8014.S6 (History)]
  [PL 8014.S62 (Collections)]
  UF   Southern African short stories
  BT   Southern African fiction

Short stories, Southern African (English)
  [PR 9348 (Collections)]
  UF   Short stories, English--Southern
African authors
       Southern African short stories
(English)
  BT   Southern African fiction (English)

Short stories, Ugandan (English) *(May Subd Geog)*
  [PR 9402.4 (History)]
  [PR 9402.8 (Collections)]
  UF   Short stories, English--Ugandan
authors
       Ugandan short stories (English)
  BT   Ugandan fiction (English)

Short stories, Swahili *(May Subd Geog)*
  [PL 8703.5-PL 8704]
  UF   Swahili short stories

  BT   Swahili fiction

Short stories, Venda *(May Subd Geog)*
  [PL 8771.5-PL 8771.9]
  UF   Venda short stories
  BT   Venda fiction

Short stories, West African (English) *(Not Subd Geog)*
  [PR 9348 (Collections)]
  UF   Short stories, English--West African
authors
       West African short stories (English)
  BT   West African fiction (English)

Short stories, West African (French) *(Not Subd Geog)*
  [PQ 3988 (Collections)]
  UF   Short stories, French--West African authors
       West African short stories (French)
  BT   West African fiction (French)

Shorthand, Swahili
  [Z 95]
  UF   Swahili shorthand

Show business
  USE   Performing arts

Shukulumbwe (African people)
  USE   Ila (African people)

Shuli (African people)
  USE   Acoli (African people)

Shuli language
  USE   Acoli language

Shupaman (African people)
  USE   Bamun (African people)

Sickle cell anemia *(May Subd Geog)*
  [RC 641.7.S5]
  BT   Tropical medicine

Sidama (African people)
  USE   Sidamo (African people)

Sidaminya (African people)
  USE   Sidamo (African people)

Sidamo (African people) *(May Subd Geog)*
  [DT 380.4.S5]
  UF   Sadama (African people)
       Sadaminya (African people)
       Sidama (African people)
       Sidaminya (African people)   *(Continued)*

UF = Used for; BT = Broader term; RT = Related term; SA = See also; NT = Narrower term

Sidamo (African people) *(Continued)*
  BT Ethnology--Ethiopia

Sidamo language *(May Subd Geog)*
  [PJ 2517]
  BT Sidamo languages

Sidamo languages *(May Subd Geog)*
  [PJ 2491-PJ 2517]
  BT Cushitic languages
  NT Gedeo language
      Sidamo language

Siena (African people)
  USE Senufo (African people)

Sieges
  USE *subdivision* History--Siege--[date] *under
names of countries, cities, etc., e.g.* Ladysmith
(South Africa)--History--Siege, 1899-1900

Sierra Leone *(Not Subd Geog)*
  [DT 516-DT 516.9]
 --Description and travel
 -- --1981-
 --Drama
  NT Krio drama
 --Economic conditions
  [HC 1065]
 -- --To 1896
 -- --1896-1961
 -- --1961-
 --History
 -- --To 1896
  NT Waima (Sierra Leone), Battle of, 1893
 --Languages
  NT Gola language
      Kissi language
      Kono language
      Krio language
      Limba language
      Loko language
      Mende language
      Northern Bullom language
      Sherbro language
      Susu language
      Timne language
      Vai language
 --Literatures
  USE Sierra Leone literature
 --Politics and government
 -- --To 1808
 -- --1808-1896
 -- --1896-1961
 -- --1961-
 --Social conditions

 -- --To 1961
 -- --1961-

Sierra Leone college verse (English)
  USE College verse, Sierra Leone (English)

Sierra Leone literature *(May Subd Geog)*
  [PL 8014.S]
  UF Sierra Leone--Literatures
  BT West African literature
  NT Krio literature

Sierra Leone literature (English) *(May Subd Geog)*
  [PR 9393]
  UF English literature--Sierra Leone authors
  BT West African literature (English)
  NT Sierra Leone poetry (English)

Sierra Leone poetry (English) *(May Subd Geog)*
  [PR 9393.2 (History)]
  [PR 9393.6-PR 9393.65 (Collections)]
  UF English poetry--Sierra Leone authors
  BT Sierra Leone literature (English)
      West African poetry (English)
  NT College verse, Sierra Leone (English)

Sikisi (African people)
  USE Kipsigis (African people)

Sikololo language
  USE Lozi language

Silabe language
  USE Soninke language

Silenge language
  USE Chopi language

Silozi language
  USE Lozi language

SiLuyana language
  USE Luyana language

Simba (African people)
  USE Himba (African people)

Simba dialect
  USE Himba dialect

Simen Mountains (Ethiopia) *(Not Subd Geog)*
  UF Semien Mountains (Ethiopia)
      Simien Mountains (Ethiopia)
      Simyen Mountains (Ethiopia)
  BT Mountains--Ethiopia
  RT Simen Mountains National Park (Ethiopia)

(May Subd Geog) = Place names may follow the heading

Simen Mountains National Park (Ethiopia) *(Not Subd Geog)*
  UF Simen National Park (Ethiopia)
      Simien Mountains National Park
(Ethiopia)
      Simien National Park (Ethiopia)
  BT National parks and reserves--Ethiopia
  RT Simen Mountains (Ethiopia)

Simen National Park (Ethiopia)
  USE Simen Mountains National Park
(Ethiopia)

Simien Mountains (Ethiopia)
  USE Simen Mountains (Ethiopia)

Simien Mountains National Park (Ethiopia)
  USE Simen Mountains National Park
(Ethiopia)

Simien National Park (Ethiopia)
  USE Simen Mountains National Park
(Ethiopia)

Simyen Mountains (Ethiopia)
  USE Simen Mountains (Ethiopia)

Sindebele language
  USE Ndebele language (Zimbabwe)

Sindja (African people)
  USE Zinza (African people)

Single party systems
  USE One party systems

Sira (African people)
  USE Shira (African people)

Sisai language
  USE Sisala language

Sisala (African people) *(May Subd Geog)*
  [DT 510.43.S57 (Ghana)]
  UF Isala (African people)
  BT Ethnology--Burkina Faso
      Ethnology--Ghana

Sisala language *(May Subd Geog)*
  [PL 8682.S55]
  UF Hissala language
      Issala language
      Sisai language
  BT Burkina Faso--Languages
      Ghana--Languages
      Grusi languages

Siska (African people)
  USE Tumbuka (African people)

SiSwati language
  USE Swazi language

Siswazi (African people)
  USE Swazi (African people)

Sisya (African people)
  USE Tumbuka (African people)

Siti language
  USE Vagala language

Sitigo language
  USE Vagala language

Skeletal remains
  USE Man, Prehistoric

Skeleton Coast (Namibia) *(Not Subd Geog)*
  [DT 720.S : old class]
  [DT 1670.S64 : new class]
  UF Coast of Death (Namibia)
      Death, Coast of (Namibia)
      Kaokoveld Coast (Namibia)
  BT Coasts--Namibia

Skin, Color of
  USE Color of man

Skin pigmentation
  USE Color of man

Slachters Nek Rebellion, 1815
  [DT 844.3 : old class]
  [DT 1839 : new class]
  BT South Africa--History--To 1836

Slave Coast
  USE Africa, West

Slave dealers
  USE Slave traders

Slave keeping
  USE Slavery

Slave-trade *(May Subd Geog)*
  [HT 1321-HT 1427 (Africa)]
  BT Slavery
  NT Slave traders
      Slavery (International law)
  --Africa, Central
    [DT 351 (History)]

UF = Used for; BT = Broader term; RT = Related term; SA = See also; NT = Narrower term

Slave traders *(May Subd Geog)*
    UF   Slave dealers
         Slavers
         Traders, Slave
    BT   Slave-trade
         Slavery
 --**Africa, Central**
    [DT 351]

Slavers
    USE   Slave traders

Slavery *(May Subd Geog)*
    [HT 1321-HT 1427 (Africa)]
    UF   Abolition of slavery
         Antislavery
         Ownership of slaves
         Slave keeping
    NT   Slave-trade
         Slave traders

Slavery (International law)
    [JX 4447]
    BT   Slave-trade

Slavery and slaves in literature
    [PN 56.S]
    UF   Slaves in literature
    BT   Literature

Slaves in literature
    USE   Slavery and slaves in literature

Slaves' writings
    UF   Writings of slaves
    BT   Literature

Slaves' writings, English *(May Subd Geog)*
    [PR 1178.S]
    UF   English slaves' writings
    BT   English literature

Slum clearance
    USE   Slums

Slumber songs
    USE   Lullabies

Slums *(May Subd Geog)*
    UF   Slum clearance
    NT   Squatter settlements
 --**Africa**
    [HV 4617]
 --**Angola**
    [HV 4623.9]

So (African people)
    USE   Tepeth (African people)

So (Chad people)
    USE   Sao (Chad people)

Soba (African people)
    USE   Suba (African people)

Sobo (African people) *(May Subd Geog)*
    [DT 515.45.S]
    UF   Urhobo (African people)
    BT   Ethnology--Nigeria
    NT   Isoko (African people)

Soce (African people)
    USE   Mandingo (African people)

Social anthropology
    USE   Ethnology

Social customs
    USE   Manners and customs

Social democracy
    USE   Socialism

Social life and customs
    USE   Manners and customs

Social service and race relations *(May Subd Geog)*
    UF   Race relations and social service
    BT   Race relations

Socialism *(May Subd Geog)*
    Here are entered works on a variety of social and
    political doctrines or movements which advocate collective
    ownership of the means of production, a more equitable
    distribution of wealth, and democratic processes for
    achieving these ends, and which, in Marxist theory,
    represent the transitional stage between capitalism and
    communism.
    UF   Marxism
         Social democracy
         Socialist movements
    RT   Communism
    NT   Collective settlements
 --**Africa, Sub-Saharan**
    [HX 436.5]
 --**Tanzania**
    [HX 448.5]

Socialist movements
    USE   Socialism

(May Subd Geog) = Place names may follow the heading

Société forestière et industrielle de la
Doumé Strike, 1963
[HD 9767.C34S63]
BT Strikes and lockouts--Lumber trade--
Cameroon

Sofala language
USE Chindau language

Soga (African people) *(May Subd Geog)*
[DT 433.245.S]
BT Bantu-speaking peoples
Ethnology--Uganda
--Kings and rulers

Soga language *(May Subd Geog)*
[PL 8682.S6]
UF Lusoga language
DT Bantu languages
Uganda--Languages

Soga philology
[PL 8682.S6]
UF Philology, Soga
BT Bantu philology

Soghaua (African people)
USE Zaghawa (African people)

Sokile (African people)
USE Nyakyusa (African people)

Sokoto Caliphate
USE Fula Empire

Sokoto Empire
USE Fula Empire

Sokoto Jihad, 1803-1830
[DT 530.5.F84]
UF Fulani Jihad, 1803-1930
BT Africa, West--History--To 1884
Fula (African people)--History--19th
century

Sokoto River (Nigeria) *(Not Subd Geog)*
UF Kebbi River (Nigeria)
BT Rivers--Nigeria

Soldiers *(May Subd Geog)*
UF Military life
Military personnel
Servicemen, Military
Soldiers' life

Soldiers, Black *(May Subd Geog)*
UF Black soldiers
BT Blacks
--Namibia
[UB 419.N]
--South Africa
[UB 419.S6]
NT South African War, 1899-1902--
Participation, Black

Soldiers' life
USE Soldiers

Soldiers' writings
BT Literature

Soldiers' writings, Nigerian (English) *(May Subd
Geog)*
[PR 9387.6]
UF Nigerian soldiers' writings (English)

Solongo dialect *(May Subd Geog)*
[PL 8682.S]
UF Kisolongo dialect
Musserongo dialect
BT Angola--Languages
Kongo language

Soma language
USE Somba language

Somali children's stories
USE Children's stories, Somali

Somali-Ethiopian Conflict, 1977-1979
[DT 387.952]
UF Ethiopian-Somali Conflict, 1977-1979
BT Ethiopia--History--1974-
Somalia--History

Somali-Ethiopian Conflict, 1979-
[DT 387.952]
UF Ethiopian-Somali Conflict, 1979-
BT Ethiopia--History--1974-
Somalia--History

Somali fiction *(May Subd Geog)*
[PJ 2533.5-PJ 2534]
BT African fiction
Somali literature
NT Children's stories, Somali

Somali folk literature
USE Folk literature, Somali

UF = Used for; BT = Broader term; RT = Related term; SA = See also; NT = Narrower term

Somali folk songs
USE Folk songs, Somali

Somali language *(May Subd Geog)*
[PJ 2531-PJ 2534]
BT Somali languages
Somalia--Languages

Somali languages *(May Subd Geog)*
[PJ 2525]
UF Sam languages
BT Cushitic languages
Kenya--Languages
Somalia--Languages
NT Rendile language
Somali language

Somali literature *(May Subd Geog)*
[PJ 2533.5-PJ 2534]
UF Somalia--Literatures
BT African literature
NT Folk literature, Somali
Somali fiction
Somali poetry

Somali philology
[PJ 2531-PJ 2534]
UF Philology, Somali

Somali poetry *(May Subd Geog)*
[PJ 2533.5-PJ 2534]
BT African poetry
Somali literature
NT Revolutionary poetry, Somali

Somali proverbs
USE Proverbs, Somali

Somali Republic
USE Somalia

Somali revolutionary poetry
USE Revolutionary poetry, Somali

Somali students *(May Subd Geog)*
BT Students
--Foreign countries
BT Students, Foreign

Somalia *(Not Subd Geog)*
[DT 401-DT 409]
*Formed with the merger of British Somaliland and
Italian Somaliland.*
UF British Somaliland
Italian Somaliland
Somali Republic

UF Somaliland, British
Somaliland, Italian
--Description and travel
-- --1981-
--Economic conditions
[HC 850]
-- --1960-
--Foreign relations *(May Subd Geog)*
-- --1960-
--History
NT Maxamad Cabdulle Xasan's Rebellion, British
Somaliland, 1900-1920
Somali-Ethiopian Conflict, 1977-1979
Somali-Ethiopian Conflict, 1979-
--Languages
NT Boni language
Somali language
Somali languages
--Literatures
USE Somali literature
--Politics and government
-- --1960-
--Social conditions
-- --1960-

Somaliland, British
USE Somalia

Somaliland, French
USE Djibouti

Somaliland, Italian
USE Somalia

Somalis *(May Subd Geog)*
UF Somals
BT Ethnology--Somalia
Hamites
--Ethiopia
[DT 380.4.S65]

Somals
USE Somalis

Somba (African people) *(May Subd Geog)*
[DT 541.45.S65 (Benin)]
UF Batammaliba (African people)
Sombhla (African people)
Tamberma (African people)
Tammaliba (African people)
BT Ethnology--Benin
Ethnology--Togo

Somba language *(May Subd Geog)*
[PL 8682.S64]
UF Betammadibe language

(May Subd Geog) = Place names may follow the heading

UF Betammaribe language
    Ditamaba language
    Ditammari language
    Soma language
    Some language
    Tamaba language
    Tamari language
    Tamberma language
BT Benin--Languages
    Gur languages
    Togo--Languages

Sombhla (African people)
  USE Somba (African people)

Some language
  USE Somba language

Sonay language
  USE Songhai language

Songay Empire
  USE Songhai Empire

Songbooks, Afrikaner
  [M 1834]
  UF Community songbooks, Afrikaner
      Afrikaner songbooks
  NT School songbooks, Afrikaner

Songe (African people) *(May Subd Geog)*
  [DT 650.S55]
  UF Basonge (African people)
      Bassonge (African people)
  BT Bantu-speaking peoples
      Ethnology--Zaire
      Luba (African people)

Songe art
  USE Art, Songe

Songe language *(May Subd Geog)*
  [PL 8683]
  UF Kalebwe language (Songe)
      Kisonge language
      Luba language, Northeastern
      Lusonge language
      Northeastern Luba language
      Songi language
      Songye language
      Yembe language
  BT Bantu languages
      Zaire--Languages

Songhai (African people) *(May Subd Geog)*
  [DT 530.5.S65 (French West Africa)]
  [DT 547.45.S65 (Niger)]
  UF Songhay (African people)
      Songhoi (African people)
      Songhoy (African people)
      Songoi (African people)
      Sonrai (African people)
  BT Ethnology--Africa, French-speaking West
      Ethnology--Mali
      Ethnology--Niger
  NT Dendi (African people)
  --History
  NT Songhai Empire

Songhai Empire *(Not Subd Geog)*
  [DT 532.27]
  UF Gaô Empire
      Songay Empire
      Songhay Empire
      Sonrai Empire
  BT Songhai (African people)--History
  NT Wogo (African people)

Songhai language *(May Subd Geog)*
  [PL 8685]
  UF Sonay language
  BT Africa, West--Languages
      Nilo-Saharan languages
  NT Dendi dialect
      Zarma dialect

Songhay (African people)
  USE Songhai (African people)

Songhay Empire
  USE Songhai Empire

Songhoi (African people)
  USE Songhai (African people)

Songhoy (African people)
  USE Songhai (African people)

Songi language
  USE Songe language

Songo
  USE Ayo (Game)

Songo (Central African Republic people)
  USE Mbati (Central African Republic people)

Songoi (African people)
  USE Songhai (African people)

UF = Used for; BT = Broader term; RT = Related term; SA = See also; NT = Narrower term

Songola (African people) *(May Subd Geog)*
  [DT 650.S]
  UF Binja (African people)
      Goa (African people)
      Songoora (African people)
      Tchongoa (African people)
      Usongora (African people)
      Wasongola (African people)
  BT Bantu-speaking peoples
      Ethnology--Zaire

Songola language
  USE Ombo language

Songoora (African people)
  USE Songola (African people)

Songs *(May Subd Geog)*
  BT Music
      Poetry
  SA *subdivision Songs and music under ethnic*
groups; and subdivision Music under ethnic groups for
music of the group
  NT Ballads
      Folk songs
      Lullabies
      Popular music

Songs, Bantu *(May Subd Geog)*
  UF Bantu songs

Songs, Fang *(May Subd Geog)*
  UF Fang songs

Songs, Kinyarwanda *(May Subd Geog)*
  UF Kinyarwanda songs

Songs, Lingala *(May Subd Geog)*
  UF Lingala songs

Songs, Malagasy *(May Subd Geog)*
  UF Malagasy songs

Songs, Ndebele (Zimbabwe) *(May Subd Geog)*
  UF Ndebele songs (Zimbabwe)

Songs, Nembe *(May Subd Geog)*
  UF Nembe songs

Songs, Popular
  USE Popular music

Songs, Shona *(May Subd Geog)*
  UF Shona songs

Songs, Tivi *(May Subd Geog)*
  UF Tivi songs

Songs, Tsogo *(May Subd Geog)*
  UF Tsogo songs

Songs, Yoruba *(May Subd Geog)*
  UF Yoruba songs

Songwriters
  USE Composers

Songye language
  USE Songe language

Sonike language
  USE Soninke language

Soninke (African people) *(May Subd Geog)*
  [DT 549.45.S66 (Senegal)]
  BT Ethnology--Africa, French-speaking West
      Ethnology--Senegal
  --History
  NT Mamadou Lamine, Rebellion of, 1885-1887

Soninke language *(May Subd Geog)*
  [PL 8686]
  UF Aswanik language
      Dyakanke language
      Gadyaga language
      Marka language
      Sarakole language
      Sarakolle language
      Sarawule language
      Serahuli language
      Silabe language
      Sonike language
      Sooninke language
      Toubakai language
      Wakore language
  BT Africa, West--Languages
      Mande languages
      Senegal--Languages

Sonjo (African people) *(May Subd Geog)*
  [DT 443.3.S]
  BT Bantu-speaking peoples
      Ethnology--Tanzania

Sonrai (African people)
  USE Songhai (African people)

Sonrai Empire
  USE Songhai Empire

(May Subd Geog) = Place names may follow the heading

Sonyo (African people) *(May Subd Geog)*
  [DT 352.43.S]
  BT Ethnology--Africa, Central

Sooninke language
  USE Soninke language

Sopono (Cult)
  [BL 2480.Y6]
  BT Cults--Nigeria
     Yoruba (African people)--Religion

Sorko (African people)
  USE Bozo (African people)

Sorko language
  USE Bozo language

Sorogo language
  USE Bozo language

Soso language
  USE Susu language

Sosse (African people)
  USE Mandingo (African people)

Sotho (African people) *(May Subd Geog)*
  [DT 797 (Botswana : old class)]
  [DT 2458.S78 (Botswana : new class)]
  [DT 786.5 (Lesotho : old class)]
  [DT 2596.L (Lesotho : new class)]
  [DT 764.S (South Africa : old class)]
  [DT 1768.S68 (South Africa : new class)]
  UF Basotho (African people)
    Basuto (African people)
    Souto (African people)
    Suthu (African people)
    Suto (African people)
  BT Bantu-speaking peoples
    Ethnology--Botswana
    Ethnology--Lesotho
    Ethnology--South Africa
  NT Kgaga (African people)
    Pedi (African people)
    Tswana (African people)
--Medicine
  BT Medicine, Primitive--Botswana
    Medicine, Primitive--Lesotho
    Medicine, Primitive--South Africa

Sotho, Northern (African people)
  USE Pedi (African people)

Sotho atlases
  USE Atlases, Sotho

Sotho courts
  USE Courts, Sotho

Sotho children's stories
  USE Children's stories, Sotho

Sotho fiction *(May Subd Geog)*
  [PL 8689.5-PL 8689.9]
  BT Botswana--Fiction
    Lesotho--Fiction
    Sotho literature
    South African fiction
  NT Children's stories, Sotho

Sotho folk literature
  USE Folk literature, Sotho

Sotho-Free State War, 1865-1866
  [DT 777 : old class]
  [DT 2133 : new class]
  UF Basuto War, 1865-1866
    Free State-Sotho War, 1865-1866
    Second Basuto War, 1865-1866
    Second Free State-Sotho War, 1865-1866
    Second Sotho-Free State War, 1865-1866
    Sotho War, 1865-1866
  BT Lesotho--History--To 1966
    Orange Free State (South Africa)--History--
1854-1900

Sotho imprints *(May Subd Geog)*
  [Z 7108.S65]
  UF Imprints, Sotho

Sotho language *(May Subd Geog)*
  [PL 8689]
  UF Sesotho language
    Sesuto language
    Southern Sotho language
    Suto language
    Sutu language
  BT Botswana--Languages
    Lesotho--Languages
    Sotho-Tswana languages
    South Africa--Languages
  RT Venda language

Sotho language, Northern
  USE Northern Sotho language

Sotho law
  USE Law, Sotho

UF = Used for; BT = Broader term; RT = Related term; SA = See also; NT = Narrower term

Sotho literature *(May Subd Geog)*
  [PL 8689.5-PL 8689.9]
  BT Botswana literature
      Lesotho--Literatures
      South African literature
  NT Folk literature, Sotho
      Sotho fiction
      Sotho poetry

Sotho poetry *(May Subd Geog)*
  [PL 8689.5 (History)]
  [PL 8689.7 (Collections)]
  BT Botswana--Poetry
      Lesotho--Poetry
      Sotho literature
      South African poetry

Sotho-Tswana languages *(May Subd Geog)*
  [PL 8691]
  UF Suto-Chuana languages
  BT Bantu languages
  NT Lozi language
      Northern Sotho language
      Sotho language
      Tswana language

Sotho War, 1865-1866
  USE Sotho-Free State War, 1865-1866

Soubiya language
  USE Subiya language

South Africa *(Not Subd Geog)*
  [DT 730-DT 944 : old class]
  [DT 1701-DT 2405 : new class]
  Here are entered works on the Republic of South
  Africa. Works on the area south of the countries of
  Zaire and Tanzania are entered under Africa,
  Southern.
  UF Africa, South
      Republic of South Africa
      Union of South Africa
  NT Robben Island (South Africa)
  --Afrikaner-English relations
  USE South Africa--English-Afrikaner
relations
  --Antiquities
  NT Mapungubwe Site (South Africa)
      Nelson Bay Cave (South Africa)
  --Armed Forces *(May Subd Geog)*
  -- --Medals, badges, decorations, etc.
  NT Honoris Crux
  --Church history
  NT Ethiopian movement (South Africa)

--Civilization
-- --20th century
-- --British influences
  BT Great Britain--Civilization
--Description and travel
-- --To 1800
-- --1801-1900
-- --1901-1950
-- --1951-1965
-- --1966-
--Economic conditions
  [HC 905]
-- --To 1918
-- --1918-1961
-- --1961-
--English-Afrikaner relations
  UF South Africa--Afrikaner-English relations
  BT Afrikaners
      British--South Africa
--Foreign relations *(May Subd Geog)*
-- --1948-1961
-- --1961-1978
-- --1978-1989
-- --1989-
--History
-- --To 1836
  NT Slachters Nek Rebellion, 1815
-- --Frontier Wars, 1811-1878
  [DT 777 : old class]
  [DT 1837 : new class]
  UF Axe, War of the (South Africa), 1847
      Frontier Wars (South Africa), 1811-1878
      Kaffir Wars, 1811-1878
      Kafir Wars, 1811-1878
      Xhosa Wars, 1811-1878
      War of the Axe (South Africa), 1847
  NT Blood River (South Africa), Battle of, 1838
      Korana War, 1st, 1868-1870
      Korana War, 2nd, 1878-1879
      Ngcayecibi, War of, South Africa, 1877-1878
      South Africa Medal (1834-1853)
-- --Great Trek, 1836-1840
  UF Great Trek
  BT Afrikaners
-- --1836-1909
  NT Zulu War, 1879
-- --Xhosa Cattle-Killing, 1856-1857
  UF Cattle-Killing Movement (South Africa),
1856-1857
      Xhosa Cattle-Killing (South Africa), 1856-
1857
-- --Korana War, 1868-1870
  USE Korana War, 1st, 1868-1870
-- --War of Ngcayecibi, 1877-1878
  USE Ngcayecibi, War of, South Africa, 1877-1878

                (May Subd Geog) = Place names may follow the heading

-- --Korana War, 1878-1879
USE Korana War, 2nd, 1878-1879
-- --Usutu Uprising, 1888
 UF Usutu Uprising (South Africa), 1888
 BT Zululand (South Africa)--History
-- --South African War, 1899-1902
USE South African War, 1899-1902
-- --1909-1961
-- --Rebellion, 1914-1915
 [DT 779.5 : old class]
 [DT 1933 : new class]
 UF Afrikaner Rebellion, 1914-1915
     Maritz's Rebellion, 1914-1915
-- --Sharpeville Massacre, 1960
USE Massacres--South Africa--Sharpeville
-- --1961-
 NT Angola--History--South African
Incursions, 1978-
-- --Soweto Uprising, 1976
 [DT 763.6 : old class]
 [DT 1959 : new class]
 UF Soweto Uprising (South Africa), 1976
 BT Anti-apartheid movements--South Africa
     Riots--South Africa
--History, Military
-- --1961-
 NT Angola--History--South African
Invasion, 1975-1976
--Languages
 NT Afrikaans language
     Kham language
     Korana language
     Nama language
     Ndebele language (South Africa)
     Nguni languages
     Ronga language
     San languages
     Shona language
     Sotho language
     Tsonga language
     Tswana language
     Venda language
     Xhosa language
     Zulu language
--Literatures
USE South African literature
--Native races
USE Indigenous peoples--South Africa
--Politics and government
-- --To 1836
-- --1836-1909
-- --20th century
 NT African National Congress
-- --1909-1948
-- --1948-
-- --1948-1961

-- --1961-1978
-- --1978-1989
-- --1989-
--Race relations
 NT Colored people (South Africa)--Relocation
     Ethiopian movement (South Africa)
--Social conditions
-- --1961-

South Africa 1853 Medal
 USE South Africa Medal (1834-1853)

South Africa House (London, England)
 [DA 687.S75]

South Africa in motion pictures
 [PN 1995.9.S]
 BT Motion pictures

South Africa Medal (1834-1853)
 [DT 777 : old class]
 [DT 1837 : new class]
 UF 1853 Medal (South Africa)
     South Africa 1853 Medal
 BT South Africa--History--Frontier Wars, 1811-
1878

South African almanacs
 USE Almanacs, South African

South African art
 USE Art, South African

South African arts
 USE Arts, South African

South African atlases
 USE Atlases, South African

South African authors
 USE Authors, South African

South African children's literature
 USE Children's literature, South African

South African children's stories (English)
 USE Children's stories, South African (English)

South African children's writings (English)
 USE Children's writings, South African
(English)

South African coins
 USE Coins, South African

UF = Used for; BT = Broader term; RT = Related term; SA = See also; NT = Narrower term

South African cookery
USE Cookery, South African

South African drama *(May Subd Geog)*
[PL 8014.S6 (History)]
[PL 8014.S62 (Collections)]
BT African drama
South African literature
NT Shona drama

South African drama (Afrikaans)
USE Afrikaans drama

South African drama (English) *(May Subd Geog)*
[PR 9361.2-PR 9361.7 (History)]
[PR 9366.2-PR 9366.8 (Collections)]
UF English drama--South African authors
BT African drama (English)
South African literature (English)
NT One-act plays, South African (English)
Young adult drama, South African
(English)

South African essays (Afrikaans)
USE Afrikaans essays

South African essays (English) *(May Subd Geog)*
[PR 9363.5 (History)]
[PR 9367.7 (Collections)]
UF English essays--South African authors
BT South African literature (English)

South African fiction *(May Subd Geog)*
[PL 8014.S6 (History)]
[PL 8014.S62 (Collections)]
BT South African literature
Southern African fiction
NT Shona fiction
Short stories, South African
Sotho fiction
Venda fiction
Xhosa fiction
Zulu fiction

South African fiction (Afrikaans)
USE Afrikaans fiction

South African fiction (English) *(May Subd Geog)*
[PR 9362.2-PR 9362.6 (History)]
[PR 9367.3-PR 9367.36 (Collections)]
UF English fiction--South African authors
BT South African literature (English)
Southern African fiction (English)
NT Children's stories, South African
(English)

NT Short stories, South African (English)

South African Homelands (South Africa)
USE Homelands (South Africa)

South African Incursions into Angola, 1978-
USE Angola--History--South African Incursions,
1978-

South African Invasion of Angola, 1975-1976
USE Angola--History--South African Invasion,
1975-1976

South African literature *(May Subd Geog)*
[PL 8014.S6 (History)]
[PL 8014.S62 (Collections)]
UF South Africa--Literatures
BT Southern African literature
NT Children's literature, South African
Shona literature
Sotho literature
South African drama
South African fiction
South African poetry
Sotho literature
Venda literature
Xhosa literature
Zulu literature

South African literature (Afrikaans)
USE Afrikaans literature

South African literature (English) *(May Subd Geog)*
[PR 9350-PR 9369.3]
UF English literature--South African authors
BT Southern Africa literature (English)
NT Children's writings, South African
(English)
Protest literature, South African (English)
South African drama (English)
South African essays (English)
South African fiction (English)
South African poetry (English)
South African prose literature (English)
--Black authors
[PR 9364.5.B55 (Collections)]
UF Black literature, South African (English)

South African national characteristics
USE National characteristics, South African

South African National Gallery
NT Hyman Liberman Memorial Door (South African
National Gallery)

(**May Subd Geog**) = Place names may follow the heading

South African newspapers *(May Subd Geog)*
[PN 5471-PN 5480]
UF Newspapers, South African

South African novelists
USE Novelists, South African

South African one-act plays (English)
USE One-act plays, South African (English)

South African painting
USE Painting, South African

South African periodicals *(May Subd Geog)*
[PN 5471-PN 5480]
UF Periodicals, South African

South African poetry *(May Subd Geog)*
[PL 8014.S6 (History)]
[PL 8014.S62 (Collections)]
BT South African literature
Southern African poetry
NT Shona poetry
Sotho poetry
Tsonga poetry
Tswana poetry
Xhosa poetry
Zulu poetry

South African poetry (Afrikaans)
USE Afrikaans poetry

South African poetry (English) *(May Subd Geog)*
[PR 9360.2-PR 9360.9 (History)]
[PR 9365.1-PR 9365.9 (Collections)]
UF English poetry--South African authors
BT African poetry (English)
South African literature (English)
NT Protest poetry, South African
(English)
Revolutionary poetry, South African
(English)
--Black authors
[PR 9365.55 (Collections)]
UF Black poetry, South African (English)

South African poets
USE Poets, South African

South African pottery
USE Pottery, South African

South African prints
USE Prints, South African

South African propaganda

USE Propaganda, South African

South African prose literature (Afrikaans)
USE Afrikaans prose literature

South African prose literature (English) *(May Subd Geog)*
[PR 9362.2-PR 9362.6 (History)]
[PR 9367.2-PR 9367.25 (Collections)]
UF English prose literature--South African
authors
BT African prose literature (English)
South African literature (English)
NT Reportage literature, South African
(English)

South African protest literature (English)
USE Protest literature, South African (English)

South African protest poetry (English)
USE Protest poetry, South African (English)

South African reportage literature (English)
USE Reportage literature, South African
(English)

South African Republic
USE Transvaal (South Africa)

South African revolutionary poetry (English)
USE Revolutionary poetry, South African
(English)

South African sculpture
USE Sculpture, South African

South African short stories
USE Short stories, South African

South African short stories (English)
USE Short stories, South African (English)

South African War, 1899-1902 *(May Subd Geog)*
[DT 930-DT 939.5 : old class]
[DT 1890-DT 1920 : new class]
UF Anglo-Boer War, 1899-1902
Boer War, 1899-1902
South Africa--History--South African War,
1899-1902
Transvaal War, 1899-1902
NT Afrikaner loyalists
Jameson's Raid, 1895-1896
Kimberley (South Africa)--History--Seige,
1899-1900
Ladysmith (South Africa)--History--Siege,
1899-1900   *(Continued)*

UF = Used for; BT = Broader term; RT = Related term; SA = See also; NT = Narrower term

South African War, 1899-1902   *(Continued)*
   NT Mafikeng (South Africa)--History--
Siege, 1899-1900
  --Atrocities
  --Blacks
  --Campaigns *(May Subd Geog)*
  -- --South Africa
   NT Elandslaagte, South Africa, Battle of,
1899
      Magersfontein, South Africa, Battle
of, 1899
      Spioenkop, Battle of, 1900
      Stormberg, Battle of, 1899
  --Causes
  --Concentration camps *(May Subd Geog)*
  -- --South Africa
   NT Irene Concentration Camp (South
Africa)
  --Participation, Black
   BT Soldiers, Black
  --Prisoners and prisons
  --Prisoners and prisons, British
  --Regimental histories *(May Subd Geog)*

South African watercolor painting
   USE Watercolor painting, South African

South African wit and humor *(May Subd Geog)*
   [PN 6222.S (Collections)]
   UF Wit and humor, South African

South African wit and humor, Pictorial *(May
Subd Geog)*
   [NC 1740.S]
   UF Wit and humor, Pictorial (South
African)

South African women authors
   USE Women authors, South African

South African young adult drama (English)
   USE Young adult drama, South African
(English)

South Africans *(May Subd Geog)*
   BT Ethnology--South Africa

South Africans, Afrikaans-speaking
   USE Afrikaners

South Bauchi languages
   USE Southern Bauchi languages

South Cushitic languages
   USE Cushitic languages, Southern

South-West Africa
   USE Namibia

Southern Africa
   USE Africa, Southern

Southern African fiction
   [PL 8014.S6 (History)]
   [PL 8014.S62 (Collections)]
   UF Africa, Southern--Fiction
   BT African fiction
      Southern African literature
   NT Short stories, Southern African
      South African fiction
      Zimbabwean fiction

Southern African fiction (English)
   [PR 9344 (History)]
   [PR 9347.5 (Collections)]
   UF English fiction--Southern African authors
   BT African fiction (English)
      Southern African literature (English)
   NT Short stories, Southern African (English)
      South African fiction (English)
      Zambian fiction (English)
      Zimbabwean fiction (English)

Southern African literature
   [PL 8014.S6 (History)]
   [PL 8014.S62 (Collections)]
   UF Africa, Southern--Literatures
   BT African literature
   NT Botswana literature
      Malawi literature
      Mozambican literature
      South African literature
      Southern African fiction
      Southern African poetry
      Zambian literature
      Zimbabwean literature

Southern African literature (English)
   [PR 9340-PR 9347.5]
   UF English literature--Southern African
authors
   BT African literature (English)
   NT Malawi literature (English)
      South African literature (English)
      Southern African fiction (English)
      Zambian literature (English)
      Zimbabwean literature (English)

Southern African newspapers
   [PN 5450.5.S6]
   UF Newspapers, Southern African

(May Subd Geog) = Place names may follow the heading

Southern African periodicals
  [PN 5450.5.S6]
  UF Periodicals, Southern African

Southern African poetry
  [PL 8014.S6 (History)]
  [PL 8014.S62 (Collections)]
  UF Africa, Southern--Poetry
  BT African poetry
      Southern African literature
  NT South African poetry
      Zambian poetry
      Zimbabwean poetry

Southern African short stories
  USE Short stories, Southern African

Southern African short stories (English)
  USE Short stories, Southern African
(English)

Southern Bauchi languages (May Subd Geog)
  [PL 8068.B37]
  UF Bauchi languages, Southern
      South Bauchi languages
  BT Chadic languages
      Nigeria--Languages

Southern Bullom (African people)
  USE Sherbro (African people)

Southern Bullom language
  USE Sherbro language

Southern Cushitic languages
  USE Cushitic languages, Southern

Southern Highlands (Tanzania) (Not Subd Geog)
  BT Mountains--Tanzania
      Plateaus--Tanzania

Southern Luba language
  USE Sanga language

Southern Lunda (African people)
  USE Lunda, Southern (African people)

Southern Mande languages (May Subd Geog)
  [PL 8490.M3595S68]
  UF Mande languages, Southern
  BT Ivory Coast--Languages
      Liberia--Languages
      Mande languages
  NT Dan language
      Gagu language

  NT Kweni language
      Mano language

Southern Nilotic languages
  USE Nandi languages

Southern Rhodesia
  USE Zimbabwe

Southern Samo language
  USE Sembla language

Southern Sotho language
  USE Sotho language

Southern Sudan question, 1955-1972
  USE Sudan--History--Civil War, 1955-1972

Southwest Africa
  USE Namibia

Souto (African people)
  USE Sotho (African people)

Sovereigns
  USE Kings and rulers

Soweto Uprising (South Africa), 1976
  USE South Africa--History--Soweto Uprising,
1976

Spain (Not Subd Geog)
  --Colonies
    BT Colonies
  -- --Administration
      UF Spain--Colonies--Politics and government
  -- --Boundaries (May Subd Geog)
  -- --Commerce (May Subd Geog)
  -- --Constitutional history
  -- --Constitutional law
  -- --Defenses
  -- --Description and travel
  -- --Discovery and exploration
  -- --Economic conditions
  -- --Economic policy
  -- --Emigration and immigration
  -- --Geography (Not Subd Geog)
  -- --History
  -- --Industries
  -- --Manufactures
  -- --Native races
      USE Indigenous peoples--Spain--Colonies
  -- --Officials and employees
  -- --Politics and government
      USE Spain--Colonies--Administration
  -- --Population   (Continued)

UF = Used for; BT = Broader term; RT = Related term; SA = See also; NT = Narrower term

Spain
--Colonies   *(Continued)*
-- --Public lands
-- --Public works
-- --Race relations
-- --Religion
-- --Religious life and customs
-- --Rural conditions
-- --Social conditions
-- --Social life and customs
-- --Social policy
-- --Africa

Spanish America
    USE Latin America

Spanish Guinea
    USE Equatorial Guinea

Speeches, addresses, etc., Malagasy *(May Subd Geog)*
    [PN 6129.M]
    UF Malagasy orations
        Malagasy speeches

Spiders *(May Subd Geog)*
--Folklore
    NT Anansi (Legendary character)

Spioenkop, Battle of, 1900
    [DT 934.S65 : old class]
    [DT 1908.S : new class]
    UF Battle of Spioenkop (South Africa),
1900
        Spion Kop, Battle of (South Africa),
1900
    BT South African War, 1899-1902--
Campaigns--South Africa

Spion Kop, Battle of (South Africa), 1900
    USE Spioenkop, Battle of, 1900

Squatter settlements *(May Subd Geog)*
    UF Settlements, Squatter
        Shack towns
        Shantytowns
        Uncontrolled settlements
    BT Slums
--Botswana
    [HD 7375.9.A3]
--South Africa
-- --Cape Coast
    [HD 7375.4.C33]

St. Floris National Park (Central African
Republic)

    USE Parc national de Saint-Floris (Central
African Republic)

St. Helena
    USE Saint Helena

Stage
    USE Drama
         Theater

Standing on one foot
    USE One-leg resting position

Stanley Falls (Zaire) *(Not Subd Geog)*
    UF Boyama Falls (Zaire)
    BT Congo River
        Waterfalls--Zaire

State and comunication
    USE Communication policy

State and transportation
    USE Transportation and state

State farms *(May Subd Geog)*
    UF Institution farms, State-owned
    BT Farms
--Zambia
    NT Kambilombilo State Farm (Zambia)

State forests
    USE Forest reserves

State parks
    USE Parks

Statistics
    USE *subdivision* Statistics *under names of countries,
cities, etc. and under ethnic groups, e.g.,* Senegal--
Statistics

Statuettes
    USE Bronzes

Stiegler's Gorge Dam (Tanzania) *(Not Subd Geog)*
    BT Dams--Tanzania

Stone age *(May Subd Geog)*
    RT Archaeology
    NT Neolithic period
--Zimbabwe
    [GN 865.Z]

Stonework, Decorative
    USE Sculpture

(May Subd Geog) = Place names may follow the heading

Stools *(May Subd Geog)*
--Ghana
  BT Akan (African people)--Kings and
rulers
      Ashanti (African people)--Kings and
rulers

Stories
  USE Fiction

Stories, Short
  USE Short stories

Stormberg, Battle of, 1899
  [DT 777 : old class]
  [DT 1908.S87 : new class]
  UF Battle of Stormberg (South Africa),
1899
  BT South African War, 1899-1902--
Campaigns--South Africa

Stormberg Range (South Africa) *(Not Subd Geog)*
  UF Stormberge (South Africa)
  BT Mountains--South Africa

Stormberge (South Africa)
  USE Stormberg Range (South Africa)

Storytellers *(May Subd Geog)*
  UF Griots
      Raconteurs
      Tellers of stories
  RT Oral tradition
--Africa, West
  [GR 350.3]

Strait of Mandab
  USE Mandab, Strait of

Straits *(May Subd Geog)*
  BT Landforms
--Africa
  NT Mandab, Strait of
--Madagascar
  NT Mozambique Channel
--Mozambique
  NT Mozambique Channel

Stratigraphic groups
  USE Groups (Stratigraphy)

Stream valleys
  USE Valleys

Streams
  USE Rivers

Streets *(May Subd Geog)*
  UF Avenues
      Boulevards
      Thoroughfares
  BT Roads
--South Africa
  NT Avenue, The (Stellenbosch, South Africa)
--Zimbabwe
  NT First Street (Harare, Zimbabwe)

Strikes and lockouts *(May Subd Geog)*
  UF Combinations of labor
      Lockouts
      Work stoppages
  RT Trade-unions
--Civil service *(May Subd Geog)*
  UF Government employee strikes
      Public employee strikes
      Public sector strikes
      Public worker strikes
  BT Civil service
-- --Ghana
  NT Civil Service Strike, Ghana, 1978
--Copper mining *(May Subd Geog)*
  BT Strikes and lockouts--Miners
-- --Zambia
  NT Copper Miners' Strike, Zambia, 1935
      Copper Miners' Strike, Zambia, 1940
--Lumber trade *(May Subd Geog)*
-- --Cameroon
  NT Société forestière et industrielle de la
Doumé Strike, 1963
--Miners *(May Subd Geog)*
  NT Strikes and lockouts--Copper mining
-- -- South Africa
  NT Witwatersrand Strike, 1922
--Cameroon
--Ghana
--South Africa
  NT General Strike, Transvaal, South Africa,
1913
--Tanzania
  NT General Strike, Zanzibar, Zanzibar, 1948
--Zambia

Strip weaving, West African
  USE West African strip weaving

Structural basins
  USE Basins (Geology)

Student life and customs
  USE Students

UF = Used for; BT = Broader term; RT = Related term; SA = See also; NT = Narrower term

Students *(May Subd Geog)*
  UF School life
      Student life and customs
  BT Education
      Universities and colleges
  NT African students
      Afrikaner students
      College students
      Ghanaian students
      Namibian students
      Senegalese students
      Somali students
      Students, Black
      Tanzanian students
      Togolese students

Students, Black *(May Subd Geog)*
  [LC 2781.7 (General)]
  UF Black students
  BT Blacks--Education
      Students
  NT College students, Black
 --**South Africa**
  [LC 2808.S7]

Students, Foreign *(May Subd Geog)*
  UF Foreign students
      International students
      Students, International
  NT African students--Foreign countries
      Namibian students--Foreign countries
      Senegalese students--Foreign countries
      Somali students--Foreign countries
      Tanzanian students--Foreign countries
      Togolese students--Foreign countries

Students, International
  USE Students, Foreign

Students' writings
  USE College prose
      College verse
      School prose
      School verse

Suaheli language
  USE Swahili language

Sub-Sahara Africa
  USE Africa, Sub-Saharan

Suba (African people) *(May Subd Geog)*
  [DT 433.545.S83]
  UF Abasuba (African people)
      Soba (African people)

  BT Bantu-speaking peoples
      Ethnology--Kenya

Subia language
  USE Subiya language

Subiya folk literature
  USE Folk literature, Subiya

Subiya language *(May Subd Geog)*
  [PL 8692.S86]
  UF ciIkuhane language
      eciSubiya language
      Ikuhane language
      Ikwahani language
      Soubiya language
      Subia language
      Subya language
      Supia language
  BT Bantu languages
      Botswana--Languages
      Zambia--Languages

Subsahara Africa
  USE Africa, Sub-Saharan

Subya language
  USE Subiya language

Succession, Intestate
  USE Inheritance and succession

Sudan *(Not Subd Geog)*
  [DT 154.1-DT 154.9]
  UF Anglo-Egyptian Sudan
 --**Antiquities**
  NT Akashah Site (Sudan)
      Meroe (Sudan)
      Musawwarat al-Sufrah Site (Sudan)
      Napata (Ancient city)
      Shaqadud Cave (Sudan)
      Tabo Site (Sudan)
 --**Economic conditions**
  [HC 835]
 -- --1973-
 --**History**
 -- --To 1820
 -- --1820-
 -- --1862-1899
  NT Fashoda Crisis, 1898
      Gordon Relief Expedition, 1884-1885
      Omdurman, Battle of, 1898
 -- --1899-1956
 -- --**Civil War, 1955-1972**
  [DT 157.67]
  UF Civil war--Sudan

(May Subd Geog) = Place names may follow the heading

UF Southern Sudan question, 1955-1972
-- -- --Reconstruction
-- --Coup d'état, 1985
 [DT 157.33]
 BT Coups d'état--Sudan
--Languages
 NT Acoli language
     Aja language (Sudan)
     Anuak language
     Baka language
     Bari language
     Beja language
     Bongo language
     Bor dialect (Dinka)
     Bor language (Lwo)
     Dinka language
     Dongola-Kenuz dialect
     Feroge languages
     Fur language
     Gólo language
     Hausa language
     Ingassana language
     Kakwa dialect
     Kara language
     Kordofanian languages
     Kresh language
     Krongo language
     Kunama language
     Latuka language
     Lwo language (Sudan)
     Maba language
     Maban language
     Ma'di language (Uganda and Sudan)
     Mahas-Fiyadikka language
     Meroitic language
     Moro language (Sudan)
     Moru language
     Mundu language
     Murle language
     Ndogo-Sere languages
     Nirere dialect
     Nubian languages
     Nuer language
     Orig dialect (Sudan)
     Padang dialect
     Päri language (Sudan)
     Shilluk language
     Tagoi language
     Toposa language
     Uduk language
     Yulu language
     Zande language
     Zande languages
--Literatures
 NT Hausa literature

--Politics and government
-- --1956-1985
-- --1985-

Sudan (Region) *(Not Subd Geog)*
    Here are entered works on a region of north central
Africa south of the Sahara and Libyan deserts and north of
the rainy tropics, extending across the African continent
from the west coast to the mountains of Ethiopia.

Sudan, French
 USE Mali

Sudanese *(May Subd Geog)*
 UF Sudanis
 BT Ethnology--Sudan
--Uganda
 [DT 433.245.S92]

Sudanese alien labor
 USE Alien labor, Sudanese

Sudanese cookery
 USE Cookery, Sudanese

Sudanese literature (English) *(May Subd Geog)*
 [PR 9408.S82]
 UF English literature--Sudanese authors
 BT African literature (English)

Sudanese national characteristics
 USE National characteristics, Sudanese

Sudanese Republic
 USE Mali

Sudanis
 USE Sudanese

Suk (African people) *(May Subd Geog)*
 [DT 433.545.S85 (Kenya)]
 UF Bawgott (African people)
     Hill Suk (African people)
     Pakot (African people)
     Plains Suk (African people)
     Pokot (African people)
 BT Ethnology--Kenya
     Ethnology--Uganda
     Nilo-Hamitic tribes

Suk language *(May Subd Geog)*
 [PL 8692.S9]
 UF Pokot language
 BT Kalenjin language
     Kenya--Languages
     Uganda--Languages

UF = Used for; BT = Broader term; RT = Related term; SA = See also; NT = Narrower term

Suku (African people) *(May Subd Geog)*
  [DT 650.S]
  UF Basuku (African people)
  BT Bantu-speaking peoples
      Ethnology--Zaire
 --Religion
  [BL 2480.S8]

Suku (Tanzanian people)
  USE Sukuma (African people)

Suku language (Tanzania)
  USE Sukuma language

Suku language (Zaire) *(May Subd Geog)*
  [PL 8693]
  UF Kisuku language
  BT Kongo language
      Zaire--Languages

Sukulumbwe (African people)
  USE Ila (African people)

Sukuma (African people) *(May Subd Geog)*
  [DT 443.3.S86]
  UF Basukuma (African people)
      Suku (Tanzanian people)
  BT Bantu-speaking peoples
      Ethnology--Tanzania

Sukuma language *(May Subd Geog)*
  [PL 8694.S94]
  UF Gwe language
      Kesukuma language
      Suku language (Tanzania)
  BT Bantu languages
      Tanzania--Languages

Sukuma law
  USE Law, Sukuma

Sukuma proverbs
  USE Proverbs, Sukuma

Summer Rainfall Agriculture Project
  USE Moisture Utilization in Semi-Arid
Tropics: Summer Rainfall Agriculture Project

Sundi (African people) *(May Subd Geog)*
  [DT 650.S94]
  UF Manyanga (African people)
      Nsundi (African people)
  BT Ethnology--Zaire

Sungu (African people)
  USE Tetela (African people)

Supergroups (Stratigraphy)
  USE Groups (Stratigraphy)

Supia language
  USE Subiya language

Susoo language
  USE Susu language

Susu language *(May Subd Geog)*
  [PL 8695]
  UF Soso language
      Susoo language
  BT Guinea--Languages
      Mande languages
      Sierra Leone--Languages

Suthu (African people)
  USE Sotho (African people)

Suto (African people)
  USE Sotho (African people)

Suto-Chuana languages
  USE Sotho-Tswana languages

Suto language
  USE Sotho language

Sutu language
  USE Sotho language

Suwa (Arab people) *(May Subd Geog)*
  [DT 571.S]
  BT Ethnology--Cameroon

Swahili (African people)
  USE Swahili-speaking peoples

Swahili children's poetry
  USE Children's poetry, Swahili

Swahili children's stories
  USE Children's stories, Swahili

Swahili college and school drama
  USE College and school drama, Swahili

Swahili drama *(May Subd Geog)*
  [PL 8703.5-PL 8704]
  BT African drama
      Swahili literature
  NT College and school drama, Swahili
      Radio plays, Swahili

(May Subd Geog) = Place names may follow the heading

Swahili epic poetry
    USE Epic poetry, Swahili

Swahili essays *(May Subd Geog)*
    [PL 8703.5-PL 8704]
    BT Swahili literature

Swahili fiction *(May Subd Geog)*
    [PL 8703.5-PL 8704]
    BT Kenya--Fiction
        Swahili literature
        Tanzania--Fiction
    NT Children's stories, Swahili
        Short stories, Swahili

Swahili folk literature
    USE Folk literature, Swahili

Swahili hymns
    USE Hymns, Swahili

Swahili imprints *(May Subd Geog)*
    [Z 7108.S8]
    UF Imprints, Swahili

Swahili language *(May Subd Geog)*
    [PL 8701-PL 8704]
    UF Kiswahili language
        Suaheli language
    BT Bantu languages
        Kenya--Languages
        Tanzania--Languages
    NT Cifundi dialect
        Comorian language
        Kingwana language
        Mtang'ata dialect

Swahili literature *(May Subd Geog)*
    [PL 8703.5-PL 8704]
    BT Kenyan literature
        Tanzanian literature
    NT Folk literature, Swahili
        Swahili drama
        Swahili essays
        Swahili fiction
        Swahili poetry
        Swahili prose literature
        Teenagers' writings, Swahili
        Youths' writings, Swahili

Swahili philology
    [PL 8701-8704]
    UF Philology, Swahili

Swahili poetry *(May Subd Geog)*
    [PL 8703.5-PL 8704]

    BT Kenya--Poetry
        Swahili literature
        Tanzanian poetry
    NT Children's poetry, Swahili
        Epic poetry, Swahili

Swahili prose literature *(May Subd Geog)*
    [PL 8703.5-PL 8704]
    BT Tanzanian prose literature
        Swahili literature

Swahili proverbs
    USE Proverbs, Swahili

Swahili radio plays
    USE Radio plays, Swahili

Swahili riddles
    USE Riddles, Swahili

Swahili short stories
    USE Short stories, Swahili

Swahili shorthand
    USE Shorthand, Swahili

Swahili-speaking peoples *(May Subd Geog)*
    [DT 365.45.S93 (Eastern Africa)]
    [DT 433.545.S (Konya)]
    UF Swahili (African people)
    BT Bantu-speaking peoples
        Ethnology--Africa, Eastern
        Ethnology--Kenya
        Ethnology--Tanzania
    NT Bajun (African people)

Swahili-speaking women
    USE Women, Swahili-speaking

Swahili teenagers' writings
    USE Teenagers' writings, Swahili

Swahili wit and humor *(May Subd Geog)*
    [PL 8704 (History and major collections)]
    [PN 6222.S (Minor collections)]
    UF Wit and humor, Swahili

Swahili youths' writings
    USE Youths' writings, Swahili

Swati (African people)
    USE Swazi (African people)

Swati language
    USE Swazi language

UF = Used for; BT = Broader term; RT = Related term; SA = See also; NT = Narrower term

Swazi (African people) *(May Subd Geog)*
   [DT 971.42 : old class]
   [DT 2746.S : new class]
   UF Amaswazi (African people)
      Isiswazi (African people)
      Siswazi (African people)
      Swati (African people)
      Tekela (African people)
      Tekeza (African people)
   BT Bantu-speaking peoples
      Ethnology--Swaziland
      Nguni (African people)
 --Marriage customs and rites
   UF Marriage customs and rites, Swazi
(African people)
 --Medicine
   BT Medicine, Primitive--Swaziland
 --Rites and ceremonies

Swazi alien labor
  USE Alien labor, Swazi

Swazi language *(May Subd Geog)*
   [PL 8705]
   UF SiSwati language
      Swati language
   BT Nguni languages
      Swaziland--Languages

Swaziland *(Not Subd Geog)*
   [DT 971 : old class]
   [DT 2701-DT 2825 : new class]
 --Economic conditions
   [HC 925]
 --Languages
   NT Swazi language
 --Politics and government
 -- --To 1968
 -- --1968-

Swciri language
  USE Mwamba language

Swedes *(May Subd Geog)*
 --Ethiopia
   [DT 380.4.S94]
 --Zaire
   NT Zaire--History--Civil War, 1960-1965--
Participation, Swedish

Swiss agricultural assistance
  USE Agricultural assistance, Swiss

Syena (African people)
  USE Senufo (African people)

Syènara language *(May Subd Geog)*
   BT Mali--Languages
      Senufo languages
   NT Tuwunro dialect

Syenere language
  USE Senari language

T

Taabwa (African people)
  USE Tabwa (African people)

Tabele (African people)
  USE Ndebele (African people)

Tabele language
  USE Ndebele language (Zimbabwe)

Tabi language
  USE Ingassana language

Table Mountain (Cape of Good Hope, South Africa)
(Not Subd Geog)
   BT Mountains--South Africa

Table Mountain (Natal, South Africa) *(Not Subd Geog)*
   BT Mountains--South Africa

Tablelands
  USE Plateaus

Tabo Site (Sudan) *(Not Subd Geog)*
   [DT 159.9.T33]
   BT Sudan--Antiquities

Tabwa (African people) *(May Subd Geog)*
   [DT 443.3.T32 (Tanzania)]
   UF Batabwa (African people)
      Batambwa (African people)
      Itawa (African people)
      Rungu (African people)
      Taabwa (African people)
      Waitawba (African people)
   BT Ethnology--Tanzania
      Ethnology--Zambia

Tabwa art
  USE Art, Tabwa

Tadjoura, Gulf of (Djibouti) *(Not Subd Geog)*
   UF Golfe de Tadjoura (Djibouti)
      Gulf of Tadjoura (Djibouti)
      Gulf of Tajura (Djibouti)
      Tajura, Gulf of (Djibouti)

(May Subd Geog) = Place names may follow the heading

BT Inlets--Djibouti

Tagba language (Ivory Coast)
  USE Tagbana language

Tagbana (African people) *(May Subd Geog)*
  [DT 545.45.T]
  UF Babaála (African people)
      Kangable (African people)
      Tagwana (African people)
      Takponin (African people)
  BT Ethnology--Ivory Coast
      Senufo (African people)
 --Religion
  [BL 2480.T25]

Tagbana language *(May Subd Geog)*
  [PL 8706.T]
  UF Tagba language (Ivory Coast)
      Taqbona language
      Tagouana language
      Tagwana language
      Takponin language
  BT Gur languages
      Ivory Coast--Languages

Tagbo language
  USE Mambila language

Tagbona language
  USE Tagbana language

Tagoi language *(May Subd Coog)*
  [PL 8706.T34]
  UF Tagoy language
  BT Kordofanian languages
      Sudan--Languages
  NT Orig dialect (Sudan)

Tagouana language
  USE Tagbana language

Tagoy language
  USE Tagoi language

Tagwana (African people)
  USE Tagbana (African people)

Tagwana language
  USE Tagbana language

Taimoro (Malagasy people) *(May Subd Geog)*
  [DT 469.M277T]
  UF Antaimoro (Malagasy people)
      Antamorona (Malagasy people)
      Antamuro (Malagasy people)

  UF Anteimoro (Malagasy people)
      Antemoro (Malagasy people)
      Temoro (Malagasy people)
      Temuru (Malagasy people)
  BT Ethnology--Madagascar

Taita (African people) *(May Subd Geog)*
  [DT 433.545.T34 (Kenya)]
  UF Teita (African people)
      Wataita (African people)
  BT Ethnology--Kenya
      Ethnology--Tanzania
 --Religion
  [BL 2480.T27]

Taita Hills (Kenya) *(Not Subd Geog)*
  UF Teita Hills (Kenya)
  BT Mountains--Kenya

Taita language *(May Subd Geog)*
  [PL 8707]
  UF Sagalla dialect
      Teita language
  BT Bantu languages
      Kenya--Languages
      Tanzania--Languages
  NT Dabida dialect

Tajura, Gulf of (Djibouti)
  USE Tadjoura, Gulf of (Djibouti)

Takponin (African people)
  USE Tagbana (African people)

Takponin language
  USE Tagbana language

Talansi (African people)
  USE Tallensi (African people)

Talen (African people)
  USE Tallensi (African people)

Talene (African people)
  USE Tallensi (African people)

Talense (African people)
  USE Tallensi (African people)

Tallensi (African people) *(May Subd Geog)*
  [DT 510.43.T35]
  UF Talansi (African people)
      Talen (African people)
      Talene (African people)
      Talense (African people)
  BT Ethnology--Ghana   *(Continued)*

UF = Used for; BT = Broader term; RT = Related term; SA = See also; NT = Narrower term

Tallensi (African people)   *(Continued)*
--Religion
  [BL 2480.T3]

Tama (African people)
  USE Majangir (African people)

Tamaba language
  USE Somba language

Tamari language
  USE Somba language

Tamberma (African people)
  USE Somba (African people)

Tamberma language
  USE Somba language

Tamboka language
  USE Tumbuka language

Tambuka (African people)
  USE Tumbuka (African people)

Tammaliba (African people)
  USE Somba (African people)

Tampele language
  USE Tampulma language

Tamplima dialect
  USE Tampulma language

Tampole language
  USE Tampulma language

Tampolem dialect
  USE Tampulma language

Tamprusi dialect
  USE Tampulma language

Tampulma language *(May Subd Geog)*
  [PL 8223.G995T3]
  UF Tampele language
      Tamplima dialect
      Tampole language
      Tampolem dialect
      Tamprusi dialect
  BT Ghana--Languages
      Grusi languages

Tan-Zam Railway
  [HE 3460.T35]
  UF Freedom Railway

  UF Great Uhuru Railway
      Tanzania-Zambia Railway
      Uhuru Railway
  BT Railroads--Africa, East
      Railroads--Tanzania
      Railroads--Zambia

Tana, Lake (Ethiopia) *(Not Subd Geog)*
  [DT 390.T8]
  UF Lake Tana (Ethiopia)
      Lake Tsana (Ethiopia)
      Tsana, Lake (Ethiopia)
  BT Lakes--Ethiopia

Tanala (Malagasy people) *(May Subd Geog)*
  [DT 469.M277T35]
  UF Antanala (Malagasy people)
  BT Ethnology--Madagascar

Tandanke language
  USE Bedik language

Tandroy (Malagasy people)
  USE Antandroy (Malagasy people)

Tandruy (Malagasy people)
  USE Antandroy (Malagasy people)

Tanga (African people) *(May Subd Geog)*
  [DT 571.T]
  UF Banoho (African people)
      Bapuku (African people)
      Batanga-Nda (African people)
      Noho (African people)
      Puku (African people)
  BT Bantu-speaking peoples
      Ethnology--Cameroon

Tanga women
  USE Women, Tanga

Tanganika, Lac
  USE Tanganyika, Lake

Tanganyika *(Not Subd Geog)*
  [DT 436-DT 449]
    Here are entered works limited in subject coverage to
  the historical, political or cultural aspects of Tanganyika
  for the period before the merger in 1964. Works on other
  subjects relating to Tanganyika for any pre-merger period
  are entered under the name of the present jurisdiction,
  Tanzania.
  --History
  NT Maji Maji Uprising, 1905-1907

(May Subd Geog) = Place names may follow the heading

Tanganyika, Lake *(Not Subd Geog)*
  UF Lac Tanganika
      Lake Tanganyika
      Tanganika, Lac
  BT Lakes--Africa, East

Tangwena (African people) *(May Subd Geog)*
  [DT 962.42 : old class]
  [DT 2913.T36 : new class]
  BT Barwe (African people)
      Ethnology--Zimbabwe

Tankay (Malagasy people)
  USE Bezanozano (Malagasy people)

Tannekwe (African people) *(May Subd Geog)*
  [DT 797 : old class]
  [DT 2458.T35 : new class]
  BT Ethnology--Botswana
      Khoikhoi (African people)
      San (African people)

Tanzania *(Not Subd Geog)*
  [DT 436-DT 449]
  Here are entered works on the jurisdiction of Tanzania formed in 1964 by the merger of Tanganyika and Zanzibar for all periods and subjects. Works on the island of Zanzibar for all periods and subjects are entered under Zanzibar. Works limited in subject coverage to the historical, political or cultural aspects of Tanganyika for the period before the merger in 1964 are entered under Tanganyika. Works on other subjects relating to Tanganyika for any pre-merger period are entered under the name of the present jurisdiction, Tanzania.
  UF United Republic of Tanzania
  --Antiquities
    NT Laetoli Site (Tanzania)
  --Description and travel
  -- --1981
  --Economic conditions
  [HC 885]
  -- --To 1964
  -- --1964-
  --Fiction
    NT Ganda fiction
        Swahili fiction
  --History
    NT Uganda-Tanzania War, 1978-1979
  -- --To 1964
  --Languages
    NT Asu language
        Bembe language (Lake Tanganyika)
        Bondei language
        Chaga language
        Cushitic languages, Southern

    NT Ganda language
        Gogo language
        Holoholo language
        Iraqw language
        Jita language
        Kaguru language
        Kalenjin language
        Kerebe language
        Kuria language
        Kwafi language
        Luo language (Kenya and Tanzania)
        Makonde language
        Masai language
        Meru language
        Mtanq'ata dialect
        Mwamba language
        Mwera language
        Nandi languages
        Ngonde language
        Nika language
        Nilamba language
        Nyamwezi language
        Pangwa language
        Pogoro language
        Sagara language
        Sandawe language
        Shambala language
        Shambala languages
        Sukuma language
        Swahili language
        Taita language
        Taveta language
        Yao language
        Zanaki language
        Ziba language
        Zigula language
  --Literatures
  USE Tanzanian literature
  --Poetry
  USE Tanzanian poetry
  --Politics and government
  -- --1964-
  --Social conditions
  -- --1964-

Tanzania-Uganda War, 1978-1979
  USE Uganda-Tanzania War, 1978-1979

Tanzania-Zambia Railway
  USE Tan-Zam Railway

Tanzanian atlases
  USE Atlases, Tanzanian

Tanzanian cookery
  USE Cookery, Tanzanian

UF = Used for; BT = Broader term; RT = Related term; SA = See also; NT = Narrower term

Tanzanian literature *(May Subd Geog)*
  [PL 8014.T34 (History)]
  [PL 8014.T342 (Collections)]
  UF Tanzania--Literatures
  BT East African literature
  NT Ganda literature
      Masai literature
      Meru literature
      Swahili literature
      Tanzanian poetry
      Tanzanial prose literature

Tanzanian literature (English) *(May Subd Geog)*
  [PR 9399]
  UF English literature--Tanzanian authors
  BT East African literature (English)
  NT Tanzanian poetry (English)

Tanzanian newspapers *(May Subd Geog)*
  [PN5499.T35]
  UF Newspapers, Tanzanian

Tanzanian periodicals *(May Subd Geog)*
  [PN5499.T35]
  UF Periodicals, Tanzanian

Tanzanian poetry *(May Subd Geog)*
  [PL 8014.T34 (History)]
  [PL 8014.T342 (Collections)]
  UF Tanzania--Poetry
  BT Tanzanian literature
  NT School verse, Tanzanian
      Swahili poetry

Tanzanian poetry (English) *(May Subd Geog)*
  [PR 9399.2 (History)]
  [PR 9399.6-PR 9399.65 (Collections)]
  UF English poetry--Tanzanian authors
  BT East African poetry (English)
      Tanzanian literature (English)

Tanzanian prose literature *(May Subd Geog)*
  [PL 8014.T34 (History)]
  [PL 8014.T342 (Collections)]
  BT African prose literature
      Tanzanian literature
  NT School prose, Tanzanian
      Swahili prose literature

Tanzanian school prose
  USE School prose, Tanzanian

Tanzanian school verse
  USE School verse, Tanzanian

Tanzanian students *(May Subd Geog)*
  BT Students
  --Foreign countries
  BT Students, Foreign

Taoudenni Basin (Mali) *(Not Subd Geog)*
  UF Bassin de Taoudenni (Mali)
  BT Basins (Geology)--Mali

Taposa language
  USE Toposa language

Tapoumbi (Togolese and Ghanaian people)
  USE Bassari (Togolese and Ghanaian people)

Tara Baaka language
  USE Baka language

Taste (Aesthetics)
  USE Aesthetics

Tatoga (African people)
  USE Mangati (African people)

Tatton Farm (Kenya) *(Not Subd Geog)*
  BT Farms--Kenya

Tattooing *(May Subd Geog)*
  [GN 419.3 (Ethnology)]
  BT Body-marking
      Ethnology
      Manners and customs
  --Angola

Taturu (African people)
  USE Nyaturu (African people)

Tauara (African people)
  USE Tawara (African people)

Taveita language
  USE Taveta language

Taveta (African people) *(May Subd Geog)*
  [DT 433.545.T38]
  UF Tubeta (African people)
      Watabeta (African people)
  BT Ethnology--Kenya

Taveta art
  USE Art, Taveta

Taveta language *(May Subd Geog)*
  [PL 8715]
  UF KiTaveta language
      KiTubeta language

(May Subd Geog) = Place names may follow the heading

UF Taveita language
    Tubeta language
BT Shambala languages
    Kenya--Languages
    Tanzania--Languages

Tawara (African people) *(May Subd Geog)*
[DT 458.3.T38 (Mozambique : old class)]
[DT 3328.T38 (Mozambique : new class)]
[DT 962.42 (Zimbabwe : old class)]
[DT 2913.T38 (Zimbabwe : new class)]
UF Matawara (African people)
    Taura (African people)
    Watawara (African people)
BT Ethnology--Mozambique
    Ethnology--Zimbabwe
    Shona (African people)

Tchad
  USE Chad

Tchad, Lake
  USE Lake Chad

Tchambe (Togolese and Ghanaian people)
  USE Bassari (Togolese and Ghanaian people)

Tchi (African people)
  USE Twi (African people)

Tchien language *(May Subd Geog)*
  UF Gien language
      Kien language
      Tie language
  BT Kru languages
      Liberia--Languages

Tchiri River (Malawi and Mozambique)
  USE Shire River (Malawi and Mozambique)

Tchokwe (African people)
  USE Chokwe (African people)

Tchongoa (African people)
  USE Songola (African people)

Tchopi (African people)
  USE Chopi (African people)

Teacher education
  USE Teachers--Training of

Teacher training
  USE Teachers--Training of

Teachers *(May Subd Geog)*
UF Faculty (Education)
BT Education
NT College teachers
    Teachers, Black
--**Training of** *(May Subd Geog)*
UF Teacher education
    Teacher training
    Teachers, Training of
SA *subdivision* Training of *under classes of*
teachers, e.g. Teachers, Black--Training of

Teachers, Black *(May Subd Geog)*
UF Black teachers
BT Teachers
NT College teachers, Black
--**Training of** *(May Subd Geog)*
-- --**Africa**
[LB 1727.A35]

Teachers, College
  USE College teachers

Teachers, Training of
  USE Teachers--Training of

Teachers, University
  USE College teachers

Tebele (African people)
  USE Ndebele (African people)

Tebele language
  USE Ndebele language (Zimbabwe)

Tebu (African people)
  USE Tibbu (African people)

Technical assistance, Scandinavian *(May Subd Geog)*
UF Scandinavian technical assistance
--**Tanzania**
NT Nordic Tanganyika Project

Teda (African people)
  USE Tibbu (African people)

Teda folk songs
  USE Folk songs, Teda

Teda language *(May Subd Geog)*
[PL 8724]
BT Chad--Languages
    Kanuri language
    Nigeria--Languages

UF = Used for; BT = Broader term; RT = Related term; SA = See also; NT = Narrower term

Téén dialect *(May Subd Geog)*
    UF Tenhe dialect
    BT Ivory Coast--Languages
        Lorhon language

Teenagers' writings
    BT Youths' writings

Teenagers' writings, Swahili *(May Subd Geog)*
    [PL 8704.A2 (Collections)]
    UF Swahili teenagers' writings
    BT Swahili literature

Tegdaoust (Mauritania)
    USE Aoudaghost (City)

Teita (African people)
    USE Taita (African people)

Teita Hills (Kenya)
    USE Taita Hills (Kenya)

Teita language
    USE Taita language

Teke (African people) *(May Subd Geog)*
    [DT 546.245.T43]
    UF Bateke (African people)
        Sa (African people)
        Tio (African people)
        Yansi (African people)
    BT Bantu-speaking peoples
        Ethnology--Congo (Brazzaville)

Teke folk songs
    USE Folk songs, Teke

Teke language *(May Subd Geog)*
    [PL 8725]
    UF Balali language
        Ilali language
        Itio language
        Kiteke language
        Lali language
        Lari language
    BT Bantu languages
        Congo (Brazzaville)--Languages

Tekela (African people)
    USE Swazi (African people)

Tekeza (African people)
    USE Swazi (African people)

Tekrourien (African people)
    USE Toucouleurs

Television broadcasting *(May Subd Geog)*
    UF Television industry
    BT Mass media
    NT Blacks in television broadcasting

Television industry
    USE Television broadcasting

Tell Houlouf (Cameroon)
    USE Houlouf Site (Cameroon)

Tellers of stories
    USE Storytellers

Tem (African people) *(May Subd Geog)*
    [DT 582.45.T45 (Togo)]
    UF Kotokoli (African people)
        Temba (African people)
    BT Ethnology--Africa, West
        Ethnology--Togo

Tem language *(May Subd Geog)*
    [PL 8725.15]
    UF Cotocoli language
        Kotokoli language
        Tim language
    BT Africa, West--Languages
        Gur languages
        Togo--Languages
    NT Kabre dialect

Temba (African people)
    USE Tem (African people)

Tembo language (Kivu, Zaire) *(May Subd Geog)*
    UF KiTembo language
    BT Bantu languages
        Zaire--Languages

Tembu (African people) *(May Subd Geog)*
    [DT 764.T46 : old class]
    [DT 1768.T46 : new class]
    UF Amatembu (African people)
        Thembu (African people)
    BT Ethnology--South Africa
        Nguni (African people)

Temne (African people) *(May Subd Geog)*
    [DT 516.45.T45]
    UF Timani (African people)
        Timne (African people)
    BT Ethnology--Sierra Leone

Temne language
    USE Timne language

(May Subd Geog) = Place names may follow the heading

Temoro (Malagasy people)
  USE Taimoro (Malagasy people)

Temuru (Malagasy people)
  USE Taimoro (Malagasy people)

Tenda (African people) *(May Subd Geog)*
  [DT 474.6.T46 (West Africa)]
  BT Ethnology--Africa, West
     Ethnology--Guinea
     Ethnology--Guinea-Bissau
     Ethnology--Senegal
  NT Badyaranké (African people)
     Bassari (Senegalese and Guinean
people)
     Bedik (African people)

Tenda language
  USE Bedik language

Tendanke language
  USE Bedik language

Tende language
  USE Kuria language

Ténéré (Niger) *(Not Subd Geog)*
  [DT 547.9.T46]
  BT Deserts--Niger
     Plains--Niger
     Sahara

Tenne dialect
  USE Téén dialect

Tenure of land
  USE Land tenure

Tepes (African people)
  USE Tepeth (African people)

Tepeth (African people) *(May Subd Geog)*
  [DT 433.245.T (Uganda)]
  UF So (African people)
     Tepes (African people)
  BT Ethnology--Sudan
     Ethnology--Uganda

Tepo language *(May Subd Geog)*
  [PL 8725.3]
  UF Kroumen language
     Tewi language
  BT Ivory Coast--Languages
     Kru languages

Tera language *(May Subd Geog)*
  [PL 8725.5]
  UF Terawa language
  BT Chadic languages
     Nigeria--Languages

Terawa language
  USE Tera language

Terra-cotta sculpture *(May Subd Geog)*
  BT Sculpture
  --Mali
  [NB 1265]

Terra-cotta sculpture, Mandingo *(May Subd Geog)*
  [NB 1265]
  UF Mandingo terra-cotta sculpture

Terra-cotta sculpture, Nigerian *(May Subd Geog)*
  [NB 1265]
  UF Nigerian terra-cotta sculpture

Terra-cotta sculpture, Nok *(May Subd Geog)*
  [NB 1265]
  UF Nok terra-cotta sculpture

Terrorism *(May Subd Geog)*
  UF Political violence
  BT Insurgency
  --Africa, Sub-Saharan
  [HV 6433.A]

Teso (African people) *(May Subd Geog)*
  [DT 433.545.T (Kenya)]
  [DT 433.245.T (Uganda)]
  UF Ateso (African people)
     Bakedi (African people)
     Bakidi (African people)
     Bateso (African people)
     Elgumi (African people)
     Etossio (African people)
     Ikumama (African people)
     Iteso (African people)
     Itesyo (African people)
     Kedi (African people)
     Wamia (African people)
  BT Ethnology--Kenya
     Ethnology--Uganda
     Nilo-Hamitic tribes

Teso language *(May Subd Geog)*
  [PL 8726]
  UF Ateso language
     Iteso language
  BT Kenya--Languages
     Nilo-Hamitic languages   *(Continued)*

UF = Used for; BT = Broader term; RT = Related term; SA = See also; NT = Narrower term

Teso language *(Continued)*
  BT Uganda--Languages
  NT Karamojong language

Tete language *(May Subd Geog)*
  [PL 8727]
  UF Nyai language
      Nyungwe language
      Tette language
  BT Bantu languages
      Zaire--Languages
  RT Nyanja language
      Sena language

Tetela (African people) *(May Subd Geog)*
  [DT 650.T]
  UF Batetela (African people)
      Otetela (African people)
      Sungu (African people)
  BT Bantu-speaking peoples
      Ethnology--Zaire
 --Religion
  [BL 2480.B37]

Tetela language *(May Subd Geog)*
  [PL 8728]
  UF Otetela language
  BT Bantu languages
      Zaire--Languages

Tetela proverbs
  USE Proverbs, Tetela

Tette language
  USE Tete language

Teuso (African people)
  USE Ik (African people)

Teuso languages *(May Subd Geog)*
  [PL 8731]
  UF Kuliak languages
  BT Nilo-Saharan languages
      Uganda--Languages

Tewi language
  USE Tepo language

Textile fabrics *(May Subd Geog)*
  UF Cloth
      Fabrics
  BT Decorative arts
      Weaving
 --Ghana
  [NK 8889.6.G5]

 --Ivory Coast
  [NK 8889.6.I8]
 --Nigeria
  [NK 8889.6.N4]

Textile fabrics, Bini *(May Subd Geog)*
  [NK 8889.6.N4]
  UF Bini textile fabrics

Textile fabrics, Black *(May Subd Geog)*
  [NK 8889]
  UF Black textile fabrics

Textile fabrics, Senufo *(May Subd Geog)*
  [NK 8889.6.I8]
  UF Senufo textile fabrics

Tharaka (African people) *(May Subd Geog)*
  [DT 433.545.T]
  UF Atharaka (African people)
      Kitharaka (African people)
      Saraka (African people)
      Sharoka (African people)
  BT Ethnology--Kenya

The Avenue (Stellenbosch, South Africa)
  USE Avenue, The (Stellenbosch, South Africa)

The Comoros
  USE Comoros

The Congo
  USE Congo (Brazzaville)

The Gambia
  USE Gambia

Theater *(May Subd Geog)*
  Here are entered works on drama as acted on the stage.
  Works on drama as a literary form are entered under Drama.
  UF Stage
  BT Performing arts
  RT Actors
  NT Black theater
      Children's plays
      Masks
 --Ghana
  [PN 2990.8]

Theater, Black
  USE Black theater

Theatricals, College
  USE College and school drama

(May Subd Geog) = Place names may follow the heading

Thembu (African people)
USE Tembu (African people)

Theology
UF Christian theology
Theology, Christian
BT Christianity
NT Black theology

Theology, Black
USE Black theology

Theology, Christian
USE Theology

Thonga (African people)
USE Tsonga (African people)

Thonga language
USE Tsonga language

Thoroughfares
USE Roads
Streets

Tiamus (African people)
USE Njemps (African people)

Tibbu (African people) *(May Subd Geog)*
[DT 346.T4]
UF Tebu (African people)
Teda (African people)
Tibu (African people)
BT Ethnology--Sahara

Tibesti Massif
USE Tibesti Mountains

Tibesti Mountains *(Not Subd Geog)*
[DT 546.49.T (Chad)]
UF Tibesti Massif
Tu Mountains
BT Mountains--Chad
Mountains--Niger

Tibu (African people)
USE Tibbu (African people)

Tie language
USE Tchien language

Tigrai language
USE Tigrinya language

Tigray (African people)
USE Tigrinya (African people)

Tigray language
USE Tigrinya language

Tigré language *(May Subd Geog)*
[PJ 9131]
BT Ethiopian languages

Tigrenna language
USE Tigrinya language

Tigrensis language
USE Tigrinya language

Tigrigna language
USE Tigrinya language

Tigrina (African people)
USE Tigrinya (African people)

Tigrina language
USE Tigrinya language

Tigrinya (African people) *(May Subd Geog)*
[DT 380.4.T54]
UF Tigray (African people)
Tigrina (African people)
BT Ethnology--Ethiopia

Tigrinya language *(May Subd Geog)*
[PJ 9111]
UF Tigrai language
Tigray language
Tigrenna language
Tigrensis language
Tigrigna language
Tigrina language
Tna language
BT Ethiopian languages

Tigrinya proverbs
USE Proverbs, Tigrinya

Tikali (African people)
USE Tikar (African people)

Tikali language
USE Tikar language

Tikar (African people) *(May Subd Geog)*
[DT 571.T]
UF Tikali (African people)
BT Ethnology--Cameroon
NT Mfumte (African people)
Yamba (African people)

UF = Used for; BT = Broader term; RT = Related term; SA = See also; NT = Narrower term

Tikar language *(May Subd Geog)*
  [PL 8733]
  UF Tikali language
  BT Benue-Congo languages
      Cameroon--Languages

Tim language
  USE Tem language

Timani (African people)
  USE Temne (African people)

Timbavati Game Reserve (South Africa) *(Not Subd Geog)*
  BT Game reserves--South Africa

Timboctú (Mali)
  USE Tombouctou (Mali)

Timbuctoo (Mali)
  USE Tombouctou (Mali)

Timbuctú (Mali)
  USE Tombouctou (Mali)

Timbuka (African people)
  USE Tumbuka (African people)

Timbuktu (Mali)
  USE Tombouctou (Mali)

Timne (African people)
  USE Temne (African people)

Timne language *(May Subd Geog)*
  [PL 8735]
  UF Temne language
  BT Niger-Congo languages
      Sierra Leone--Languages

Tindiga (African people) *(May Subd Geog)*
  [DT 443.3.T (Tanzania)]
  UF Hadzapi (African people)
      Kindiga (African people)
      Watindega (African people)
  BT Ethnology--Africa, East
      Ethnology--Tanzania
 --Material culture

Tio (African people)
  USE Teke (African people)

Tiriki (African people) *(May Subd Geog)*
  [DT 433.545.T]
  BT Bantu-speaking peoples
      Ethnology--Kenya

Tiv (African people)
  USE Tivi (African people)

Tivi (African people) *(May Subd Geog)*
  [DT 515.45.T58]
  UF Mba-tivi (African people)
      Michi (African people)
      Munshi (African people)
      Munsi (African people)
      Tiv (African people)
      Tiwi (African people)
  BT Ethnology--Nigeria
 --Religion
  [BL 2480.T5]

Tivi language *(May Subd Geog)*
  [PL 8738]
  UF Tiwi language (Nigeria)
  BT Benue-Congo languages
      Nigeria--Languages

Tivi law
  USE Law, Tivi

Tivi songs
  USE Songs, Tivi

Tivi women
  USE Women, Tivi

Tiwi (African people)
  USE Tivi (African people)

Tiwi language (Nigeria)
  USE Tivi language

Tjimba (African people)
  USE Himba (African people)

Tjimba dialect
  USE Himba dialect

Tlahaping (African people)
  USE Tlhaping (African people)

Tlapi (African people)
  USE Tlhaping (African people)

Tlhaping (African people) *(May Subd Geog)*
  [DT 797 (Botswana : old class)]
  [DT 2458.T55 (Botswana : new class)]
  [DT 764.T (South Africa : old class)]
  [DT 1768.T57 (South Africa : new class)]
  [DT 962.42 (Zimbabwe : old class)]
  [DT 2913.T55 (Zimbabwe : new class)]

(May Subd Geog) = Place names may follow the heading

UF Bachapin (African people)
    Batlapin (African people)
    Tlahaping (African people)
    Tlapi (African people)
BT Ethnology--Botswana
    Ethnology--South Africa
    Ethnology--Zimbabwe
    Tswana (African people)

Tlokwa (African people) *(May Subd Geog)*
    [DT 797 (Botswana : old class)]
    [DT 2458.T (Botswana : new class)]
    [DT 786.5 (Lesotho : old class)]
    [DT 2596.T (Lesotho : new class)]
UF Batlokwa (African people)
    Batloqua (African people)
    Dokwa (African people)
    Tokwa (African people)
BT Ethnology--Botswana
    Ethnology--Lesotho

Tna language
    USE Tigrinya language

To-bedawie language
    USE Beja language

Tobago
    USE Trinidad and Tobago

Tobote (Togolese and Ghanaian people)
    USE Bassari (Togolese and Ghanaian people)

Tobote language *(May Subd Geog)*
    [PL 8738.5]
UF Basari language (Togo and Ghana)
    Bassari language (Togo and Ghana)
BT Ghana--Languages
    Gur languages
    Togo--Languages

Tobote proverbs
    USE Proverbs, Tobote

Tofingbe dialect *(May Subd Geog)*
    [PL 8164.Z9T6]
BT Benin--Languages
    Ewe languages

Tofinnu (African people) *(May Subd Geog)*
    [DT 541.45.T63]
BT Ethnology--Benin

Tofoke (African people)
    USE Topoke (African people)

Togo *(Not Subd Geog)*
    [DT 582-DT 582.9]
UF Togoland (British)
    Togoland (French)
--Economic conditions
    [HC 1020]
--History
-- --1922-1960
--Languages
NT Adangme language
    Aja dialect
    Anufo dialect
    Dompago dialect
    Ewe language
    Kabre dialect
    Konkomba language
    Kposo language
    Mina dialect
    Somba language
    Tem language
    Tobote language
--Literatures
    USE Togolese literature
--Poetry
NT Ewe poetry
--Politics and government
-- --1922-1960
-- --1960-

Togo, Lake (Togo) *(Not Subd Geog)*
    UF Lake Togo (Togo)
    BT Lagoons--Togo

Togoland (British)
    USE Ghana
         Togo

Togoland (French)
    USE Togo

Togolese literature *(May Subd Geog)*
    [PL 8014.T]
    UF Togo--Literatures
    BT West African literature
    NT Ewe literature

Togolese literature (French) *(May Subd Geog)*
    [PQ 3988.5.T6 (History)]
    [PQ 3988.5.T62 (Collections)]
    UF French literature--Togolese authors
    BT West African literature (French)
    NT Togolese poetry (French)

Togolese newspapers *(May Subd Geog)*
    [PN 5499.T6]
    UF Newspapers, Togolese

UF = Used for; BT = Broader term; RT = Related term; SA = See also; NT = Narrower term

Togolese periodicals *(May Subd Geog)*
  [PN 5499.T6]
  UF Periodicals, Togolese

Togolese poetry (French) *(May Subd Geog)*
  [PQ 3988.5.T6 (History)]
  [PQ 3988.5.T62 (Collections)]
  UF French poetry--Togolese authors
  BT Togolese literature (French)
      West African poetry (French)

Togolese students *(May Subd Geog)*
  BT Students
  --Foreign countries
  BT Students, Foreign

Toi (African people)
  USE Didinga (African people)

Toka (Zambesi people)
  USE Tonga (Zambesi people)

Tokoror (African people)
  USE Toucouleurs

Tokwa (African people)
  USE Tlokwa (African people)

Toma (African people) *(May Subd Geog)*
  [DT 474.6.T]
  BT Ethnology--Africa, West

Toma language
  USE Loma language

Tomba language
  USE Ntomba language

Tombo (African people)
  USE Dogon (African people)

Tombo language
  USE Dogon language

Tombouctou (Mali) *(Not Subd Geog)*
  [DT 551.9.T55]
  UF Timboctú (Mali)
      Timbuctoo (Mali)
      Timbuctú (Mali)
      Timbuktu (Mali)
      Tombutu (Mali)
      Tumbuktu (Mali)

Tombucas (African people)
  USE Tumbuka (African people)

Tombutu (Mali)
  USE Tombouctou (Mali)

Tombwa (African people)
  USE Holoholo (African people)

Tone (Phonetics)
  [P 223]
  UF Language and languages--Tone
      Lexical tone (Phonetics)
      Tone languages
  NT African languages--Tone
      Attie language--Tone
      Bantu languages--Tone
      Baoulé language--Tone
      Dyula language--Tone
      Efik language--Tone
      Etsako language--Tone
      Kalenjin language--Tone
      Nama language--Tone
      Nguni languages--Tone
      Shona language--Tone
      Xhosa language--Tone

Tone languages
  USE Tone (Phonetics)

Tonga (Malawi people)
  USE Tumbuka (African people)

Tonga (Mozambique people) *(May Subd Geog)*
  [DT 458.3.T : old class]
  [DT 3328.T : new class]
  UF Inhambane (Mozambique people)
      Shengwe (Mozambique people)
  BT Ethnology--Mozambique

Tonga (Zambesi people) *(May Subd Geog)*
  [DT 962.42 (Zambia : old class)]
  [DT 3058.T65 (Zambia : new class)]
  UF Gwembe (Zambesi people)
      Plateau Tonga (Zambesi people)
      Toka (Zambesi people)
      Tonka (Zambesi people)
      Valley Tonga (Zambesi people)
  BT Bantu-speaking peoples
      Ethnology--Botswana
      Ethnology--Zambia
      Ethnology--Zimbabwe
  --Material culture

Tonga children's stories (Zambesi)
  USE Children's stories, Tonga (Zambesi)

(May Subd Geog) = Place names may follow the heading

Tonga fiction (Zambesi) *(May Subd Geog)*
  [PL 8741.5-PL 8741.9]
  BT Botswana--Fiction
      Tonga literature (Zambesi)
      Zambia--Fiction
      Zimbabwean fiction
  NT Children's stories, Tonga (Zambesi)

Tonga folk literature (Zambesi)
  USE Folk literature, Tonga (Zambesi)

Tonga language (Gitonga)
  USE Tonga language (Inhambane)

Tonga language (Inhambane) *(May Subd Geog)*
  [PL 8739]
  UF Gi-Tonga language
      Gitonga language
      Tonga language (Gitonga)
  BT Bantu languages
      Mozambique--Languages

Tonga language (Nyasa) *(May Subd Geog)*
  [PL 8740]
  UF Chi-Tonga language (Nyasa)
  BT Bantu language
      Malawi--Languages
  RT Tumbuka language

Tonga language (Tsonga)
  USE Tsonga language

Tonga language (Zambesi) *(May Subd Geog)*
  [PL 8741]
  UF Chi-Tonga language (Zambesi)
      Ci-Tonga language
  BT Bantu languages
      Botswana--Languages
      Zambia--Languages
      Zimbabwe--Languages
  NT Ila language
      Lenje language

Tonga law
  USE Law, Tonga

Tonga literature (Zambesi) *(May Subd Geog)*
  [PL 8741.5-PL 8741.9]
  BT Botswana literature
      Zambia literature
      Zimbabwean literature
  NT Folk literature, Tonga (Zambesi)
      Tonga fiction (Zambesi)

Tonga women (Zambesi)
  USE Women, Tonga (Zambesi)

Tongaland (South Africa)
  USE Maputaland (South Africa)

Tongbo language
  USE Mambila language

Toni (African people)
  USE Eton (African people)

Tonka (Zambesi people)
  USE Tonga (Zambesi people)

Tooro (African people) *(May Subd Geog)*
  [DT 433.245.T]
  UF Toro (African people)
  BT Bantu-speaking peoples
      Ethnology--Uganda

Tooro language *(May Subd Geog)*
  [PL 8743]
  UF Lutoro language
      Toro language
  BT Bantu languages
      Uganda--Languages
  RT Nyoro-Tooro language

Topoke (African people) *(May Subd Geog)*
  [DT 650.T65]
  UF Tofoke (African people)
  BT Bantu-speaking peoples
      Ethnology--Zaire

Toposa (African people)
  USE Nyangatom (African people)

Toposa language *(May Subd Geog)*
  UF Abo language (Sudan)
      Akeroa language
      Dabossa language
      Huma language (Sudan)
      Kare language (Sudan)
      Khumi language (Sudan)
      Taposa language
      Topotha language
  BT Nilo-Hamitic languages
      Sudan--Languages

Topotha language
  USE Toposa language

Torbi language
  USE Mambila language

Toro (African people)
  USE Tooro (African people)

UF = Used for; BT = Broader term; RT = Related term; SA = See also; NT = Narrower term

Toro language
USE Tooro language

Torobo (African people)
USE Dorobo (African people)

Torodo (African people)
USE Toucouleurs

Touaregs
USE Tuaregs

Toubakai language
USE Soninke language

Toubou (African people)
USE Daza (African people)

Toubou language
USE Daza language

Toubouri language
USE Tuburi language

Toucouleur Empire
[DT 532.3]
BT Toucouleurs--History

Toucouleurs *(May Subd Geog)*
[DT 549.45.T68 (Senegal)]
UF Futa Toro (African people)
Futankobe (African people)
Tekrourien (African people)
Tokoror (African people)
Torodo (African people)
Tukulor (African people)
BT Ethnology--Senegal
Ethnology--Sudan (Region)
RT Fula (African people)
--History
NT Toucouleur Empire
-- --19th century
NT Bambara Jihad, 1852-1863

Toumak language
USE Tumak language

Toupouri language
USE Tuburi language

Toura (African people)
USE Tura (African people)

Toura language
USE Tura language

Tours, Adventure
USE Safaris

Toussia (African people)
USE Tusia (African people)

Toussia language
USE Tusia language

Trade, International
USE *name of place subdivided by Commerce and further subdivided by place, if appropriate, e.g. Zimbabwe--Commerce--United States*

Trade languages
USE Lingua francas

Trade-unions *(May Subd Geog)*
UF Industrial unions
Labor, Organized
Labor organizations
Labor unions
Organizations, Labor
Organized labor
Unions, Industrial
Unions, Labor
Unions, Trade
Working-men's associations
RT Strikes and lockouts

Trade-unions, Black *(May Subd Geog)*
UF Black trade-unions
--South Africa
[HD 6870.5]

Traders, Slave
USE Slave traders

Tradition, Oral
USE Oral tradition

Traditions
USE Folklore
Legends
Manners and customs
Rites and ceremonies

Trans-African Highway
[HE 367.Z6T7]
UF Axe routier transafrican
Transafrican Highway
BT Roads--Africa

Transafrican Highway
USE Trans-African Highway

(May Subd Geog) = Place names may follow the heading

Transkei (South Africa) *(Not Subd Geog)*
  [DT 846.T7 : old class]
  [DT 2400.T83 : new class]
  BT Homelands (South Africa)

Transportation *(May Subd Geog)*
  NT Railroads
      Roads

Transportation and state *(May Subd Geog)*
  UF State and transportation
      Transportation policy
  --Africa
  NT United Nations Transport and
Communications Decade in Africa, 1978-1988

Transportation policy
  USE Transportation and state

Transvaal (Colony)
  USE Transvaal (South Africa)

Transvaal (South Africa) *(Not Subd Geog)*
  [DT 911-DT 944 : old class]
  [DT 2291-DT 2405 : new class]
  UF South African Republic
      Transvaal (Colony)
  Description and travel
  -- --To 1910
  --General Strike
  USE General Strike, Transvaal, South
Africa, 1913
  --History
  -- --To 1880
  -- --War of 1880-1881
      [DT 928 : old class]
      [DT 2354-DT 2359 : new class]
      UF Boer War, 1880-1881
          Transvaal War, 1880-1881
      NT Majuba Hill (South Africa), Battle of,
1881
  -- --1880-1910
      NT Jameson's Raid, 1895-1896
  -- --1910-
  --Politics and government
  -- --To 1880
  -- --1880-1910
  -- --1910-

Transvaal Ndebele language
  USE Ndebele language (South Africa)

Transvaal Sotho (African people)
  USE Pedi (African people)

Transvaal Sotho language
  USE Northern Sotho language

Transvaal War, 1880-1881
  USE Transvaal (South Africa)--History--War of
1880-1881

Transvaal War, 1899-1902
  USE South African War, 1899-1902

Tribal government *(May Subd Geog)*
  UF Government, Tribal
  BT Ethnology
      Tribes
  --Botswana
      [JC 29.B]
  --Nigeria
      [JC 29.N53]
  --Togo
      [JC 29.T]

Tribal marking
  USE Body-marking

Tribal names
  USE Names, Ethnological

Tribes *(May Subd Geog)*
  BT Family
  RT Clans
      Kinship
  SA *names of individual tribes or groups of tribes,*
e.g. Khoikhoi (African people); Nilo-Hamitic
tribes
  NT Detribalization
      Tribal government
  --Africa
      [DT 15]
  --Africa, Southern
      [DT 737 : old class]
      [DT 1054 : new class]

Trickster *(May Subd Geog)*
  BT Folklore
  --Africa, West
      NT Anansi (Legendary character)
  --Nigeria
      NT Esu (Legendary character)

Trinidad and Tobago *(Not Subd Geog)*
  UF Tobago
  --Civilization
  -- --African influences
      BT Africa--Civilization

UF = Used for; BT = Broader term; RT = Related term; SA = See also; NT = Narrower term

Tropical Africa
  USE Africa, Sub-Saharan

Tropical diseases
  USE Tropical medicine

Tropical medicine *(May Subd Geog)*
  [RC 960-RC 962]
  UF Diseases, Tropical
      Hygiene, Tropical
      Medicine, Tropical
      Public health, Tropical
      Sanitation, Tropical
      Tropical diseases
  NT AIDS (Disease)
      Malaria
      Sickle cell anemia
  --**Africa, Southern**
    [RC 962.A]

Tsana, Lake (Ethiopia)
  USE Tana, Lake (Ethiopia)

Tsavo National Park (Kenya) *(Not Subd Geog)*
  NT Game reserves--Kenya
      National parks and reserves--Kenya
      Parks--Kenya

Tschagga language
  USE Chaga language

Tschi language
  USE Twi language

Tschiokwe language
  USE Chokwe language

Tschopi (African people)
  USE Chopi (African people)

Tschwi (African people)
  USE Twi (African people)

Tshere language
  USE Gabri language

Tshi (African people)
  USE Twi (African people)

Tshi language
  USE Twi language

tshi-sala-Mpasu language
  USE Salampasu language

Tshiboko language
  USE Chokwe language

Tshiluba language (Luba-Katanga)
  USE Luba-Katanga language

Tshiluba language (Luba-Lulua)
  USE Luba-Lulua language

Tshiri language
  USE Gabri language

Tshivenda language
  USE Venda language

Tshobwa (African people)
  USE Shoowa (African people)

Tshogo (African people)
  USE Hutu (African people)

Tshokossi (African people)
  USE Chokossi (African people)

Tshokwe (African people)
  USE Chokwe (African people)

Tshokwe language
  USE Chokwe language

Tshopi (African people)
  USE Chopi (African people)

Tshwana language
  USE Tswana language

Tsimihety (Malagasy people) *(May Subd Geog)*
  [DT 469.M277T]
  BT Ethnology--Madagascar

Tsimihety dialect *(May Subd Geog)*
  [PL 5379]
  BT Malagasy language

Tsiri language
  USE Gabri language

Tsiribihina River (Madagascar) *(Not Subd Geog)*
  [DT 469.M37T77]
  BT Rivers--Madagascar

Tsogho (African people)
  USE Mitsogho (African people)

Tsogo folk songs
  USE Folk songs, Tsogo

(May Subd Geog) = Place names may follow the heading

Tsogo language *(May Subd Geog)*
  UF Apindji language
       Mitsogo language
  BT Bantu languages
       Gabon--Languages

Tsogo literature *(May Subd Geog)*
  BT Gabon literature
  NT Tsogo poetry

Tsogo poetry *(May Subd Geog)*
  BT Gabon--Poetry
       Tsogo literature

Tsogo songs
  USE Songs, Tsogo

Tsonga (African people) *(May Subd Geog)*
  [DT 458.3.T47 (Mozambique : old class)]
  [DT 3328.T48 (Mozambique : new class)]
  [DT 764.T (South Africa : old class)]
  [DT 1768.T55 (South Africa : new class)]
  UF Hlengwe (African people)
       Ronga (African people)
       Shangaan (African people)
       Shangana (African people)
       Thonga (African people)
  BT Bantu-speaking peoples
       Ethnology--Malawi
       Ethnology--Mozambique
       Ethnology--South Africa

Tsonga children's poetry
  USE Children's poetry, Tsonga

Tsonga folk songs
  USE Folk songs, Tsonga

Tsonga hymns
  USE Hymns, Tsonga

Tsonga imprints *(May Subd Geog)*
  [Z 7108.T]
  UF Imprints, Tsonga

Tsonga language *(May Subd Geog)*
  [PL 8745]
  UF Changana language
       Gwamba language
       Shangaan language
       Shitsonga language
       Thonga language
       Tonga language (Tsonga)
       Xitsonga language
  BT Bantu languages
       Malawi--Languages

  BT Mozambique--Language
       South Africa--Languages
  RT Ronga language
       Tswa language

Tsonga poetry *(May Subd Geog)*
  [PL 8745.5 (History)]
  [PL 8745.7 (Collections)]
  BT Malawi--Poetry
       Mozambique--Poetry
       South African poetry
  NT Children's poetry, Tsonga

Tswa language *(May Subd Geog)*
  [PL 8746.T]
  UF Kitswa language
       Sheetswa language
       Shitswa language
       Xitswa language
  BT Bantu languages
       Mozambique--Languages
       Zimbabwe--Languages
  RT Ronga language
       Tsonga language

Tswana (African people) *(May Subd Geog)*
  [DT 797 (Botswana : old class)]
  [DT 2458.T89 (Botswana : new class)]
  [DT 764.T75 (South Africa : old class)]
  [DT 1768.T89 (South Africa : new class)]
  [DT 962.42 (Zimbabwe : old class)]
  [DT 2913.T78 (Zimbabwe : new class)]
  UF Bechuana (African people)
       Beetjuans (African people)
       Chuana (African people)
       Coana (African people)
       Cuana (African people)
  BT Ethnology--Botswana
       Ethnology--South Africa
       Ethnology--Zimbabwe
       Sotho (African people)
  NT Bafokeng (African people)
       Kgatla (African people)
       Tlhaping (African people)
  --Religion
  [BL 2480.T76]

Tswana folk songs
  USE Folk songs, Tswana

Tswana hymns
  USE Hymns, Tswana

Tswana imprints *(May Subd Geog)*
  [Z 7108.T]
  UF Imprints, Tswana

UF = Used for; BT = Broader term; RT = Related term; SA = See also; NT = Narrower term

Tswana language *(May Subd Geog)*
  [PL 8747]
  UF Bechuana language
      Beetjuans language
      Chuana language
      Chwana language
      Coana language
      Cuana language
      Cwana language
      Sechuana language
      Secoana language
      Secwana language
      Setswana language
      Tshwana language
  BT Africa, Southern--Languages
      Botswana--Languages
      Sotho-Tswana languages
      South Africa--Languages
      Zimbabwe--Languages
  NT Kgalagadi dialect
--Dictionaries
  NT Picture dictionaries, Tswana

Tswana laudatory poetry
  USE Laudatory poetry, Tswana

Tswana law
  USE Law, Tswana

Tswana picture dictionaries
  USE Picture dictionaries, Tswana

Tswana poetry *(May Subd Geog)*
  [PL 8746.5 (History)]
  [PL 8747.7 (Collections)]
  BT Botswana--Poetry
      South African poetry
      Zimbabwean poetry
  NT Laudatory poetry, Tswana

Tswi language
  USE Twi language

Tu-bedawie language
  USE Beja language

Tu Mountains
  USE Tibesti Mountains

Tuaregs *(May Subd Geog)*
  [DT 547.45.T83 (Niger)]
  [DT 346.T7 (Sahara)]
  UF Touaregs
      Tuariks
  BT Ethnology--Niger
      Ethnology--Sahara

  NT Ajjer (African people)
--History
  NT Senussite Rebellion, 1916-1918
--Jewelry
  UF Jewelry, Tuareg

Tuariks
  USE Tuaregs

Tubeta (African people)
  USE Taveta (African people)

Tubeta language
  USE Taveta language

Tubu language
  USE Daza language

Tuburi language *(May Subd Geog)*
  [PL 8748.T]
  UF Ndore language
      Toubouri language
      Toupouri language
      Tupuri language
  BT Cameroon--Languages
      Chad--Languages
      Chadic languages

Tugen (African people) *(May Subd Geog)*
  [DT 433.545.T83]
  UF Kamasia (African people)
      Kamasya (African people)
      Tuken (African people)
  BT Ethnology--Kenya

Tuislande (South Africa)
  USE Homelands (South Africa)

Tuken (African people)
  USE Tugen (African people)

Tukubba (African people)
  USE Kuba (African people)

Tukulor (African people)
  USE Toucouleurs

Tumak language *(May Subd Geog)*
  [PL 8748.T84]
  UF Maga language
      Sara Toumak language
      Toumak language
      Tummok language
      Tumok language
  BT Chad--Languages
      Chadic languages

(May Subd Geog) = Place names may follow the heading

Tumas River (Namibia) *(Not Subd Geog)*
  BT Rivers--Namibia

Tumba (African people)
  USE Luba (African people)

Tumbuka (African people) *(May Subd Geog)*
  [DT 864 : old class]
  [DT 3192.T85 : new class]
  UF Batumbuka (African people)
      Nyasa (African people)
      Siska (African people)
      Sisya (African people)
      Tambuka (African people)
      Timbuka (African people)
      Tombucas (African people)
      Tonga (Malawi people)
      Watumbuka (African people)
  BT Bantu-speaking peoples
      Ethnology--Malawi
  NT Phoka (African people)
      Yombe (African people)

Tumbuka imprints *(May Subd Geog)*
  [Z 7108.T]
  UF Imprints, Tumbuka

Tumbuka language *(May Subd Geog)*
  [PL 8749]
  UF Tamboka language
  BT Bantu languages
      Malawi--Languages
  RT Nyanja language
      Tonga language (Nyasa)

Tumbuktu (Mali)
  USE Tombouctou (Mali)

Tumbwe (African people)
  USE Holoholo (African people)

Tummok language
  USE Tumak language

Tumok language
  USE Tumak language

Tunen language
  USE Banen language

Tungue Bay (Mozambique) *(Not Subd Geog)*
  UF Bahia de Tungue (Mozambique)
      Baía de Tungue (Mozambique)
  BT Bays--Mozambique

Tungue Bay (Mozambique), Battle of, 1887
  [DT 861 : old class]
  [DT 3211 : new class]
  UF Battle of Tungue Bay (Mozambique), 1887
  BT Zanzibar--History

Tupende (African people)
  USE Pende (African people)

Tupuri language
  USE Tuburi language

Tura (African people) *(May Subd Geog)*
  [DT 545.45.T]
  UF Toura (African people)
      Weingme (African people)
  BT Ethnology--Ivory Coast

Tura language *(May Subd Geog)*
  [PL 8750.T82]
  UF Toura language
  BT Ivory Coast--Languages
      Kweni language

Turkana, Lake (Kenya and Ethiopia)
  USE Rudolf, Lake (Kenya and Ethiopia)

Turkana (African people) *(May Subd Geog)*
  [DT 433.545.T87 (Kenya)]
  UF Elgume (African people)
  BT Ethnology--Ethiopia
      Ethnology--Kenya
      Nilo-Hamitic tribes
  --Religion
  [BL 2480.T87]

Turkana language *(May Subd Geog)*
  [PL 8750.T83]
  BT Ethiopia--Languages
      Kenya--Languages
      Nilo-Hamitic languages

Turruba (African people)
  USE Luba (African people)

Turu (African people)
  USE Nyaturu (African people)

Tusi (African people)
  USE Tutsi (African people)

Tusia (African people) *(May Subd Geog)*
  [DT 555.45.T87]
  UF Toussia (African people)
      Win (African people)
  BT Ethnology--Burkina Faso

UF = Used for; BT = Broader term; RT = Related term; SA = See also; NT = Narrower term

Tusia language *(May Subd Geog)*
    [PL 8750.T]
    UF   Toussia language
          Win language
    BT   Burkina Faso--Languages
          Gur languages

Tusona *(May Subd Geog)*
    UF   Kasona
    BT   Folk art--Zambia
          Rites and ceremonies--Zambia

Tussi (African people)
    USE Tutsi (African people)

Tutchokue language
    USE Chokwe language

Tuti (African people)
    USE Batwa (African people)

Tutsi (African people) *(May Subd Geog)*
    [DT 443.3.T (Tanzania)]
    UF   Batutsi (African people)
          Tusi (African people)
          Tussi (African people)
          Tuti (African people)
          Watussi (African people)
    BT   Ethnology--Burundi
          Ethnology--Rwanda
          Ethnology--Tanzania
          Rundi (African people)

Tuwunro dialect *(May Subd Geog)*
    BT   Mali--Languages
          Syènara language

Twa (African people)
    USE Batwa (African people)

Twi (African people) *(May Subd Geog)*
    [DT 510.43.T]
    UF   Tchi (African people)
          Tschwi (African people)
          Tshi (African people)
    BT   Ethnology--Ghana

Twi ballads
    USE Ballads, Twi

Twi Fante (African people)
    USE Akan (African people)

Twi-Fanti language
    USE Akan language

Twi language *(May Subd Geog)*
    [PL 8751]
    Here are entered works limited to dialects of the
    Akuapem, Ashanti, and related peoples who accept the name
    Twi. Works dealing collectively with the above dialects and
    the dialect of the Fanti people are entered under Akan
    language.
    UF   Akuapem language
          Akwapim language
          Asante language
          Ashanti language
          Chwee language
          Chwi language
          Odschi language
          Oji language
          Otji language
          Tschi language
          Tshi language
          Tswi language
    BT   Akan language
          Ghana--Languages

Twi proverbs
    USE Proverbs, Twi

Tyap language
    USE Katab language

Tyebali dialect
    USE Tyembara dialect

Tyembara dialect *(May Subd Geog)*
    UF   Tyebali dialect
    BT   Ivory Coast--Languages
          Senari language
   --Texts

Tyokossi (African people)
    USE Chokossi (African people)

Tyrants
    USE Dictators

U

U.N.E.C.A.
    USE United Nations. Economic Commission for
Africa

U.S.A.
    USE United States

Ubangi-Shari
    USE Central African Republic

Ubangui-Chari
  USE Central African Republic

Ubani dialect
  USE Ibani dialect

Ubium (African people) *(May Subd Geog)*
  [DT 515.45.U24]
  BT Ethnology--Nigeria
     Ibibio (African people)

Udlam language
  USE Uldeme language

Udok (African people)
  USE Uduk (African people)

Uduk (African people) *(May Subd Geog)*
  [DT 155.2.U38 (Sudan)]
  UF Kebeirka (African people)
     Kwanim pas (African people)
     Othan (African people)
     Udok (African people)
  BT Ethnology--Ethiopia
     Ethnology--Sudan
 --Religion
  [BL 2480.U38]

Uduk language *(May Subd Geog)*
  [PL 8753]
  BT Ethiopia--Languages
     Nilo-Saharan languages
     Sudan--Languages

Udzo language
  USE Ijo language

Uebi Scebeli River (Ethiopia and Somalia)
  USE Shebeli River (Ethiopia and Somalia)

Uganda *(Not Subd Geog)*
  [DT 433.2-DT 433.29]
 --Economic conditions
  [HC 870]
 -- --1979-
 --Emigration and immigration
  [HB 2126.U4]
 --Fiction
  NT Ganda fiction
 --Foreign relations *(May Subd Geog)*
 -- --Israel
  NT Entebbe Airport Raid, 1976
 --History
 -- --To 1890
 -- --1890-1962
 -- --1962-1971

 -- --1971-1979
  NT Uganda-Tanzania War, 1978-1979
 -- --1979-
 --Languages
  NT Acoli language
     Alur language
     Bari language
     Bukusu dialect
     Ganda language
     Gisu language
     Kakwa dialect
     Kalenjin language
     Karamojong language
     Kiga language
     Lango language
     Logbara language
     Luyia language
     Ma'di language (Uganda and Sudan)
     Mamvu language
     Mbete language
     Nandi languages
     Nubi language
     Nyankole language
     Nyankore-Kiga language
     Nyoro language
     Nyoro-Tooro language
     Soga language
     Suk language
     Tebo language
     Teuso languages
     Tooro language
     Ziba language
 --Literatures
  USE Ugandan literature
 --Poetry
  NT Nyankole poetry
 --Politics and government
 -- --1890-1962
 -- --1962-1971
 -- --1971-1979
 -- --1979-
 --Social conditions
 -- --1971-1979
 -- --1979-

Uganda-Tanzania War, 1978-1979
  [DT 433.283]
  UF Tanzania-Uganda War, 1978-1979
  BT Tanzania--History
     Uganda--History--1971-1979

Ugandan fiction (English) *(May Subd Geog)*
  [PR 9402.4 (History)]
  [PR 9402.8 (Collections)]
  UF English fiction--Ugandan authors
  BT Ugandan literature (English) *(Continued)*

UF = Used for; BT = Broader term; RT = Related term; SA = See also; NT = Narrower term

Ugandan fiction (English) *(Continued)*
  NT Short stories, Ugandan (English)

Ugandan literature *(May Subd Geog)*
  [PL 8014.U]
  UF Uganda--Literatures
  BT East African literature
  NT Ganda literature
      Nyankole literature

Ugandan literature (English) *(May Subd Geog)*
  [PR 9402]
  UF English literature--Ugandan authors
  BT East African literature (English)
  NT Ugandan fiction (English)
      Ugandan poetry (English)

Ugandan poetry (English) *(May Subd Geog)*
  [PR 9402.2 (History)]
  [PR 9402.6-PR 9402.65 (Collections)]
  UF English poetry--Ugandan authors
  BT East African poetry (English)
      Ugandan literature (English)

Ugandan short stories (English)
  USE Short stories, Ugandan (English)

Uhuru Railway
  USE Tan-Zam Railway

Ujalli (African people)
  USE Ujari (African people)

Ujamaa vijijini
  USE Ujamaa villages

Ujamaa villages *(May Subd Geog)*
  [HX 771.3.A3]
  UF Ujamaa vijijini
      Villages, Ujamaa
  BT Collective settlements--Tanzania

Ujang (African people)
  USE Majangir (African people)

Ujari (African people) *(May Subd Geog)*
  [DT 515.45.U35]
  UF Ajalli (African people)
      Ujalli (African people)
  BT Ethnology--Nigeria
      Igbo (African people)

Ukimbu (African people)
  USE Kimbu (African people)

Ukubandwa
  [BL 2470.B94U3]
  BT Burundi--Religious life and customs
      Rites and ceremonies--Burundi

Ukwese language
  USE Kwese language

Uldeme (African people) *(May Subd Geog)*
  [DT 571.U43]
  UF Ouldémé (African people)
  BT Ethnology--Cameroon

Uldeme language *(May Subd Geog)*
  [PL 8753.5]
  UF Ouldémé language
      Udlam language
      Uzan language
  BT Cameroon--Languages
      Chadic languages

UluBukusu dialect
  USE Bukusu dialect

Uluf (African people)
  USE Felup (African people)

Uluguru Mountains (Tanzania) *(Not Subd Geog)*
  BT Mountains--Tanzania

Ulunyankole (African people)
  USE Nyankole (African people)

Ulunyankore (African people)
  USE Nyankole (African people)

Umbelosi River (Swaziland and Mozambique)
  USE Umbeluzi River (Swaziland and Mozambique)

Umbeluzi River (Swaziland and Mozambique) *(Not Subd Geog)*
  UF Rio Umbeluzi (Swaziland and Mozambique)
      Umbelosi River (Swaziland and Mozambique)
      Umbuluzi River (Swaziland and Mozambique)
  BT Rivers--Mozambique
      Rivers--Swaziland

Umbete (African people)
  USE Mbete (African people)

Umbuluzi River (Swaziland and Mozambique)
  USE Umbeluzi River (Swaziland and Mozambique)

Umbundu (African people)
  USE Mbundu (African people)

(May Subd Geog) = Place names may follow the heading

Umbundu folk literature
USE Folk literature, Umbundu

Umbundu language *(May Subd Geog)*
[PL 8755]
UF Benguela language
Mbundu language (Benguela District,
Angola)
BT Angola--Languages
Bantu languages
NT Mussele dialect

Umbundu literature *(May Subd Geog)*
[PL 8755.5-PL 8755.9]
BT Angolan literature
NT Folk literature, Umbundu

Umbundu proverbs
USE Proverbs, Umbundu

Umbundu riddles
USE Riddles, Umbundu

Umgeni River (South Africa)
USE Mgeni River (South Africa)

Umwausi (African people)
USE Ushi (African people)

Uncontrolled settlements
USE Squatter settlements

Undergraduates
USE College students

Ungas *(May Subd Geog)*
[DT 963.42 : old class]
[DT 3058.U65 : new class]
UF Waungas (African people)
BT Ethnology--Zambia

Union of South Africa
USE South Africa

Unions, Industrial
USE Trade-unions

Unions, Labor
USE Trade-unions

Unions, Trade
USE Trade-unions

**United Nations. Economic Commission for
Africa**
[HC 8000]

UF E.C.A.
Economic Commission for Africa (United
Nations)
U.N.E.C.A.

United Nations Industrial Development Decade for
Africa, 1980-1990
USE Industrial Development Decade for Africa,
1980-1990

**United Nations Transport and Communications Decade
in Africa, 1978-1988**
[HE 8465]
BT Communication policy--Africa
Transportation and state--Africa

United Republic of Cameroon
USE Cameroon

United Republic of Tanzania
USE Tanzania

United States *(Not Subd Geog)*
UF U.S.A.
USA
--Civilization
NT Africa--Civilization--American influences
Africa, West--Civilization--American
influences
Liberia--Civilization--American influences
Political culture--Africa--American
influences
-- --African influences
BT Africa--Civilization

Universities and colleges *(May Subd Geog)*
UF Colleges
BT Education
NT Students
Universities and colleges, Black
--Students
USE College students

Universities and colleges, Black *(May Subd Geog)*
UF Black colleges
Black universities and colleges
Colleges, Black
BT Blacks--Education
Universities and colleges
--South Africa
[LC 2808.S7]

University Campus Site (Maputo, Mozambique) *(Not
Subd Geog)*
BT Mozambique--Antiquities

UF = Used for; BT = Broader term; RT = Related term; SA = See also; NT = Narrower term

University drama
  USE College and school drama

University graduates
  USE College graduates

University students
  USE College students

University teachers
  USE College teachers

Upper Karoo (South Africa)
  USE Northern Karroo (South Africa)

Upper Volta
  USE Burkina Faso

Urhobo (African people)
  USE Sobo (African people)

Urulera (African people)
  USE Hutu (African people)

Urundi
  USE Burundi

Urunyaruanda language
  USE Kinyarwanda language

Urunyarwanda language
  USE Kinyarwanda language

Urunyoro language
  USE Nyoro language

Uruund language
  USE Ruund language

USA
  USE United States

Usage and customs (Law)
  USE Customary law

Usages
  USE Manners and customs

Ushi (African people) *(May Subd Geog)*
  [DT 963.42 : old class]
  [DT 3058.U85 : new class]
  NT Aushi (African people)
     Avausi (African people)
     Ba-Ushi (African people)
     Bahusi (African people)
     Baousi (African people)

  NT Baoussi (African people)
     Batushi (African people)
     Baushi (African people)
     Bausi (African people)
     Umwausi (African people)
     Vouaousi (African people)
     Waushi (African people)
     Wausi (African people)
  BT Bemba (African people)
     Ethnology--Zambia

Usongora (African people)
  USE Songola (African people)

Usutu Uprising (South Africa), 1888
  USE South Africa--History--Usutu Uprising, 1888

Uwana language *(May Subd Geog)*
  [PL 8758]
  BT Africa, West--Languages
     Hausa language

'Uwaynat Mountain (Sudan) *(Not Subd Geog)*
  UF Gebel 'Uweinat (Sudan)
     Jabal al-'Uwaynat (Sudan)
     Jebel Oweinat (Sudan)
     Jebel 'Uwaynat (Sudan)
     Jebel 'Uweinat (Sudan)
  BT Mountains--Sudan

Uzan language
  USE Uldeme language

Uzigula (African people)
  USE Zigula (African people)

Uzo language
  USE Ijo language

∇

Va Ngangela (African people)
  USE Ngangela (African people)

Vaal Triangle (South Africa)
  UF Vaaldriehoek (South Africa)

Vaaldriehoek (South Africa)
  USE Vaal Triangle (South Africa)

Vabembe (East African people)
  USE Bembe (East African people)

Vacamwe (African people)
  USE Kamwe (African people)

(May Subd Geog) = Place names may follow the heading

Vachopi (African people)
USE Chopi (African people)

Vagala language *(May Subd Geog)*
[PL 8759]
UF Kira language
Konosara language
Konosarola language
Paxala language
Siti language
Sitigo language
Vagla language
BT Ghana--Languages
Grusi languages

Vagla language
USE Vagala language

Vai (African people) *(May Subd Geog)*
[DT 630.5.V2]
UF Vei (African people)
Vy (African people)
BT Ethnology--Liberia
Ethnology--Sierra Leone

Vai language *(May Subd Geog)*
[PL 8761]
UF Vei language
BT Liberia--Languages
Mande languages
Sierra Leone--Languages
NT Kono language

Vakuanano (African people)
USE Mbundu (African people)

Vakuanyama (African people)
USE Kuanyama (African people)

Valega (African people)
USE Waregas

Valenge (African people)
USE Chopi (African people)

Vallée de l'Omo (Ethiopia and Kenya)
USE Omo River Valley (Ethiopia and Kenya)

Valley Tonga (Zambesi people)
USE Tonga (Zambesi people)

Valleys *(May Subd Geog)*
UF River valleys
Stream valleys
BT Landforms
NT Floodplains

--Africa
NT Dambos
Great Rift Valley
--Africa, West
NT Niger River Valley
--Cameroon
NT Benue River Valley (Cameroon and Nigeria)
--Ethiopia
NT Omo River Valley (Ethiopia and Kenya)
--Kenya
NT Omo River Valley (Ethiopia and Kenya)
--Nigeria
NT Benue River Valley (Cameroon and Nigeria)
--South Africa
NT Kaapsedrifrivier Valley (South Africa)
--Zambia
NT Kafue River Valley (Zambia)

Valsbaai (Cape of Good Hope, South Africa)
USE False Bay (Cape of Good Hope, South Africa)

VaLuchazi (African people)
USE Luchazi (African people)

Valunda (African people)
USE Lunda, Northern (African people)

Vandau language
USE Chindau language

Vandists (Cult)
[BL 2470.C6]
BT Cults--Zaire

Vazezuru (African people)
USE Zezuru (African people)

Vazimbas *(May Subd Geog)*
[DT 469.M445V]
UF Bazimba (Malagasy people)
BT Ethnology--Madagascar

Vehicular languages
USE Lingua francas

Vei (African people)
USE Vai (African people)

Vei language
USE Vai language

Veld *(May Subd Geog)*
UF Veldt
BT Grasslands--South Africa

UF = Used for; BT = Broader term; RT = Related term; SA = See also; NT = Narrower term

Veldt
  USE Veld

Venda (African people) *(May Subd Geog)*
  [DT 920 : old class]
  [DT 1768.V45 : new class]
  UF Bavenda (African people)
      Bawenda (African people)
  BT Bantu-speaking peoples
      Ethnology--South Africa

Venda (South Africa)
  [DT 944.V46 : old class]
  [DT 2400.V45 : new class]
  BT Homelands (South Africa)

Venda fiction *(May Subd Geog)*
  [PL 8771.5-PL 8771.9]
  BT South African fiction
      Venda literature
  NT Short stories, Venda

Venda language *(May Subd Geog)*
  [PL 8771]
  UF Benda language
      Ci-venda language
      Tshivenda language
      Wenda language
  BT Bantu languages
      South Africa--Languages
  RT Sotho language

Venda law
  USE Law, Venda

Venda literature *(May Subd Geog)*
  [PL 8771.5-PL 8771.9]
  BT South African literature
  NT Venda fiction

Venda short stories
  USE Short stories, Venda

Venezuela *(Not Subd Geog)*
  --Civilization
  -- --**African influences**
  BT Africa--Civilization

Vere (African people) *(May Subd Geog)*
  [DT 545.45.V47]
  UF Verre (African people)
      Waré (African people)
      Warebo (African people)
      Were (African people)
      Yaware (African people)
      Yere (African people)

  BT Ethnology--Ivory Coast

Verre (African people)
  USE Vere (African people)

Vezo (Malagasy people) *(May Subd Geog)*
  [DT 469.M277.V]
  UF Vezu (Malagasy people)
  BT Ethnology--Madagascar

Vezu (Malagasy people)
  USE Vezo (Malagasy people)

Viemo language
  USE Vige language

Vige language *(May Subd Geog)*
  [PL 8773.V43]
  UF Viemo language
      Vigué language
      Viguié language
      Vigye language
  BT Burkina Faso--Languages
      Gur languages
      Ivory Coast--Languages

Vigué language
  USE Vige language

Viguié language
  USE Vige language

Vigye language
  USE Vige language

Vili (African people) *(May Subd Geog)*
  [DT 611.45.V (Angola : old class)]
  [DT 1308.V (Angola : new class)]
  [DT 650.B375 (Zaire)]
  UF Bavili (African people)
      Loango (African people)
  BT Bantu-speaking peoples
      Ethnology--Angola
      Ethnology--Zaire

Vili language *(May Subd Geog)*
  [PL 8774]
  UF Ki-vili language
      Ki-vumbu language
      Kivili language
      Kivumbu language
      Lu-wumbu language
      Luwumbu language
  BT Angola--Languages
      Bantu languages
      Zaire--Languages

(May Subd Geog) = Place names may follow the heading

Villages, Ujamaa
    USE Ujamaa villages

Virgin Islands of the United States *(Not Subd Geog)*
  --Civilization
  -- --African influences
    BT Africa--Civilization

Viri language
    USE Birri language

Virunga *(Not Subd Geog)*
    UF Mfumbiro
        Mufumbiro
        Virungu
    BT Mountains--Rwanda
        Mountains--Uganda
        Mountains--Zaire
        Volcanoes--Rwanda
        Volcanoes--Uganda
        Volcanoes--Zaire
    NT Karisimbi (Rwanda and Zaire)
        Nyamlagira (Zaire)

Virunga, Parc National des (Zaire)
    USE Parc National des Virunga (Zaire)

Virungu
    USE Virunga

Visual arts
    USE Art

Vlum dialect
    USE Vulum dialect

Vocal music, Popular
    USE Popular music

Volcanoes *(May Subd Geog)*
    BT Landforms
  --Ethiopia
    NT Ertale Volcano (Ethiopia)
  --Kenya
    NT Kenya, Mount (Kenya)
  --Réunion
    NT Fournaise, Piton de la (Réunion)
  --Rwanda
    NT Karisimbi (Rwanda and Zaire)
        Virunga
  --Tanzania
    NT Kilimanjaro, Mount (Tanzania)
  --Uganda
    NT Virunga

--Zaire
    NT Karisimbi (Rwanda and Zaire)
        Nyamlagira (Zaire)
        Virunga

Vollamo language
    USE Walamo language

Volof (African people)
    USE Wolof (African people)

Volof language
    USE Wolof language

Volta River (Ghana) *(Not Subd Geog)*
    BT Rivers--Ghana

Voltaic languages
    USE Gur languages

Vouaghénia (African people)
    USE Genya (African people)

Vouaousi (African people)
    USE Ushi (African people)

Vouté language
    USE Mbum language

Vridi-Canal (Abidjan, Ivory Coast) *(Not Subd Geog)*
    UF Abidjan (Ivory Coast). Vridi-Canal

Vuahuha (African people)
    USE Holoholo (African people)

Vuaregga (African people)
    USE Waregas

Vulum dialect *(May Subd Geog)*
    [PL 8535.95.V8]
    UF Mulwi dialect
        Vlum dialect
    BT Chad--Languages
        Musgu language

Vute language
    USE Mbum language

Vy (African people)
    USE Vai (African people)

W

Waata language
    USE Boni language

UF = Used for; BT = Broader term; RT = Related term; SA = See also; NT = Narrower term

Wabarwe (African people)
  USE Barwe (African people)

Wabembe (East African people)
  USE Bembe (East African people)

Wabena (African people)
  USE Bena (African people)

Waboni language
  USE Boni language

Wabuma (African people)
  USE Boma (African people)

Wabuyu (African people)
  USE Hemba (African people)

Wachaga (African people)
  USE Chaga (African people)

Wachanzi (African people)
  USE Yanzi (African people)

Wacongomani (African people)
  USE Kongo (African people)

Wadigo (African people)
  USE Digo (African people)

Wadschagga (African people)
  USE Chaga (African people)

Wae (African people)
  USE We (African people)

Waembu (African people)
  USE Embu (African people)

Wafipa (African people)
  USE Fipa (African people)

Waganda (African people)
  USE Ganda (African people)

Wagaya language
  USE Luo language (Kenya and Tanzania)

Wagenia (African people)
  USE Genya (African people)

Waggenia (African people)
  USE Genya (African people)

Wagiliama (African people)

  USE Giryama (African people)

Wagogo (African people)
  USE Gogo (African people)

Wahaya (African people)
  USE Haya (African people)

Wahera (African people)
  USE Hera (African people)

Wahehe (African people)
  USE Hehe (African people)

Wahima (African people)
  USE Hima (African people)

Wahondjo (Zairian people)
  USE Nande (Zairian people)

Waima (Sierra Leone), Battle of, 1893
  [DT 516.7]
    UF Battle of Waima (Sierra Leone), 1893
        Waima Incident (Sierra Leone), 1893
    BT Sierra Leone--History--To 1896

Waima Incident (Sierra Leone), 1893
  USE Waima (Sierra Leone), Battle of, 1893

Wainya (African people)
  USE Genya (African people)

Wairu (African people)
  USE Bairo (African people)

Waitawba (African people)
  USE Tabwa (African people)

Wakaguru (African people)
  USE Kaguru (African people)

Wakamba (African people)
  USE Kamba (African people)

Wakaranga (African people)
  USE Karanga (African people)

Wakikuyu (African people)
  USE Kikuyu (African people)

Wakilindi (African people)
  USE Kilindi (African people)

Wakore language
  USE Soninke language

(May Subd Geog) = Place names may follow the heading

Wakua (African people)
    USE Makua (African people)

Wakumu (Zairian people)
    USE Kumu (Zairian people)

Wala (African people) *(May Subd Geog)*
    [DT 510.43.W]
    UF Ala (African people)
        Ouala (African people)
        Wali (African people)
    BT Dagari (African people)
        Ethnology--Ghana

Walai language
    USE Masa language (Chadic)

Walala (African people)
    USE Lala (African people)

Walamo language *(May Subd Geog)*
    [PJ 2582]
    UF Vollamo language
        Welamo language
        Wolamo language
        Wolataita language
    BT Omotic languages

Walega (African people)
    USE Lendu (African people)

Walendu (African people)
    USE Lendu (African people)

Walese (African people)
    USE Lese (African people)

Wali (African people)
    USE Wala (African people)

Wali dialect
    USE Wule dialect

Walisi (African people)
    USE Lese (African people)

Walof (African people)
    USE Wolof (African people)

Walomwe (African people)
    USE Lomwe (African people)

Walu language
    USE Ngizim language

Waluba (African people)
    USE Luba (African people)

Waluchazi (African people)
    USE Luchazi (African people)

Wama River (Tanzania) *(Not Subd Geog)*
    BT Rivers--Tanzania

Wamakua (African people)
    USE Makua (African people)

Wamatengo (African people)
    USE Matengo (African people)

Wambouti (African people)
    USE Mbuti (African people)

Wambulu (African people)
    USE Iraqw (African people)

Wameru (African people)
    USE Meru (African people)

Wamia (African people)
    USE Teso (African people)

Wamwera (African people)
    USE Mwera (African people)

Wanande (Zairian people)
    USE Nande (Zairian people)

Wanda language
    USE Mwamba language

Wandala (African people)
    USE Mandari (African people)

Wandala language
    USE Mandara language

Wandorobo (African people)
    USE Dorobo (African people)

Wanena (African people)
    USE Pangwa (African people)

Wanga (African people) *(May Subd Geog)*
    [DT 433.545.W]
    UF Bahanga (African people)
    BT Bantu-speaking peoples
        Ethnology--Kenya

Wanga dialect
    USE Hanga dialect (Kenya)

UF = Used for; BT = Broader term; RT = Related term; SA = See also; NT = Narrower term

Wangala (African people)
  USE Banqalas

Wangana (African people)
  USE Huana (African people)

Wangonde (African people)
  USE Ngonde (African people)

Wangoni (African people)
  USE Ngoni (African people)

Wanika (African people)
  USE Nika (African people)

Wanyambungi (African people)
  USE Bashi (African people)

Wanyamwezi (African people)
  USE Nyamwezi (African people)

Wanyanga (African people)
  USE Nyanga (African people)

Wanyaturu (African people)
  USE Nyaturu (African people)

Wanyika (African people)
  USE Nika (African people)

Wapangwa (African people)
  USE Pangwa (African people)

Wapare (African people)
  USE Pare (African people)

Wapogoro (African people)
  USE Pogoro (African people)

Wapokomo (African people)
  USE Pokomo (African people)

War of Ngcayecibi (South Africa), 1877-1878
  USE Ngcayecibi, War of, South Africa,
1877-1878

War of the Axe (South Africa), 1847
  USE South Africa--History--Frontier Wars,
1811-1878

War of the Hoe Handle, 1928-1931
  USE Kongo Wara, 1928-1931

Warangi (African people)
  USE Rangi (African people)

Waré (African people)
  USE Vere (African people)

Warebo (African people)
  USE Vere (African people)

Waregas *(May Subd Geog)*
      [DT 650.W37 (Zaire)]
      UF Balegga (African people)
          Barega (African people)
          Kalega (African people)
          Rega (African people)
          Valega (African people)
          Vuaregga (African people)
      BT Ethnology--Central African Republic
          Ethnology--Zaire

Wari
  USE Ayo (Game)

Waribe (African people)
  USE Ribe (African people)

Warri
  USE Ayo (Game)

Warundi (African people)
  USE Rundi (African people)

Waruwa (African people)
  USE Hemba (African people)

Wasanye language
  USE Boni language

Washambala (African people)
  USE Shambala (African people)

Washambara (African people)
  USE Shambala (African people)

Wasongola (African people)
  USE Songola (African people)

Wassandaui (African people)
  USE Sandawe (African people)

Wassandaui language
  USE Sandawe language

Wassiba (African people)
  USE Haya (African people)

Wassindja (African people)
  USE Zinza (African people)

(May Subd Geog) = Place names may follow the heading

Wata language
USE Boni language

Watabala language
USE Boni language

Watabeta (African people)
USE Taveta (African people)

Wataita (African people)
USE Taita (African people)

Watawara (African people)
USE Tawara (African people)

Water resources development (May Subd Geog)
--South Africa
NT Orange River Project

Watercolor painting (May Subd Geog)
BT Painting

Watercolor painting, South African (May Subd Geog)
[ND 2088.6.S6]
UF South African watercolor painting

Waterfalls (May Subd Geog)
UF Cataracts
Falls (Waterfalls)
BT Rivers
--Gabon
NT Poubara, Chute de (Gabon)
--Zaire
NT Stanley Falls (Zaire)

Watindega (African people)
USE Tindiga (African people)

Watshua (African people)
USE Batwa (African people)

Wattua (African people)
USE Batwa (African people)

Watumbuka (African people)
USE Tumbuka (African people)

Watussi (African people)
USE Tutsi (African people)

Waungas (African people)
USE Ungas

Waushi (African people)
USE Ushi (African people)

Wausi (African people)
USE Ushi (African people)

Wawemba (African people)
USE Bemba (African people)

Wawi dialect
USE Dida dialect

Wayao (African people)
USE Yao (African people)

Wayao language
USE Yao language

Wazaramo (African people)
USE Zaramo (African people)

Wazezuru (African people)
USE Zezuru (African people)

We (African people) (May Subd Geog)
[DT 571.W]
UF Kuwe (African people)
Qué (African people)
Wae (African people)
BT Ethnology--Cameroon

We (Ivory Coast people)
USE Wobe (African people)

Weather
RT Meteorology
NT Droughts
Weather control
--Research
USE Meteorology--Research

Weather control (May Subd Geog)
UF Artificial weather control
Cloud modification
BT Meteorology
Weather
--South Africa
NT Bethlehem Weather Modification Experiment

Weather Modification Experiment at Bethlehem
USE Bethlehem Weather Modification Experiment

Weather research
USE Meteorology--Research

Weaving (May Subd Geog)
NT Hand weaving
Men weavers
Textile fabrics

UF = Used for; BT = Broader term; RT = Related term; SA = See also; NT = Narrower term

Weaving, Hand
  USE Hand weaving

Weaving, West African narrow band
  USE West African strip weaving

Webi River (Ethiopia and Somalia)
  USE Shebeli River (Ethiopia and Somalia)

Webi Shebeli River (Ethiopia and Somalia)
  USE Shebeli River (Ethiopia and Somalia)

Wedlock
  USE Marriage

Wee (Ivory Coast people)
  USE Wobe (African people)

Weenyo (African people)
  USE Wobe (African people)

Weingmé (African people)
  USE Tura (African people)

Welamo language
  USE Walamo language

Welmera (Ethiopia) *(Not Subd Geog)*
  [DT 398.W]

Wemba language
  USE Bemba language

Wenda language
  USE Venda language

Wenya (African people)
  USE Genya (African people)

Were (African people)
  USE Vere (African people)

Wereleopards
  USE Leopard men

Werize languages
  USE Werizoid languages

Werizoid languages *(May Subd Geog)*
  [PJ 2485]
  UF Dullay languages
      Werize languages
  BT Cushitic languages

Werleopards
  USE Leopard men

West Africa
  USE Africa, West

West Africa, Francophone
  USE Africa, French-speaking West

West Africa, German
  USE Cameroon

West Africa, Portuguese
  USE Angola

West African band weaving
  USE West African strip weaving

West African cookery
  USE Cookery, West African

West African Economic Community
  USE Communauté économique de l'Afrique de
l'Ouest

West African fiction *(Not Subd Geog)*
  [PL 8014.W37]
  UF Africa, West--Fiction
  BT African fiction
      West African literature

West African fiction (English) *(Not Subd Geog)*
  [PR 9344 (History)]
  [PR 9347.5 (Collections)]
  UF English fiction--West African authors
  BT African fiction (English)
      West African literature (English)
  NT Cameroon fiction (English)
      Ghanaian fiction (English)
      Liberian fiction (English)
      Nigerian fiction (English)
      Short stories, West African (English)

West African fiction (French) *(Not Subd Geog)*
  [PQ 3984 (History)]
  [PQ 3987.5 (Collections)]
  UF French fiction--West African authors
  BT African fiction (French)
      West African literature (French)
  NT Cameroon fiction (French)
      Ivory Coast fiction (French)
      Niger fiction (French)
      Senegalese fiction (French)
      Short stories, West African (French)

West African literature *(Not Subd Geog)*
  [PL 8014.W37]
  UF Africa, West--Literatures

(May Subd Geog) = Place names may follow the heading

BT African literature
NT Burkinabe literature
    Cameroon literature
    Gambian literature
    Ghanaian literature
    Guinean literature
    Liberian literature
    Mandingo literature
    Mauritanian literature
    Niger literature
    Nigerian literature
    Senegalese literature
    Sierra Leone literature
    Togolese literature
    West African fiction
    West African poetry

West African literature (English) *(Not Subd Geog)*
    [PR 9340-PR 9347.5]
    UF English literature--West African authors
    BT African literature (English)
    NT Cameroon literature (English)
        Ghanaian literature (English)
        Liberian literature (English)
        Nigerian literature (English)
        Sierra Leone literature (English)
        West African fiction (English)
        West African poetry (English)

West African literature (French) *(Not Subd Geog)*
    [PQ 3980-PQ 3989.2]
    UF French literature--West African authors
    BT African literature (French)
    NT Benin literature (French)
        Burkinabe literature (French)
        Cameroon literature (French)
        Guinean literature (French)
        Ivory Coast literature (French)
        Niger literature (French)
        Senegalese literature (French)
        Togolese literature (French)
        West African fiction (French)
        West African poetry (French)

West African Monsoon Experiment
    [QC 939.M7]
    BT Meterology--Research

West African mythology
    USE Mythology, West African

West African narrow band weaving
    USE West African strip weaving

West African poetry *(Not Subd Geog)*
    [PL 8014.W37]
    UF Africa, West--Poetry
    BT African poetry
        West African literature
    NT Mandingo poetry
        Nigerian poetry

West African poetry (English) *(Not Subd Geog)*
    [PR 9342 (History)]
    [PR 9346 (Collections)]
    UF English poetry--West African authors
    BT African poetry (English)
        West African literature (English)
    NT Cameroon poetry (English)
        Ghanaian poetry (English)
        Liberian poetry (English)
        Nigerian poetry (English)
        Sierra Leone poetry (English)

West African poetry (French) *(Not Subd Geog)*
    [PQ 3982 (History)]
    [PQ 3986 (Collections)]
    UF French fiction--West African authors
    BT West African literature (French)
    NT Benin poetry (French)
        Burkinabe poetry (French)
        Cameroon poetry (French)
        Guinean poetry (French)
        Niger poetry (French)
        Senegalese poetry (French)
        Togolese poetry (French)

West African publications, Acquisition of
    USE Acquisition of West African publications

West African short stories (English)
    USE Short stories, West African (English)

West African short stories (French)
    USE Short stories, West African (French)

West African strip weaving *(May Subd Geog)*
    [NK 8989.A44]
    UF Band weaving, West African
        Kente cloth
        Narrow band weaving, West African
        Strip weaving, West African
        Weaving, West African narrow band
        West African band weaving
        West African narrow band weaving
    BT Hand weaving--Africa, West
    RT Men weavers--Africa, West

UF = Used for; BT = Broader term; RT = Related term; SA = See also; NT = Narrower term

West Africans *(May Subd Geog)*
    UF Africans, West
    BT Ethnology--Africa, West

West Cushitic languages
    USE Omotic languages

West Indies *(Not Subd Geog)*
    Here are entered works on the extended archipelago
that separates the Caribbean Sea from the rest of the
Atlantic Ocean, and consists of the Bahamas and the
Greater and Lesser Antilles.
    UF Antilles
        Antilles, Greater
        Caribbean Islands
        Greater Antilles
        Islands--Caribbean Area
        Islands of the Caribbean
  --Civilization
  -- --African influences
    BT Africa--Civilization

West Indies, French *(Not Subd Geog)*
    UF Antilles, French
        French Antilles
        French West Indies
  --Civilization
  -- --African influences
    BT Africa--Civilization

West Indies Region
    USE Caribbean Area

West Rand Group (South Africa) *(Not Subd Geog)*
    BT Groups (Stratigraphy)--South Africa

Western Africa
    USE Africa, West

Western Bobo Wule dialect
    USE Boomu dialect

Western civilization
    USE Civilization, Western

Western Europe
    USE Europe

Western Kongo dialect
    USE Koongo dialect (Western Kongo)

Western Luba (African people)
    USE Lulua (African people)

Western Luba language
    USE Luba-Lulua language

Western Province (Zambia) *(Not Subd Geog)*
    [DT 963.9.W : old class]
    [DT 3140.W48 : new class]
    UF Barotseland (Northern Rhodesia)
        Barotseland Protectorate

Whiro (African people)
    USE Bairo (African people)

White Highlands (Kenya)
    USE Kenya Highlands (Kenya)

Whites *(May Subd Geog)*
    Here are entered works of a sociological nature that
discuss white people as an element in the population,
especially in countries where they are a minority.
    BT Ethnology
  --Africa
    [DT 16.W45]
  --South Africa
    [DT 764.W47 : old class]
    [DT 1768.W55 : new class]
  --Zimbabwe
    [DT 962.42 : old class]
    [DT 2913.W : new class]

Whittling
    USE Wood-carving

Widerkum (African people)
    USE Ngemba (African people)

Wildlife refuges *(May Subd Geog)*
    UF Refuges, Wildlife
        Sanctuaries, Wildlife
        Wildlife sanctuaries
    BT Natural areas
    RT Game reserves
  --Namibia
    NT Etosha National Park (Namibia)

Wildlife sanctuaries
    USE Wildlife refuges

Wimbum language
    USE Limbum language

Win (African people)
    USE Tusia (African people)

Win language
    USE Tusia language

Wiro (African people)
    USE Bairo (African people)

(May Subd Geog) = Place names may follow the heading

Wisa (Zambian people)
USE Bisa (Zambian people)

Wisa language
USE Bisa language

Wit and humor
   UF Humor
       Jests
       Jokes
   BT Literature
   NT Humorous stories
       Riddles
       Satire
       Wit and humor, Pictorial

Wit and humor, Afrikaans
USE Afrikaans wit and humor

Wit and humor, Amharic
USE Amharic wit and humor

Wit and humor, Kenyan
USE Kenyan wit and humor

Wit and humor, Kinyarwanda
USE Kinyarwanda wit and humor

Wit and humor, Nigerian
USE Nigerian wit and humor

Wit and humor, Nigerian (English)
USE Nigerian wit and humor (English)

Wit and humor, Rundi
USE Rundi wit and humor

Wit and humor, Shona
USE Shona wit and humor

Wit and humor, South African
USE South African wit and humor

Wit and humor, Swahili
USE Swahili wit and humor

Wit and humor, Pictorial
   UF Humorous illustrations
       Illustrations, Humorous
       Pictorial wit and humor
       Pictures, Humorous
   BT Wit and humor

Wit and humor, Pictorial (Congo)

USE Congo wit and humor, Pictorial

Wit and humor, Pictorial (Ghanaian)
USE Ghanaian wit and humor, Pictorial

Wit and humor, Pictorial (Kenyan)
USE Kenyan wit and humor, Pictorial

Wit and humor, Pictorial (Nigerian)
USE Nigerian wit and humor, Pictorial

Wit and humor, Pictorial (Réunion)
USE Réunion wit and humor, Pictorial

Wit and humor, Pictorial (South African)
USE South African wit and humor, Pictorial

Witwatersrand Strike, 1922
   [HD 5441.M612 1922.W5]
   BT Strikes and lockouts--Miners--South Africa

Wo (Senegalese and Guinean people)
USE Bassari (Senegalese and Guinean people)

Wo language
USE Bassari language

Wobe (African people) *(May Subd Geog)*
   [DT 545.45.G47]
   UF Gere (Kru-speaking African people)
       Guere (Kru-speaking African people)
       Ngere (Kru-speaking African people)
       Nguere (Kru-speaking African people)
       Ouobé (African people)
       We (Ivory Coast people)
       Wee (Ivory Coast people)
       Weenyo (African people)
       Ethnology--Ivory Coast
       Ethnology--Liberia

Wobe language *(May Subd Geog)*
   [PL 8783]
   UF Gere language (Kru)
       Guere language (Kru)
       Ouobe language
   BT Bete language
       Ivory Coast--Languages
       Liberia--Languages

Wobe proverbs
USE Proverbs, Wobe

Wodaabe (African people)
USE Bororo (African people)

UF = Used for; BT = Broader term; RT = Related term; SA = See also; NT = Narrower term

Wogo (African people) *(May Subd Geog)*
  [DT 547.W]
  BT Ethnology--Niger
       Songhai Empire

Wolamo language
  USE Walamo language

Wolataita language
  USE Walamo language

Wolof (African people) *(May Subd Geog)*
  [DT 509.45.W64 (Gambia)]
  [DT 549.45.W64 (Senegal)]
  UF Jolof (African people)
      Oulaf (African people)
      Volof (African people)
      Walof (African people)
      Yallof (African people)
  BT Ethnology--Gambia
      Ethnology--Mauritania
      Ethnology--Senegal
  NT Lebou (African people)
 --Children
  BT Children--Gambia
      Children--Mauritania
      Children--Senegal

Wolof folk literature
  USE Folk literature, Wolof

Wolof folk poetry
  USE Folk poetry, Wolof

Wolof language *(May Subd Geog)*
  [PL 8785]
  UF Jaloof language
      Jolof language
      Ouolof language
      Volof language
      Yolof language
  BT Gambia--Languages
      Mauritania--Languages
      Niger-Congo languages
      Senegal--Languages
  NT Lebou dialect

Wolof literature *(May Subd Geog)*
  [PL 8785.5-PL 8785.9]
  BT Gambian literature
      Mauritanian literatures
      Senegalese literature
  NT Folk literature, Wolof
      Wolof poetry

Wolof poetry *(May Subd Geog)*
  [PL 8785.5 (History)]
  [PL 8785.8 (Collections)]
  BT Wolof literature
      Gambia--Poetry
      Mauritiana--Poetry
      Senegal--Poetry
  NT Folk poetry, Wolof

Women *(May Subd Geog)*
  UF Females, Human
      Human females
  BT Anthropology
  NT Married women

Women, Ashanti *(May Subd Geog)*
  [DT 507]
  UF Ashanti women

Women, Bafokeng *(May Subd Geog)*
  [DT 1768.B35 : new class]
  UF Bafokeng women

Women, Bambara *(May Subd Geog)*
  [DT 551.45.B35]
  UF Bambara women

Women, Barabaig *(May Subd Geog)*
  [DT 443.3.B37]
  UF Barabaig women

Women, Bariba *(May Subd Geog)*
  [DT 541.45.B37]
  UF Bariba women

Women, Basa *(May Subd Geog)*
  [DT 571.B37]
  UF Basa women

Women, Beti *(May Subd Geog)*
  [DT 571.B4]
  UF Beti women

Women, Black *(May Subd Geog)*
  UF Black women
 --Africa
  [HQ 1787]

Women, Black, in literature
  [PN 56.3.B55]
  BT Literature

Women, Bobo *(May Subd Geog)*
  [DT 555.45.B63]
  UF Bobo women

(May Subd Geog) = Place names may follow the heading

Women, Daza *(May Subd Geog)*
    [DT 346.D38]
    UF Daza women

Women, Dogon *(May Subd Geog)*
    [DT 551.45.D64 (Mali)]
    UF Dogon women

Women, Fula *(May Subd Geog)*
    [DT 571.F84]
    UF Fula women

Women, Grebo *(May Subd Geog)*
    [DT 630.5.G6]
    UF Grebo women

Women, Gusii *(May Subd Geog)*
    [DT 433.545.G86]
    UF Gusii women

Women, Hausa *(May Subd Geog)*
    [DT 515.45.H38]
    UF Hausa women

Women, Hima *(May Subd Geog)*
    [DT 650.H64]
    UF Hima women

Women, Igbo *(May Subd Geog)*
    [DT 515.45.I33]
    UF Igbo women

Women, Kabre *(May Subd Geog)*
    [DT 582.45.K33]
    UF Kabre women

Women, Kamba *(May Subd Geog)*
    [DT 433.545.K36]
    UF Kamba women

Women, Karamojong *(May Subd Geog)*
    [DT 433.245.K35]
    UF Karamojong women

Women, Kela *(May Subd Geog)*
    [DT 650.K39]
    UF Kela women

Women, Kikuyu *(May Subd Geog)*
    [DT 433.545.K55]
    UF Kikuyu women

Women, Kuria *(May Subd Geog)*
    [DT 443.3.K87 (Tanzania)]
    UF Kuria women

Women, Lango *(May Subd Geog)*
    [DT 433.245.L]
    UF Lango women

Women, Lebou *(May Subd Geog)*
    [DT 549.45.L42]
    UF Lebou women

Women, Mandingo *(May Subd Geog)*
    [DT 509.45.M34]
    UF Mandingo women

Women, Manga *(May Subd Geog)*
    [DT 547.45.M2]
    UF Manga women

Women, Masai *(May Subd Geog)*
    [DT 443.3.M37 (Tanzania)]
    UF Masai women

Women, Mawri *(May Subd Geog)*
    [DT 547.45.M38]
    UF Mawri women

Women, Nuer *(May Subd Geog)*
    [DT 155.2.N85]
    UF Nuer women

Women, Rondile *(May Subd Geog)*
    [DT 433.545.R45]
    UF Rendile women

Women, Swahili-speaking *(May Subd Geog)*
    [DT 433.545.S (Kenya)]
    UF Swahili-speaking women

Women, Tanga *(May Subd Geog)*
    [DT 571.T]
    UF Tanga women

Women, Tivi *(May Subd Geog)*
    [DT 515.45.T58]
    UF Tivi women

Women, Tonga (Zambesi) *(May Subd Geog)*
    [DT 962.42 (Zambia : old class)]
    [DT 3058.T65 (Zambia : new class)]
    UF Tonga women (Zambesi)

Women, Yoruba *(May Subd Geog)*
    [DT 515.45.Y67 (Nigeria)]
    UF Yoruba women

Women, Zaramo *(May Subd Geog)*
    [DT 443.3.W39]
    UF Zaramo women

UF = Used for; BT = Broader term; RT = Related term; SA = See also; NT = Narrower term

Women, Zulu *(May Subd Geog)*
   [DT 878.Z9 : old class]
   [DT 1768.Z95 : new class]
   UF   Zulu women

Women authors
   Here are entered works on women authors as a class
of persons.
   UF   Authors, Women
   BT   Authors

Women authors, African
   [PR 9340.5 (English literature)]
   UF   African women authors

Women authors, Black *(May Subd Geog)*
   [PN 56.3.B55]
   UF   Black women authors

Women authors, South African *(May Subd Geog)*
   [PR 9358]
   UF   South African women authors

Women heads of households *(May Subd Geog)*
   UF   Heads of households, Women
 --**Africa**
   [HQ 1787]
 --**Botswana**
   [HQ 1803]
 --**Zambia**
   [HQ 1801.5]

Women in development *(May Subd Geog)*
   Here are entered works about women's participation
in various economic, rural, educational, agricultural,
etc. development activities in developing countries.
   UF   Development and women
 --**Africa**
   [HQ 1240.5.A35]

Wood-carving *(May Subd Geog)*
   UF   Whittling
   BT   Decoration and ornament
        Sculpture

Wood-carving, Ashanti *(May Subd Geog)*
   [NK 9789.6.G5]
   UF   Ashanti wood-carving

Wood-carving, Betsileo *(May Subd Geog)*
   [NK 9788.9.M3]
   UF   Betsileo wood-carving

Wood-carving, Chokwe *(May Subd Geog)*
   [NK 9789.6.A5]
   UF   Chokwe wood-carving

Wood-carving, Hemba *(May Subd Geog)*
   [NK 9789.6.C6]
   UF   Hemba wood-carving

Wood-carving, Igala *(May Subd Geog)*
   [NK 9789.6.N5]
   UF   Igala wood-carving

Wood-carving, Igbo *(May Subd Geog)*
   [NK 9789.6.N5]
   UF   Igbo wood-carving

Wood-carving, Mbembe *(May Subd Geog)*
   [NK 9789.6.N5]
   UF   Mbembe wood-carving

Wood-carving, Sakalava *(May Subd Geog)*
   [NK 9788.9.M3]
   UF   Sakalava wood-carving

Woods (Forests)
   USE   Forests and forestry

Woodstock (Cape Town, South Africa) *(Not Subd Geog)*
   UF   Cape Town (South Africa). Woodstock

Word books
   USE   Picture dictionaries

Work stoppages
   USE   Strikes and lockouts

Working-men's associations
   USE   Trade-unions

World literature
   USE   Literature

World War, 1914-1919 *(May Subd Geog)*
   UF   1st World War
        European War, 1914-1918
        First World War
        World War I
 --**Campaigns** *(May Subd Geog)*
 -- --**Africa**
   NT   Senussite Rebellion, 1916-1918

World War, 1939-1945 *(May Subd Geog)*
   UF   2nd World War
        European War, 1939-1945
        Second World War
        World War II
 --**Blacks**
 --**Campaigns**

(May Subd Geog) = Place names may follow the heading

-- --Africa, French-speaking West
   NT Operation Menace
-- --Ethiopia
   NT Cheren, Battle of, 1941
-- --Senegal
   NT Dakar, Battle of, 1940
-- --Sudan
   NT Alam Halfa, Battle of, 1942

World War I
   USE World War, 1914-1918

World War II
   USE World War, 1939-1945

Wotsschua (African people)
   USE Batwa (African people)

Writers
   USE Authors

Writings of slaves
   USE Slaves' writings

Wule dialect *(May Subd Geog)*
   [PL 8118.D3595W04]
   UF Wali dialect
       Wulewule dialect
       Wuli dialect
   BT Burkina Faso--Languages
       Dagari language

Wulewule dialect
   USE Wule dialect

Wuli dialect
   USE Wule dialect

X

Xegwe (African people)
   USE Batwa (African people)

Xegwi (African people)
   USE Batwa (African people)

Xhosa (African people) *(May Subd Geog)*
   [DT 764.X6 : old class]
   [DT 1768.X57 : new class]
   UF Amaxosa (African people)
       Kaffirs (African people)
       Kafirs (African people)
       Koosa (African people)
       Xosa (African people)
   BT Ethnology--South Africa
       Nguni (African people)

--Missions *(May Subd Geog)*
   [BV 3630.X65]
   UF Missions to Xhosa (African people)
--Religion
   [BL 2480.X55]

Xhosa authors
   USE Authors, Xhosa

Xhosa beadwork
   USE Beadwork, Xhosa

Xhosa Cattle-Killing (South Africa), 1856-1857
   USE South Africa--History--Xhosa Cattle-
Killing, 1856-1857

Xhosa fiction *(May Subd Geog)*
   [PL 8795.5-PL 8795.9]
   BT South African fiction
       Xhosa literature

Xhosa folk poetry
   USE Folk poetry, Xhosa

Xhosa hymns
   USE Hymns, Xhosa

Xhosa imprints *(May Subd Geog)*
   [Z 7108.X]
   UF Imprints, Xhosa

Xhosa language *(May Subd Geog)*
   [PL 8795]
   UF isiXhosa language
       Kaffer language
       Kaffir language
       Kafir language
       Xosa language
   BT Nguni languages
       South Africa--Languages
   NT Fanakalo
--Tone
   BT Tone (Phonetics)

Xhosa literature *(May Subd Geog)*
   [PL 8795.5-PL 8795.9]
   BT South African literature
   NT Xhosa fiction
       Xhosa poetry
   RT Authors, Xhosa

Xhosa poetry *(May Subd Geog)*
   [PL 8795.5 (History)]
   [PL 8795.7 (Collections)]
   BT South Africa poetry
       Xhosa literature   *(Continued)*

UF = Used for; BT = Broader term; RT = Related term; SA = See also; NT = Narrower term

Xhosa poetry   *(Continued)*
   NT   Folk poetry, Xhosa
        Protest poetry, Xhosa

Xhosa protest poetry
   USE   Protest poetry, Xhosa

Xhosa Wars, 1811-1878
   USE   South Africa--History--Frontier Wars,
1811-1878

Xilenge language
   USE   Chopi language

Xironga language
   USE   Ronga language

Xitsonga language
   USE   Tsonga language

Xitswa language
   USE   Tswa language

Xó (The Fon word)
   [PL 8164.Z9F6]
   BT   Fon dialect--Etymology

!Xo language *(May Subd Geog)*
   [PL 8104.Z9X6]
   UF   Gxon language
        Hua-owani language
        !Ko language (Botswana and Namibia)
        Koon language
        Magong language
        !Xong language (Botswana and Namibia)
   BT   Botswana--Languages
        Namibia--Languages
        San languages

!Xong language (Botswana and Namibia)
   USE   !Xo language

Xosa (African people)
   USE   Xhosa (African people)

Xosa language
   USE   Xhosa language

!Xu (African people)
   USE   !Kung (African people)

!Xu (!Kung) language
   USE   !Xu language

!Xu language *(May Subd Geog)*
   [PL 8104.Z9X9]

   UF   !Hu language
        !Khung language
        !Ku language
        !Kung language
        Qung language
        !Xu (!Kung) language
   BT   Angola--Languages
        Botswana--Languages
        Namibia--Languages
        San languages

Y

Yaayuwee dialect *(May Subd Geog)*
   [PL 8205]
   BT   Cameroon--Languages
        Gbaya language

Yabuba language
   USE   Dan language

Yacouba (African people)
   USE   Dan (African people)

Yacouba language
   USE   Dan language

Yadinga (African people)
   USE   Babinga (African people)

Yagga (African people)
   USE   Yaka (African people)

Yaghwatadaxa language *(May Subd Geog)*
   UF   Yawotatacha language
   BT   Chadic languages
        Nigeria--Languages

Yaka (African people) *(May Subd Geog)*
   [DT 650.B38 (Zaire)]
   UF   Bayaka (African people)
        Bayéké (African people)
        Djakka (African people)
        Giaka (African people)
        Iaka (African people)
        Jaca (African people)
        Joca (African people)
        Mayaka (African people)
        Ngiaka (African people)
        Yagga (African people)
   BT   Bantu-speaking peoples
        Ethnology--Angola
        Ethnology--Zaire
--Funeral customs and rites
   UF   Funeral rites and ceremonies, Yaka (African
people)

(May Subd Geog) = Place names may follow the heading

--Missions
  [BV 3630.B69]
  UF Missions to Yaka (African people)
--Rites and ceremonies

Yaka language
  USE Punu language

Yaka mythology
  USE Mythology, Yaka

Yaka language (Zaire and Angola) (May Subd Geog)
  UF Iaka language
     Kiyaka language
  BT Angola--Languages
     Kongo language
     Zaire--Languages

Yaka proverbs (Zaire and Angola)
  USE Proverbs, Yaka (Zaire and Angola)

Yakö language (May Subd Geog)
  [PL 8797]
  UF Kö language
     Lukö language
     Yakurr language
  BT Benue-Congo languages
     Nigeria--Languages

Yakoro language
  USE Bekwarra language

Yakoma language (May Subd Geog)
  [PL 8799]
  BT Central African Republic--Languages
     Congo (Brazzaville)--Languages
     Niger-Congo languages
  RT Ngbandi language
     Sango language

Yakuba (African people)
  USE Dan (African people)

Yakuba language
  USE Dan language

Yakurr language
  USE Yakö language

Yakusu (African people)
  USE Lokele (African people)

Yallof (African people)
  USE Wolof (African people)

Yalonke (African people)
  USE Yalunka (African people)

Yalunka (African people) (May Subd Geog)
  [DT 516.45.Y34 (Sierra Leone)]
  UF Dialonke (African people)
     Djallonke (African people)
     Dyalonka (African people)
     Yalonke (African people)
  BT Ethnology--Guinea
     Ethnology--Sierra Leone

Yamá language
  USE Kara language

Yamba (African people) (May Subd Geog)
  [DT 571.Y (Cameroon)]
  [DT 515.45.Y (Nigeria)]
  UF Kaka (African people)
     Mbem (African people)
  BT Ethnology--Cameroon
     Ethnology--Nigeria
     Tikar (African people)

Yamba language (Cameroon and Nigeria) (May Subd
Geog)
  [PL 8800.Y33]
  UF Kaka language (Grasslands Bantu)
     Mbem language
  BT Cameroon--Languages
     Grasslands Bantu languages
     Nigeria--Languages

Yambe (Zela deity) (Not Subd Geog)
  [BL 2480.Z37]
  BT Gods, Zela
     Religion, Primitive--Zaire
     Zela (African people)--Religion

Yambeta language (May Subd Geog)
  [PL 8800.Y35]
  BT Banen language
     Cameroon--Languages

Yambo (African people)
  USE Anuak (African people)

Yambo language
  USE Anuak language

Yamegi language
  USE Kara language

Yanchi language
  USE Yanzi language

UF = Used for; BT = Broader term; RT = Related term; SA = See also; NT = Narrower term

Yani (Guinea)
  USE Niani (Guinea)

Yans language
  USE Yanzi language

Yansi (African people)
  USE Teke (African people)
       Yanzi (African people)

Yansi language
  USE Yanzi language

Yanzi (African people) *(May Subd Geog)*
  [DT 650.Y3]
  UF Bayansi (African people)
      Mbiem (African people)
      Wachanzi (African people)
      Yansi (African people)
  BT Bantu-speaking peoples
      Ethnology--Zaire
 --Religion
  [BL 2480.Y34]

Yanzi language *(May Subd Geog)*
  [PL 8800.Y4]
  UF iYans language
      iYanzi language
      KiYanzi language
      Yanchi language
      Yans language
      Yansi language
  BT Bantu languages
      Zaire--Languages
  NT Mpur dialect
 --Names
  USE Names, Yanzi

Yanzi law
  USE Law, Yanzi

Yanzi names
  USE Names, Yanzi

Yanzi philosophy
  USE Philosophy, Yanzi

Yao (African people) *(May Subd Geog)*
  [DT 429.5.Y (East Africa)]
  [DT 864 (Malawi : old class)]
  [DT 3192.Y36 (Malawi : new class)]
  [DT 458.3.Y (Mozambique : old class)]
  [DT 3328.Y36 (Mozambique : new class)]
  UF Wayao (African people)
  BT Bantu-speaking people

BT Ethnology--Africa, East
    Ethnology--Malawi
    Ethnology--Mozambique
    Ethnology--Tanzania

Yao language *(May Subd Geog)*
  [PL 8801-PL 8804]
  UF Adjaua language
      Ajawa language
      Chi-yao language
      Wayao language
  BT Bantu languages
      Malawi--Languages
      Mozambique--Languages
      Tanzania--Languages

Yaounde (African people)
  USE Ewondo (African people)

Yariba (African people)
  USE Yoruba (African people)

Yariba language
  USE Yoruba language

Yatenga (Burkina Faso : Region) *(Not Subd Geog)*
  [DT 555.9.Y]

Yatenga (Kingdom)
  [DT 532.33]
  BT Africa, West--History--To 1884
      Mossi (African people)--History

Yaunde (African people)
  USE Ewondo (African people)

Yaunde-Fang languages *(May Subd Geog)*
  [PL 8807]
  UF Fang languages
  BT Bantu languages
      Cameroon--Languages
      Equatorial Guinea--Languages
      Gabon--Languages
  NT Bulu language
      Ewondo language
      Fang language

Yaunde language
  USE Ewondo language

Yaware (African people)
  USE Vere (African people)

Yawotatacha language
  USE Yaghwatadaxa language

(May Subd Geog) = Place names may follow the heading

Yebu (African people) *(May Subd Geog)*
  [DT 515.45.Y]
  UF Ijebu (African people)
  BT Ethnology--Nigeria
      Yoruba (African people)

Yebu language *(May Subd Geog)*
  [PL 8811]
  UF Idzebu language
      Ijabu language
      Ijebu language
  BT Nigeria--Languages
      Yoruba language

Yedina (African people)
  USE Buduma (African people)

Yekhee language
  USE Etsako language

Yembe language
  USE Songe language

Yere (African people)
  USE Vere (African people)

Yidi (African people)
  USE Kwegu (African people)

Yola (African people)
  USE Diola (African people)

Yola language
  USE Diola language

Yolof language
  USE Wolof language

Yombe (African people) *(May Subd Geog)*
  [DT 864 (Malawi : old class)]
  [DT 3192.Y (Malawi : new class)]
  [DT 963.42 (Zambia : old class)]
  [DT 3058.Y66 (Zambia : new class)]
  UF Kiombe (African people)
  BT Bantu-speaking peoples
      Ethnology--Malawi
      Ethnology--Zambia
      Tumbuka (African people)

Yombe language *(May Subd Geog)*
  [PL 8815]
  UF Kiombe language
      Kiyombe language
      Luango language
  BT Bantu languages
      Malawi--Languages

  BT Zambia--Languages

Yooba (African people)
  USE Yoruba (African people)

Yoruba (African people) *(May Subd Geog)*
  [DT 515.45.Y67 (Nigeria)]
  [DT 474.6.Y67 (West Africa)]
  UF Yariba (African people)
      Yooba (African people)
  BT Ethnology--Africa, West
      Ethnology--Benin
      Ethnology--Nigeria
  NT Egba (African people)
      Igbona (African people)
      Yebu (African people)
  --Children *(May Subd Geog)*
    BT Children--Africa, West
        Children--Benin
        Children--Nigeria
  --Funeral rites and customs
    UF Funeral rites and ceremonies, Yoruba
(African people)
  --History
    NT Oyo Empire
  --Marriage customs and rites
    UF Marriage customs and rites, Yoruba (African
people)
  --Medicine
    BT Medicine, Primitive--Africa, West
        Medicine, Primitive--Benin
        Medicine, Primitive--Nigeria
  --Missions *(May Subd Geog)*
    [BV 3630.Y6]
    UF Missions to Yoruba (African people)
  --Music
  --Religion
    [BL 2480.Y6]
    NT Egúngún (Cult)
        Gods, Yoruba
        Ogboni (Cult)
        Sopono (Cult)
  --Rites and ceremonies

Yoruba art
  USE Art, Yoruba

Yoruba arts
  USE Arts, Yoruba

Yoruba beadwork
  USE Beadwork, Yoruba

Yoruba bronzes
  USE Bronzes, Yoruba

UF = Used for; BT = Broader term; RT = Related term; SA = See also; NT = Narrower term

Yoruba drama *(May Subd Geog)*
  [PL 8823.5-PL 8824]
  BT Benin--Drama
      Nigerian drama
      Yoruba literature

Yoruba fiction *(May Subd Geog)*
  [PL 8823.5-PL 8824]
  BT Benin--Fiction
      Nigeria--Fiction
      Yoruba literature

Yoruba folk dancing
  USE Folk dancing, Yoruba

Yoruba folk poetry
  USE Folk poetry, Yoruba

Yoruba folk songs
  USE Folk songs, Yoruba

Yoruba goddesses
  USE Goddesses, Yoruba

Yoruba gods
  USE Gods, Yoruba

Yoruba language *(May Subd Geog)*
  [PL 8821-PL 8824]
  UF Aku language
      Eyo language
      Nago language
      Yariba language
  BT Africa, West--Languages
      Benin--Languages
      Kwa languages
      Nigeria--Languages
  NT Yebu language

Yoruba law
  USE Law, Yoruba

Yoruba literature *(May Subd Geog)*
  [PL 8823.5-PL 8824]
  BT Benin literature
      Nigerian literature
  NT Yoruba drama
      Yoruba fiction
      Yoruba poetry

Yoruba philology
  [PL 8821-PL 8824]
  UF Philology, Yoruba

Yoruba philosophy
  USE Philosophy, Yoruba

Yoruba poetry *(May Subd Geog)*
  [PL 8823.5-PL 8824]
  BT Benin--Poetry
      Nigerian poetry
      Yoruba literature
  NT Folk poetry, Yoruba

Yoruba proverbs
  USE Proverbs, Yoruba

Yoruba sculpture
  USE Sculpture, Yoruba

Yoruba songs
  USE Songs, Yoruba

Yoruba women
  USE Women, Yoruba

Youlou language
  USE Yulu language

Young adult drama, English *(May Subd Geog)*
  UF English young adult drama
  BT English drama
  --South African authors
  USE Young adult drama, South African (English)

Young adult drama, South African (English) *(May Subd Geog)*
  [PR 9366.7.Y6 (Collections)]
  UF South African young adult drama (English)
      Young adult drama, English--South African authors
  BT South African drama (English)

Young adult literature, African *(Not Subd Geog)*
  UF African young adult literature
  BT African literature

Young people
  USE Youth

Youth *(May Subd Geog)*
  Here are entered works on the time of life between thirteen and twenty-five years, as well as on people in this general age range, including teenagers and young adults.
  UF Young people
  NT Youth, Black
  --Education
  USE Education
  --Nigeria
  NT Ijo (African people)--Youth
  --Zaire
  -- **--Religious life**
  NT Gen Movement

(May Subd Geog) = Place names may follow the heading

Youth, Black *(May Subd Geog)*
  UF Black youth
  BT Youth
--South Africa
  [HQ 799.S5]

Youths' writings
  BT Literature
  NT College prose
      College verse
      School prose
      School verse
      Teenagers' writings

Youths' writings, Swahili *(May Subd Geog)*
  [PL 8704.A2 (Collections)]
  UF Swahili youths' writings
  BT Swahili literature

Yulu language *(May Subd Geog)*
  [PL 8826]
  UF Youlou language
  BT Bongo-Bagirmi languages
      Central African Republic--Languages
      Sudan--Languages
      Zaire--Languages

Z

Zaaihoek Dam (South Africa)
  UF Zaaihoekdam (South Africa)
  BT Dams--South Africa

Zaaihoekdam (South Africa)
  USE Zaaihoek Dam (South Africa)

Zabarma (African people)
  USE Zarma (African people)

Zabirmawa (African people)
  USE Zarma (African people)

Zafimaniry (Malagasy people) *(May Subd Geog)*
  [DT 469.M277Z]
  BT Ethnology--Madagascar

Zagaoua (African people)
  USE Zaghawa (African people)

Zagawa (African people)
  USE Zaghawa (African people)

Zaghawa (African people) *(May Subd Geog)*
  [DT 546.445.Z33 (Chad)]
  UF Beri (African people)

  UF Berri (African people)
      Kebadi (African people)
      Merida (African people)
      Soghaua (African people)
      Zagaoua (African people)
      Zagawa (African people)
      Zeggaoua (African people)
      Zeghawa (African people)
      Zoghawa (African people)
      Zorhaua (African people)
      Zorhawa (African people)
  BT Ethnology--Chad
      Ethnology--Sudan

Zaire *(Not Subd Geog)*
  [DT 541-DT 665]
  UF Belgian Congo
      Congo (Democratic Republic)
      Congo Free State
      International Association of the Congo
  NT Idjwi Island (Zaire)
--Antiquities
  NT Katongo Site (Zaire)
      Sanga Site (Zaire)
--Book reviews
--Description and travel
-- --To 1880
-- --1881-1950
-- --1951-1980
-- --1981-
--Economic conditions
  [HC 955]
-- --1960-
--Foreign relations *(May Subd Geog)*
-- --1960-
--History
-- --To 1908
-- --1908-1960
-- --1960-
-- --Civil War, 1960-1965
  [DT 658.22]
  UF Civil war--Zaire
      Congo Crisis, 1960-1965
-- -- --Participation, Nigerian
  BT Nigerians--Zaire
-- -- --Participation, Swedish
  BT Swedes--Zaire
-- --Shaba Invasion, 1977
  [DT 658.25]
  UF Katanganese Invasion (Zaire), 1977
      Shaba Invasion (Zaire), 1977
      Shaba War (Zaire), 1977
  BT Angola--Politics and government--1975-
      Shaba (Zaire)--History

(Continued)

UF = Used for; BT = Broader term; RT = Related term; SA = See also; NT = Narrower term

Zaire
--**History** *(Continued)*
-- --**Shaba Uprising, 1978**
  [DT 658.25]
  UF Shaba Uprising (Zaire), 1978
  BT Angola--Politics and government--1975-
--**Languages**
  NT Ababua language
      Aduma language
      Alur language
      Baka language
      Balese language
      Bangubangu language
      Barambu language
      Bari language
      Bembe language (Lake Tanganyika)
      Benge language
      Bobangi language
      Bolia language
      Boma language
      Bushoong language
      Chokwe language
      Doko language (Zaire)
      Enya language
      Holoholo language
      Hungana language
      Kakwa dialect
      Kare language
      Kela language
      Kete language
      Kilega language
      Kingwana language
      Kitabwa language
      Kituba language
      Kongo language
      Kwese language
      Laadi dialect
      Lala language
      Leko dialect
      Lele dialect
      Lingala language
      Lonkengo language
      Losengo language
      Luba-Katanga language
      Luba-Lulua language
      Mamvu language
      Mangbetu language
      Mbala language (Bandundu region,
Zaire)
      Mbinsa language
      Mituku language
      Mongo language
      Mpur dialect
      Mundu language
      Nande language

  NT Ngbaka ma'bo language
      Ngombe language
      Nkundu language
      Ntaandu dialect
      Ntomba language
      Nyanga language
      Ombo language
      Pende language
      Ruund language
      Sakata language
      Salampasu language
      Sanga language
      Shi language
      Songe language
      Suku language (Zaire)
      Tembo language (Kivu, Zaire)
      Tete language
      Tetela language
      Vili language
      Yaka language (Zaire and Angola)
      Yanzi language
      Yulu language
      Zande language
      Zoombo dialect
--**Literatures**
  NT Ngbaka ma'bo literature
--**Pictorial works**
--**Poetry**
  NT Mongo poetry
--**Politics and government**
-- --1885-1908
-- --1908-1960
-- --1960-

Zaire in mass media *(May Subd Geog)*
  [P 96.Z342]
  BT Mass media

Zaire River
  USE Congo River

Zaireans
  USE Zairians

Zairian art
  USE Art, Zairian

Zairian arts
  USE Arts, Zairian

Zairian authors
  USE Authors, Zairian

Zairian civics
  USE Civics, Zairian

(May Subd Geog) = Place names may follow the heading

Zairian cookery
  USE Cookery, Zairian

Zairian ethics
  USE Ethics, Zairian

Zairian fables
  USE Fables, Zairian

Zairian literature (French) *(May Subd Geog)*
  [PQ 3988.5.Z3 (History)]
  [PQ 3988.5.Z32 (Collections)]
  UF French literature--Zairian authors
  BT African literature (French)
  NT Zairian poetry (French)

Zairian mythology
  USE Mythology, Zairian

Zairian periodicals *(May Subd Geog)*
  [PN 5499.Z3]
  UF Periodicals, Zairian

Zairian philology
  [PL 8021.C7]
  UF Philology, Zairian

Zairian poetry (French) *(May Subd Geog)*
  [PQ 3988.5.Z3 (History)]
  [PQ 3988.5.Z32 (Collections)]
  UF French poetry--Zairian authors
  BT African poetry (French)
      Zairian literature (French)

Zairian poets
  USE Poets, Zairian

Zairian sculpture
  USE Sculpture, Zairian

Zairians *(May Subd Geog)*
  UF Zaireans
  BT Ethnology--Zaire

Zak River (South Africa)
  USE Sak River (South Africa)

Zambesi River
  USE Zambezi River

Zambezi River *(Not Subd Geog)*
  UF Rio Zambeze
      Rio Zambezi
      Zambesi River
  BT Rivers--Africa, Southern

Zambia *(Not Subd Geog)*
  [DT 963-DT 963.9 : old class]
  [DT 3031-DT 3145 : new class]
  UF Northern Rhodesia
      Rhodesia, Northern
  --Description and travel
  -- --1981-
  --Economic conditions
  [HC 915]
  -- --1964-
  --Fiction
  NT Tonga fiction (Zambesi)
  --Foreign relations *(May Subd Geog)*
  -- --1964-
  --History
  -- --To 1890
  -- --1890-1924
  -- --1924-1953
  -- --1953-1964
  -- --1964-
  --Languages
  NT Ambo dialect (Zambia)
      Bemba language
      Bisa language
      Chokwe language
      Ila language
      Kitabwa language
      Lala language
      Lamba language
      Lenje language
      Luoayi language
      Luvale language
      Luyana language
      Mambwe language
      Mbunda language (Zambia)
      Nyanja language
      Sanga language
      Subiya language
      Tonga language (Zambesi)
      Yombe language
  -- --Orthography and spelling
  --Literatures
  USE Zambian literature
  --Politics and government
  -- --To 1964
  -- --1964-
  --Social conditions
  -- --1964-

Zambian art
  USE Art, Zambian

Zambian children's stories (English)
  USE Children's stories, Zambian (English)

UF = Used for; BT = Broader term; RT = Related term; SA = See also; NT = Narrower term

Zambian children's writings (English)
  USE Children's writings, Zambian (English)

Zambian cookery
  USE Cookery, Zambian

Zambian drama (English) *(May Subd Geog)*
  [PR 9405.3 (History)]
  [PR 9405.7 (Collections)]
  UF English drama--Zambian authors
  BT African drama (English)
      Zambian literature (English)

Zambian fiction (English) *(May Subd Geog)*
  [PR 9405.4 (History)]
  [PR 9405.8 (Collections)]
  UF English fiction--Zambian authors
  BT Southern African fiction (English)
      Zambian literature (English)
  NT Children's stories, Zambian (English)

Zambian literature *(May Subd Geog)*
  [PL 8014.Z]
  UF Zambia--Literatures
  BT Southern African literature
  NT Bemba literature
      Nyanja literature
      Tonga literature (Zambesi)
      Zambian poetry

Zambian literature (English) *(May Subd Geog)*
  [PR 9405]
  UF English literature--Zambian authors
  BT Southern African literature (English)
  NT Children's writings, Zambian (English)
      Zambian drama (English)
      Zambian fiction (English)
      Zambian poetry (English)

Zambian newspapers *(May Subd Geog)*
  [PN 5499.Z33]
  UF Newspapers, Zambian

Zambian periodicals *(May Subd Geog)*
  [PN 5499.Z33]
  UF Periodicals, Zambian

Zambian philosophy
  USE Philosophy, Zambian

Zambian poetry *(May Subd Geog)*
  [PL 8014.Z]
  BT Southern African poetry
      Zambian literature
  NT Bemba poetry

Zambian poetry (English) *(May Subd Geog)*
  [PR 9405.2 (History)]
  [PR 9405.65 (Collections)]
  UF English poetry--Zambian authors
  BT African poetry (English)
      Zambian literature (English)

Zanaki (African people) *(May Subd Geog)*
  [DT 443.3.Z]
  UF Sanakki (African people)
  BT Bantu-speaking peoples
      Ethnology--Tanzania

Zanaki language *(May Subd Geog)*
  UF Iki-Zanaki language
      IkiZanaki language
  BT Bantu languages
      Tanzania--Languages

Zande (African people) *(May Subd Geog)*
  [DT 352.43.Z35 (Central Africa)]
  [DT 155.2.A9 (Sudan)]
  [DT 650.Z35 (Zaire)]
  UF Azande (African people)
      Niam-Niam (African people)
      Nyam-Nyan (African people)
  BT Ethnology--Africa, Central
      Ethnology--Sudan
      Ethnology--Zaire
  --Food
  BT Food
  --Marriage customs and rites
  UF Marriage customs and rites, Zande (African
people)
  --Time management

Zande art
  USE Art, Zande

Zande folk songs
  USE Folk songs, Zande

Zande language *(May Subd Geog)*
  [PL 8828]
  UF Azande language
      Nyam-Nyam language
  BT Africa, Central--Languages
      Sudan--Languages
      Zaire--Languages
      Zande languages
  NT Nzakara dialect

Zande languages *(May Subd Geog)*
  BT Niger-Congo languages
      Sudan--Languages

(May Subd Geog) = Place names may follow the heading

NT   Barambu language
     Zande language

Zande law
  USE   Law, Zande

Zande sculpture
  USE   Sculpture, Zande

Zanza (Musical instrument)
  USE   Sanza

Zanzibar *(Not Subd Geog)*
  [DT 449.Z2-DT 449.Z29]
  Here are entered works on the island of Zanzibar
for all periods and subjects. Works on the
jurisdiction of Tanzania formed in 1964 by the merger
of Tanganyika and Zanzibar for all periods and subjects
are entered under Tanzania.
  --Economic conditions
  [HC 885]
  -- --To 1964
  -- --1964-
  --History
  NT   Tungue Bay (Mozambique), Battle of,
1887
  -- --To 1890
  -- --Revolution, 1964
  [DT 449.Z29]
  --Politics and government
  -- --To 1964
  -- --1964-
  --Social conditions
  -- --To 1964
  -- --1964-

Zanzibar (Zanzibar) *(Not Subd Geog)*
  --General Strike, 1948
  USE   General Strike, Zanzibar, Zanzibar,
1948

Zaramo (African people) *(May Subd Geog)*
  [DT 443.3.W39]
  UF   Dzalamo (African people)
       Myagatwa (African people)
       Saramo (African people)
       Wazaramo (African people)
  BT   Ethnology--Tanzania

Zaramo women
  USE   Women, Zaramo

Zarma (African people) *(May Subd Geog)*
  [DT 547.45.Z37 (Niger)]
  UF   Djerma (African people)
       Dyabarma (African people)

  UF   Dyerma (African people)
       Gole (African people)
       Zabarma (African people)
       Zabirmawa (African people)
  BT   Ethnology--Benin
       Ethnology--Niger
       Ethnology--Nigeria

Zarma dialect *(May Subd Geog)*
  [PL 8685.95Z3]
  UF   Djerma language
  BT   Benin--Languages
       Niger--Languages
       Nigeria--Languages
       Songhai language

Zarma folk songs
  USE   Folk songs, Zarma

Zazere language
  USE   Kulango language

Zeekoe River (South Africa)
  USE   Seacow River (South Africa)

Zeggaoua (African people)
  USE   Zaghawa (African people)

Zeghawa (African people)
  USE   Zaghawa (African people)

Zequha language
  USE   Zigula language

Zela (African people) *(May Subd Geog)*
  [DT 650.Z44]
  UF   Bazela (African people)
       Buzela (African people)
       Muzela (African people)
  BT   Ethnology--Zaire
  --Religion
  [BL 2480.Z37]
  NT   Gods, Zela
       Yambe (Zela deity)

Zela gods
  USE   Gods, Zela

Zelgwa language
  USE   Zulgo language

Zema (African people)
  USE   Nzima (African people)

Zema language
  USE   Nzima language

UF = Used for; BT = Broader term; RT = Related term; SA = See also; NT = Narrower term

Zezeru (African people)
  USE Zezuru (African people)

Zezuru (African people) *(May Subd Geog)*
  [DT 962.42 : old class]
  [DT 2913.Z49 : new class]
  UF Bazezuru (African people)
      Vazezuru (African people)
      Wazezuru (African people)
      Zezeru (African people)
      Zvimba (African people)
  BT Ethnology--Zimbabwe
      Shona (African people)
 --Religion
  [BL 2480.Z4]

Zezuru language
  USE Shona language

Zhu/twasi (African people)
  USE !Kung (African people)

Ziba (African people)
  USE Haya (African people)

Ziba language *(May Subd Geog)*
  [PL 8834]
  UF Haya language
      Lusiba language
      Ruhaya language
  BT Bantu languages
      Tanzania--Languages
      Uganda--Languages

Zigua language
  USE Zigula language

Zigula (African people) *(May Subd Geog)*
  [DT 443.3.Z]
  UF Uzigula (African people)
  BT Bantu-speaking peoples
      Ethnology--Tanzania

Zigula language *(May Subd Geog)*
  [PL 8831]
  UF Zeguha language
      Zigua language
  BT Bondei language
      Tanzania--Languages

Zimba language
  USE Nzima language

Zimbabwe *(Not Subd Geog)*
  [DT 962-DT 962.9 : old class]
  [DT 2871-DT 3025 : new class]

  UF Rhodesia, Southern
      Southern Rhodesia
--Antiquities
  NT Chivowa Hill Site (Zimbabwe)
      Diana's Vow Rock Shelter (Zimbabwe)
      Great Zimbabwe (City)
--Description and travel
-- --1981-
--Drama
  USE Zimbabwean drama
--Economic conditions
  [HC 910]
-- --To 1965
-- --1965-1980
-- --1980-
--Fiction
  USE Zimbabwean fiction
--Foreign relations *(May Subd Geog)*
-- --1890-1965
-- --1965-1980
-- --1980-
--History
-- --1890-1965
-- --Ndebele War, 1893
  USE Matabele War, 1893
-- --Ndebele Insurrection, 1896-1897
  [DT 962.72 : old class]
  [DT 2968 : new class]
  UF 1st Chimurenga War (Zimbabwe), 1896-1897
      Chimurenga War (Zimbabwe), 1896-1897
      First Chimurenga War (Zimbabwe), 1896-1897
      Matabele War (Zimbabwe), 1896-1897
      Ndebele Insurrection (Zimbabwe), 1896-1897
  BT Ndebele (African people)--History
      Shona (African people)--History--19th
century
-- --1965-1980
-- --Chimurenga War, 1966-1980
  [DT 962.8 : old class]
  [DT 2986 : new class]
  UF 2nd Chimurenga War (Zimbabwe), 1966-1980
      Chimurenga War (Zimbabwe), 1966-1980
      Rhodesian War (Zimbabwe), 1966-1980
      Second Chimurenga War (Zimbabwe), 1966-1980
      Zimbabwean Revolution (Zimbabwe), 1966-1980
-- --1980-
--History, Military
-- --1965-1980
--Languages
  NT Chindau language
      Lilima language
      Ndebele language (Zimbabwe)
      Nika language
      Shona language
      Tonga language (Zambesi)
      Tswa language

(May Subd Geog) = Place names may follow the heading

NT Tswana language
--Literatures
 USE Zimbabwean literature
--Poetry
 USE Zimbabwean poetry
--Politics and government
-- --1890-1965
-- --1965-1979
-- --1979-1980
-- --1980-
--Social conditions
 -- --1890-1965
-- --1965-1980
-- --1980-

Zimbabwe, Great (City)
 USE Great Zimbabwe (City)

Zimbabwean art
 USE Art, Zimbabwean

Zimbabwean atlases
 USE Atlases, Zimbabwean

Zimbabwean authors
 USE Authors, Zimbabwean

Zimbabwean children's poetry
 USE Children's poetry, Zimbabwean

Zimbabwean cookery
 USE Cookery, Zimbabwean

Zimbabwean drama *(May Subd Geog)*
 [PL 8014.Z55]
 UF Zimbabwe--Drama
 BT African drama
    Zimbabwean literature
 NT Shona drama

Zimbabwean drama (English) *(May Subd Geog)*
 [PR 9390.3 (History)]
 [PR 9390.7 (Collections)]
 UF English drama--Zimbabwean authors
 BT African drama (English)
    Zimbabwean literature (English)

Zimbabwean fiction *(May Subd Geog)*
 [PL 8014.Z55]
 UF Zimbabwe--Fiction
 BT Southern African fiction
    Zimbabwean literature
 NT Ndebele fiction (Zimbabwe)
    Shona fiction
    Tonga fiction (Zambesi)

Zimbabwean fiction (English) *(May Subd Geog)*
 [PR 9390.4 (History)]
 [PR 9390.8. (Collections)]
 UF English fiction--Zimbabwean authors
 BT Southern African fiction (English)
    Zimbabwean literature (English)
--Black authors
 UF Black fiction, Zimbabwean (English)

Zimbabwean literature *(May Subd Geog)*
 [PL 8014.Z55]
 UF Zimbabwe--Literatures
 BT Southern African literature
 NT Ndebele literature (Zimbabwe)
    Shona literature
    Tonga literature (Zambesi)
    Zimbabwean drama
    Zimbabwean fiction
    Zimbabwean poetry

Zimbabwean literature (English) *(May Subd Geog)*
 [PR 9390]
 UF English literature--Zimbabwean authors
 BT Southern African literature (English)
 NT Zimbabwean drama (English)
    Zimbabwean fiction (English)
    Zimbabwean poetry (English)

Zimbabwean newspapers *(May Subd Geog)*
 [PN 5499.Z55]
 UF Newspapers, Zimbabwean

Zimbabwean periodicals *(May Subd Geog)*
 [PN 5499.Z55]
 UF Periodicals, Zimbabwean

Zimbabwean poetry *(May Subd Geog)*
 [PL 8014.Z55]
 UF Zimbabwe--Poetry
 BT Southern African poetry
    Zimbabwean literature
 NT Children's poetry, Zimbabwean
    Ndebele poetry (Zimbabwe)
    Shona poetry
    Tswana poetry

Zimbabwean poetry (English) *(May Subd Geog)*
 [PR 9390.2 (History)]
 [PR 9390.6-PR 9390.65 (Collections)]
 UF English poetry--Zimbabwean authors
 BT African poetry (English)
    Zimbabwean literature (English)
 NT Revolutionary poetry, Zimbabwean (English)

Zimbabwean poets
 USE Poets, Zimbabwean

UF = Used for; BT = Broader term; RT = Related term; SA = See also; NT = Narrower term

Zimbabwean propaganda
  USE Propaganda, Zimbabwean

Zimbabwean Revolution (Zimbabwe), 1966-1980
  USE Zimbabwe--History--Chimurenga War,
1966-1980

Zimbabwean revolutionary poetry (English)
  USE Revolutionary poetry, Zimbabwean
(English)

Zimbabweans *(May Subd Geog)*
  BT Ethnology--Zimbabwe

Zinza (African people) *(May Subd Geog)*
  [DT 443.3.Z]
  UF Dzindza (African people)
      Jinja (African people)
      Sindja (African people)
      Wassindja (African people)
  BT Bantu-speaking peoples
      Ethnology--Tanzania
 --Religion
  [BL 2480.Z56]

Zionist churches (Africa) *(May Subd Geog)*
  [BX 9995.Z45]
  BT Christian sects--Africa

Zoghawa (African people)
  USE Zaghawa (African people)

Zombo dialect
  USE Zoombo dialect

Zonnebloem (Cape Town, South Africa)
  USE District Six (Cape Town, South Africa)

Zoombo dialect *(May Subd Geog)*
  [PL 8404.Z9Z63]
  UF Kizombo dialect
      Kizoombo dialect
      Nzombo dialect
      Nzoombo dialect
      Zombo dialect
  BT Angola--Languages
      Kongo language
      Zaire--Languages

Zorhaua (African people)
  USE Zaghawa (African people)

Zorhawa (African people)
  USE Zaghawa (African people)

Zugweya language
  USE Busa language

Zulgo (African people) *(May Subd Geog)*
  [DT 571.Z]
  BT Ethnology--Cameroon
 --Religion
  [BL 2480.Z75]

Zulgo language *(May Subd Geog)*
  [PL 8839]
  UF Zelgwa language
  BT Cameroon--Languages
      Chadic languages

Zulu (African people) *(May Subd Geog)*
  [DT 878.Z9 : old class]
  [DT 1768.Z95 : new class]
  UF Amazulu (African people)
      Isizulu (African people)
      Kafirs (African people)
      Zunda (African people)
  BT Ethnology--South Africa
      Nguni (African people)
  NT Ndebele (African people)
 --Kings and rulers
 --Medicine
  BT Medicine, Primitive--South Africa
 --Missions *(May Subd Geog)*
  [BV 3630.Z8]
  UF Missions to Zulu (African people)
 --Religion
  [BL 2480.Z8]

Zulu art
  USE Art, Zulu

Zulu catechisms
  USE Catechisms, Zulu

Zulu children's poetry
  USE Children's poetry, Zulu

Zulu fiction *(May Subd Geog)*
  [PL 8843.5-PL 8844]
  BT South African fiction
      Zulu literature

Zulu hymns
  USE Hymns, Zulu

Zulu language *(May Subd Geog)*
  [PL 8841-PL 8844]
  UF Isizulu language
      Zunda language
  BT Africa, Southern--Languages

(May Subd Geog) = Place names may follow the heading

BT Nguni languages
    South Africa--Languages
NT Ndebele language (South Africa)
    Ndebele language (Zimbabwe)

Zulu literature *(May Subd Geog)*
   [PL 8843.5-PL 8844]
BT South African literature
NT Zulu fiction
    Zulu poetry

Zulu philosophy
USE Philosophy, Zulu

Zulu poetry *(May Subd Geog)*
   [PL 8843.5-PL 8844]
BT South African poetry
    Zulu literature
NT Children's poetry, Zulu

Zulu Rebellion, 1906
   [DT 777 : old class]
   [DT 2267 : new class]
UF Bambatha Rebellion, 1906
BT Natal (South Africa) History--1893-
1910

Zulu school songbooks
USE School songbooks, Zulu

Zulu War, 1879 *(May Subd Geog)*
   [DT 777 : old class]
   [DT 1875-DT 1882 : new class]
UF Anglo-Zulu War, 1879
BT South Africa--History--1836-1909
NT Zululand (South Africa)--History--To
1879
 --**Campaigns** *(May Subd Geog)*
NT Isandlwana (South Africa), Battle of,
1879
    Rorke's Drift (South Africa), Battle
of, 1879

Zulu women
USE Women, Zulu

Zululand (South Africa) *(Not Subd Geog)*
   [DT 878.Z9 : old class]
   [DT 2400.Z85 : new class]
 --**History**
NT South Africa--History--Usutu Uprising,
1888
-- --**To 1879**
BT Zulu War, 1879
NT Ndondakusuka, Battle of, South Africa,
1856

-- --**Civil War, 1879-1884**
UF Civil war--Zululand (South Africa)

Zumari
   [ML 990.Z8]
BT Musical instruments--Kenya

Zunda (African people)
USE Zulu (African people)

Zunda language
USE Zulu language

Zungle language
USE Limbum language

Zvimba (African people)
USE Zezuru (African people)

UF = Used for; BT = Broader term; RT = Related term; SA = See also; NT = Narrower term

Source Bibliography

Africa South of the Sahara, 1990, 19th ed.   London: Europa
Publications, 1989.

African Ethnonyms and Toponyms.   Paris: Unesco, 1984. (The
General History of Africa : Studies and Documents ; 6)

Diggs, Ellen Irene.   Black Chronology from 4000 B.C. to the
Abolition of the Slave Trade.   Boston: G.K. Hall, 1983.

Freeman-Grenville, G.S.P.   Chronology of African History.
London: Oxford University Press, 1973.

Library of Congress.   Cataloging Service Bulletin, nos. 49-54
(Summer 1990-Fall 1991).   Washington, D.C.: Library of
Congress, 1990-1991.

Library of Congress.   Library of Congress Subject Headings.
13th ed.   Washington, D.C.: Library of Congress, Cataloging
Distribution Service, 1990, plus selected updated headings in
online version of LCSH in Ullas database, 1991.

Library of Congress.   Office for Subject Cataloging Policy.
Free-Floating Subdivisions : An Alphabetical Index.   2nd ed.
Washington, D.C.: Library of Congress, Cataloging Distribution
Service, 1990.

Library of Congress.   Office for Subject Cataloging Policy.
LC Subject Headings Weekly Lists, no. 01-51 (Jan. 3, 1990-Dec.
19, 1990) and no. 01-38 (Jan. 23, 1991-Sept. 18, 1991).
Washington, D.C.: Library of Congress, Cataloging Distribution
Service, 1990-1991.

Mann, Michael and David Dalby, eds.   Thesaurus of African
Languages : A Classified List and Annotated Inventory of the
Spoken Languages of Africa.   London : Hans Zell (for
International African Institute), 1987.

Murdock, George Peter.   Outline of World Cultures.   6th rev.
ed. New Haven, Conn.: Human Relations Area Files, 1983.

Voegelin, G.F. and F.M. Voegelin.   Classification and Index
of the World's Languages.   New York: Elsevier, 1977.
(Foundations of Linguistics Series)

About the Author

FREDA E. OTCHERE is senior cataloging and standards librarian at Concordia University Libraries. She is the author of *The Montreal Children's Theatre: Oral History Project* (1985).